PHILIP'S

ROAD ATLAS

2022 BIG EASY TO RE... BRITAIN

C000062069

www.philips-maps.co.uk

First published in 2020 by Philip's
a division of Octopus Publishing Group Ltd
www.octopusbooks.co.uk
Carmelite House, 50 Victoria Embankment
London EC4Y 0DZ
An Hachette UK Company
www.hachette.co.uk

Second edition 2021
First impression 2021

ISBN 978-1-84907-563-3

Cartography by Philip's
Copyright © 2021 Philip's

This product includes mapping data licensed from Ordnance Survey®, with the permission of the Controller of Her Majesty's Stationery Office. © Crown copyright 2021. All rights reserved. Licence number 100011710

Information for National Parks, Areas of Outstanding Natural Beauty, National Trails and Country Parks in Wales supplied by the Countryside Council for Wales.

Information for National Parks, Areas of Outstanding Natural Beauty, National Trails and Country Parks in England supplied by Natural England. Data for Regional Parks, Long Distance Footpaths and Country Parks in Scotland provided by Scottish Natural Heritage.

Gaelic name forms used in the Western Isles provided by Comhairle nan Eilean.

Data for the National Nature Reserves in England provided by Natural England. Data for the National Nature Reserves in Wales provided by Countryside Council for Wales. Darparwyd data'n ymwneud â Gwarchodfeydd Natur Cenedlaethol Cymru gan Gyngor Cefn Gwlad Cymru.

Information on the location of National Nature Reserves in Scotland was provided by Scottish Natural Heritage.

Data for National Scenic Areas in Scotland provided by the Scottish Executive Office. Crown copyright material is reproduced with the permission of the Controller of HMSO and the Queen's Printer for Scotland. Licence number C02W0003960.

Printed in China

*Data from Nielsen Total Consumer Market 2020 weeks 27-39

CONTENTS

II **Key to map symbols**

III **Restricted motorway junctions**

IV **Route planning maps**

XIV **Distances and journey times**

1 **Key to road map pages**

2 **Road maps of Britain**

161 **Urban approach maps**

161 Bristol *approaches*

162 Birmingham *approaches*

164 Cardiff *approaches*

165 Edinburgh *approaches*

166 Glasgow *approaches*

167 Leeds *approaches*

168 London *approaches*

172 Liverpool *approaches*

173 Manchester *approaches*

174 Newcastle *approaches*

175 **Town plans**

175 Aberdeen, Ayr, Bath

176 Birmingham, Blackpool, Bournemouth

177 Bradford, Brighton, Bristol

178 Bury St Edmunds, Cambridge, Canterbury, Cardiff

179 Carlisle, Chelmsford, Cheltenham, Chester

180 Chichester, Colchester, Coventry, Derby

181 Dorchester, Dumfries, Dundee, Durham

182 Edinburgh, Exeter, Gloucester

183 Glasgow, Grimsby, Harrogate

184 Hull, Inverness, Ipswich, Kendal

185 King's Lynn, Leeds, Lancaster

186 London

188 Leicester, Lincoln, Liverpool

189 Llandudno, Llanelli, Luton, Macclesfield

190 Manchester, Maidstone, Merthyr Tydfil

191 Middlesbrough, Milton Keynes, Newcastle upon Tyne, Newport

192 Newquay, Northampton, Norwich, Nottingham

193 Oxford, Perth, Peterborough, Plymouth

194 Poole, Portsmouth, Preston, Reading

195 St Andrews, Salisbury, Scarborough, Shrewsbury

196 Sheffield, Stoke-on-Trent (Hanley), Southampton

197 Southend-on-Sea, Stirling, Stratford-upon-Avon, Sunderland

198 Swansea, Swindon, Taunton, Telford

199 Torquay, Truro, Winchester, Windsor

200 Wolverhampton, Worcester, Wrexham, York

201 **Index to road maps of Britain**

Inside back cover: **County and unitary authority boundaries**

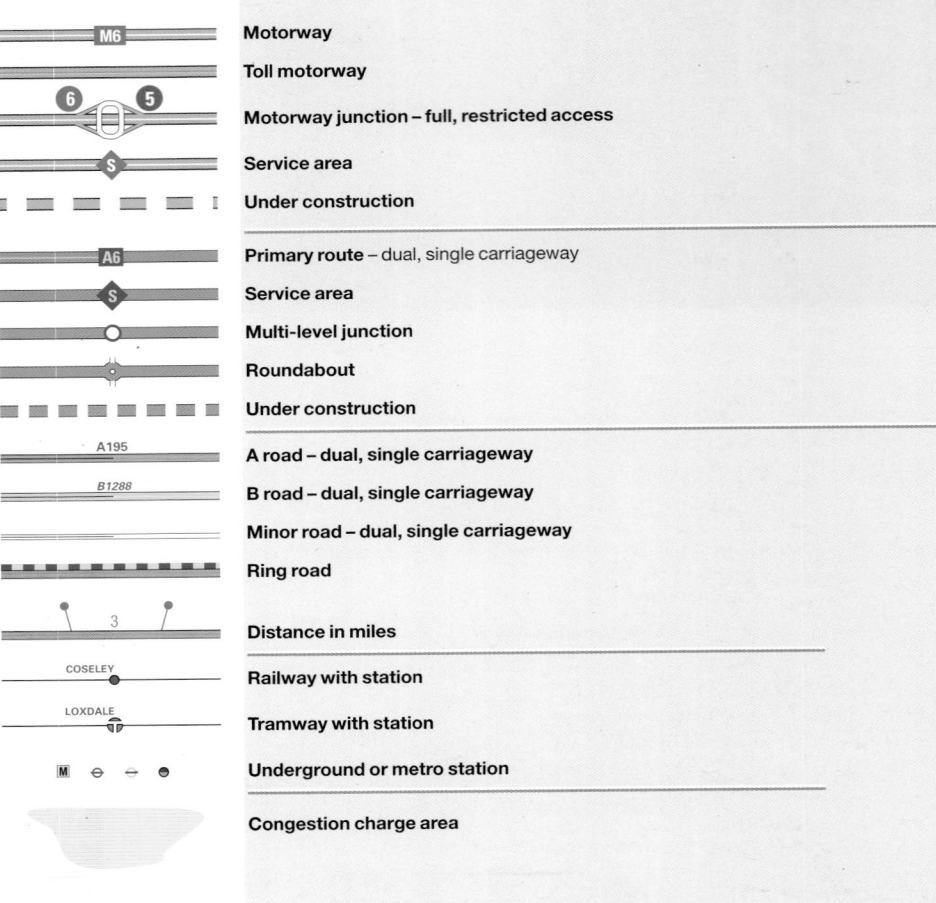

Road map symbols

M6	Motorway, toll motorway
4 S S	Motorway junction – full, restricted access
S S	Motorway service area – full, restricted access
	Motorway under construction
A453	Primary route – dual, single carriageway
S S	Service area, roundabout, multi-level junction
4 5	Numbered junction – full, restricted access
	Primary route under construction
	Narrow primary route
Derby	Primary destination
A34	A road – dual, single carriageway
	A road under construction, narrow A road
B2135	B road – dual, single carriageway
	B road under construction, narrow B road
	Minor road – over 4 metres, under 4 metres wide
	Minor road with restricted access
2	Distance in miles
	Scenic route
TOLL	Toll, steep gradient – arrow points downhill
	Tunnel
	National trail – England and Wales
	Long distance footpath – Scotland
	Railway with station
	Level crossing, tunnel
	Preserved railway with station
	National boundary
	County / unitary authority boundary
	Car ferry, catamaran
	Passenger ferry, catamaran
	Hovercraft
CALAIS	Ferry destination
Ferry	Car ferry – river crossing
	Principal airport, other airport
	National Park, Area of Outstanding Natural Beauty – England and Wales National Scenic Area – Scotland forest park / regional park / national forest
	Beach
	Linear antiquity
	Roman road
1066	Hillfort, battlefield – with date
795	Viewpoint, nature reserve, spot height – in metres
	Golf course, youth hostel, sporting venue
	Camp site, caravan site, camping and caravan site
P&R	Shopping village, park and ride
29	Adjoining page number – road maps

Road map scale
1:150 000 • 1 cm = 1.5 km • 1 inch = 2·37 miles
0 1 2 3 4 5 6 7 8 km
0 1 2 3 4 5 miles

Parts of Scotland
1:200 000 • 1 cm = 2.0 km • 1 inch = 3.16 miles
0 1 2 3 4 5 6 7 8 9 10 km
0 1 2 3 4 5 6 miles

Scottish Highlands and Islands
1:250 000 • 1 cm = 2.5 km • 1 inch = 3.95 miles
0 1 2 3 4 5 6 7 8 9 10 11 12 km
0 1 2 3 4 5 6 7 8 miles

(Orkney and Shetland Islands at 1:300 000, approximately 4.75 miles to 1 inch)

Approach map symbols

M6	Motorway
	Toll motorway
6 5	Motorway junction – full, restricted access
S	Service area
	Under construction
A6	Primary route – dual, single carriageway
S	Service area
	Multi-level junction
	Roundabout
	Under construction
A195	A road – dual, single carriageway
B1288	B road – dual, single carriageway
	Minor road – dual, single carriageway
	Ring road
3	Distance in miles
COSELEY	Railway with station
LOXDALE	Tramway with station
M	Underground or metro station
	Congestion charge area

Town plan symbols

	Motorway
	Primary route – dual, single carriageway
	A road – dual, single carriageway
	B road – dual, single carriageway
	Minor through road
	One-way street
	Pedestrian roads
	Shopping streets
	Railway with station
City Hall	Tramway with station
	Bus or railway station building
	Shopping precinct or retail park
	Park
	Building of public interest
	Theatre, cinema
P	Parking, shopmobility
Bank	Underground station
West St	Metro station
H	Hospital, Police station
PO	Post office

Tourist information

Abbey, cathedral or priory	Church	House and garden	Safari park
Ancient monument	Country park England and Wales Scotland	Motor racing circuit	Theme park
Aquarium		Museum	Tourist information
Art gallery	Farm park	Picnic area	Zoo
Bird collection or aviary	Garden	Preserved railway	Other place of interest
Castle	Historic ship	Race course	
	House	Roman antiquity	

Restricted motorway junctions

M1

M1	Northbound	Southbound
2	No exit	No access
4	No exit	No access
6A	No exit. Access from M25 only	No access. Exit to M25 only
7	No exit. Access from A414 only	No access. Exit to A414 only
17	No access. Exit to M45 only	No exit. Access from M45 only
19	No exit to A14	No access from A14
21A	No access	
23A		Exit to A42 only
24A	No exit	No access
35A	No access	No exit
43	No access. Exit to M621 only	No exit. Access from M621 only
48	No exit to A1(M) southbound	

M3

M3	Eastbound	Westbound
8	No exit	No access
10	No access	No exit
13	No access to M27 eastbound	
14	No exit	No access

M4

M4	Eastbound	Westbound
1	Exit to A4 eastbound only	Access from A4 westbound only
2	Access from A4 eastbound only	Access to A4 westbound only
21	No exit	No access
23	No access	No exit
25	No exit	No access
25A	No exit	No access
29	No exit	No access
38		No access
39	No exit or access	No exit
41	No access	No exit
41A	No exit	No access
42	Access from A483 only	Exit to A483 only

M5

M5	Northbound	Southbound
10	No exit	No access
11A	No access from A417 eastbound	No exit to A417 westbound

M6

M6	Northbound	Southbound
3A	No access.	No exit. Access from M6 eastbound only
4A	No exit. Access from M42 southbound only	No access. Exit to M42 only
5	No access	No exit
10A	No access. Exit to M54 only	No exit. Access from M54 only
11A	No exit. Access from M6 Toll only	No access. Exit to M6 Toll only
20	No exit to M56 eastbound	No access from M56 westbound
24	No exit	No access
25	No access	No exit
30	No exit. Access from M61 northbound only	No access. Exit to M61 southbound only
31A	No access	No exit
45	No access	No exit

M6 Toll

M6 Toll	Northbound	Southbound
T1		No exit
T2	No exit, no access	No access
T5	No exit	No access
T7	No access	No exit
T8	No access	No exit

M8

M8	Eastbound	Westbound
6	No exit	No access
6A	No access	No exit
7	No Access	No exit
7A	No exit. Access from A725 northbound only	No access. Exit to A725 southbound only
8	No exit to M73 northbound	No access from M73 southbound
9	No access	No exit
13	No exit southbound	Access from M73 southbound only

M9

M9	Eastbound	Westbound
2	No access	No exit
3	No access	No exit
6	No access	No exit
8	No exit	No access

M11

M11	Northbound	Southbound
4	No exit	No access
5	No access	No exit
8A	No access	No exit
9	No access	No exit
13	No access	No exit
14	No exit to A428 westbound	No exit. Access from A14 westbound only

M20

M20	Eastbound	Westbound
2	No access	No exit
3	No exit Access from M26 eastbound only	No access Exit to M26 westbound only
10	No access	No exit
11A	No access	No exit

M23

M23	Northbound	Southbound
7	No exit to A23 southbound	No access from A23 northbound
10A	No exit	No access

M25

M25	Clockwise	Anticlockwise
5	No exit to M26 eastbound	No access from M26 westbound
19	No access	No exit
21	No exit to M1 southbound. Access from M1 southbound only	No exit to M1 southbound. Access from M1 southbound only
31	No exit	No access

M27

M27	Eastbound	Westbound
10	No exit	No access
12	No access	No exit

M40

M40	Eastbound	Westbound
3	No exit	No access
7	No exit	No access
8	No exit	No access
13	No exit	No access
14	No access	No exit
16	No access	No exit

M42

M42	Northbound	Southbound
1	No exit	No access
7	No access. Exit to M6 northbound only	No exit. Access from M6 northbound only
7A	No access. Exit to M6 southbound only	No access.
8	No exit. Access from M6 southbound only.	Exit to M6 northbound only. Access from M6 southbound only

M45

M45	Eastbound	Westbound
M1 J17	Access to M1 southbound only	No access from M1 southbound
With A45	No access	No exit

M48

M48	Eastbound	Westbound
M4 J21	No exit to M4 westbound	No access from M4 eastbound
M4 J23	No access from M4 westbound	No exit to M4 eastbound

M49

M49	Southbound	Northbound
18A	No exit to M5 northbound	No access from M5 southbound

M53

M53	Northbound	Southbound
11	Exit to M56 eastbound only. Access from M56 westbound only	Exit to M56 eastbnd only. Access from M56 westbound only

M56

M56	Eastbound	Westbound
2	No exit	No access
3	No access	No exit
4	No exit	No access
7		No access
8	No exit or access	No exit
9	No access from M6 northbound	No access to M6 southbound
15	No exit to M53	No access from M53 northbound

M57

M57	Northbound	Southbound
3	No exit	No access
5	No exit	No access

M58

M58	Eastbound	Westbound
1	No exit	No access

M60

M60	Clockwise	Anticlockwise
2	No exit	No access
3	No exit to A34 northbound	No exit to A34 northbound
4	No access from M56	No exit to M56
5	No exit to A5103 southbound	No exit to A5103 northbound
14	No exit	No access
16	No exit	No access
20	No access	No exit
22		No access
25	No access	
26		No exit or access
27	No exit	No access

M61

M61	Northbound	Southbound
2	No access from A580 eastbound	No exit to A580 westbound
3	No access from A580 eastbound. No access from A666 southbound	No exit to A580 westbound
M6 J30	No exit to M6 southbound	No access from M6 northbound

M62

M62	Eastbound	Westbound
23	No access	No exit

M65

M65	Eastbound	Westbound
9	No access	No exit
11	No exit	No access

M66

M66	Northbound	Southbound
1	No access	No exit

M67

M67	Eastbound	Westbound
1A	No access	No exit
2	No access	No exit

M69

M69	Northbound	Southbound
2	No exit	No access

M73

M73	Northbound	Southbound
2	No access from M8 eastbound	No exit to M8 westbound

M74

M74	Northbound	Southbound
3	No access	No exit
3A	No access	No exit
7	No exit	No access
9	No exit or access	No access
10		No exit
11	No exit	No access
12	No access	No exit

M77

M77	Northbound	Southbound
4	No exit	No access
6	No exit	No access
7	No exit	
8	No access	No access

M80

M80	Northbound	Southbound
4A	No access	No exit
6A	No exit	No access
8	Exit to M876 northbound only.	Access from M876 southbound only. No exit

M90

M90	Northbound	Southbound
1	Access from A90 northbound only	No access. Exit to A90 south-bound only
2A	No access	No exit
7	No exit	No access
8	No access	No exit
10	No access from A912	No exit to A912

M180

M180	Eastbound	Westbound
1	No access	No exit

M621

M621	Eastbound	Westbound
2A	No exit	No access
4	No exit	No access
5	No exit	No access
6	No access	No exit

M876

M876	Northbound	Southbound
2	No access	No exit

A1(M)

A1(M)	Northbound	Southbound
2	No access	No exit
3		No access
5	No exit	No exit, no access
14	No exit	No access
40	No access	No exit
43	No exit. Access from M1 only	No access. Exit to M1 only
57	No access	No exit
65	No access	No exit

A3(M)

A3(M)	Northbound	Southbound
1	No exit	No access
4	No access	No exit

A38(M) with Victoria Rd, (Park Circus) Birmingham

Northbound	No exit
Southbound	No access

A48(M)

A48(M)	Northbound	Southbound
M4 Junc 29	Exit to M4 eastbound only	Access from M4 westbound only
29A	Access from A48 eastbound only	Exit to A48 westbound only

A57(M)

A57(M)	Eastbound	Westbound
With A5103	No access	No exit
With A34	No access	No exit

A58(M)

A58(M)	Southbound
With Park Lane and Westgate, Leeds	No access

A64(M)

A64(M)	Eastbound	Westbound
With A58 Clay Pit Lane, Leeds	No access from A58	No exit to A58

A74(M)

A74(M)	Northbound	Southbound
18	No access	No exit
22		No exit to A75

A194(M)

A194(M)	Northbound	Southbound
A1(M) J65 Gateshead Western Bypass	Access from A1(M) northbound only	Exit to A1(M) southbound only

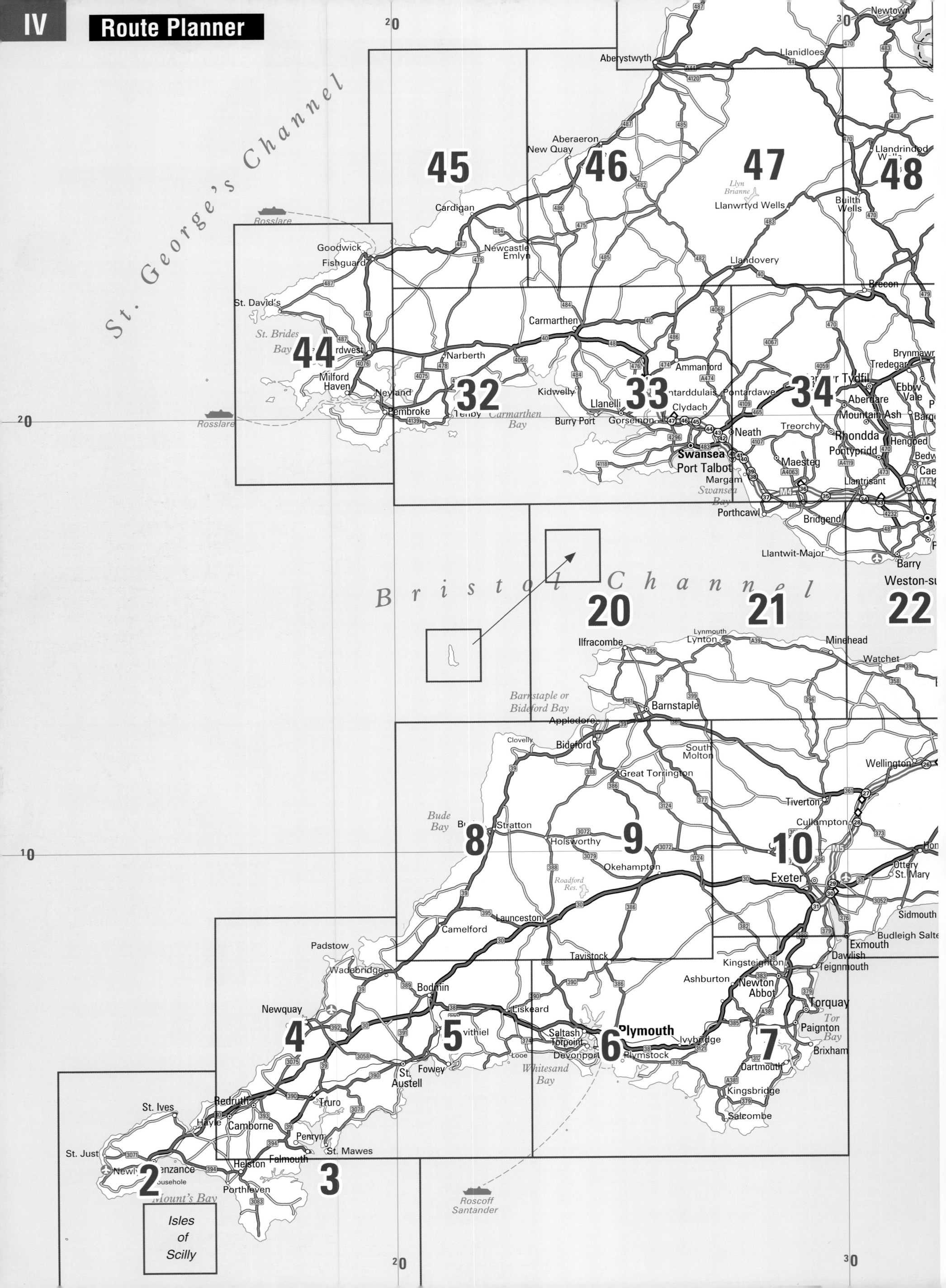

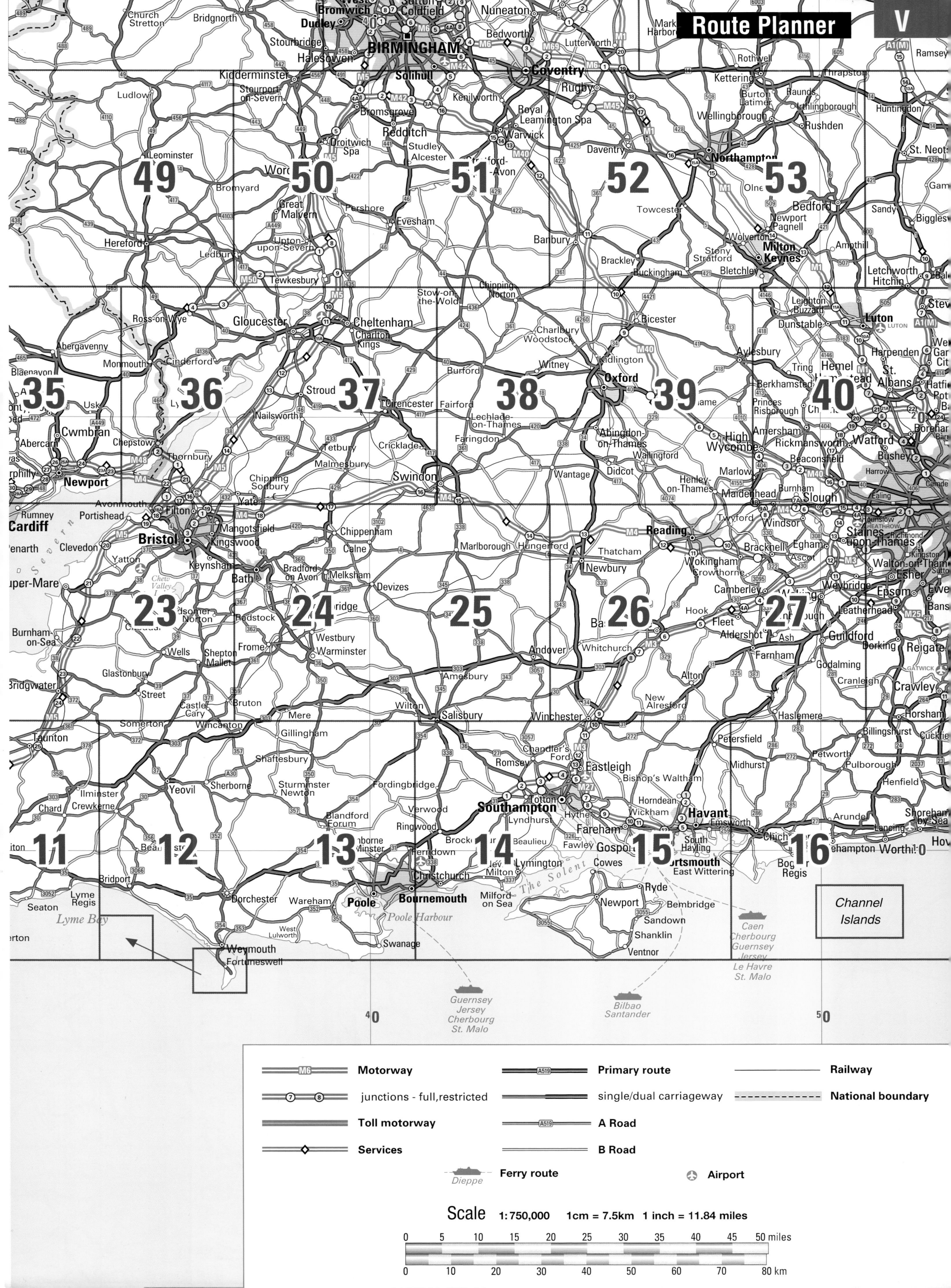

Scale   1:750,000   1cm = 7.5km   1 inch = 11.84 miles

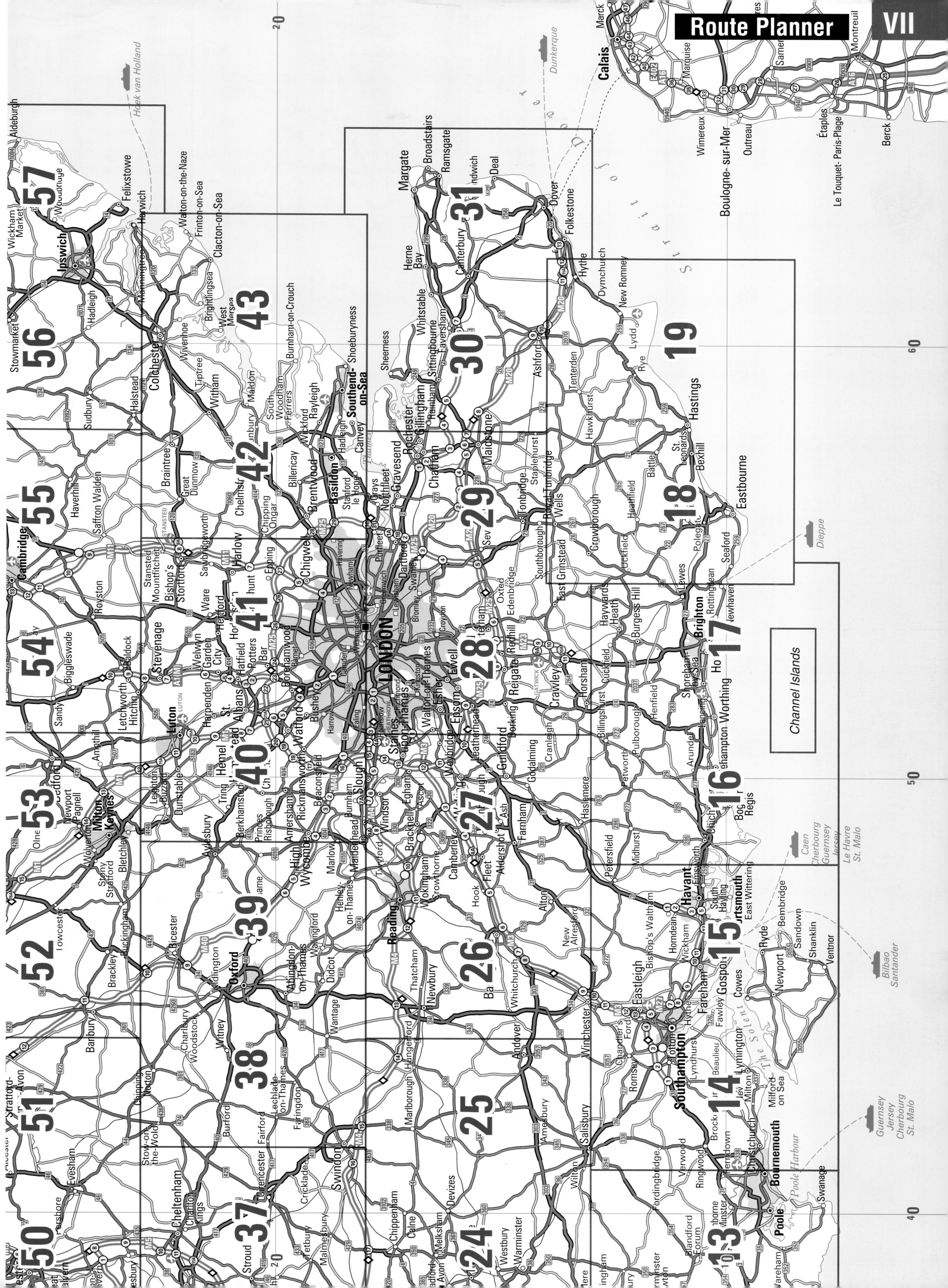

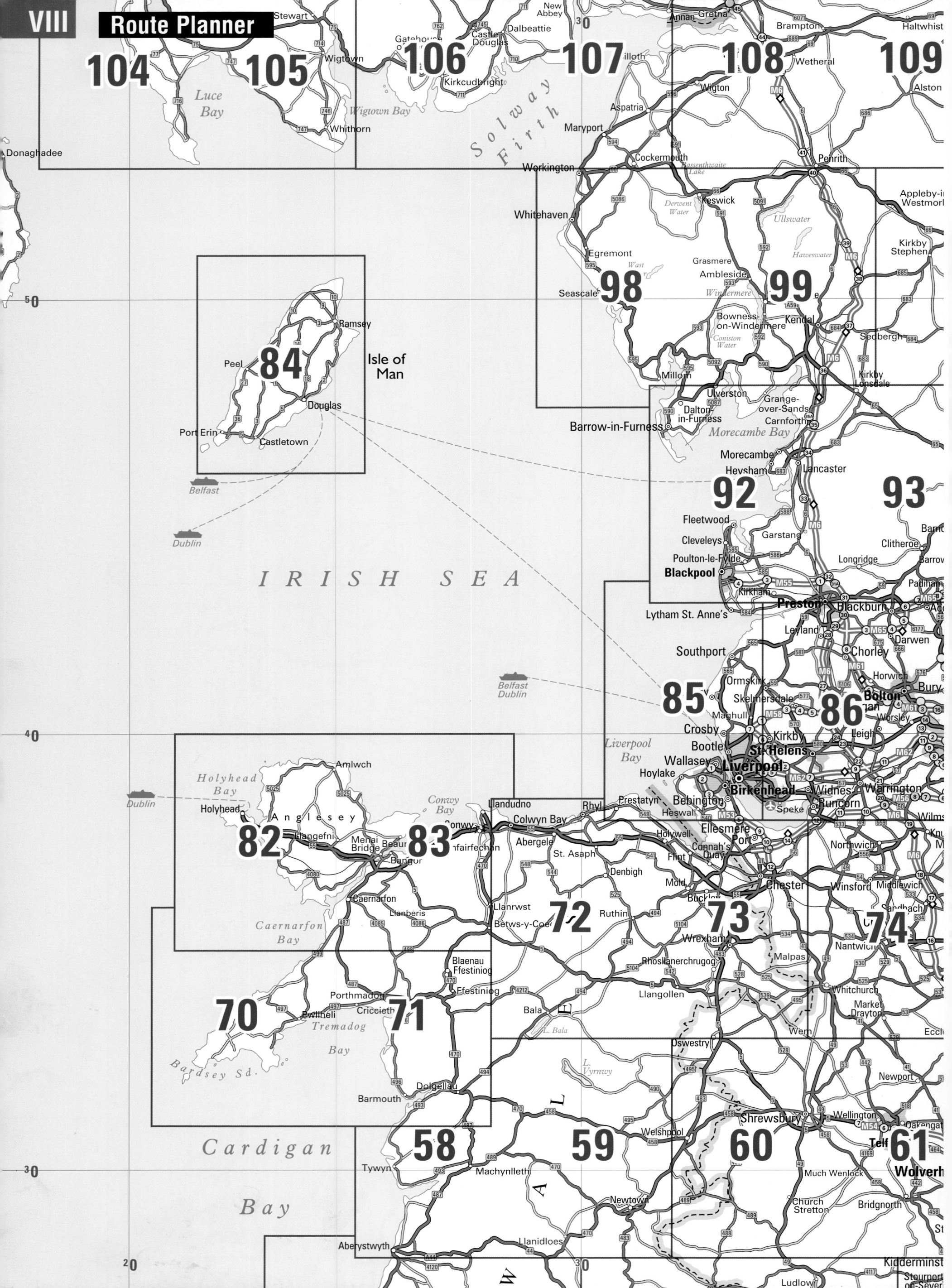

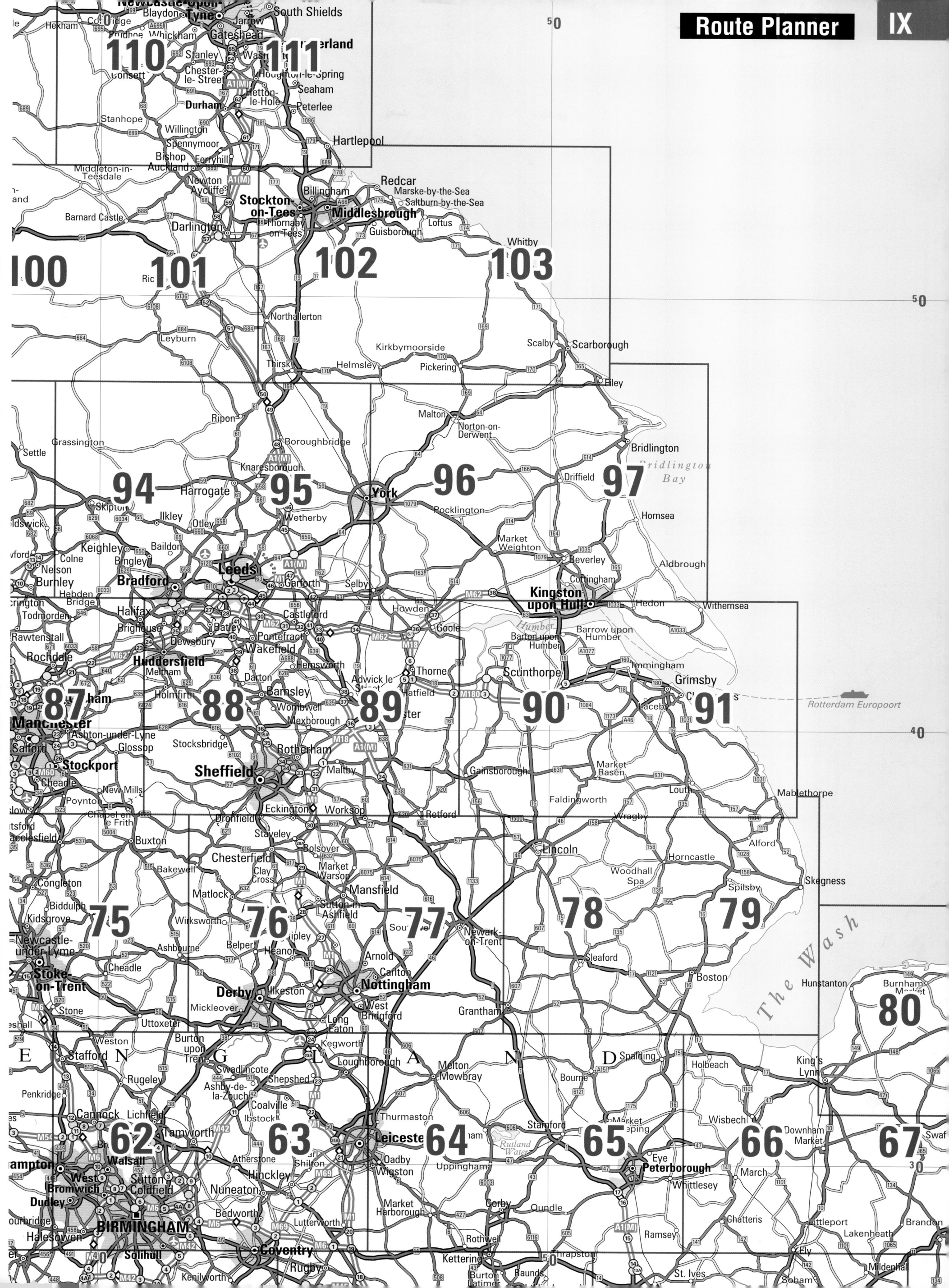

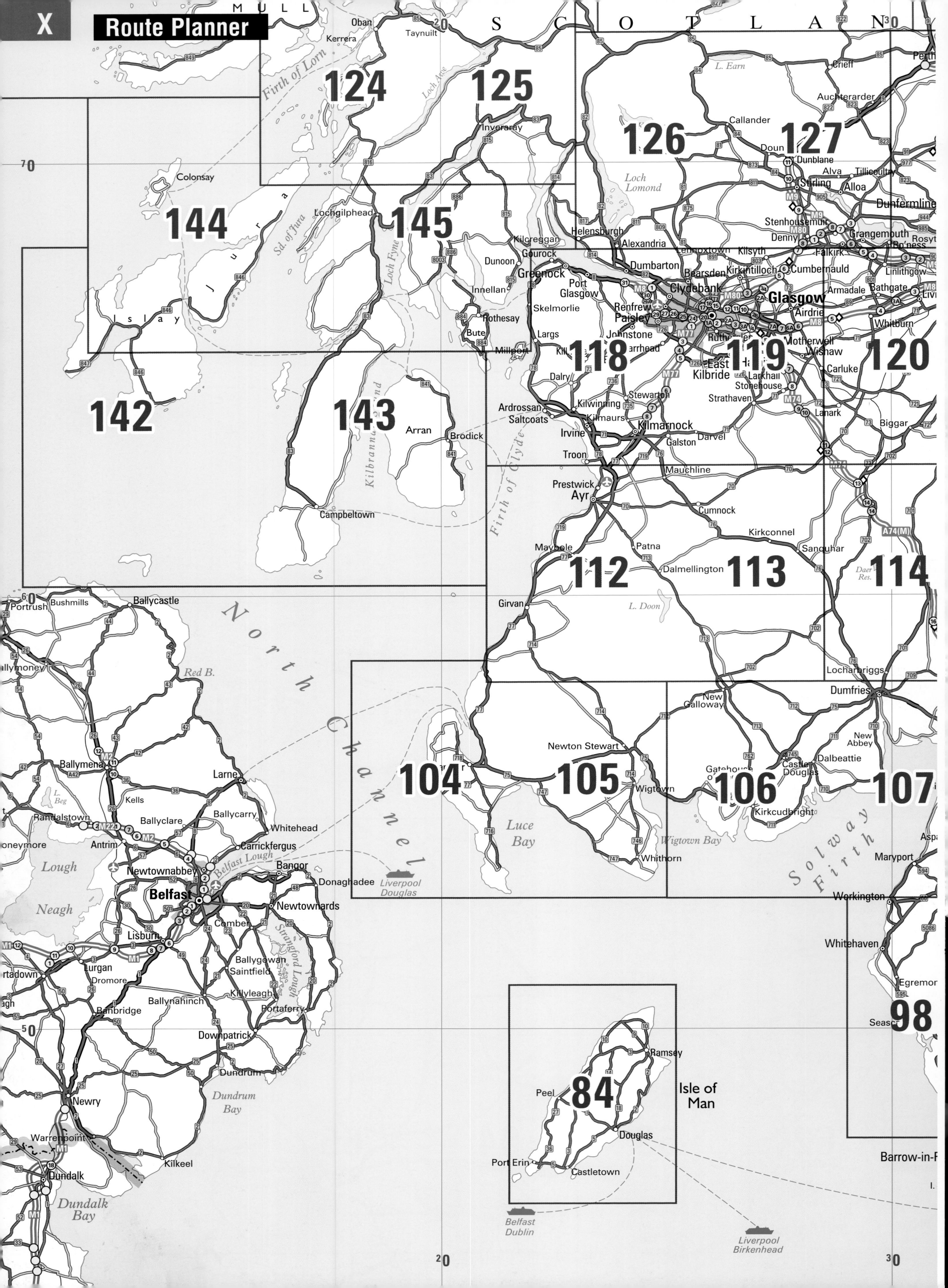

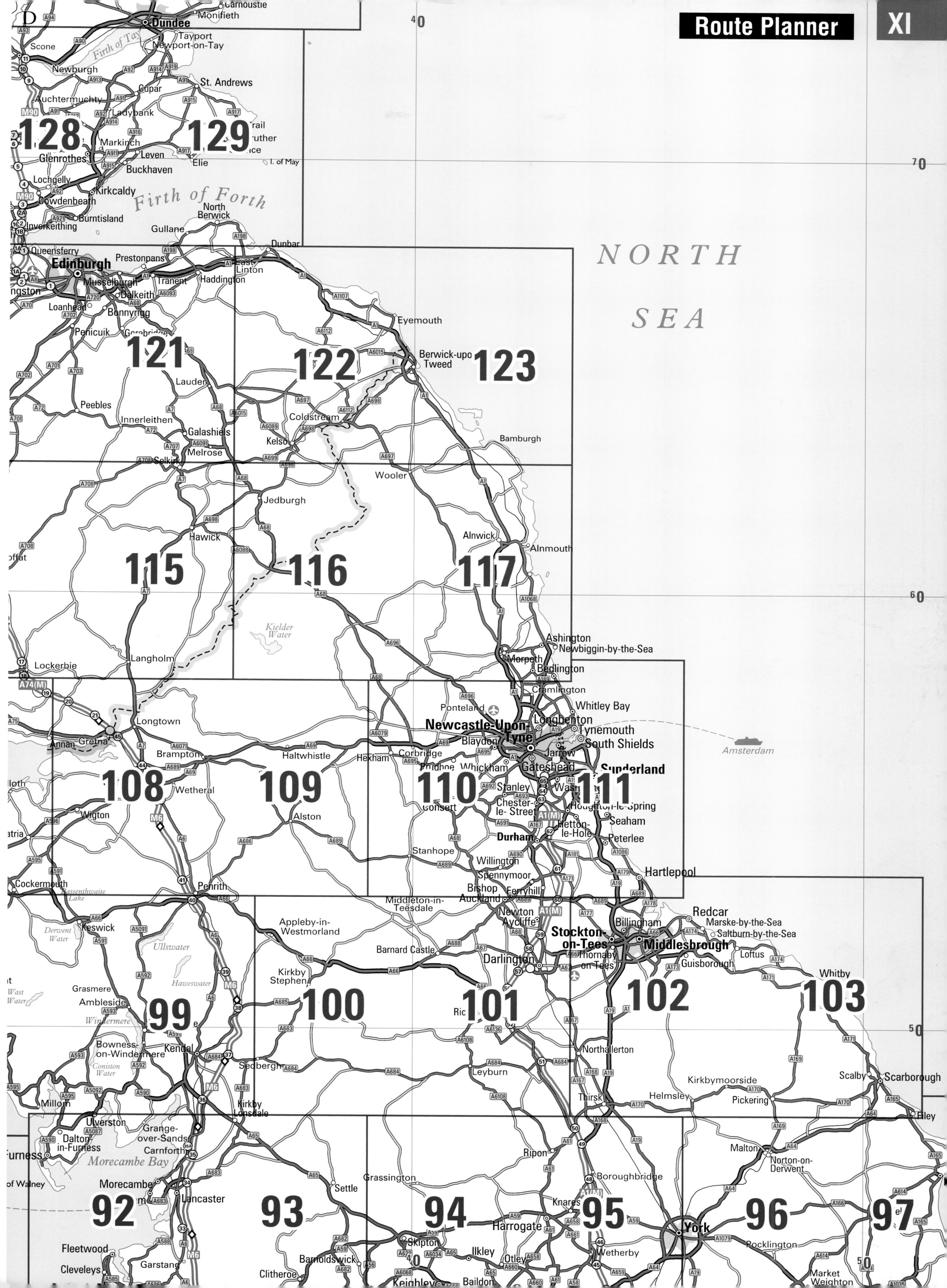

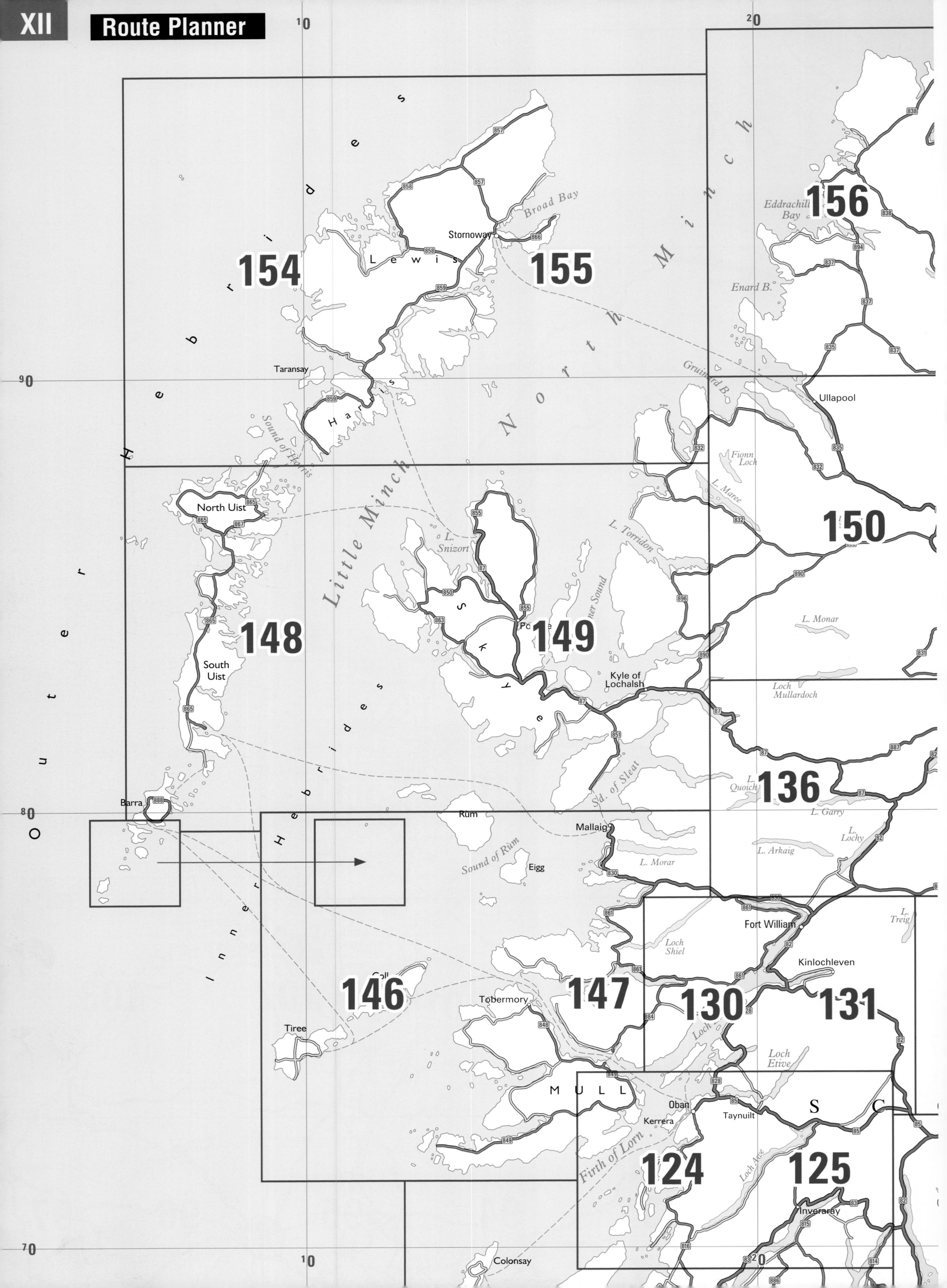

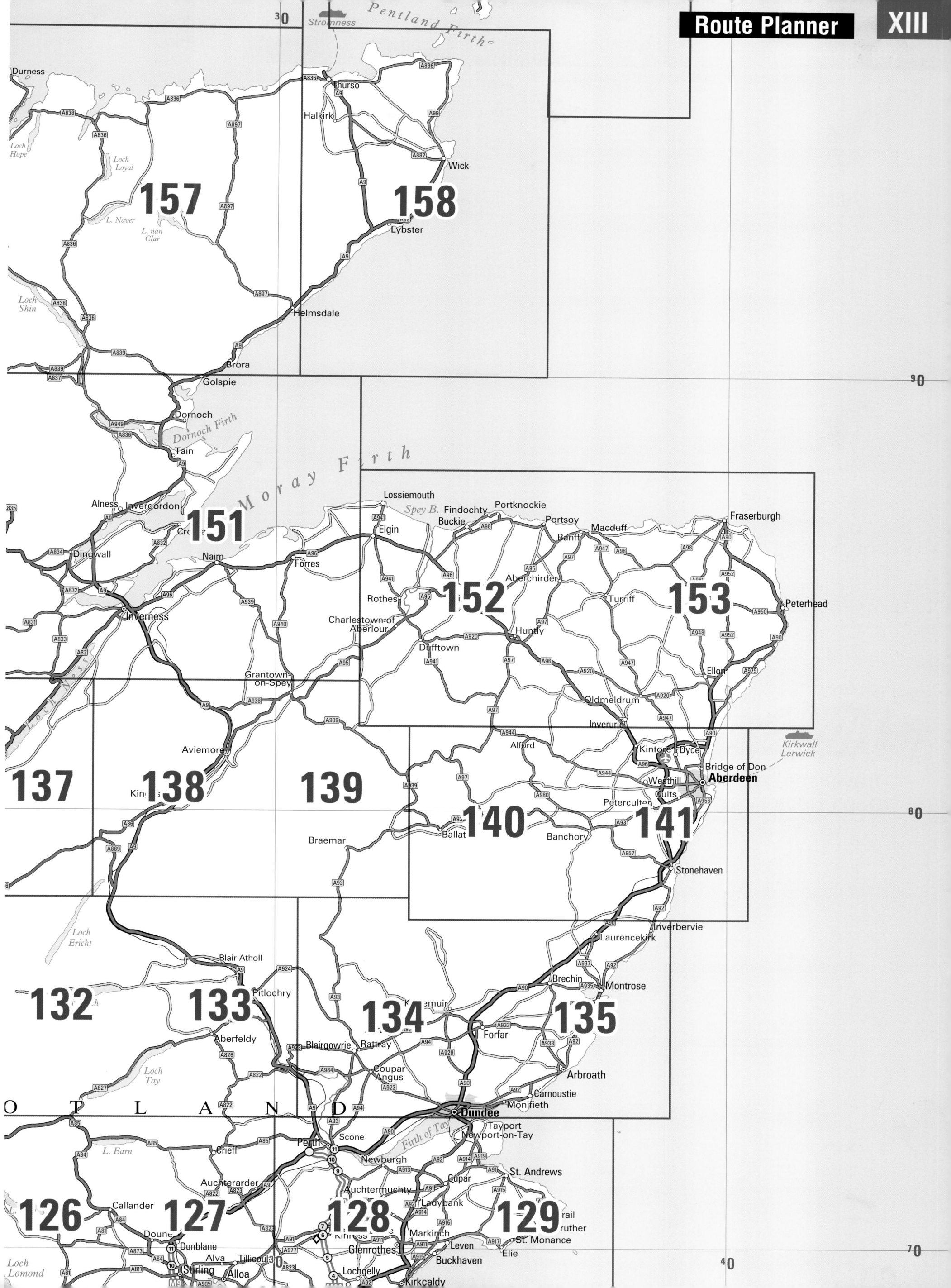

Distance table

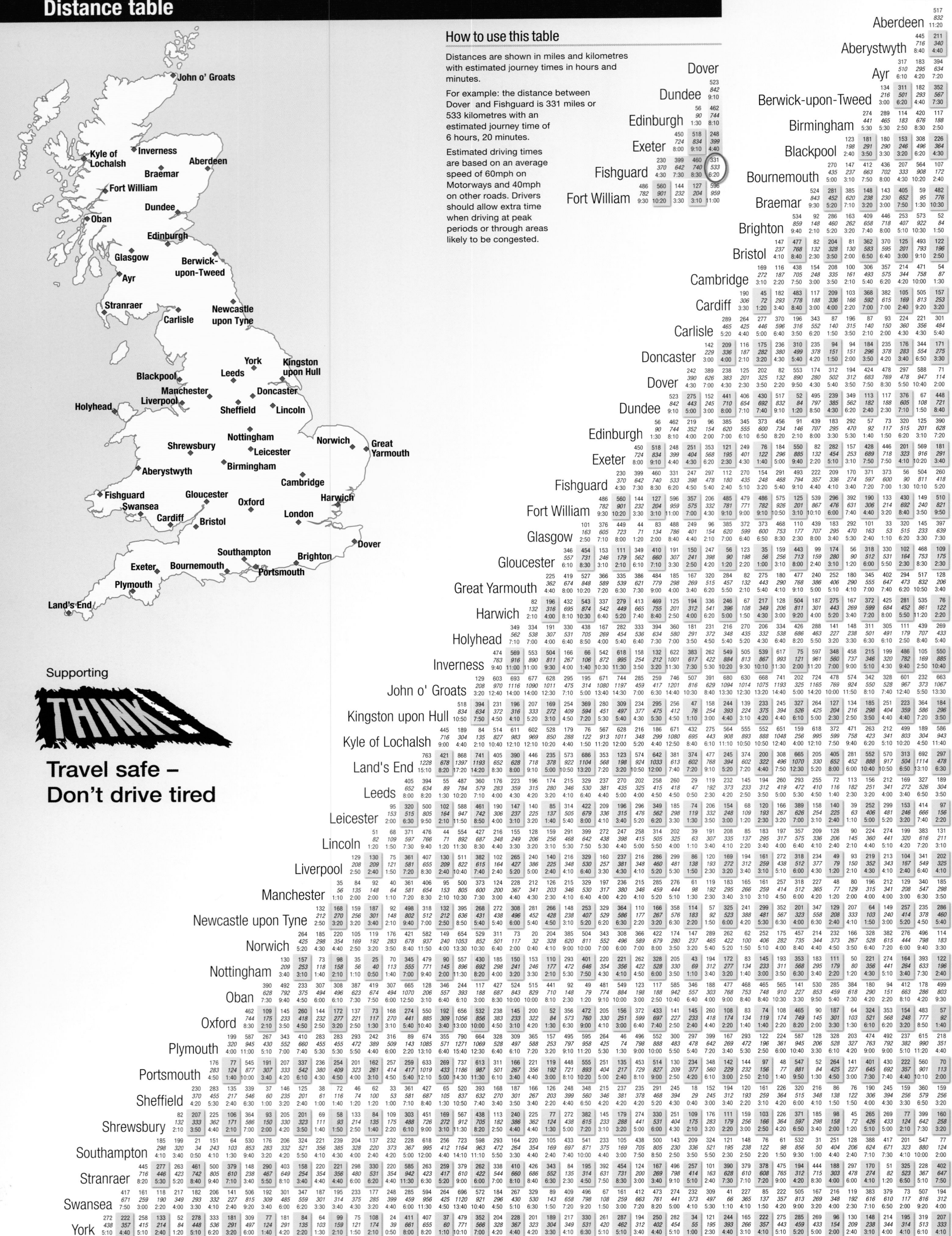

How to use this table

Distances are shown in miles and kilometres with estimated journey times in hours and minutes.

For example: the distance between Dover and Fishguard is 331 miles or 533 kilometres with an estimated journey time of 6 hours, 20 minutes.

Estimated driving times are based on an average speed of 60mph on Motorways and 40mph on other roads. Drivers should allow extra time when driving at peak periods or through areas likely to be congested.

Supporting

THINK!

Travel safe – Don't drive tired

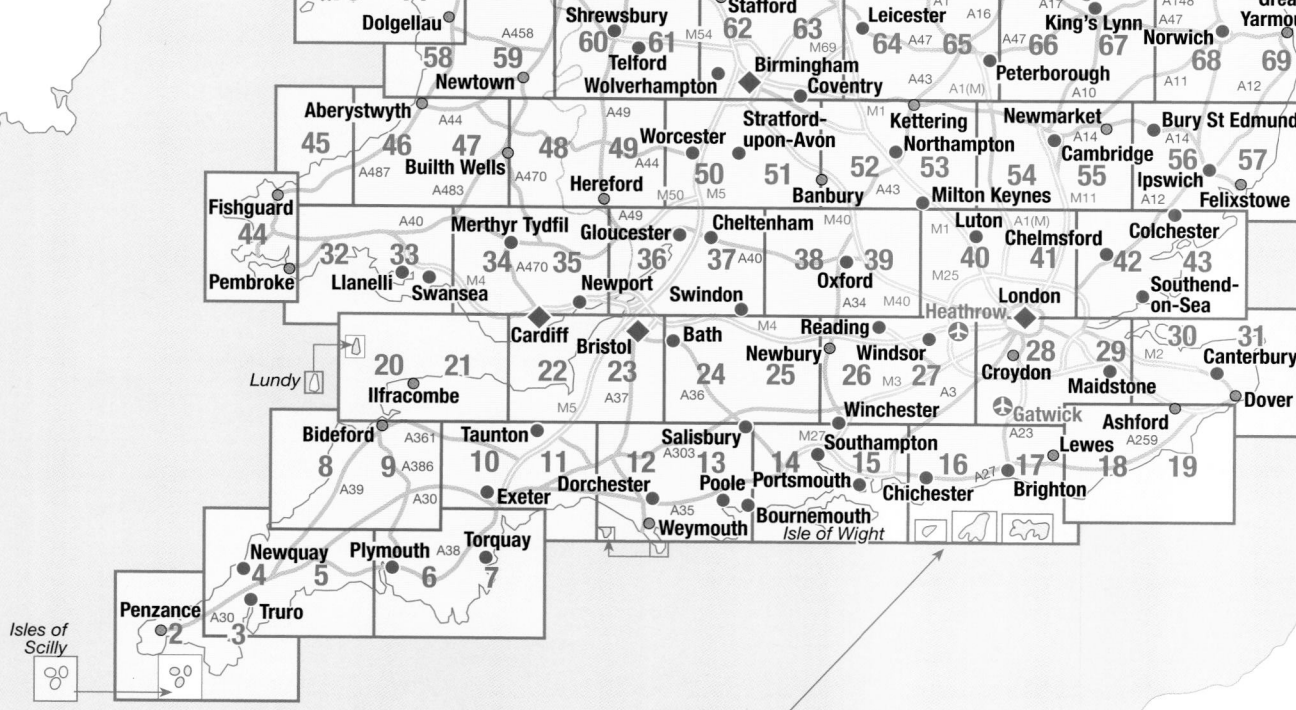

Key to road map pages

- ◆ Town plan and urban approach map
- ● Town plan

78	Map pages at 1:150000 1 cm = 1.5 km ● 1 inch = 2.37 miles
142	Map pages at 1:200000 1 cm = 2.0 km ● 1 inch = 3.16 miles
158	Map pages at 1:250000 1 cm = 2.5 km ● 1 inch = 3.95 miles

(Orkney and Shetland Islands at 1;300000, approximately 4.75 miles to 1 inch)

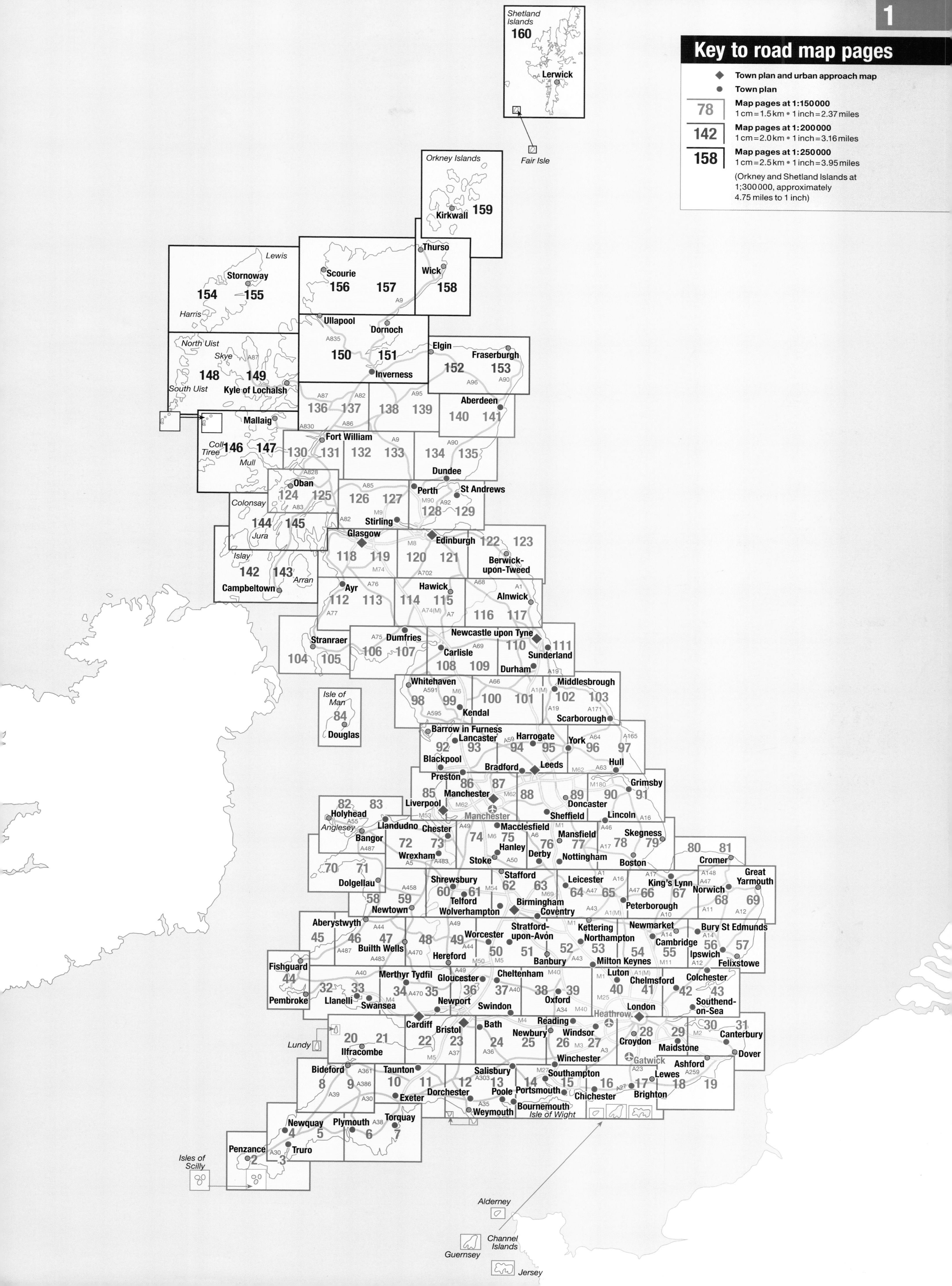

Shetland Islands
160
Lerwick

Fair Isle

Orkney Islands
Kirkwall **159**
Thurso
Wick **158**

Lewis
Stornoway
154 155
Harris
Scourie **156** **157**
North Uist
Skye
148 149
South Uist
Kyle of Lochalsh
Mallaig
Ullapool
Dornoch
150 151
Inverness
Elgin
Fraserburgh
152 153
Aberdeen
140 141

Coll
Tiree **146 147**
136 137 **138 139**
Fort William
130 131 **132 133** **134 135**
Mull
Oban
124 125
126 127
Dundee
Colonsay
144 145
Perth
St Andrews
Jura
Stirling
128 129
Islay
Glasgow
118 119
Edinburgh
120 121
122 123
Berwick-upon-Tweed
142 143
Arran
Ayr
112 113
Hawick
114 115
Alnwick
116 117
Campbeltown
Stranraer
104 105
Dumfries
106 107
Newcastle upon Tyne
110 111
Sunderland
Carlisle
108 109
Durham
Isle of Man
84
Douglas
Whitehaven
98 99
Kendal
100 101
Middlesbrough
102 103
Scarborough
Barrow in Furness
Lancaster
92 93 94 95
York
96 97
Blackpool
Harrogate
Bradford
Leeds
Hull
Preston
85 86 87 88
89 90 91
Grimsby
82 83
Liverpool
Manchester
Holyhead
Anglesey
Llandudno
Chester
72 73 74 75 76 77 78 79
Doncaster
Sheffield
Lincoln
Skegness
Bangor
Macclesfield
Mansfield
70 71
Wrexham
Hanley
Derby
Nottingham
Boston
80 81
Cromer
Dolgellau
Stoke
58 59 60 61 62 63 64 65 66 67
Stafford
Leicester
King's Lynn
Norwich
68 69
Great Yarmouth
Newtown
Telford
Birmingham
Coventry
Peterborough
Aberystwyth
Wolverhampton
45 46 47 48 49
Worcester
Stratford-upon-Avon
Kettering
Northampton
Newmarket
Cambridge
56 57
Bury St Edmunds
Ipswich
Felixstowe
Builth Wells
50 51 52 53 54 55
Hereford
Banbury
Milton Keynes
Fishguard
44
Merthyr Tydfil
32 33 34 35 36 37 38 39
Gloucester
Cheltenham
Luton
40 41 42 43
Colchester
Southend-on-Sea
Pembroke
Llanelli
Swansea
Newport
Swindon
Oxford
London
Lundy
20 21
Cardiff
22 23 24
Bath
Newbury
Windsor
Croydon
28 29 30 31
Canterbury
Ilfracombe
Reading
Maidstone
Dover
Bideford
Taunton
25 26 27
Winchester
Gatwick
Ashford
8 9 10 11 12 13 14 15 16 17 18 19
Salisbury
Southampton
Lewes
Brighton
Dorchester
Poole
Portsmouth
Chichester
Exeter
Weymouth
Bournemouth
Isle of Wight
Newquay
Plymouth
Torquay
4 5 6 7
Penzance
Truro
2 3
Isles of Scilly

Alderney
Channel Islands
Guernsey
Jersey

Isles of Scilly

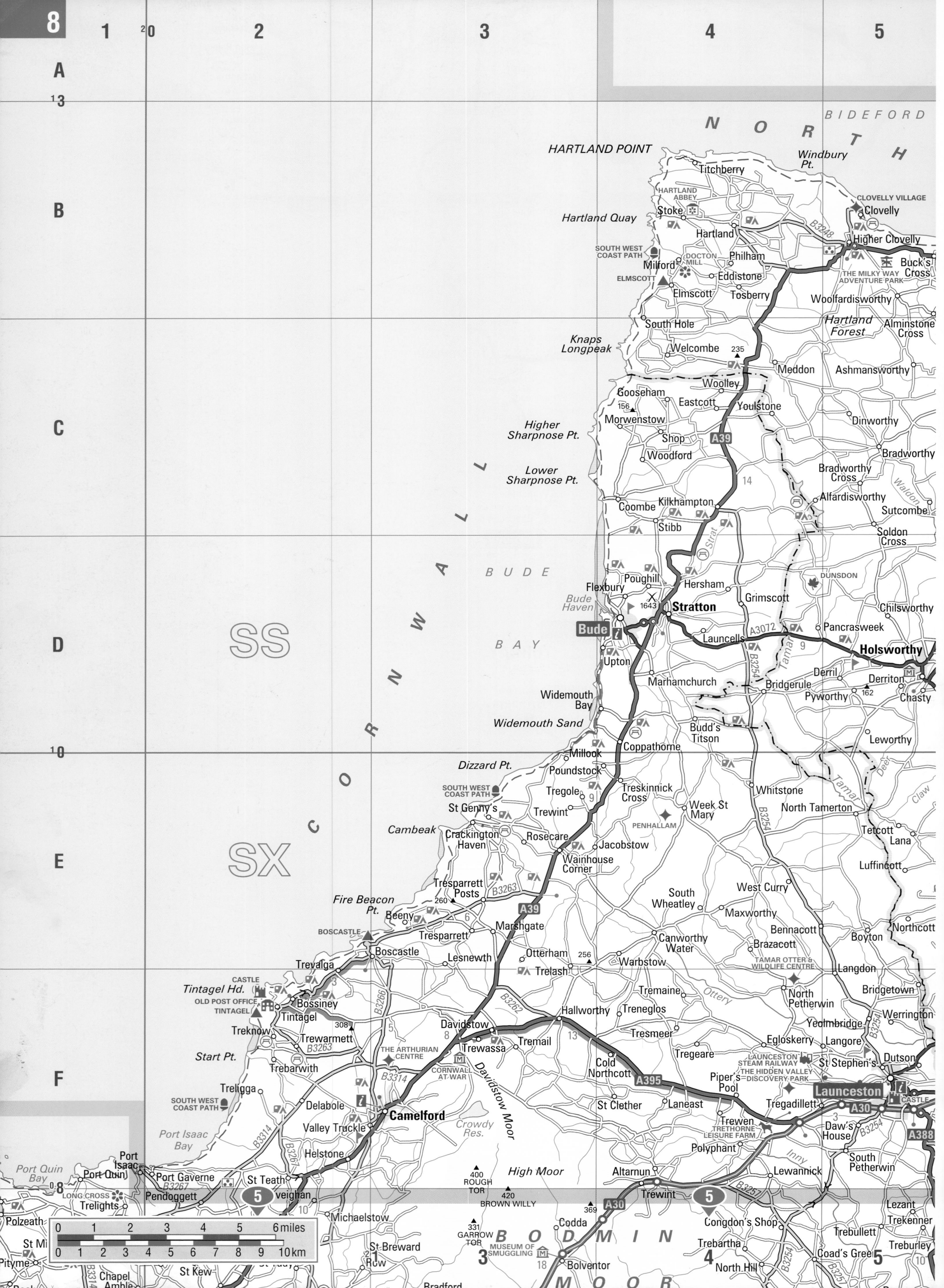

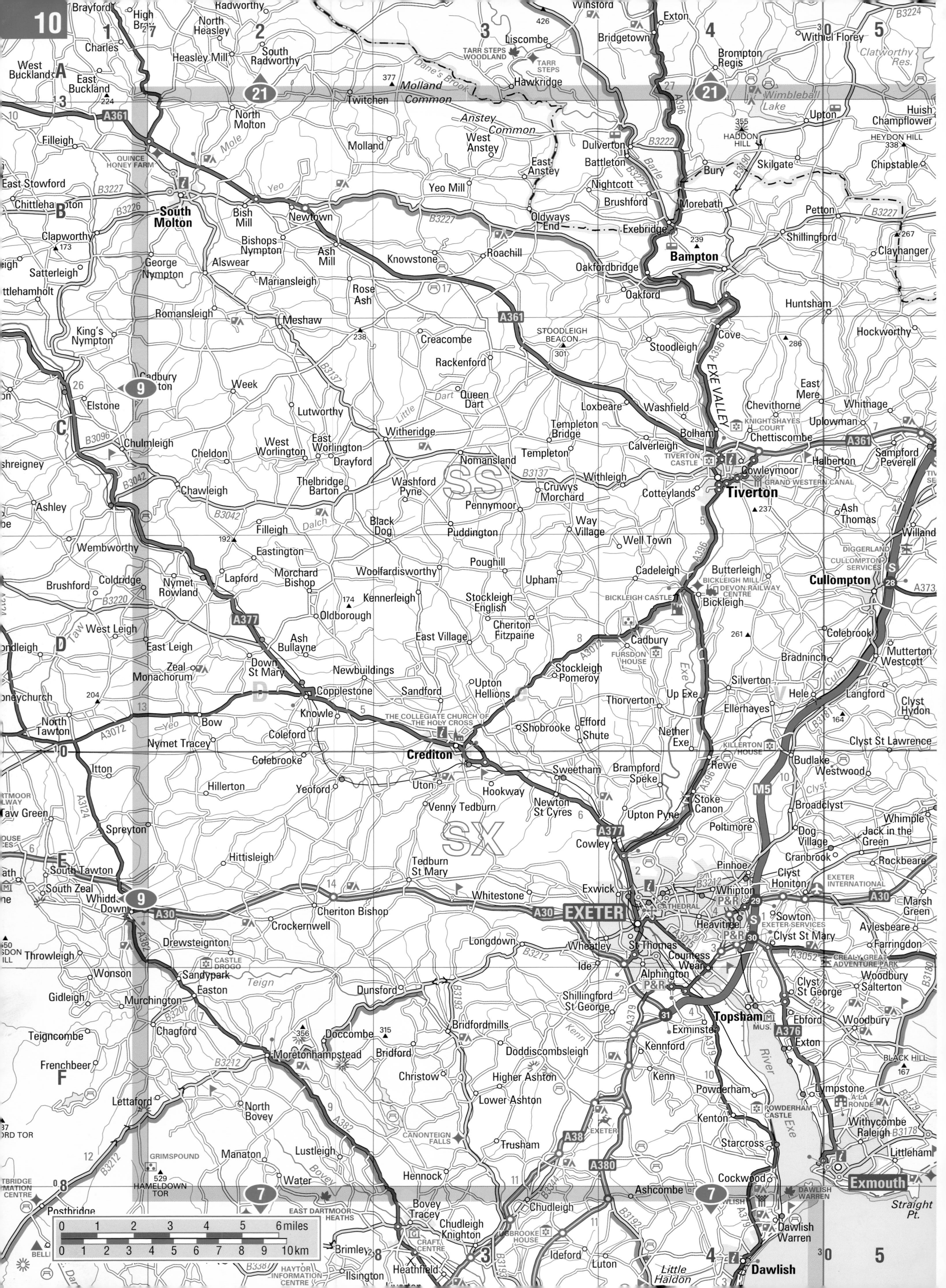

Jersey
approx 2½ miles to 1 inch

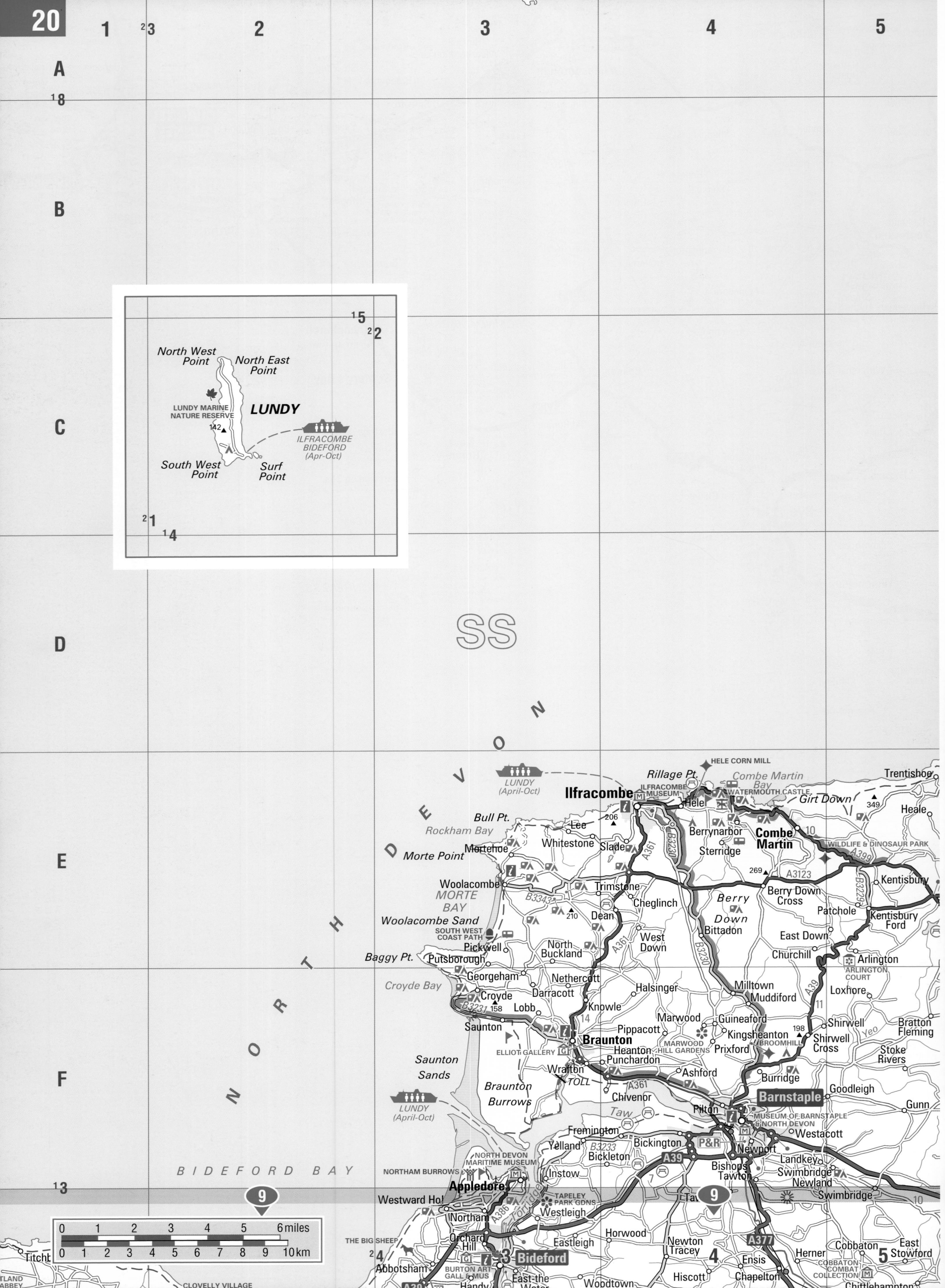

Inset map (Lundy):

North West Point
North East Point
LUNDY MARINE NATURE RESERVE
LUNDY
142 ▲
South West Point
Surf Point
ILFRACOMBE BIDEFORD (Apr-Oct)
¹5
²2
²1
¹4

SS

N O R T H   D E V O N

LUNDY (April-Oct)

Ilfracombe
Rillage Pt.
HELE CORN MILL
Combe Martin Bay
Trentishoe
ILFRACOMBE MUSEUM
WATERMOUTH CASTLE
Girt Down
Heale
349 ▲
Bull Pt.
Rockham Bay
Lee
206
Hele
Berrynarbor
Combe Martin
10
Mortehoe
Whitestone
Slade
Sterridge
WILDLIFE & DINOSAUR PARK
Morte Point
269
Berry Down Cross
Kentisbury
Woolacombe
Trimstone
Berry Down
Patchole
A3123
Kentisbury Ford
MORTE BAY
B3343
Cheglinch
Dean
210
Bittadon
East Down
Woolacombe Sand
West Down
Churchill
Arlington
SOUTH WEST COAST PATH
Pickwell
North Buckland
ARLINGTON COURT
Baggy Pt.
Putsborough
Nethercott
Halsinger
Milltown
Loxhore
11
Georgeham
Darracott
Muddiford
Croyde Bay
Croyde
158
Lobb
Knowle
Marwood
Guineaford
Shirwell
Bratton Fleming
B3231
Saunton
Pippacott
Kingsheanton
198
Shirwell Cross
Yeo
14
MARWOOD HILL GARDENS
Broomhill
Stoke Rivers
Braunton
Heanton
Prixford
ELLIOT GALLERY
Punchardon
Ashford
Burridge
Goodleigh
Saunton Sands
Wrafton
Chivenor
A361
Barnstaple
Gunn
TOLL
Pilton
MUSEUM OF BARNSTAPLE & NORTH DEVON
Westacott
LUNDY (April-Oct)
Braunton Burrows
Taw
Fremington
Bickington
A39
Newport
Landkey
B3233
Yelland
P&R
Bishops Tawton
Swimbridge Newland
BIDEFORD BAY
NORTH DEVON MARITIME MUSEUM
Instow
7
Swimbridge
9
Appledore
NORTHAM BURROWS
LTaw
9
Westward Ho!
TAPELEY PARK GDNS
Northam
Westleigh
Horwood
Newton Tracey
A377
Herner
Cobbaton
East Stowford
THE BIG SHEEP
Eastleigh
COBBATON COMBAT COLLECTION
Orchard Hill
3
Bideford
4
Ensis
5
Abbotsham
BURTON ART GALL & MUS
East-the-Water
Woodtown
Hiscott
Chapelton
CLOVELLY VILLAGE
A39
Handy
Chittlehampton

Scale bar:
0 1 2 3 4 5 6 miles
0 1 2 3 4 5 6 7 8 9 10 km

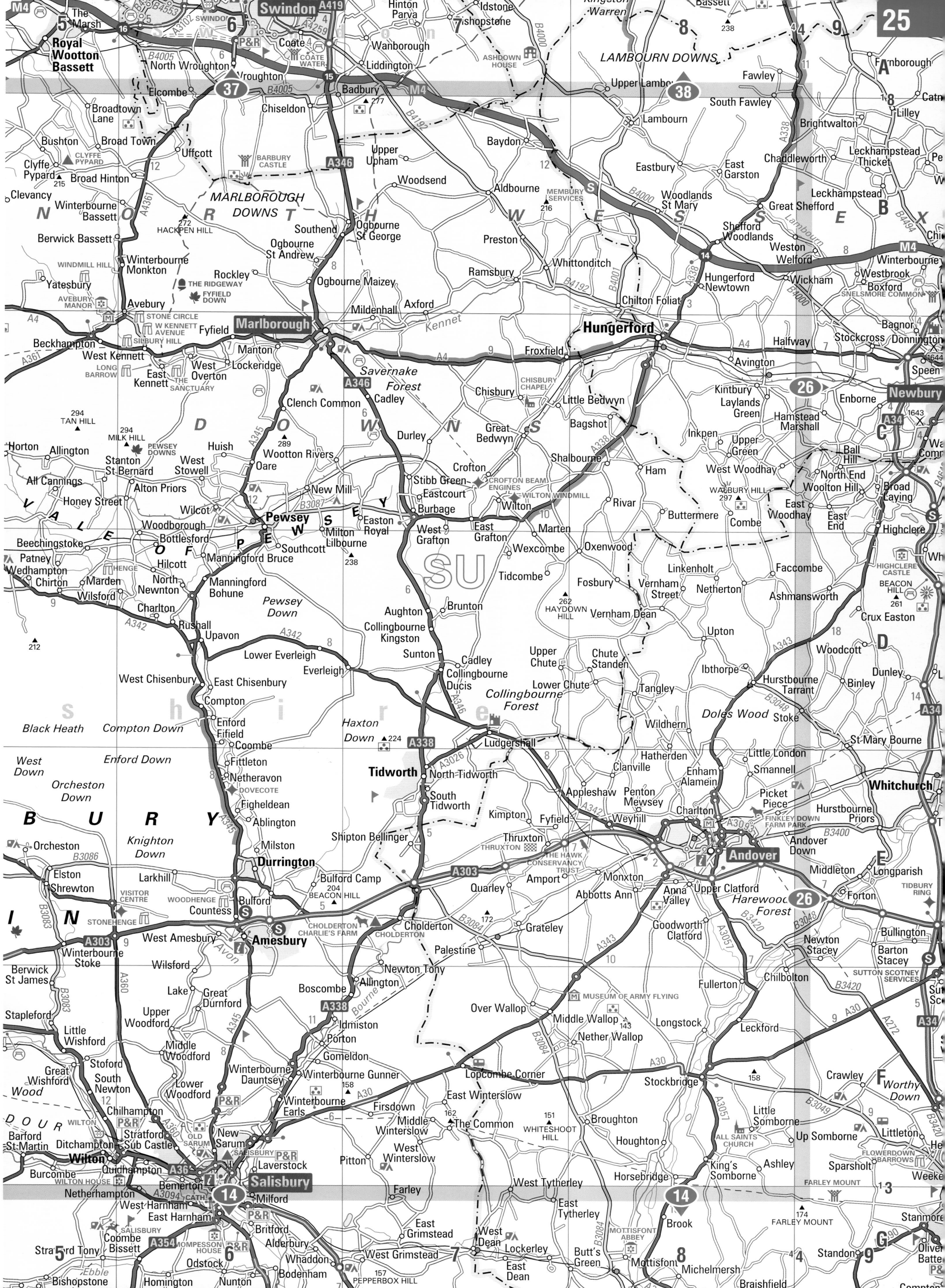

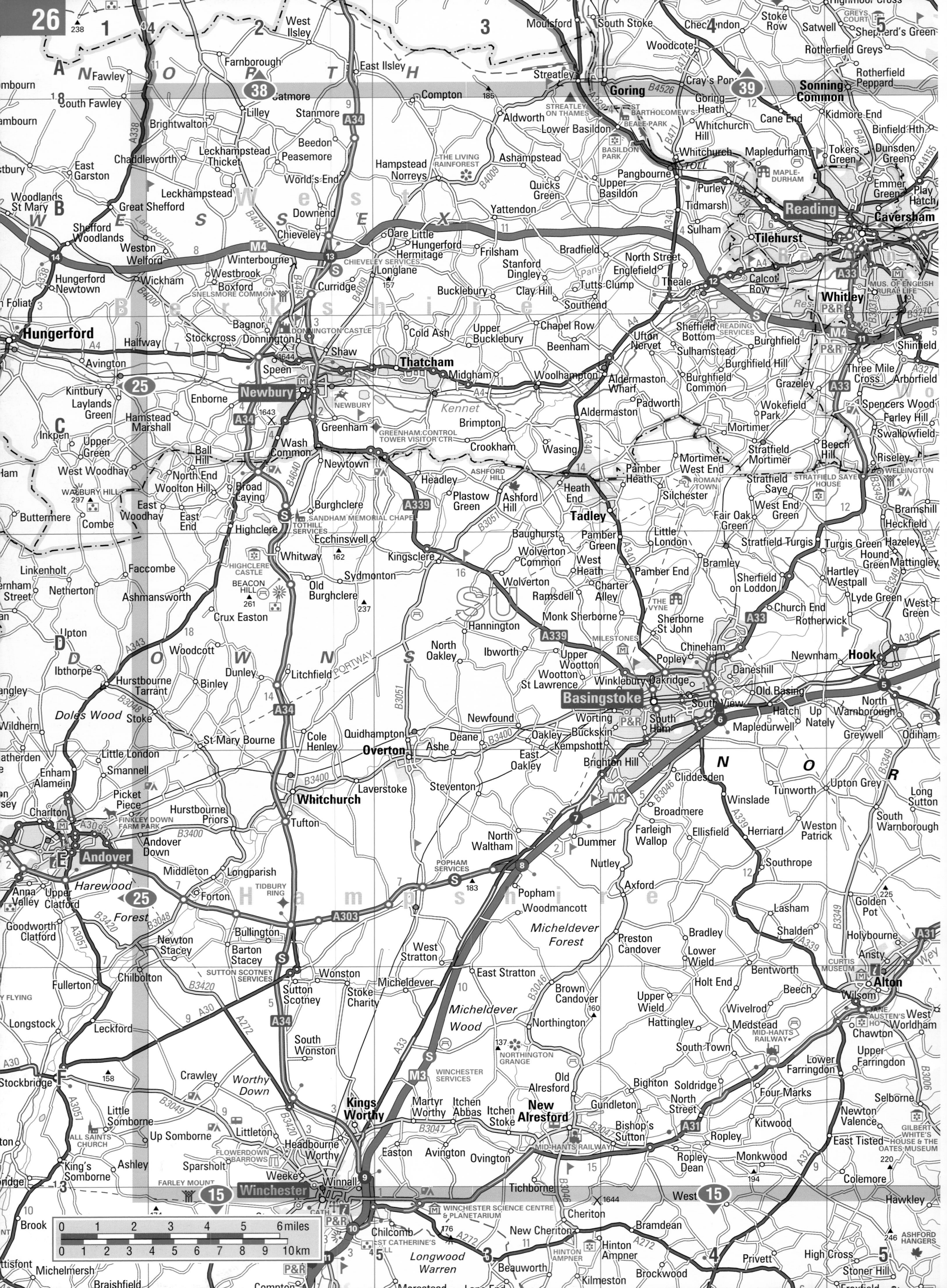

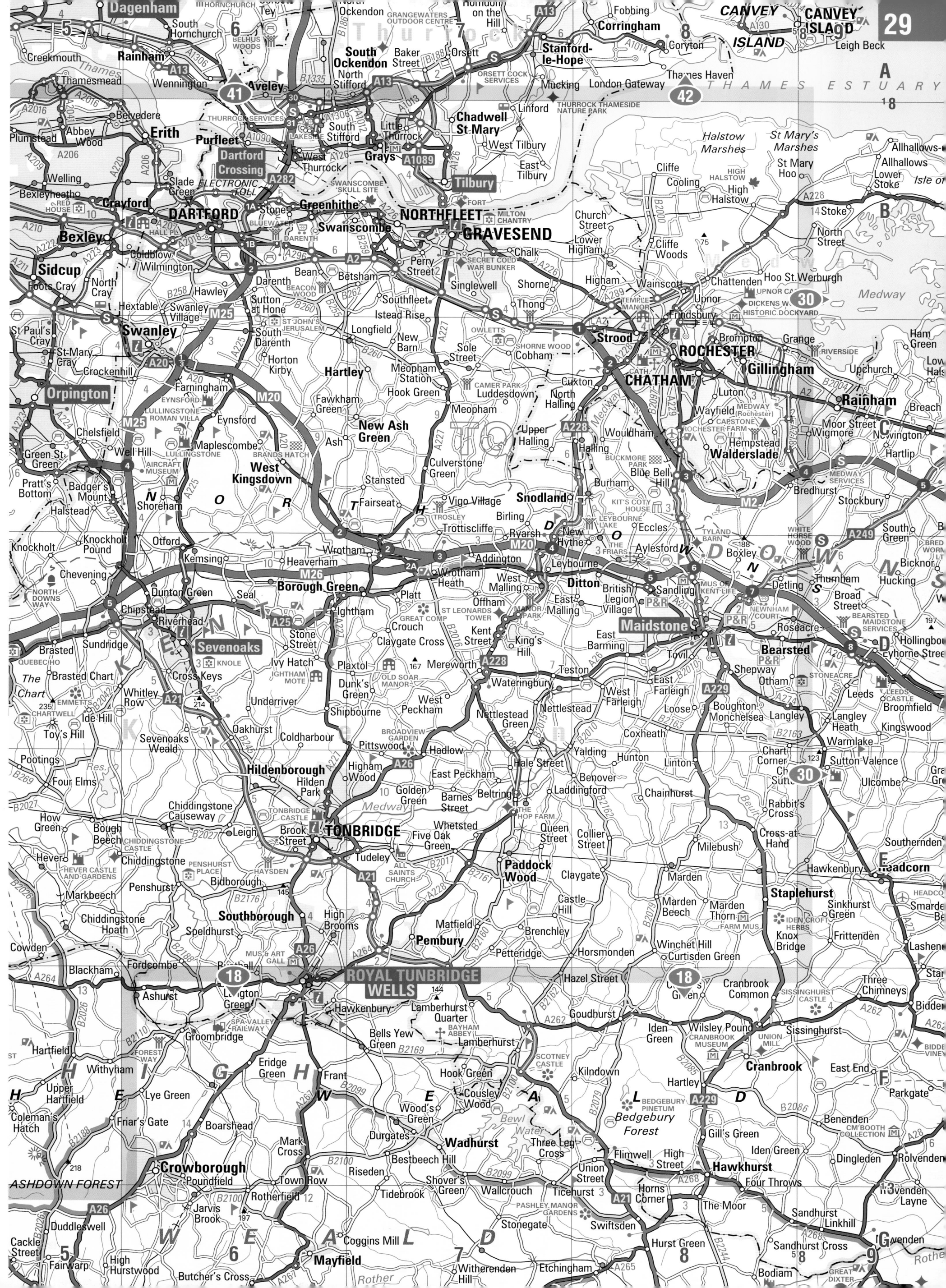

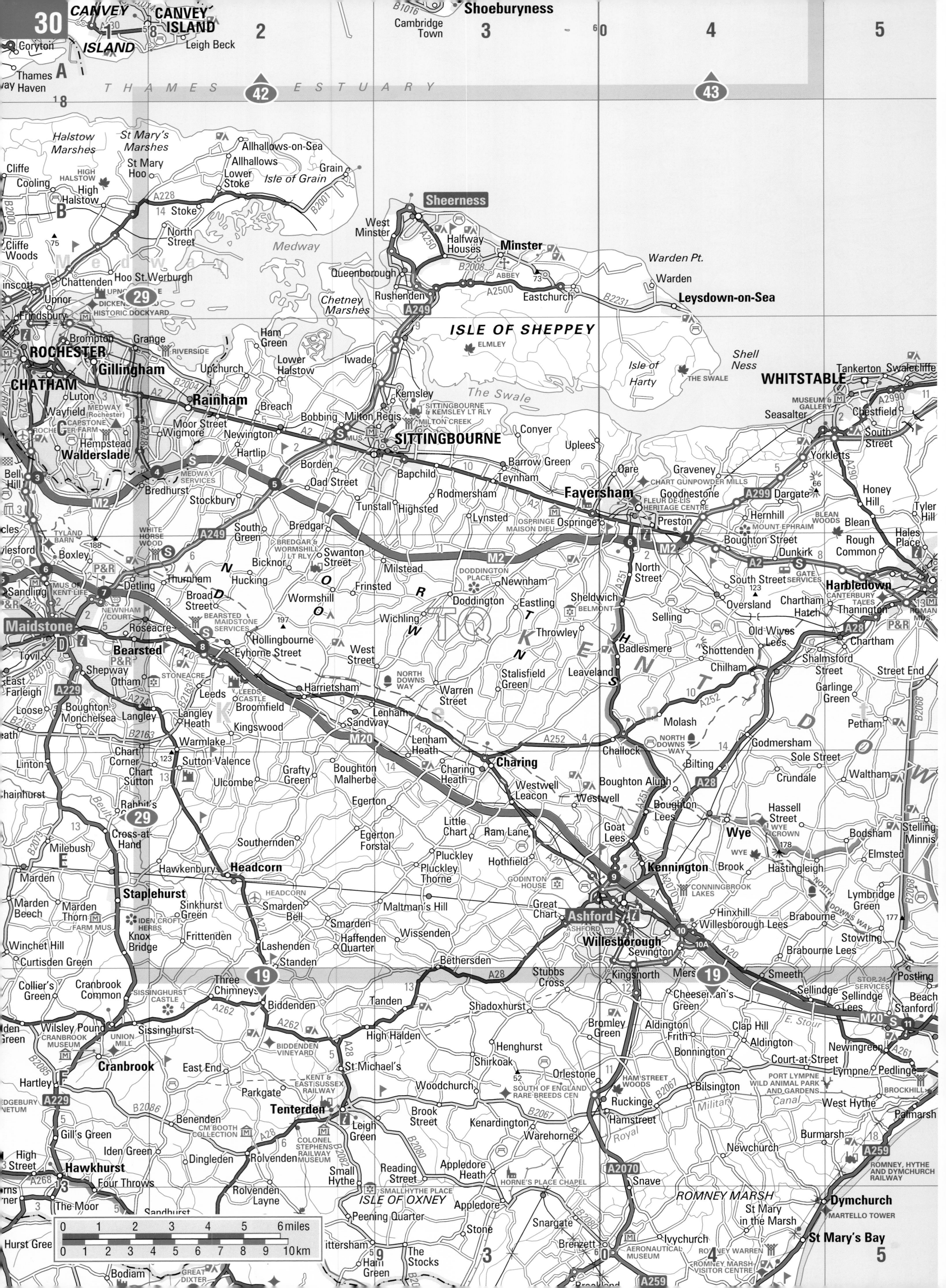

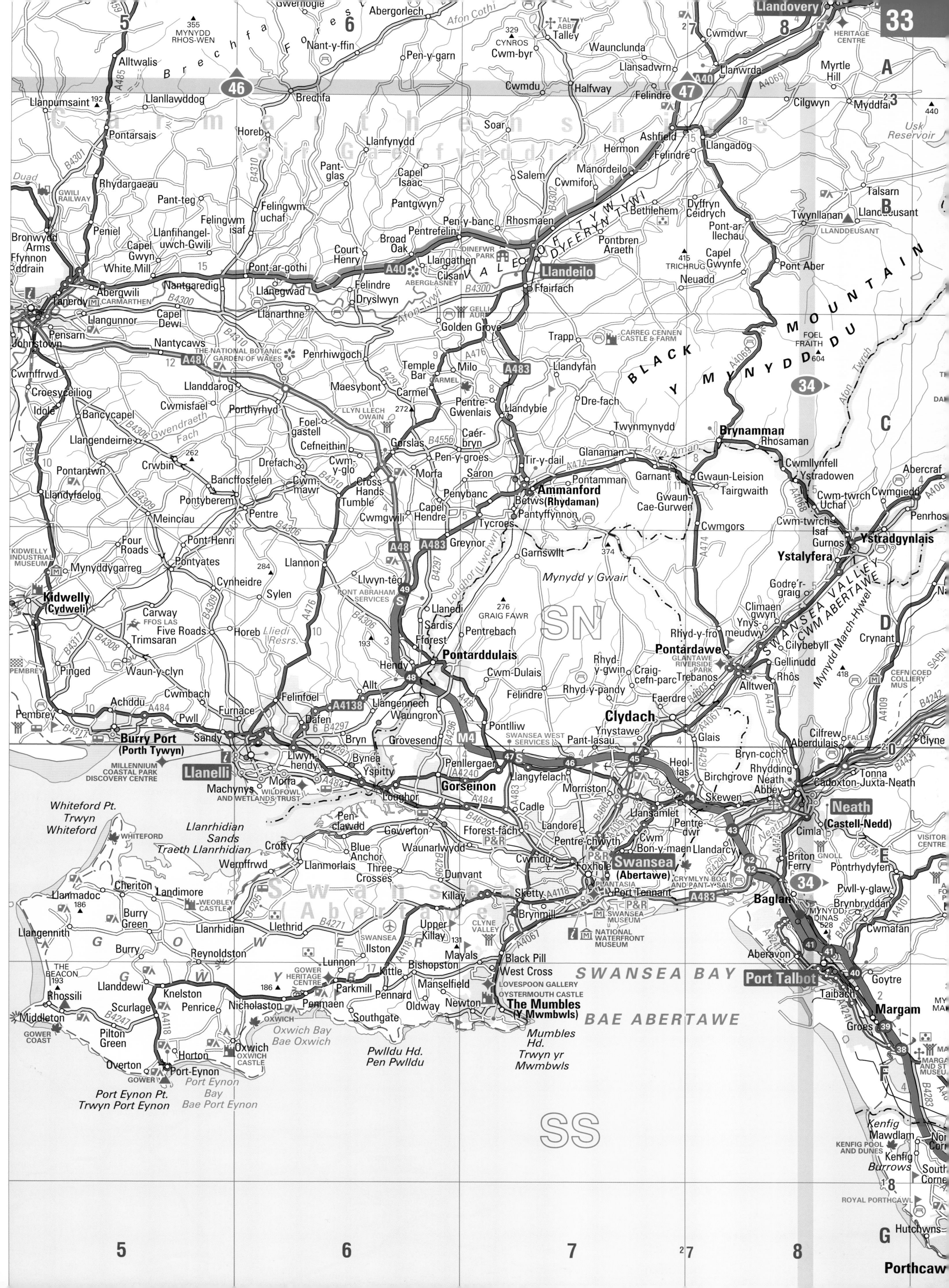

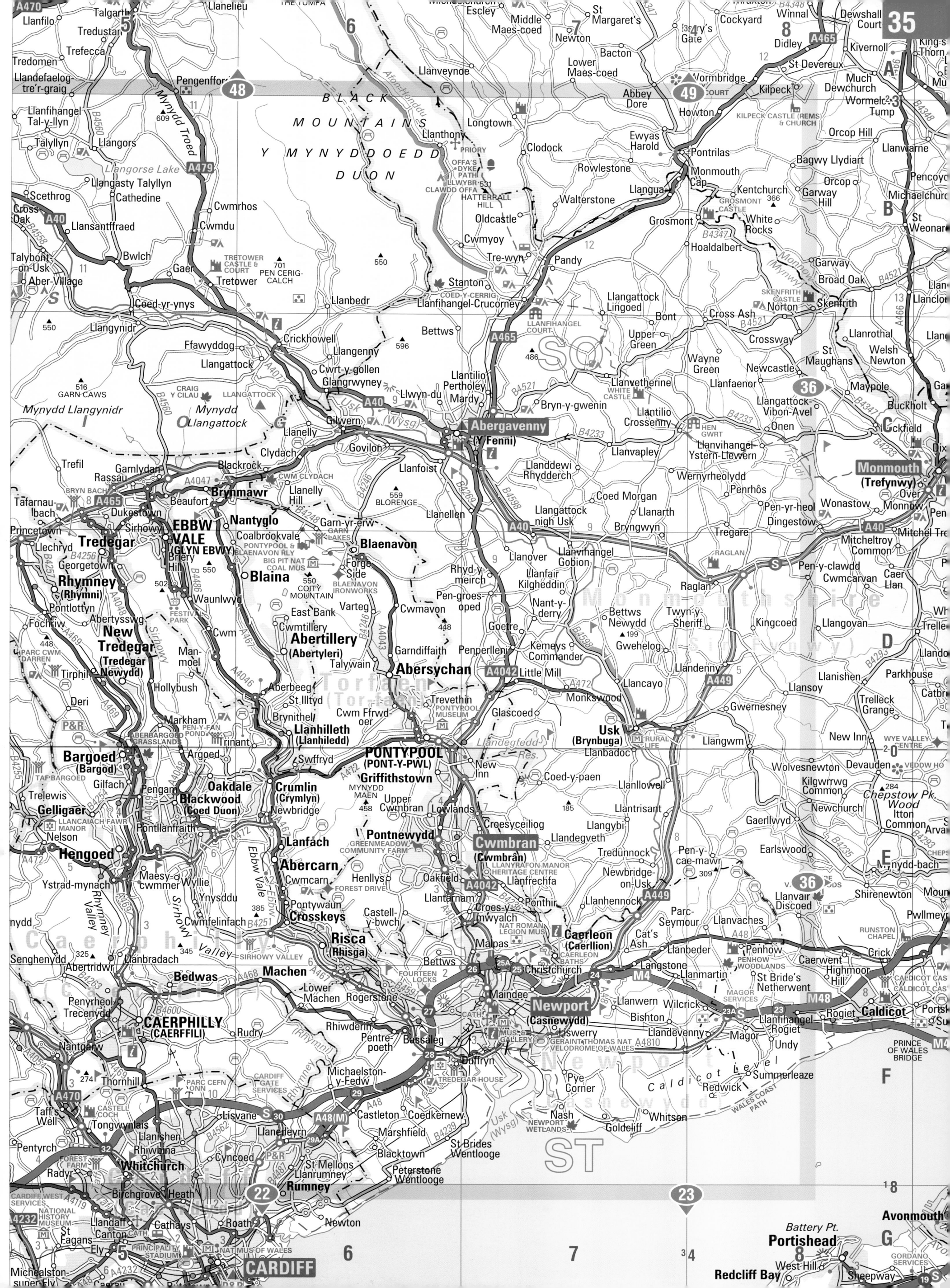

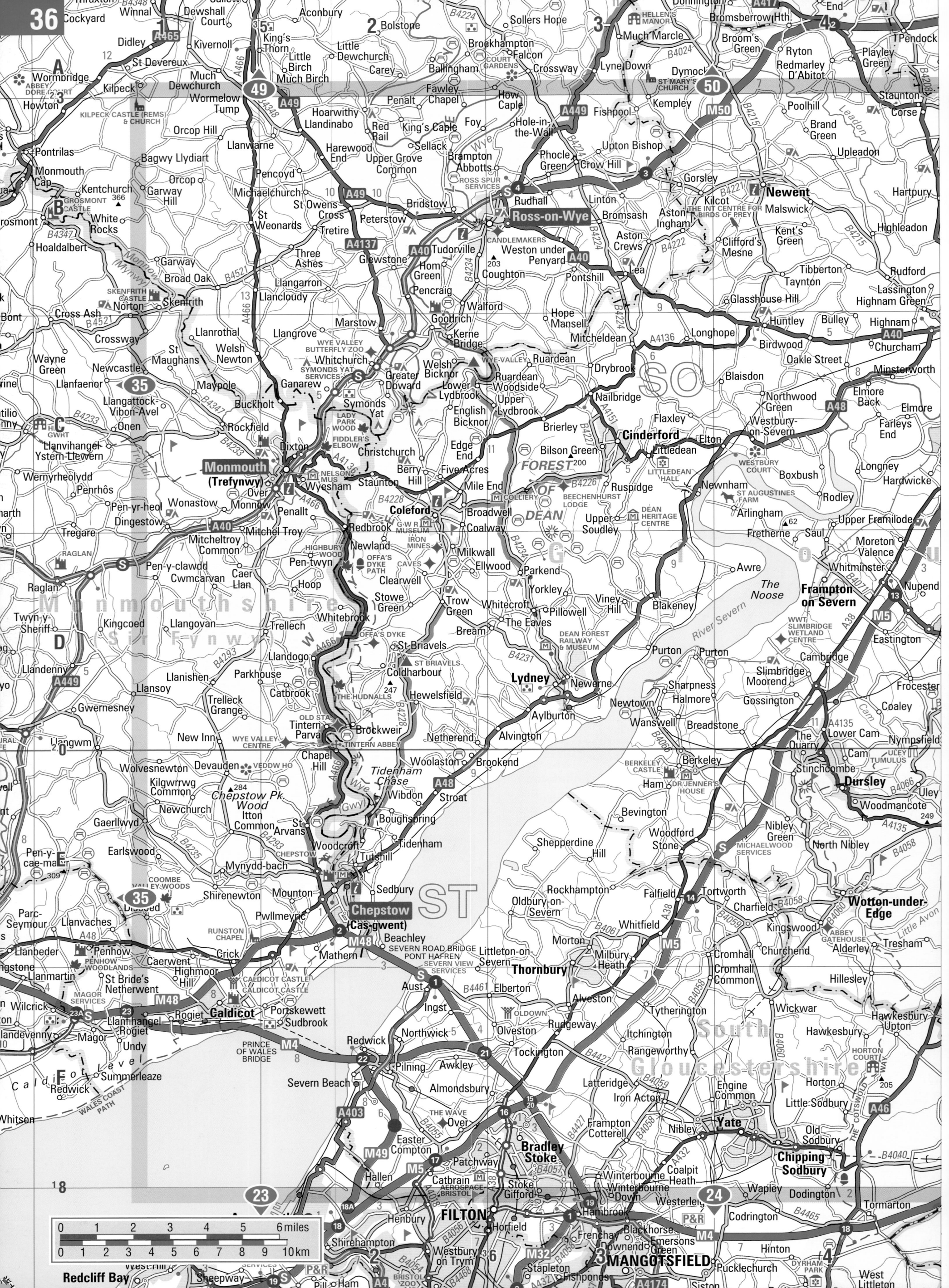

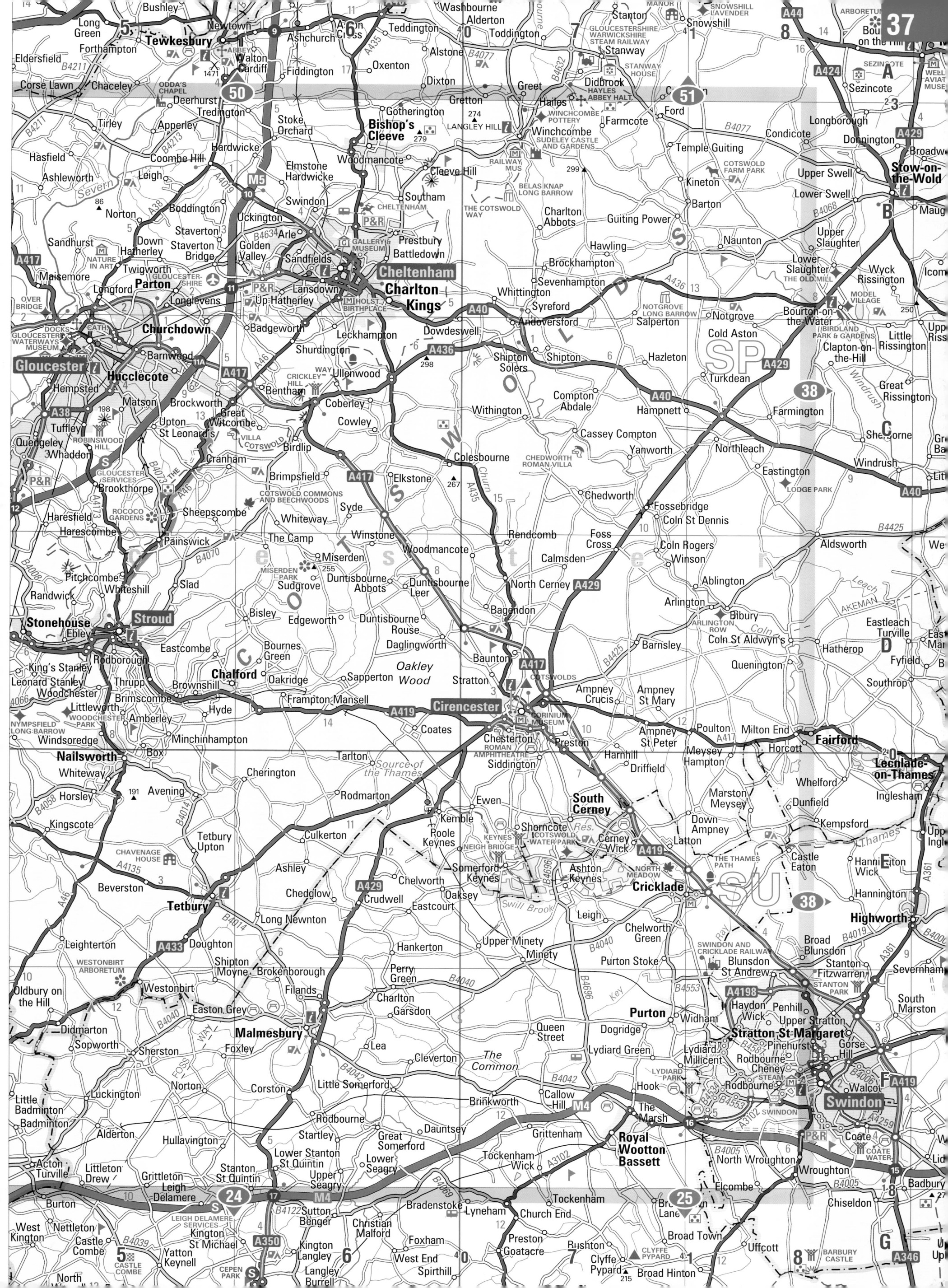

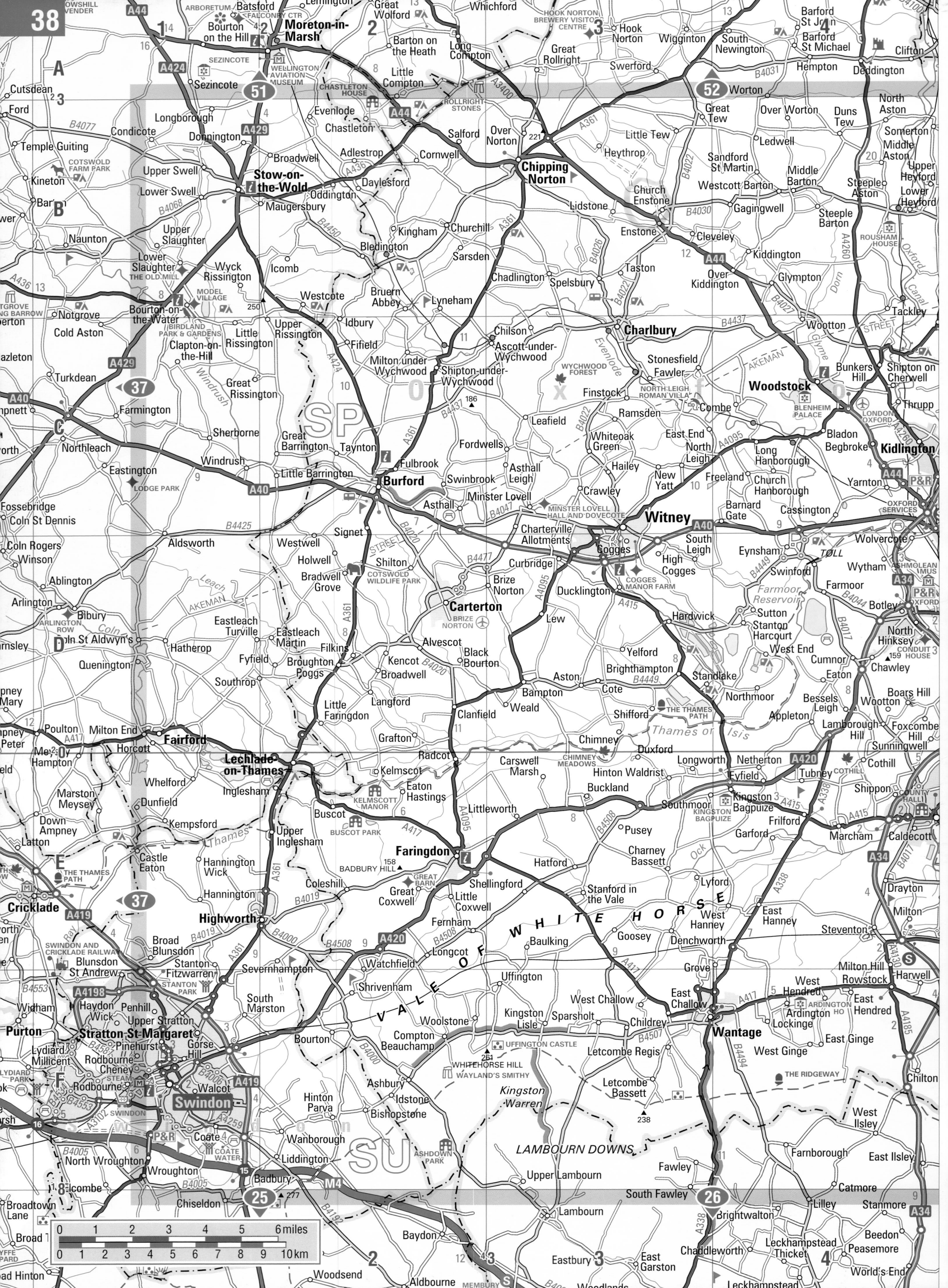

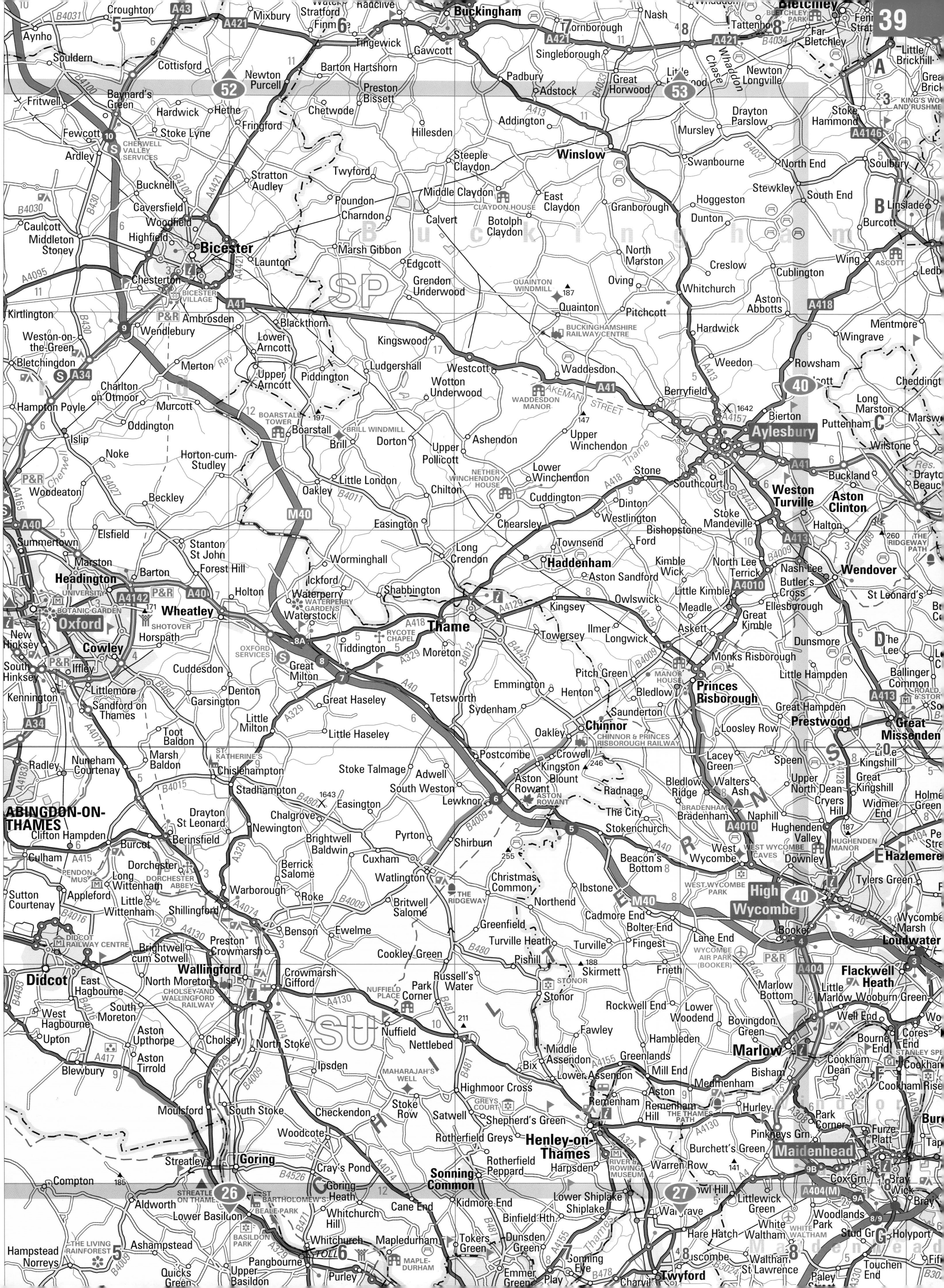

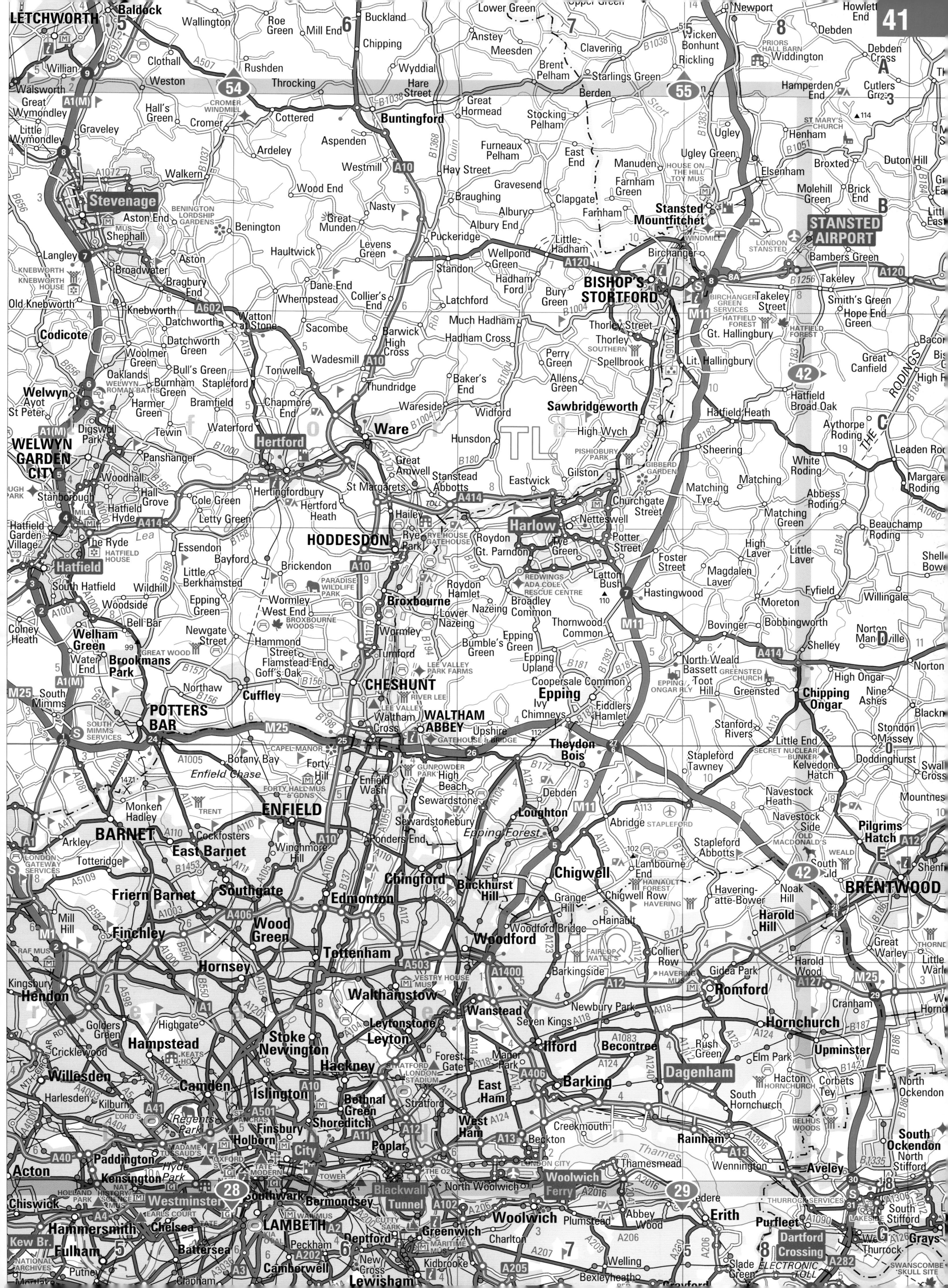

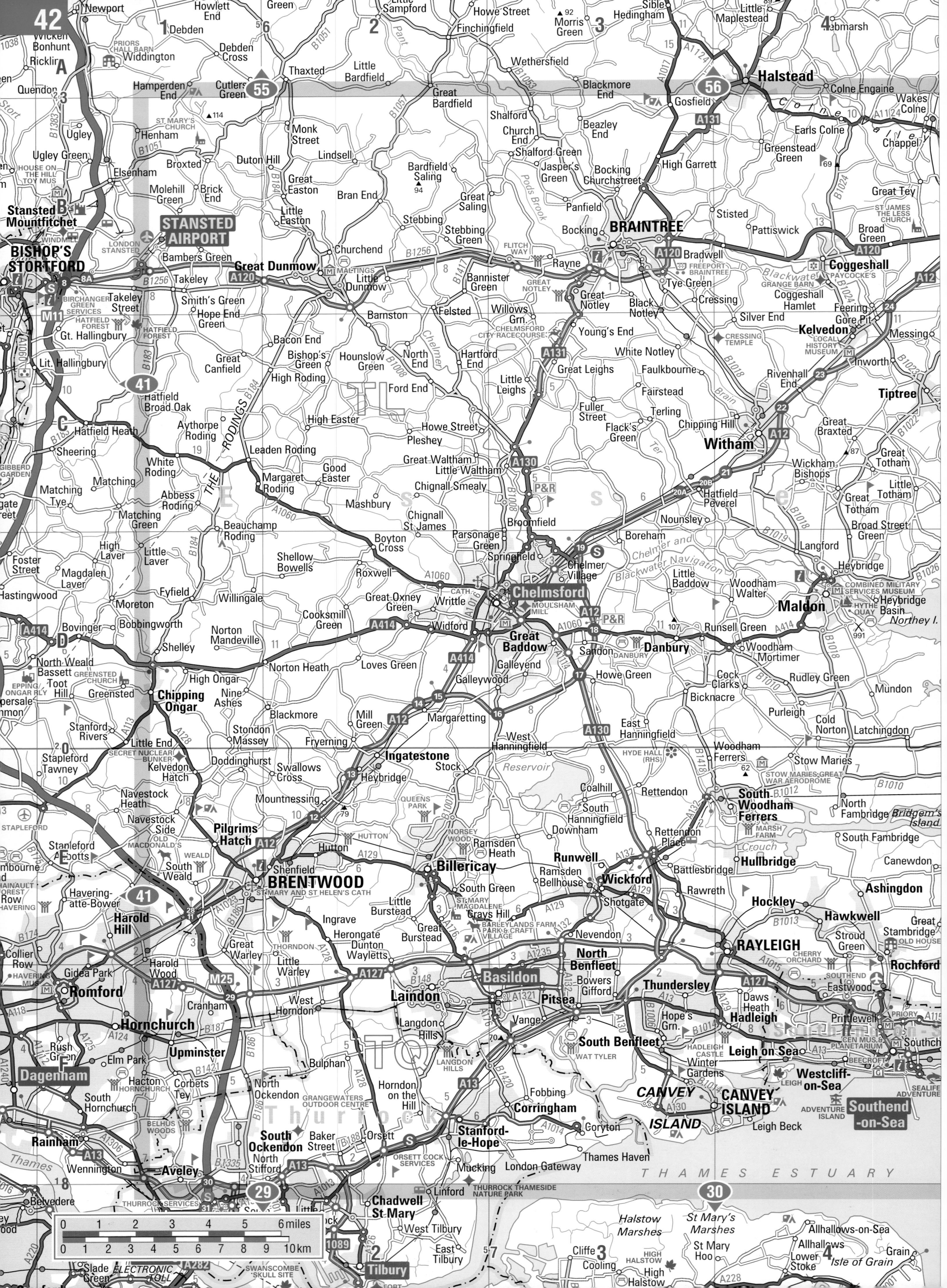

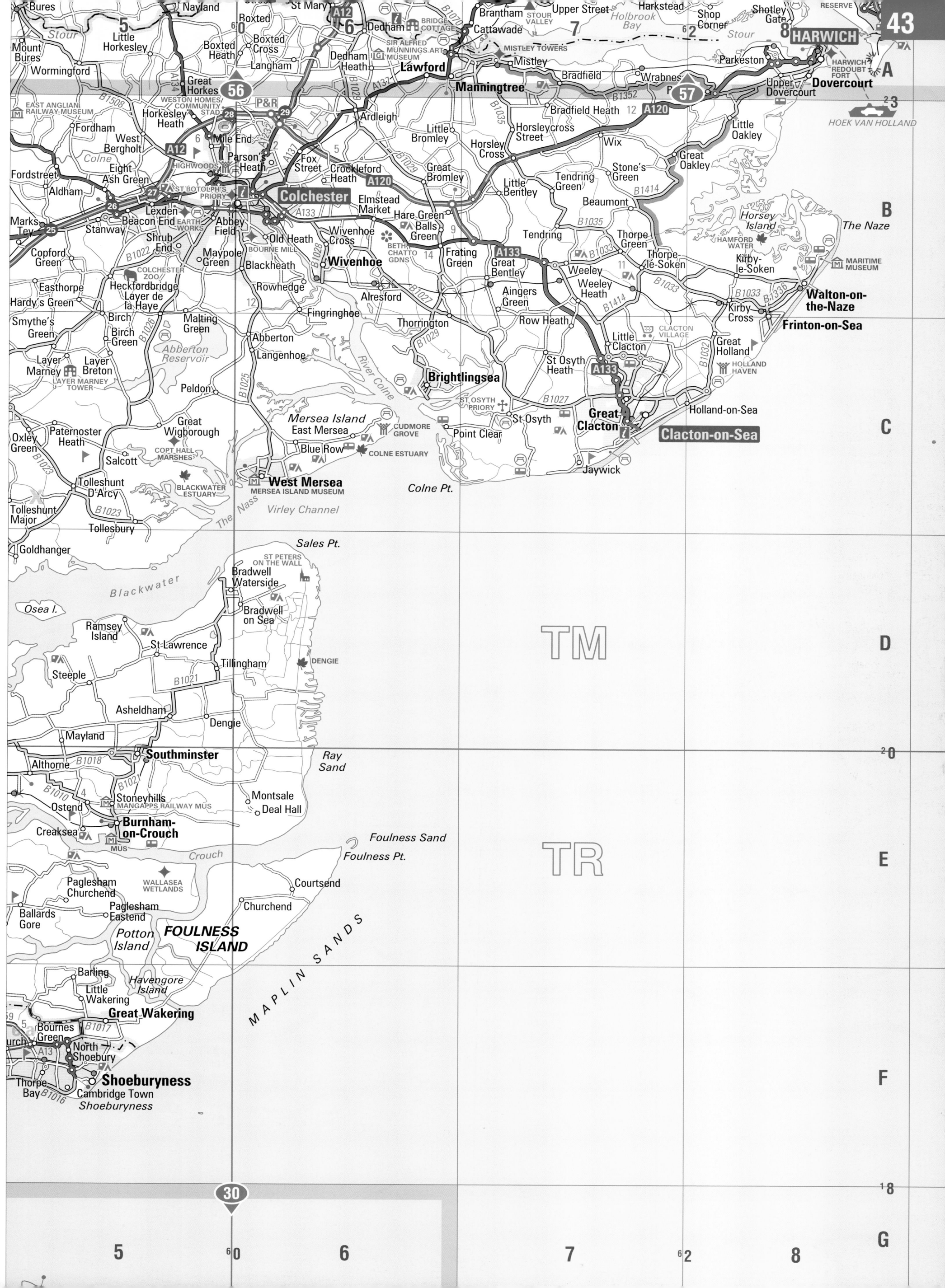

Stour
5
Bures
Little Horkesley
Mount Bures
Wormingford
Nayland
Boxted
Boxted Heath
Boxted Cross
Langham
St Mary
A12
6
Dedham
Dedham Heath
SIR ALFRED MUNNINGS MUSEUM
BRIDGE COTTAGE
Lawford
Brantham
Cattawade
Mistley Towers
Mistley
STOUR VALLEY
Upper Street
7
Holbrook Bay
Harkstead
Shop Corner
Shotley Gate
8
HARWICH
RESERVE
HARWICH REDOUBT FORT
A
Dovercourt
Upper Dovercourt

EAST ANGLIAN RAILWAY MUSEUM
Fordham
West Bergholt
Eight Ash Green
Aldham
Fordstreet
Colne
Great Horkes
B1508
56
HORKESLEY HEATH
WESTON HOMES/ COMMUNITY STAD
P&R
B1029
29
28
A12
Mile End
6
HIGHWOODS
Parson's Heath
Fox Street
Crockleford Heath
Great Bromley
Ardleigh
Little Bromley
Horsley Cross
Horsleycross Street
Wix
Bradfield
Wrabness
B1352
Bradfield Heath
12
A120
57
Little Oakley
Great Oakley
Stone's Green
Hoek van Holland
2 3
Parkeston
HOEK VAN HOLLAND

Marks Tey
25
Copford Green
Easthorpe
Stanway
Beacon End
Lexden
27
A12
ST BOTOLPH'S PRIORY
EARTH WORKS
26
Colchester
A133
Highwoods
Abbey Field
Old Heath
Wivenhoe Cross
BOURNE MILL
Elmstead Market
BETH CHATTO GDNS
Frating Green
Hare Green
Balls Green
Tendring
9
Great Bromley
Little Bentley
Tendring Green
Beaumont
B1414
Thorpe Green
Thorpe-le-Soken
B1035
B1035
Horsey Island
HAMFORD WATER
The Naze
B
MARITIME MUSEUM

Heckfordbridge
Layer de la Haye
Shrub End
Maypole Green
Blackheath
Rowhedge
Alresford
B1027
Fingringhoe
Great Bentley
Aingers Green
Weeley
Weeley Heath
11
B1033
Kirby Cross
Kirby-le-Soken
B1033
B1336
Walton-on-the-Naze
Frinton-on-Sea

Hardy's Green
Smythe's Green
Birch
Birch Green
Malting Green
B1026
Abberton Reservoir
Layer Marney
Layer Breton
LAYER MARNEY TOWER
Great Wigborough
COLCHESTER ZOO
Abberton
Langenhoe
Peldon
B1025
12
River Colne
B1029
Thorrington
Row Heath
A133
Little Clacton
Great Holland
CLACTON VILLAGE
HOLLAND HAVEN

Oxley Green
Paternoster Heath
Salcott
Tolleshunt D'Arcy
Tolleshunt Major
Goldhanger
B1023
B1023
COPT HALL MARSHES
BLACKWATER ESTUARY
The Nass
West Mersea
MERSEA ISLAND MUSEUM
Mersea Island
East Mersea
Blue Row
CUDMORE GROVE
COLNE ESTUARY
Point Clear
St Osyth
ST OSYTH PRIORY
St Osyth Heath
A133
Great Clacton
Jaywick
Holland-on-Sea
Clacton-on-Sea
C

Virley Channel
Blackwater
Osea I.
Ramsey Island
St Lawrence
Steeple
Tillingham
Sales Pt.
ST PETERS ON THE WALL
Bradwell Waterside
Bradwell on Sea
DENGIE
TM
D
2 0

Mayland
Althorne
B1018
Southminster
B1021
Asheldham
Dengie
B1010
B1021
4
Stoneyhills
MANGAPPS RAILWAY MUS
Ostend
Creaksea
Burnham-on-Crouch
MUS
Crouch
Ray Sand
Montsale
Deal Hall
Foulness Sand
Foulness Pt.
TR
E

Paglesham Churchend
WALLASEA WETLANDS
Ballards Gore
Paglesham Eastend
Potton Island
FOULNESS ISLAND
Courtsend
Churchend
MAPLIN SANDS

Barling
Little Wakering
Havengore Island
Great Wakering
B1017
MAPLIN SANDS

Bournes Green
North Shoebury
A13
Thorpe Bay
B1016
Shoeburyness
Cambridge Town
Shoeburyness
F
1 8

30
G

5
0
6
0
6
7
6 2
8

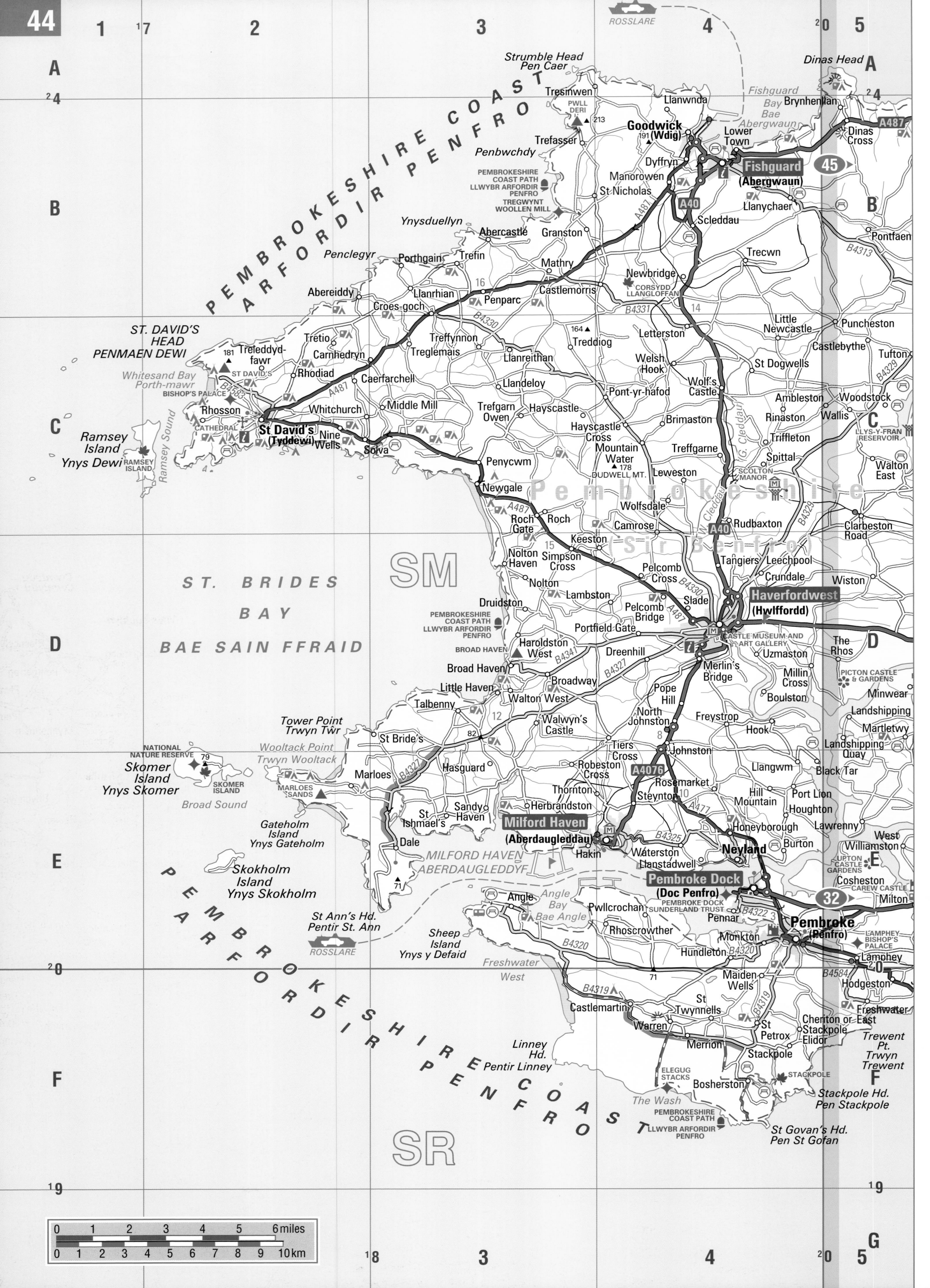

A B C D E F G

1 2 3 4 5

C A R D I G A N

B A Y

B A E

C E R E D I G I O N

SN

46

Cwmtudu
Cwmtydu

Ynys-Lochtyn

Blaencelyn
Llangrannog
Pontgarreg
Plwm

Penbryn
Parcllyn
Tresaith
Penmorfa
Pent
Felinwynt
Aberporth
Brynhoffnant
Blaenannerch
Tan-y-groes
Sarnau
ABERPORTH
WEST WALES
AIRPORT
A487
Penparc
Tremain
16
Blaenporth
Glynarthen
Rhydlewis
Penrhiw
Coed
Bettws
Ifan
Hawen
Beulah
Cemaes Head
Pen Cemaes
Cardigan I.
Ynys
Aberteifi
Gwbert
Y Ferwig
Pantgwyn
Ponthirwaun
Bryngwyn
Brongest
Troed-yr-aur
Maesllyn
Cardigan
(Aberteifi)
CASTLE
Llangoedmor
A4570
185
Capel
Tygwydd
46
POPPIT SANDS
Cippyn
St-Dogmaels
ABBEY
Bridgend
A484
COEDMOR
Llechryd
Llandygwydd
Aber-banc
Llandyfriog
PEMBROKESHIRE COAST
ARFORDIR PENFRO
Moylgrove
Penyr-
bryn
CILGERRAN
CASTLE
Cilgerran
Carreg-wen
11
Cwm-cou
PEMBROKESHIRE COAST PATH
LLWYBR ARFORDIR PENFRO
Monington
Croft
Bridell
Rhos-hill
CORACLE CENTRE
& FLOURMILL
Cenarth
Newcastle
Emlyn
(Castell Newydd
Emlyn)
Pentrecagal
Aber-
Arad
Fishguard Bay
Bae Abergwaun
Newport
Bay
Bae
Trefdraeth
Glanrhyd
197
Pontgareg
Llantood
Abercych
NATIONAL
WOOL
MUSEUM
Llange
Drefa
Berry
Hill
Nevern
Felindre
Farchog
A487
Newchapel
Penrherber
Cilwendeg
CHEESE
FARM
Cwmhiraeth
Drefe
Brynhenllan
Dinas
Cross
PEMBROKESHIRE
Parrog
Newport
(Trefdraeth)
PENGELLI
FOREST
Eglwyswrw
Boncath
CLYNFYW
Felindre
Lower
Town
A487
CARNINGLI
CASTELL
HENLLYS
FORT
TY CANOL
Llanfair-
Nant-Gwyn
Blaenffos
Bwlchygroes
Capel Iwan
Cwmpe
Fishguard
(Abergwaun)
Cilgwyn
Crosswell
DYFED SHIRE
HORSE FARM
Afon Nevern
Eglwyswen
Cwmcych
Clydey
Cwmorgan
MOELFRE
335
Lla Fychaer
Pontyglasier
Penygroes
Star
Tanglwst
Brynberian
395
44
Pontfaen
MYNYDD PRESELI
Crymych
Tegryn
Bryn-Iwan
Hermon
Trecwn
B4313
468
Pentre-galar
Hermon
Hen-feddau
fawr
247
B4299
Little
Newcastle
Puncheston
Castlebythe
536
FOEL-
CWMCERWYN
New Inn
Rosebush
32
Mynachlog-ddu
Llanfyrnach
Dinas
Trelech
32
289
enclochog
Glandwr
20
Pen-y-bont
Ambleston
Woodstock
Glandy
Cross
Pant-y-
Caws
Hebron
Blaen-
waun
Llanwinio
Talog
Rinaston
Wallis
New Moat
Llan olman
Llanglydwen
Cefn-y-pant
Cwmbach

0 1 2 3 4 5 6miles
0 1 2 3 4 5 6 7 8 9 10km

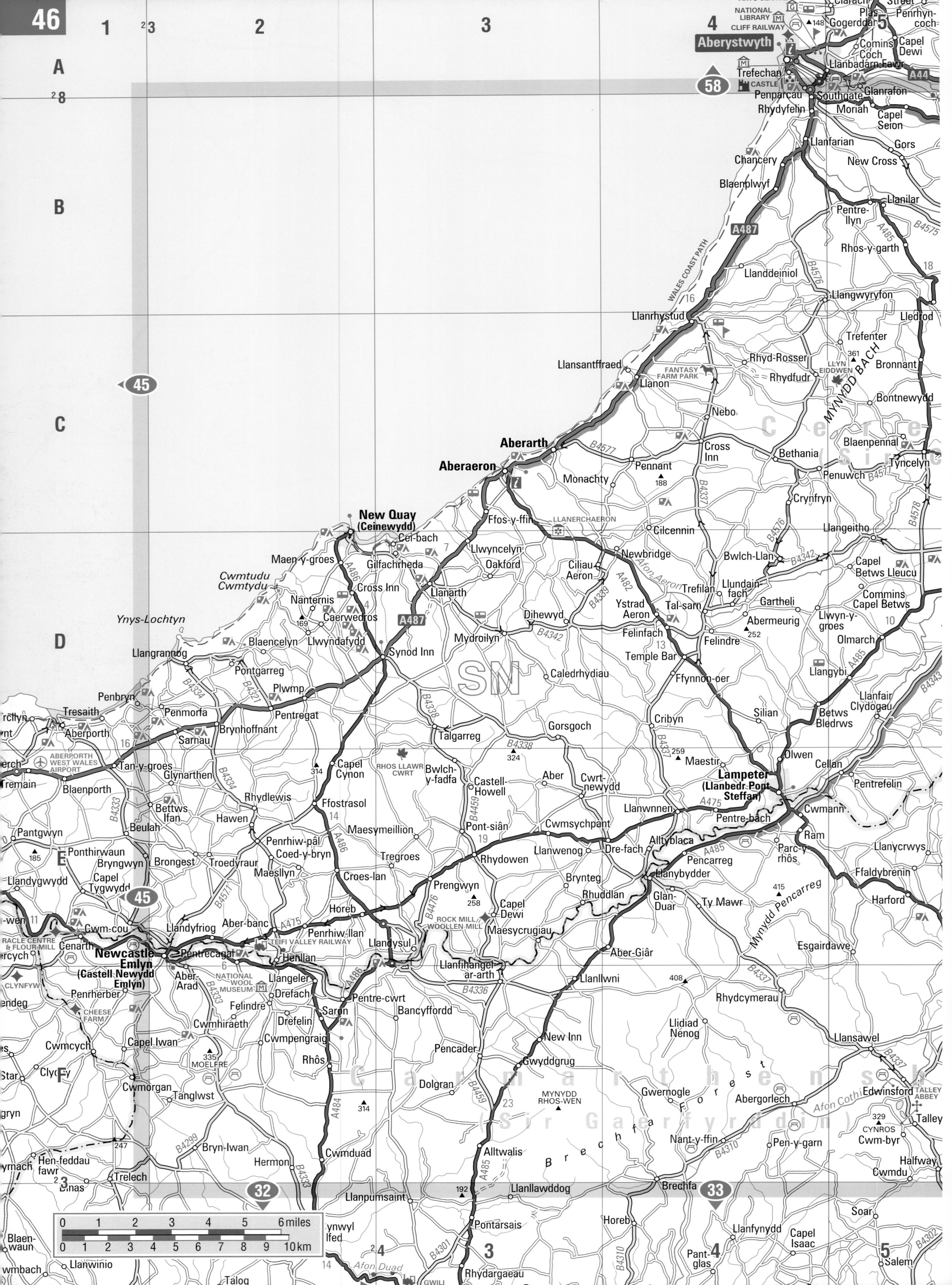

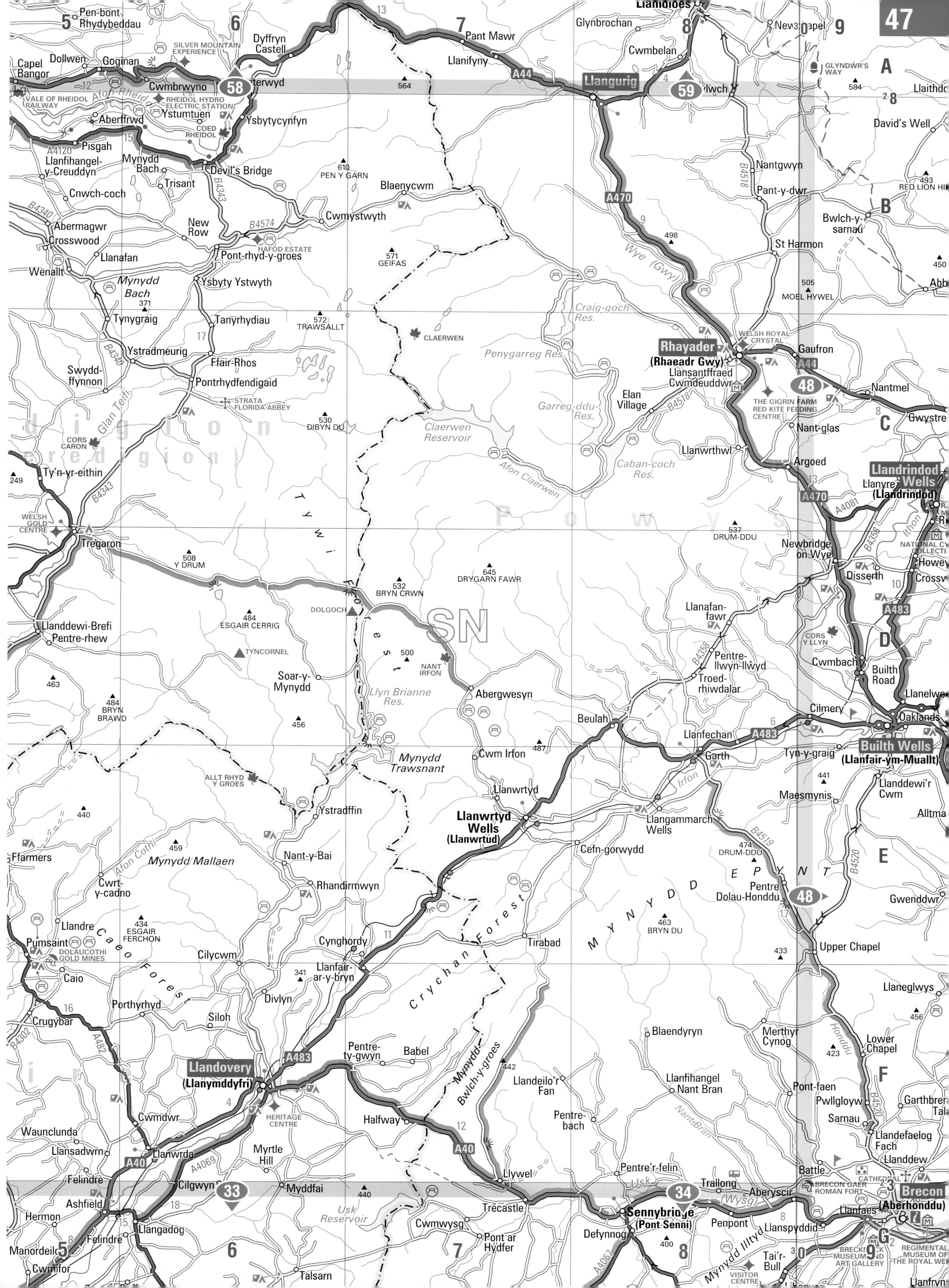

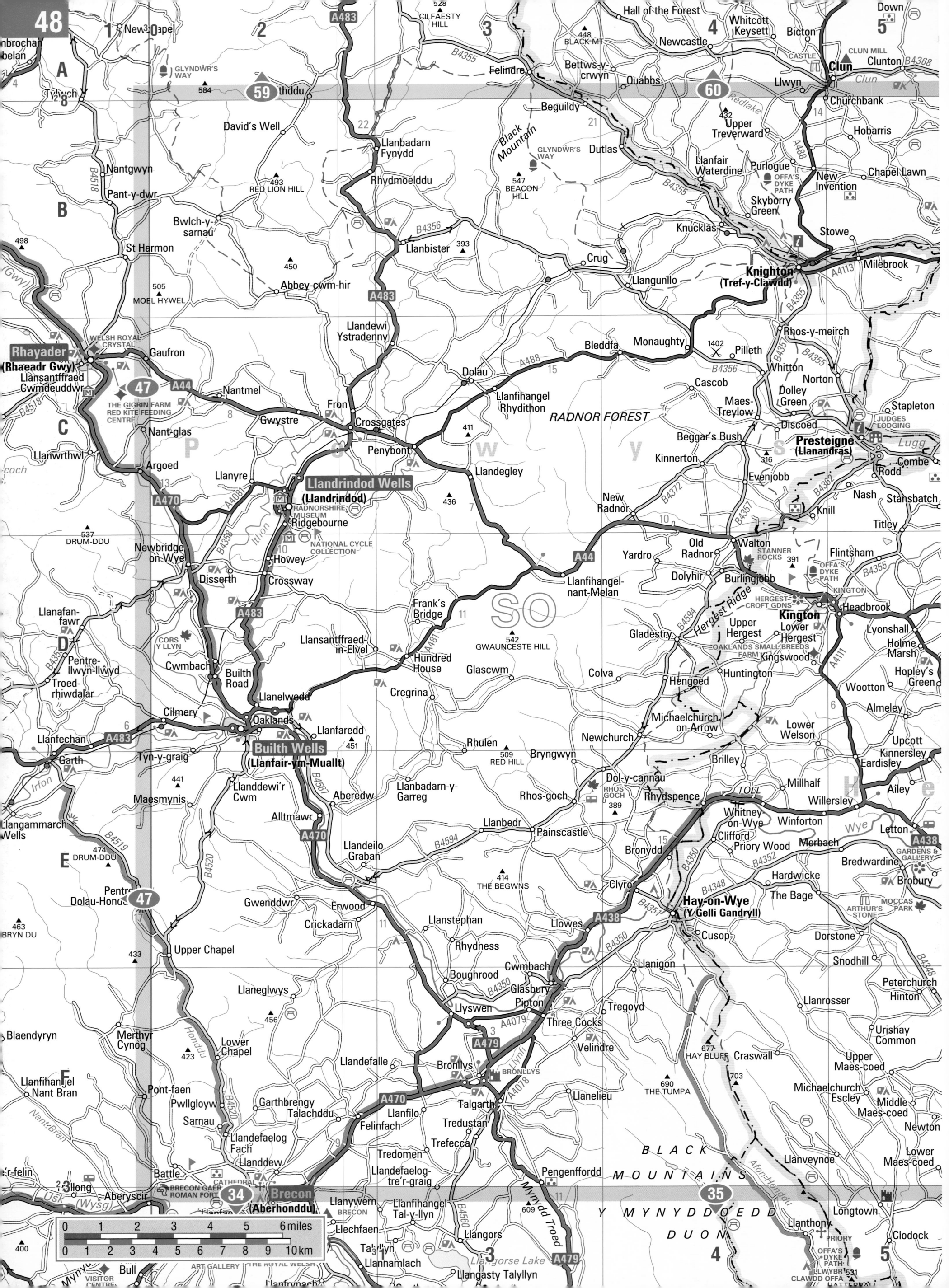

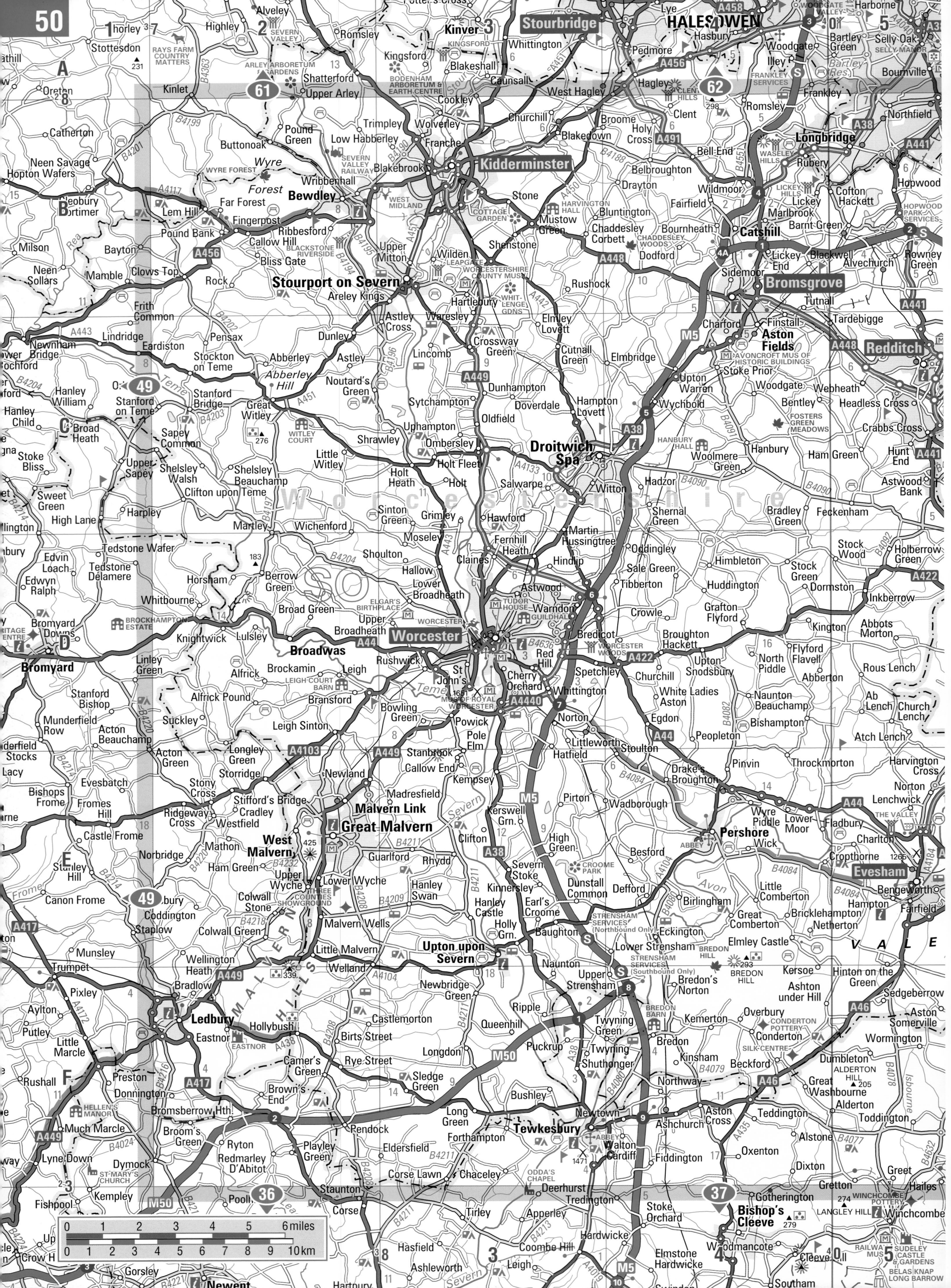

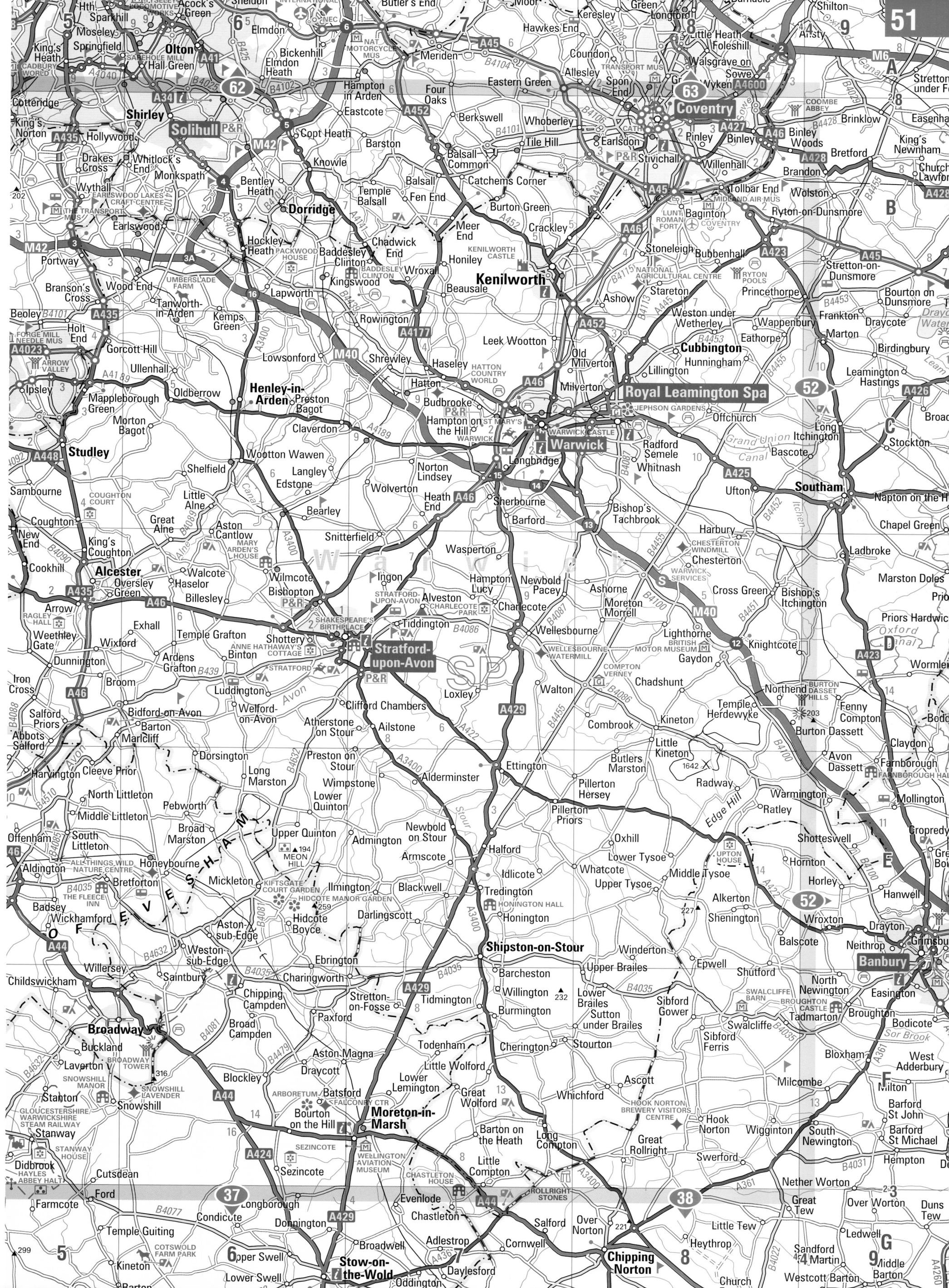

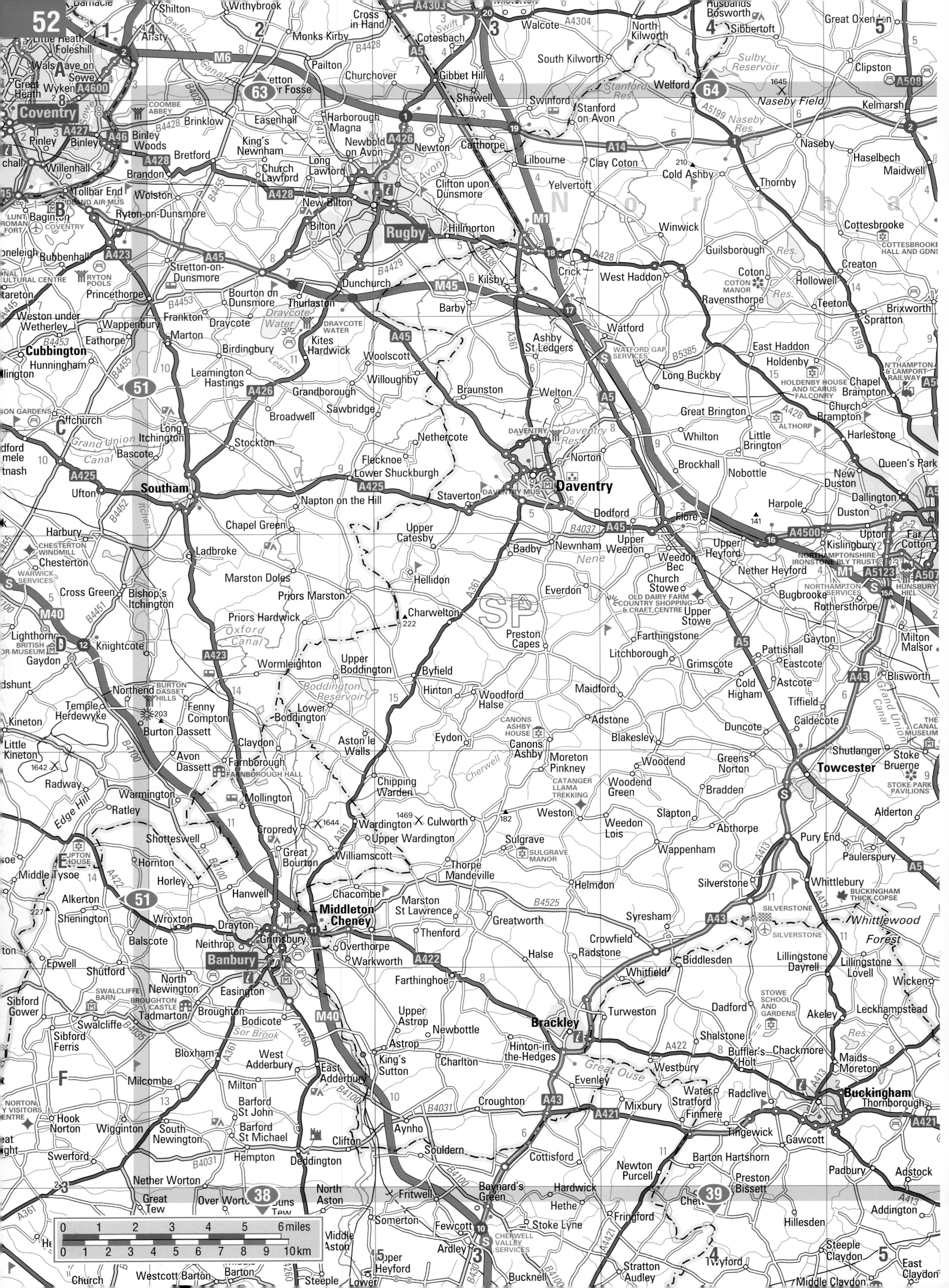

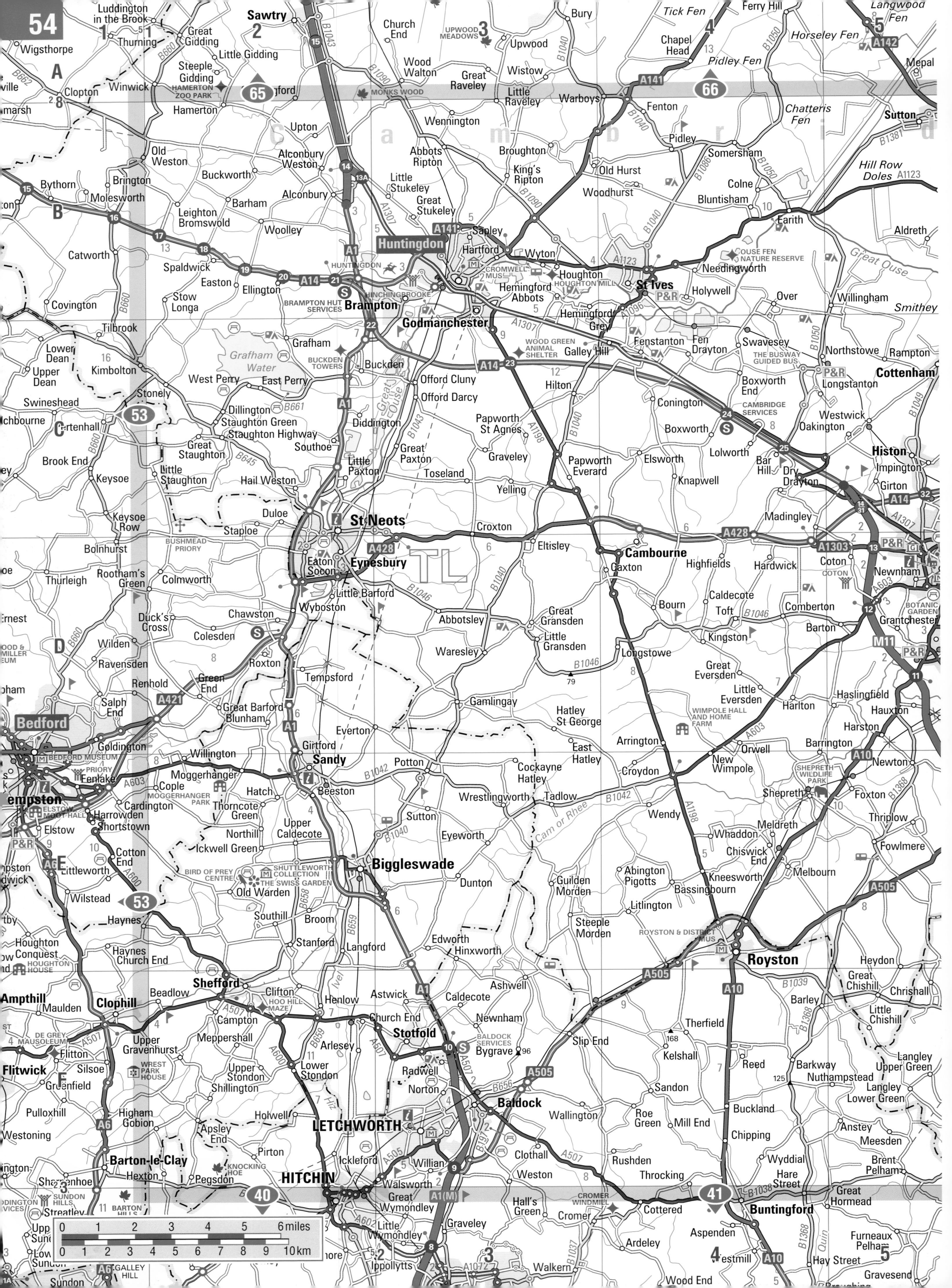

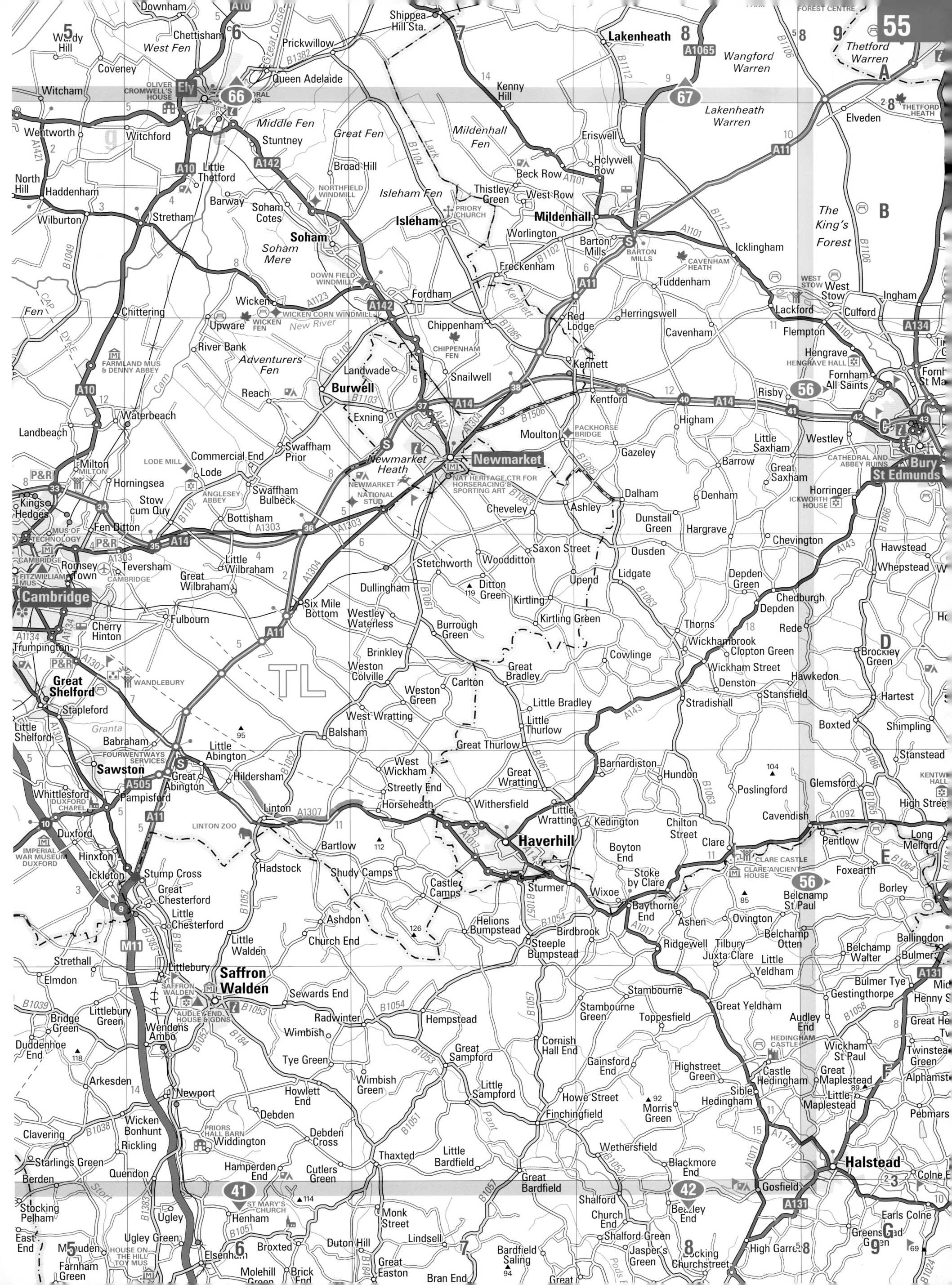

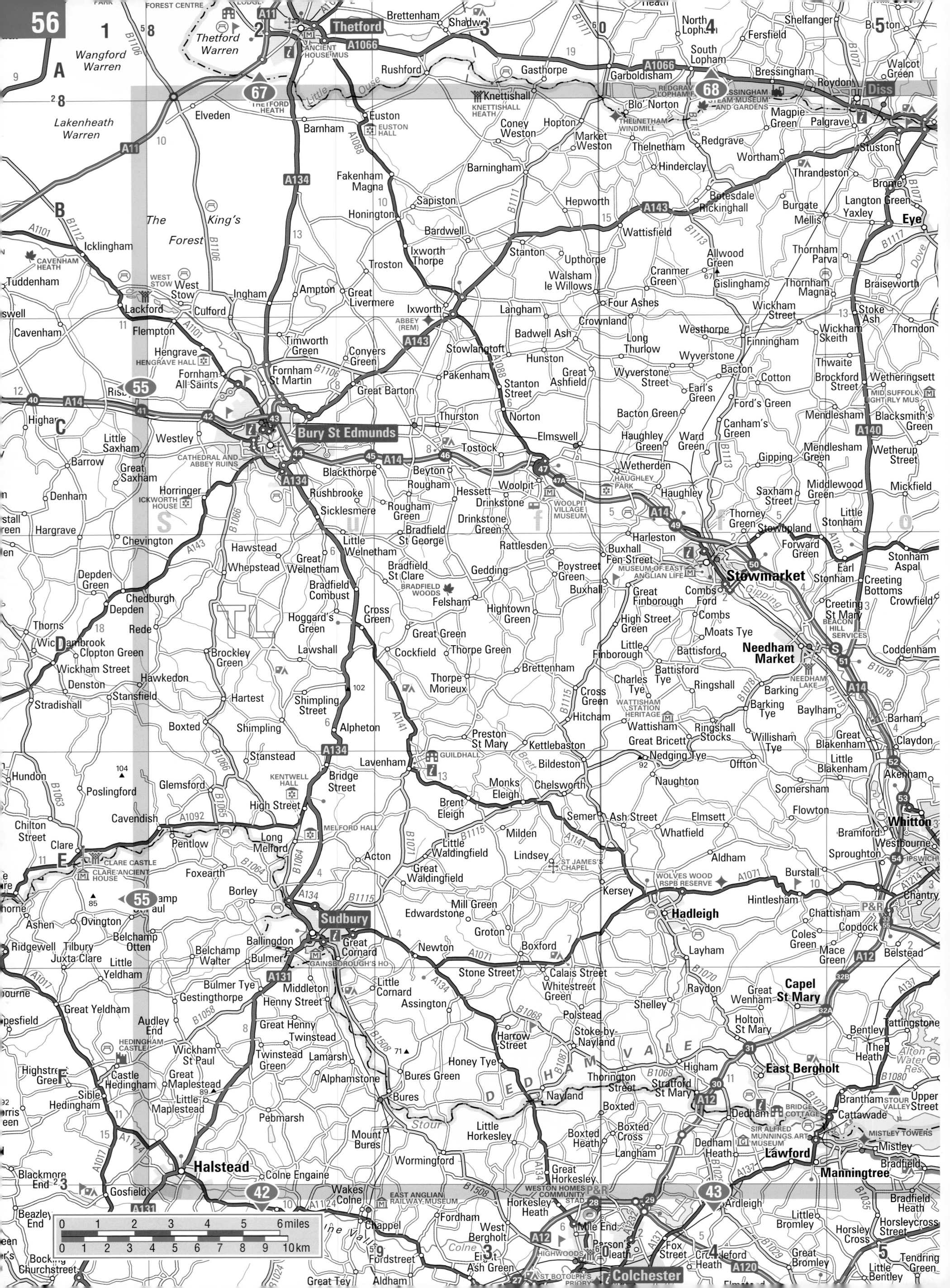

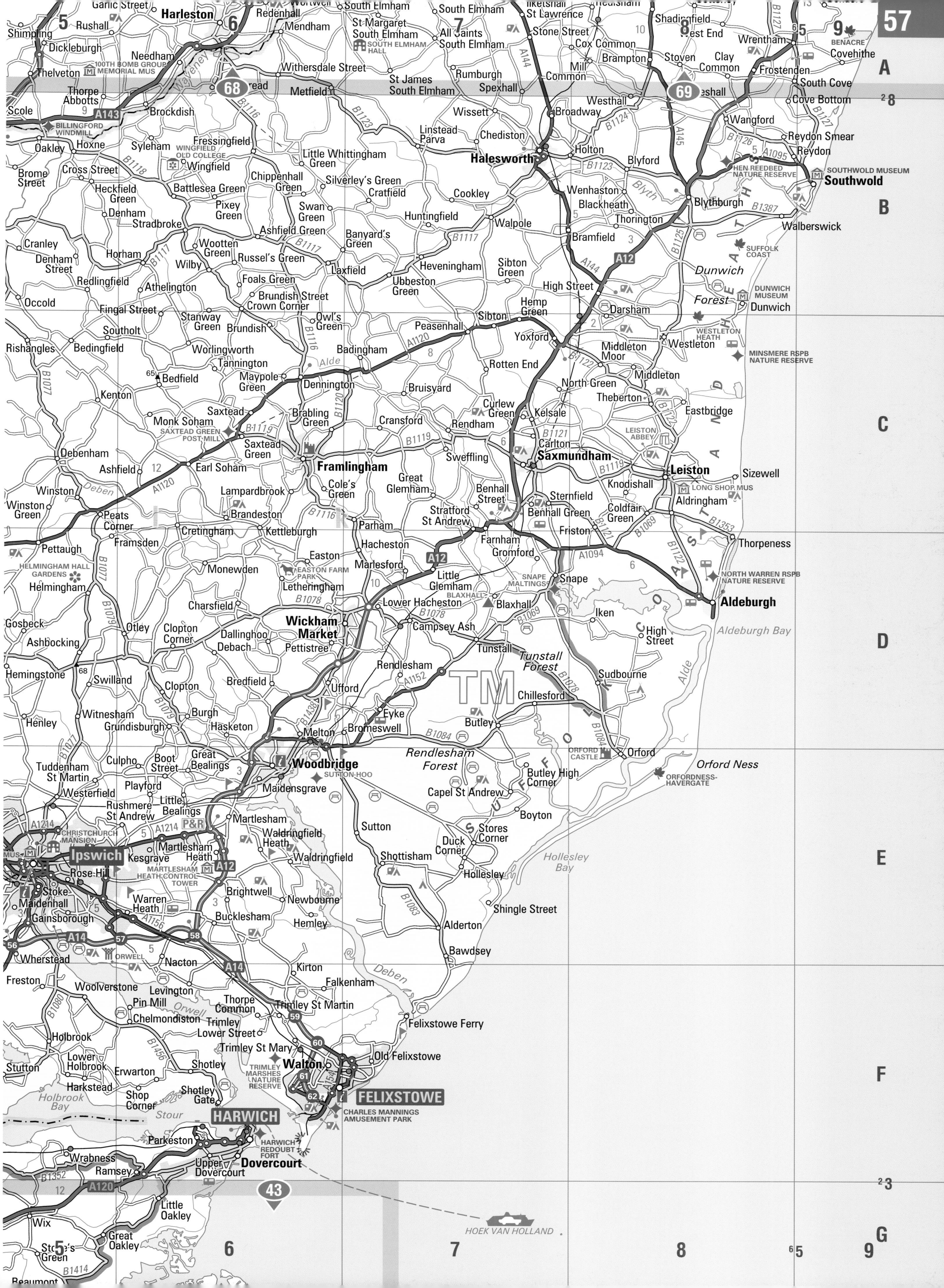

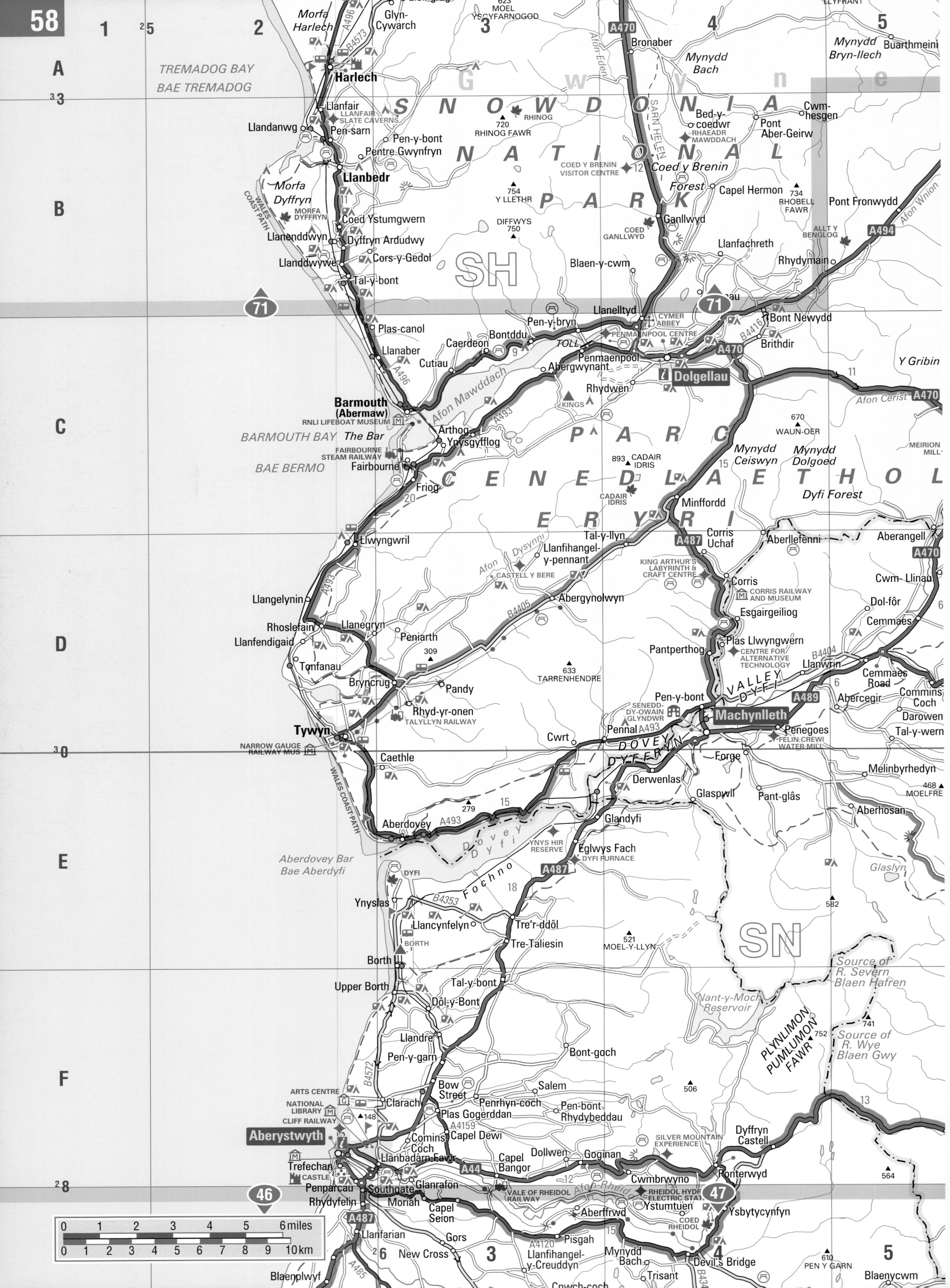

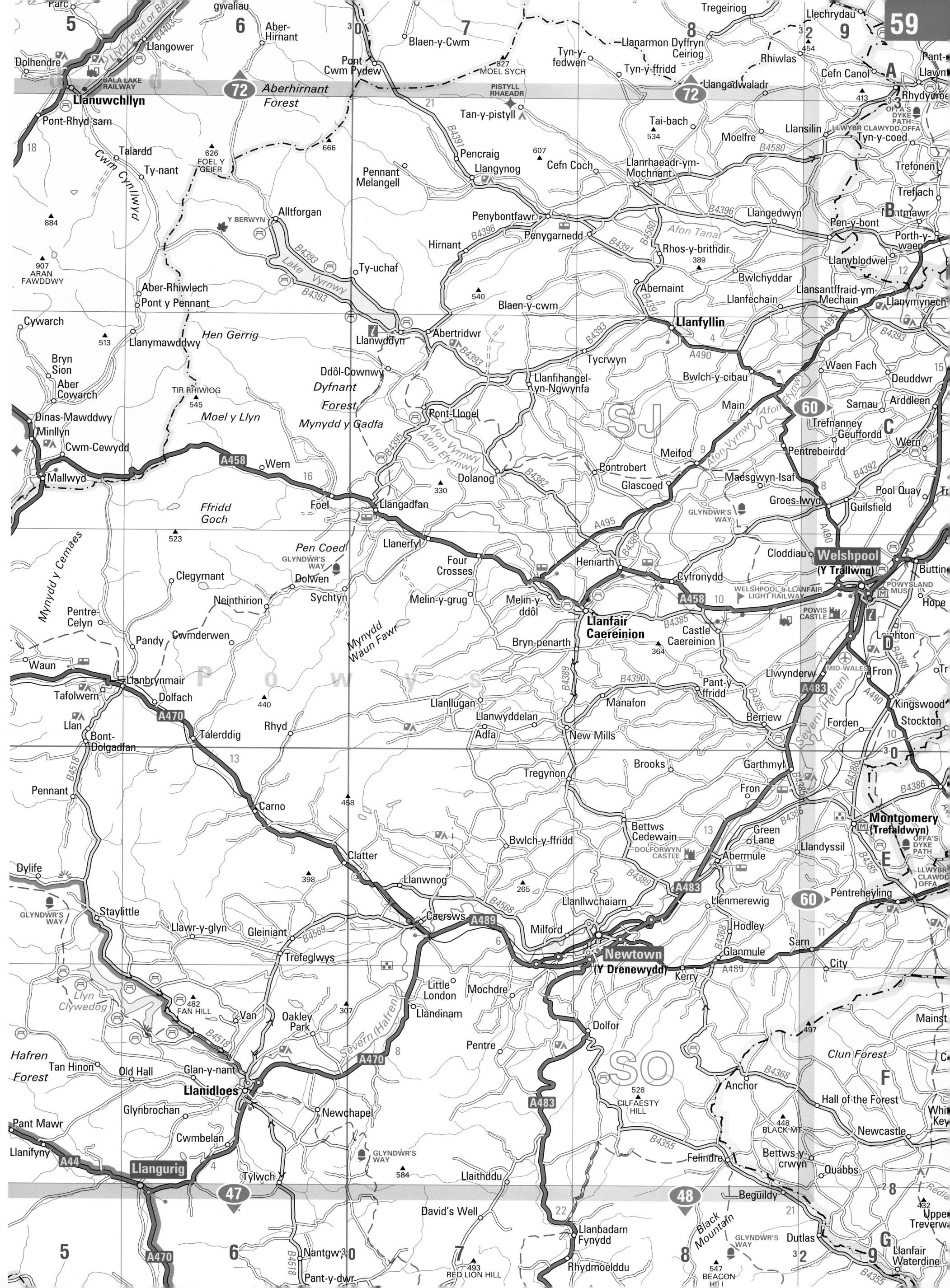

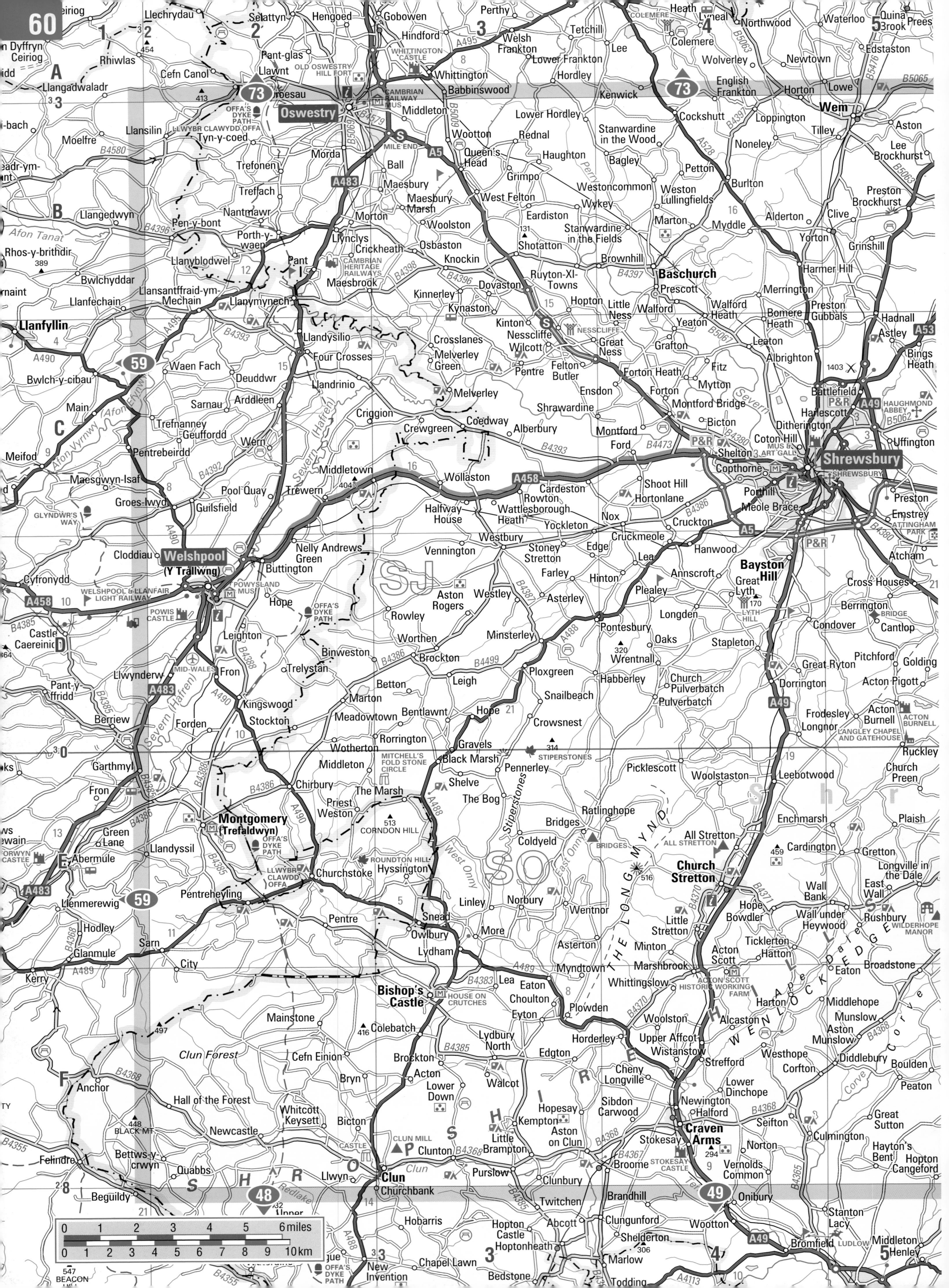

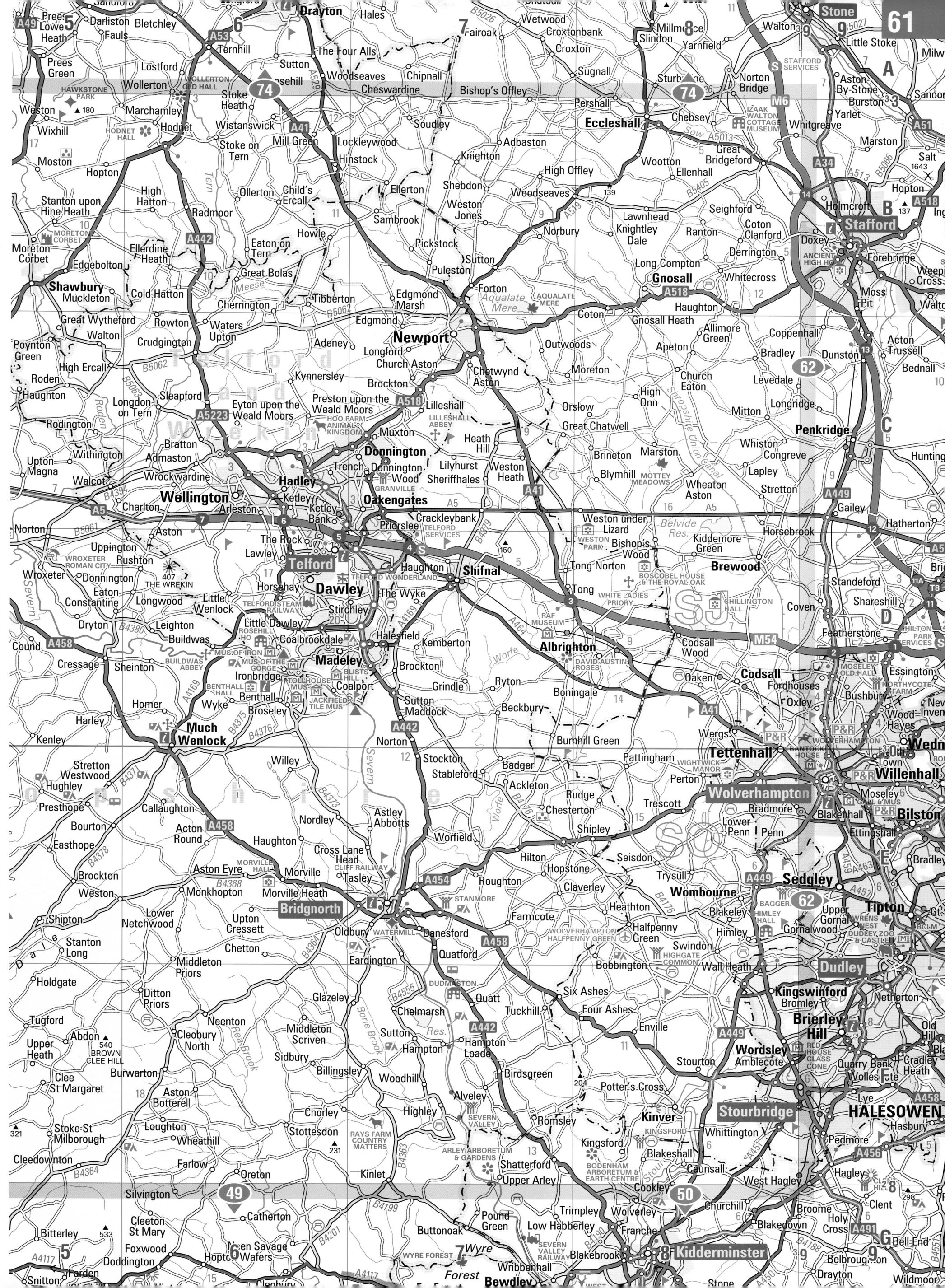

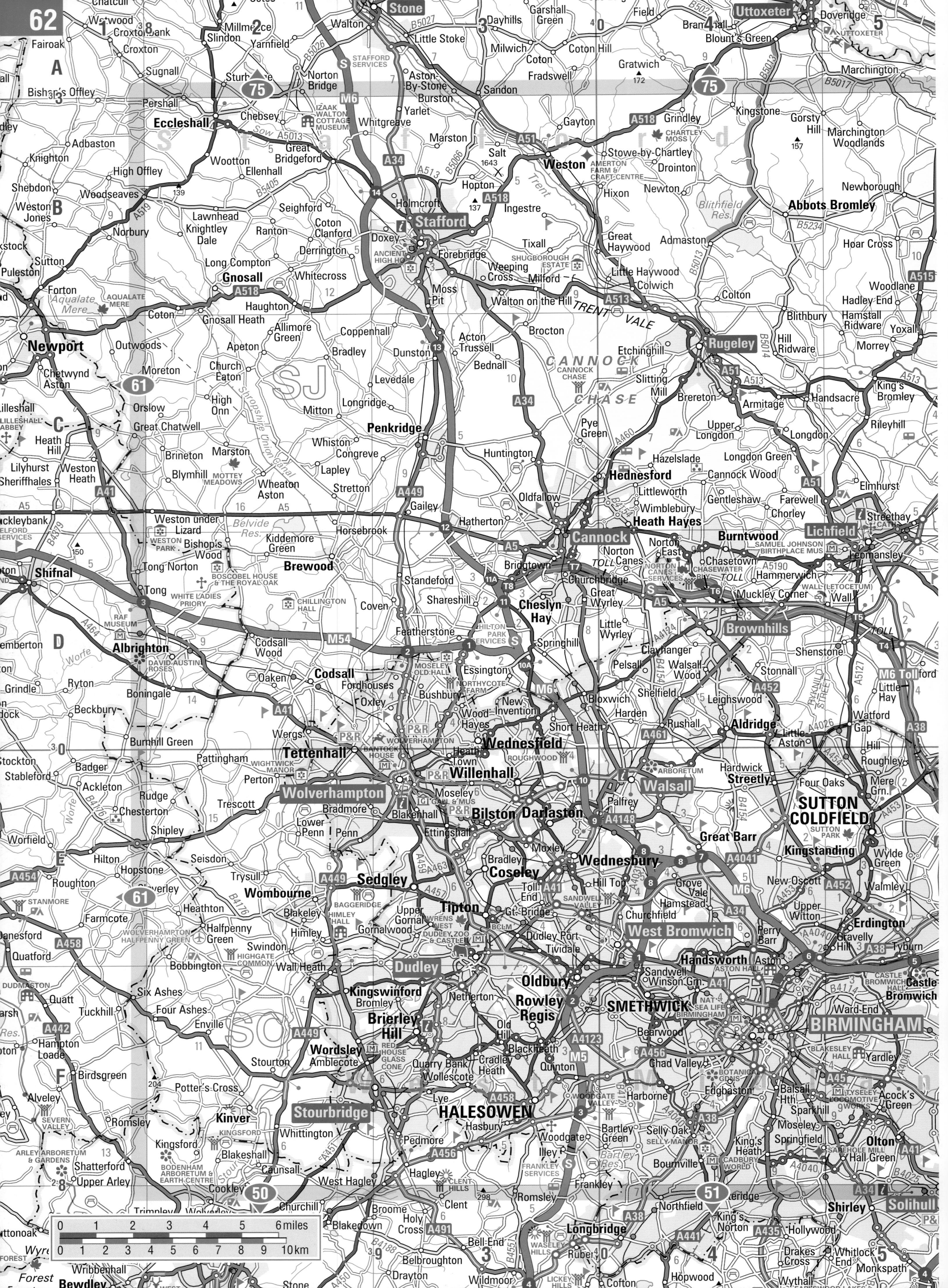

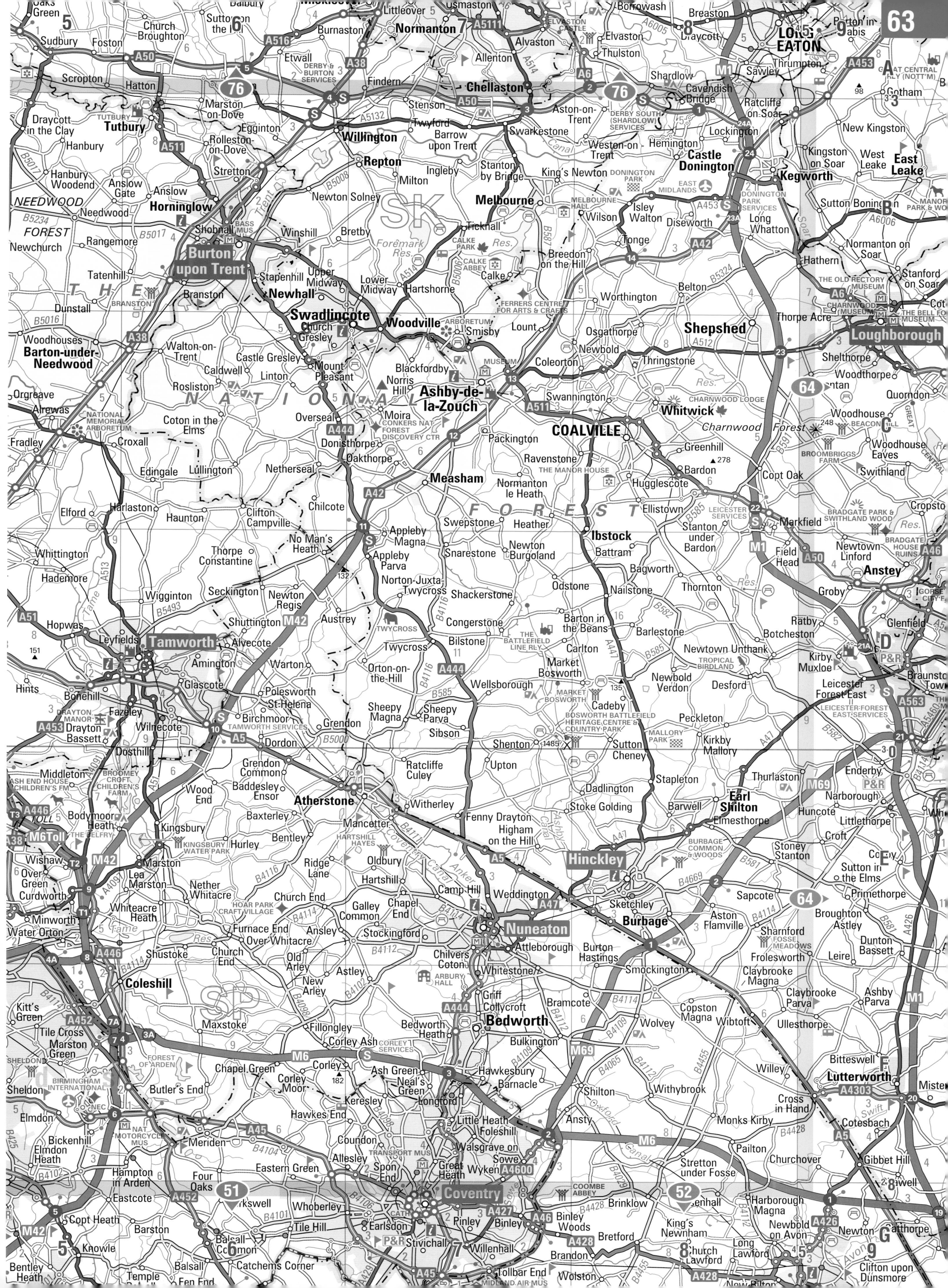

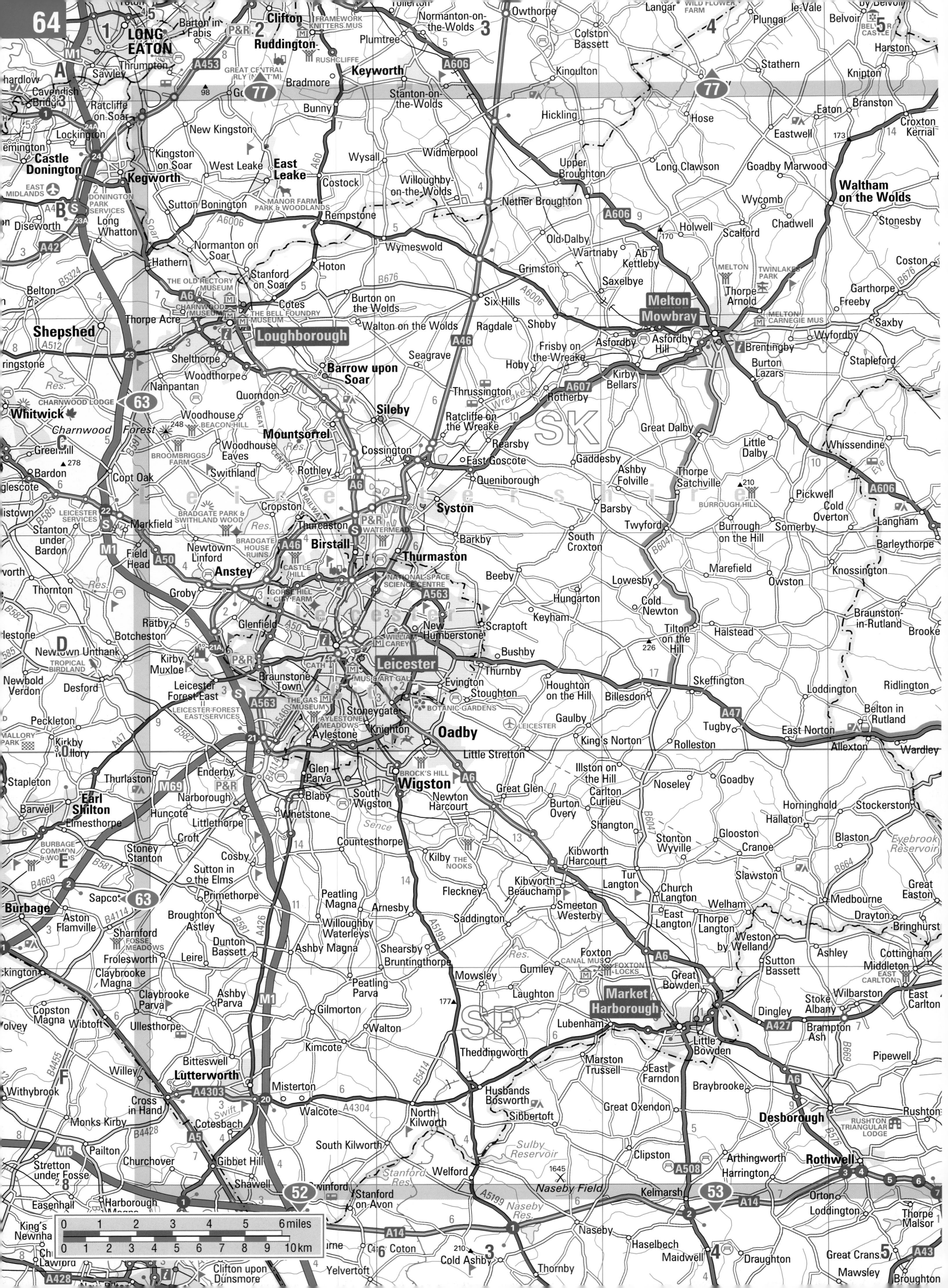

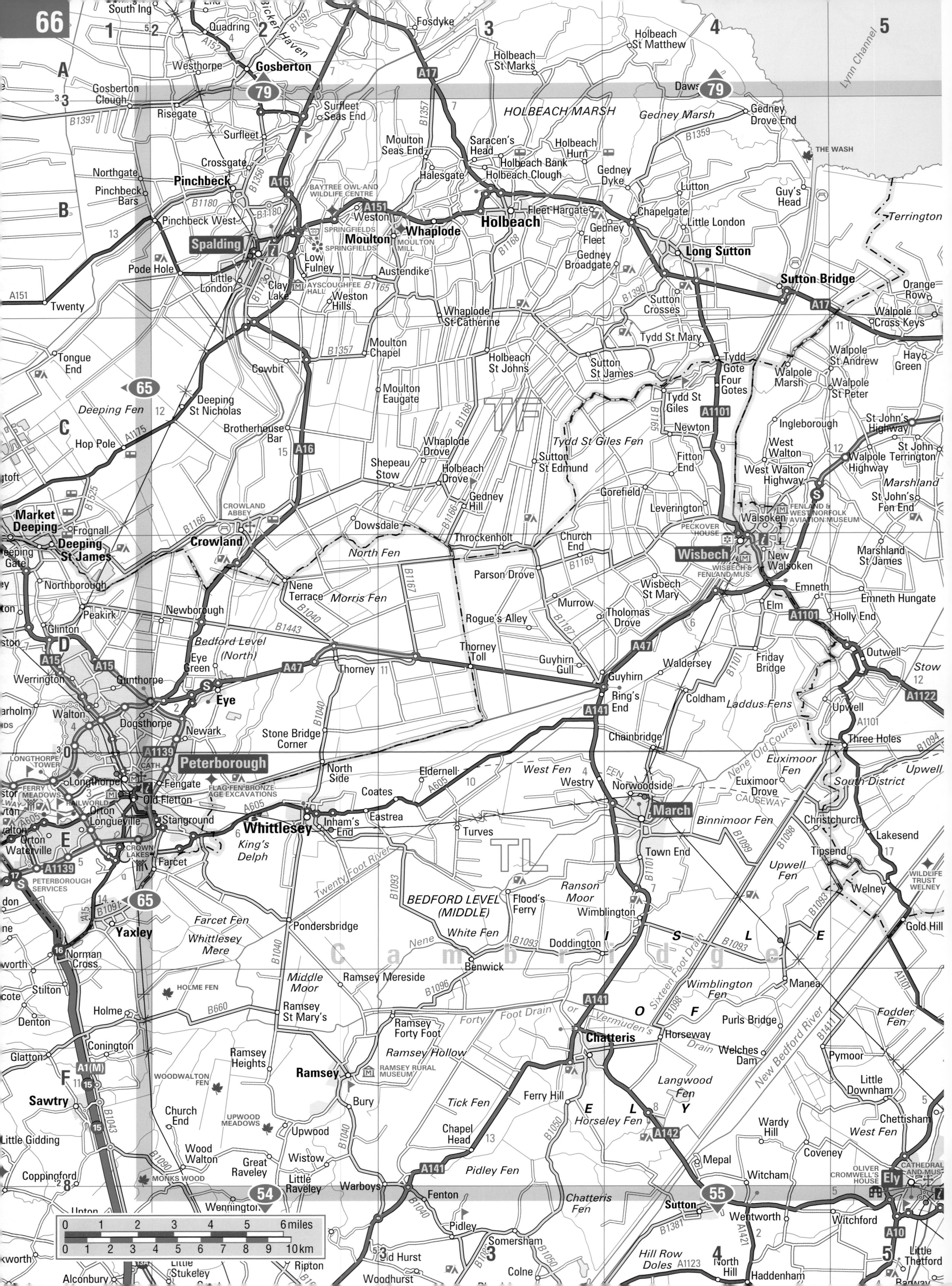

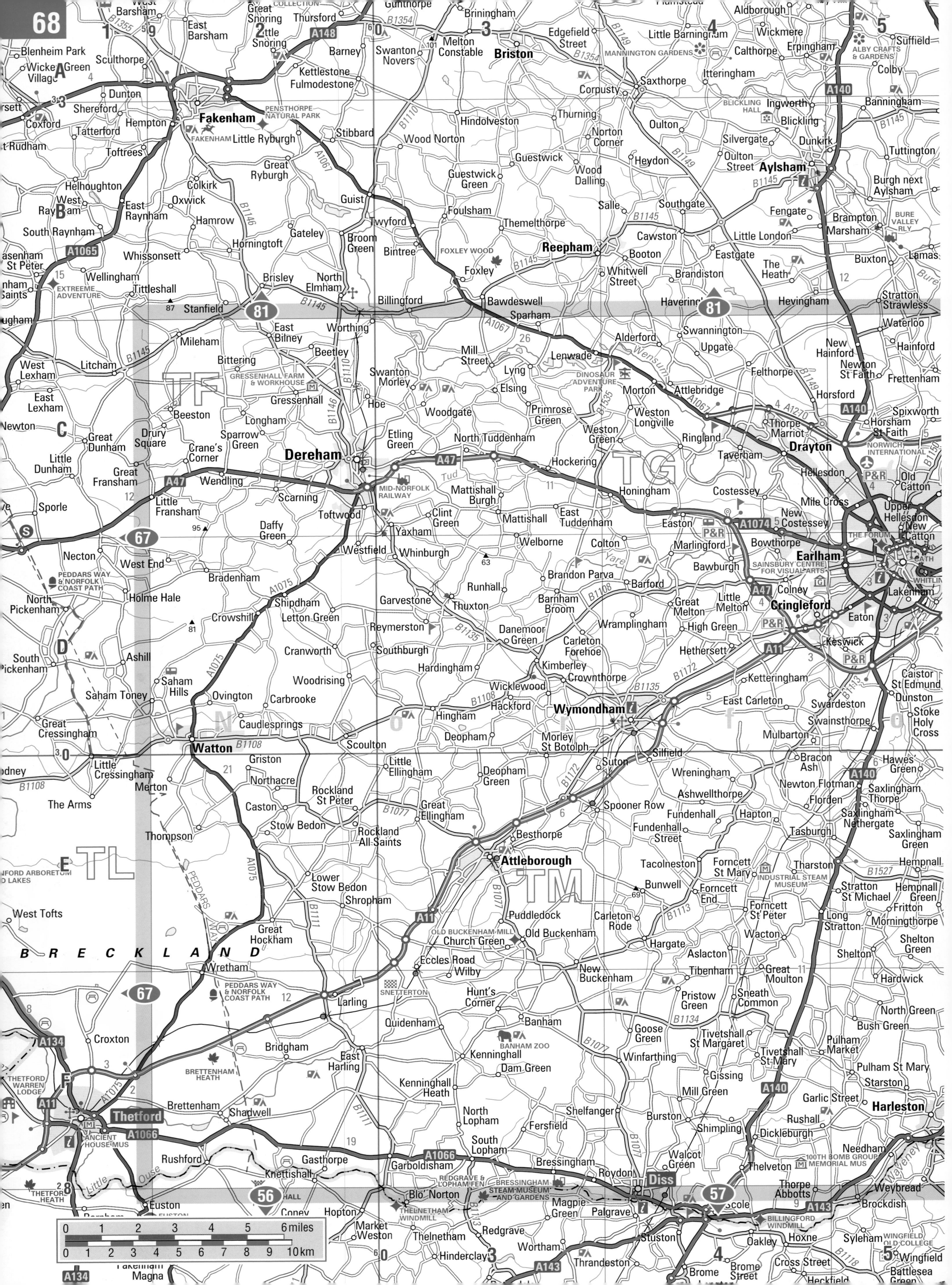

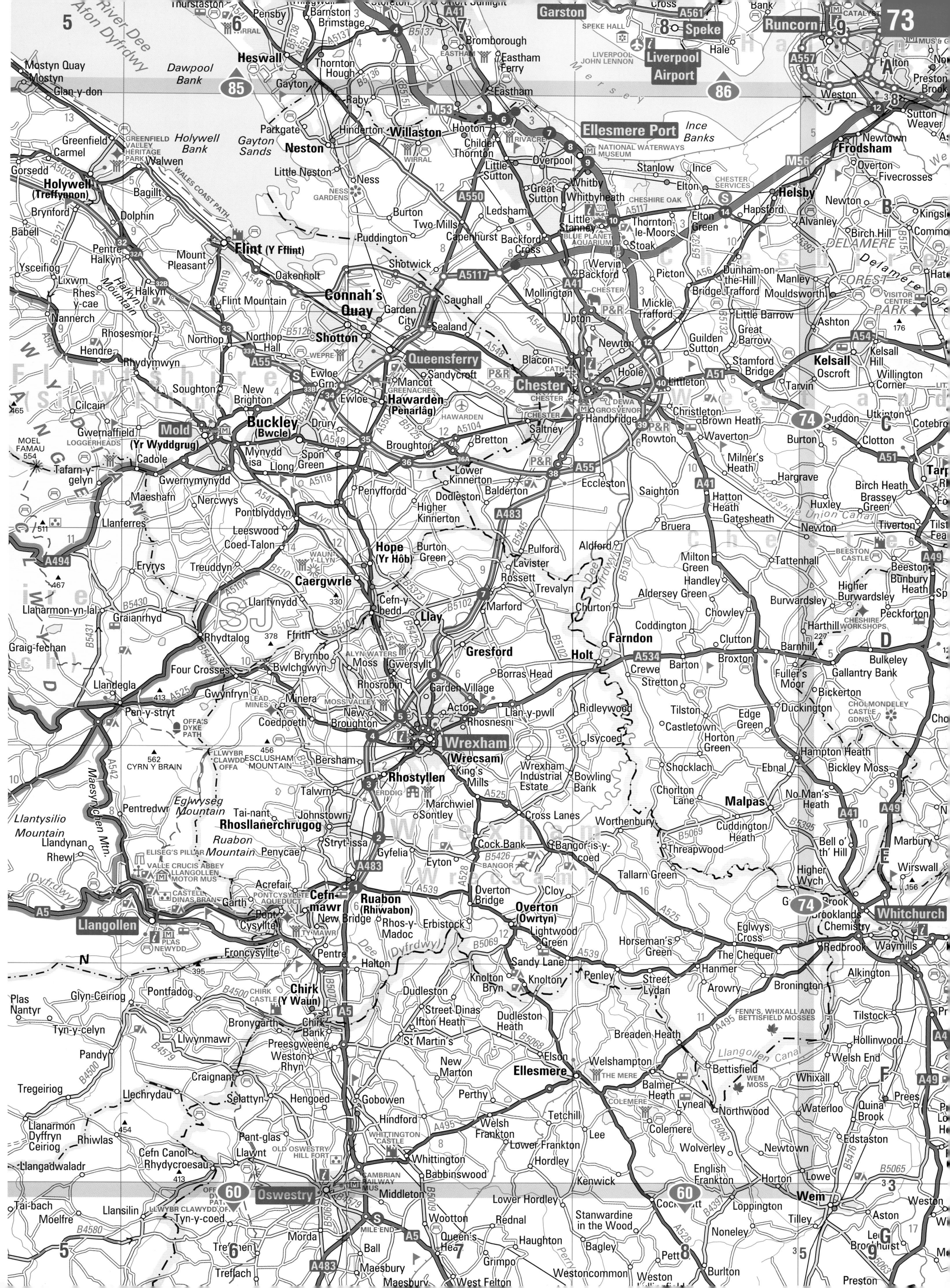

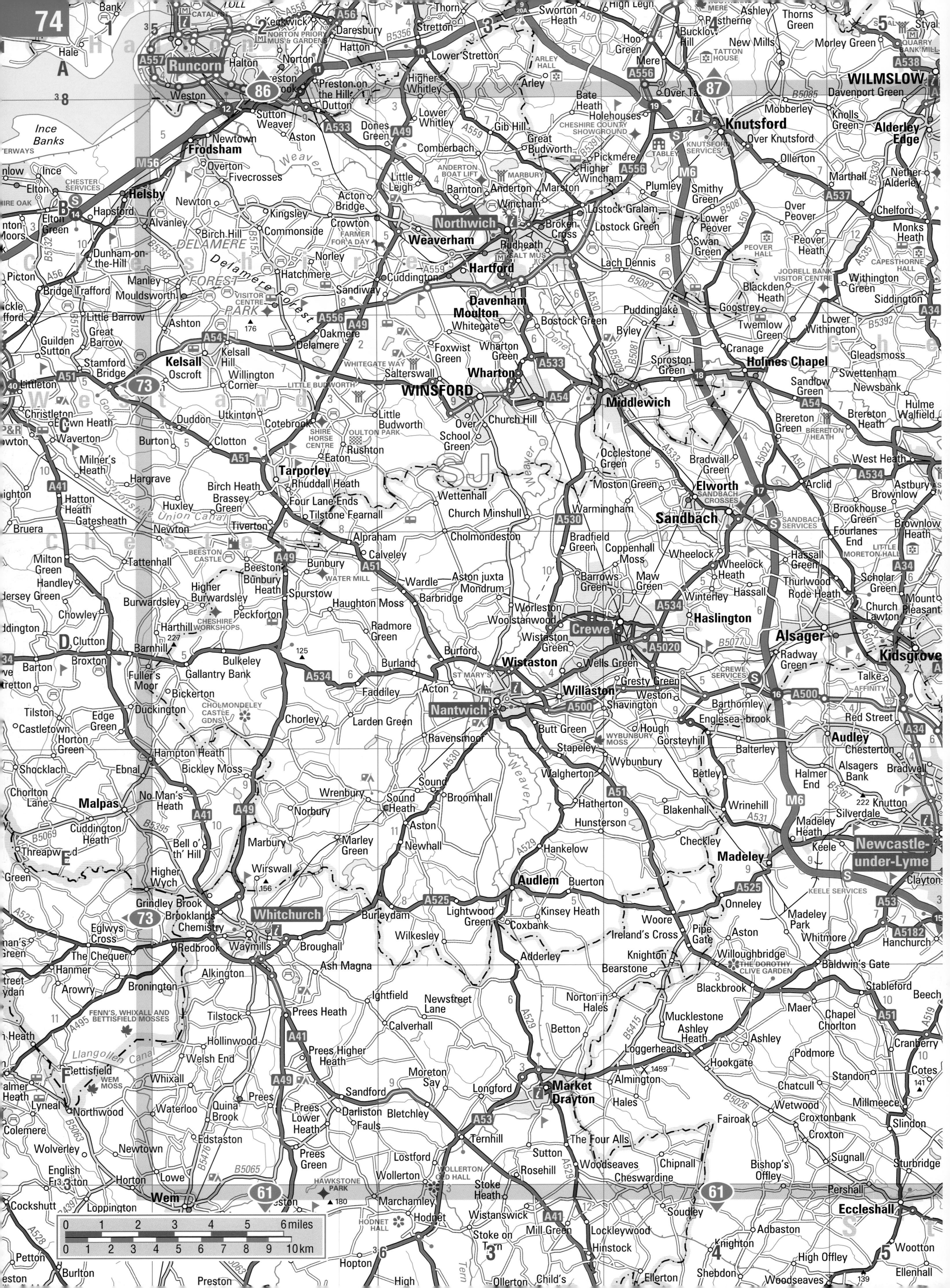

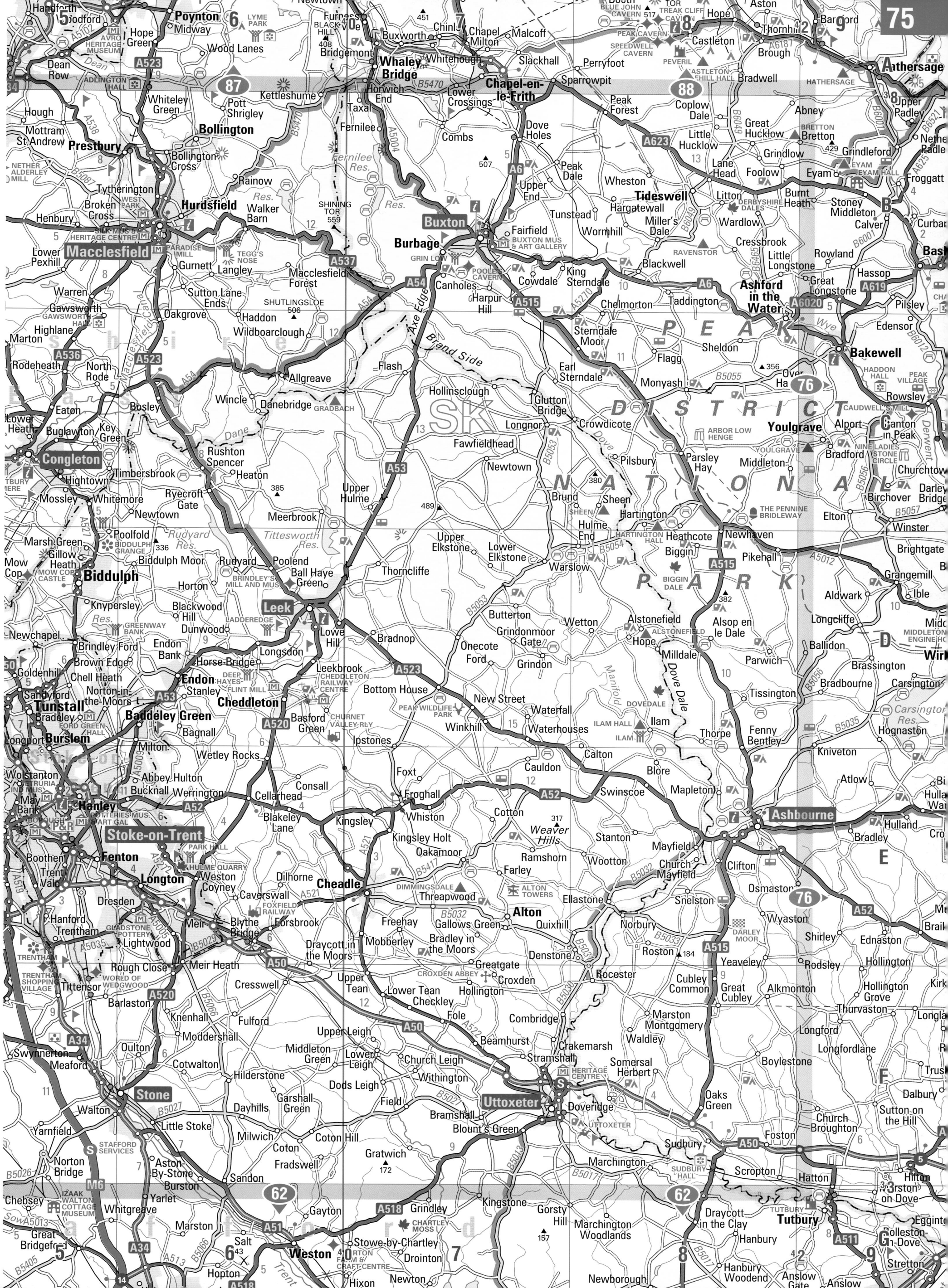

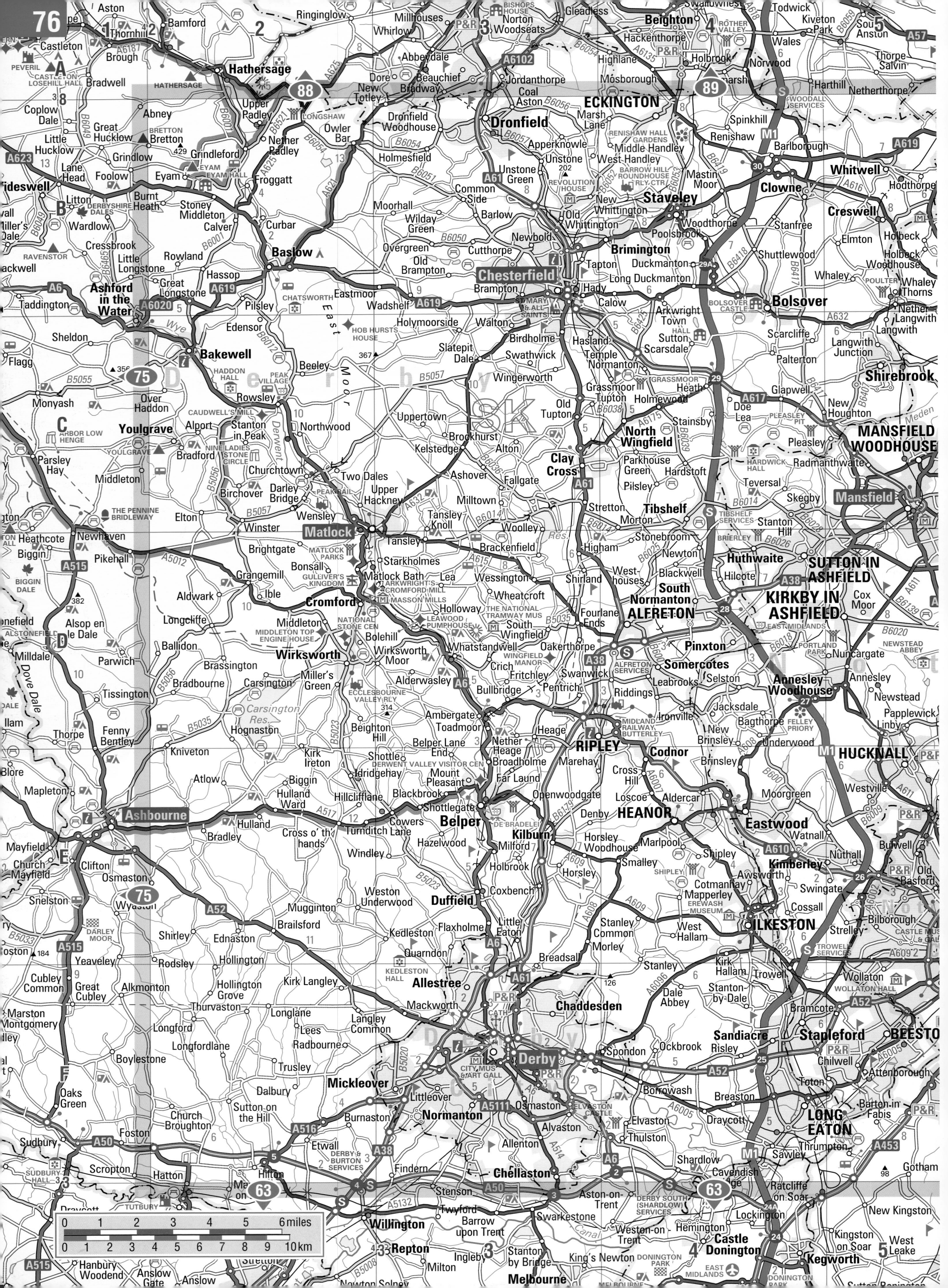

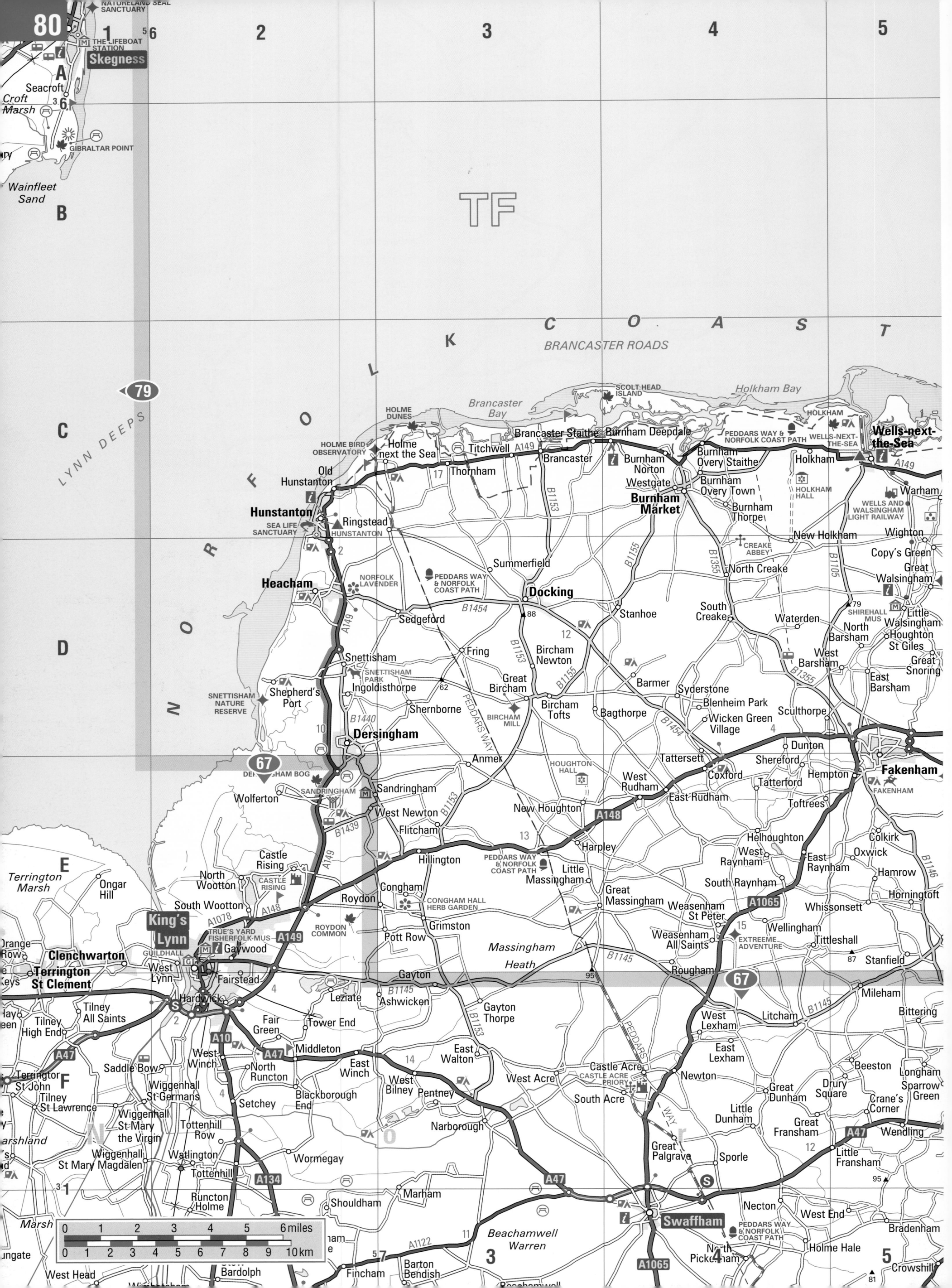

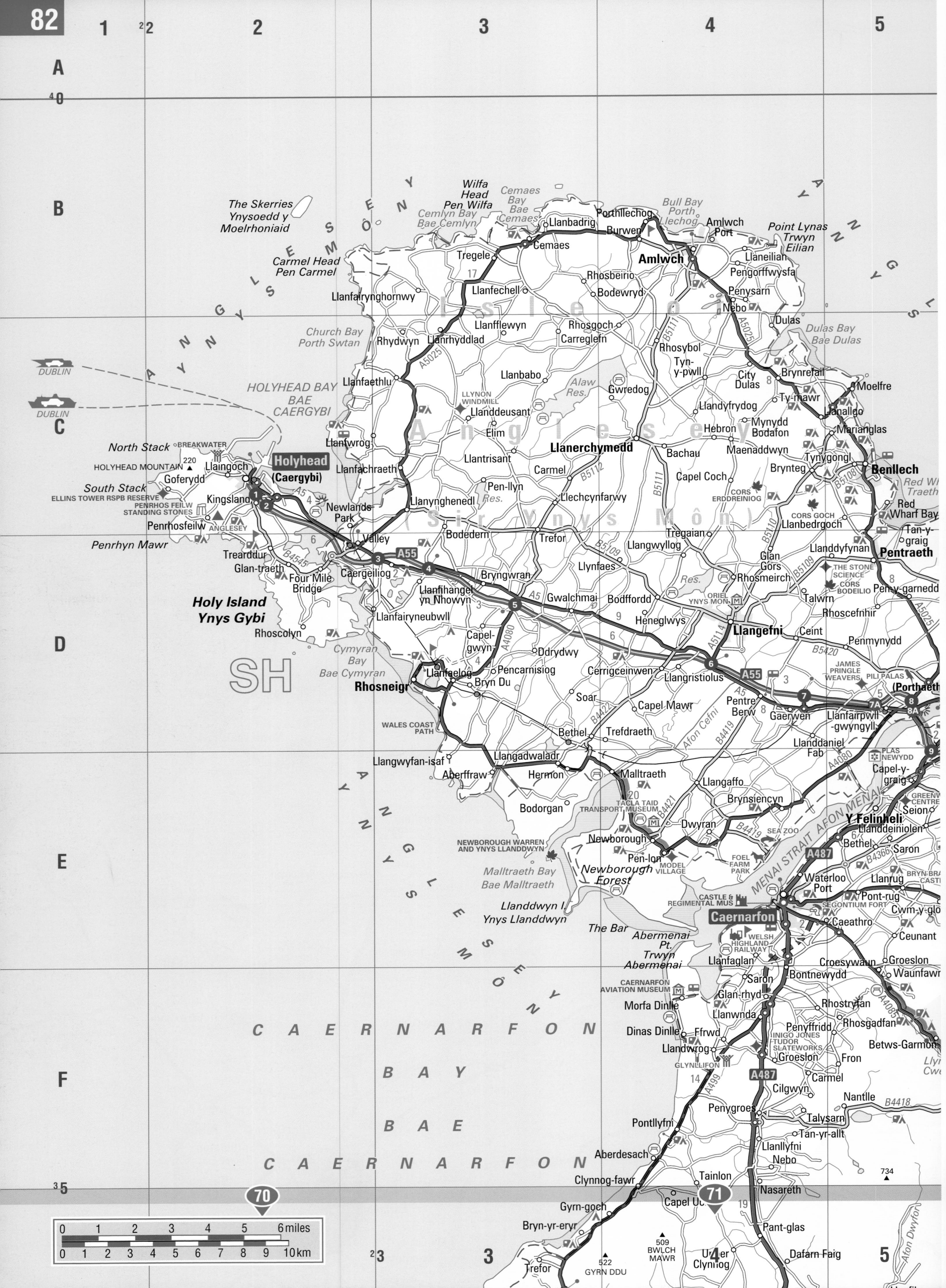

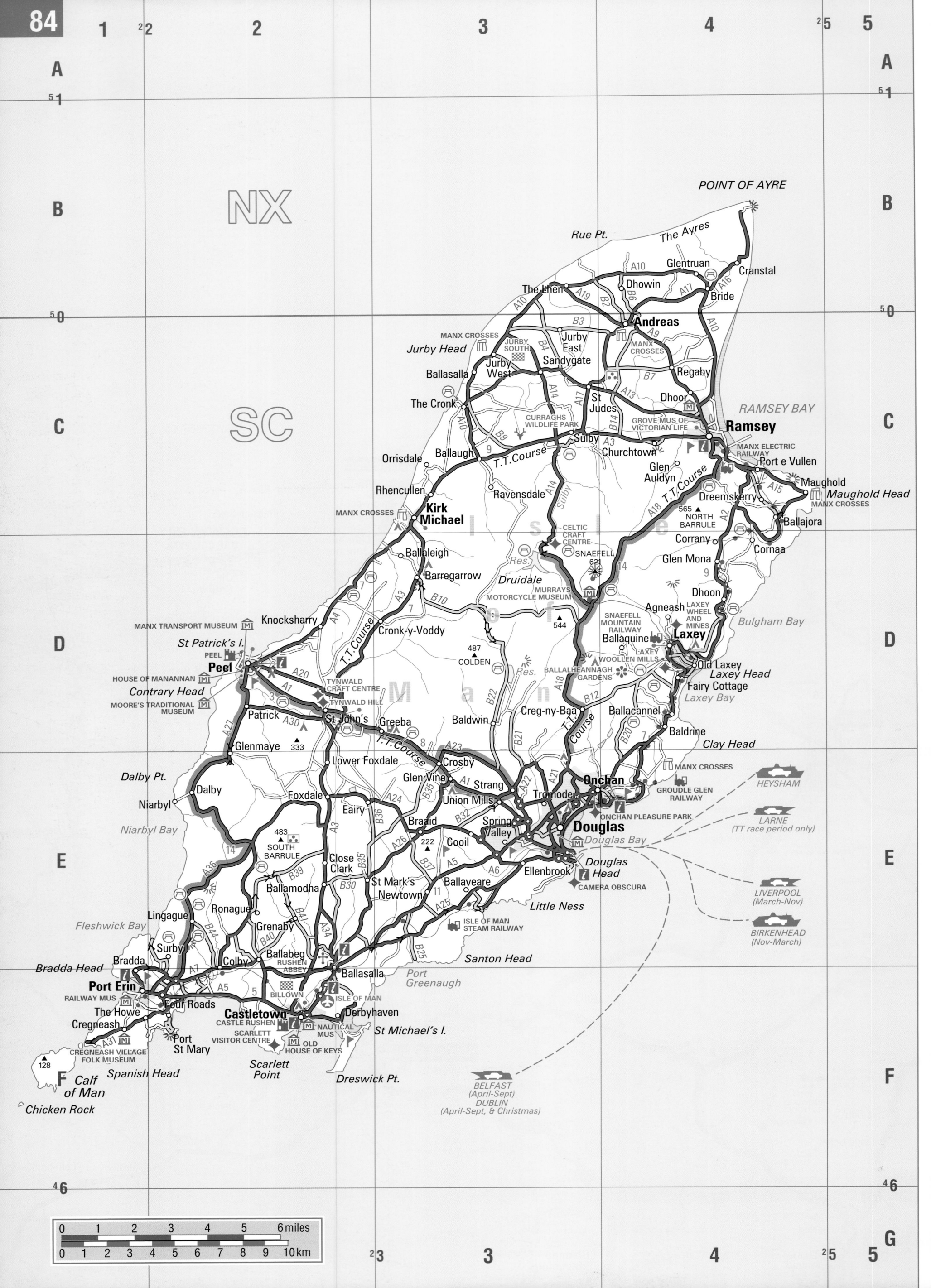

POINT OF AYRE

NX

SC

Rue Pt.   The Ayres

A10   Glentruan   Cranstal

The Lhen   A19   B2   Dhowin   Bride
                         B6   A17   A16
                    A10   A10

MANX CROSSES   JURBY SOUTH   B3   **Andreas**
Jurby Head   Jurby
              Jurby   East   A9
Ballasalla   West   Sandygate   MANX   Regaby
                         A14   CROSSES
The Cronk   A17   St   A13   B7   Dhoor
                    Judes   *RAMSEY BAY*
Orrisdale   Ballaugh   B9   CURRAGHS   GROVE MUS OF   **Ramsey**
              9   WILDLIFE PARK   VICTORIAN LIFE
                    Sulby   A3   MANX ELECTRIC
         T.T.Course   Churchtown   RAILWAY   Port e Vullen
Rhencullen   A14   Glen
              Ravensdale   Auldyn   Maughold
MANX CROSSES   A18   *T.T.Course*   Dreemskerry   *Maughold Head*
         Kirk   Sulby   A15   MANX CROSSES
         Michael   I   565   NORTH   Corrany   Ballajora
                         s   BARRULE   CELTIC
    Ballaleigh   l   CRAFT   Cornaa
                    e   CENTRE   SNAEFELL   Glen Mona
    Barregarrow   621   9
              B10   *Druidale*   MURRAYS   SNAEFELL   Dhoon
         7   MOTORCYCLE MUSEUM   MOUNTAIN   Agneash   LAXEY
MANX TRANSPORT MUSEUM   544   RAILWAY   WHEEL
    Knocksharry   o   *Res.*   Ballaquine   AND
         A4   7   WOOLLEN MILLS   **Laxey**   MINES
              T.T.Course   Cronk-y-Voddy   Ballalheannagh   LAXEY   *Bulgham Bay*
St Patrick's I.   f   487   GARDENS   Old Laxey
PEEL   A3   COLDEN   *Laxey Head*
HOUSE OF MANANNAN   A20   *Res.*   Fairy Cottage
Peel   M   B12   *Laxey Bay*
Contrary Head   A1   TYNWALD   Ballacannel
MOORE'S TRADITIONAL   CRAFT CENTRE   a   B22   Baldrine
MUSEUM   TYNWALD HILL   Baldwin   Creg-ny-Baa   7   *Clay Head*
         Patrick   3   St John's   n   B21   *T.T.*
         A30   Greeba   MANX CROSSES
    Glenmaye   A27   *T.T.Course*   M   A23   Course
Dalby Pt.   333   Crosby   *HEYSHAM*
         Dalby   Lower Foxdale   Glen   A1   Strang   A22   **Onchan**   GROUDLE GLEN
                    Vine   B35   A21   Tromode   RAILWAY
Niarbyl   Foxdale   Union Mills   *LARNE*
              A24   ONCHAN PLEASURE PARK   (TT race period only)
Niarbyl Bay   14   Eairy   B36   Braaid   B32   Spring   **Douglas**
         483   Valley   Cooil   *Douglas Bay*
         SOUTH   A26   222   A5
         BARRULE   Close   B37   *LIVERPOOL*
Port Erin   Clark   St Mark's   Ballaveare   Ellenbrook   Douglas   (March-Nov)
         B39   B30   Newtown   Head
    Lingague   Ronague   11   A6   CAMERA OBSCURA   *BIRKENHEAD*
         B44   Ballamodha   A34   A5   *Little Ness*   (Nov-March)
    Surby   Grenaby   ISLE OF MAN
Bradda Head   B40   Ballabeg   ST MARK'S   STEAM RAILWAY
    Bradda   Colby   RUSHEN   B25   *Santon Head*
RAILWAY MUS   A1   A5   ABBEY   Ballasalla
The Howe   Four Roads   5   BILLOWN   *Port*
    Cregneash   **Castletown**   ISLE OF MAN   *Greenaugh*
         CASTLE RUSHEN   Derbyhaven
A31   SCARLETT   NAUTICAL   *St Michael's I.*
CREGNEASH VILLAGE   VISITOR CENTRE   MUS
FOLK MUSEUM   Port   OLD
128   St Mary   HOUSE OF KEYS   *BELFAST*
F *Calf*   *Scarlett*   (April-Sept)
of Man   *Spanish Head*   *Point*   *Drewick Pt.*   *DUBLIN*
Chicken Rock   (April-Sept, & Christmas)

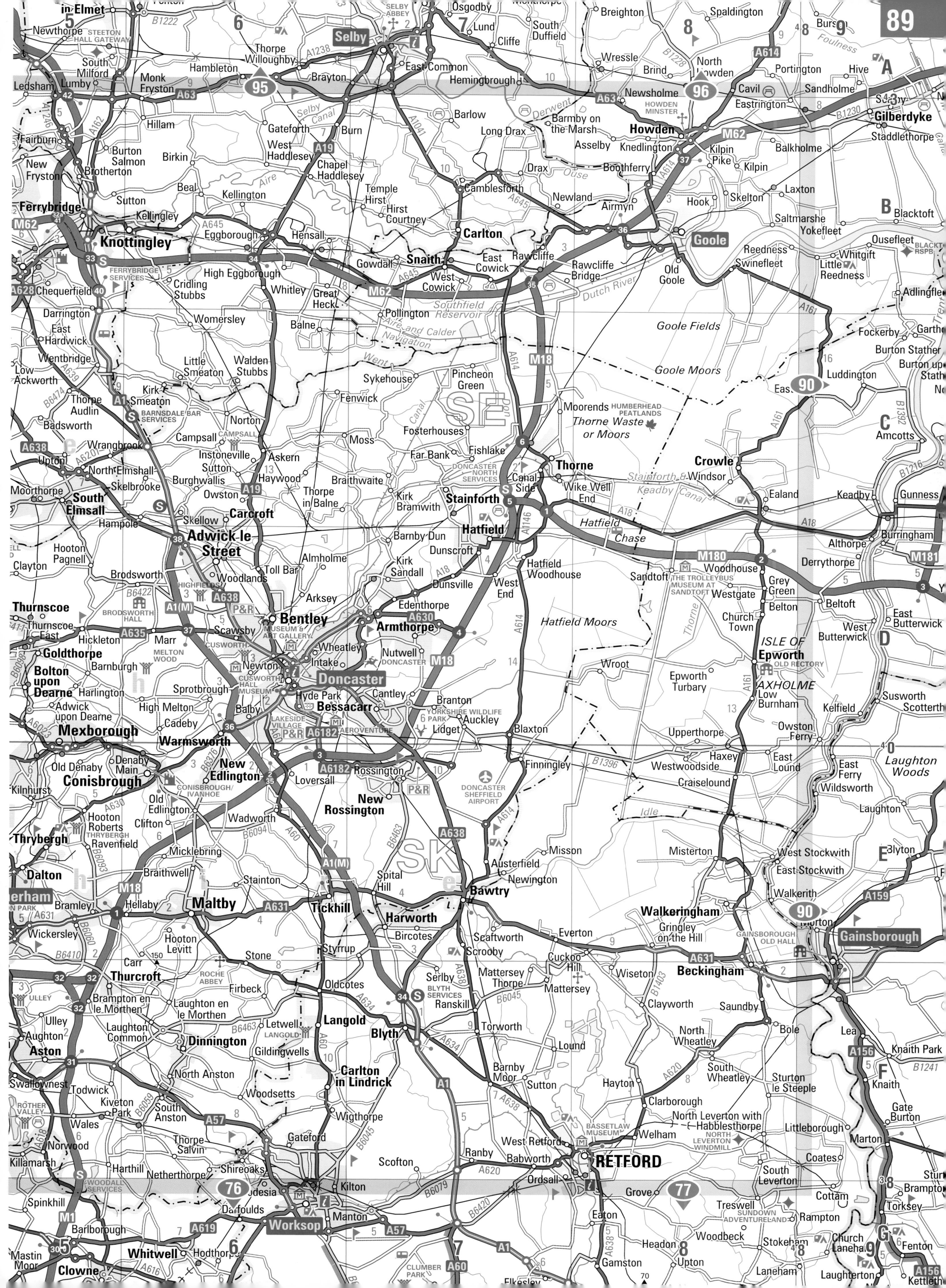

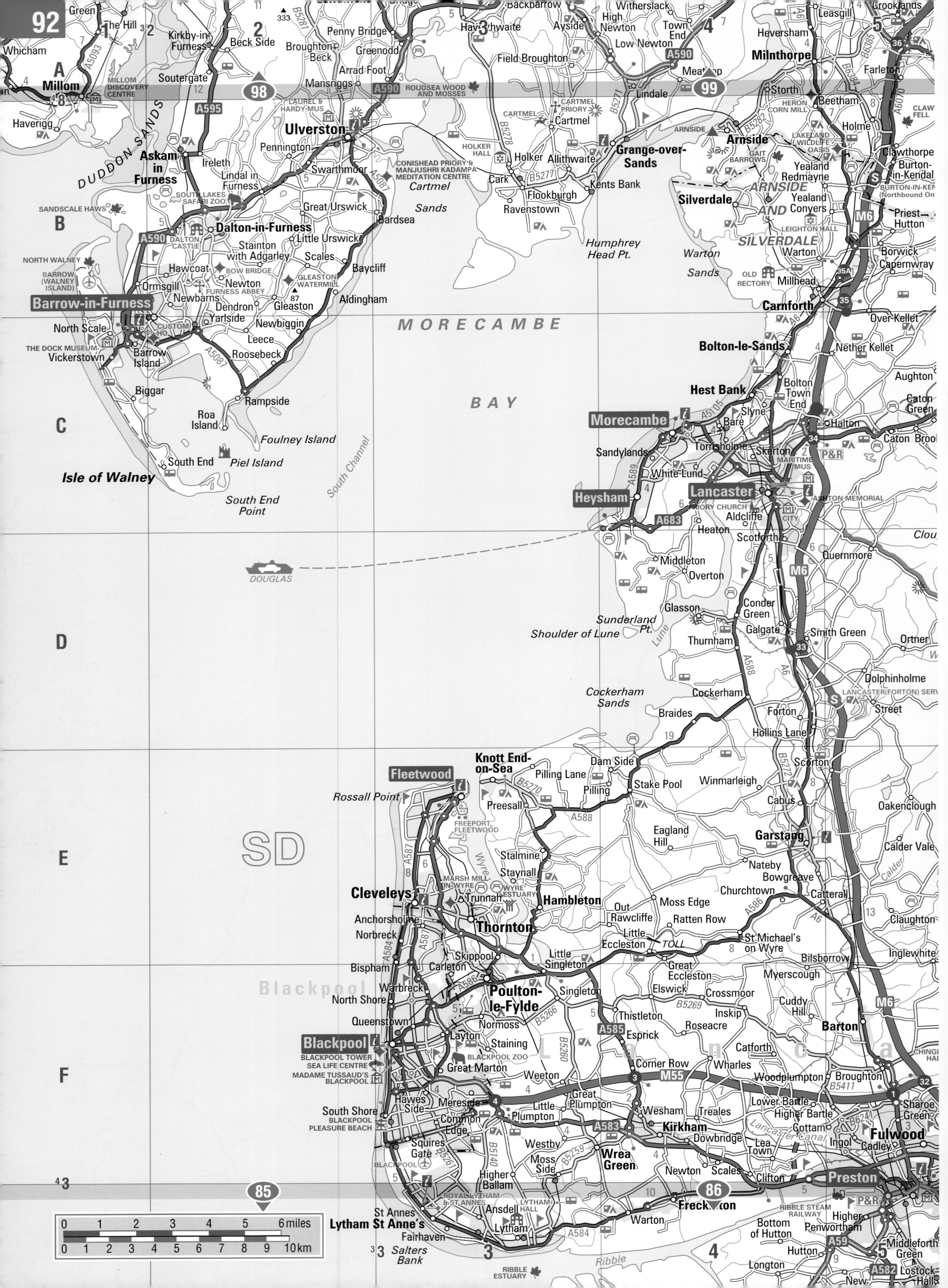

MORECAMBE

BAY

DUDDON SANDS

Millom
Haverigg
Whicham
Green
The Hill
Kirkby-in-Furness
Beck Side
Penny Bridge
Broughton Beck
Greenodd
Arrad Foot
Mansriggs
Soutergate
Ireleth
Lindal in Furness
Askam in Furness
Pennington
Swarthmoor
Ulverston
Dalton-in-Furness
Stainton with Adgarley
Great Urswick
Little Urswick
Scales
Hawcoat
Newton
Bayliff
Ormsgill
Newbarns
Dendron
Gleaston
Aldingham
Barrow-in-Furness
Yarlside
Newbiggin
North Scale
Barrow Island
Leece
Roosebeck
Vickerstown
Biggar
Rampside
Roa Island
South End
Piel Island
Isle of Walney
Foulney Island
South End Point
South Channel

Backbarrow
Haverthwaite
Ayside
Low Newton
High Newton
Field Broughton
Witherslack
Town End
Heversham
Milnthorpe
Farleton
Meathop
Lindale
Storth
Beetham
Holme
Cartmel
Grange-over-Sands
Arnside
Silverdale
Allithwaite
Kents Bank
Flookburgh
Cark
Ravenstown
Humphrey Head Pt.
Warton Sands
Yealand Redmayne
Yealand Conyers
ARNSIDE AND SILVERDALE
Warton
Leighton Hall
Millhead
Carnforth
Over-Kellet
Nether Kellet
Bolton-le-Sands
Hest Bank
Bolton Town End
Slyne
Bare
Morecambe
Torrisholme
Skerton
White Lund
Sandylands
Heysham
Lancaster
Aldcliffe
Heaton
Scotforth
Middleton
Overton
Glasson
Sunderland Pt.
Shoulder of Lune
Thurnham
Conder Green
Galgate
Smith Green
Quernmore
Dolphinholme
Forton
Street
Cockerham
Cockerham Sands
Braides
Hollins Lane
Scorton
Cabus
Garstang
Nateby
Bowgreave
Churchtown
Calder Vale
Catterall
Claughton
Oakenclough
Myerscough
Bilsborrow
Barton

DOUGLAS

SD

Knott End-on-Sea
Fleetwood
Rossall Point
Preesall
Pilling Lane
Pilling
Dam Side
Stake Pool
Winmarleigh
Eagland Hill
Stalmine
Staynall
Hambleton
Out Rawcliffe
Moss Edge
Little Rawcliffe
Ratten Row
St Michael's on Wyre
Cleveleys
Anchorsholme
Norbreck
Trunnah
Thornton
Skippool
Carleton
Little Singleton
Great Eccleston
Elswick
Crossmoor
Cuddy Hill
Bispham
Warbreck
North Shore
Poulton-le-Fylde
Singleton
Little Eccleston
Inskip
Roseacre
Blackpool
Queenstown
Normoss
Staining
Layton
Thistleton
Wharles
Catforth
Woodplumpton
Broughton
Blackpool
South Shore
Hawes Side
Mereside
Common Edge
Great Marton
Weeton
Great Plumpton
Corner Row
Wesham
Treales
Lower Bartle
Higher Bartle
Gottam
Ingol
Kirkham
Dowbridge
Fulwood
Squires Gate
Higher Ballam
Moss Side
Westby
Wrea Green
Newton
Scales
Clifton
Preston
Lytham St Anne's
St Annes
Fairhaven
Ansdell
Lytham
Warton
Freckleton
Bottom of Hutton
Penwortham
Hutton
Longton
Middleforth Green
New
Lostock
Salters Bank
RIBBLE ESTUARY
Ribble

A B C D E F

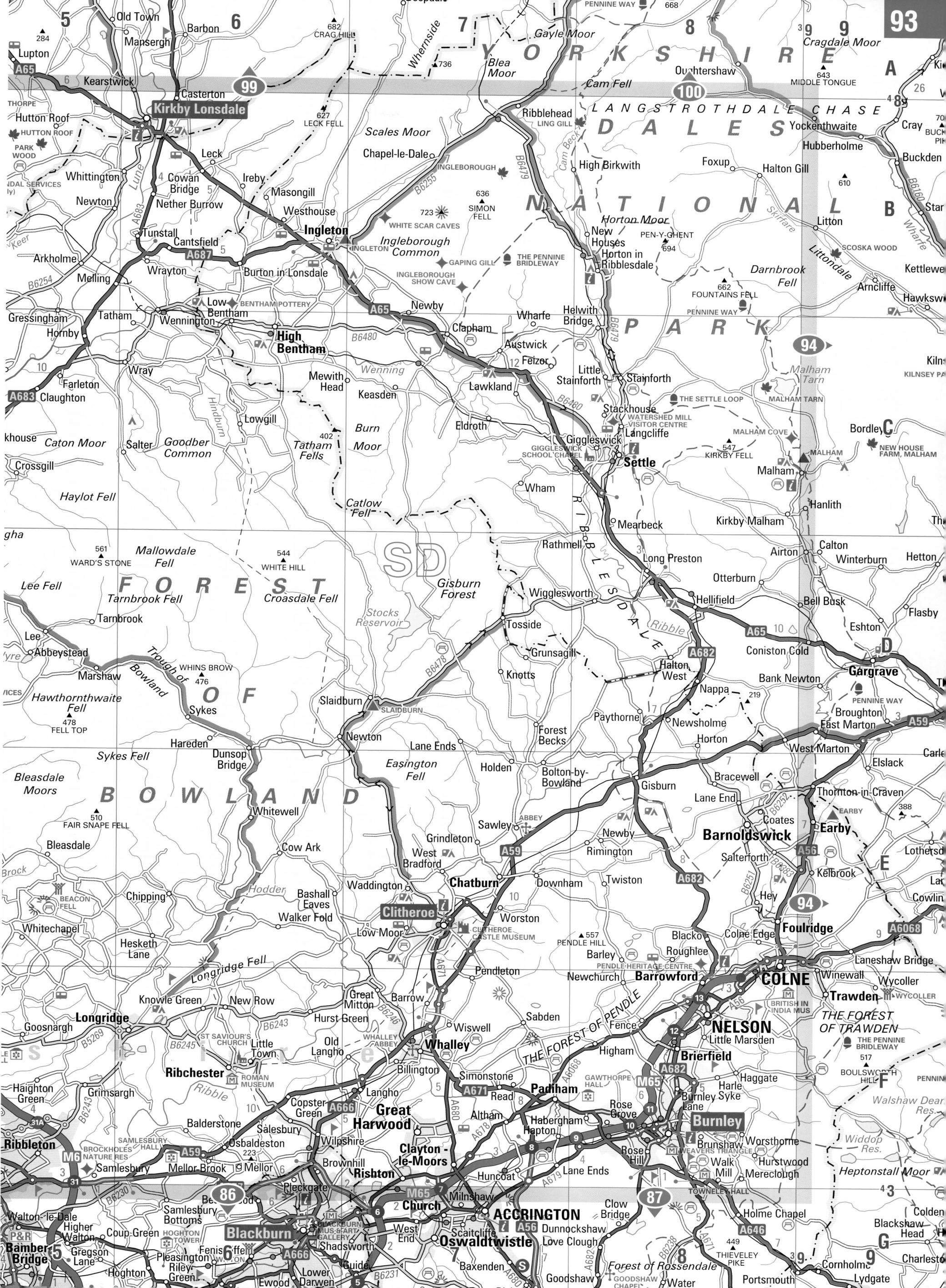

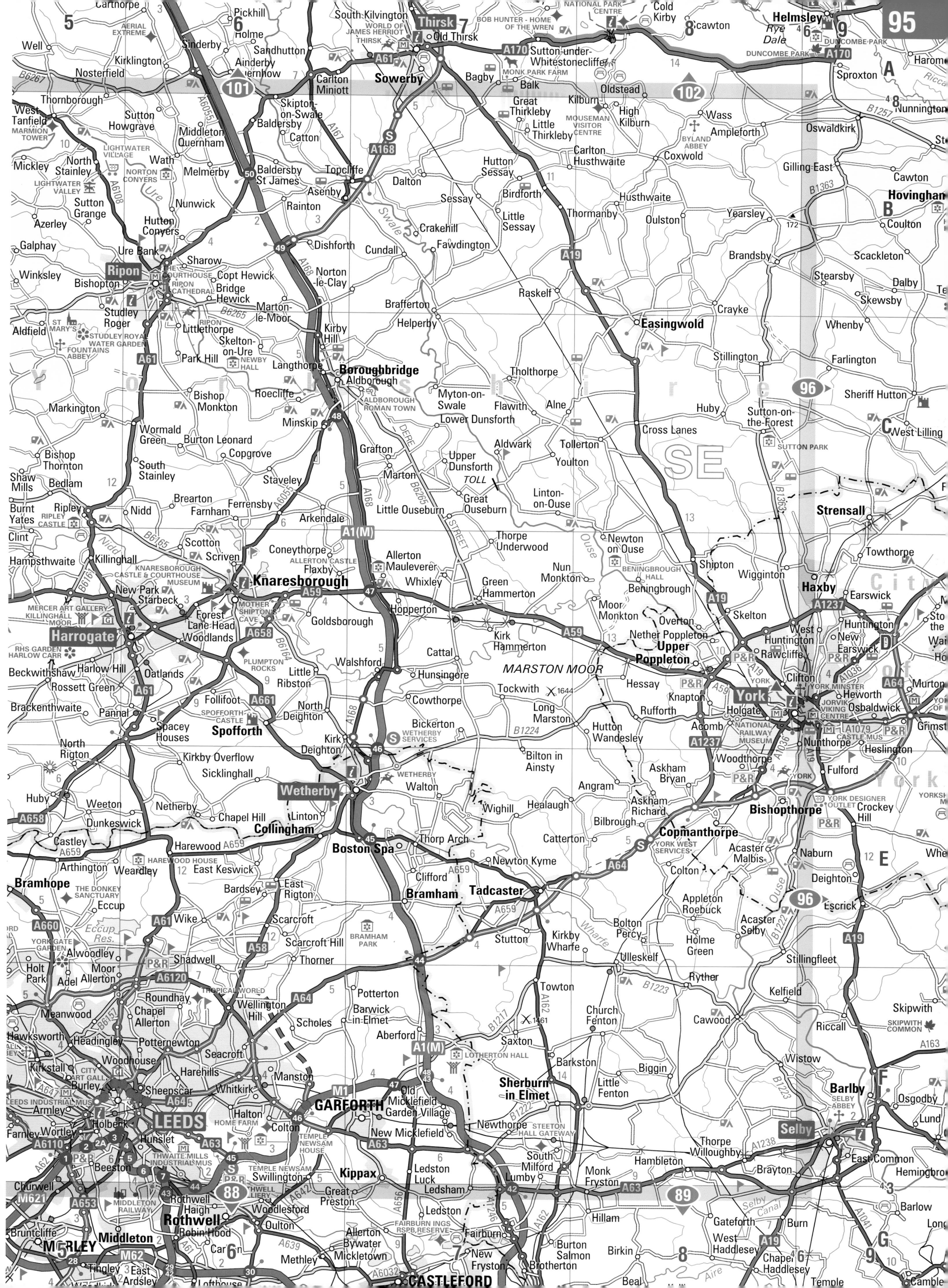

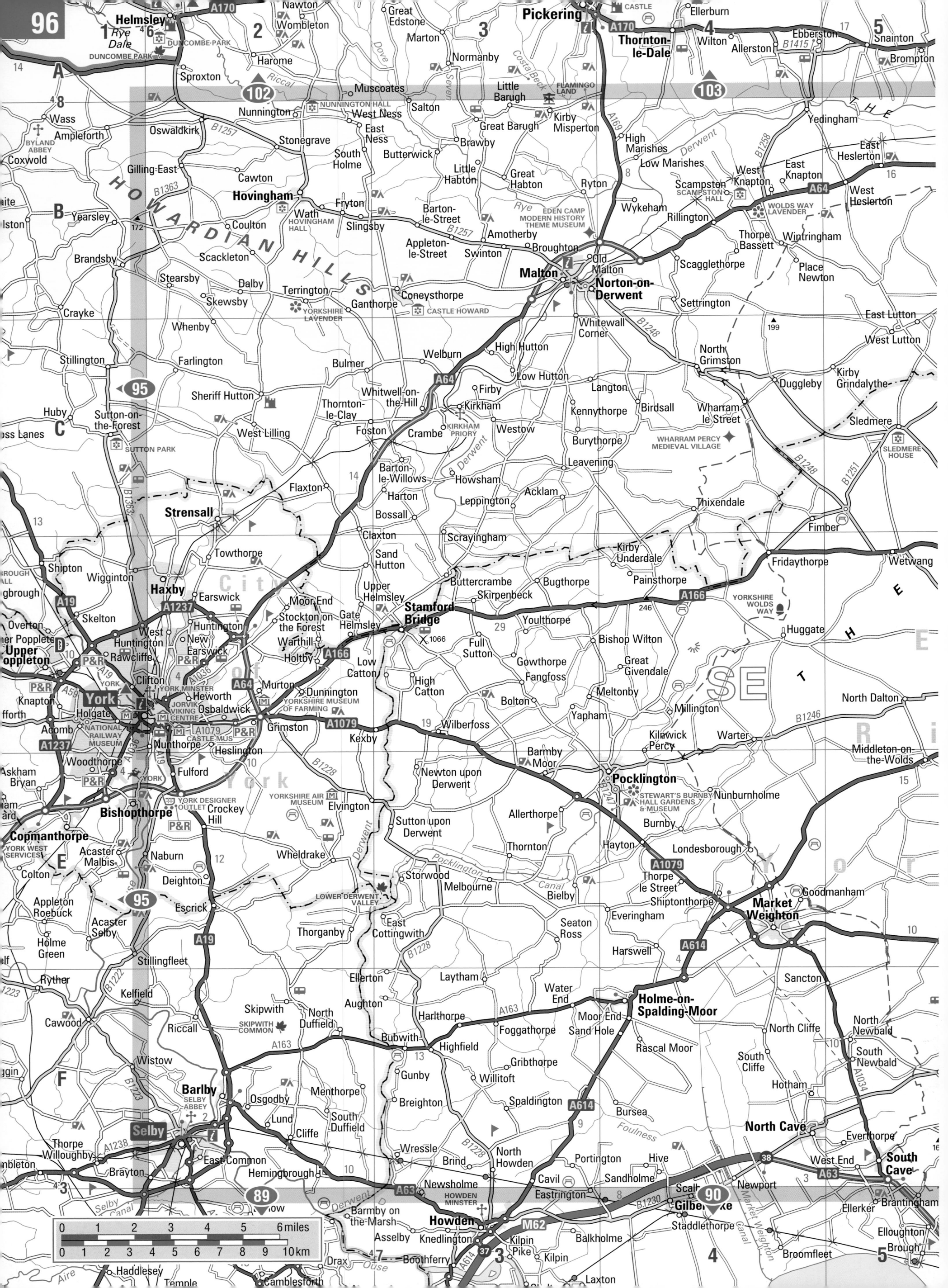

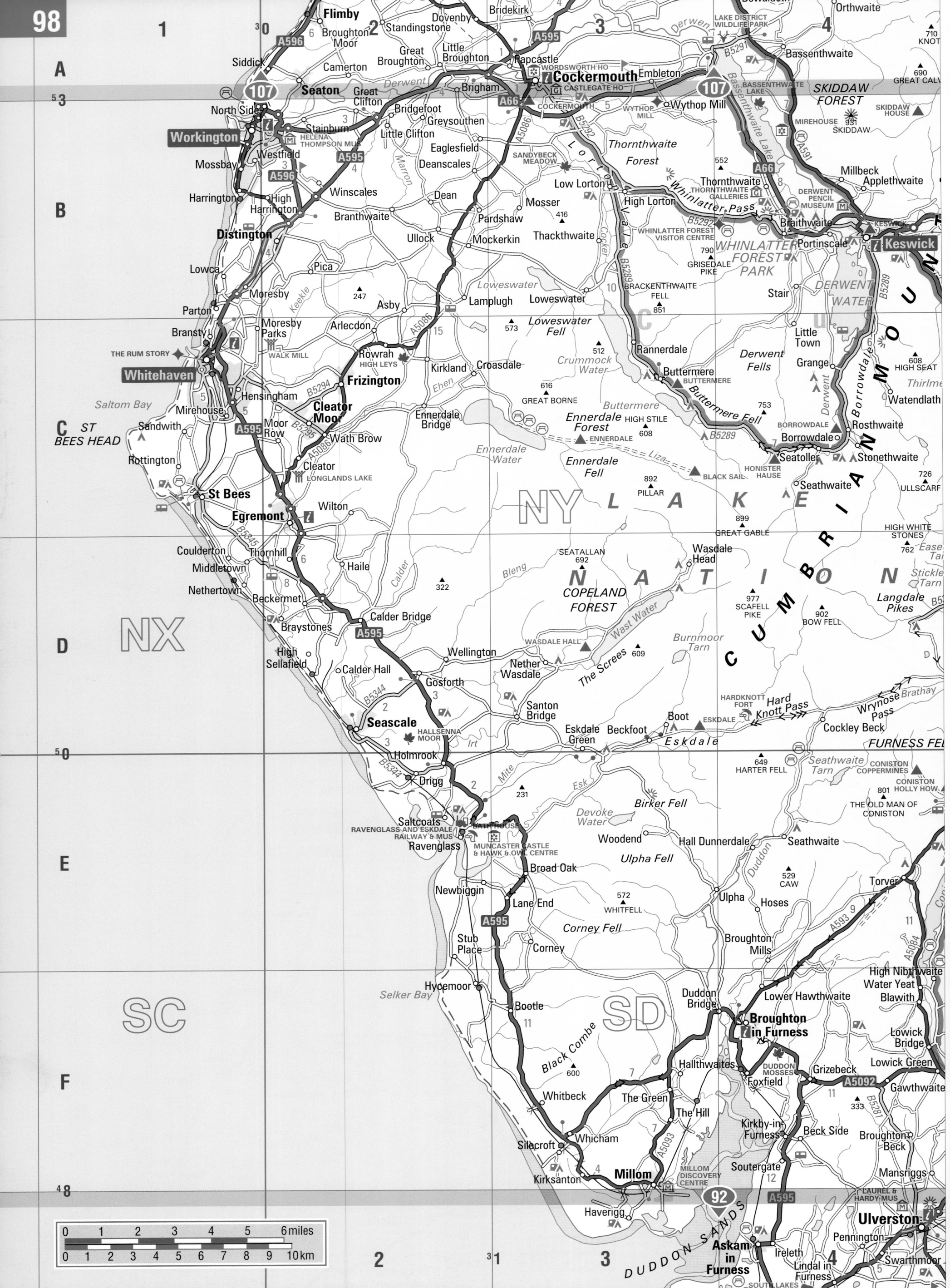

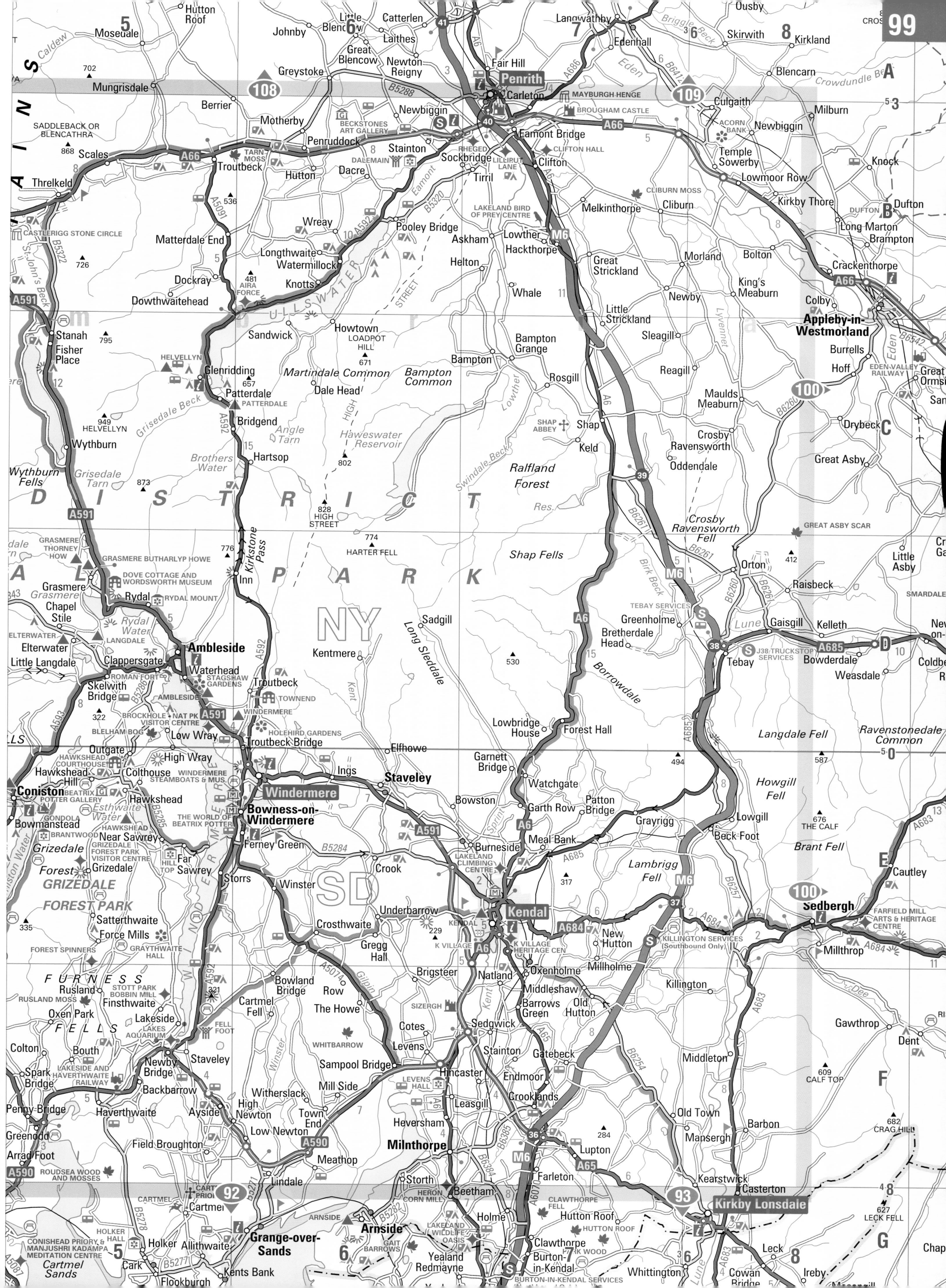

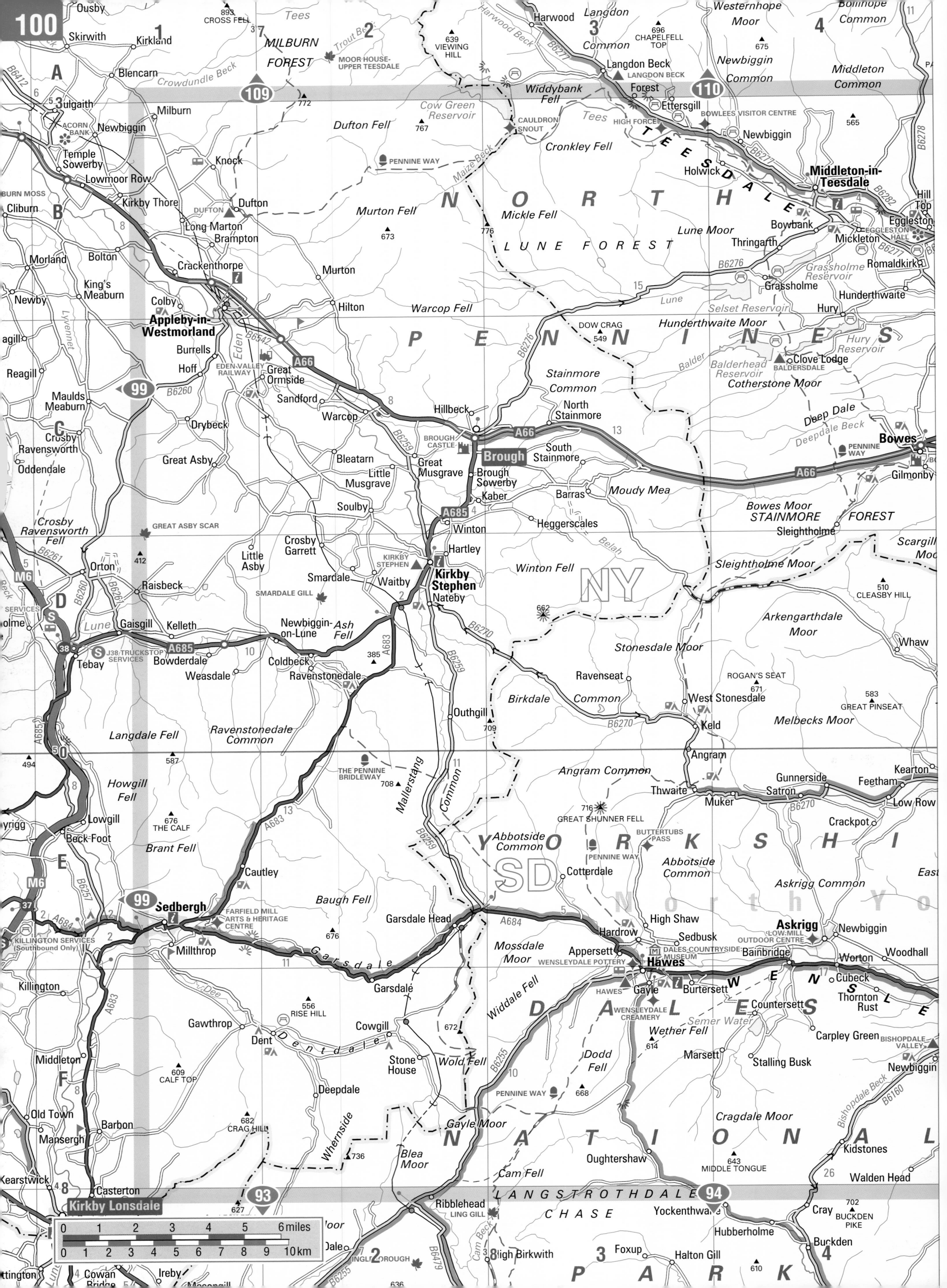

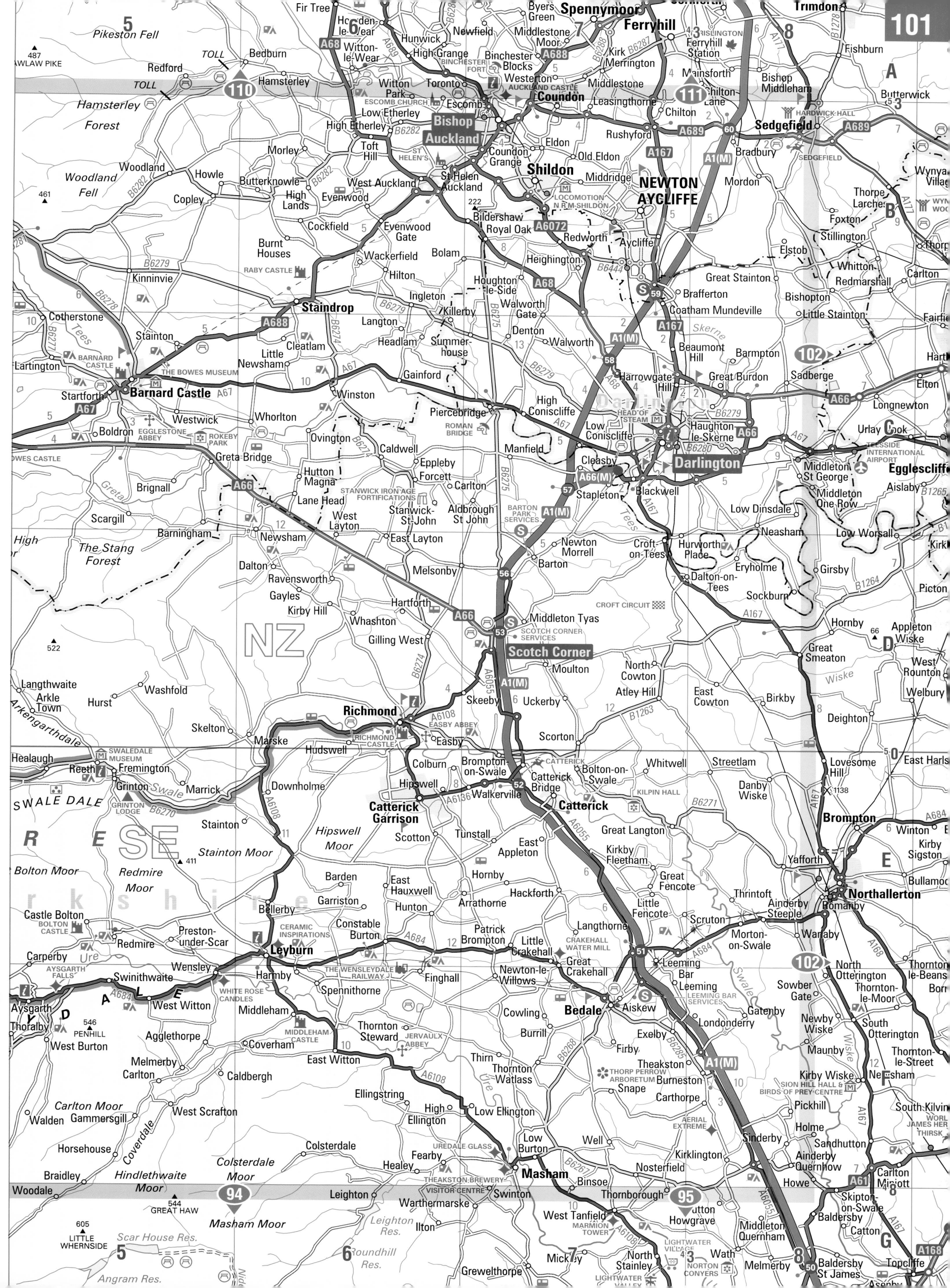

1   8   2   3   20   4   5

A

58

B

C

NW

D

E

54

F

19   3   20   4   5

CARLETON STLE

Bennane Hd.
112
Colmonell
B734 265
Knockdolian
9
Heronsford
Ballantrae Bay
Glen Tig
Ballantrae
Balkissock

Downan Pt.
Auchencrosh

439
BENERAIRD
A77

Mark
257
Glen App
17

Milleur Pt.

Corsewall Pt.
Barnhills
Portencalzie
Penwhirn
Res.
North Cairn
South Cairn
Corsewall
Cairnryan
Braid Fell
B738
Loch
Connell
Kirkcolm
Main Water of L
Dounan Bay
Ervie
The Wig
Mains of Airies
Low
Salchrie
LOCH RYAN
B798

Knocknain
Leswalt
A77
Innermessan
Slouchnawen
Bay
B738
Craigencross
Black Loch
CASTLE KENNEDY
GARDENS
White Loch
B7043
A751
A718
Glenstockadale
Stranraer
Aird
Castle Kennedy
Broadsea Bay
T   H   E   H   E   R   H   I
CASTLE OF
ST JOHN
VISITOR
CENTRE
Soulseat
Loch
Knockglass
STRANRAER
MUSEUM
Mark
A75
Black Hd.
B738
Lochans
B7077
Dunskey Ho.
182
A77
Torrs W
LITTLE
WHEELS
Awhirk
5
B7084
Portpatrick
Stoneykirk
A716
8
B7042
Luce Sa
Port of Spittal Bay

Cairngarroch
KIRKMADRINE
STONES
Sandhead
Cairngarroch Bay
Sandhead Bay
Money Hd.

Clachanmore
Hole Stone Bay
Ardwell
Ardwell
Mains
Chapel Rossan
Bay
Ardwell Pt.
Logan
Mains
10
LOGAN
BOTANIC
GARDEN
Balgowan
Pt.
Mull of Logan
LOGAN FISH POND
MARINE LIFE CENTRE
Port Nessock or Port Logan Bay
Port Logan
Cairnywellan Hd.
B7065
A716
Clanyard Bay
Low Clanyard
Kirkmaiden
Laggantalluch Hd.
Drummore
Ma
164
Damnaglaur
B7041
Crammag Hd.
Cairngaan
Port Kemin

0 1 2 3 4 5 6 miles
0 1 2 3 4 5 6 7 8 9 10km

BELFAST

LARNE

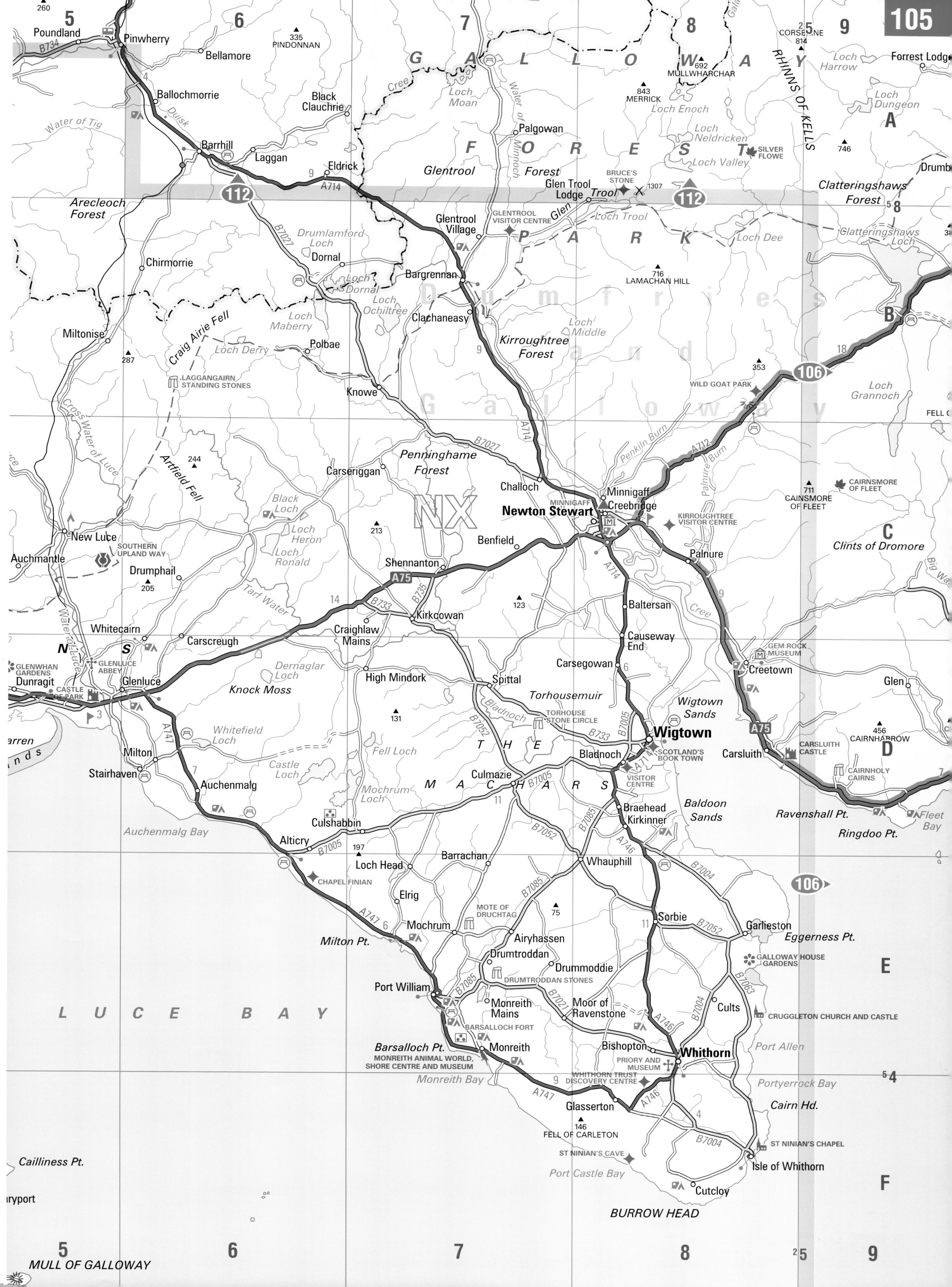

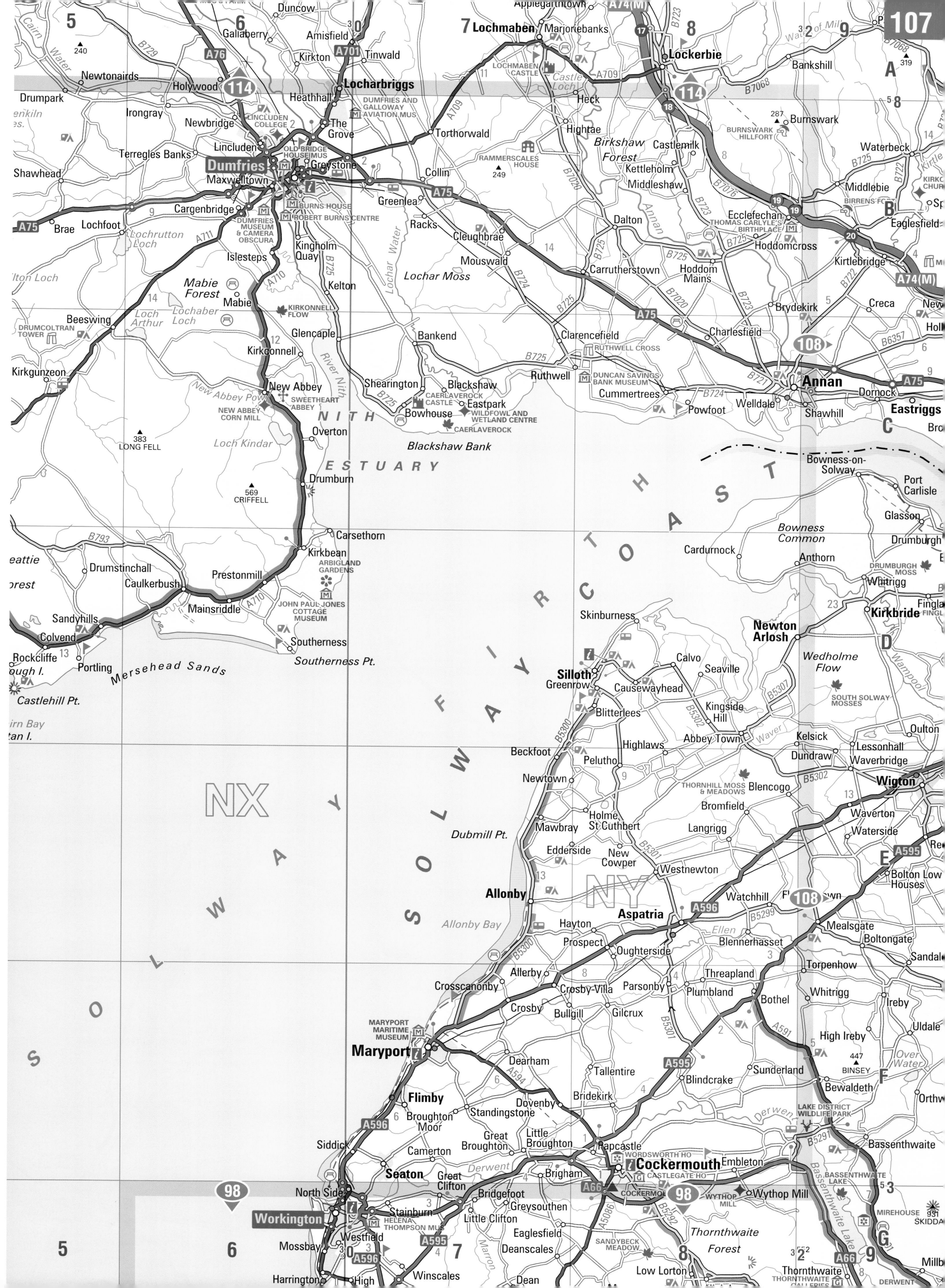

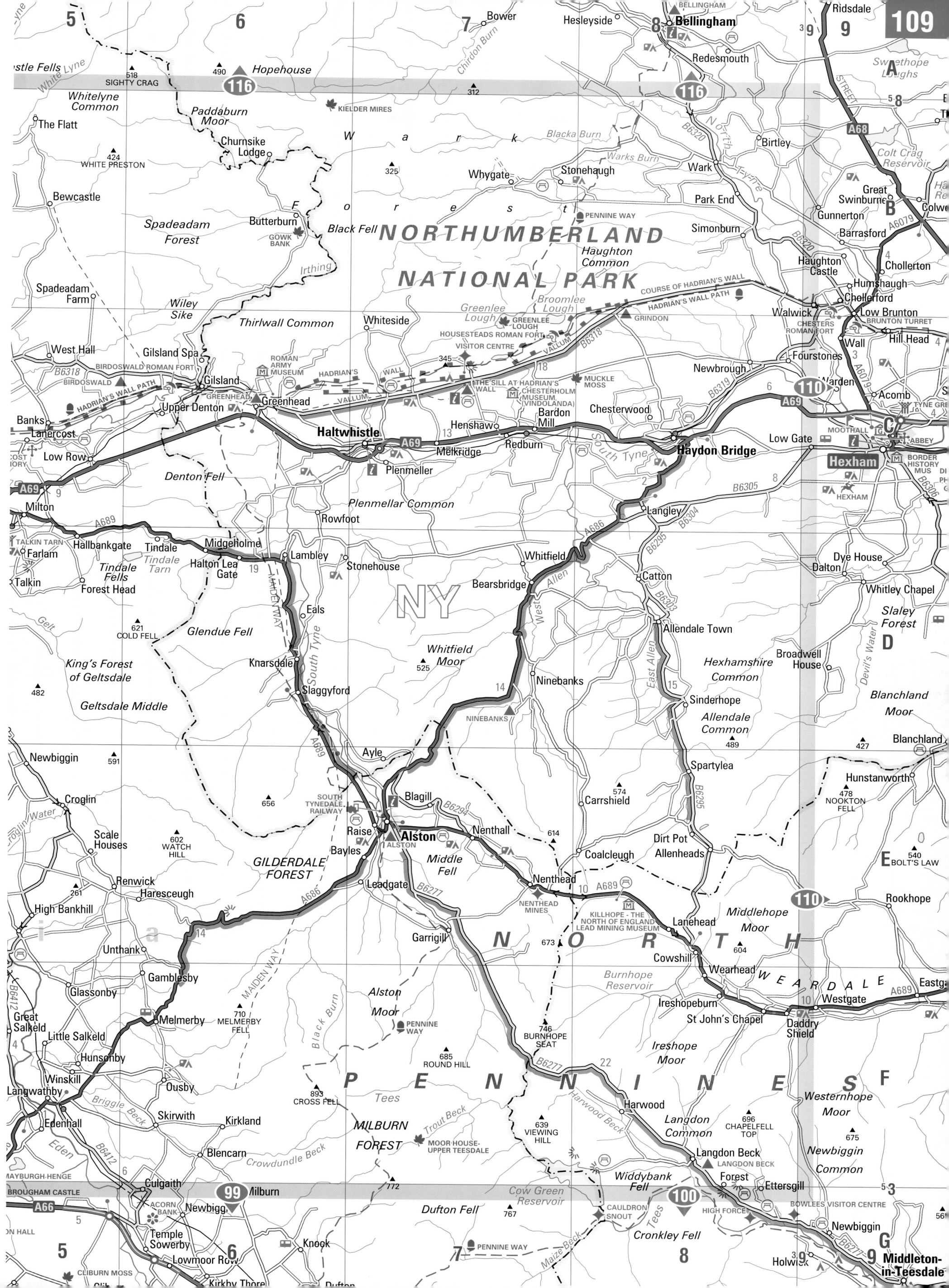

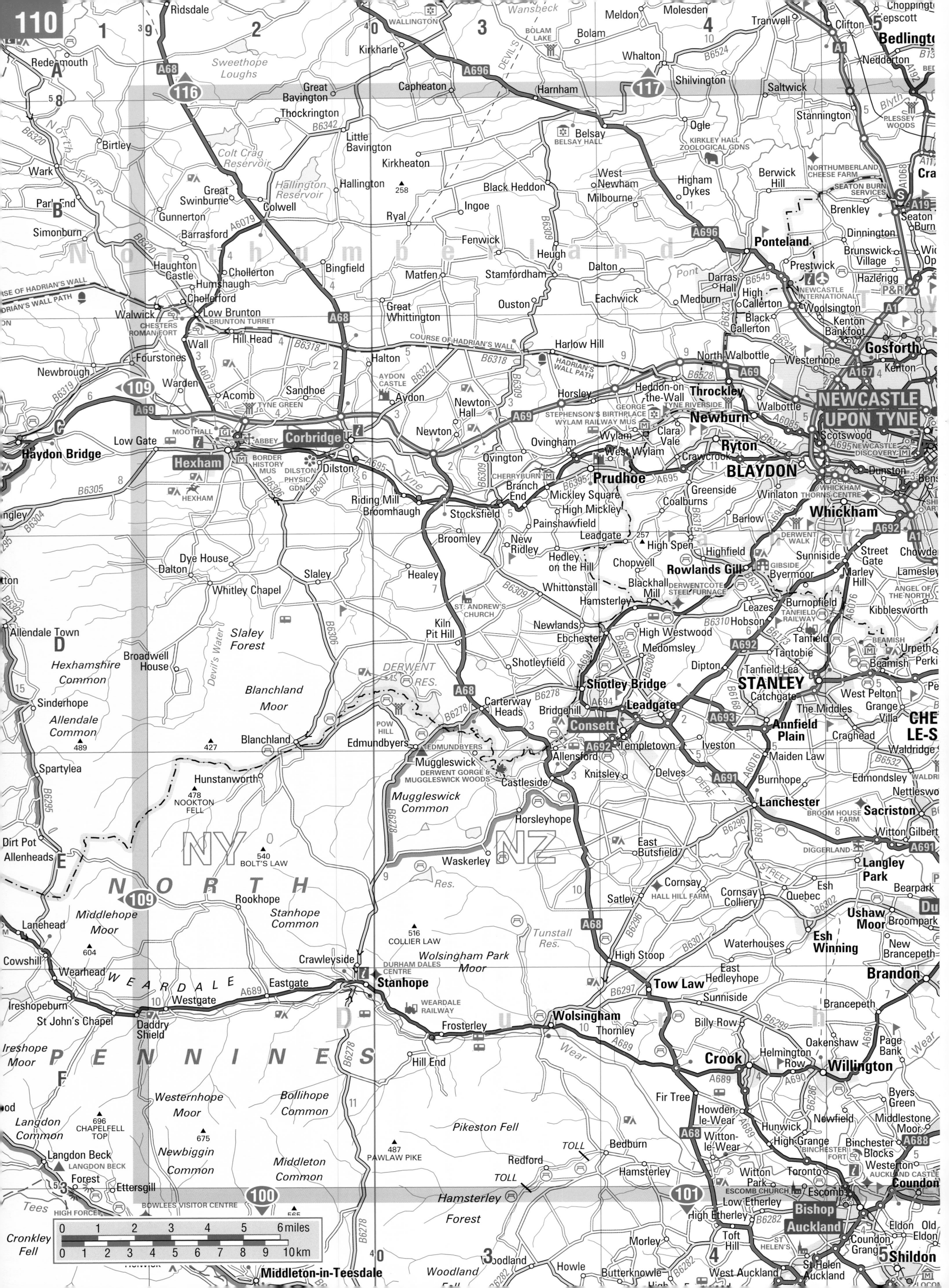

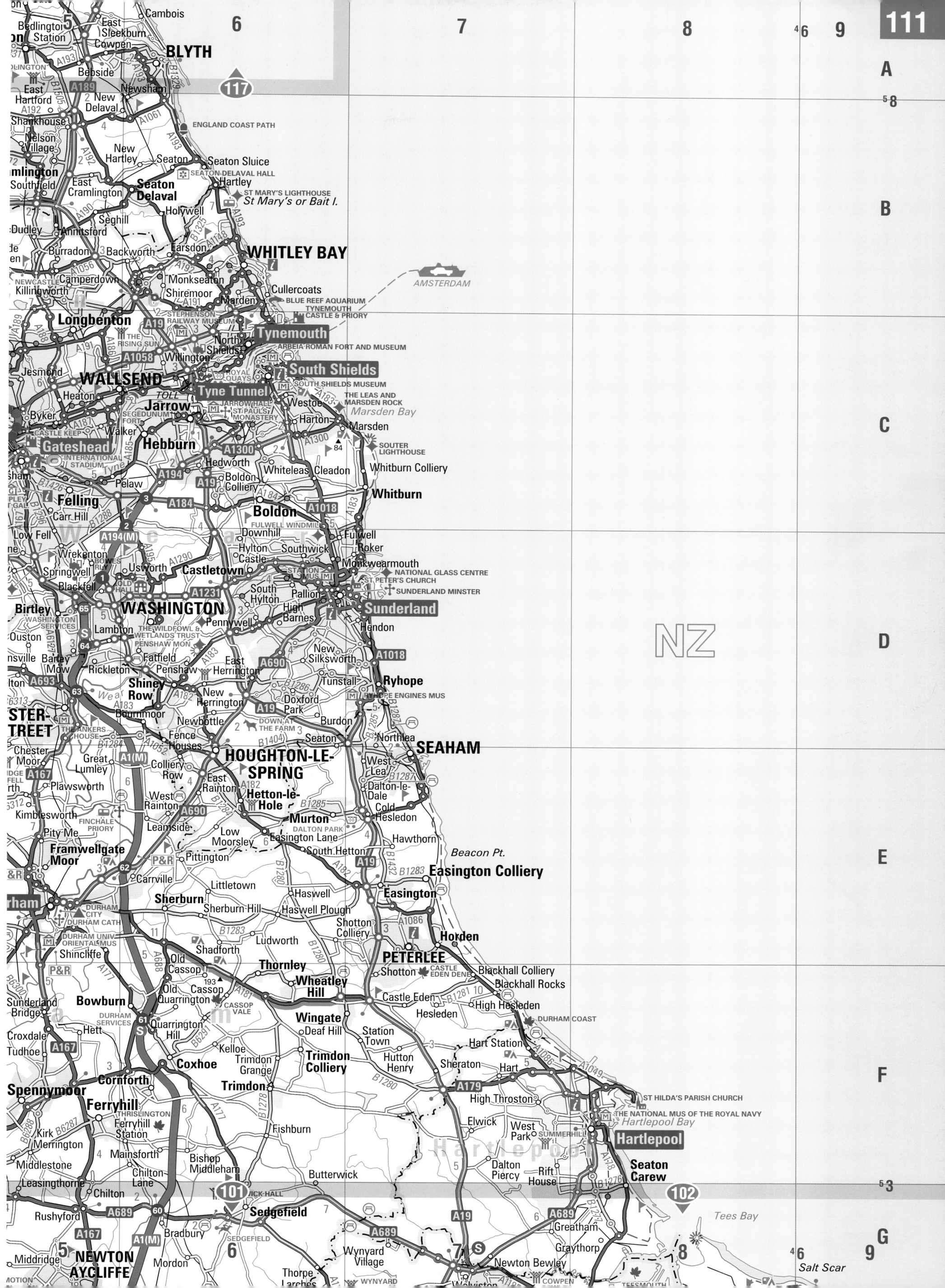

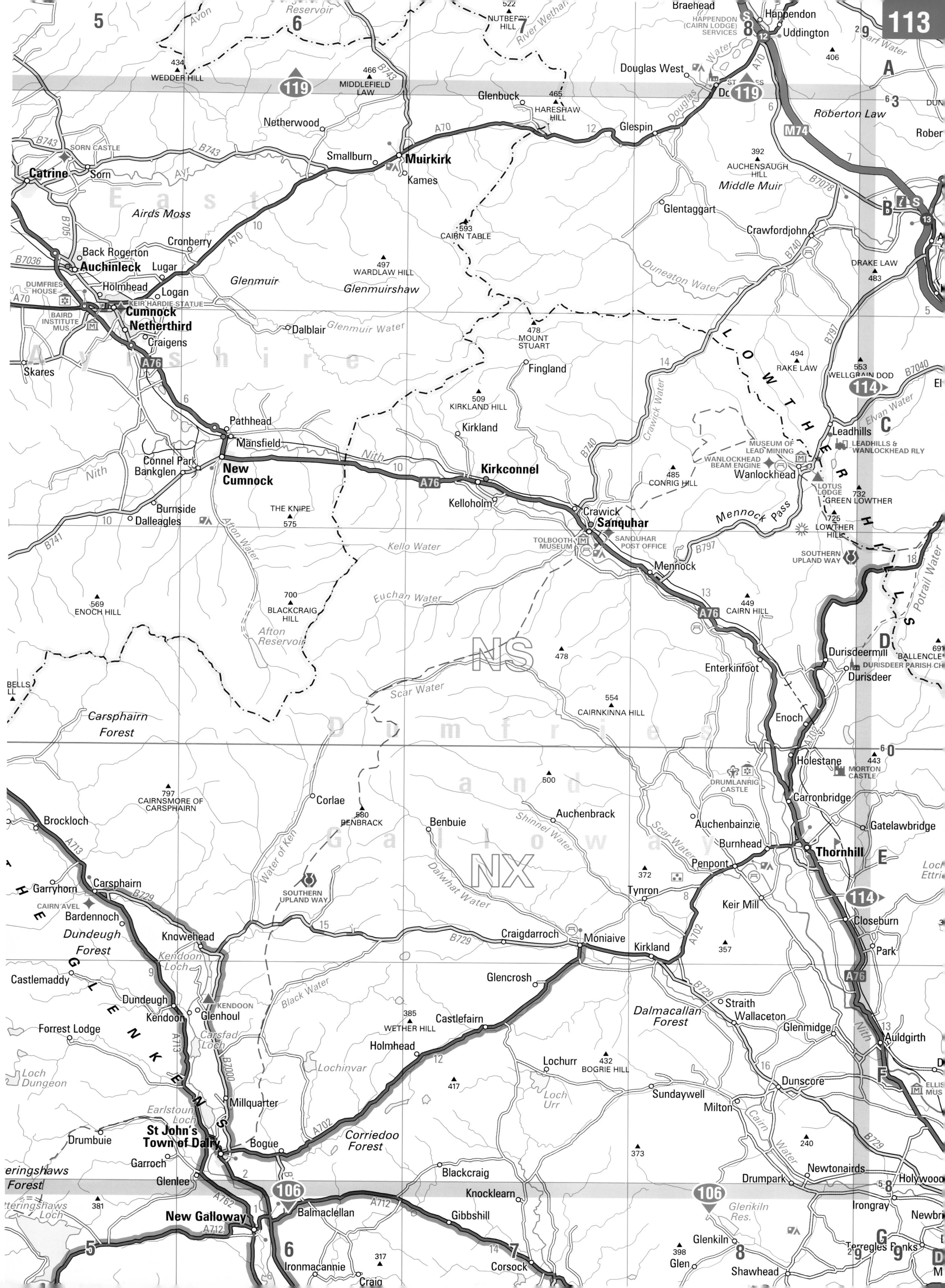

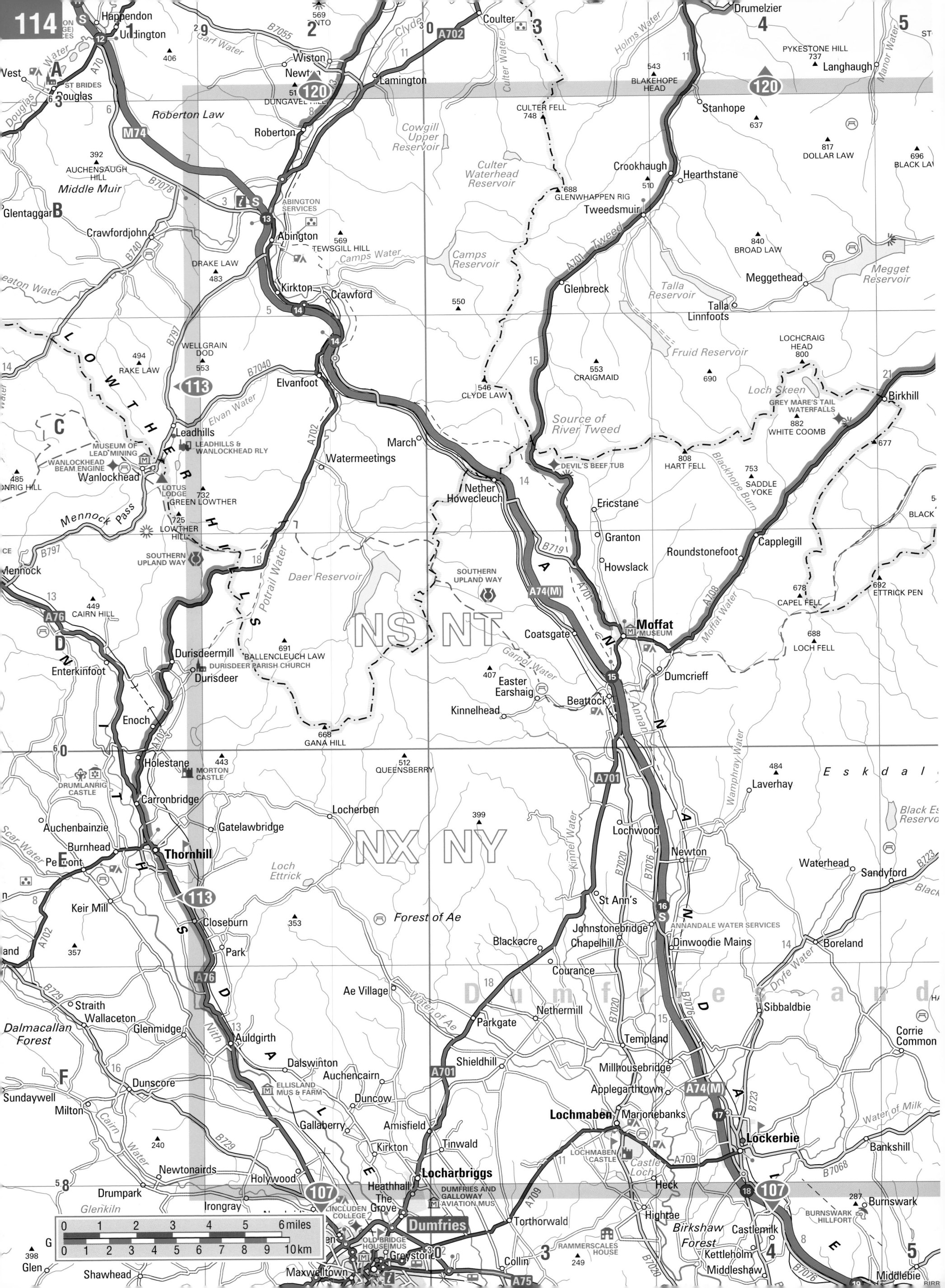

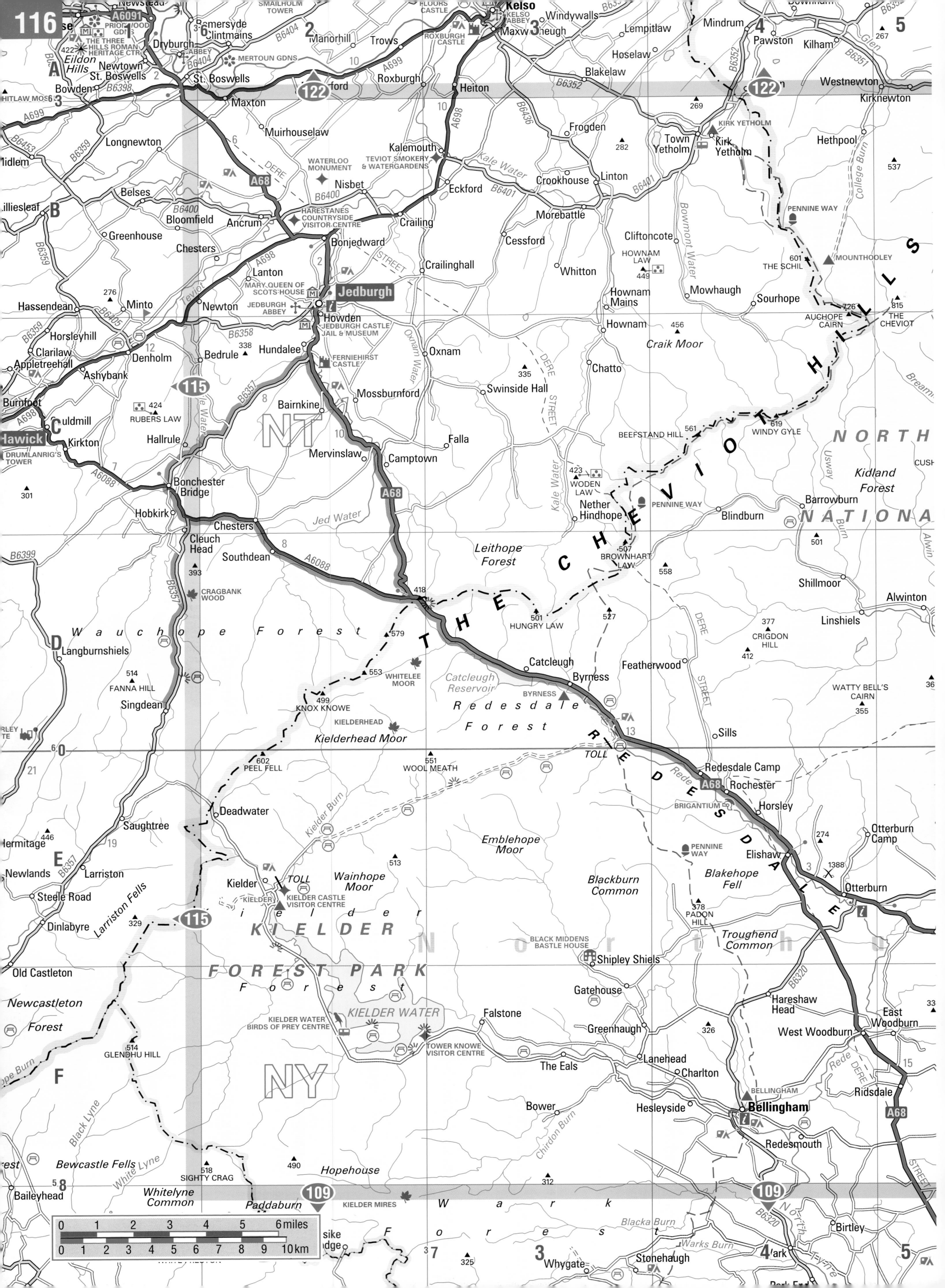

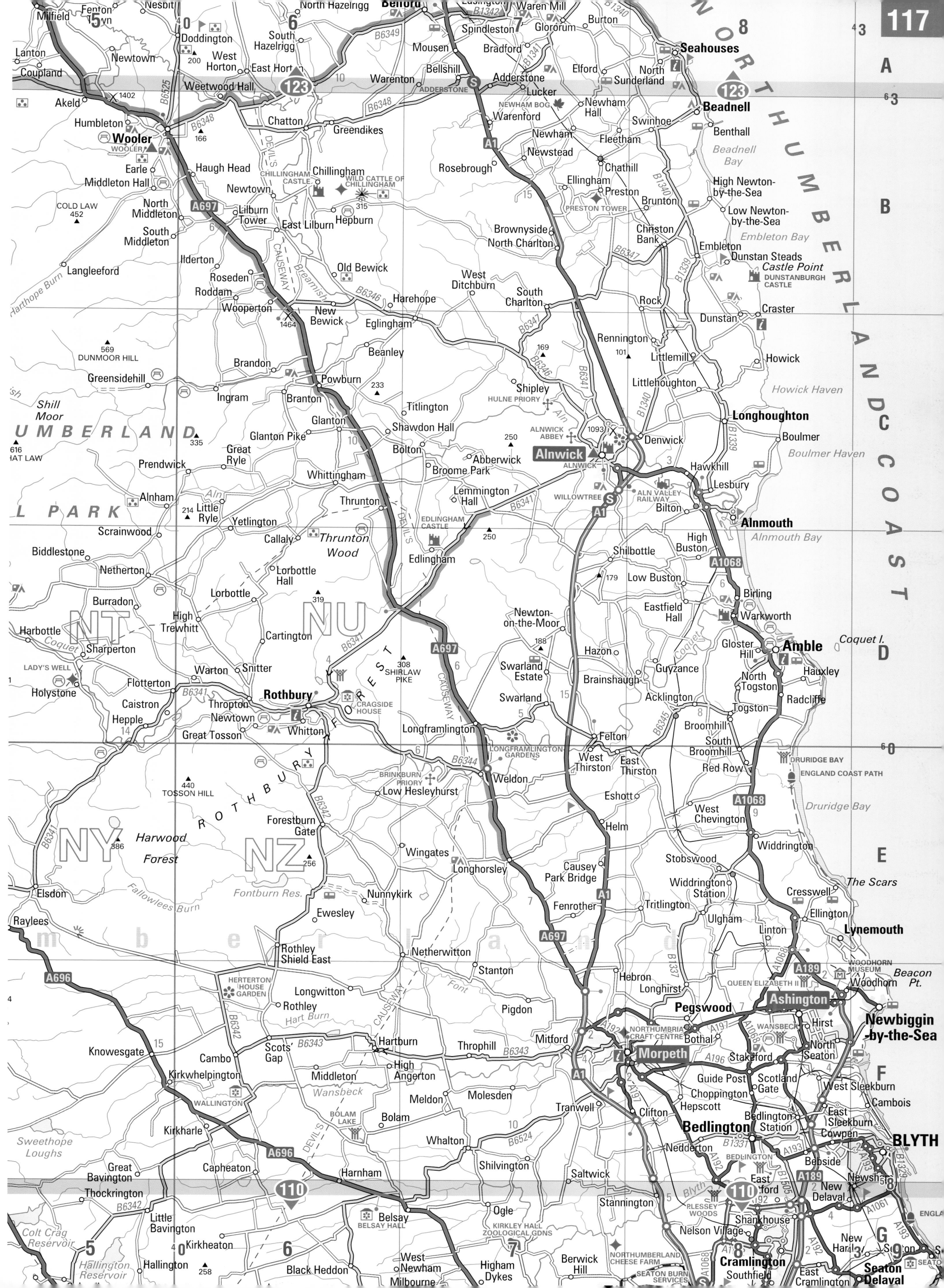

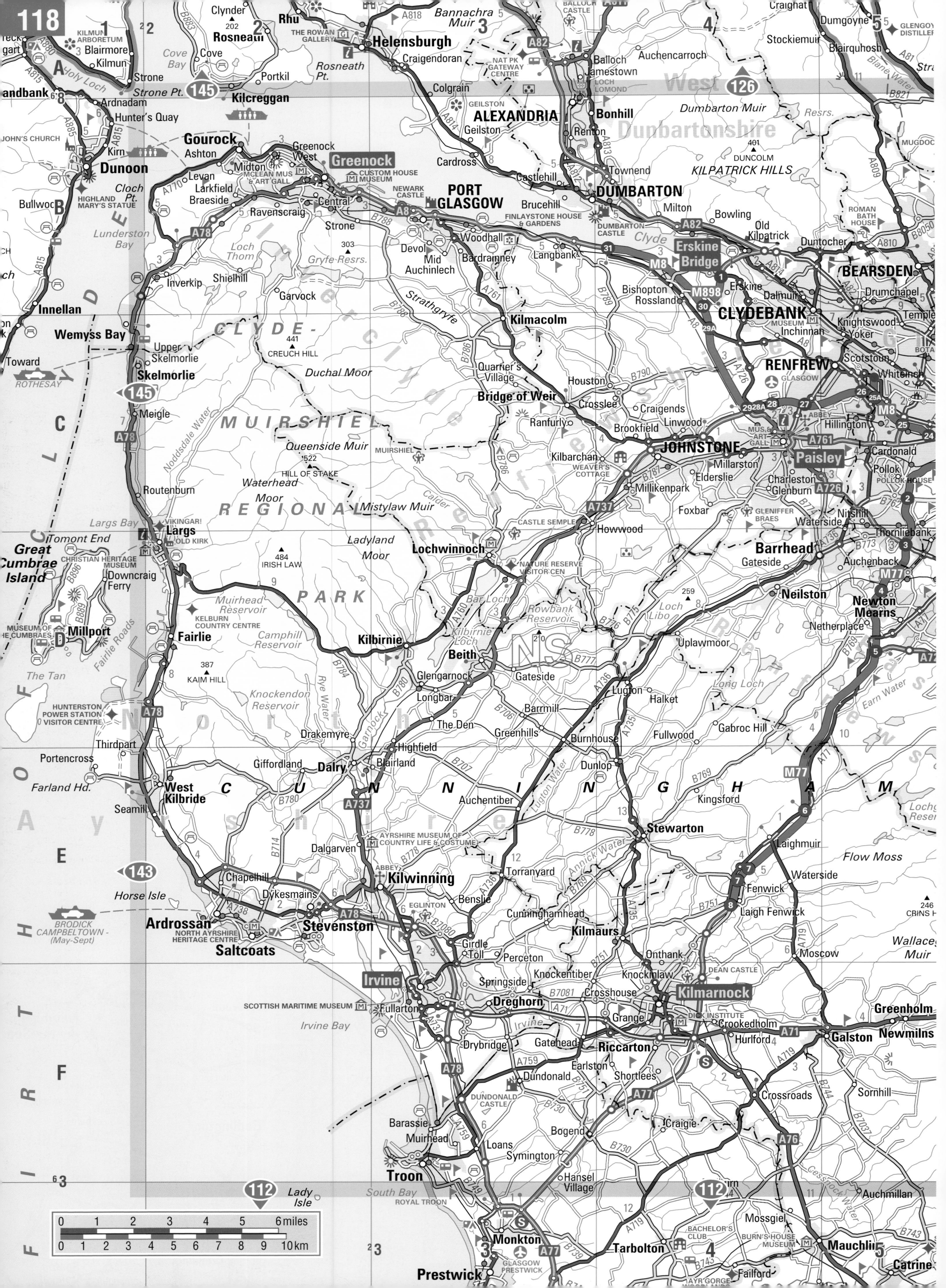

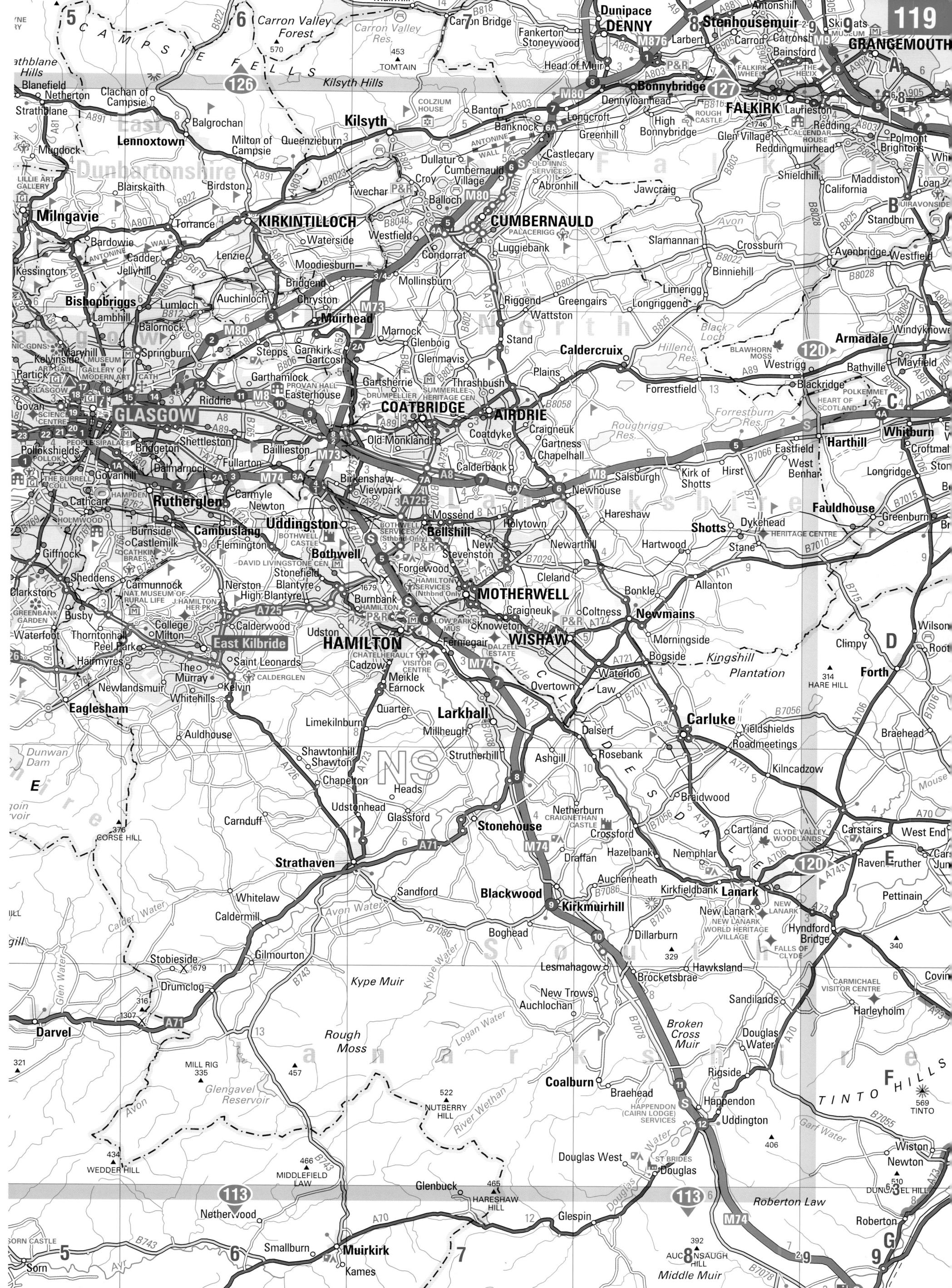

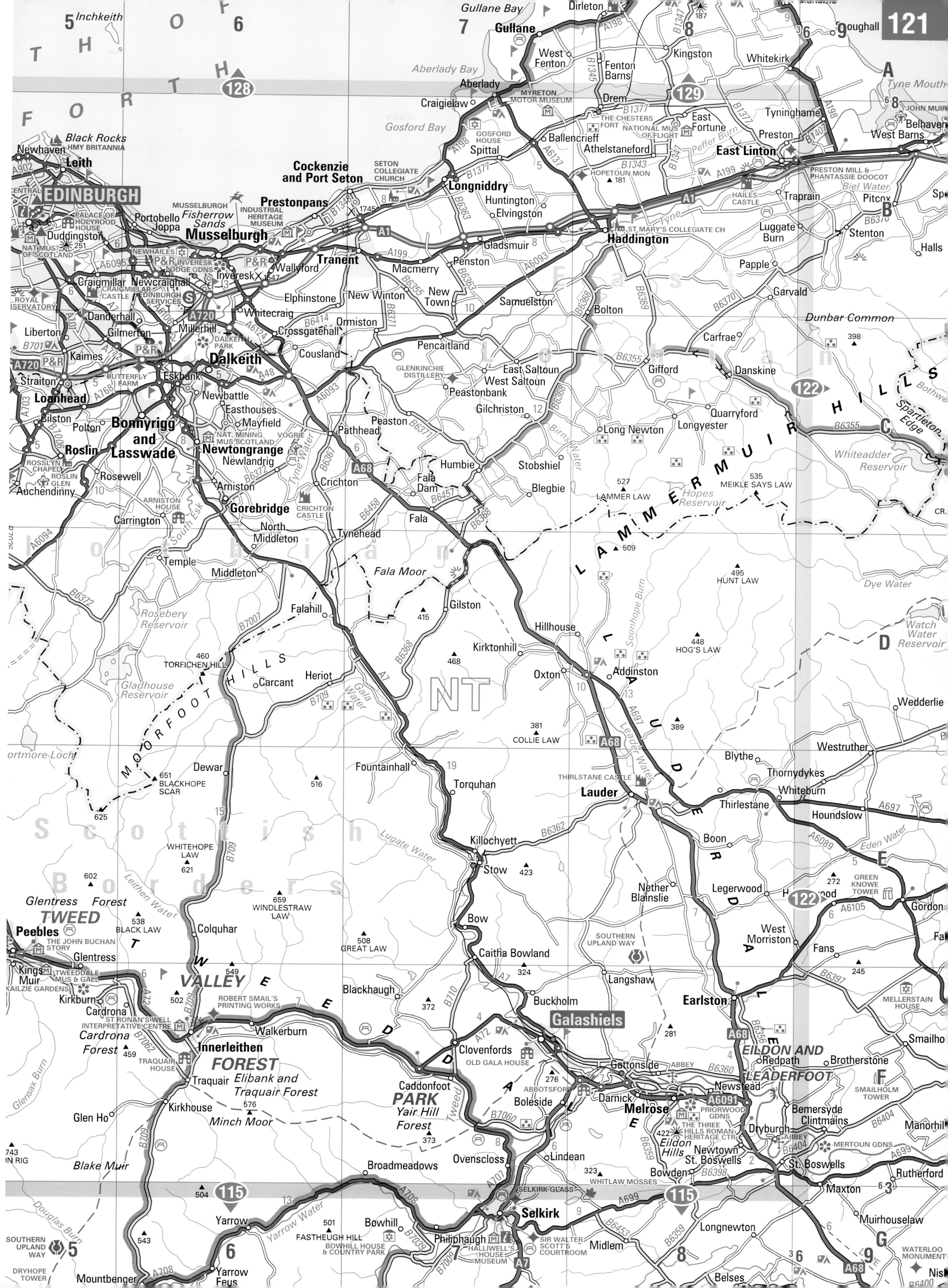

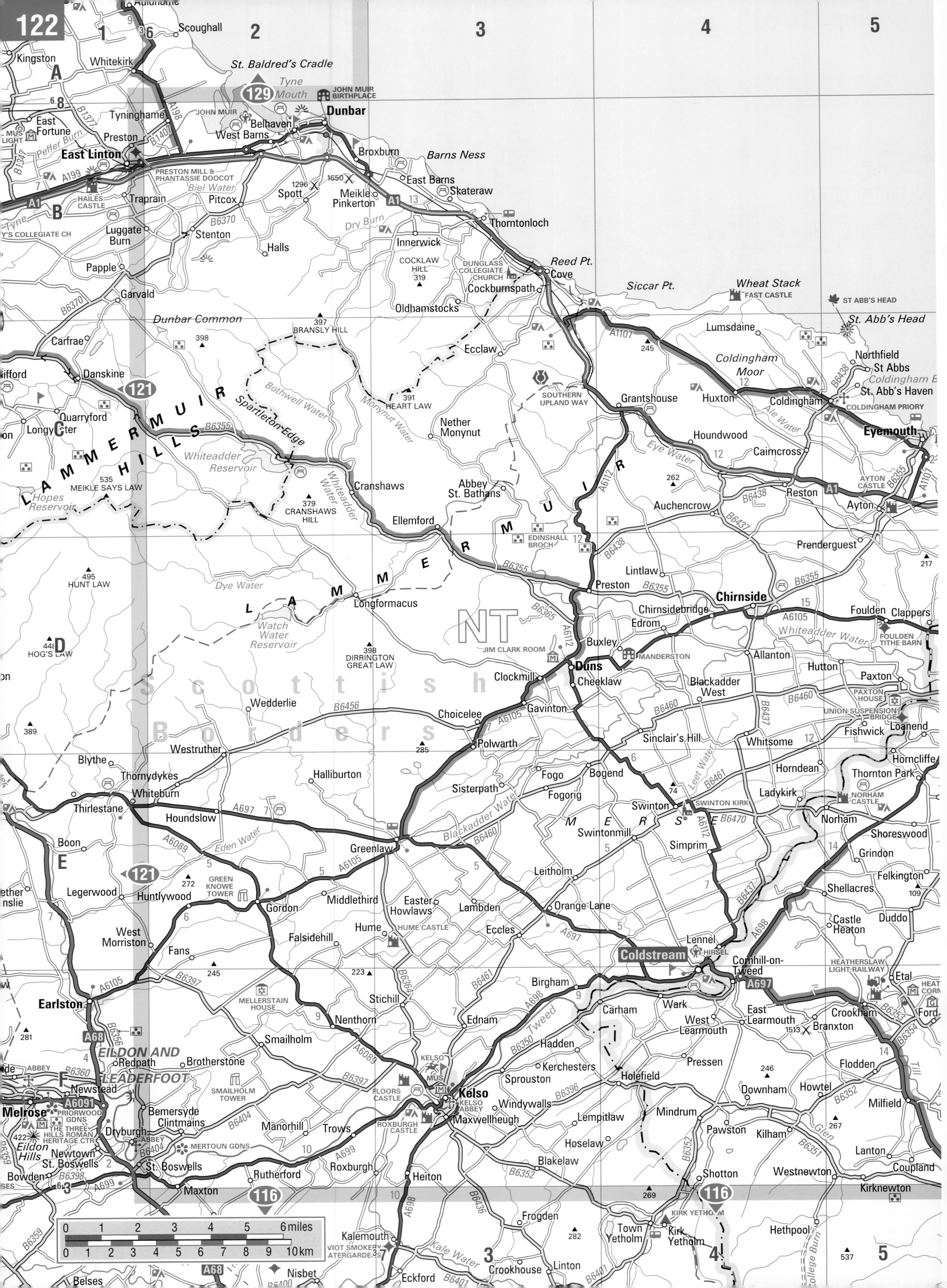

A

5   40   6   7   8   43   9

B

C

D

E

F

G

NU

NORTHUMBERLAND COAST

EYEMOUTH MUSEUM

Burnmouth

Lamberton Beach

Lamberton

1333

Highfields

Berwick-upon-Tweed
BERWICK-UPON-TWEED
BARRACKS & MAIN GUARD
BERWICK

B6461

East Ord

Tweed

Tweedmouth
Spittal

Prior
Park

Redshin Cove

A698

108

Murton
Thornton

Scremerston

West Allerdean

Shoresdean

Cheswick

B6354

Ancroft

Berrington

North Low

Goswick

Haggerston

B6525

DEVIL'S CAUSEWAY

South Low

Beal

A1

82

12

Bowsden

LINDISFARNE

*Causeway
Holy
Island
Sands*

Holy
Island

HERITAGE
CENTRE

Emmanuel Hd.

**Holy Island
(Lindisfarne)**

LINDISFARNE CASTLE

Castle Pt.

LINDISFARNE
PRIORY

Barmoor
Castle

Barmoor
Lane End

West
Kyloe

Lowick

*Kyloe
Hills*

East
Kyloe

Fenwick

Buckton

B6353

Fenham

*Guile
Pt.*

Ross

*Farne
Islands*

Staple Sound

FARNE ISLANDS

HERSLAW
MILL

LADY WATERFORD HALL

B6353

157

Kimmerston

Holburn

Detchant

Middleton

211

Elwick

*Budle
Bay*

Budle

Budle

BAMBURGH
CASTLE

Inner Sound

Bamburgh

Fenton
Town

Nesbit

North Hazelrigg

Easington

Waren Mill

B1342

Spindlestone

Glororum

Burton

B1340

Doddington

200

South
Hazelrigg

West
Horton

Mousen

Bradford

Belford

B6349

Seahouses

Elford

North
Sunderland

Newtown

East Horton

Warenton

Bellshill

B1341

Adderstone

Akeld

1402

Weetwood Hall

A697

B6525

117

10

Chatton

B6348

ADDERSTONE

S

Lucker

NEWHAM BOG

Warenford

Newham
Hall

Newham

Swinhoe

Bea 117

Benthall

Humbleton

166

Greendikes

A1

Fleetham

*Beadnell
Bay*

Wooler

WOOLER

5   40   6

Earle

Haugh Head

CHILLINGHAM
CASTLE

Chillingham

*WILD CATTLE OF
CHILLINGHAM*

Newtown

Rosebrough

7

Newstead

Chathill

Ellingham

B1340

8   43   9

Middleton Hall

Preston

High Newton-
by-the-Sea

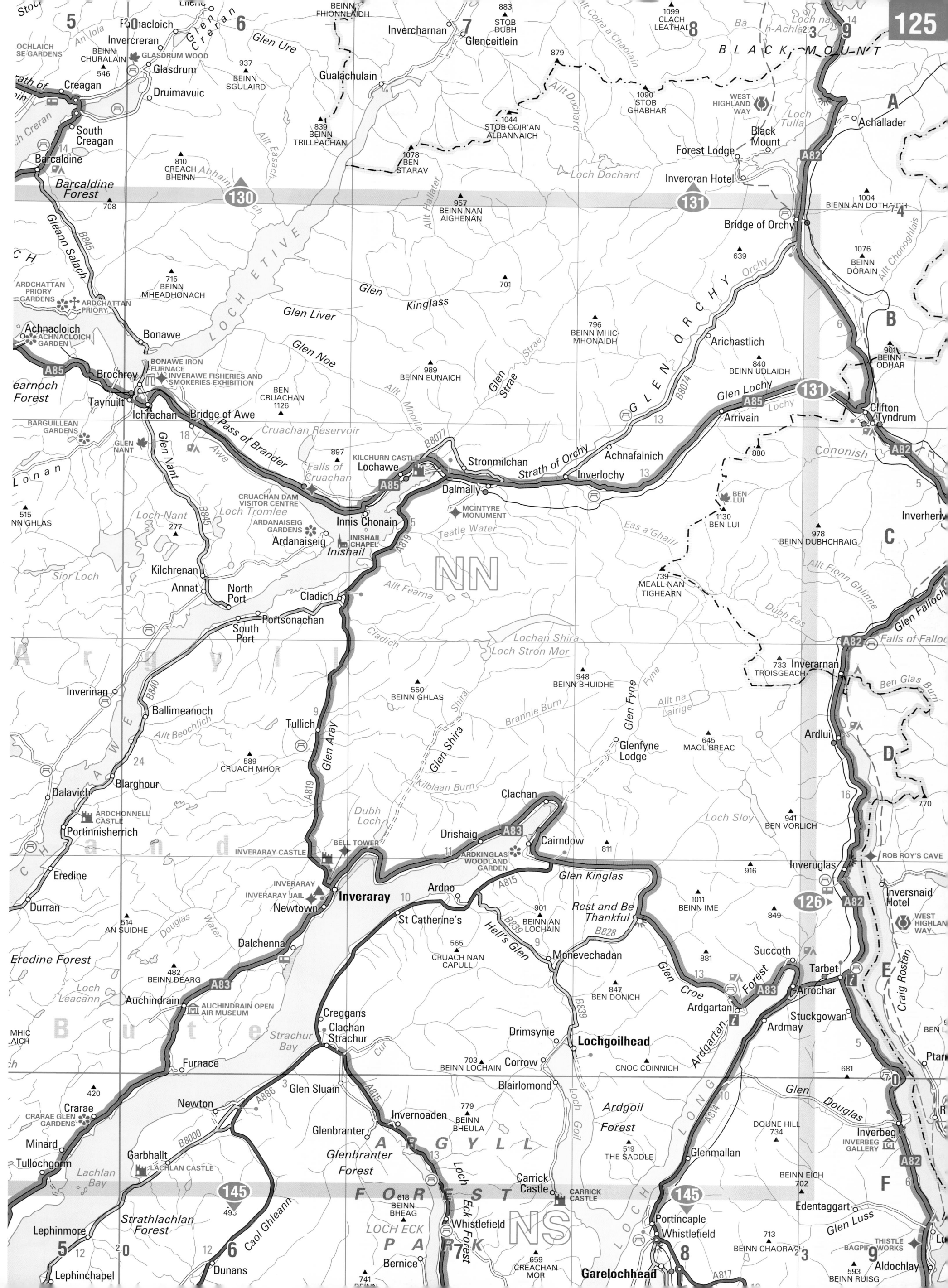

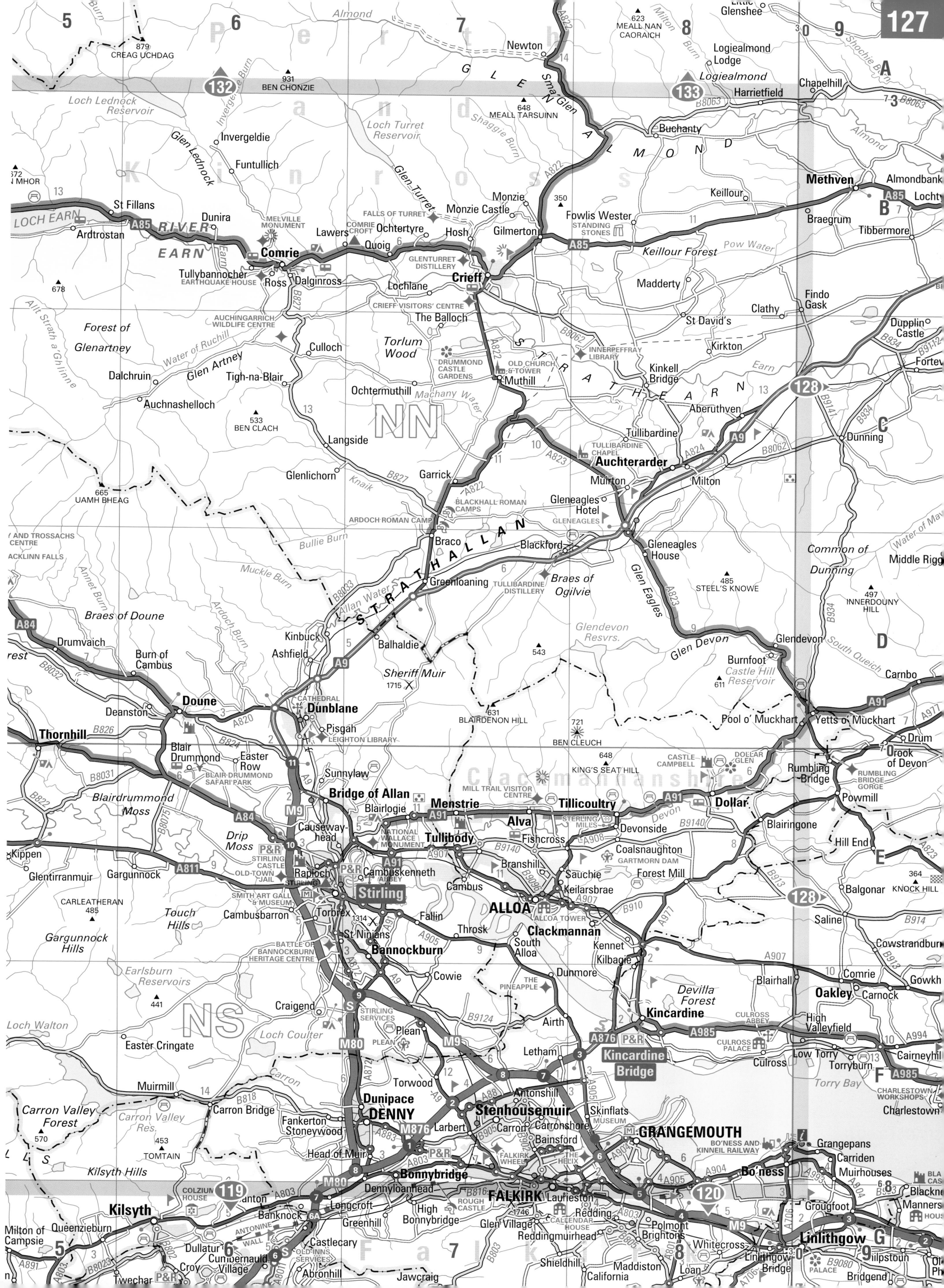

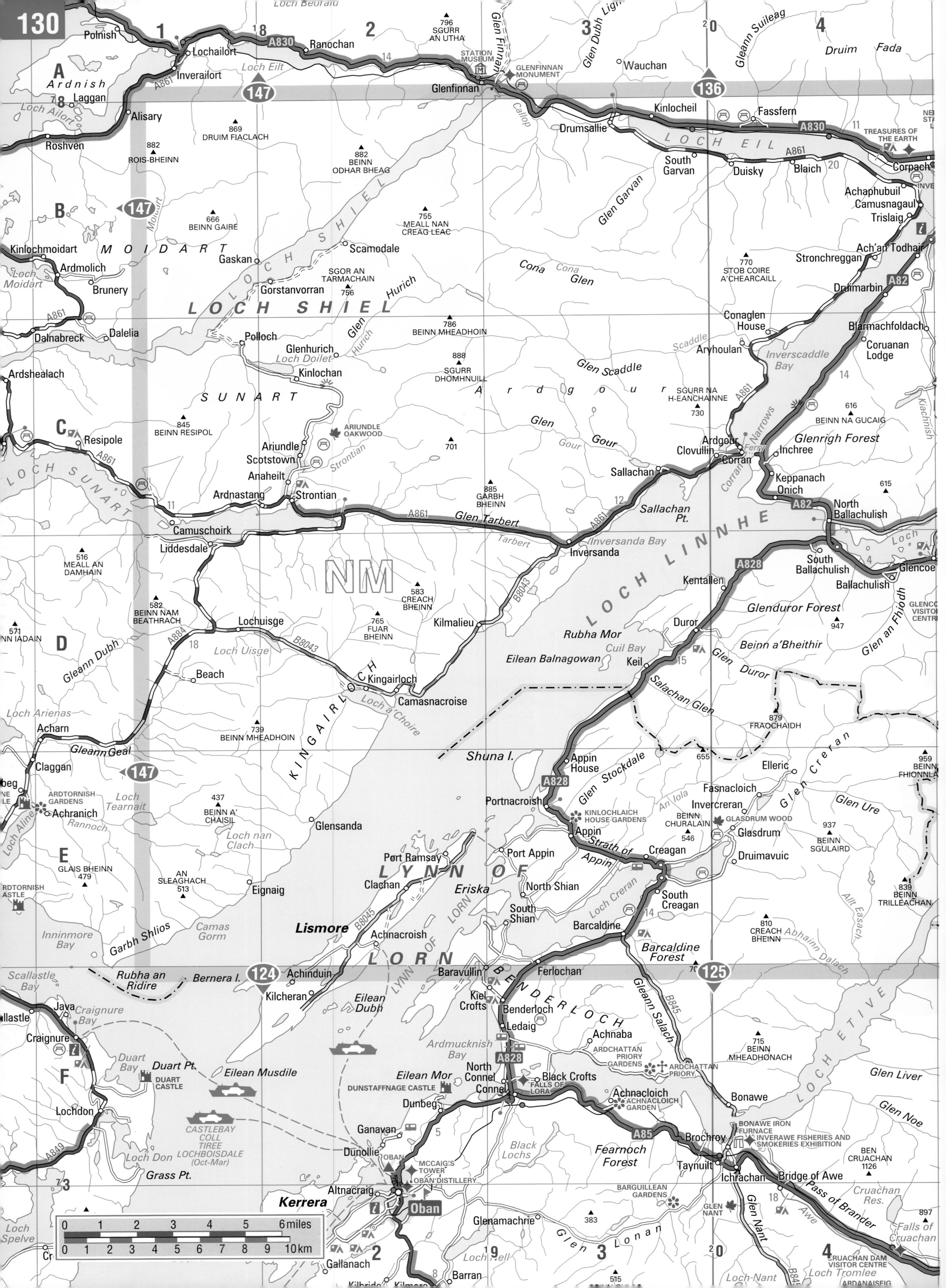

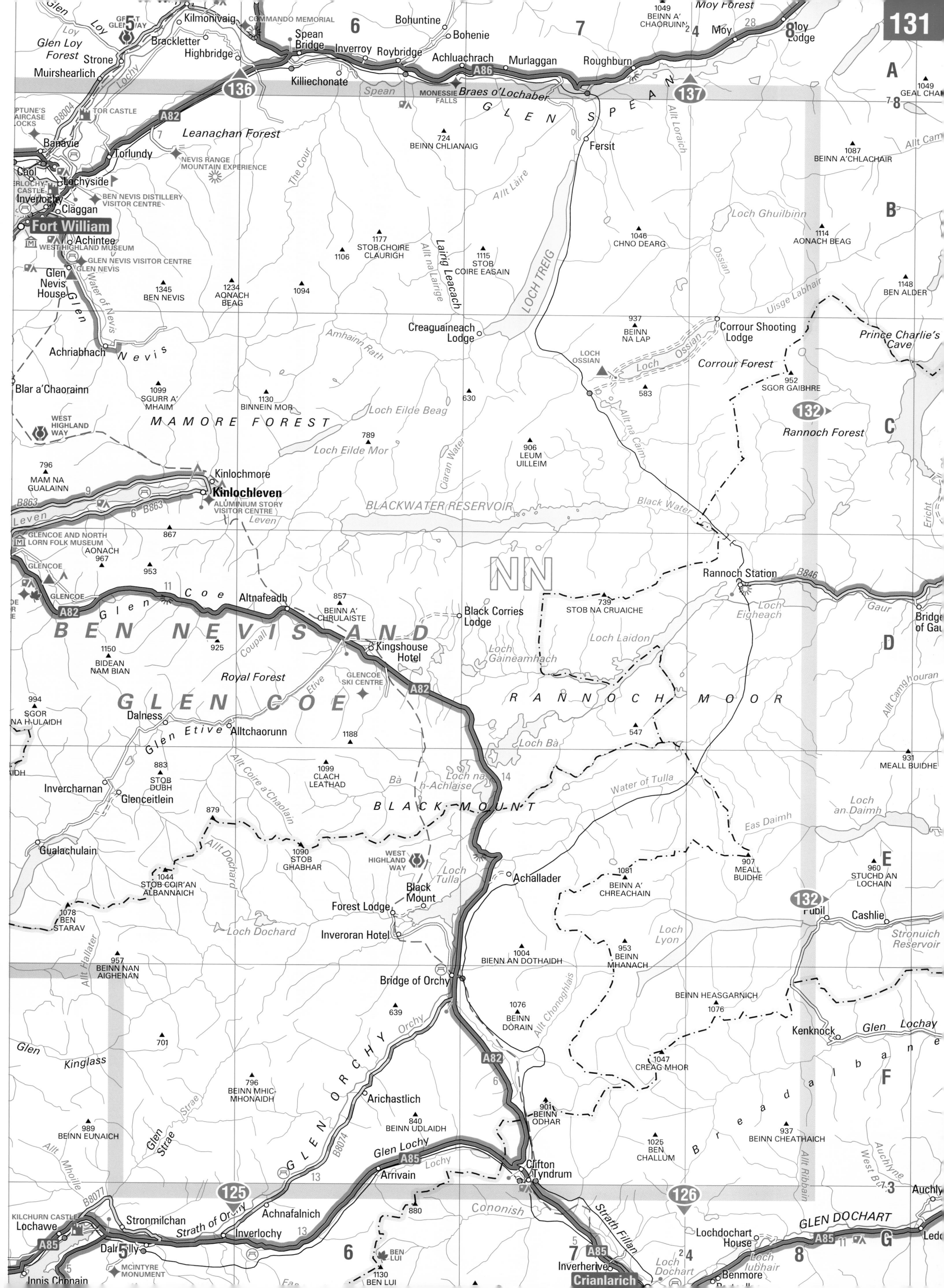

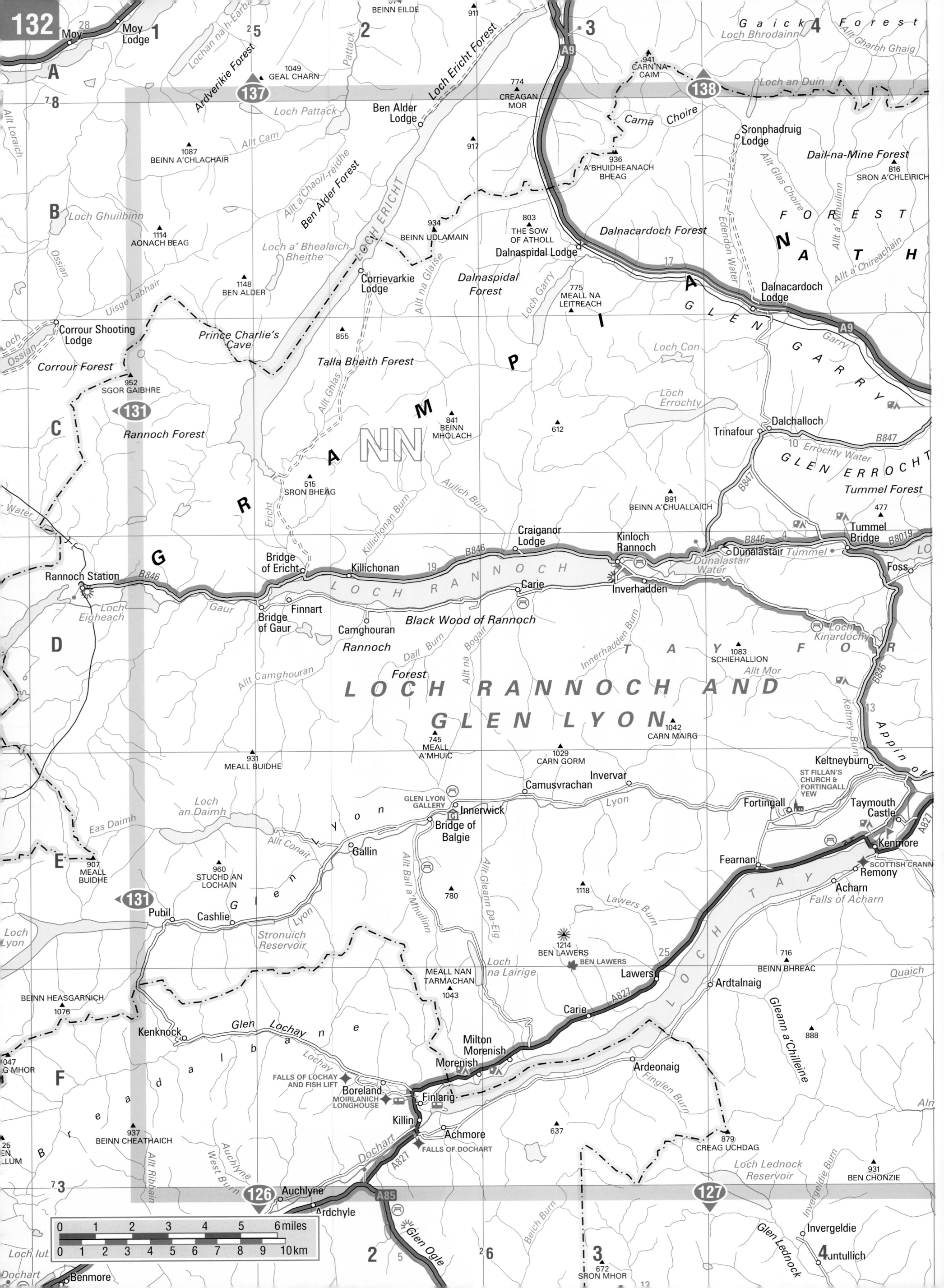

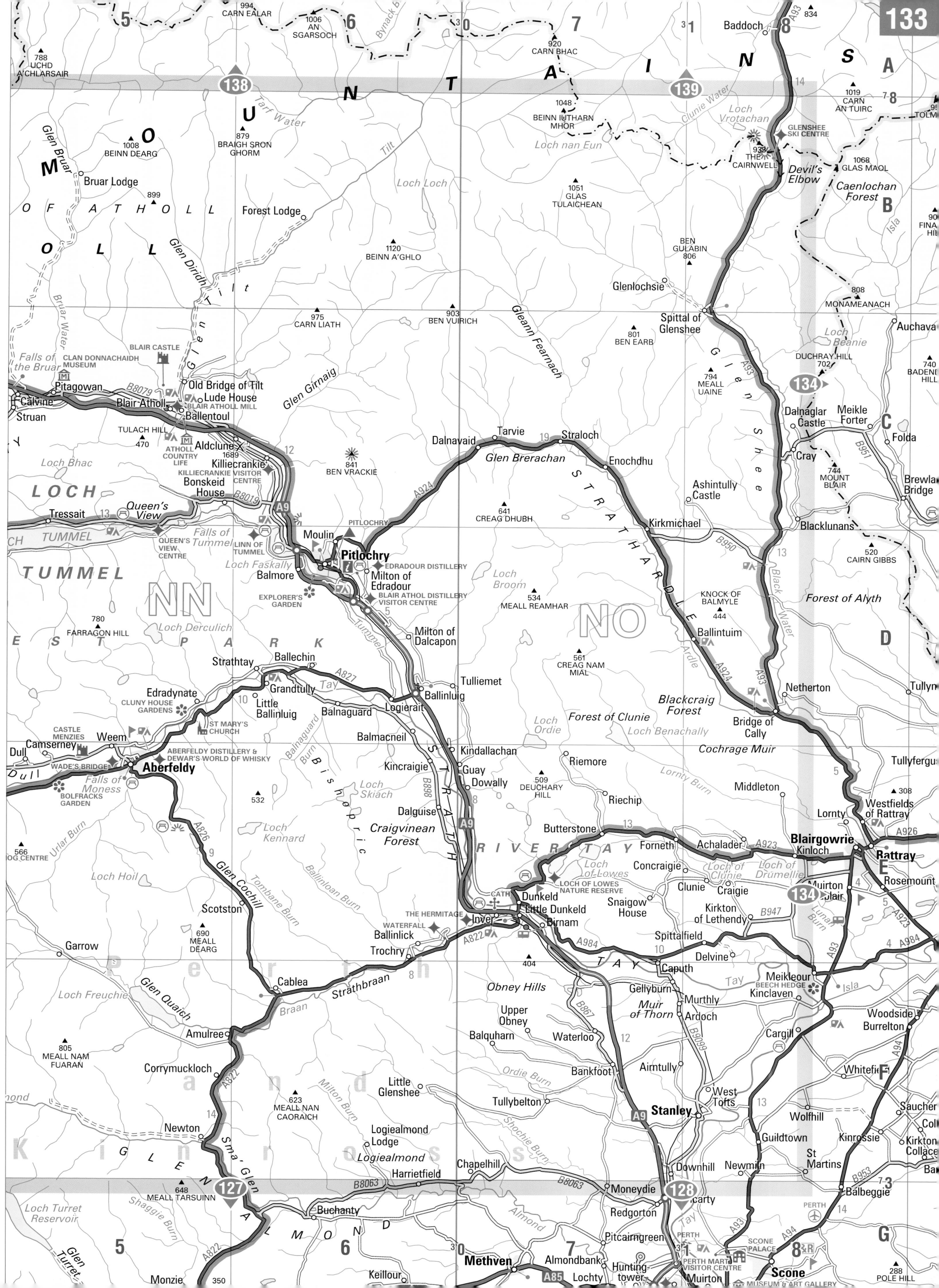

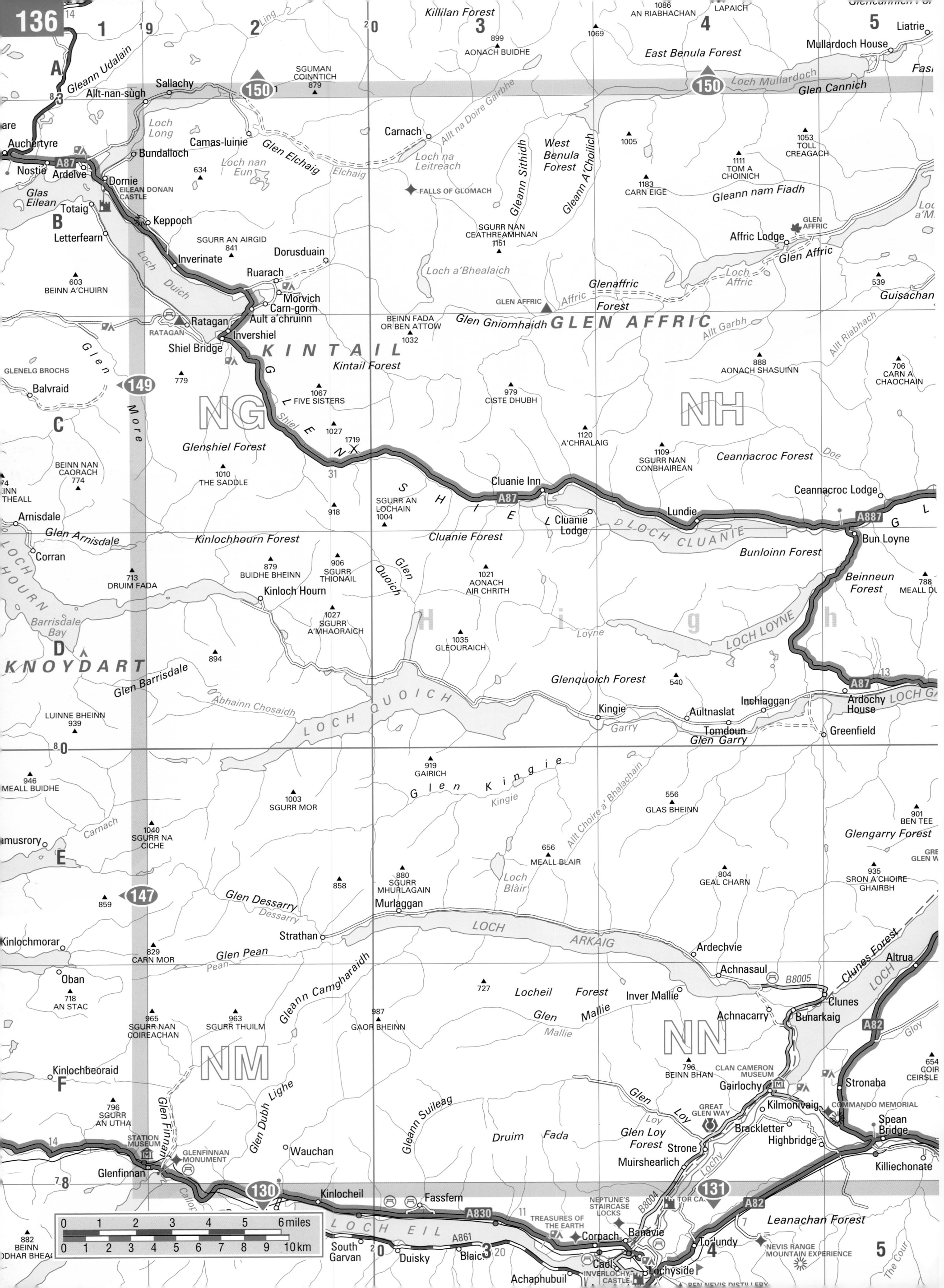

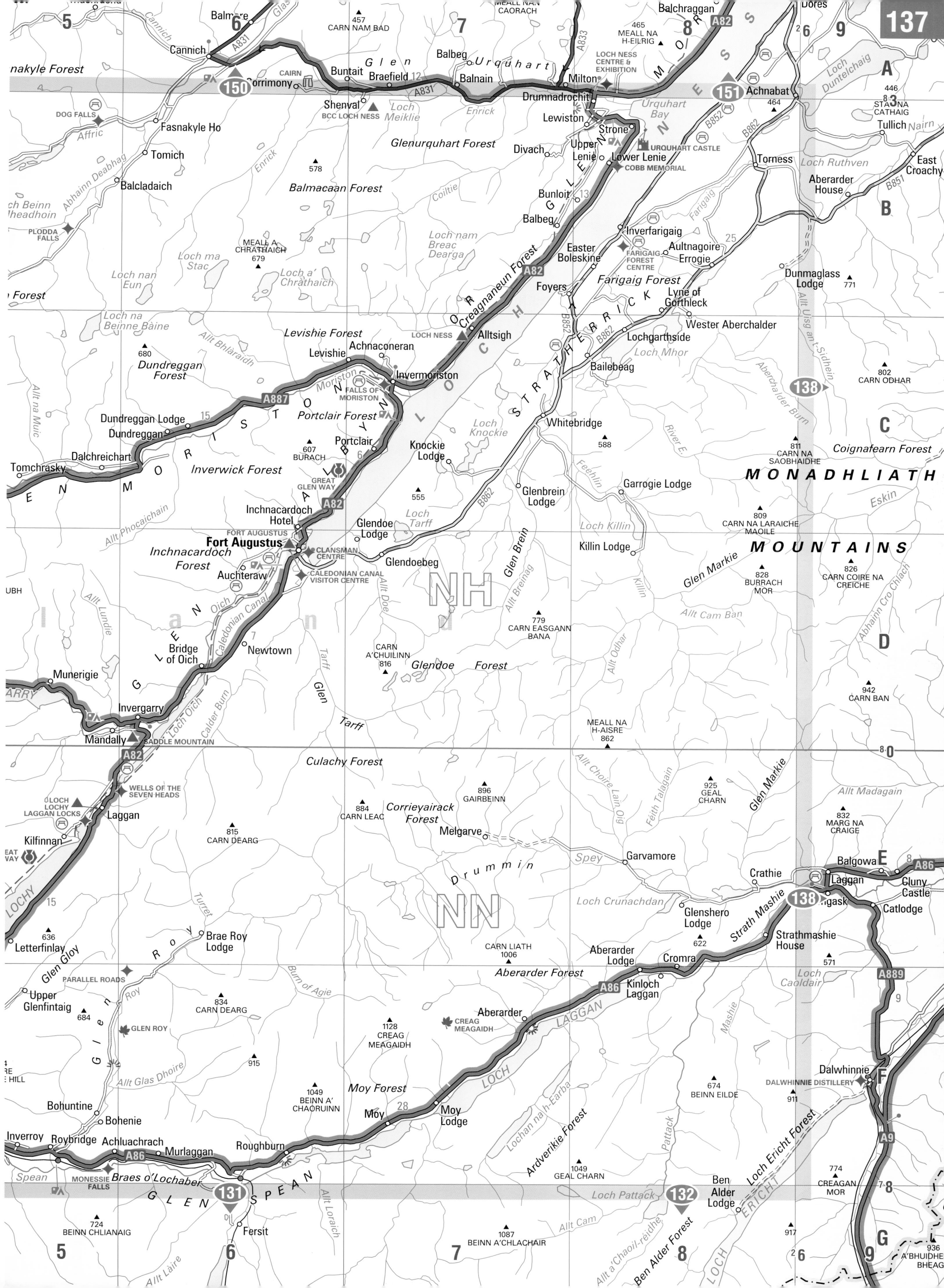

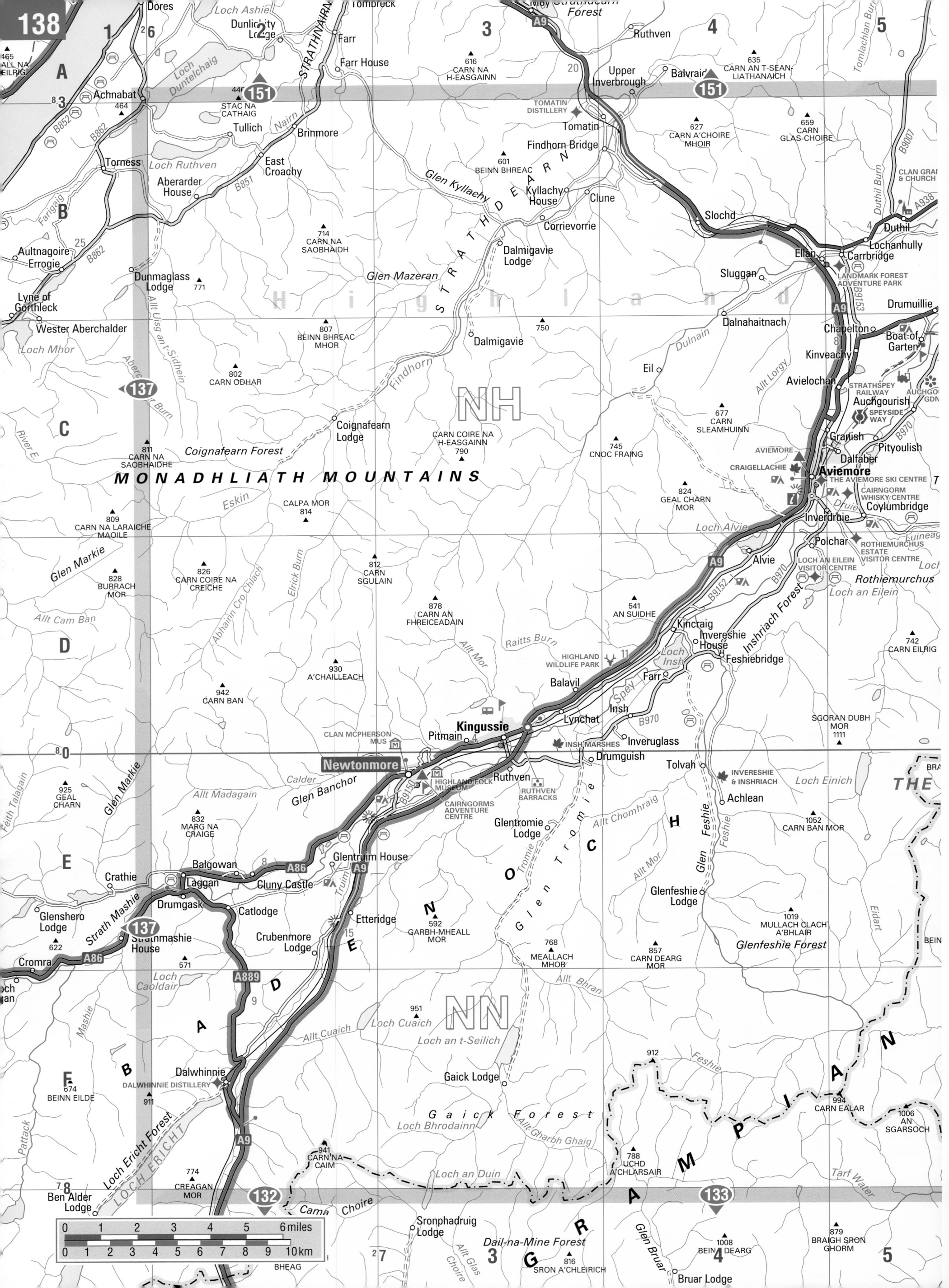

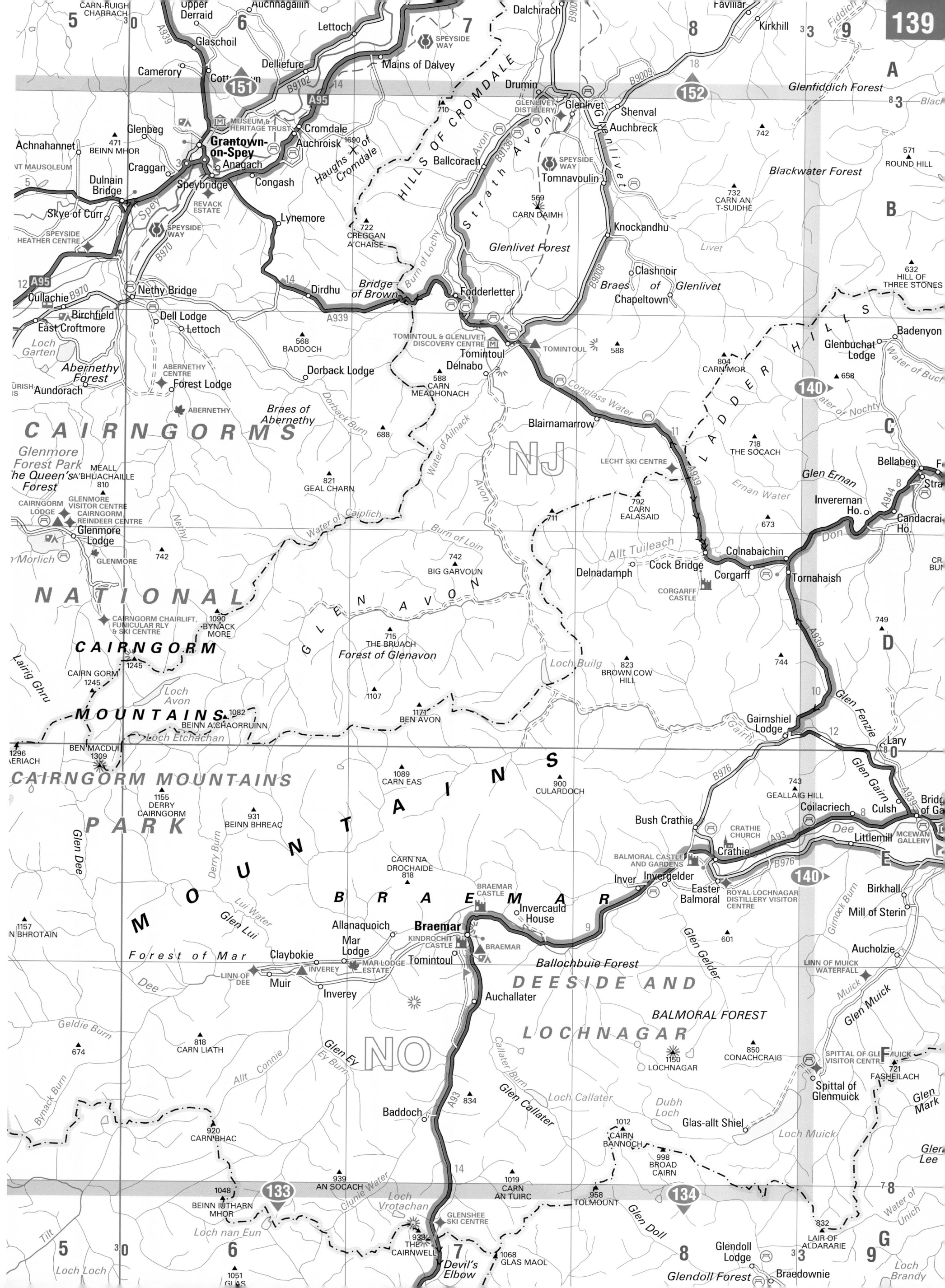

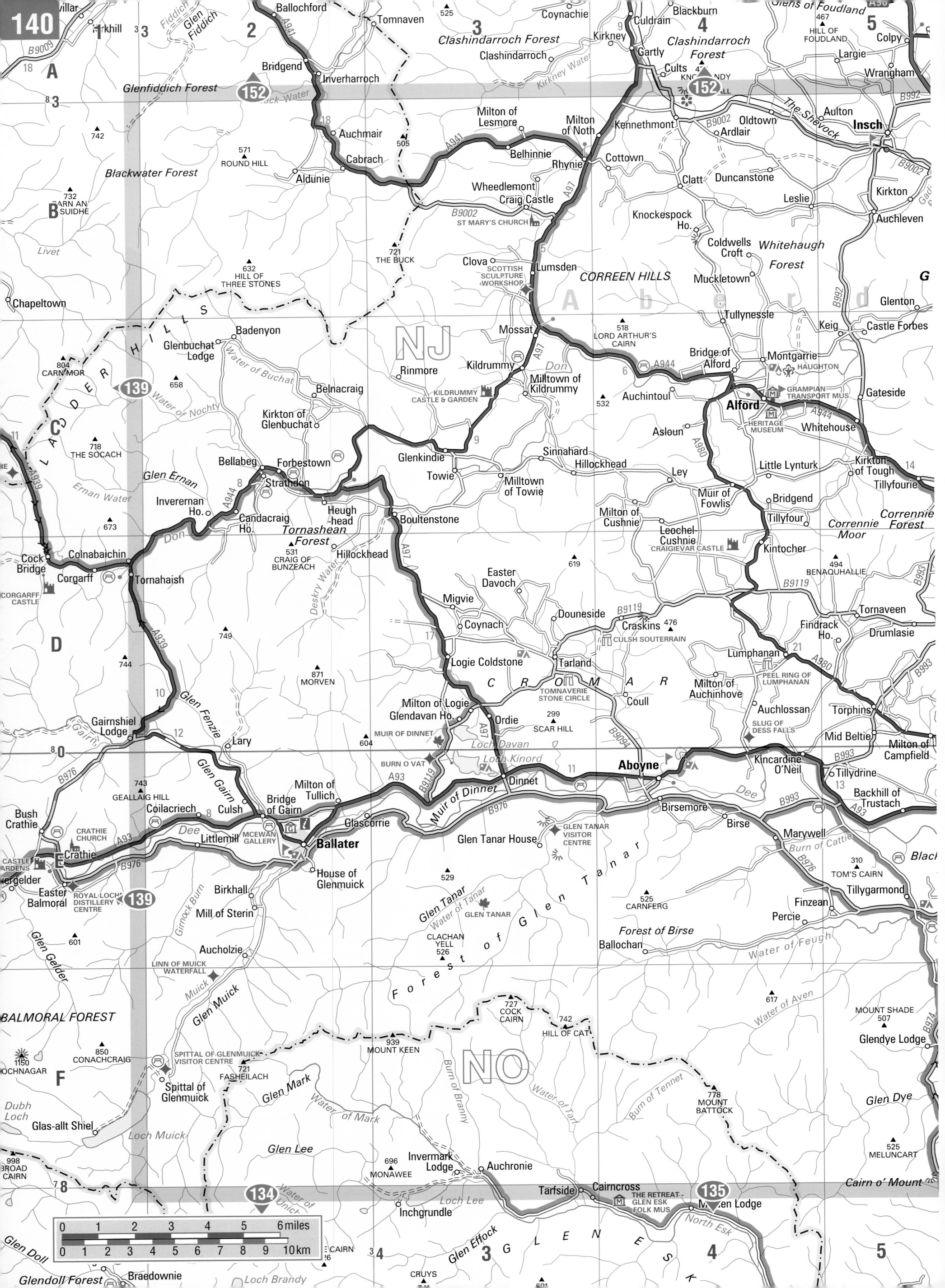

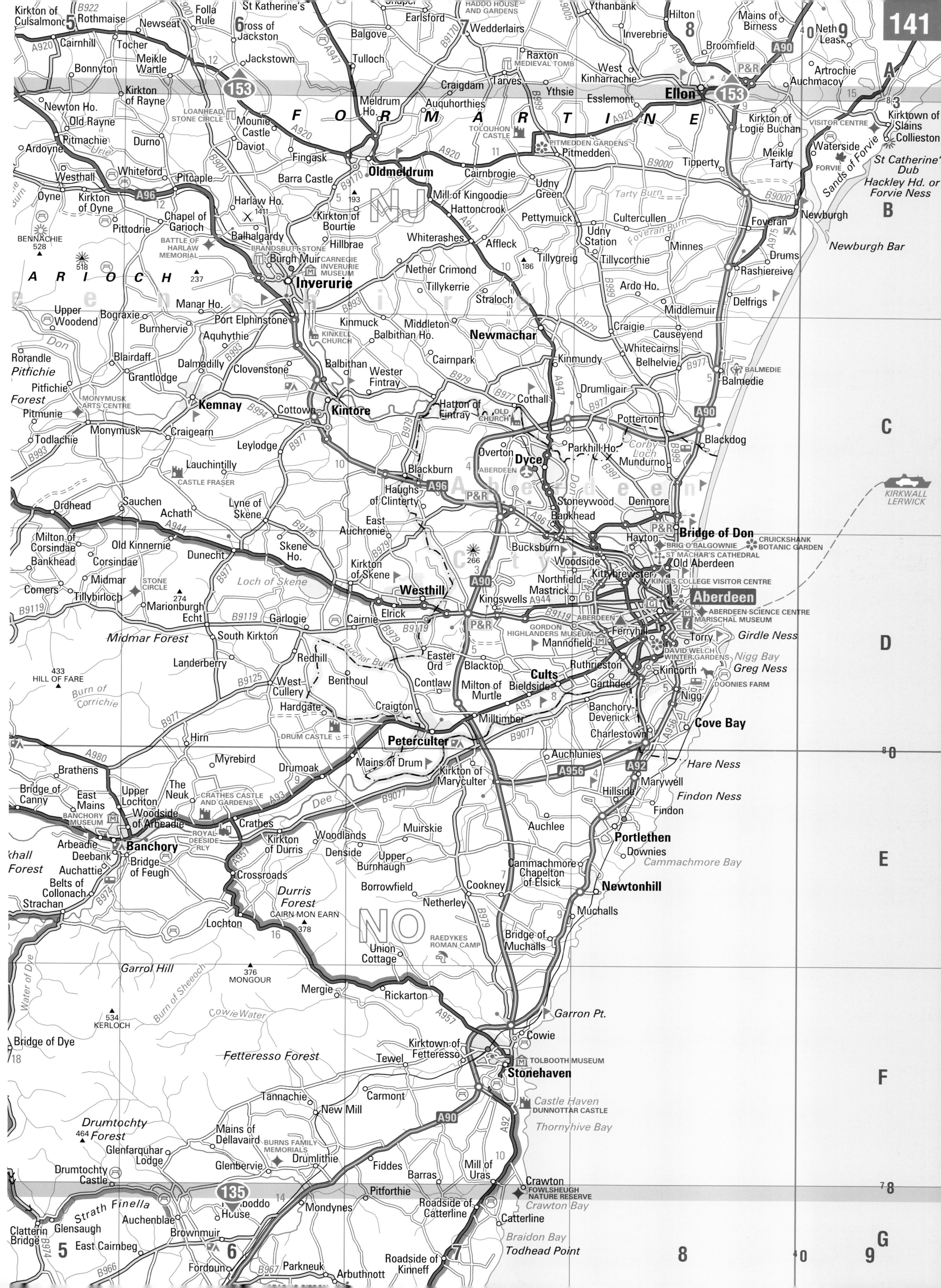

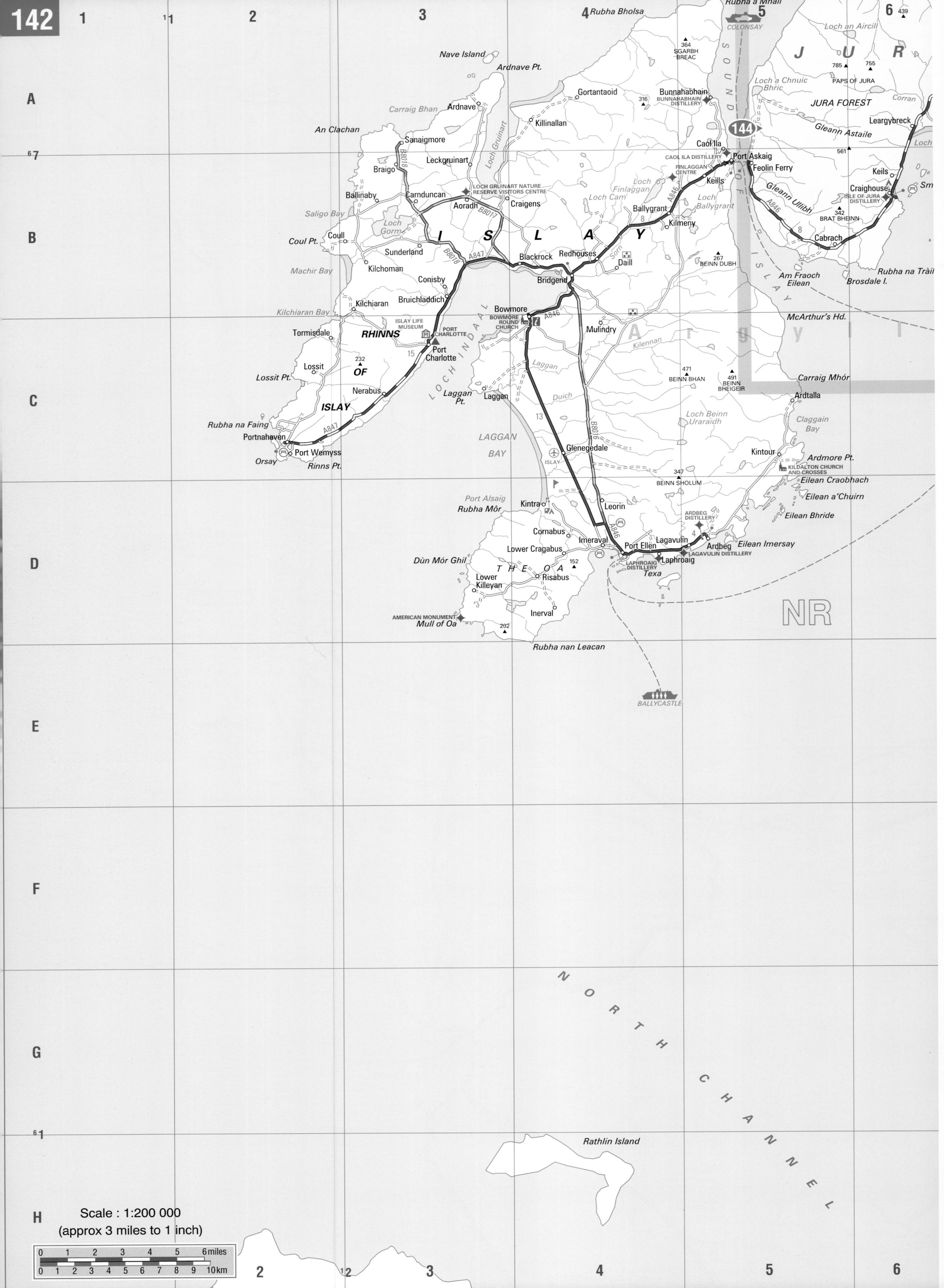

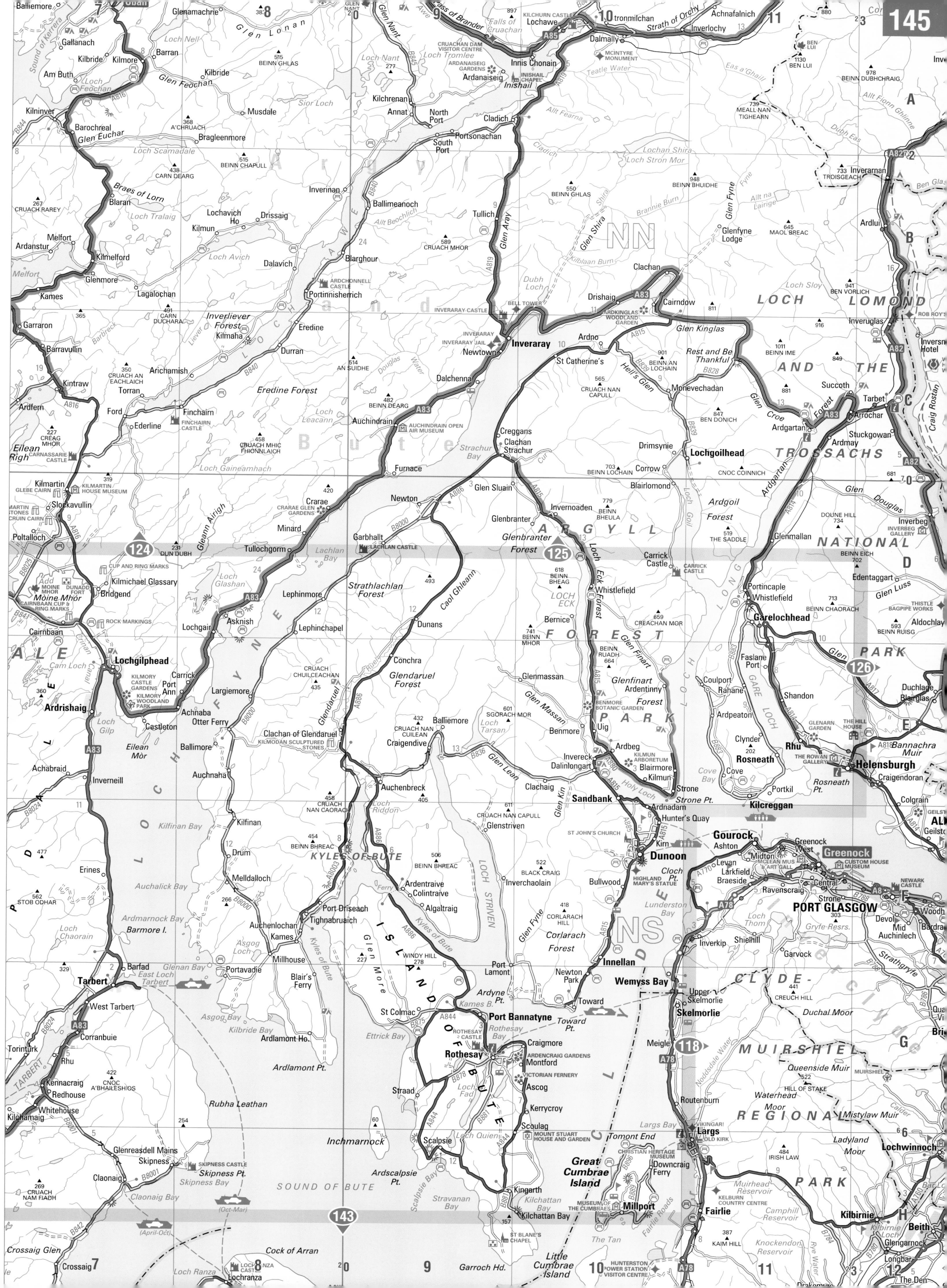

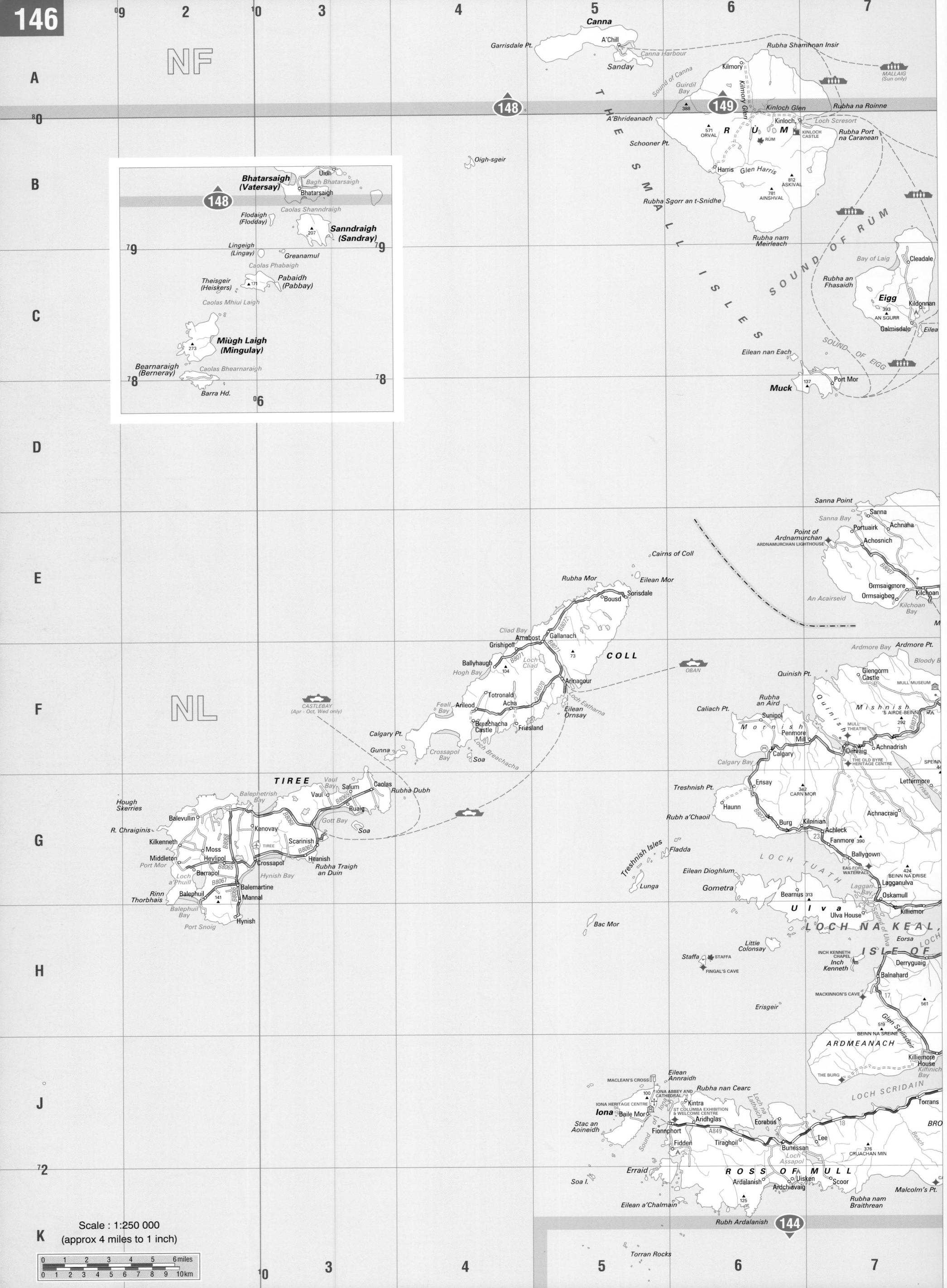

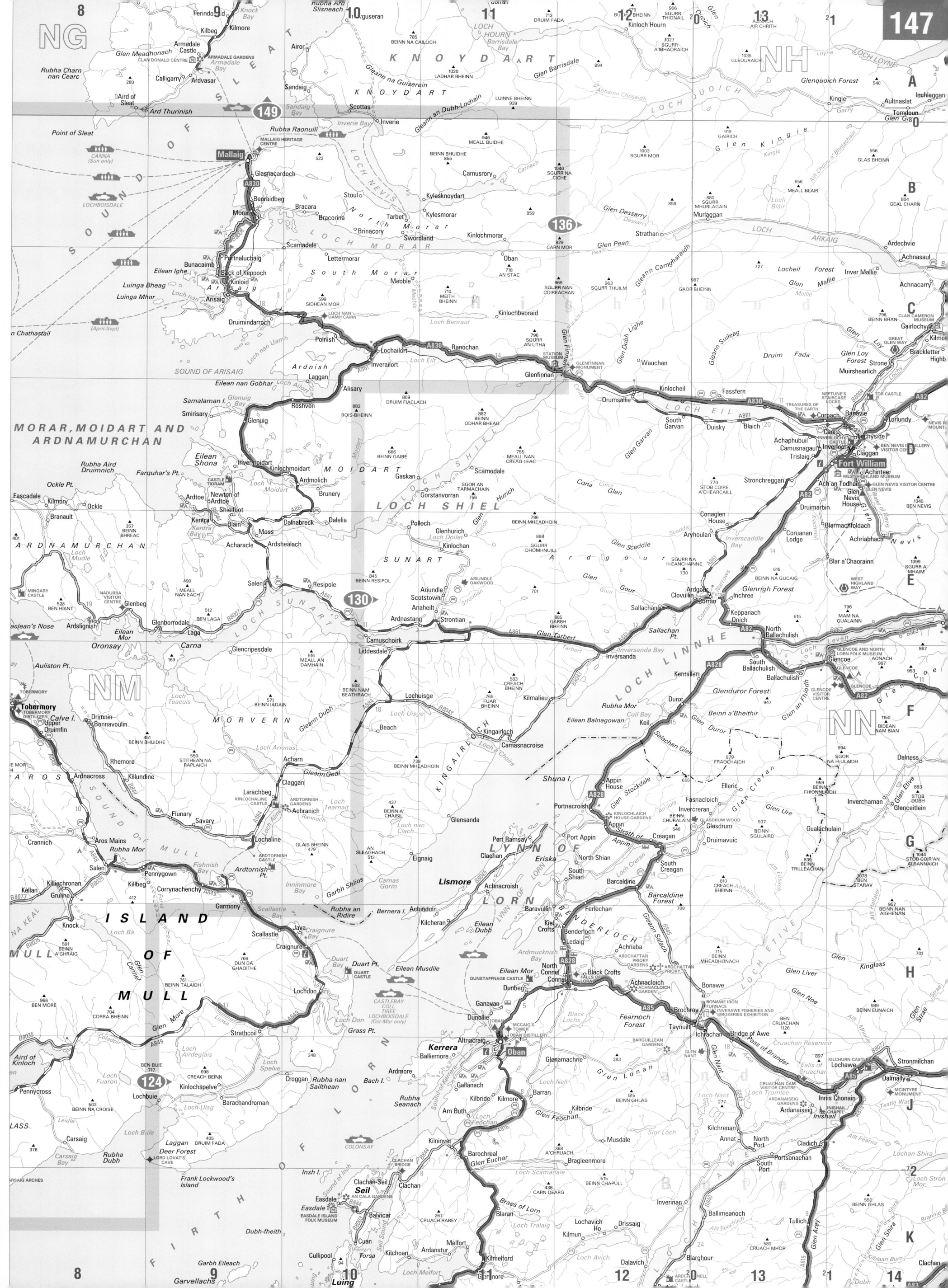

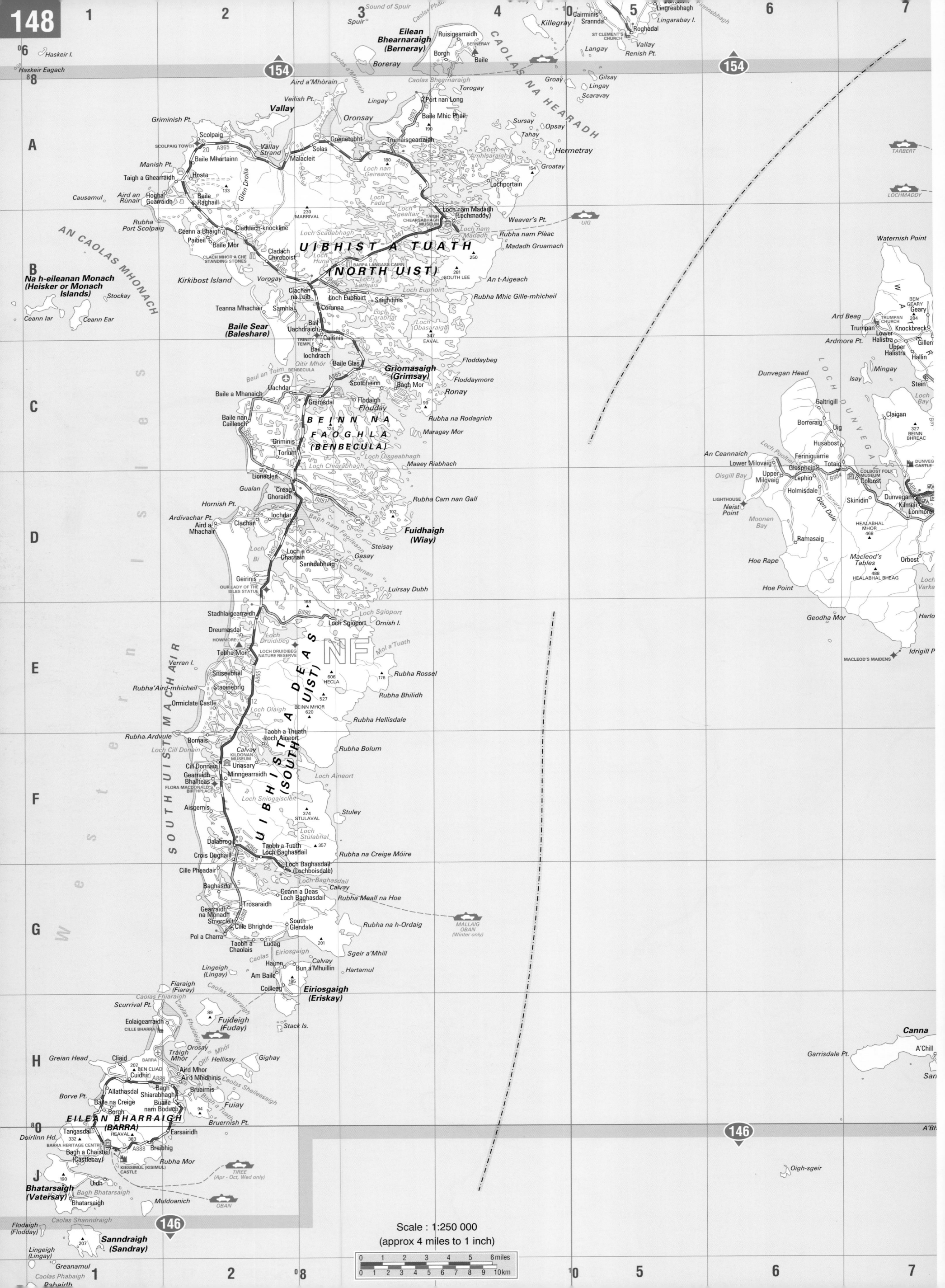

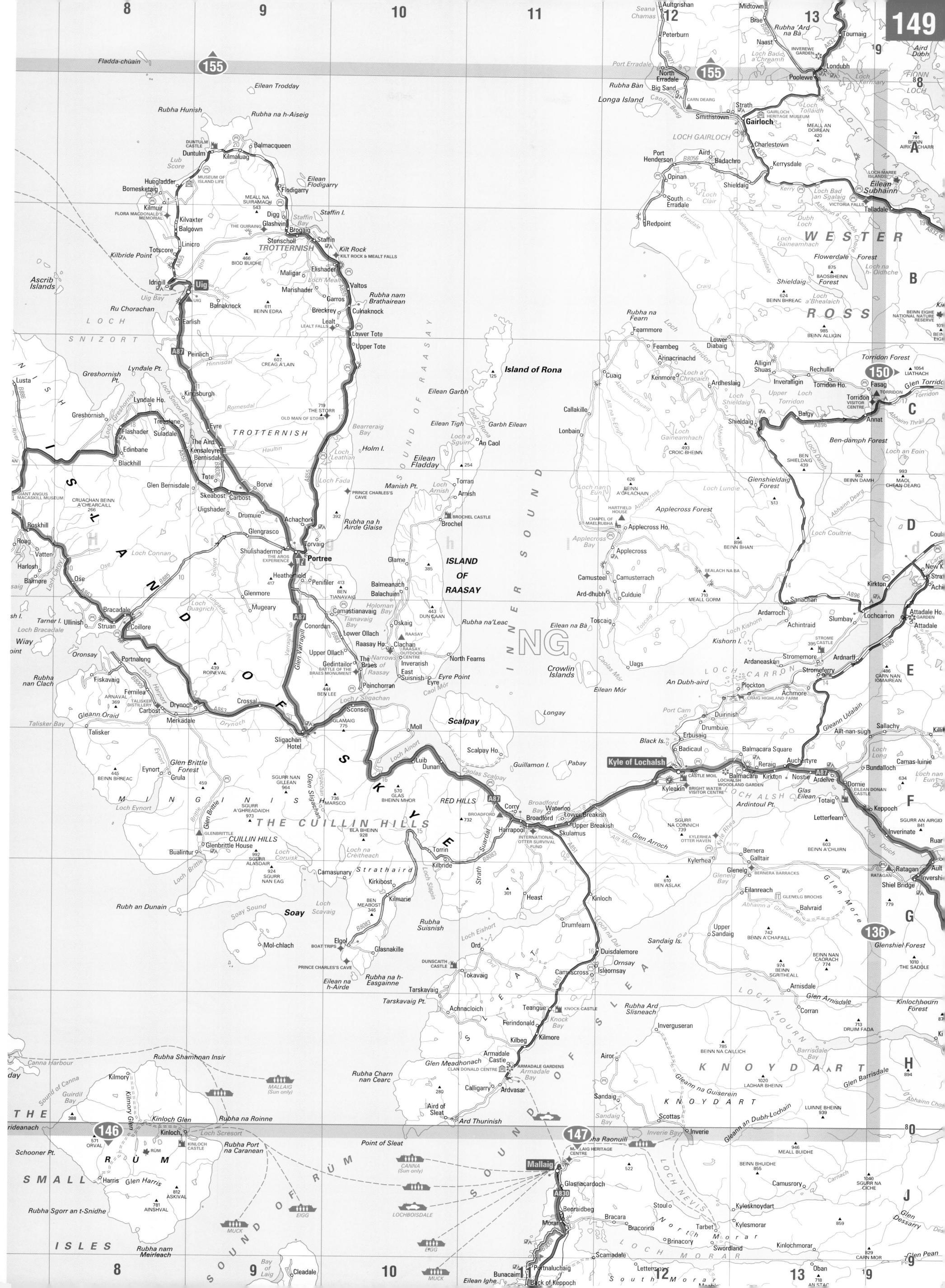

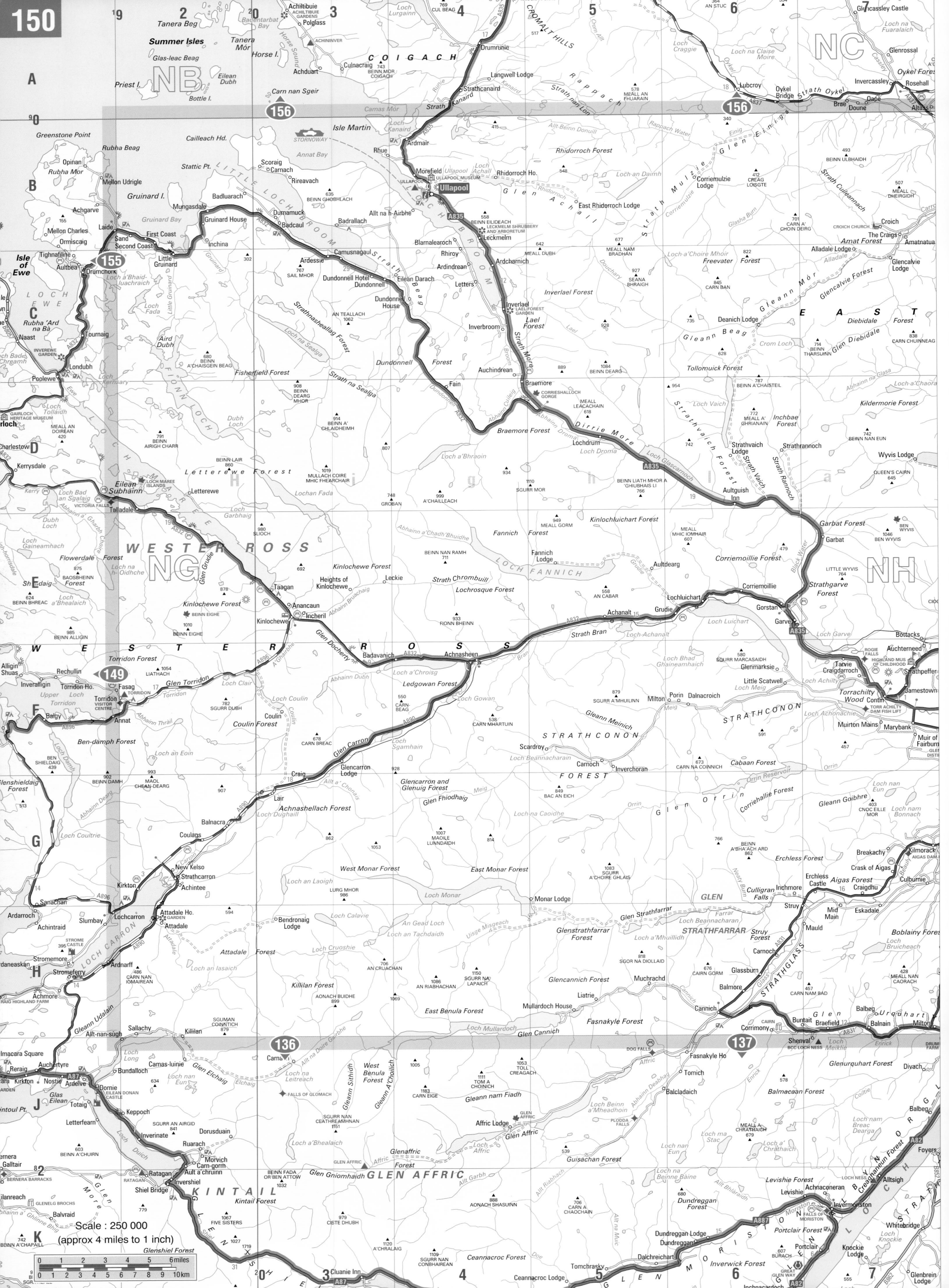

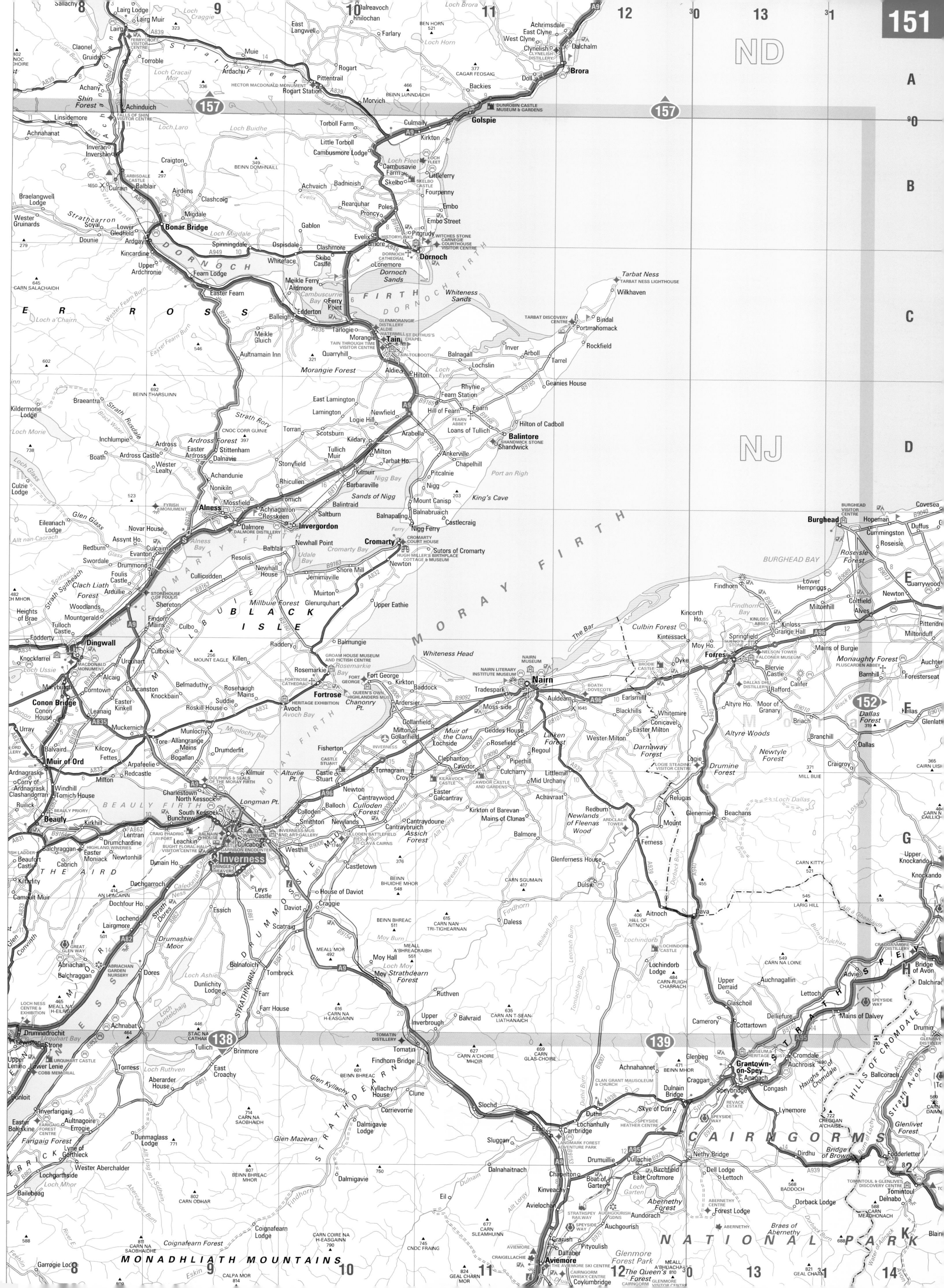

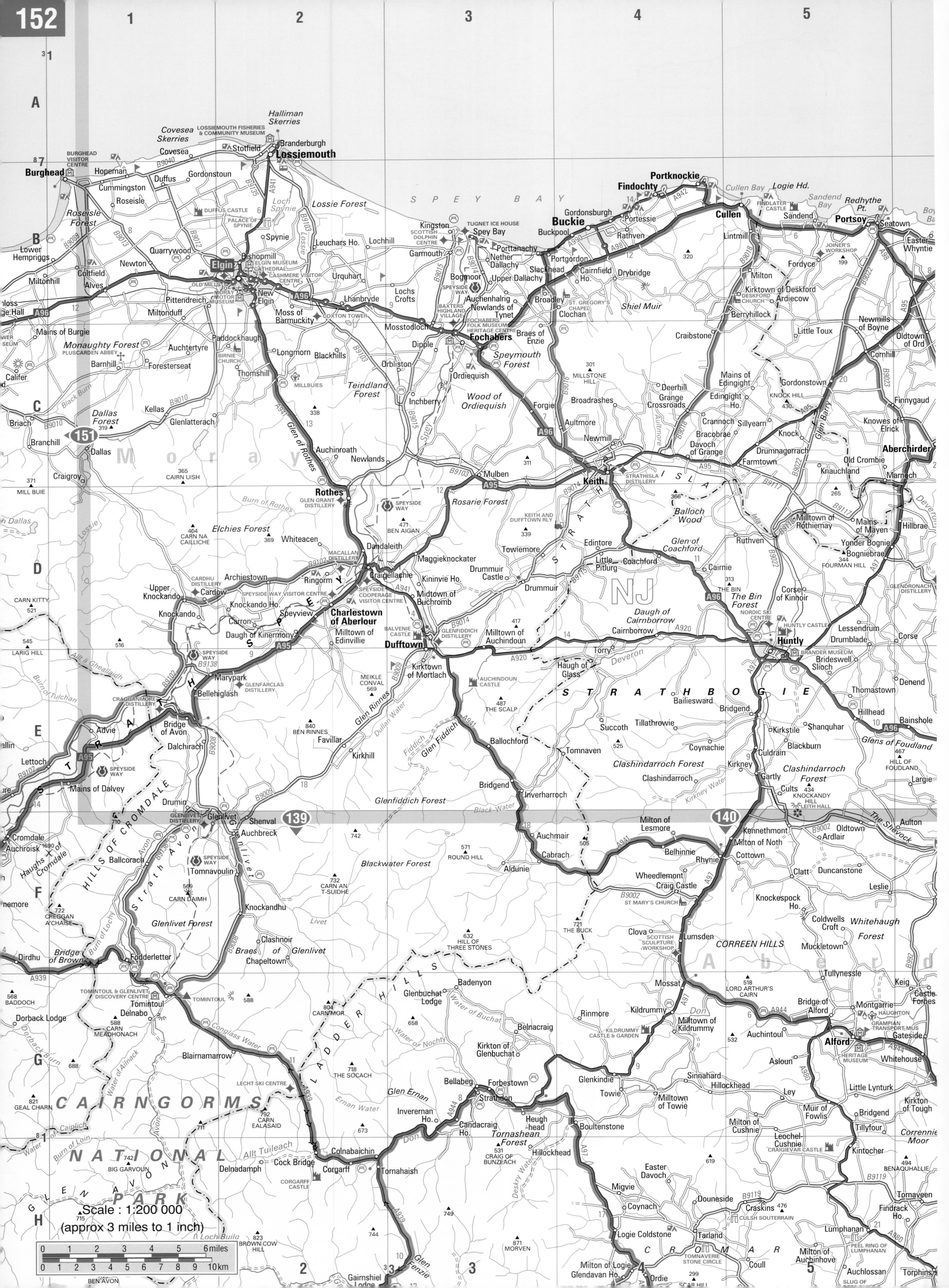

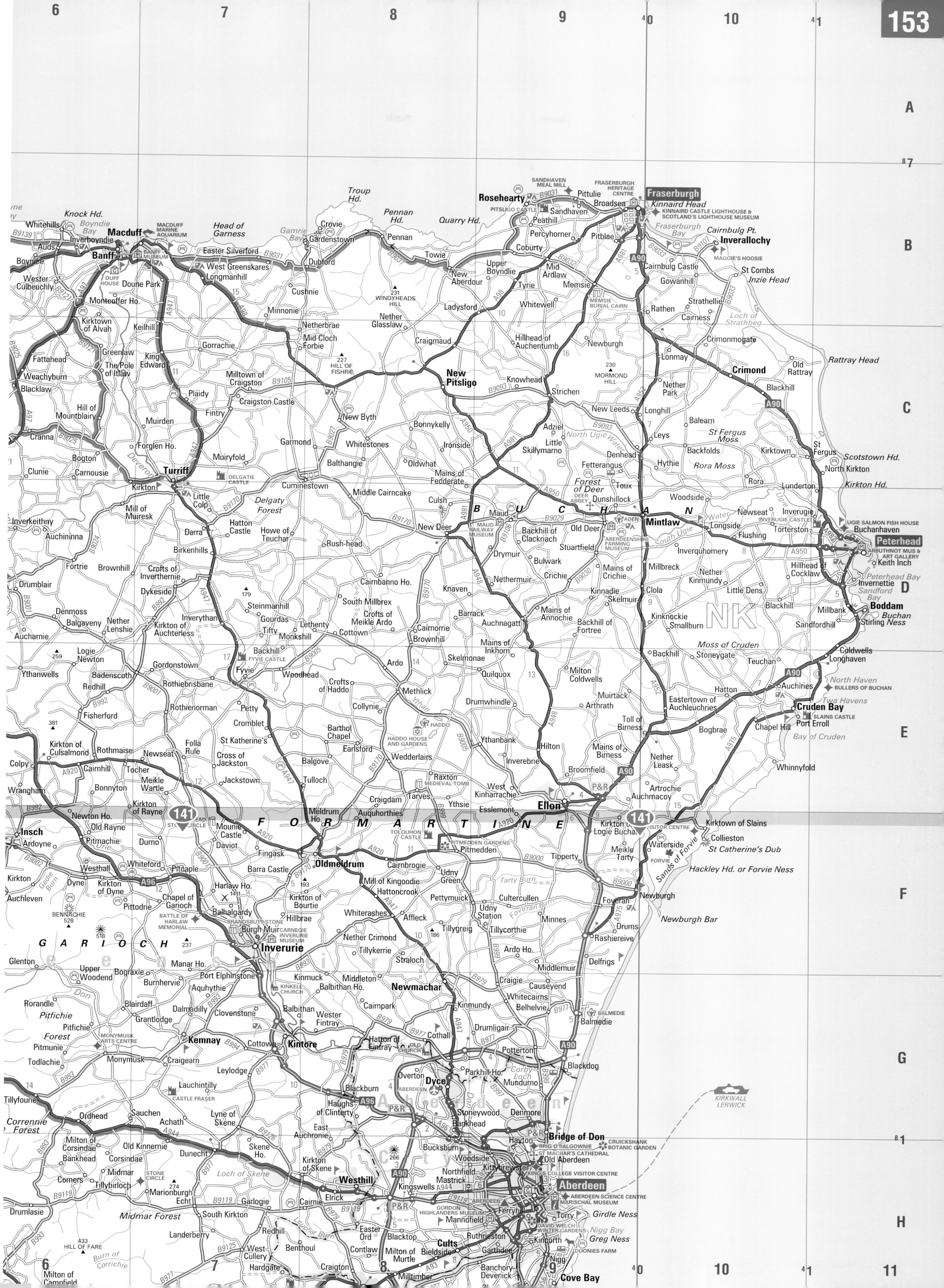

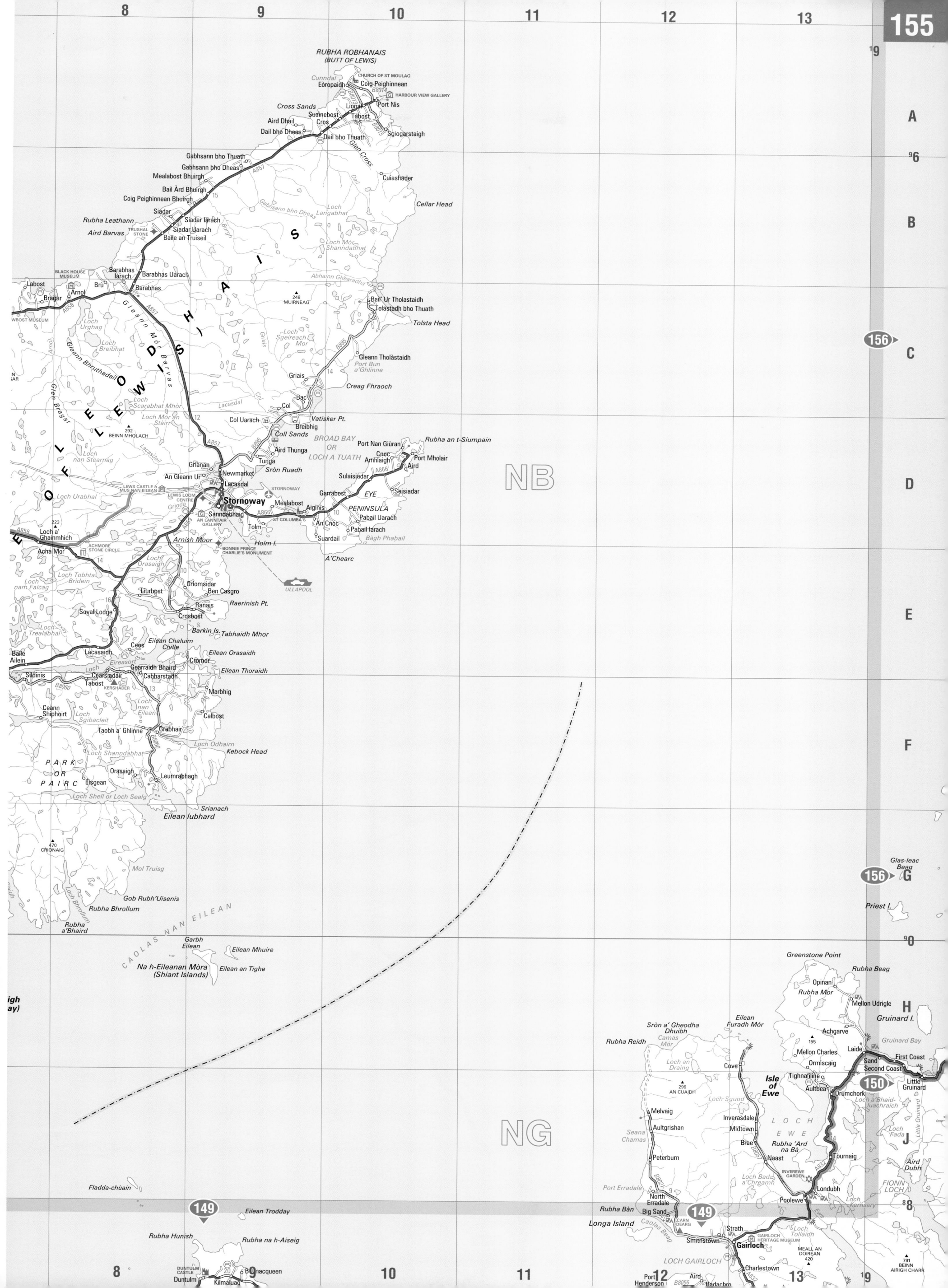

RUBHA ROBHANAIS (BUTT OF LEWIS)

ISLE OF LEWIS

LEODHAIS

Stornoway

Newmarket
Lacasdal
Sanndabhaig

BROAD BAY OR LOCH A TUATH

EYE PENINSULA

Port Nis

Eòropaidh
CHURCH OF ST MOULAG
Coig Peighinnean
HARBOUR VIEW GALLERY

Cross Sands
Suaineabost
Cros
Aird Dhail
Tàbost
Dail bho Dheas
Sgiogarstaigh
Dail bho Thuath
Gleann Cross

Gabhsann bho Thuath
Gabhsann bho Dheas
Mealabost Bhuirgh
Bail Àrd Bhuirgh
Coig Peighinnean Bhuirgh
Siàdar
Siàdar Iarach
TRUSHAL STONE
Siàdar Uarach
Baile an Truiseil
Rubha Leathann
Aird Barvas

Loch Langabhat

Cellar Head

Cuiashader

BLACK HOUSE MUSEUM
Barabhas Iarach
Barabhas Uarach
Bru
Barabhas
Labost
Bragar
Arnol
WBOST MUSEUM

Bail Ur Tholastaidh
Tolastadh bho Thuath
Tolsta Head

Loch Mòr Shanndabhat

248 MUIRNEAG

Abhainn Ghearadha

Gleann Tholàstaidh
Port Bun a'Ghlinne

Griais
Creag Fhraoch

Loch Urghag
Loch Breibhat
Loch Scarabhat Mhòr
Loch Mòr an Stàirr
Loch nan Stearnag
Loch Sgeireach Mor

Col
Bac
Col Uarach
Vatisker Pt.
Breibhig
Coll Sands
Aird Thunga
Tunga
Sròn Ruadh
Grianan
An Gleann Ur

Port Nan Giùran
Cnoc Amhlaigh
Aird
Port Mholair
Rubha an t-Siumpain

Sulaisiadar
Garrabost
Seisiadar
Mealabost
Aiglnis
St COLUMBA'S
An Cnoc
Pabail Uarach
Pabail Iarach
Bàgh Phabail
Suardail
A'Chearc

LEWS CASTLE & MUS NAN EILEAN
LEWIS LOOM CENTRE
AN LANNTAIR GALLERY
Tolm
223

Loch Urabhal
Loch a' Ghainmhich
Acha Mor
ACHMORE STONE CIRCLE
Arnish Moor
BONNIE PRINCE CHARLIE'S MONUMENT
Holm I.
ULLAPOOL

NB

Loch nam Falcag
Loch Tobhta Bridein
Loch Orasaigh
Griomsidar
Ben Casgro
Liùrbost
Ranais
Soval Lodge
Crosbost
Raerinish Pt.
Barkin Is.
Tabhaidh Mhor

Loch Trealbhal
Ceos
Eilean Chaluim Chille
Eilean Orasaigh
Cromor
Eilean Thoraidh
Baile Ailein
Lacasaidh
Gearraidh Bhaird
Cabharstadh
Sildinis
Tabost
KERSHADER
Marbhig
Calbost

Ceann Shiphoirt
Loch Sgibacleit
Loch nan Eilean
Grabhair
Loch Odhairn
Kebock Head

PARK OR PAIRC
Orasaigh
Eisgean
Leumrabhagh
Loch Shanndabhat

Loch Shell or Loch Seal
Srianach
Eilean Iubhard
470 CRIONAIG

Gob Rubh'Uisenis
Rubha Bhrollum
Rubha a'Bhaird

CAOLAS NAN EILEAN

Garbh Eilean
Na h-Eileanan Mòra (Shiant Islands)
Eilean Mhuire
Eilean an Tighe

Glas-leac Beag
Priest I.

NG

Greenstone Point
Rubha Beag
Opinan
Rubha Mòr
Mellon Udrigle
Gruinard I.
Achgarve
Sròn a' Gheodha Dhuibh
Eilean Furadh Mòr
Gruinard Bay
Rubha Reidh
Camas Mòr
Loch an Draing
Mellon Charles
Laide
Cove
Ormiscaig
Sand
First Coast
Isle of Ewe
Tighnafiline
Second Coast
Aultbea
Little Gruinard
Drumchork
296 AN CUAIDH
Melvaig
LOCH EWE
Aultgrishan
Inverasdale
Midtown
Rubha 'Ard na Bà
Tournaig
Seana Chamas
Brae
Peterburn
INVEREWE GARDEN
Loch Bad a'Chreanh
Aird Dubh
Port Erradale
North Erradale
Londubh
Poolewe
FIONN LOCH
Rubha Bàn
Big Sand
CARN DEARG
Naast
Loch Kernsary
Longa Island
Caolas Beag
Strath
Smithstown
GAIRLOCH HERITAGE MUSEUM
Gairloch
MEALL AN DOIREAN 420
791 BEINN AIRIGH CHARR
Fladda-chùain
Eilean Trodday
Rubha Hunish
Rubha na h-Aiseig
DUNTULM CASTLE
Duntulm
Kilmaluag
Shacqueen
Port Henderson
Aird
Badachro
LOCH GAIRLOCH
Charlestown

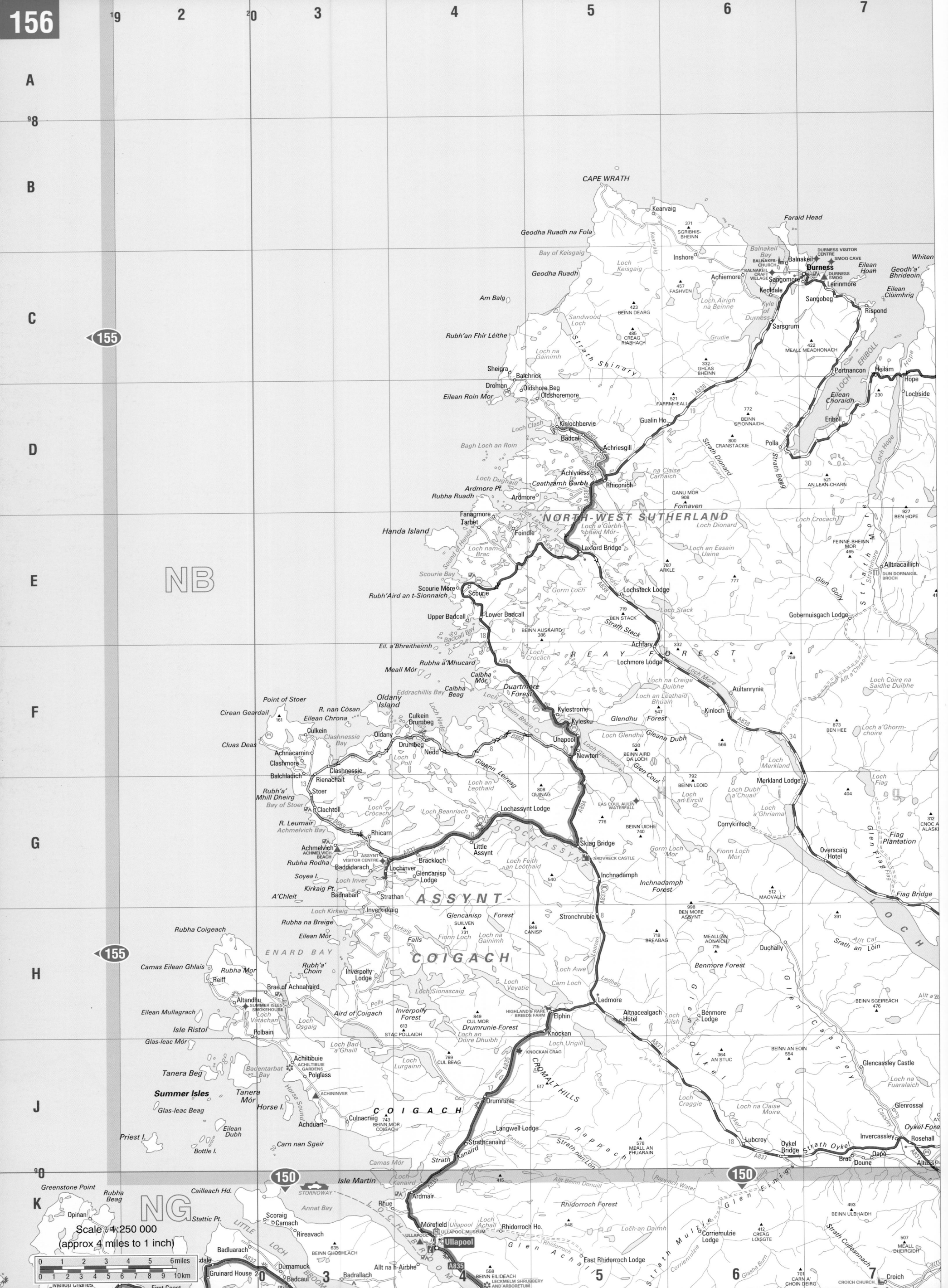

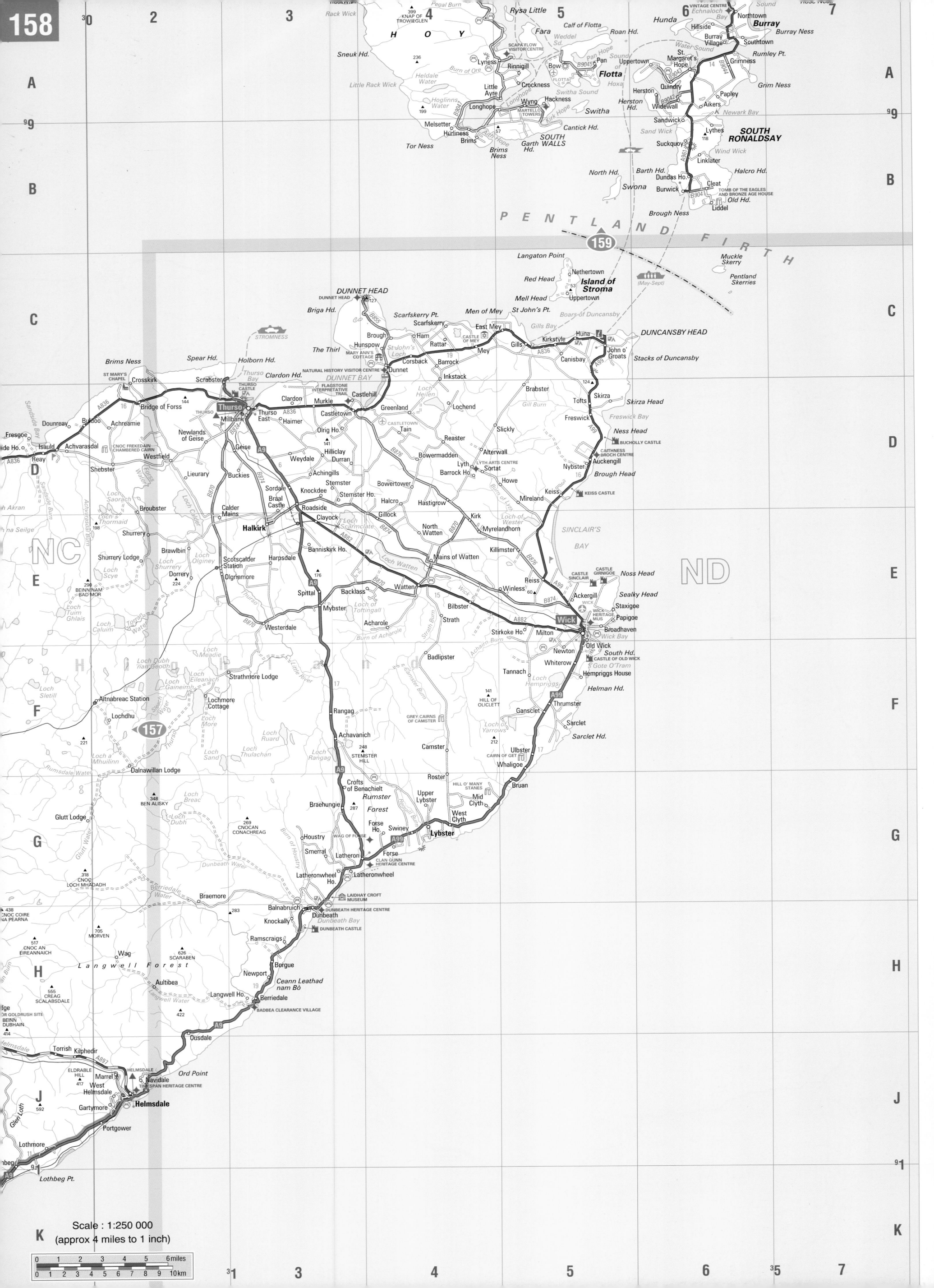

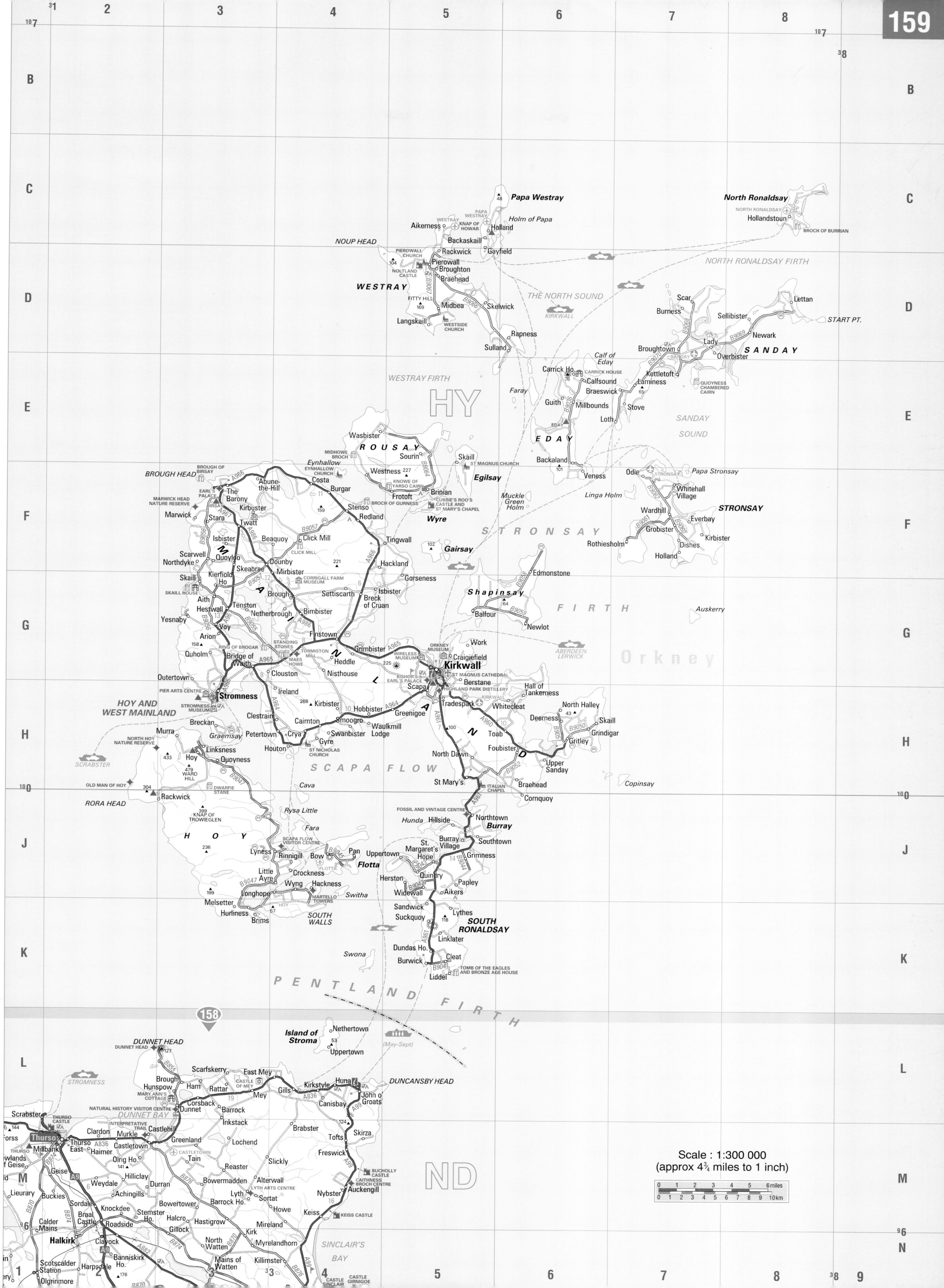

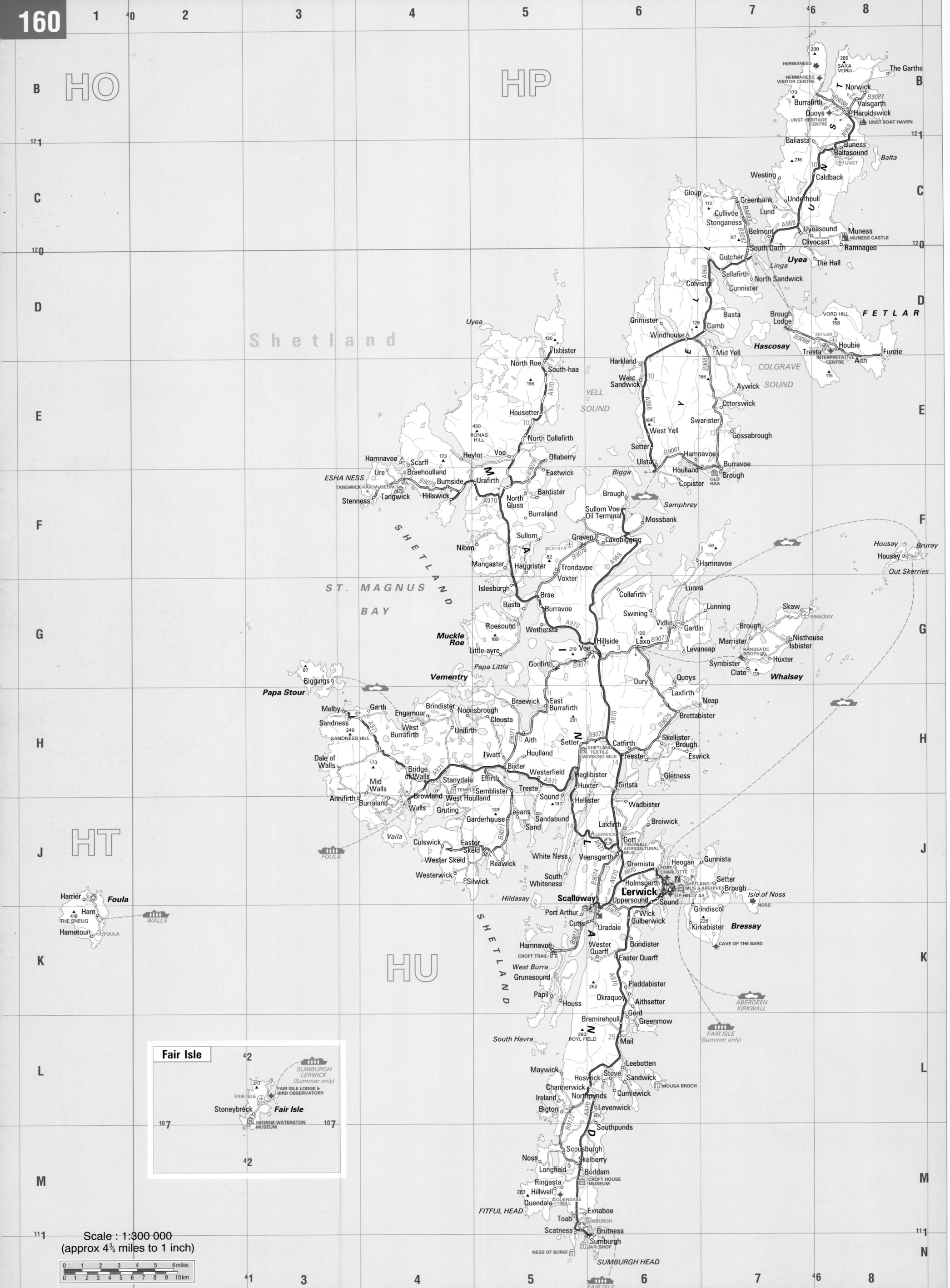

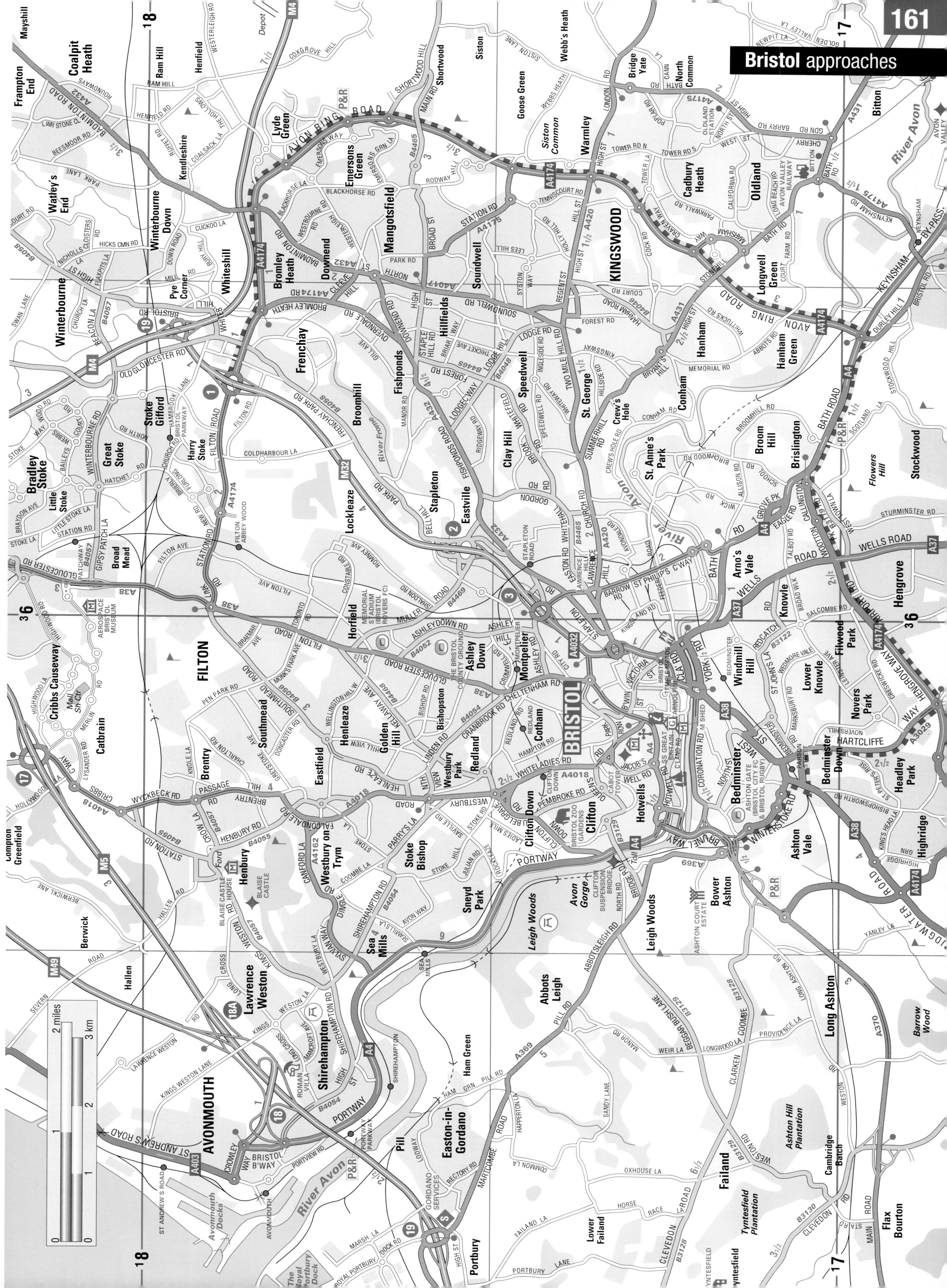

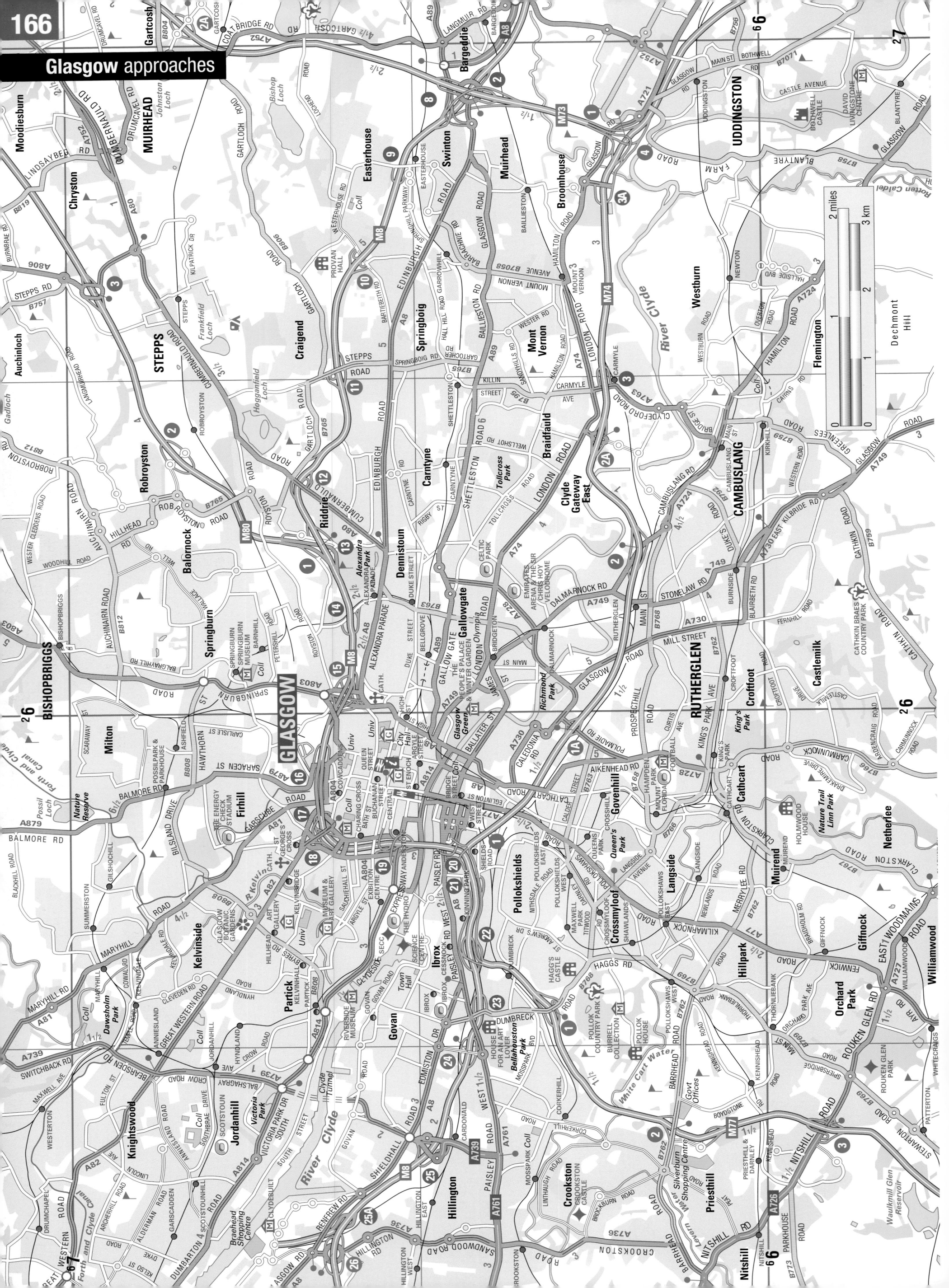

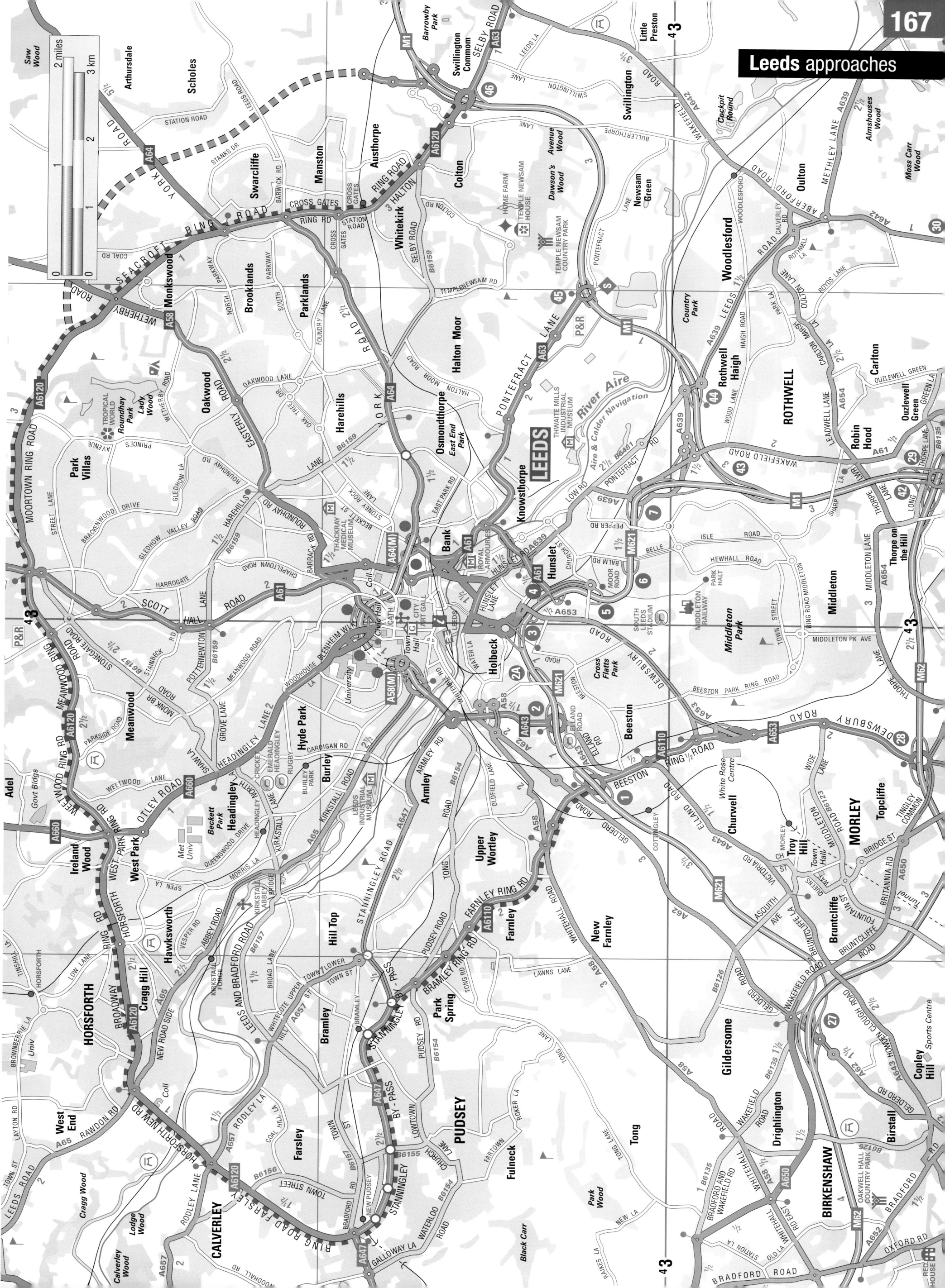

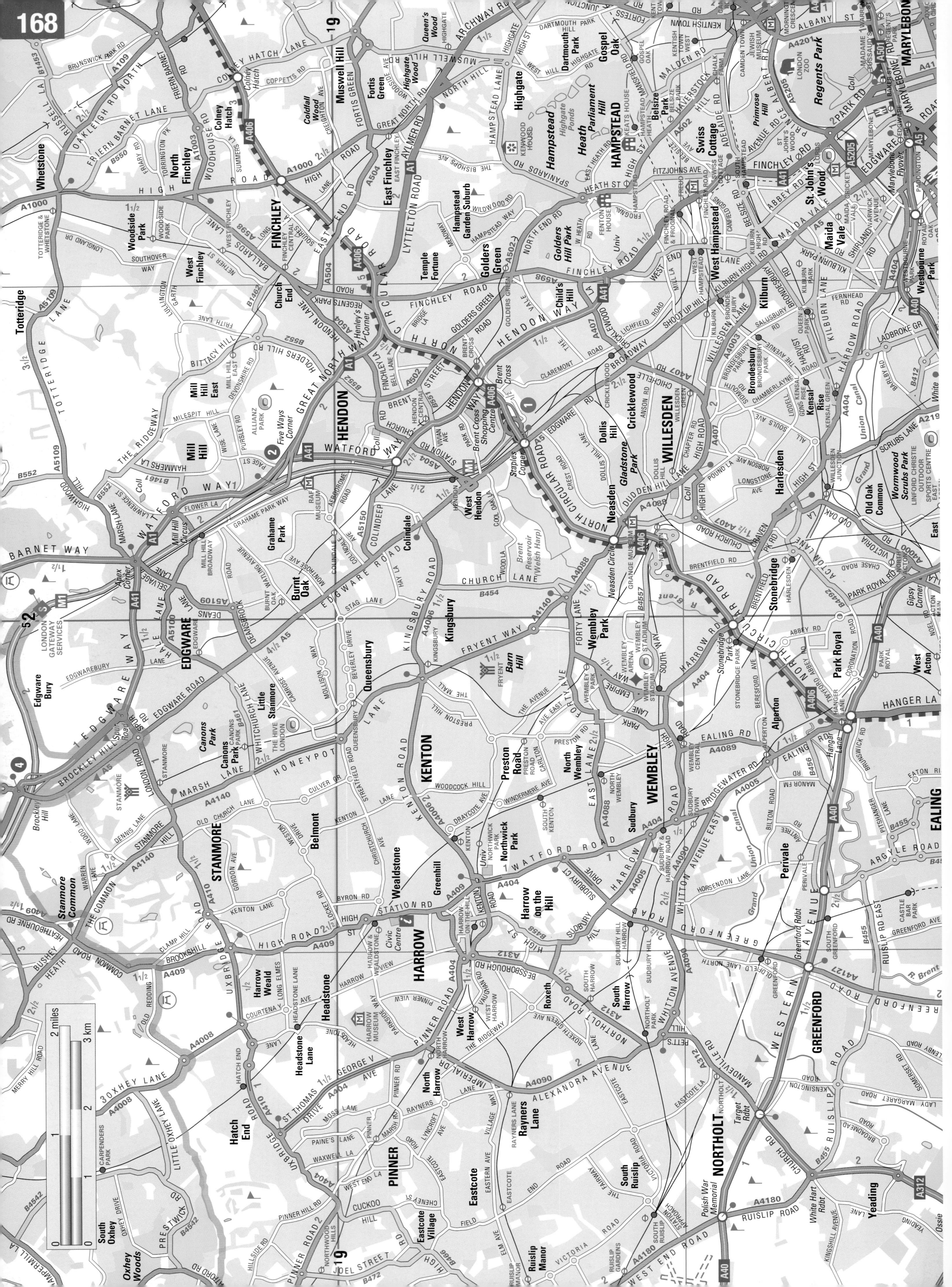

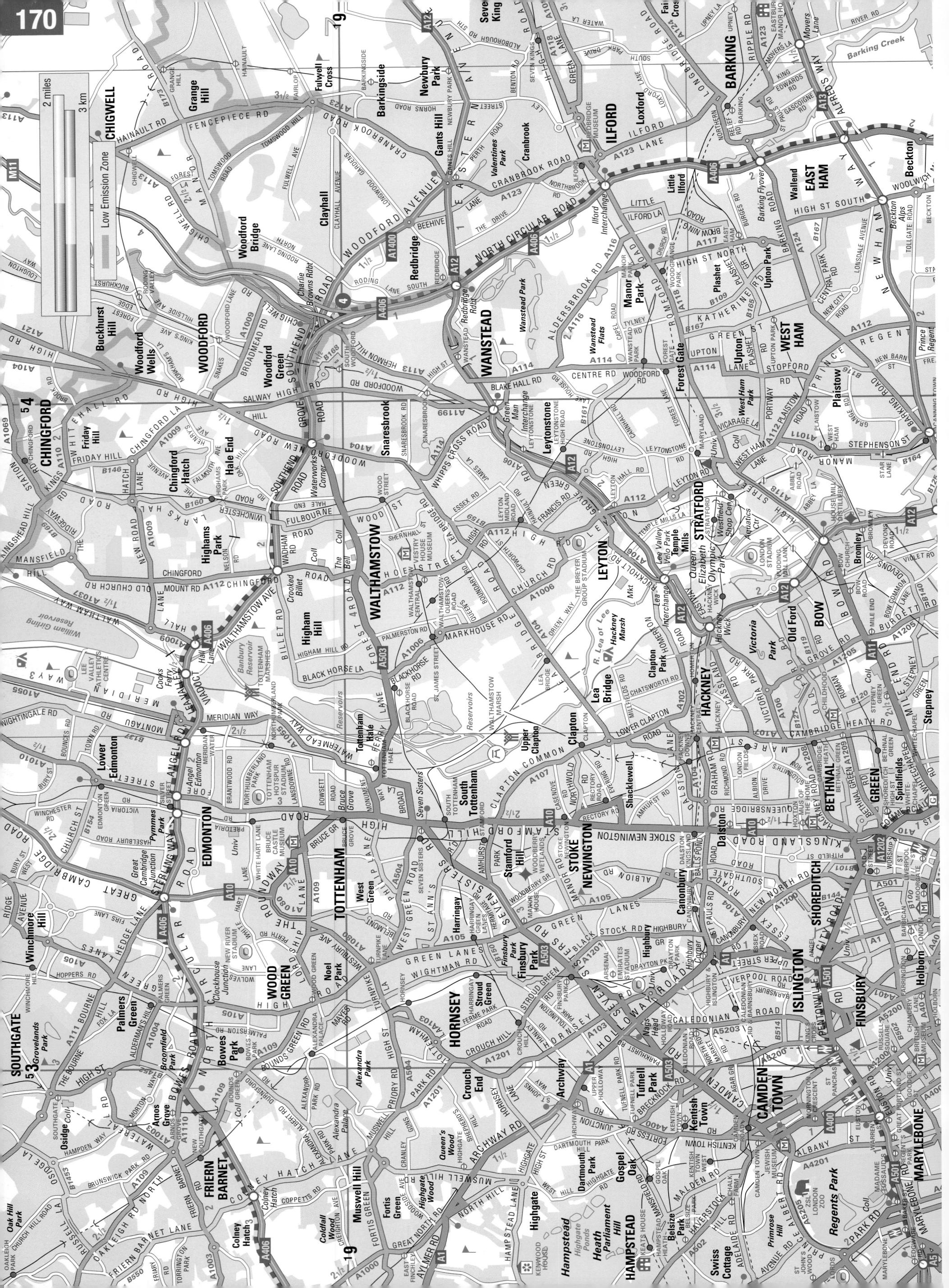

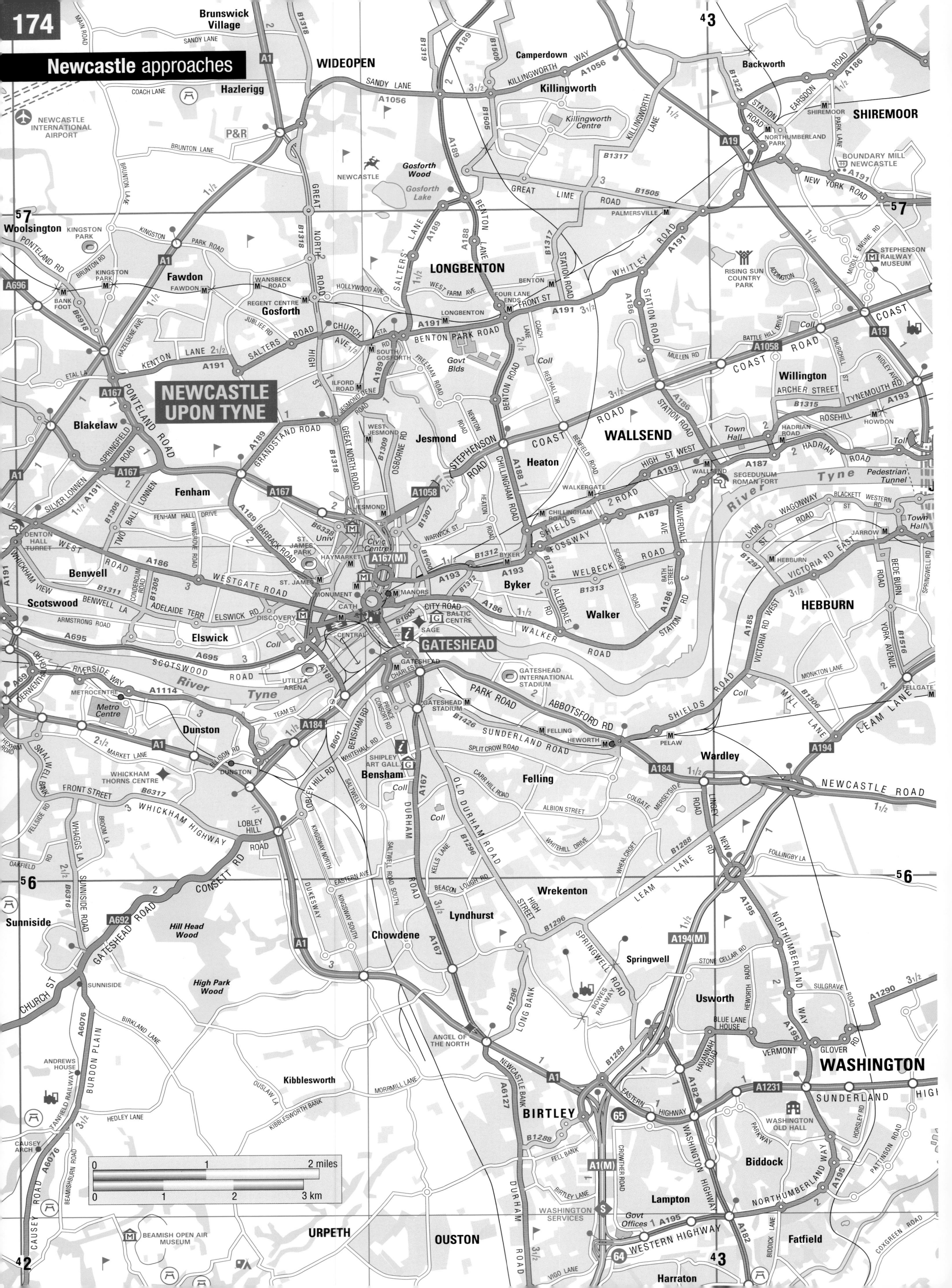

Town plan symbols

Motorway	
Primary route – dual, single carriageway	
A road – dual, single carriageway	
B road – dual, single carriageway	

Minor through road	
One-way street	
Pedestrian roads	
Shopping streets	

Railway with station
Tramway with station
Underground or Metro station

H Hospital
P Parking
Police, Post Office
Shopmobility
▲ Youth hostel

Bus or railway station building

Shopping precinct or retail park

Park

Congestion charge zone

✝ Abbey or cathedral
Ancient monument
Aquarium
Art gallery
Bird collection or aviary
Building of interest
Castle
Church of interest
Cinema
Garden
Historic ship
House
House and garden
Museum
Preserved railway
Roman antiquity
Safari park
Theatre
ℹ Tourist information
Zoo
✦ Other place of interest

Aberdeen

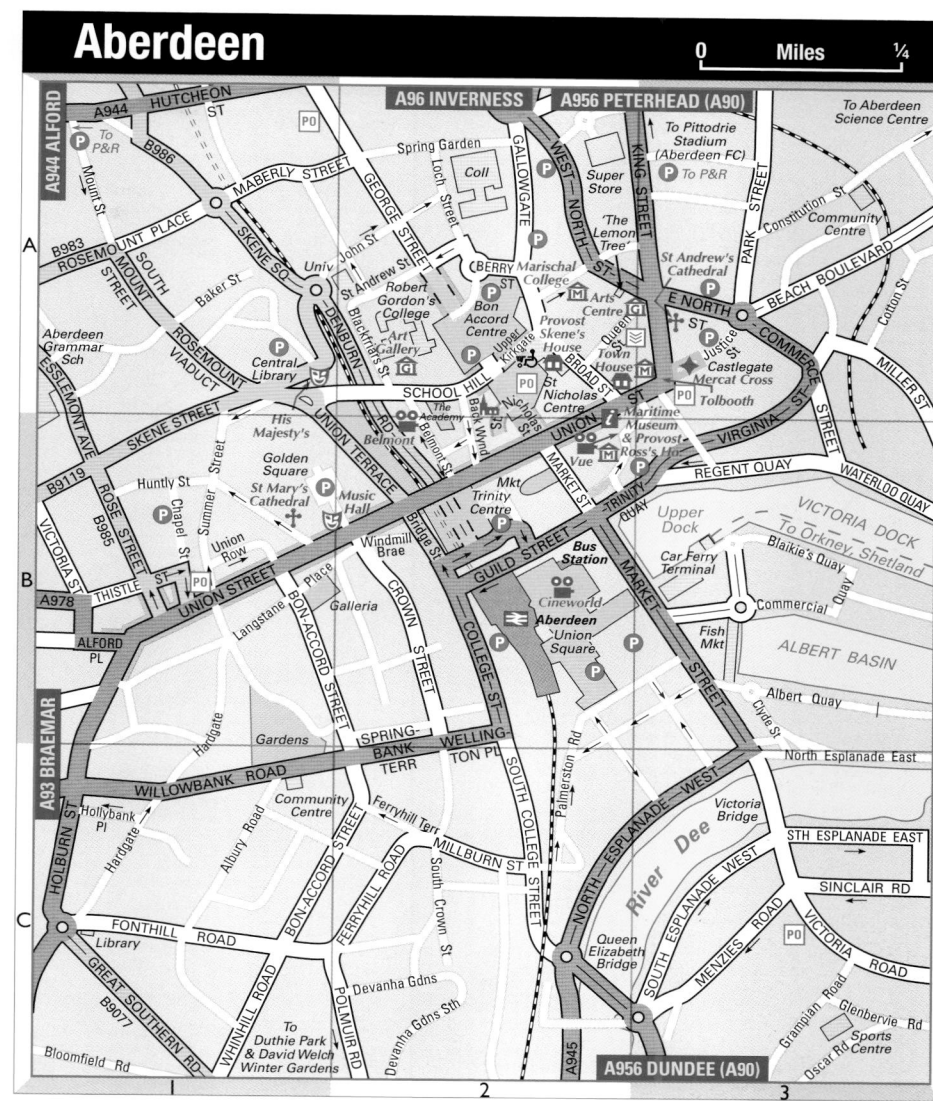

Ayr

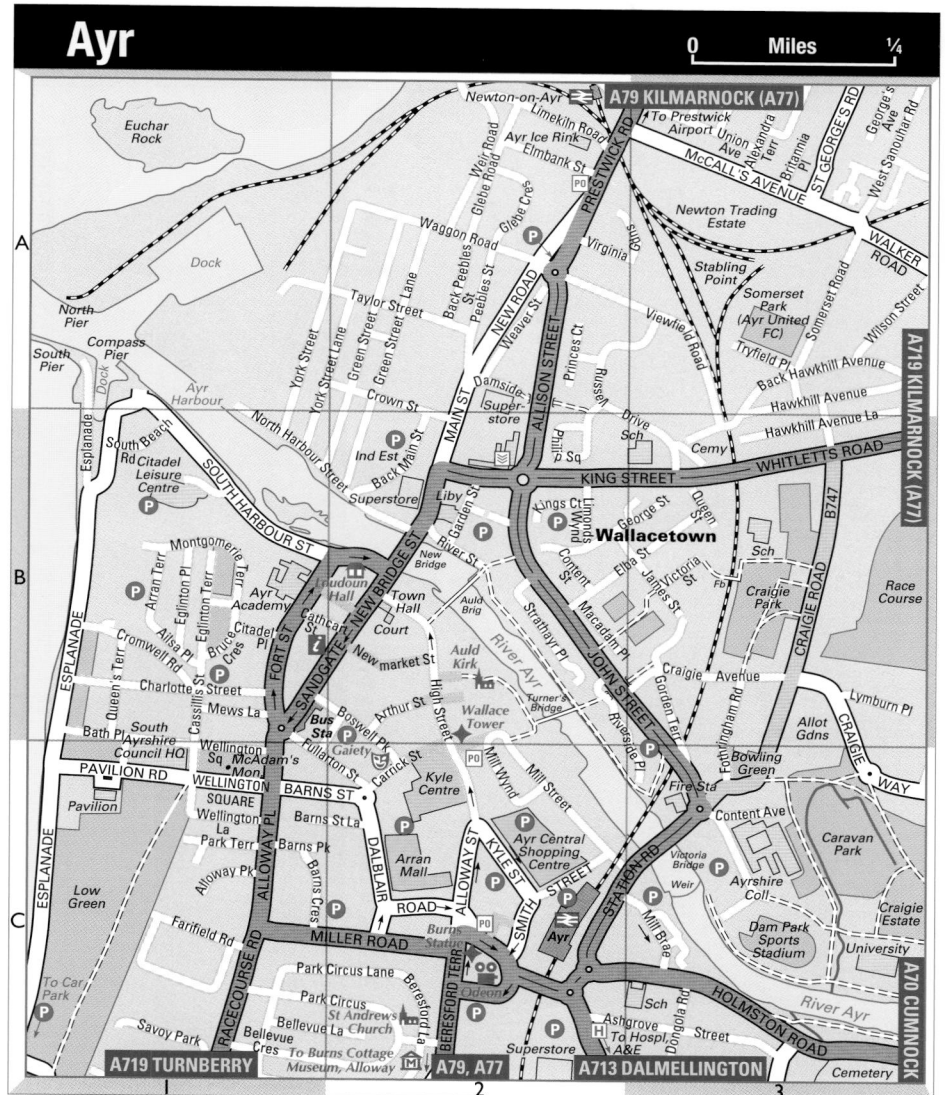

Bath

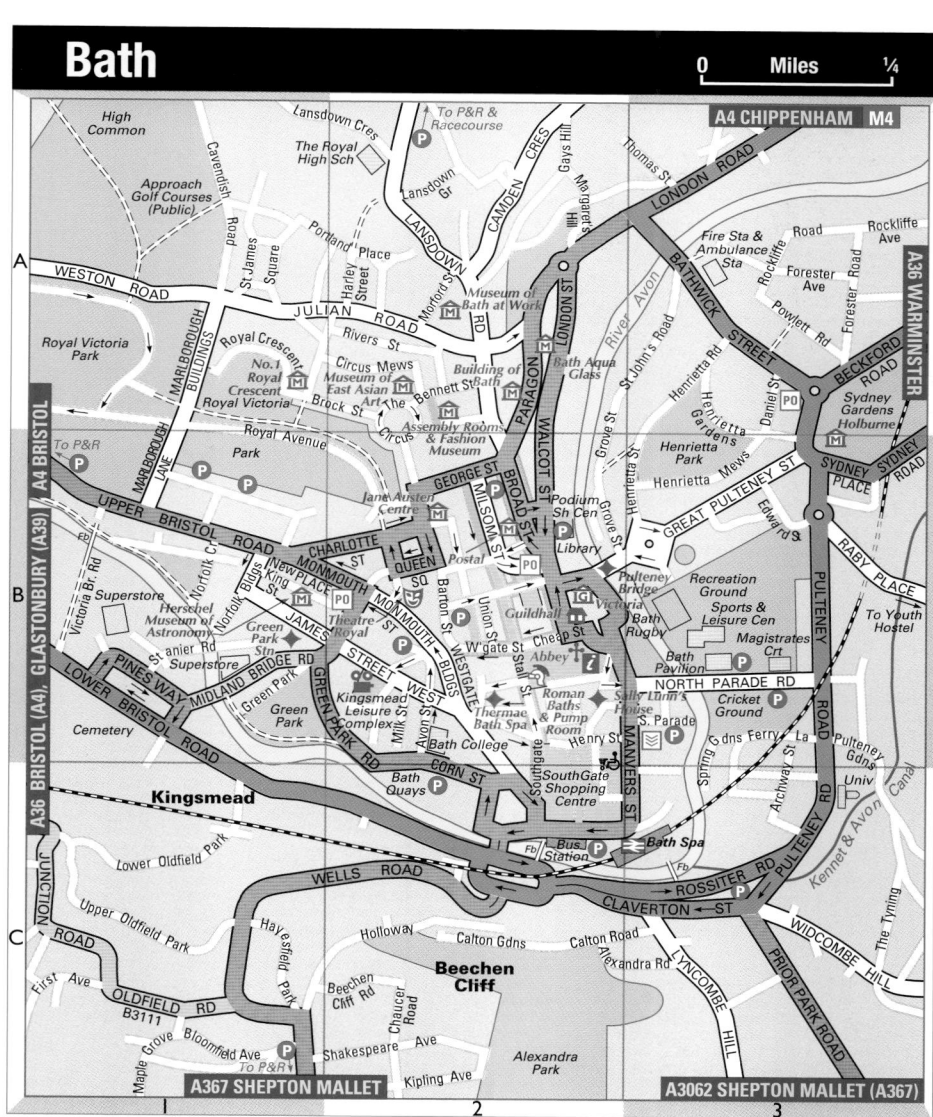

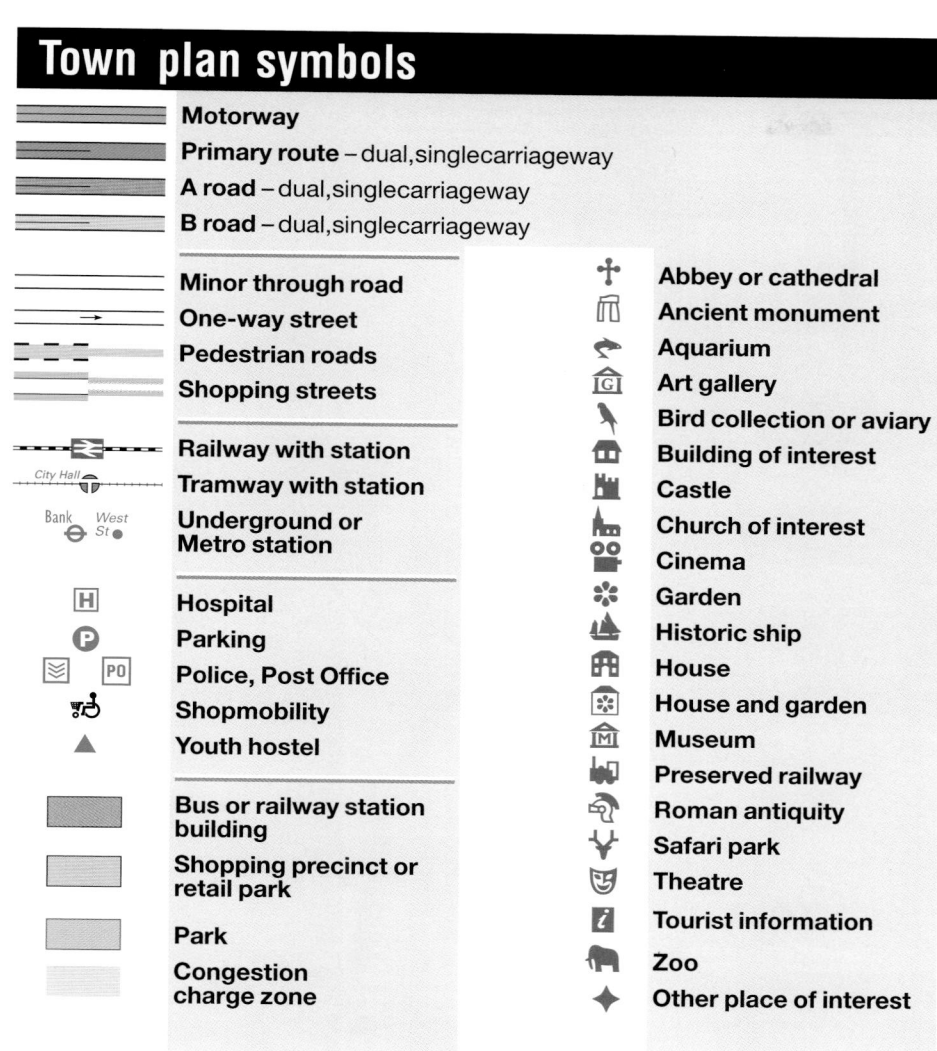

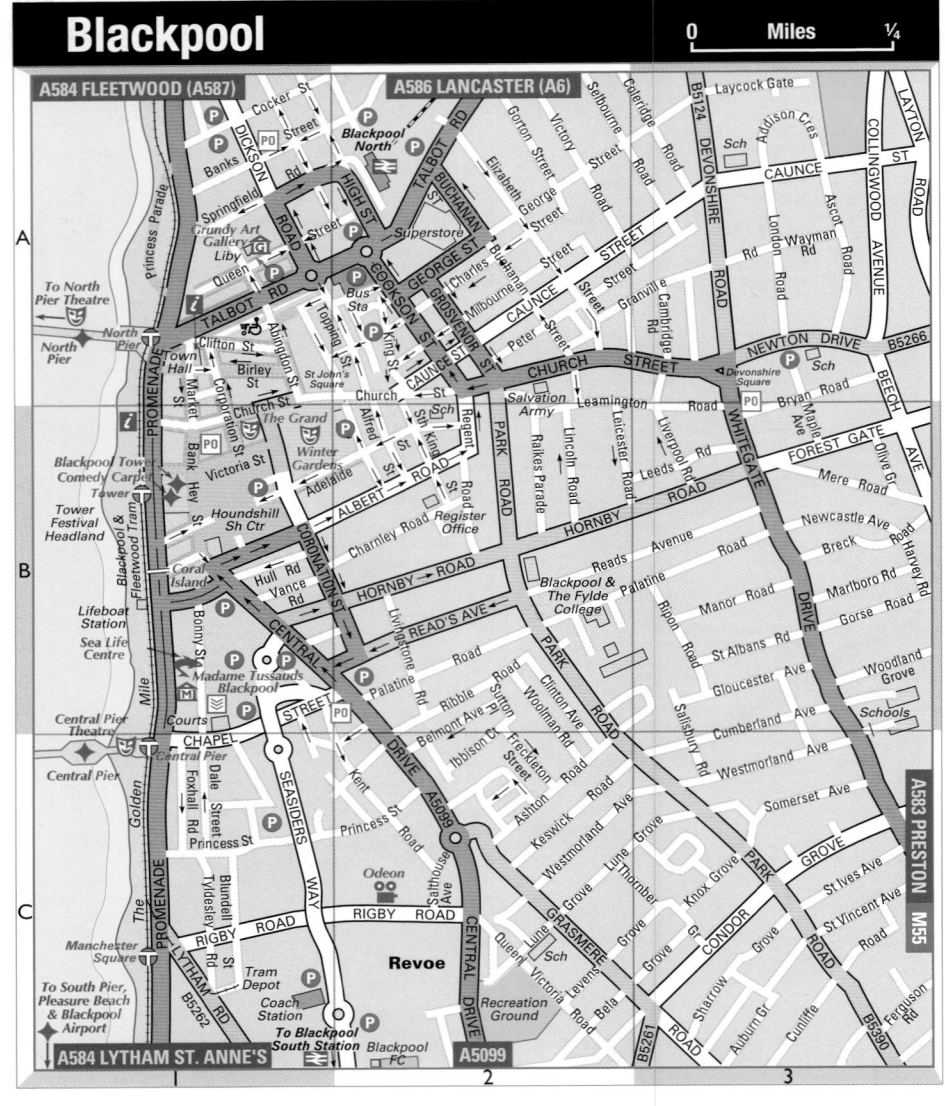

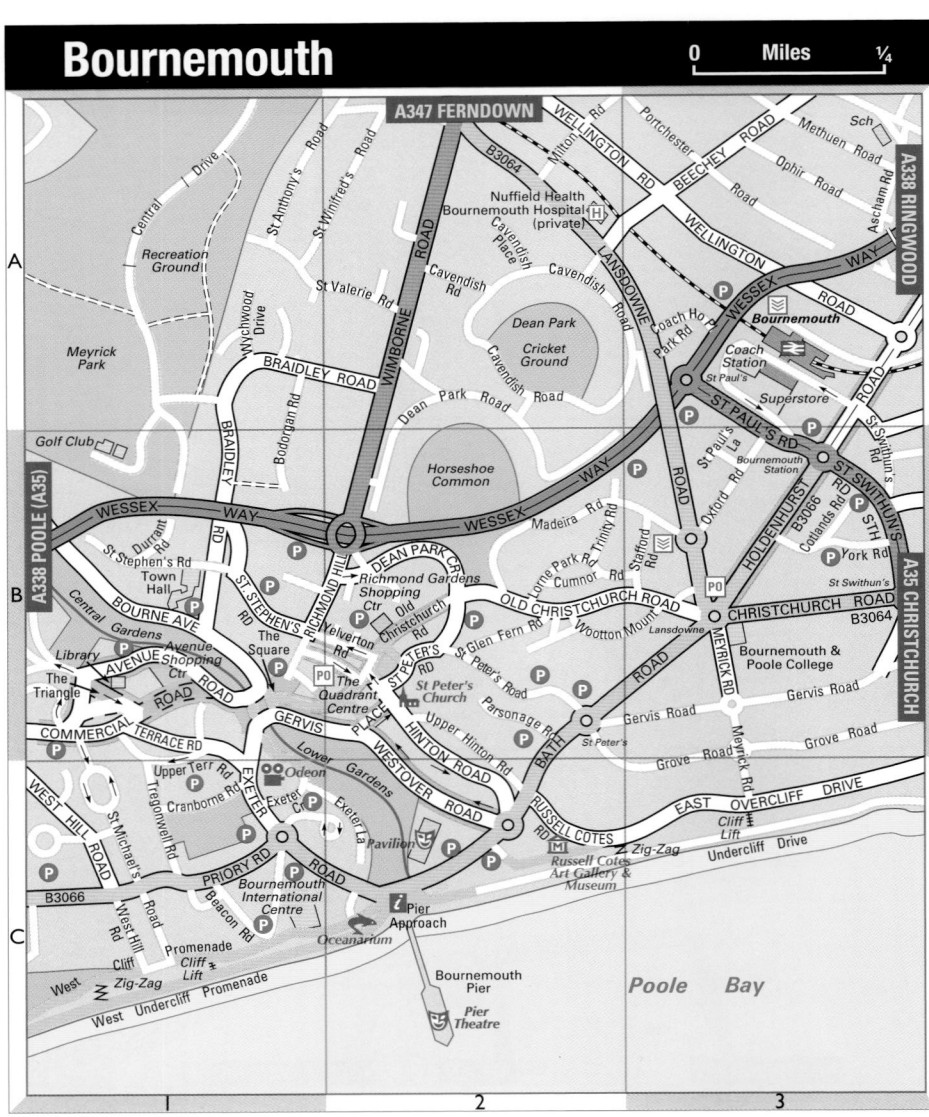

Bradford

0 Miles ¼

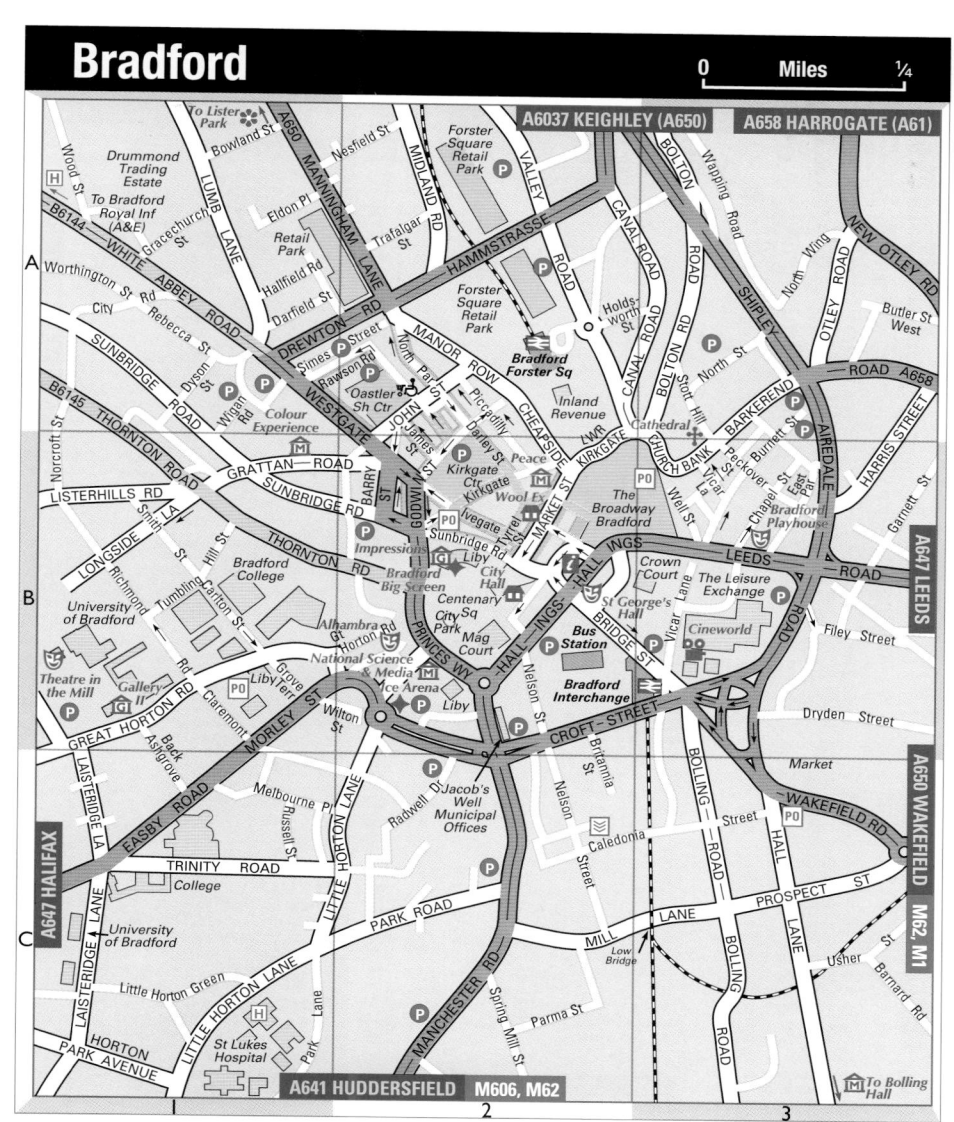

Brighton

0 Miles ¼

Bristol

0 Miles ¼

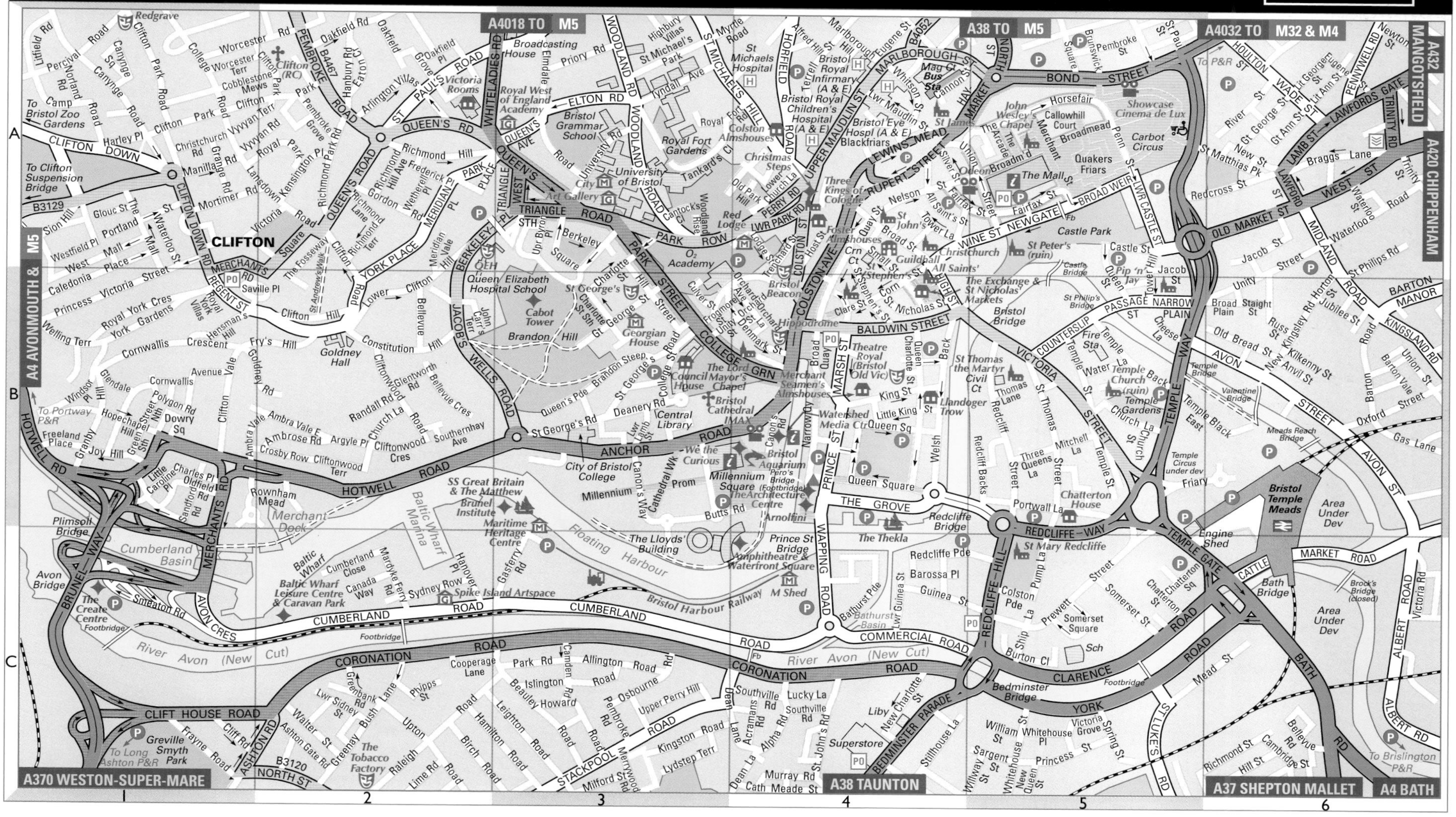

Bury St Edmunds

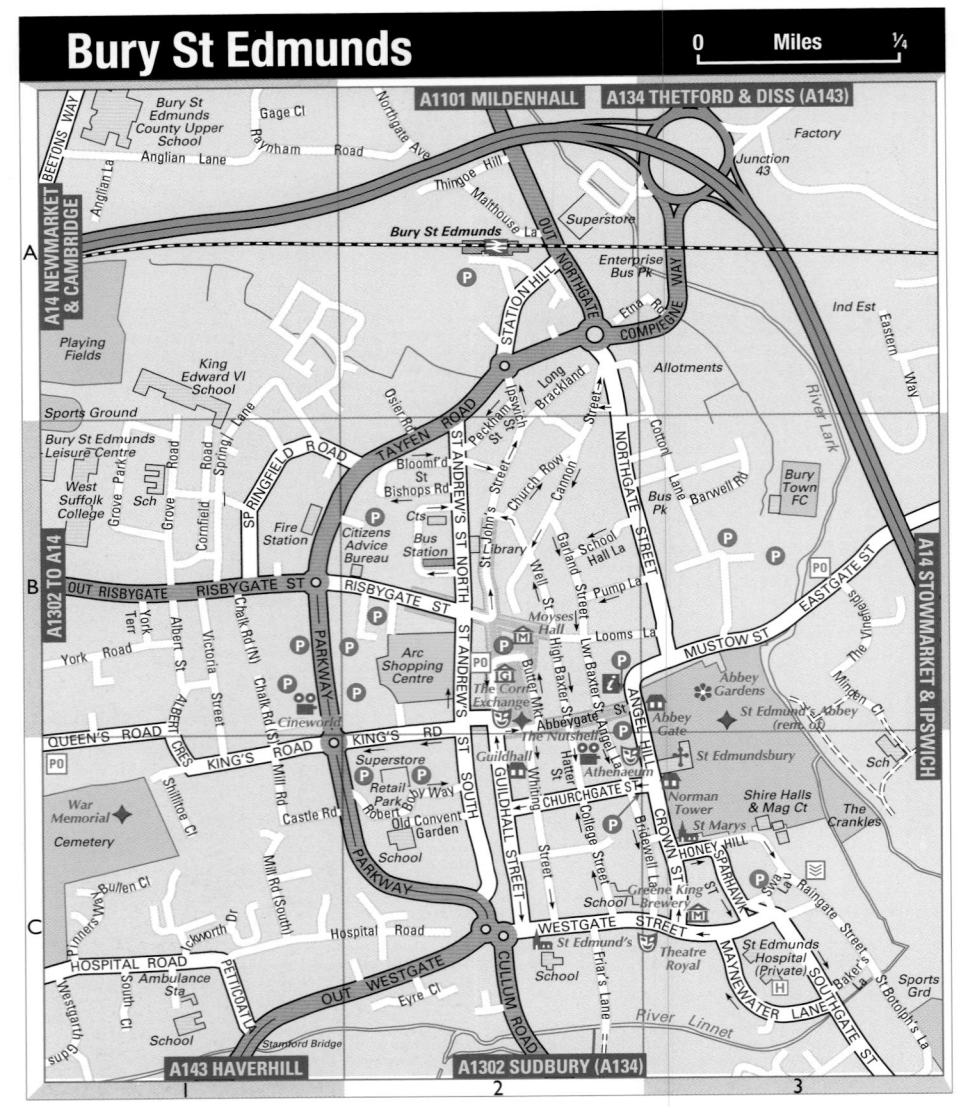

Cambridge

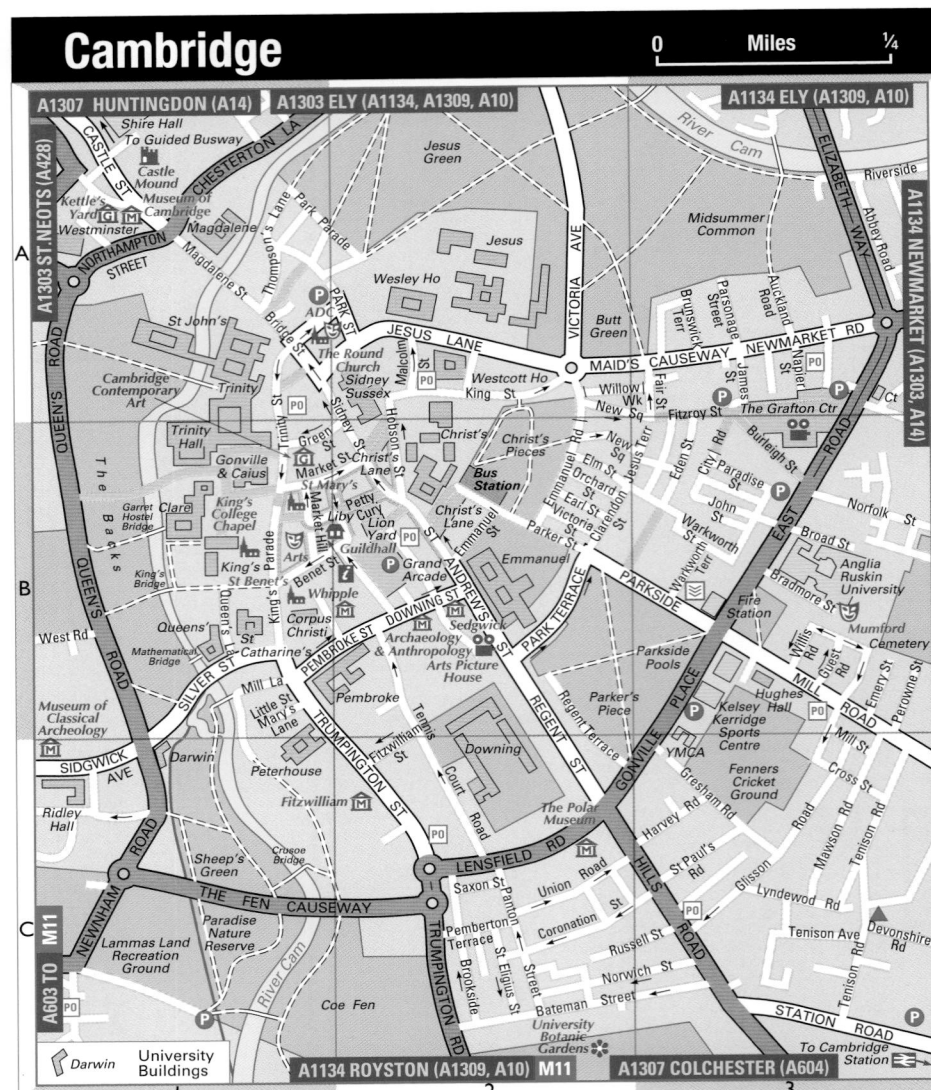

Canterbury

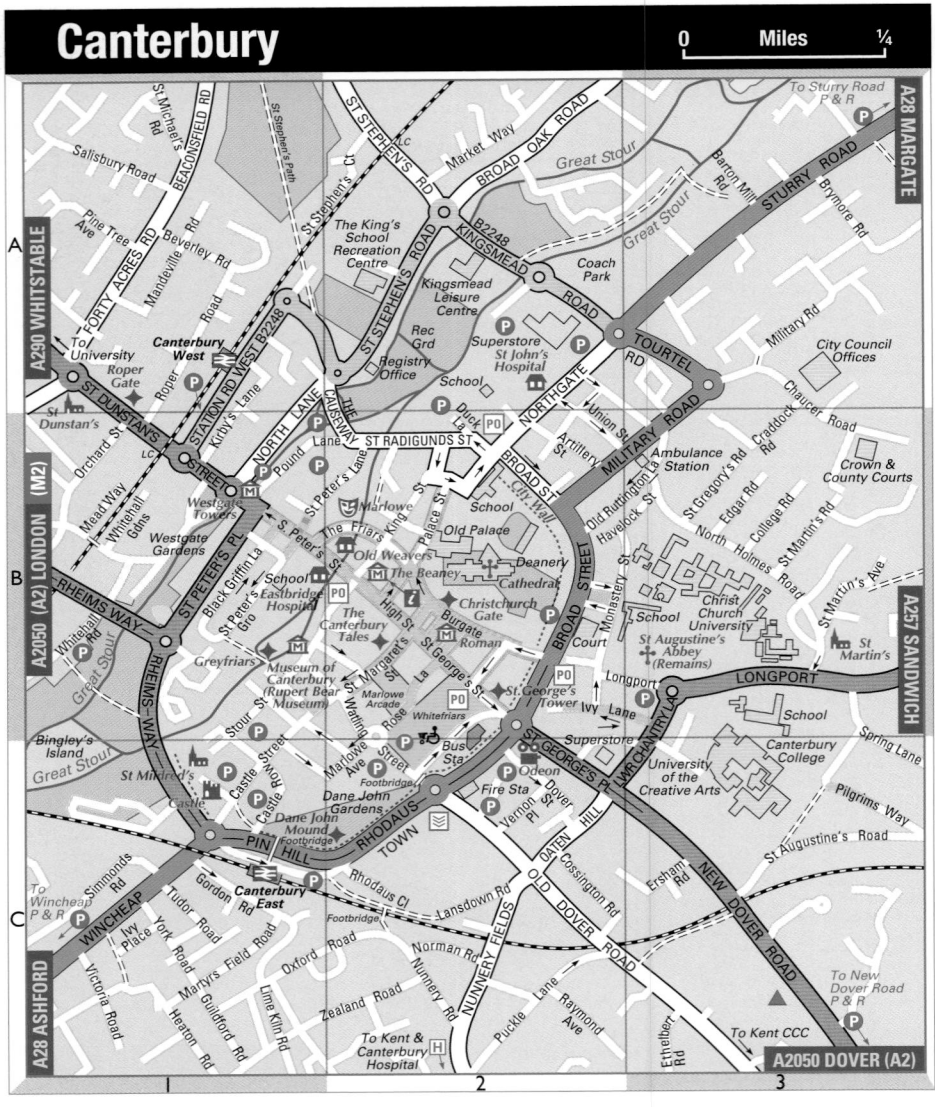

Cardiff / Caerdydd

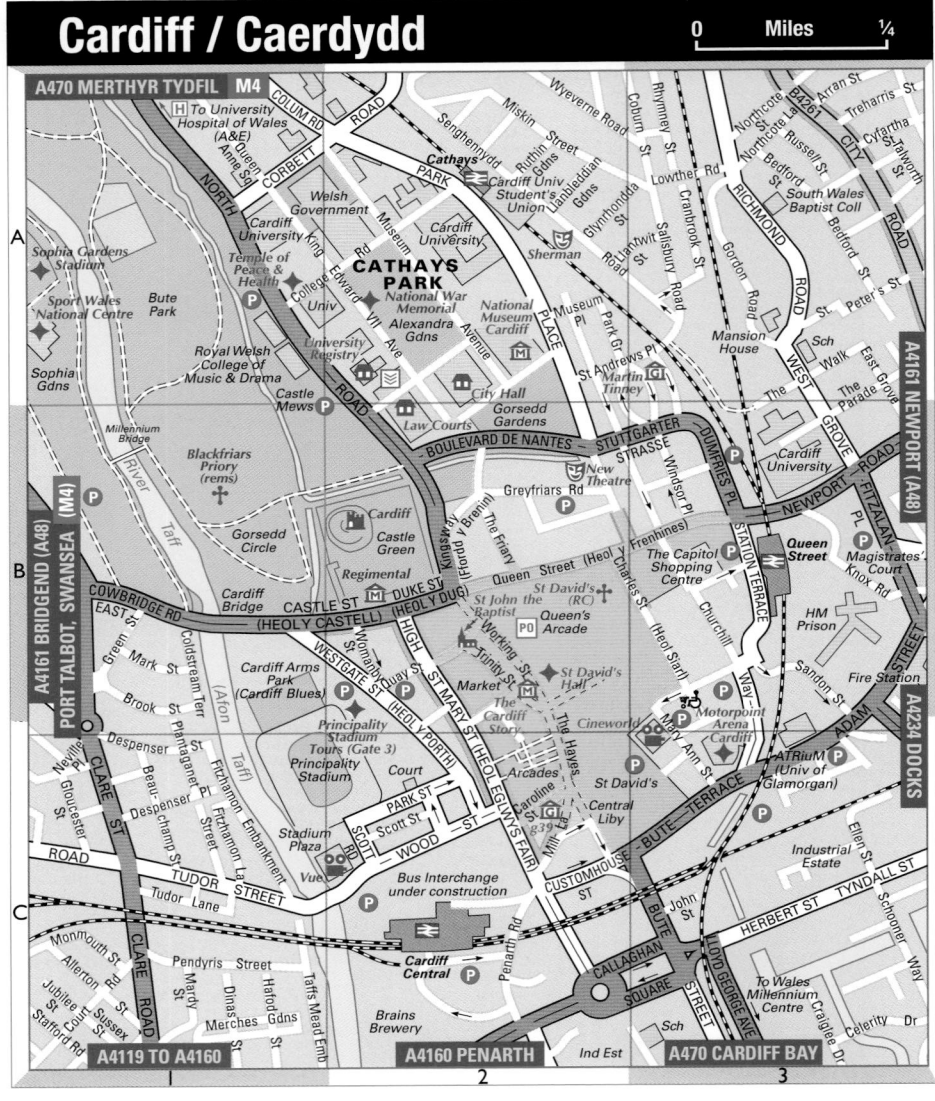

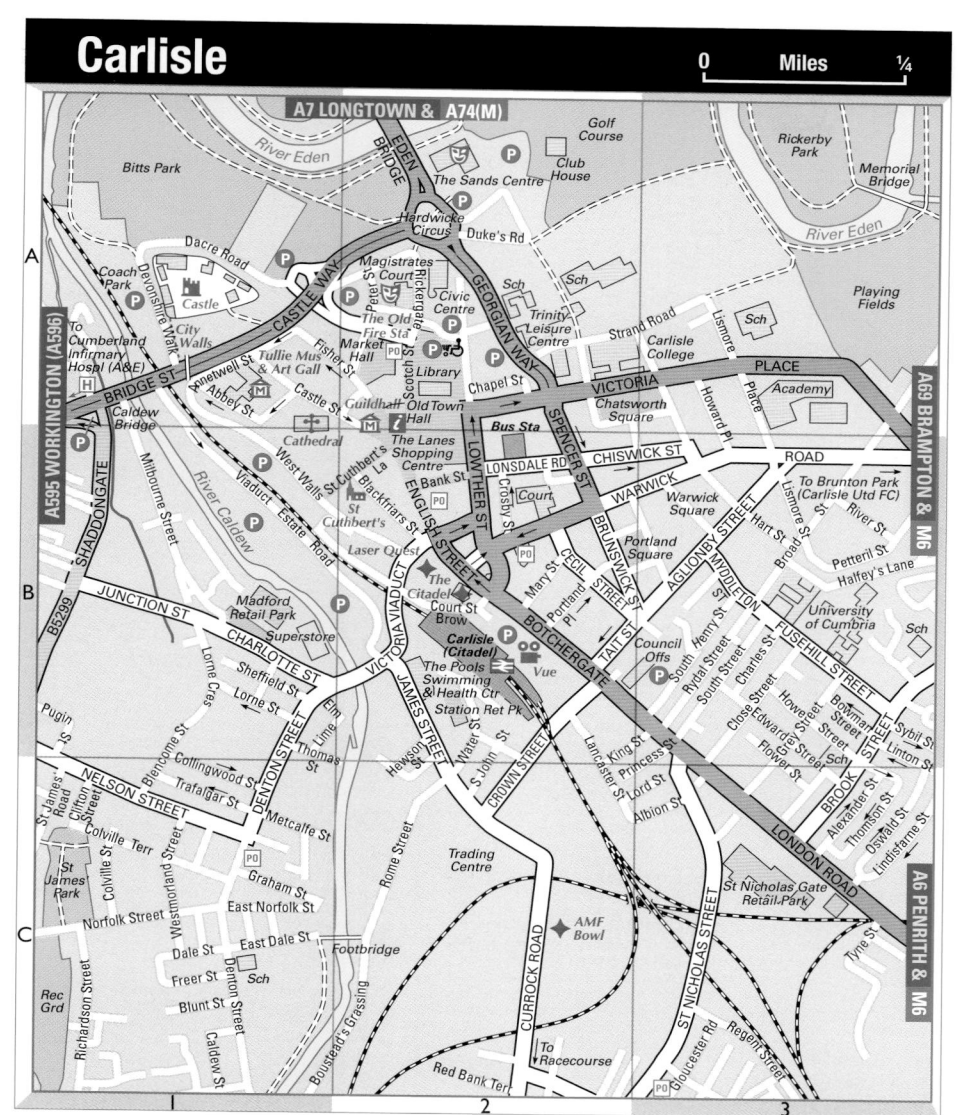

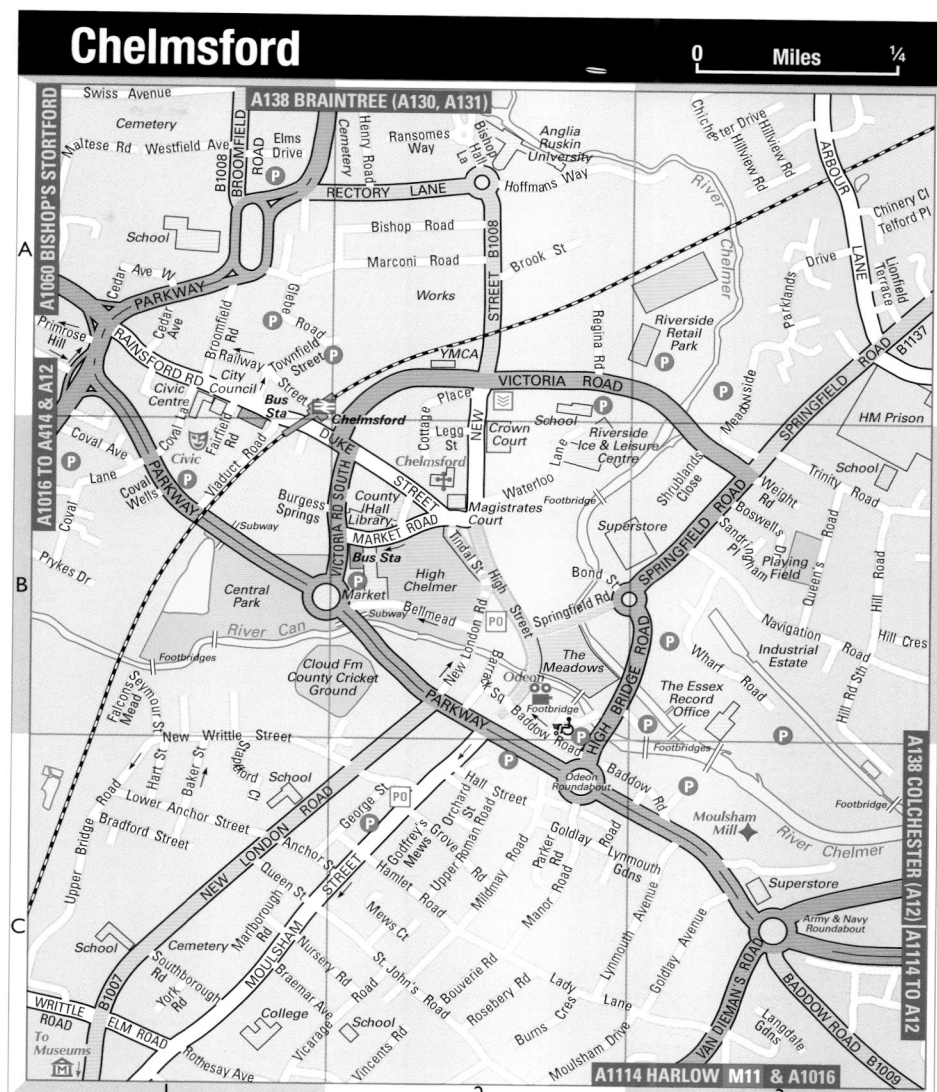

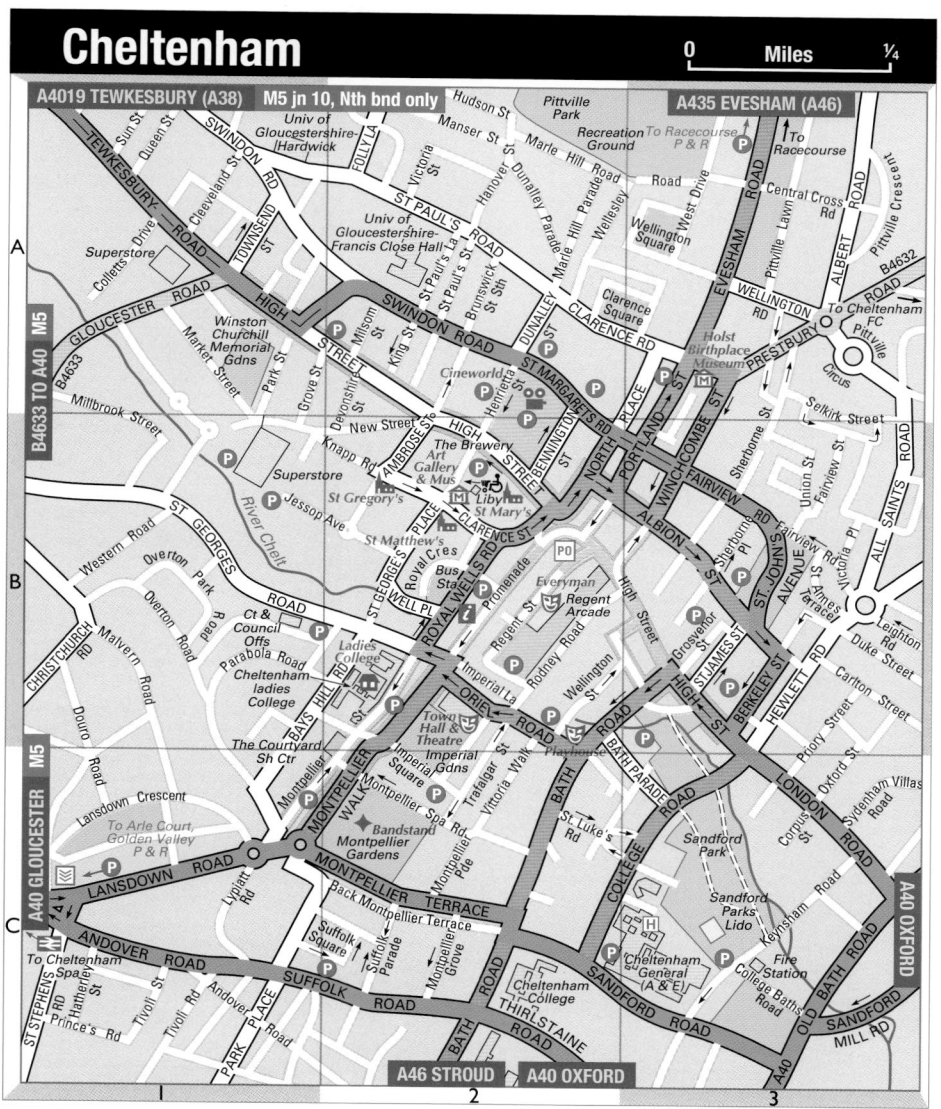

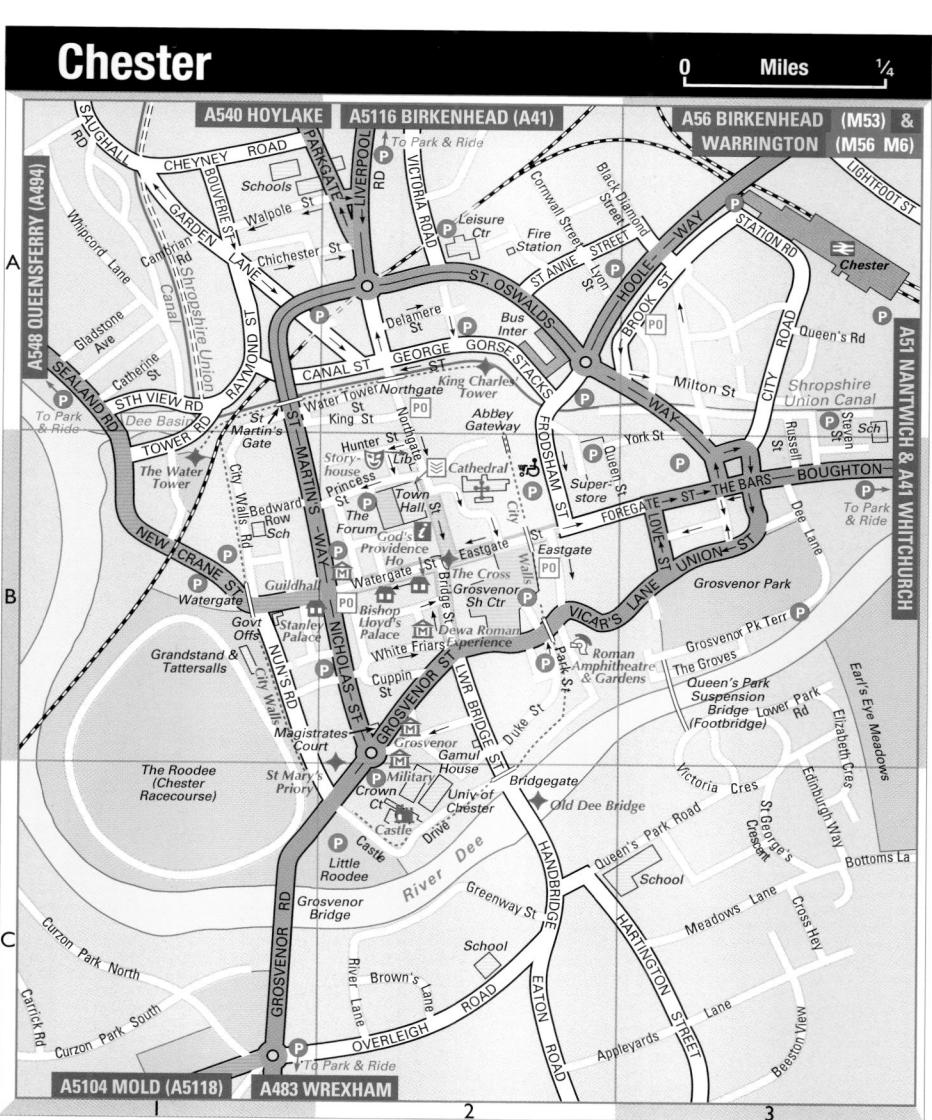

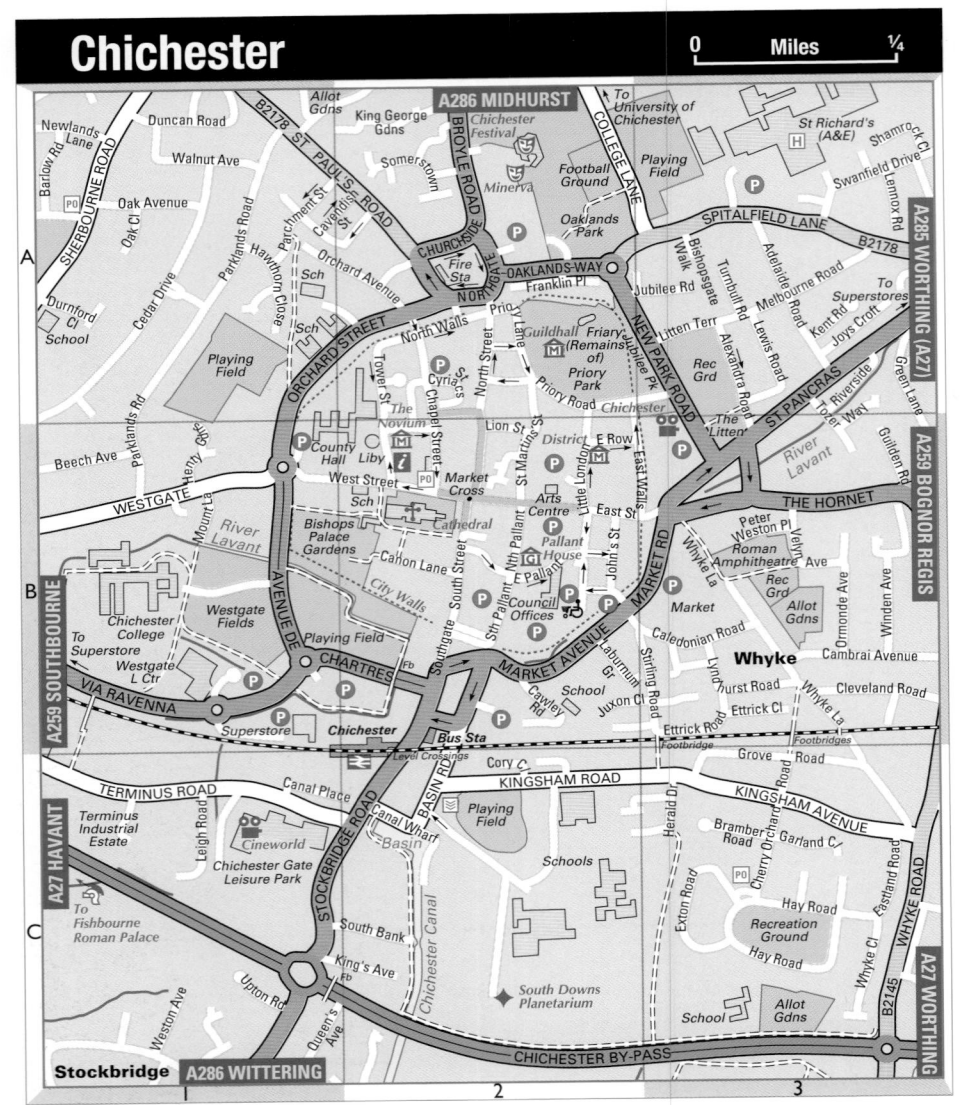

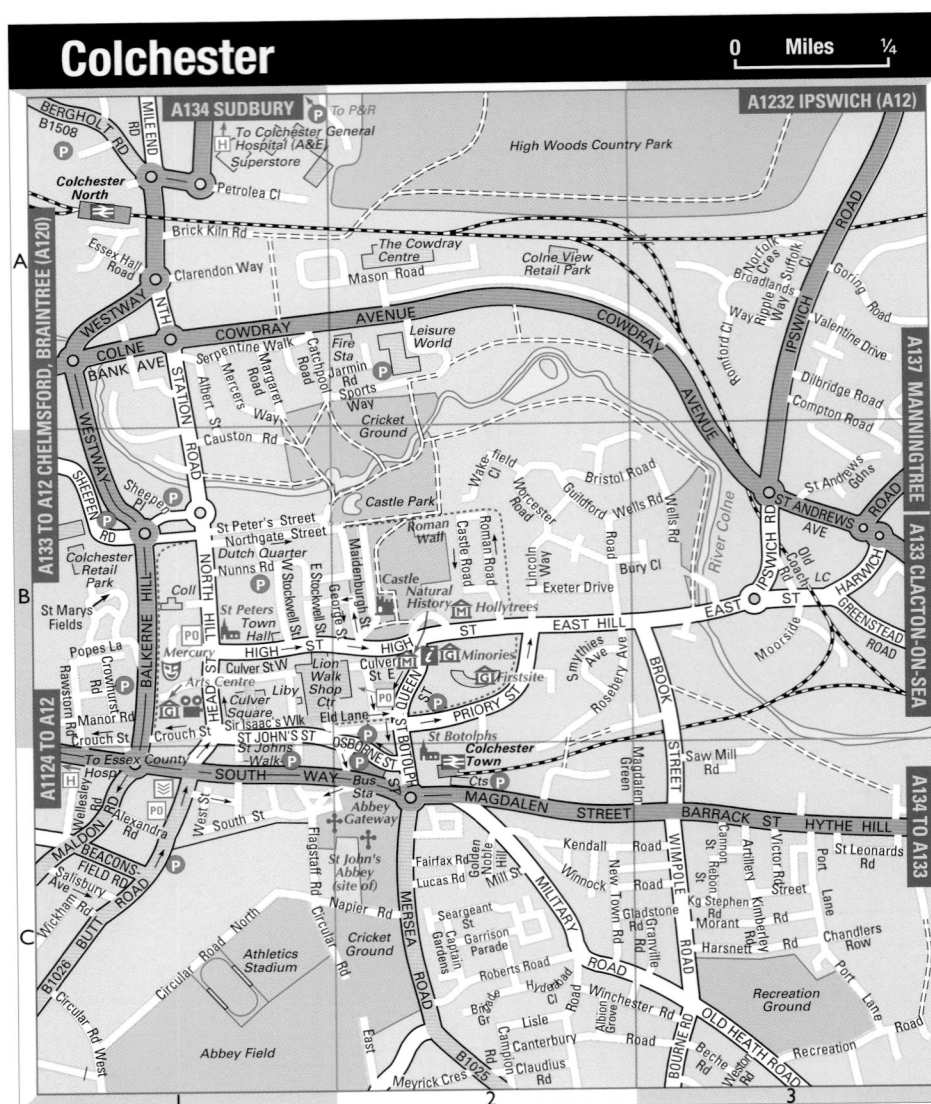

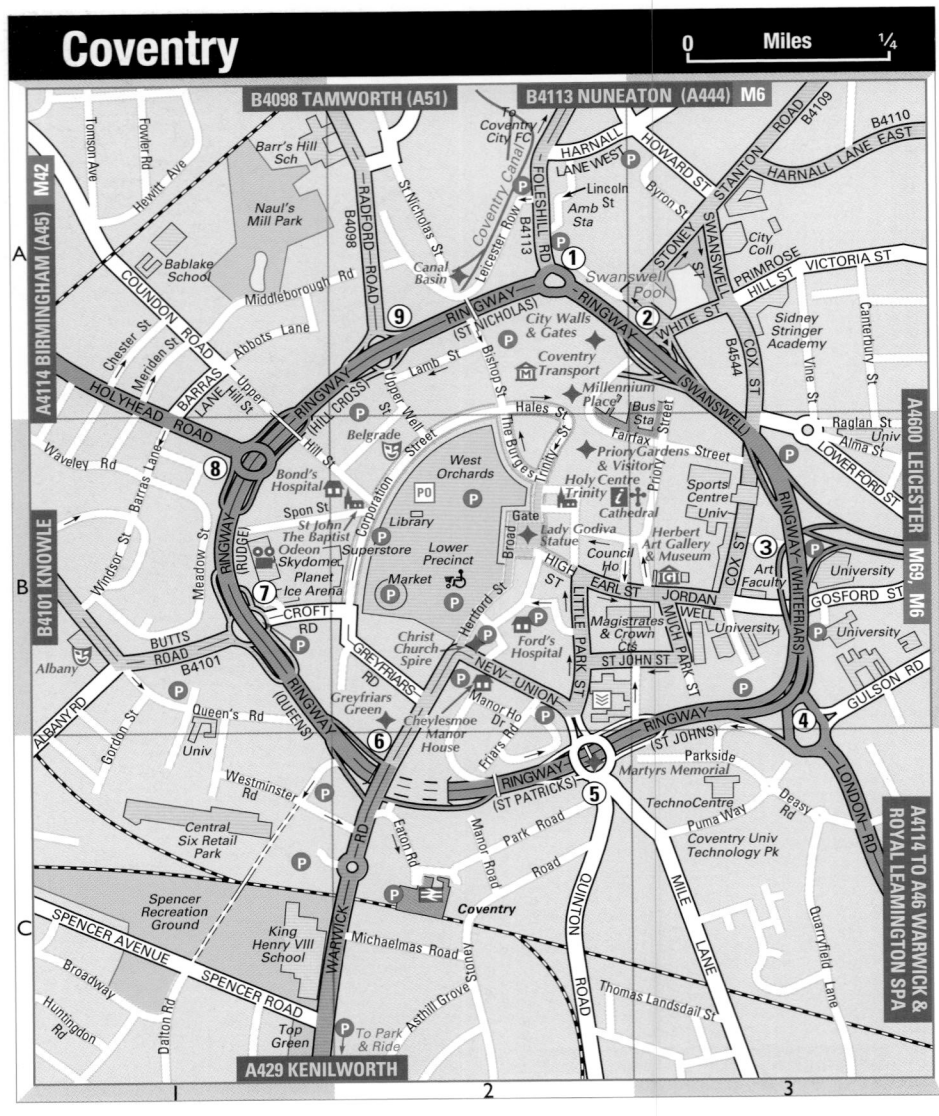

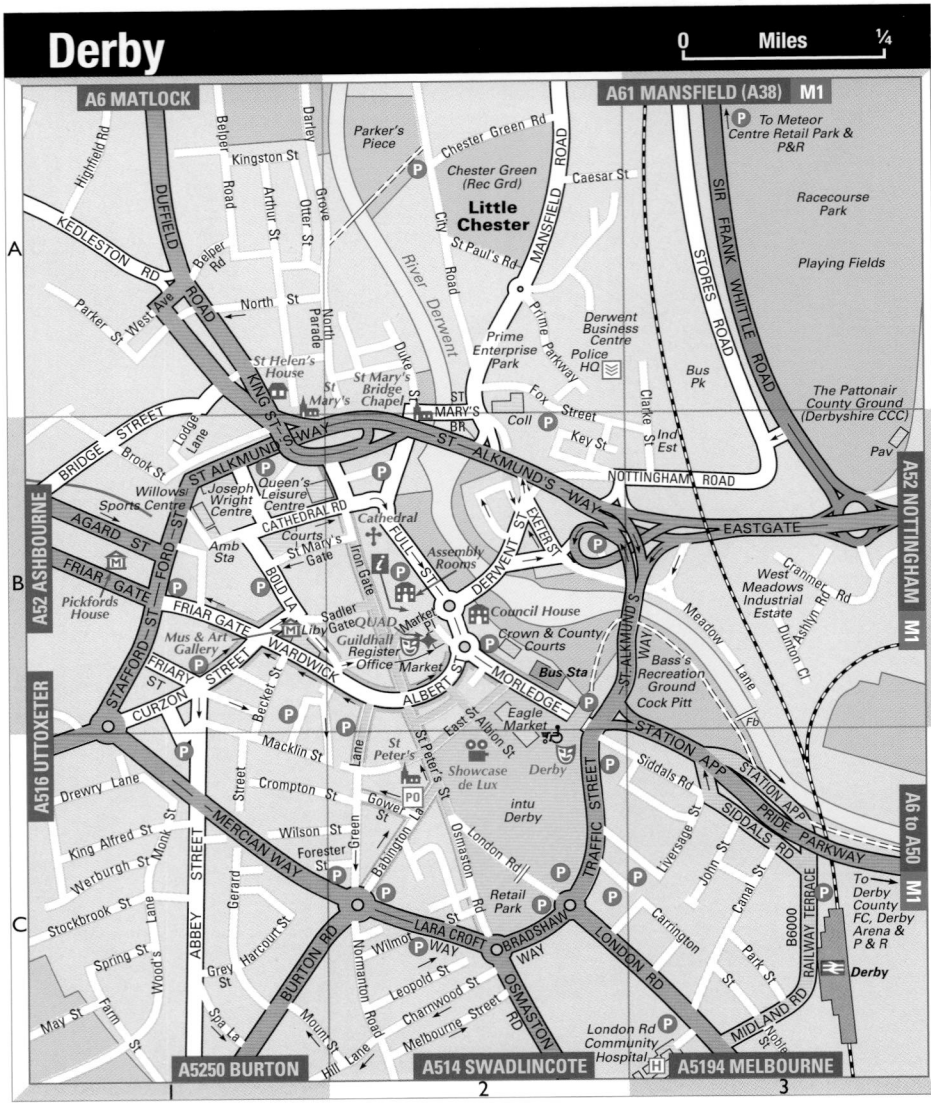

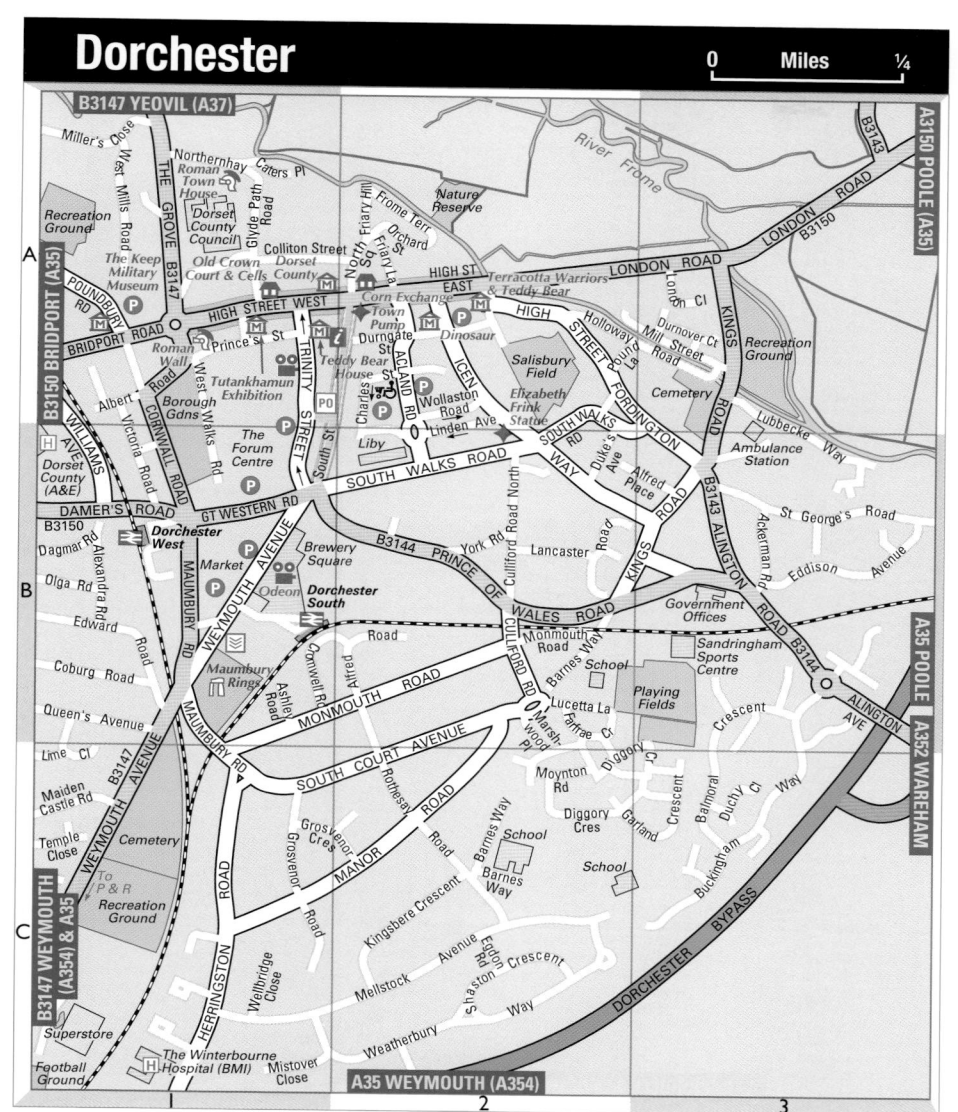

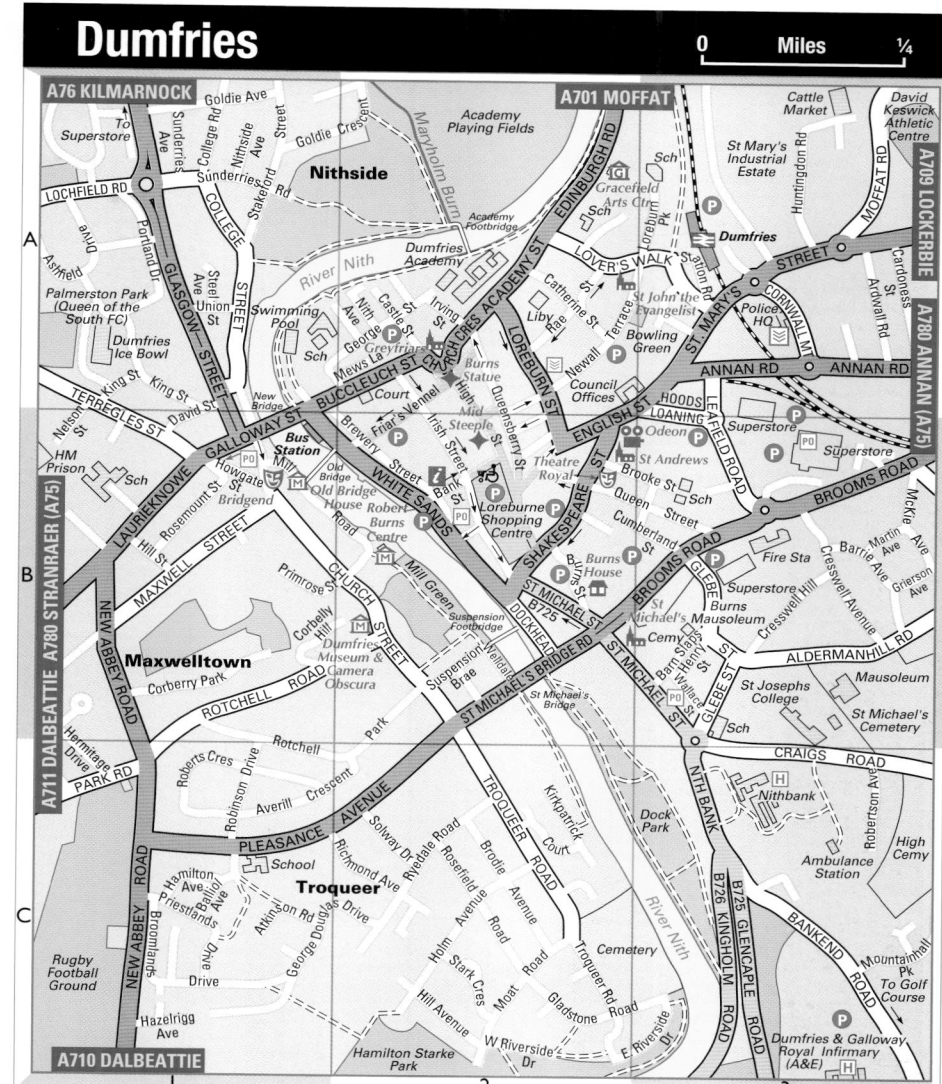

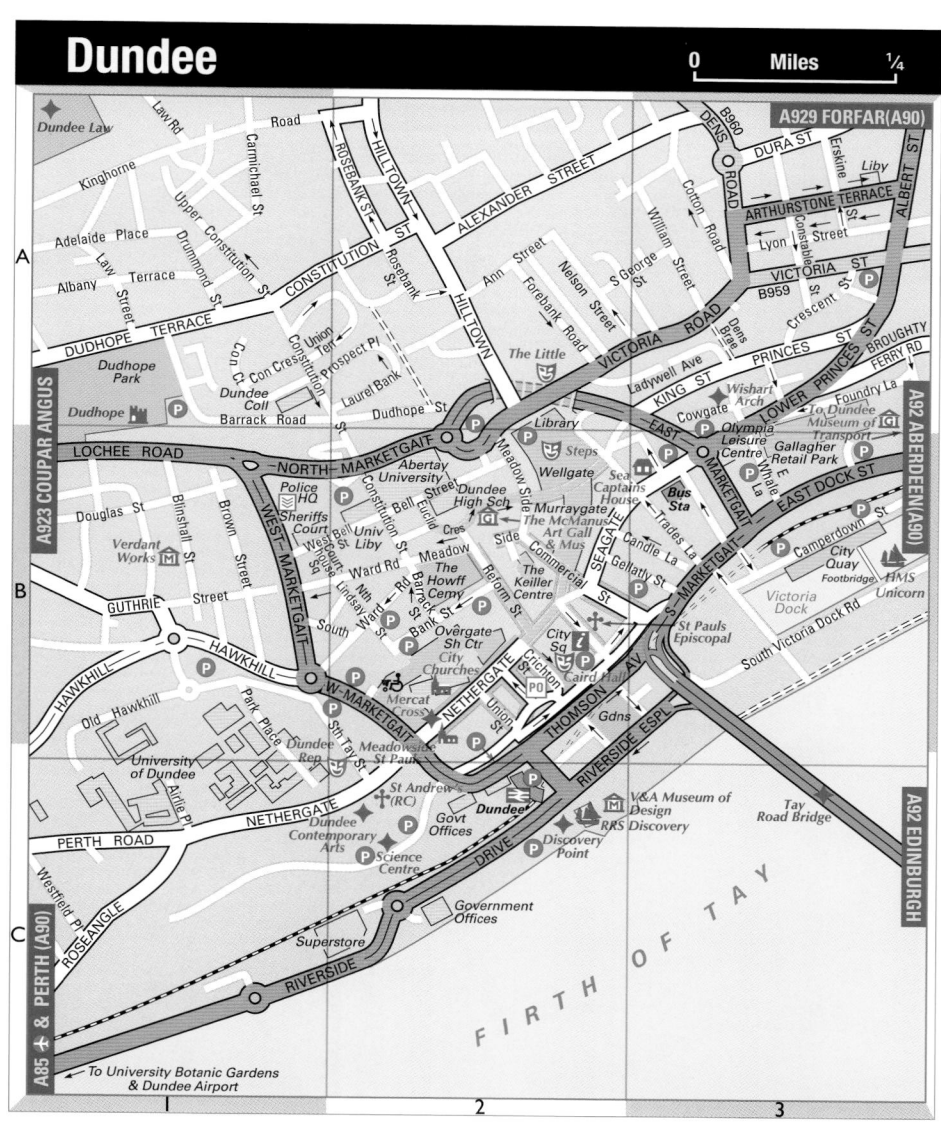

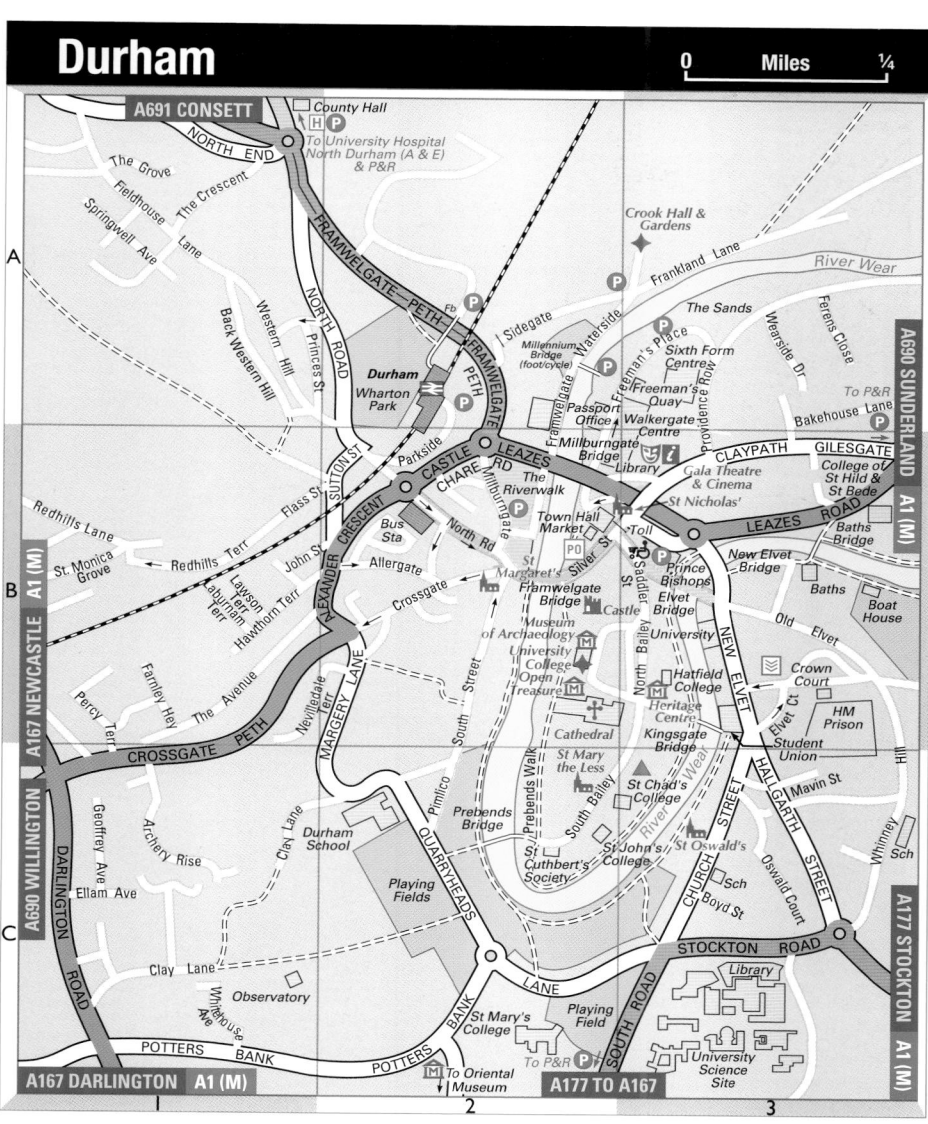

Edinburgh

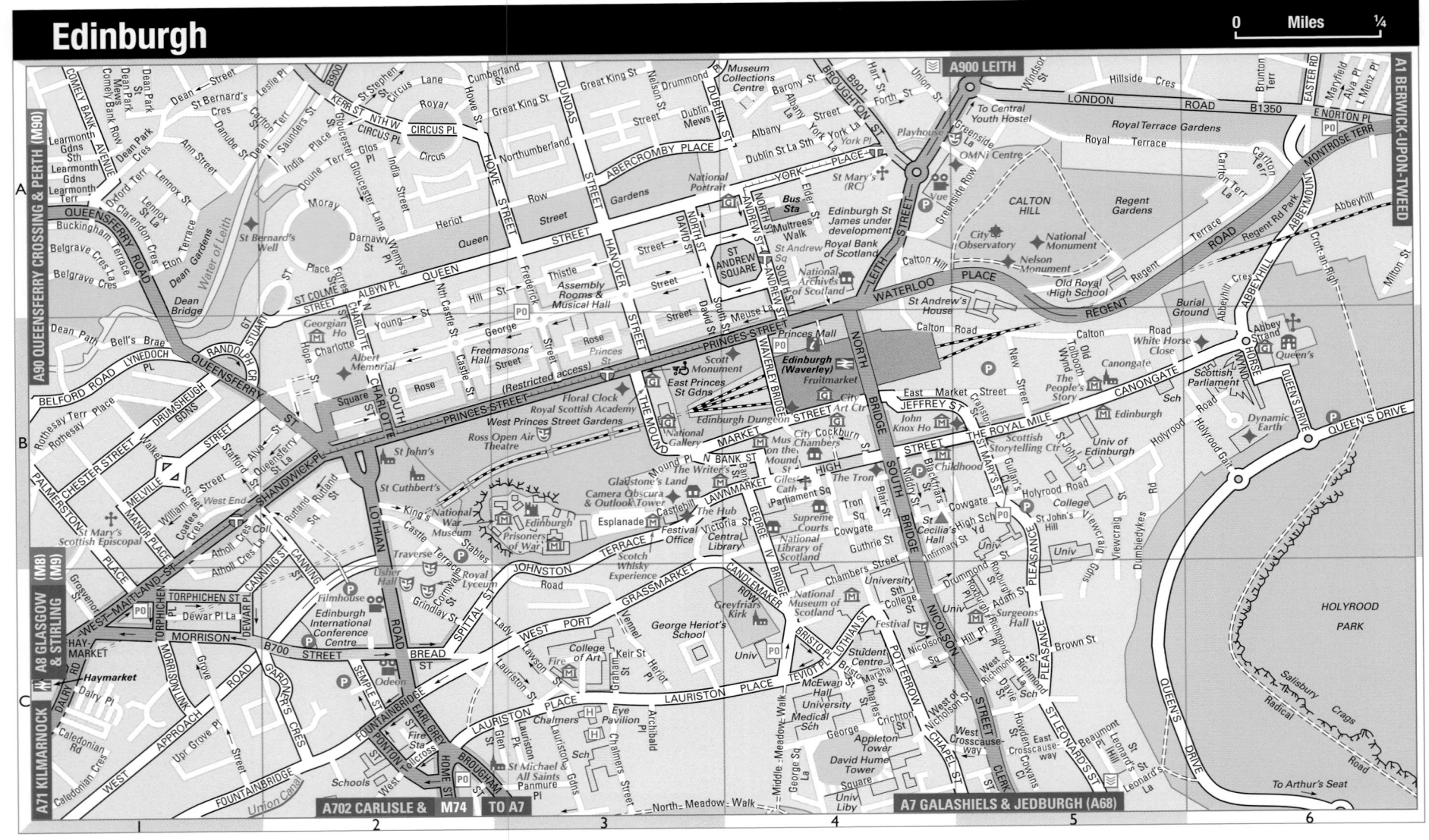

Exeter

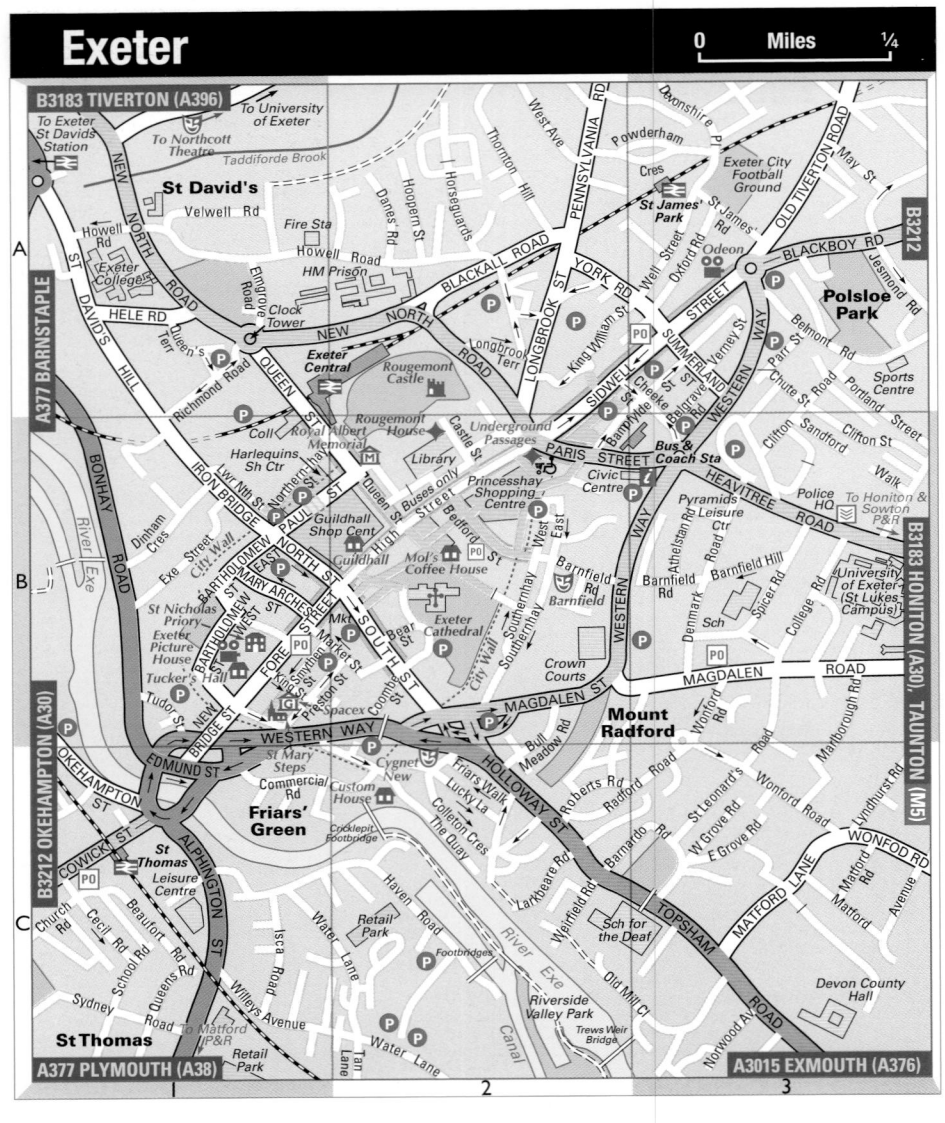

Gloucester

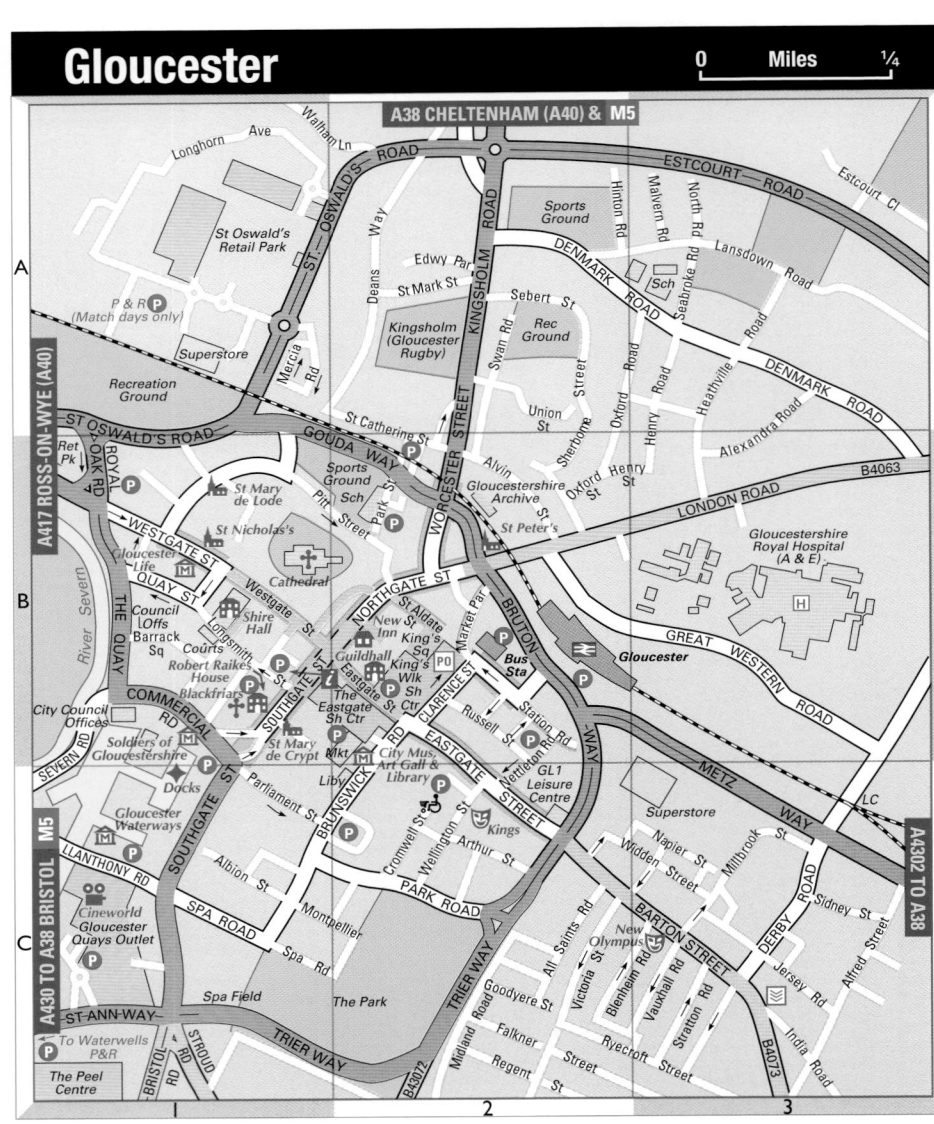

Glasgow

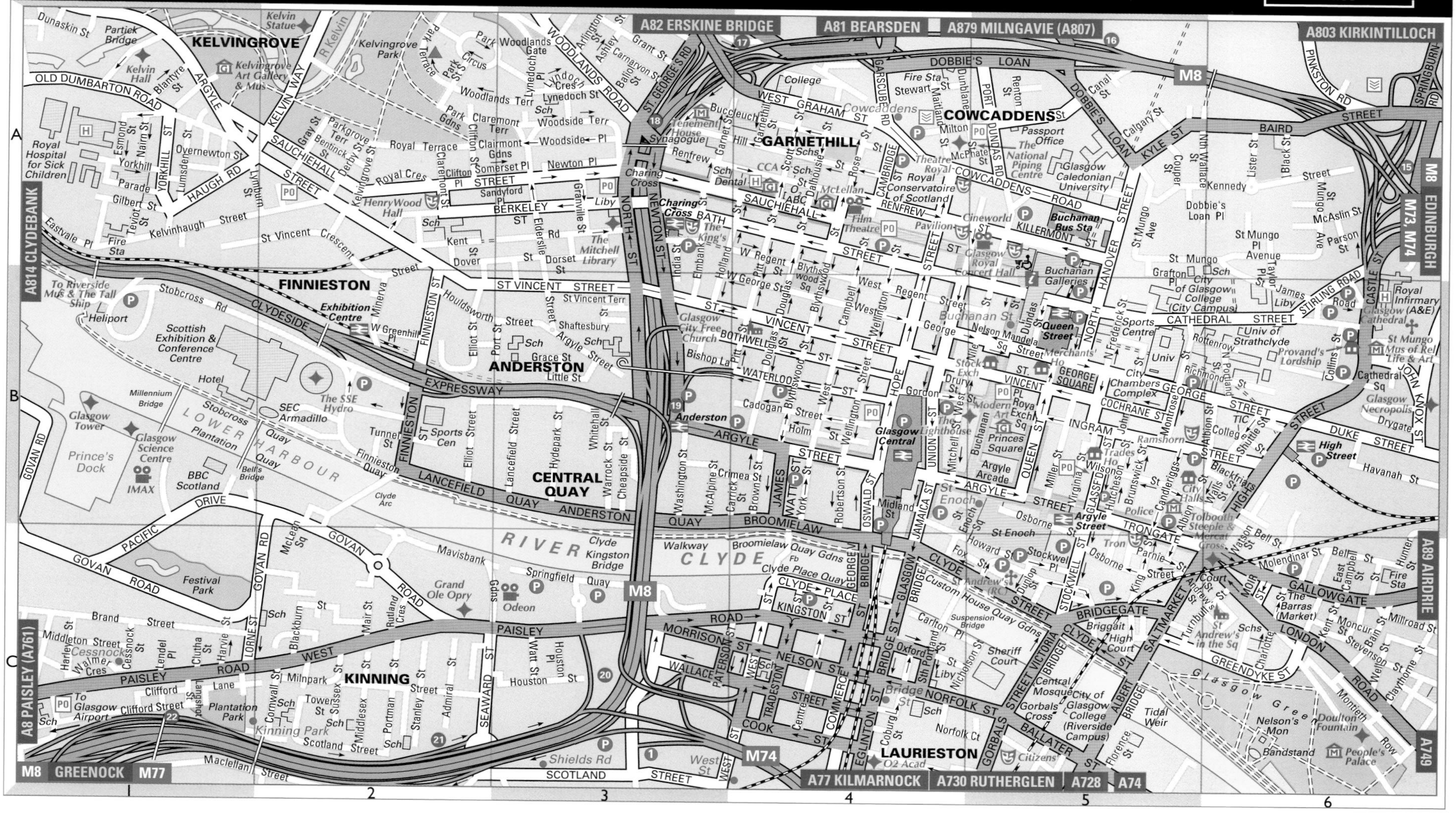

0 Miles ¼

Grimsby

0 Miles ¼

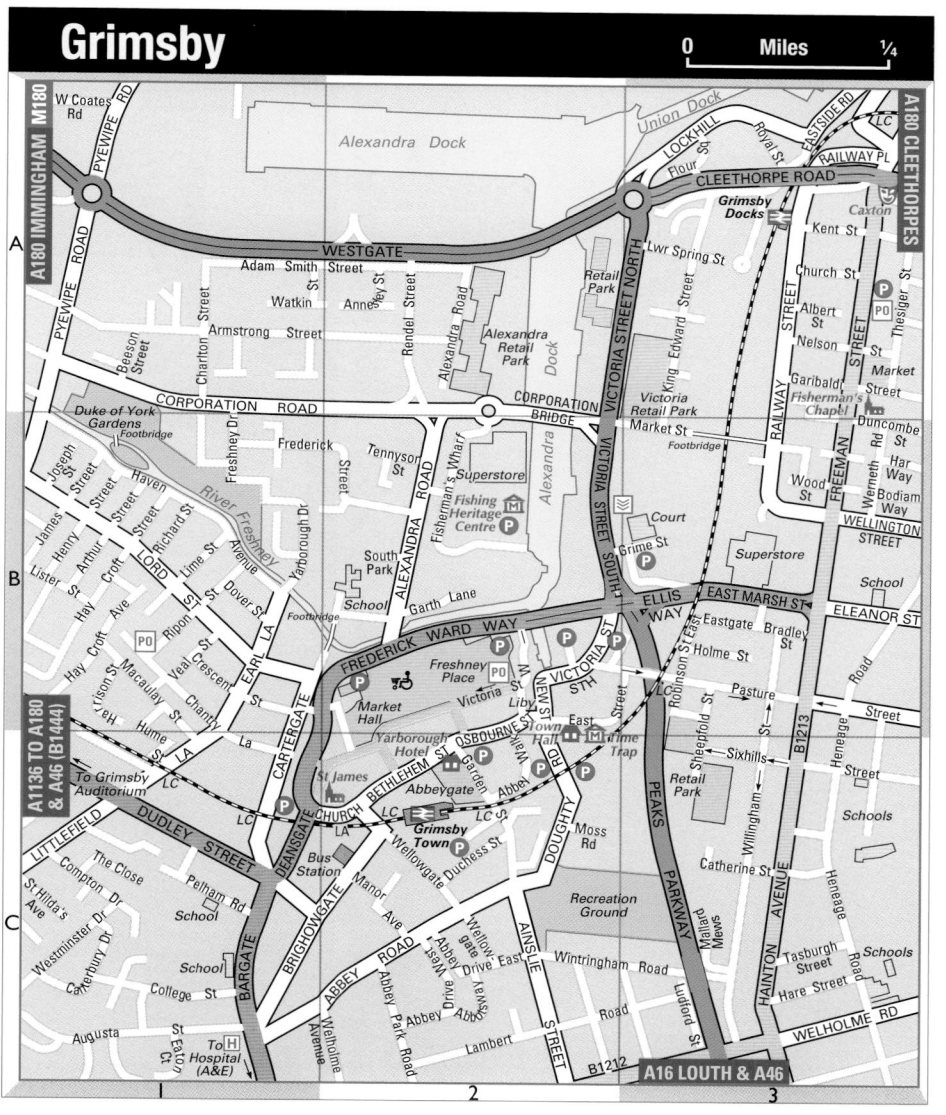

Harrogate

0 Miles ¼

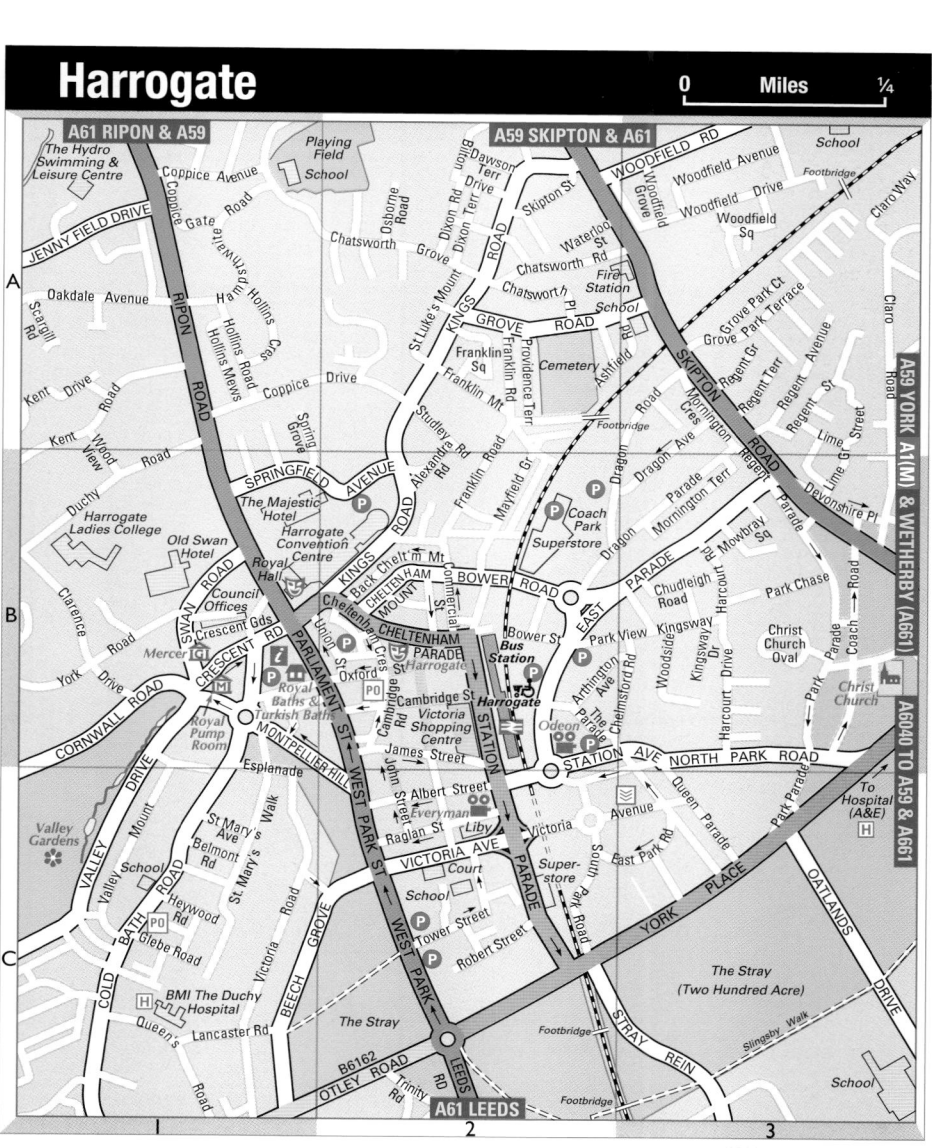

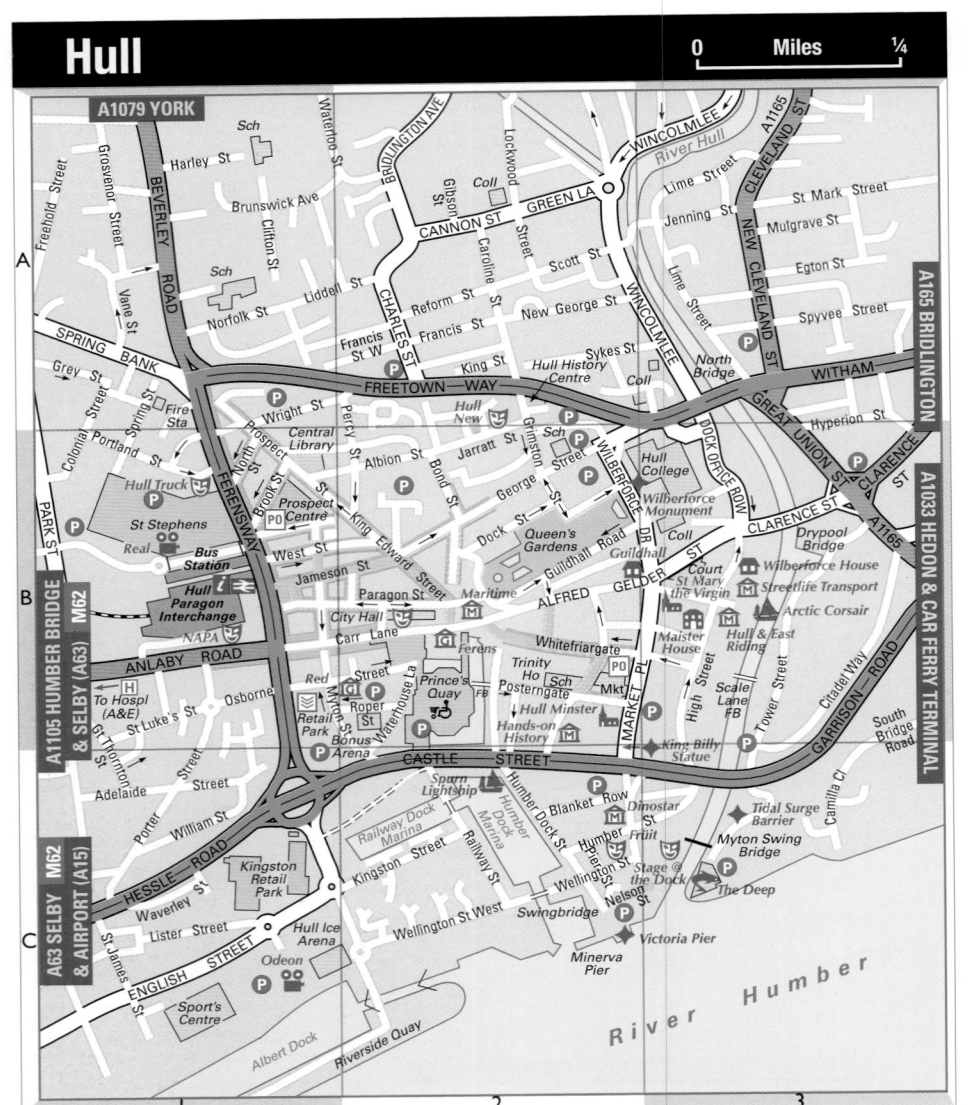

Hull

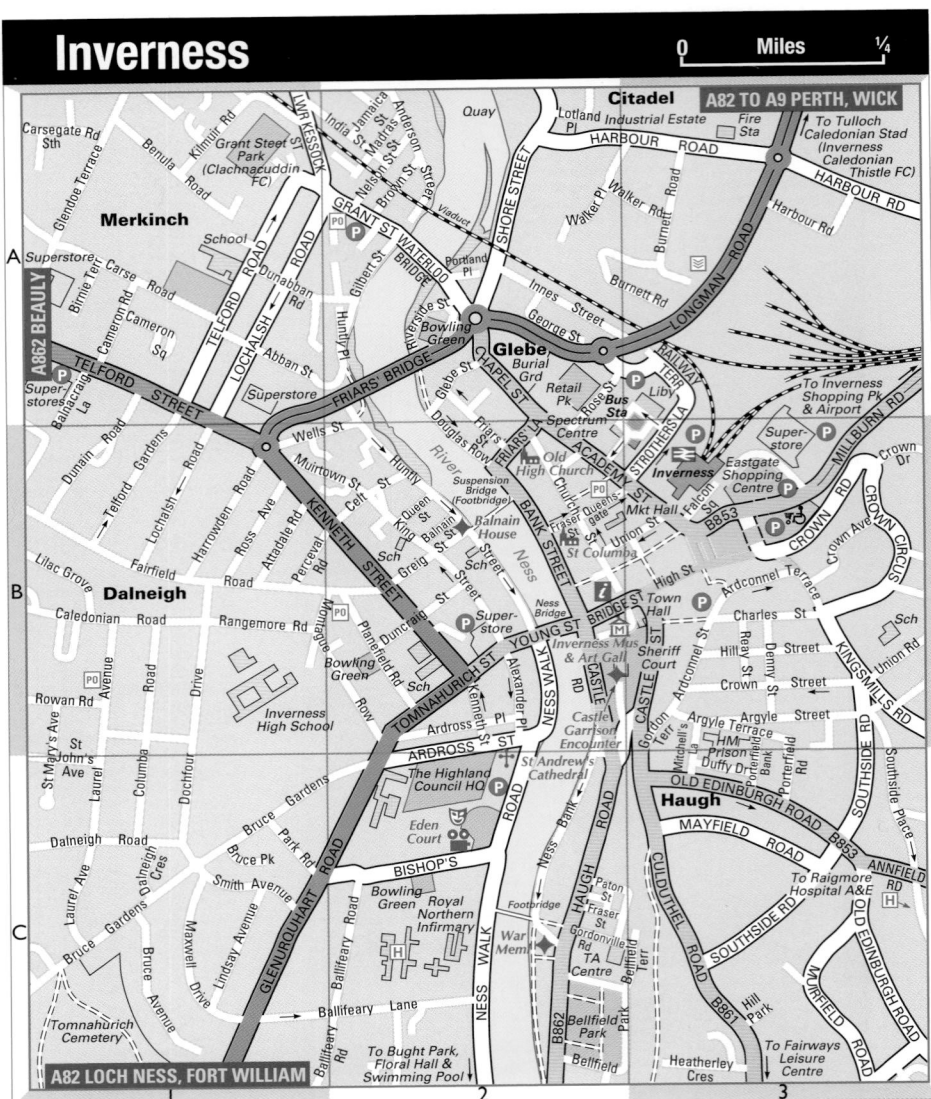

Inverness

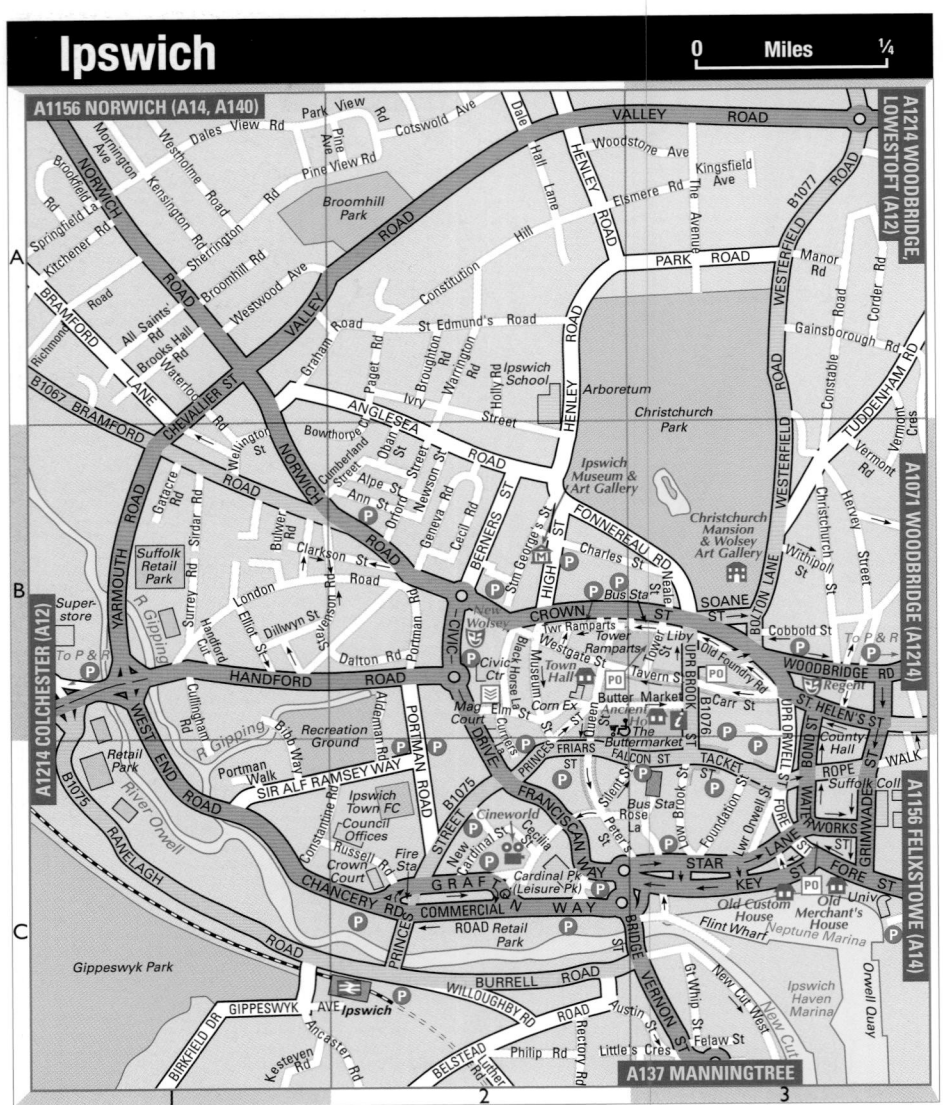

Ipswich

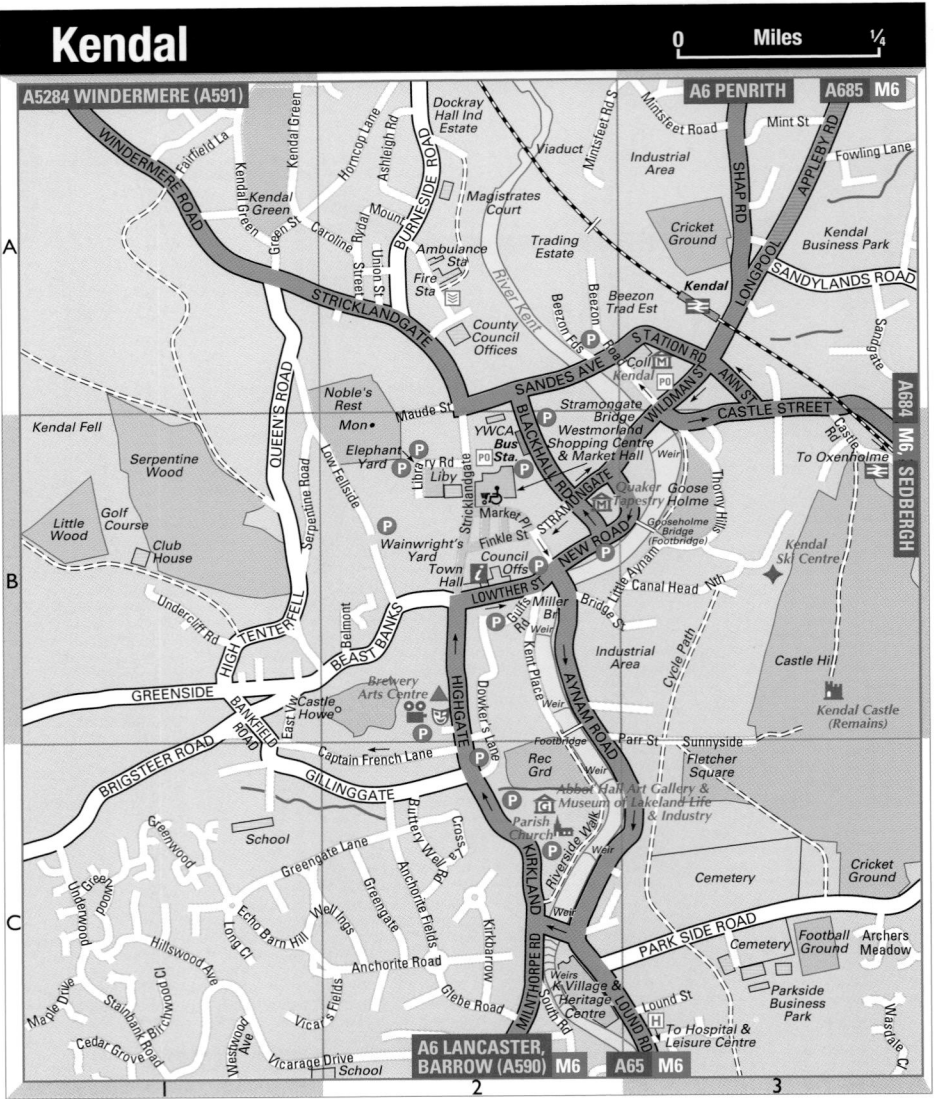

Kendal

King's Lynn

0 Miles ¼

Lancaster

0 Miles ¼

Leeds

0 Miles ¼

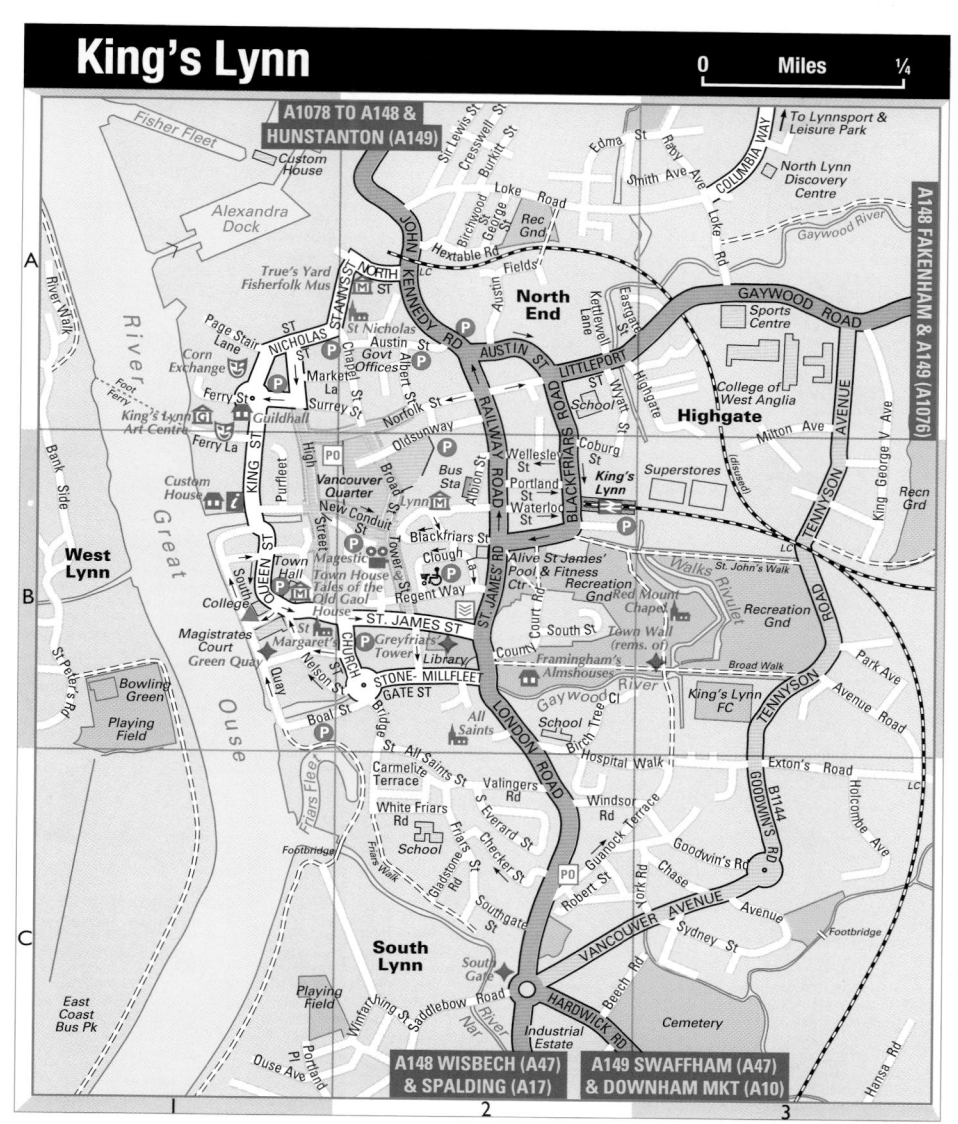

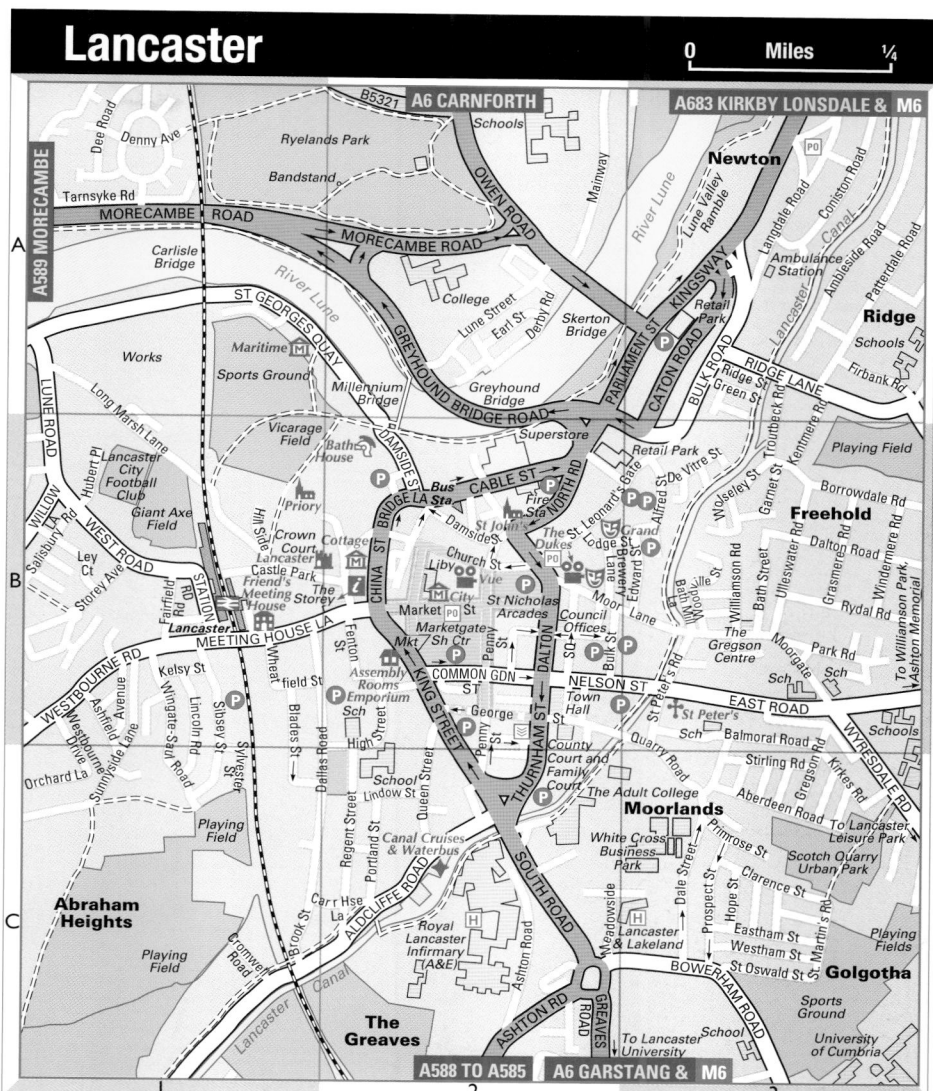

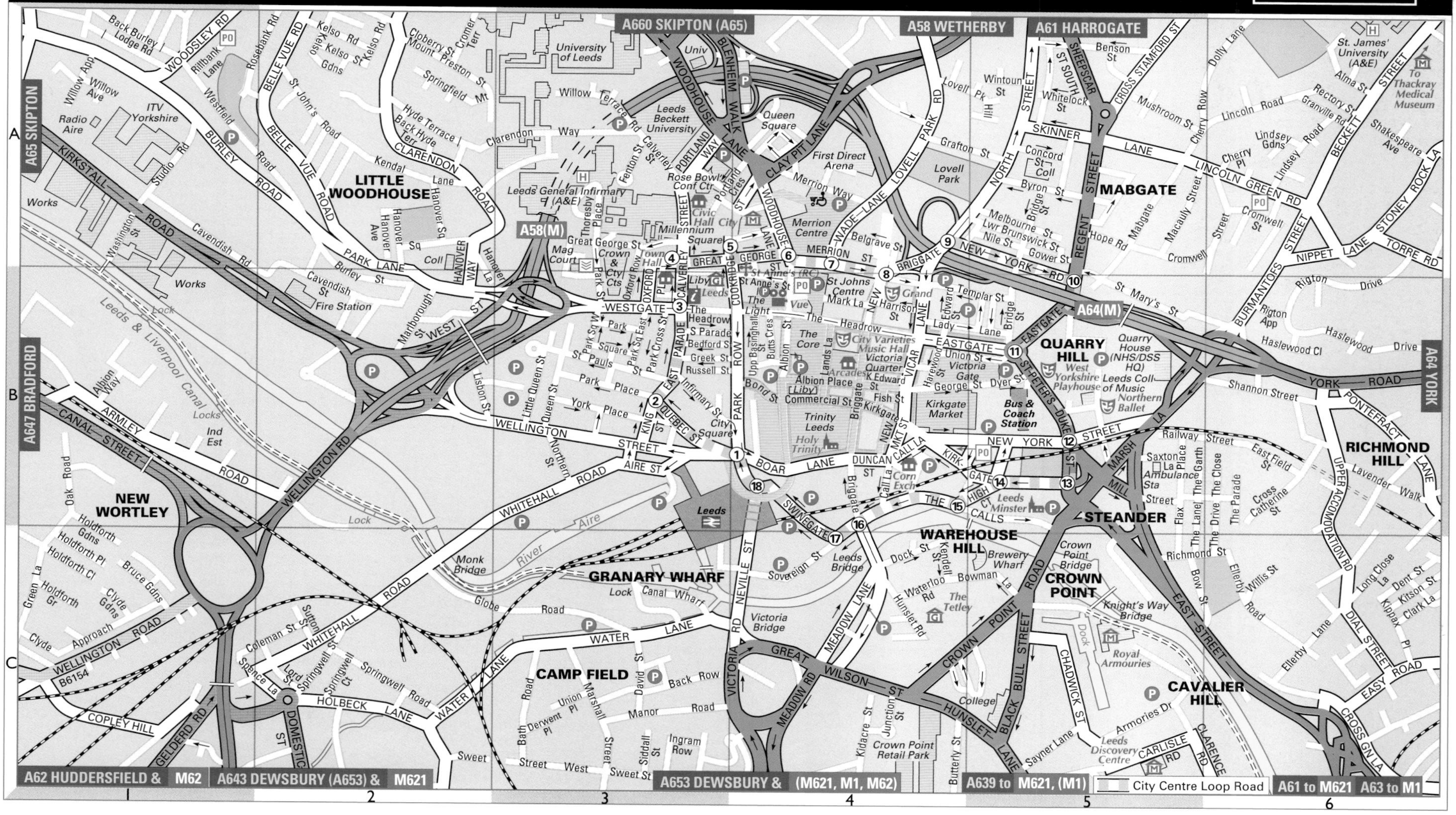

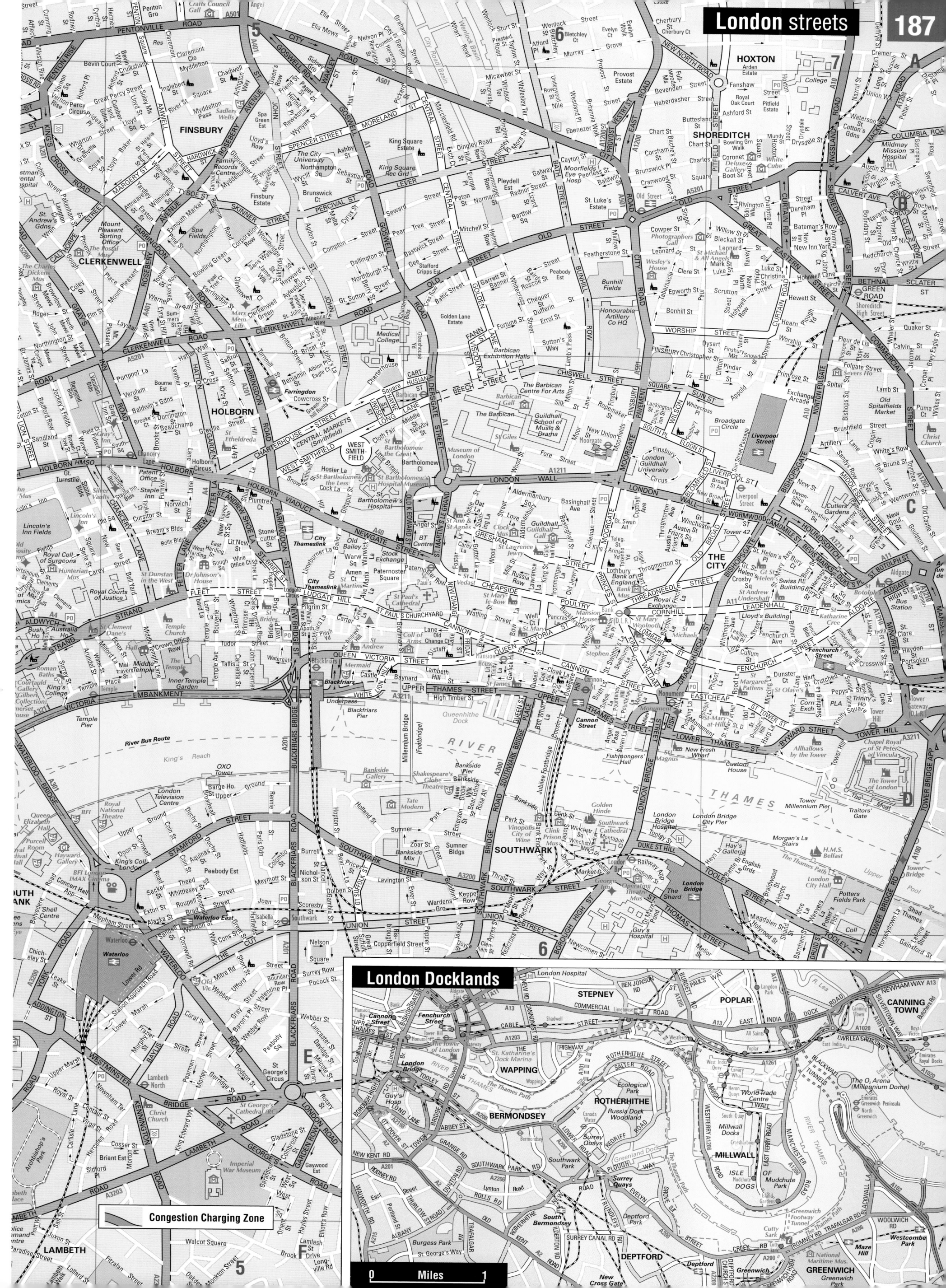

Congestion Charging Zone

London Docklands

Miles
0 — 1

Leicester

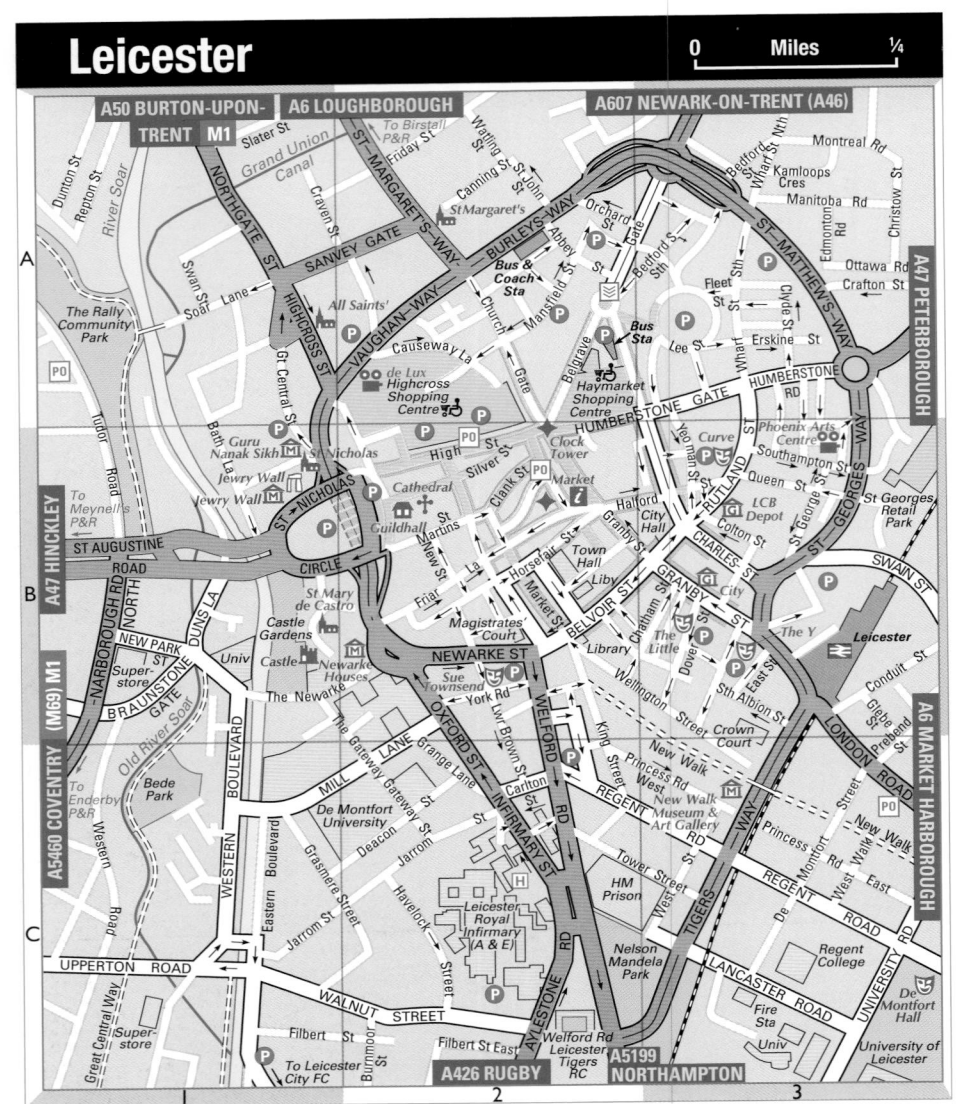

Lincoln

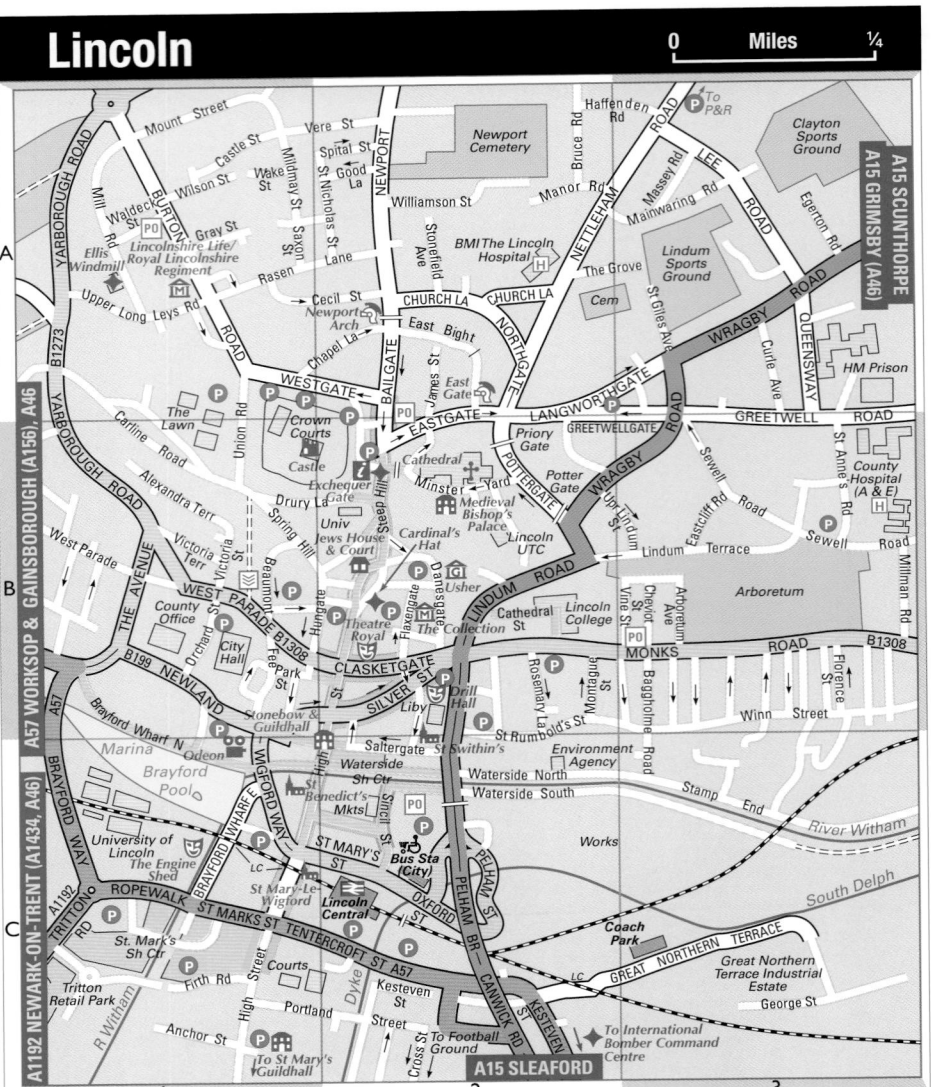

Liverpool

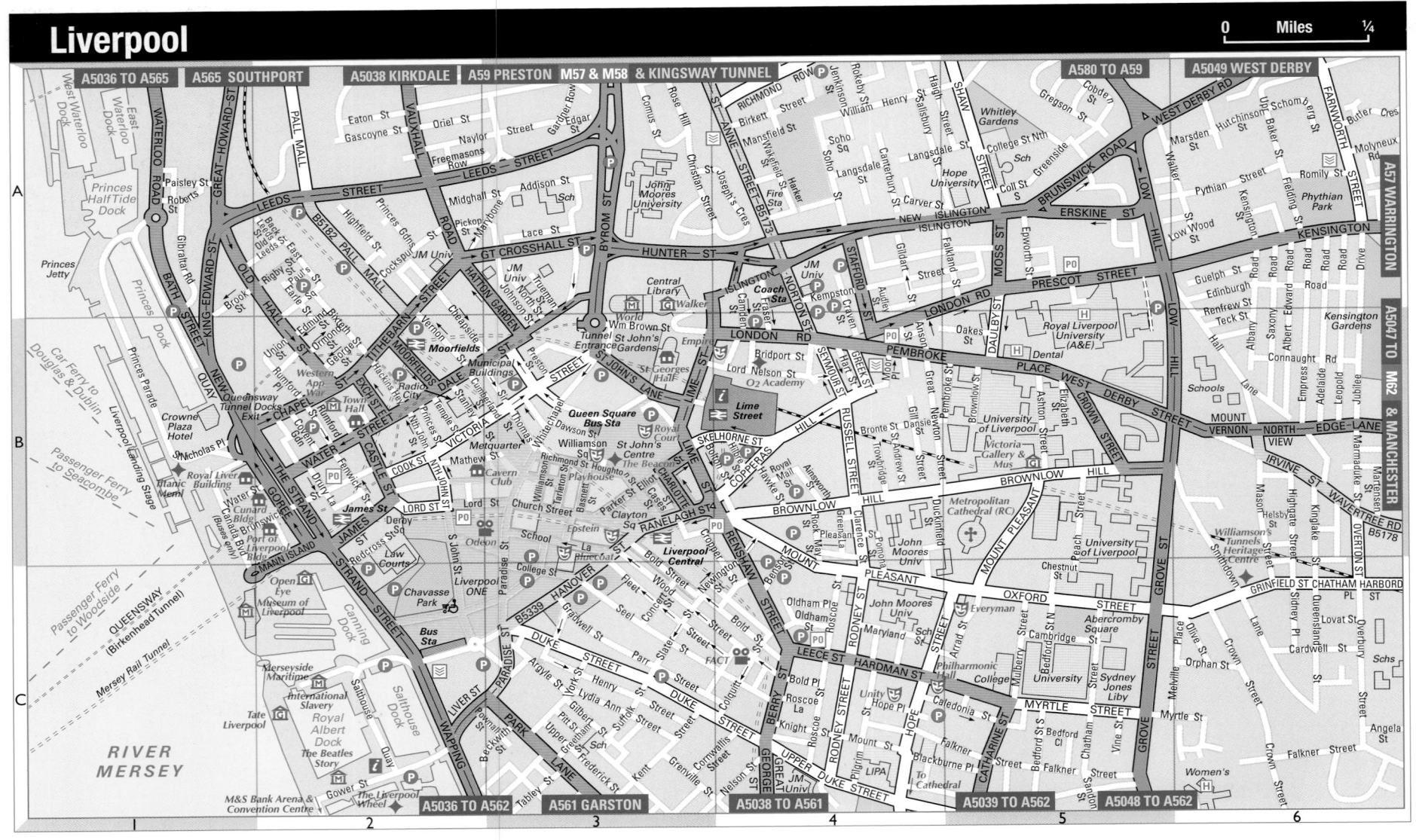

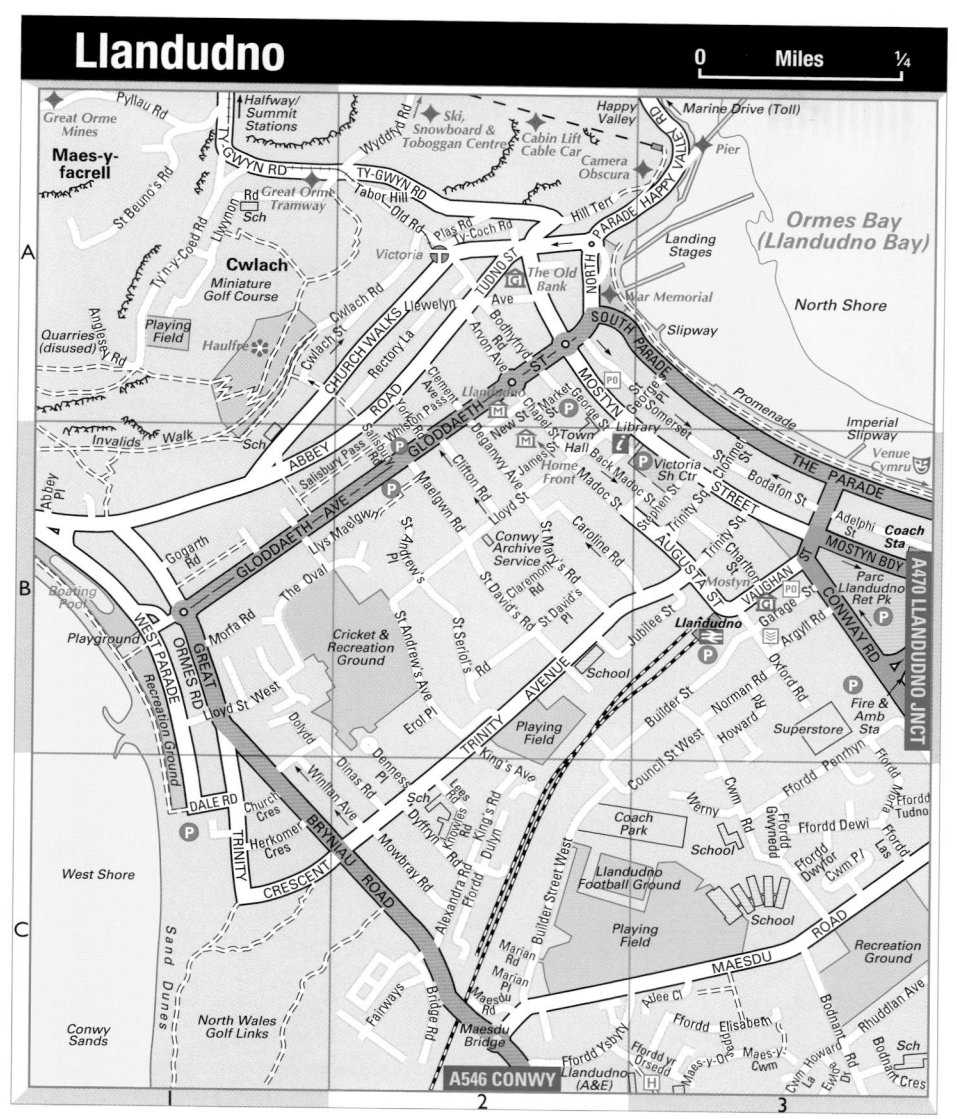

Llandudno

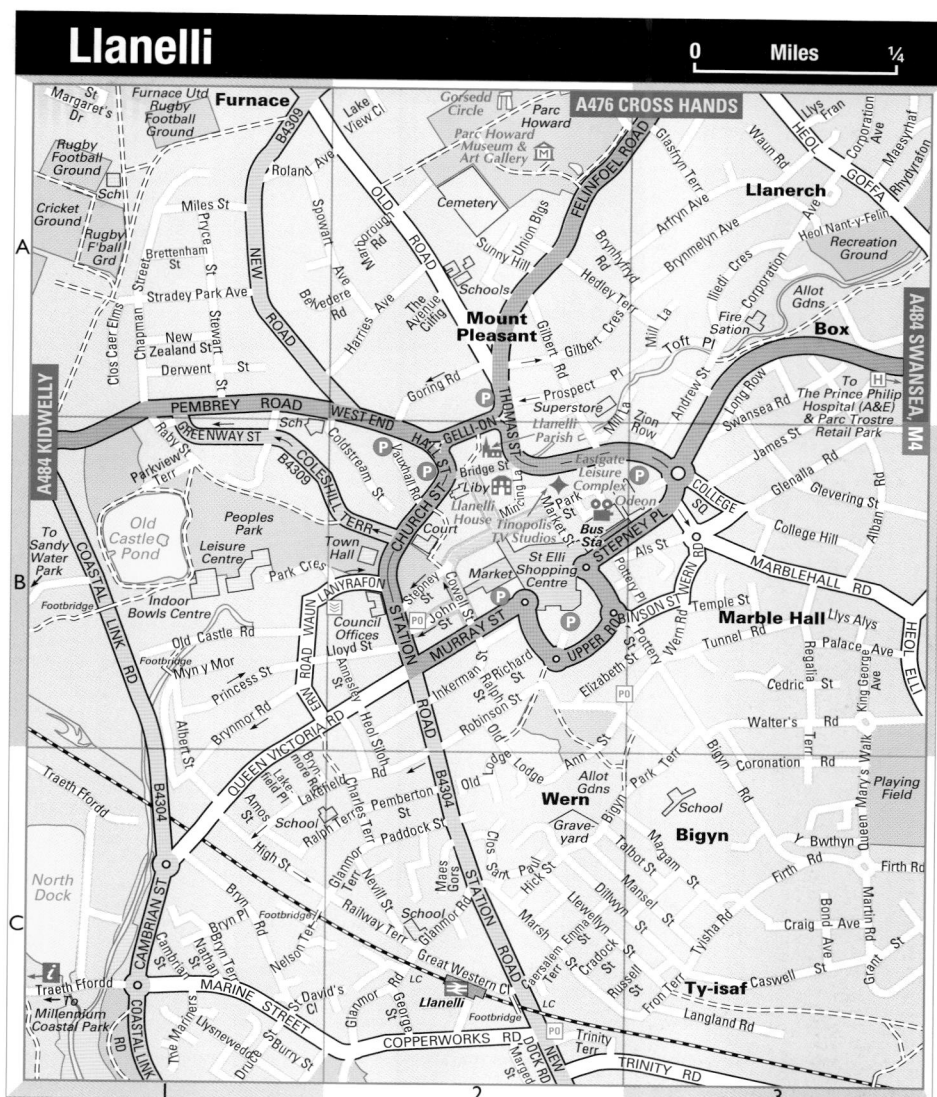

Llanelli

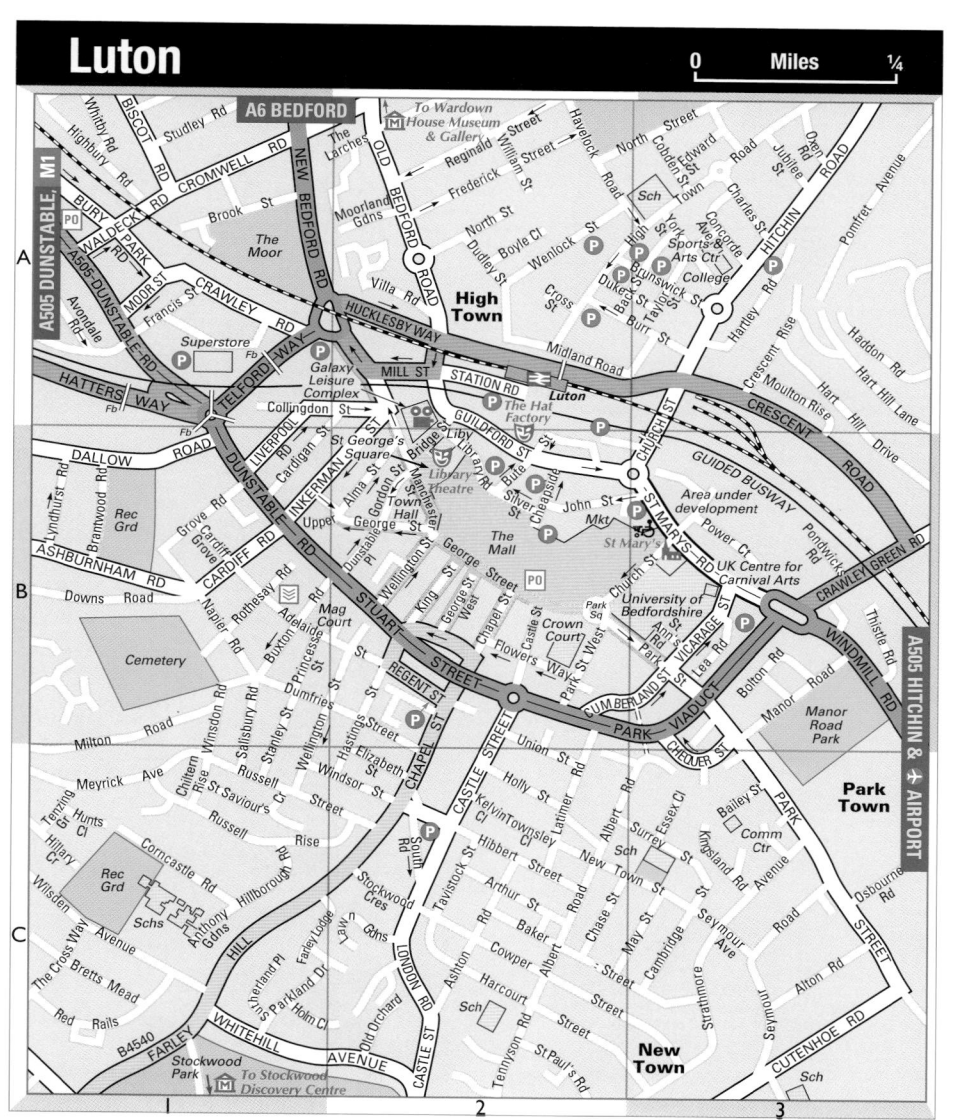

Luton

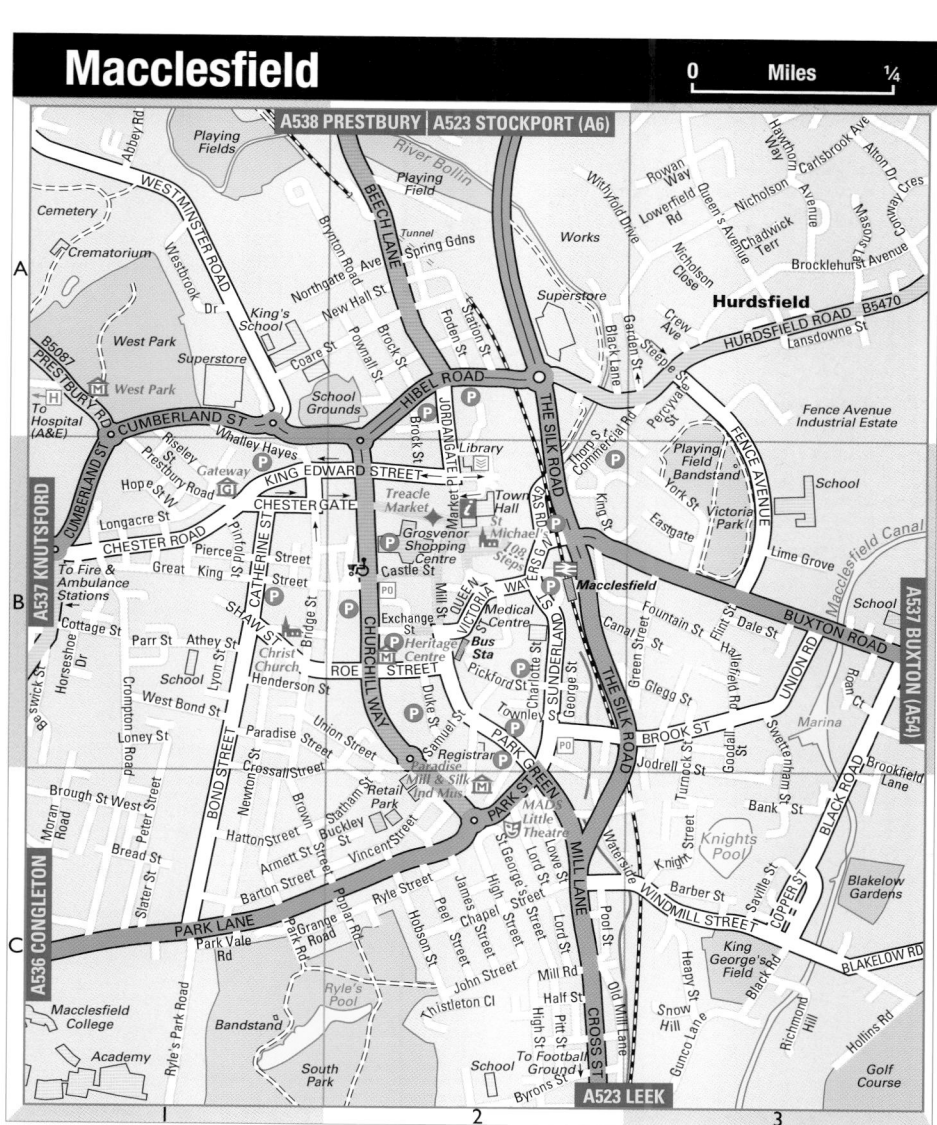

Macclesfield

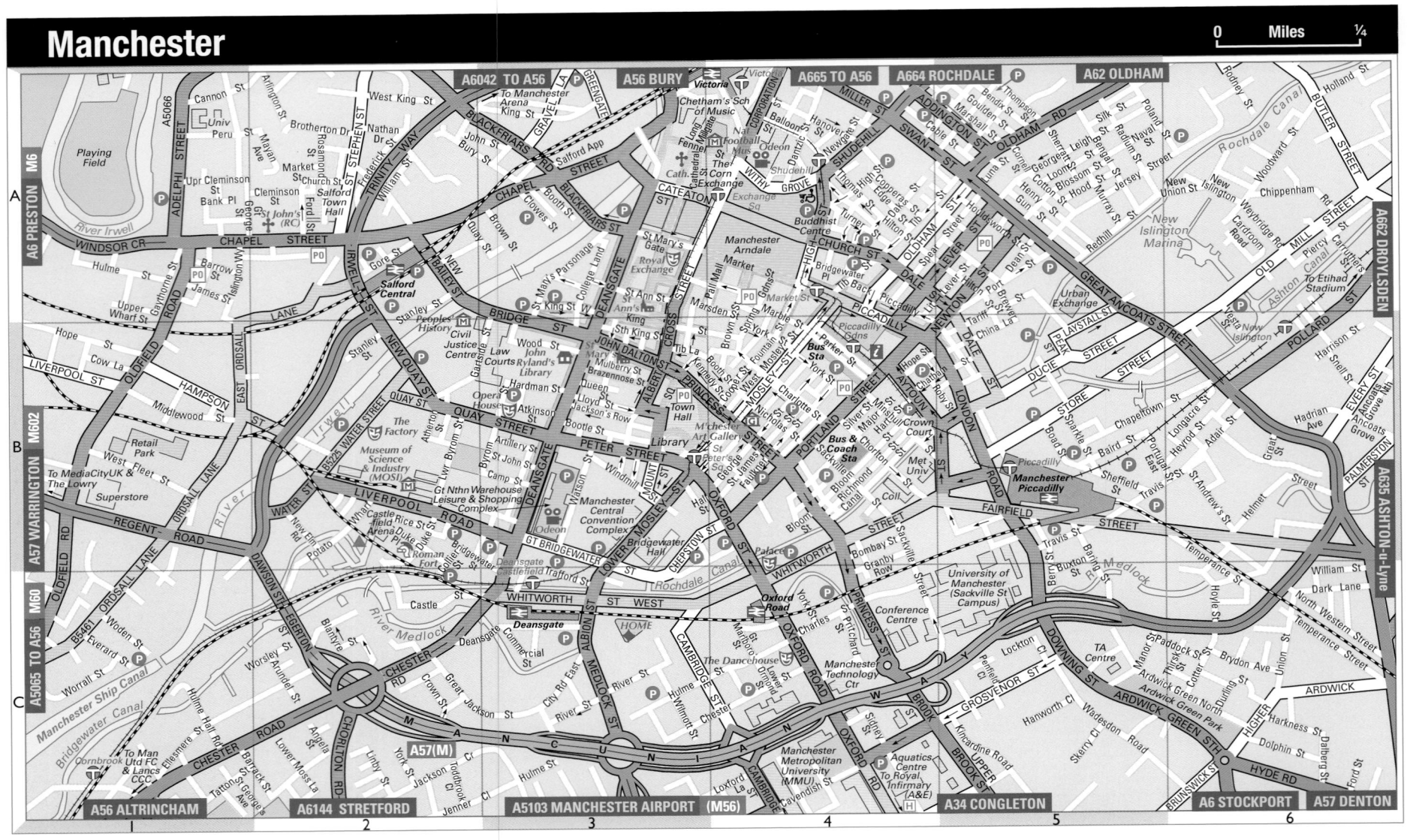

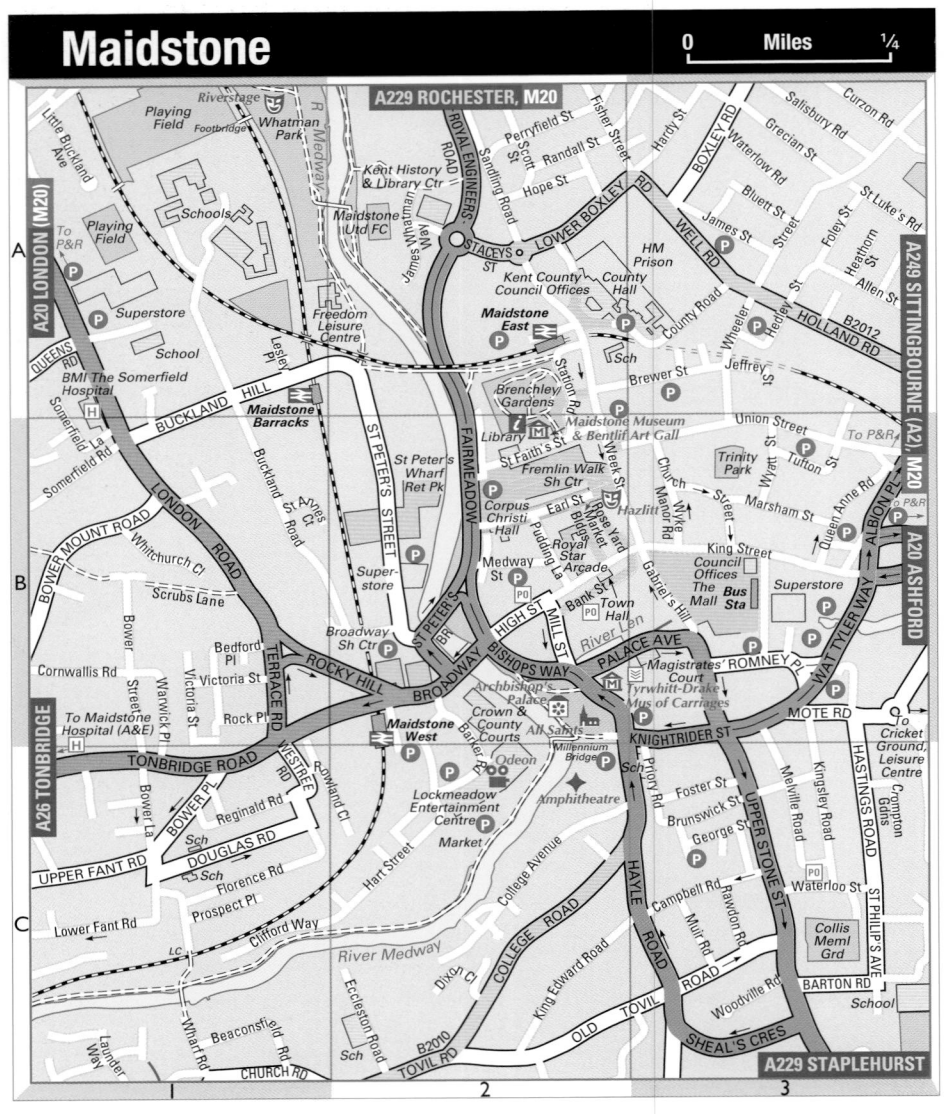

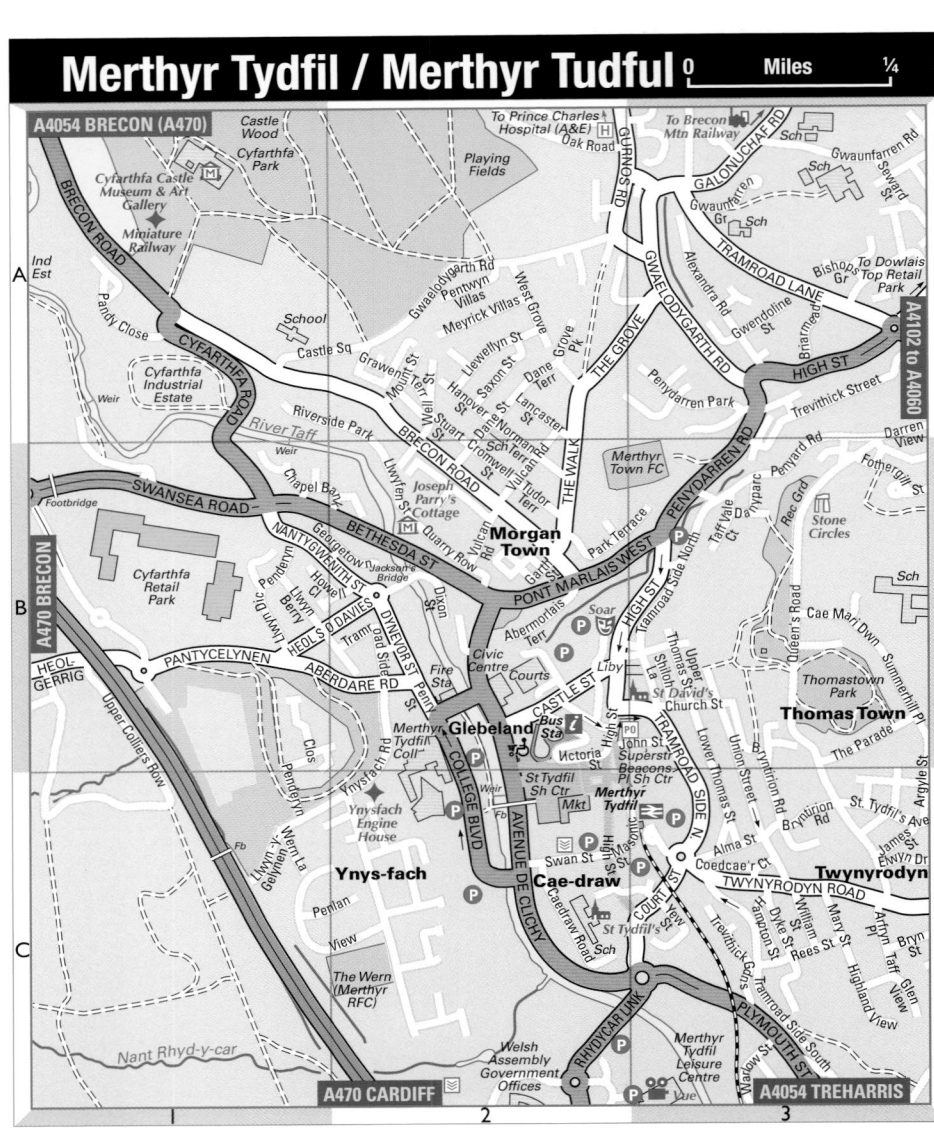

Middlesbrough

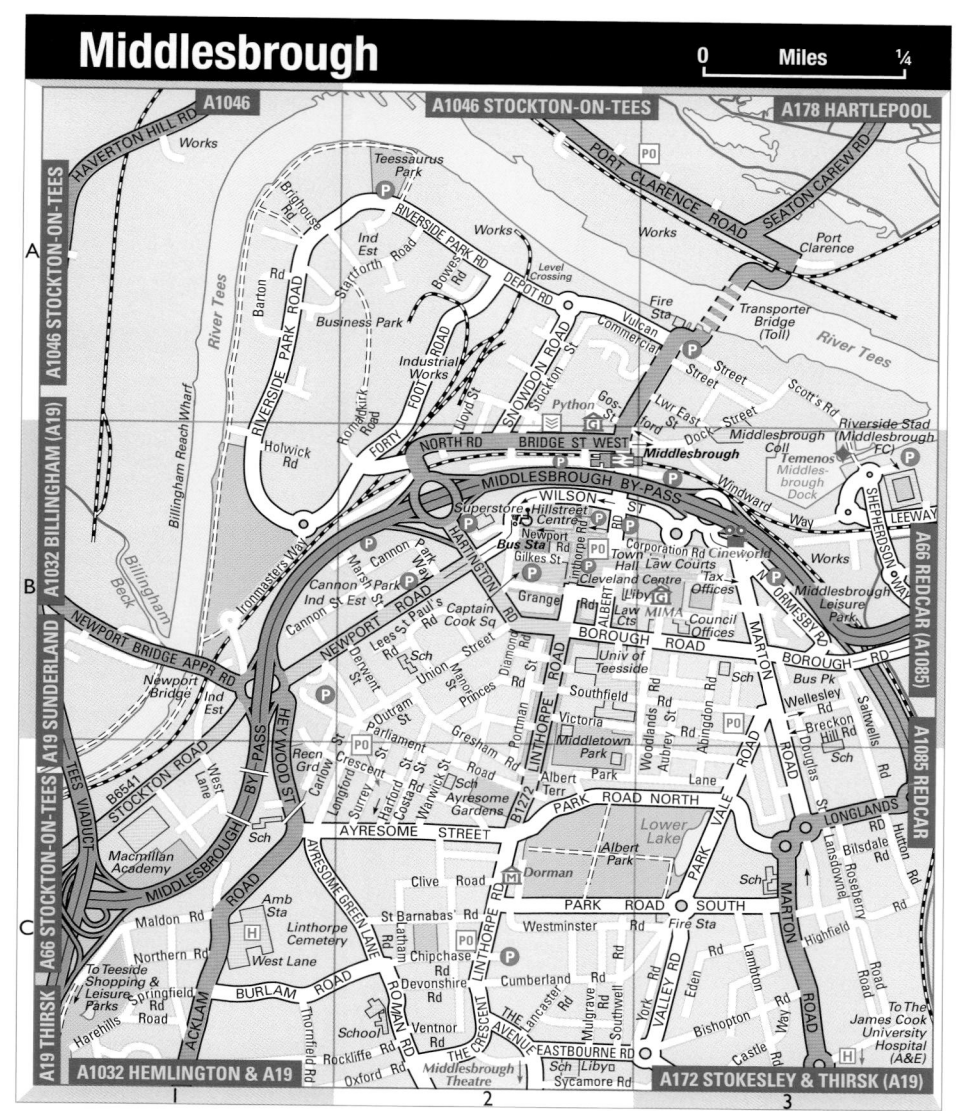

Milton Keynes

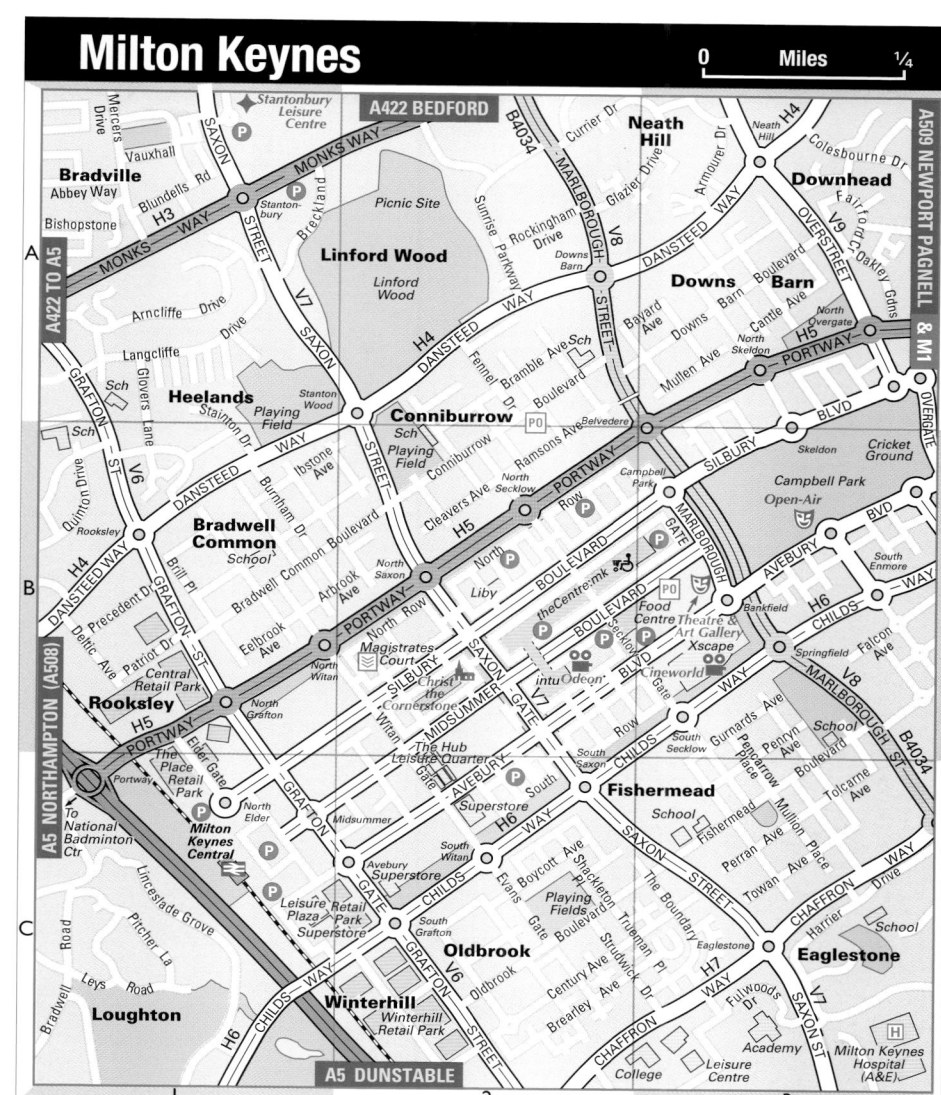

Newcastle upon Tyne

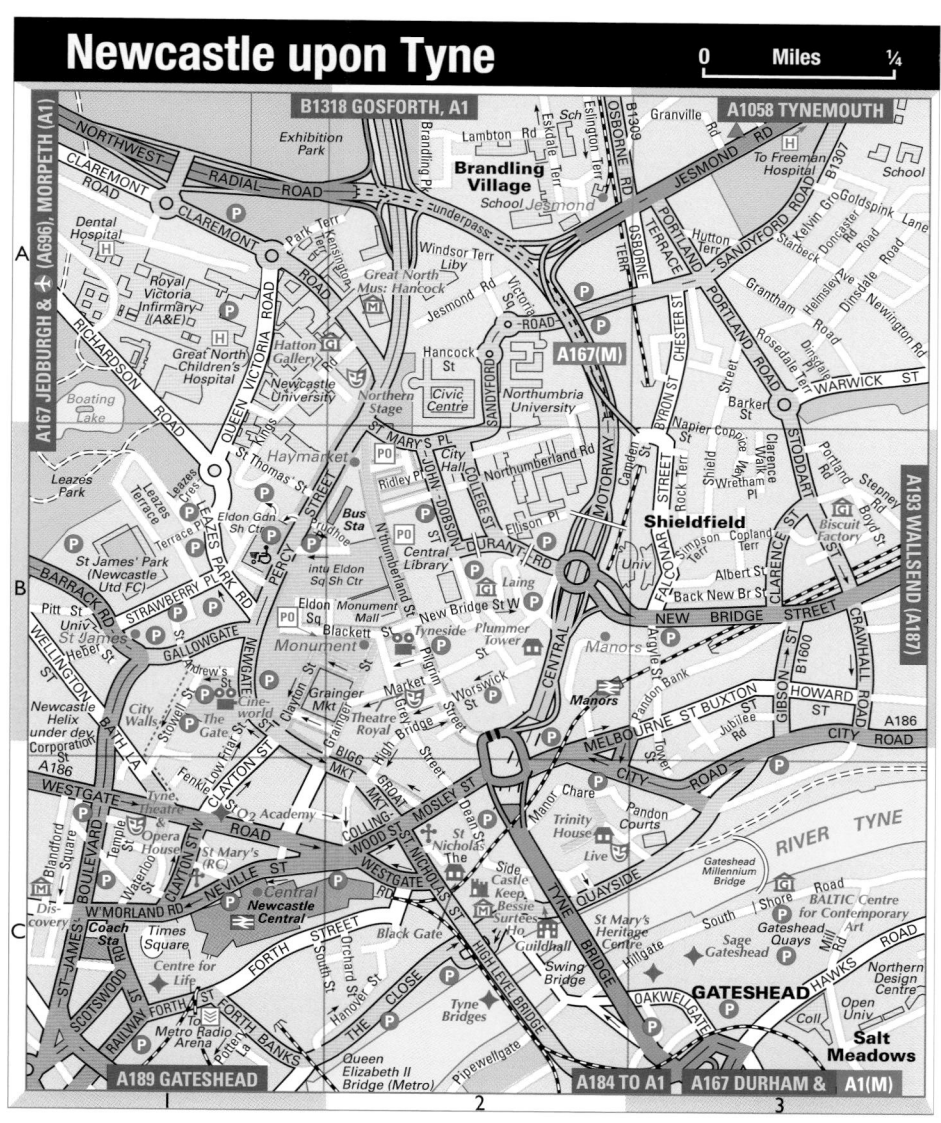

Newport / Casnewydd

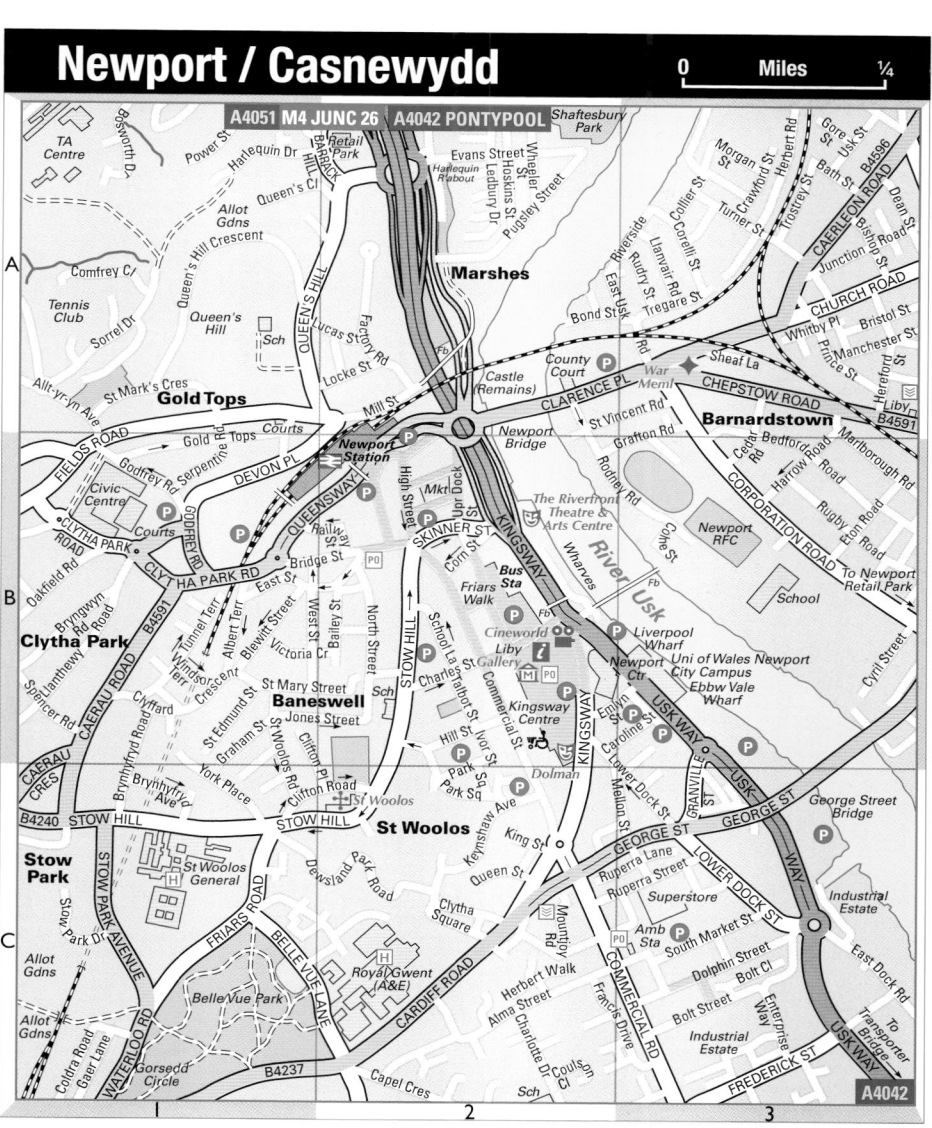

Newquay

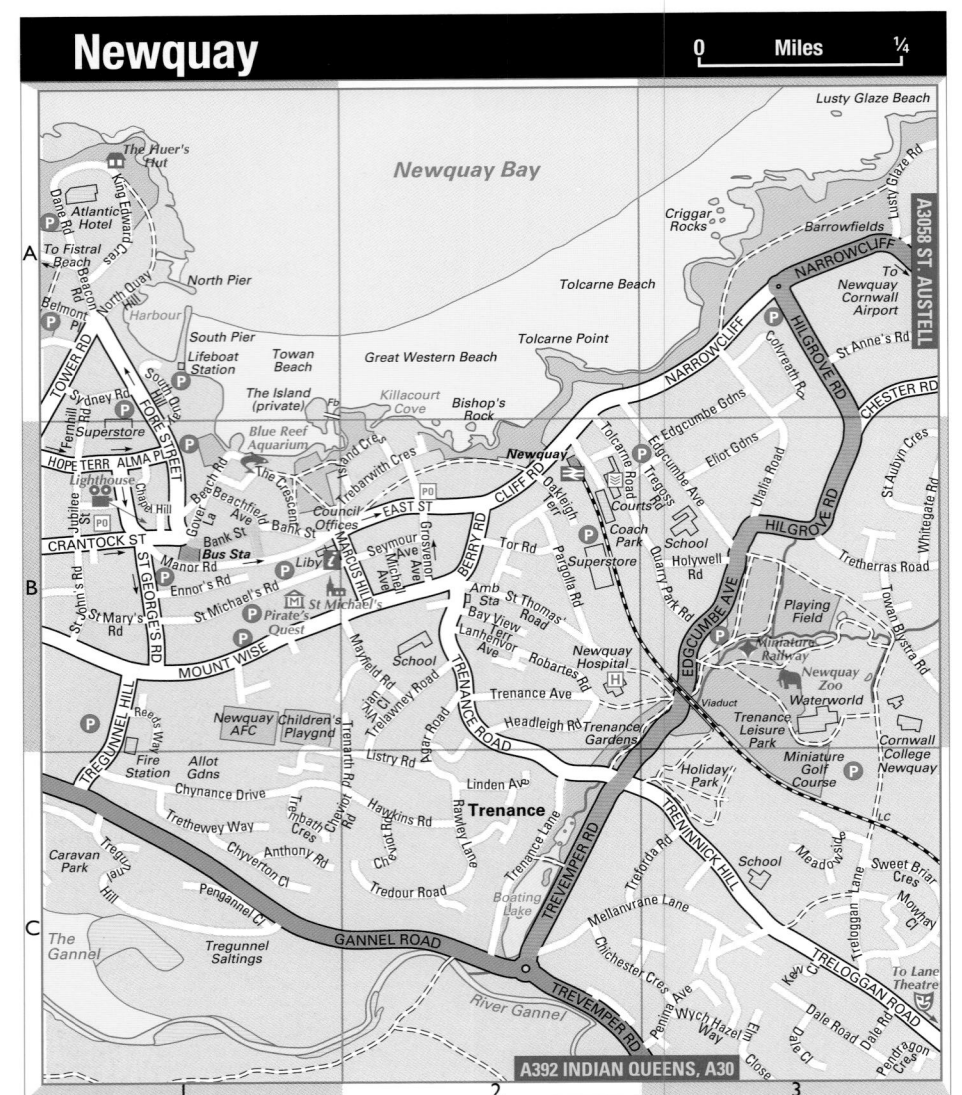

Northampton

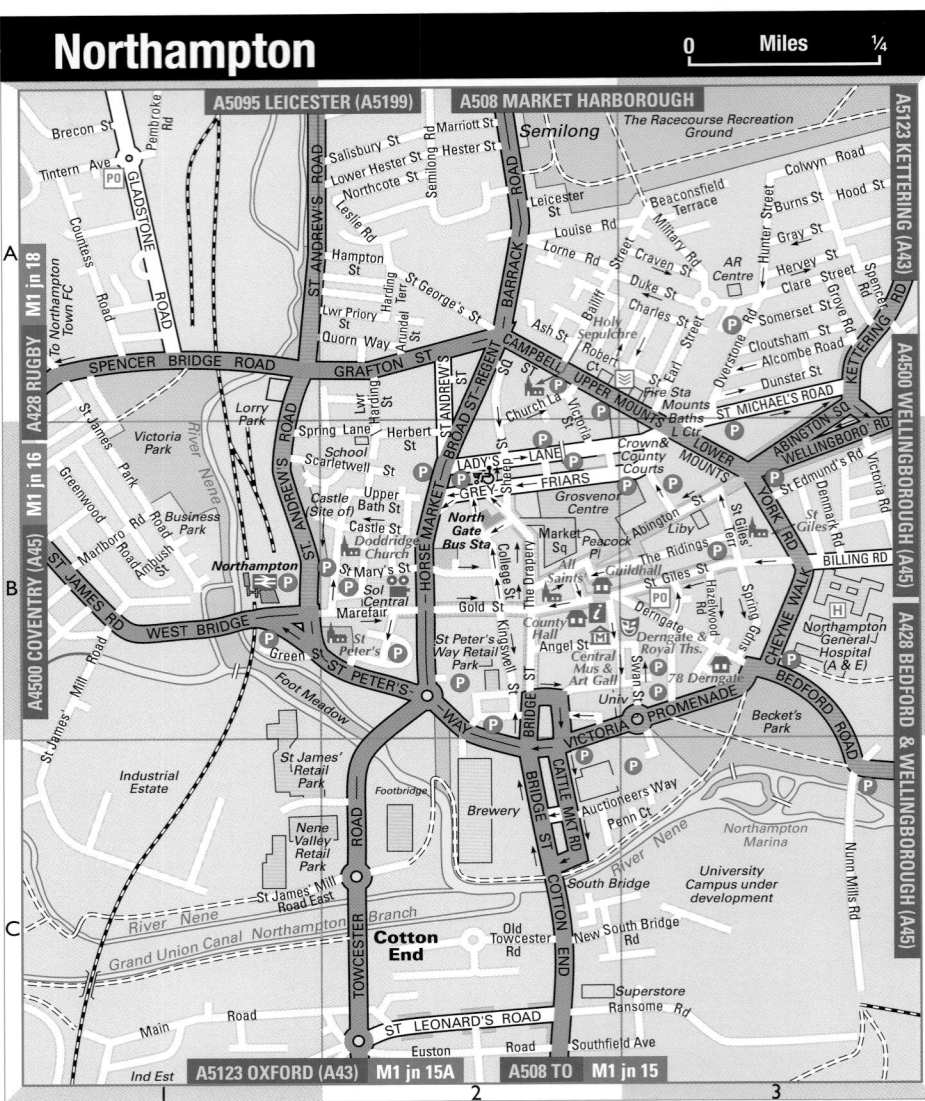

Norwich

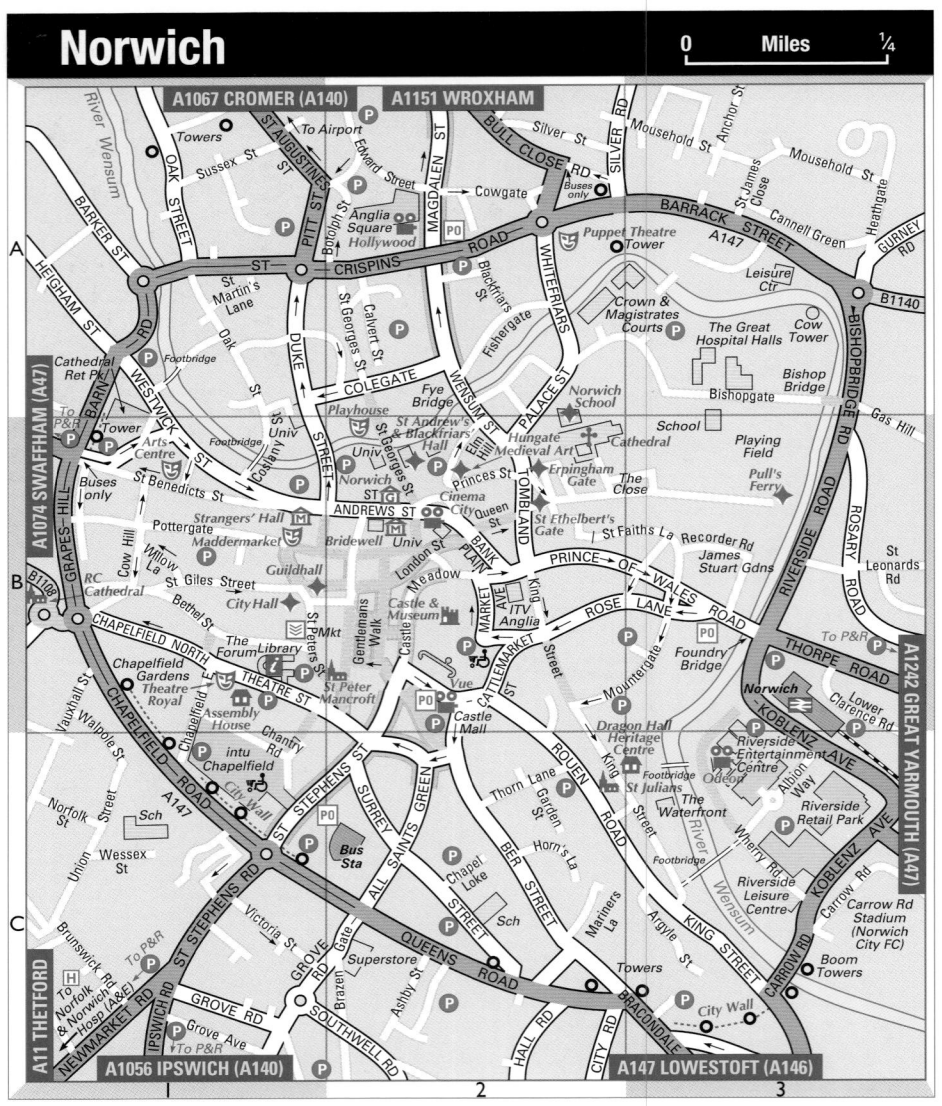

Nottingham

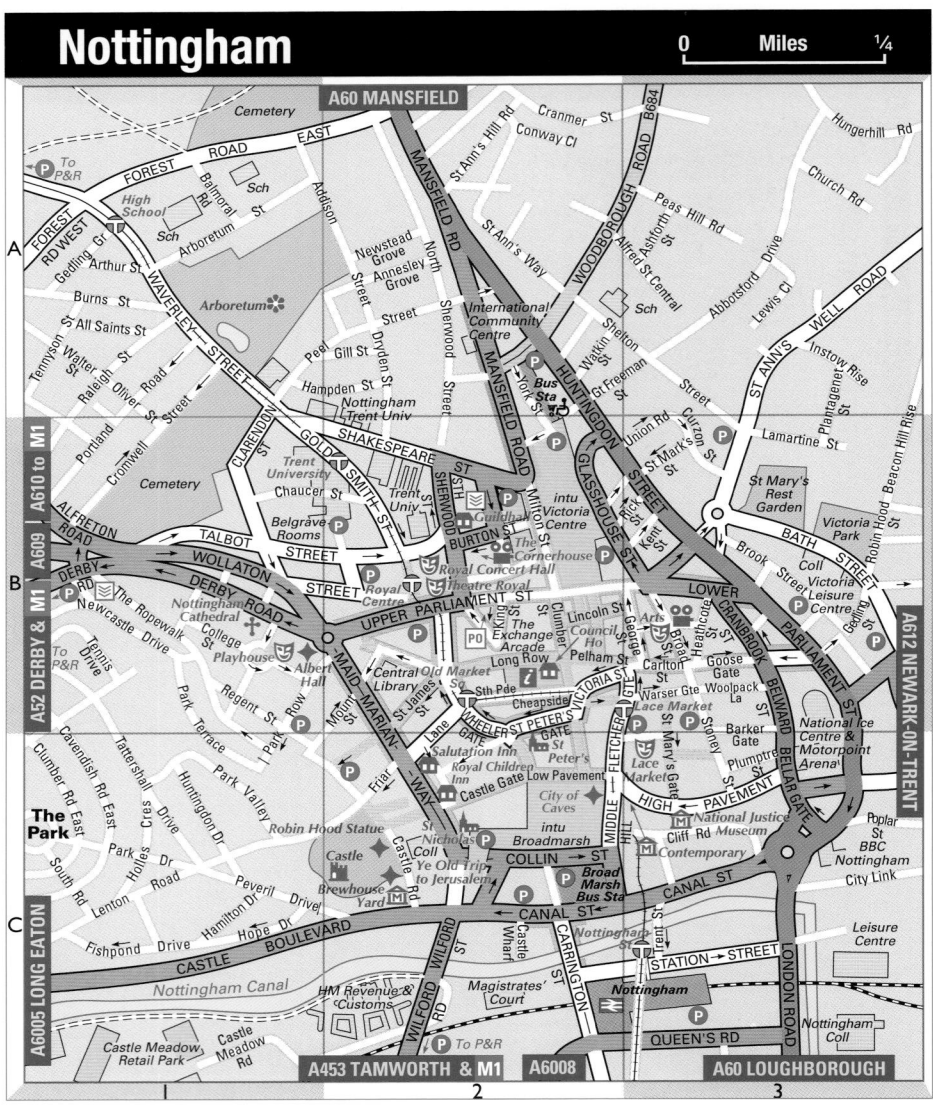

Oxford

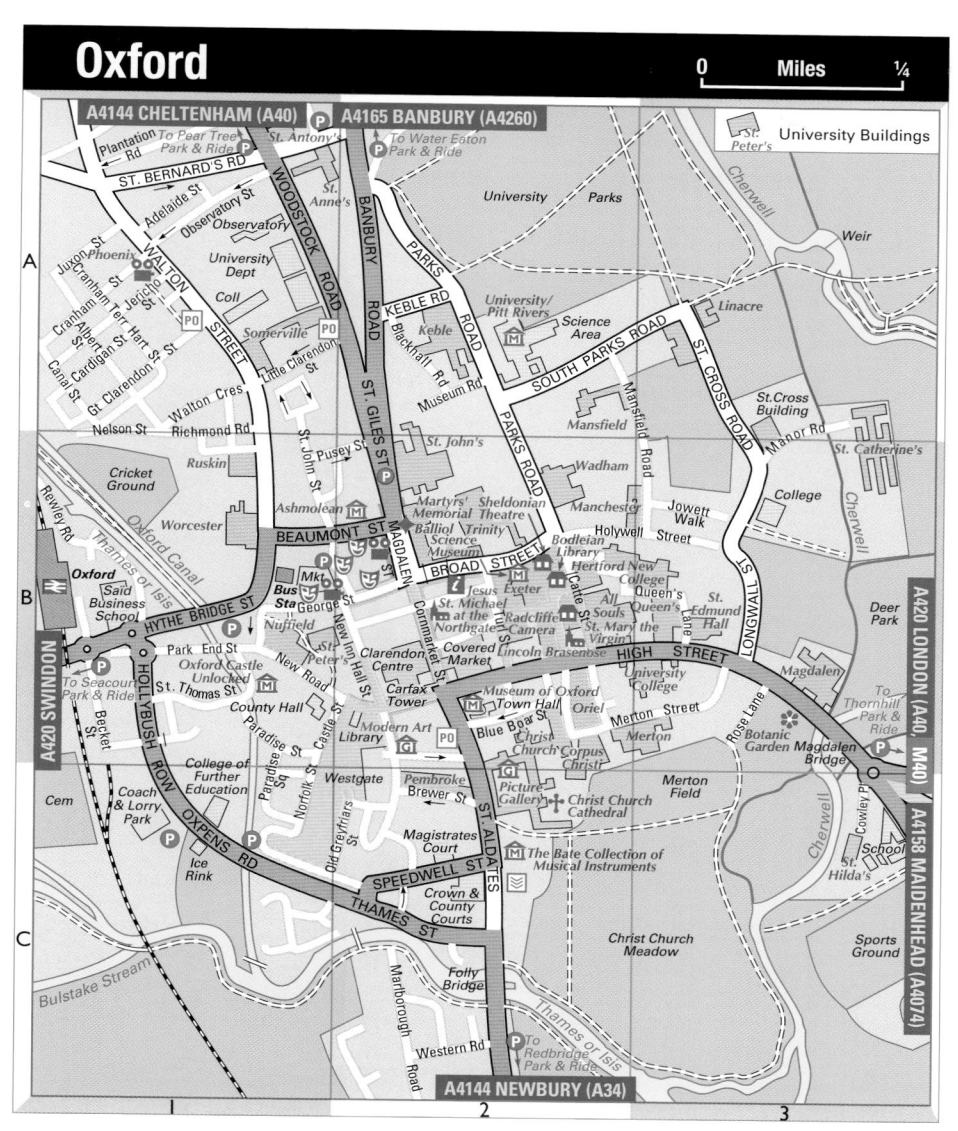

Perth

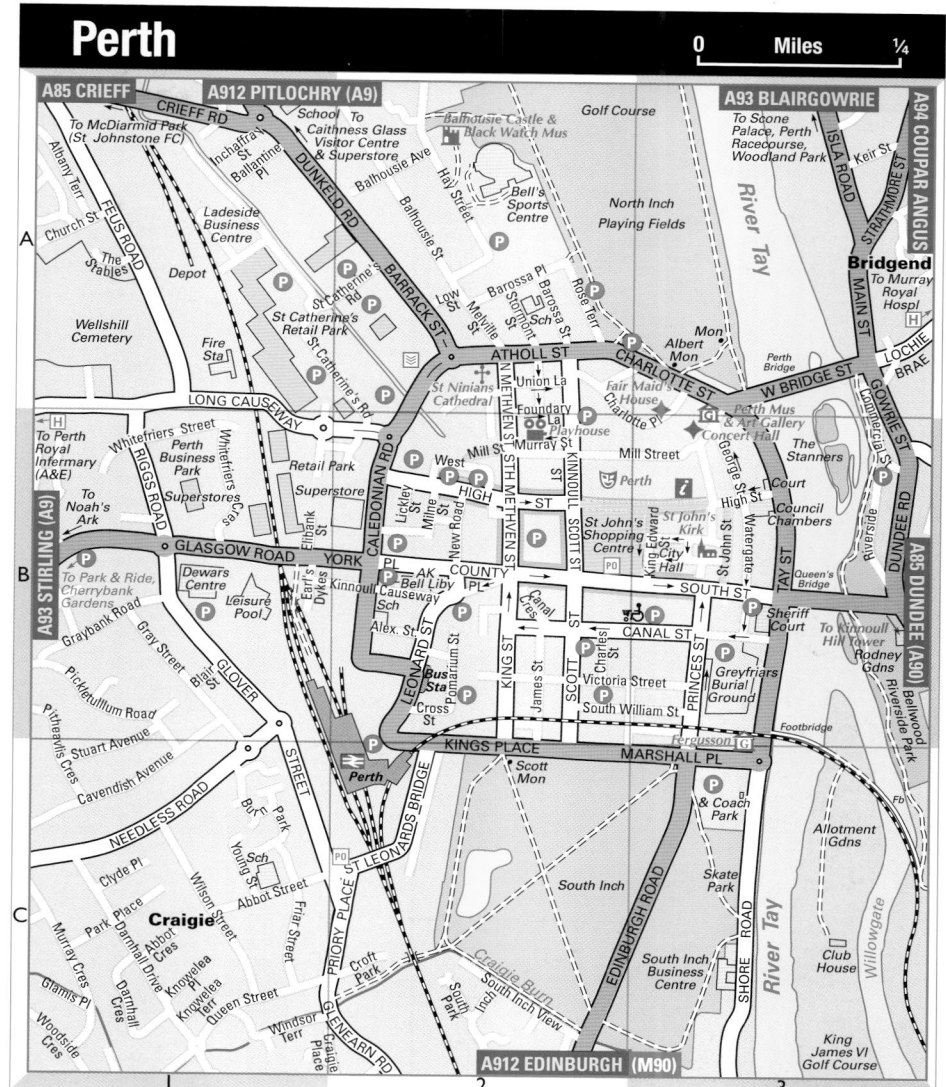

Peterborough

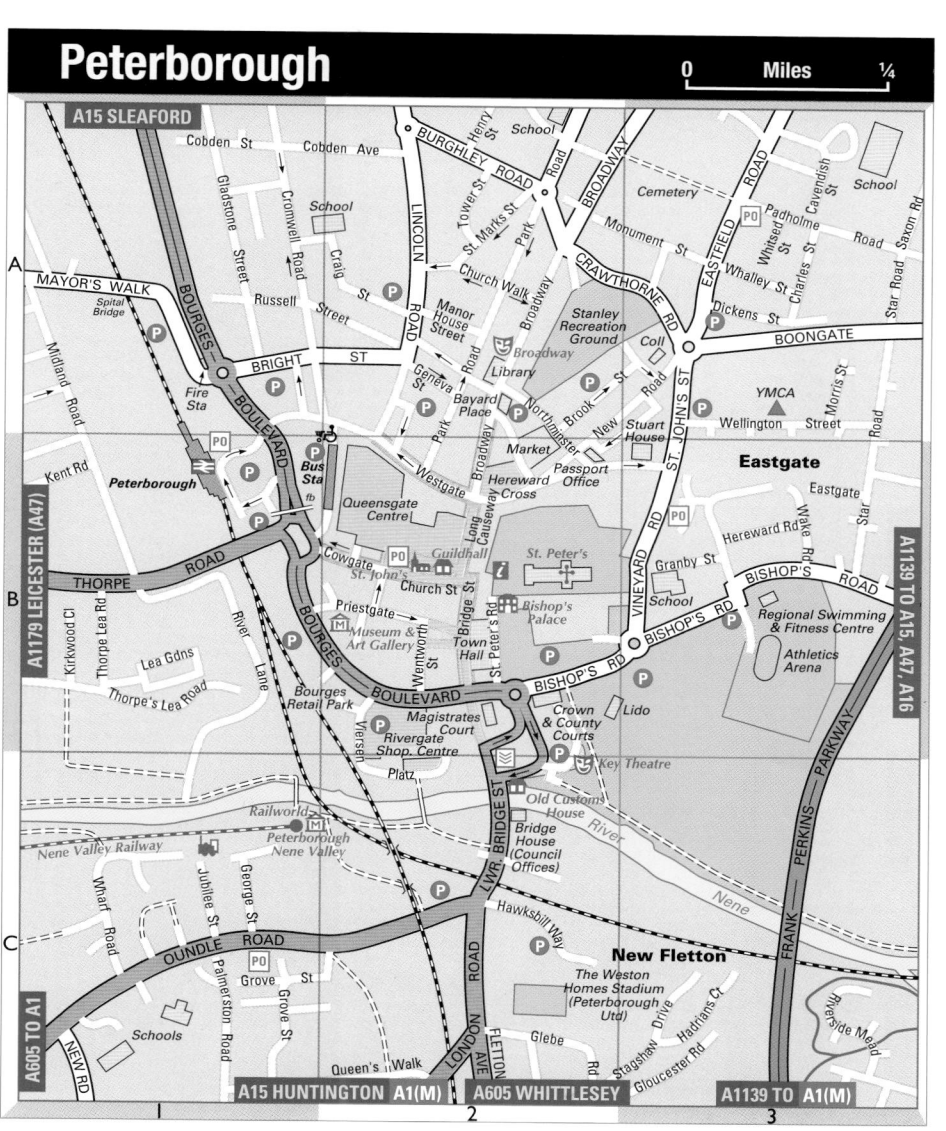

Plymouth

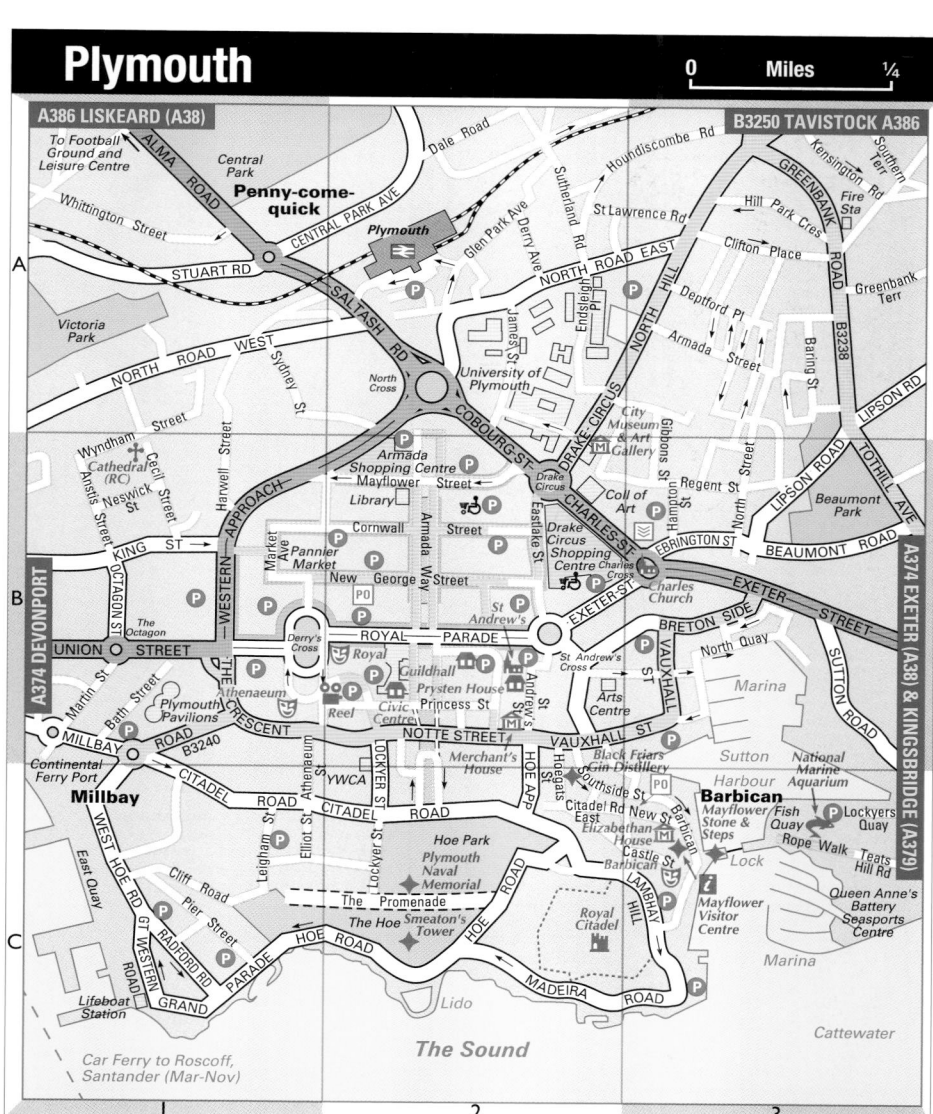

Poole

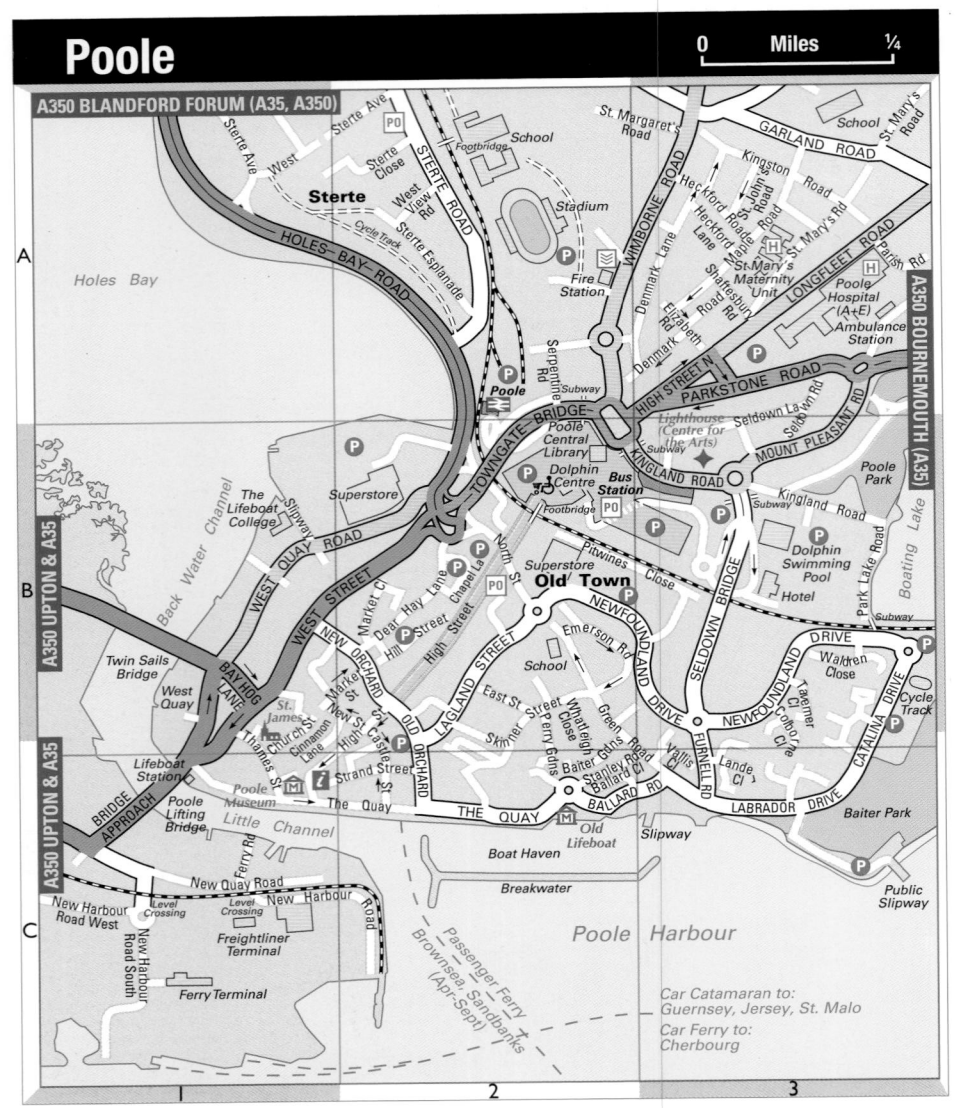

Portsmouth

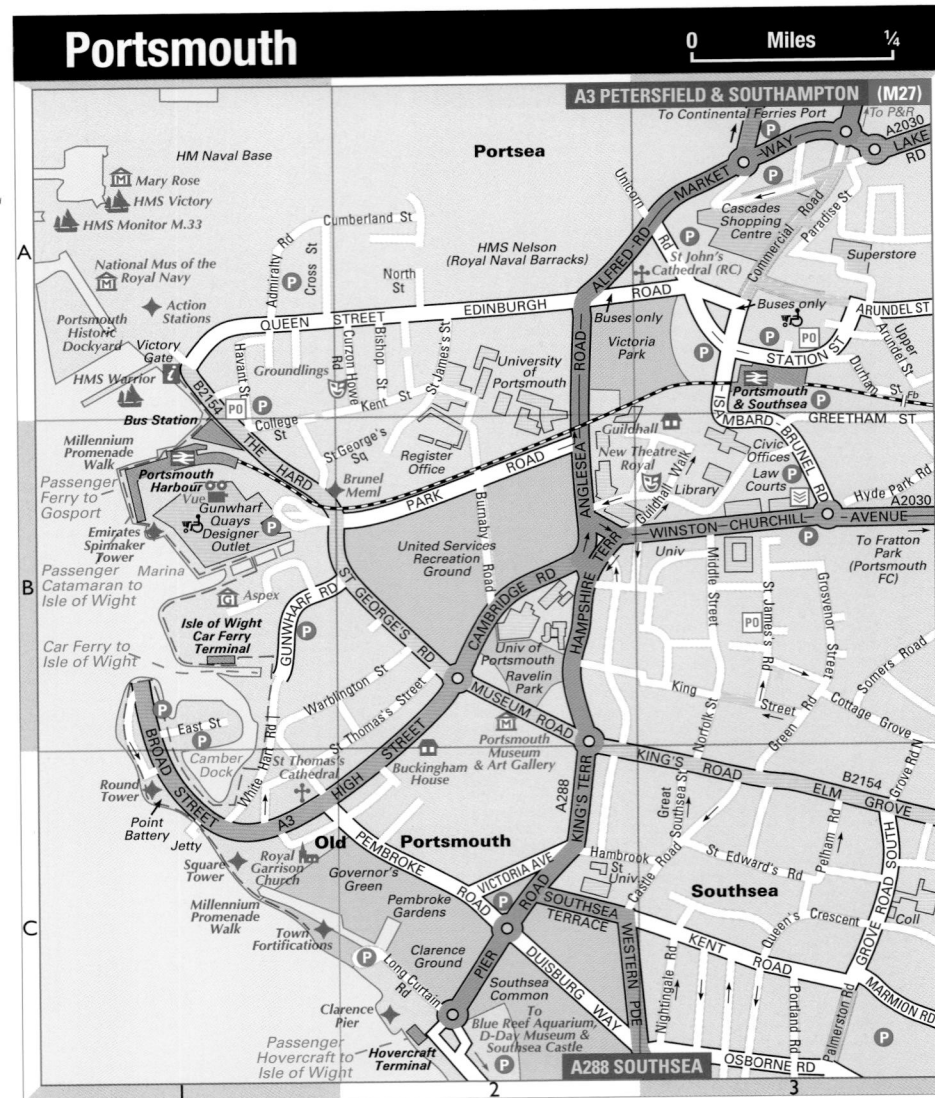

Preston

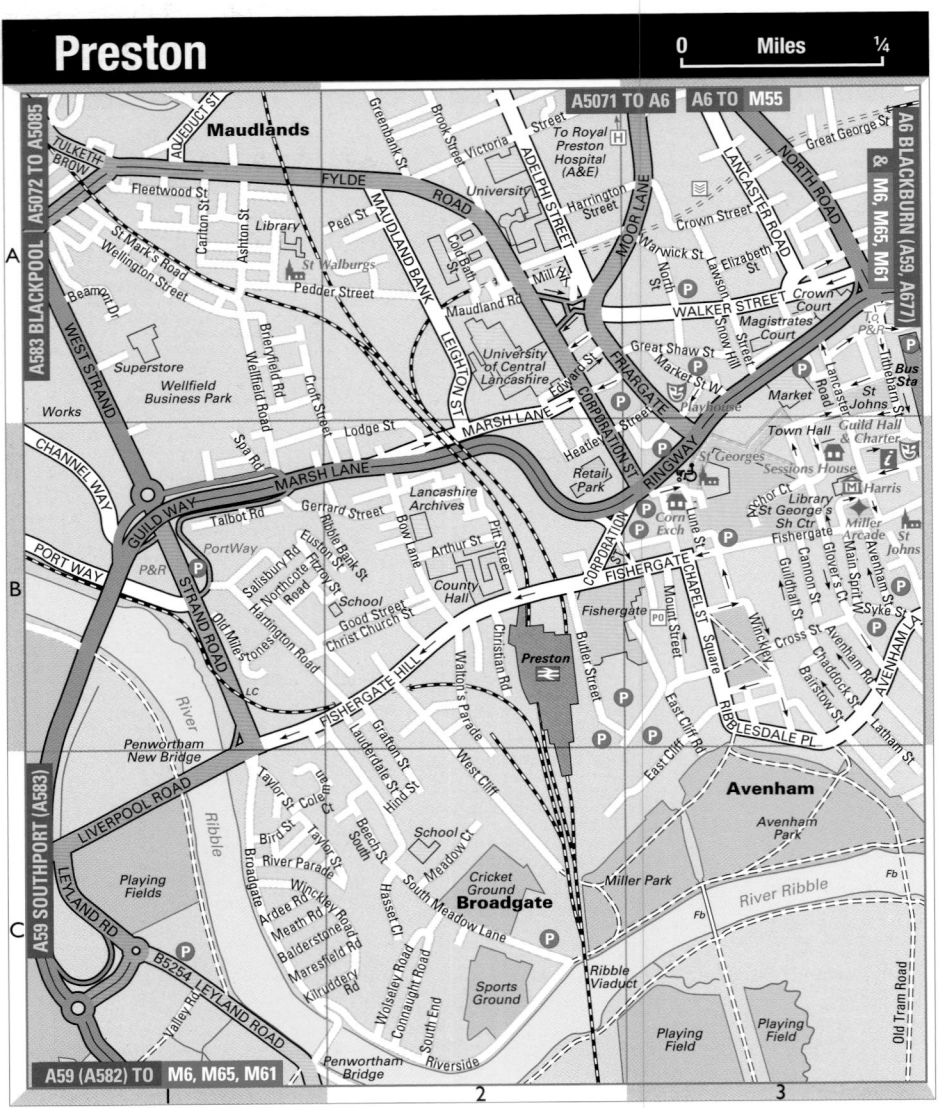

Reading

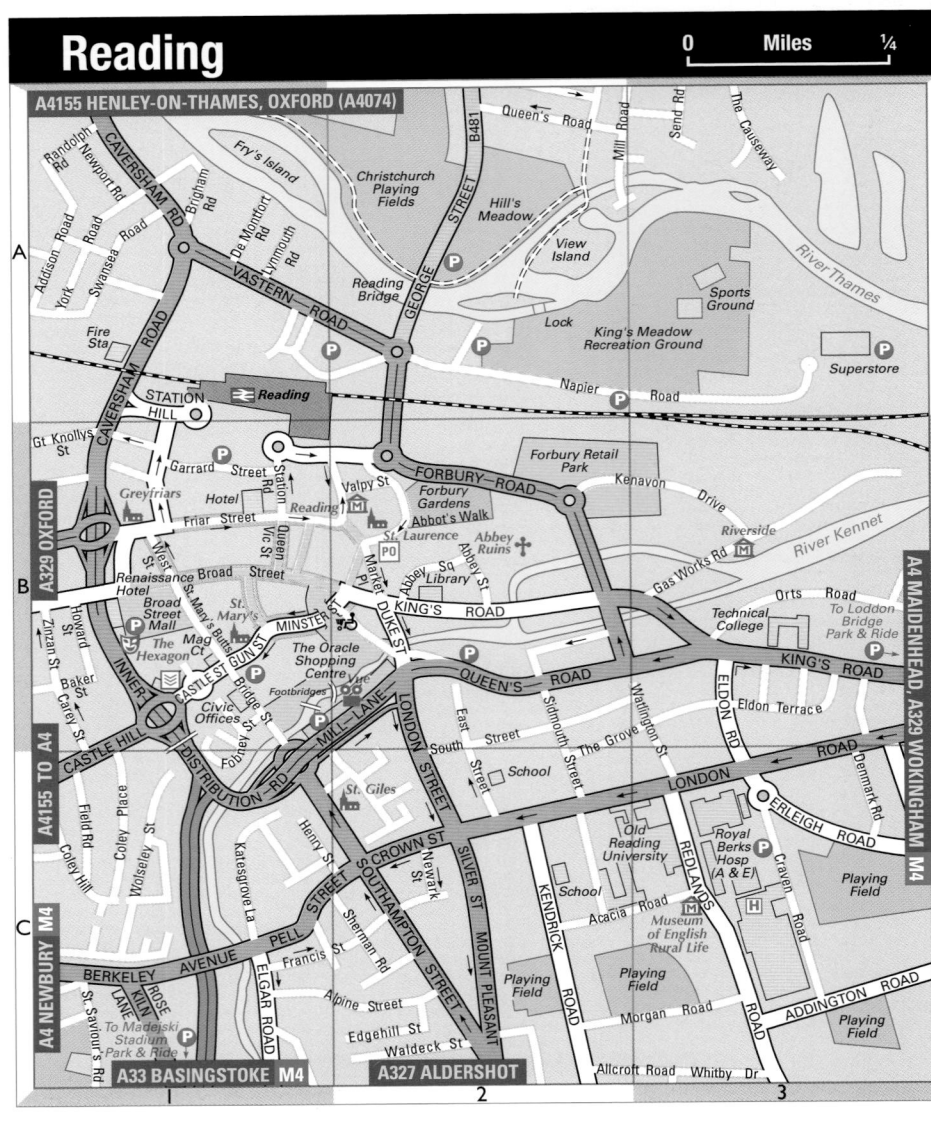

St Andrews

0 Miles ¼

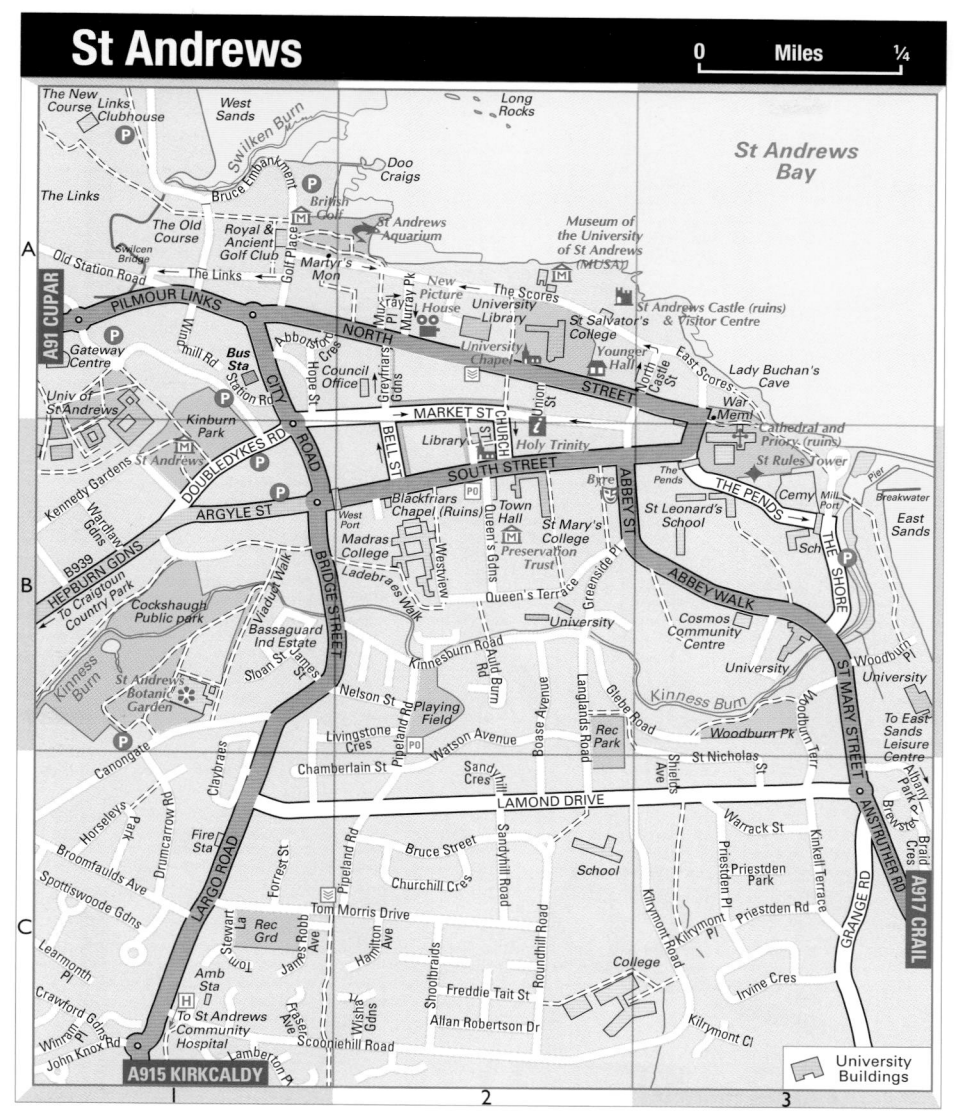

Salisbury

0 Miles ¼

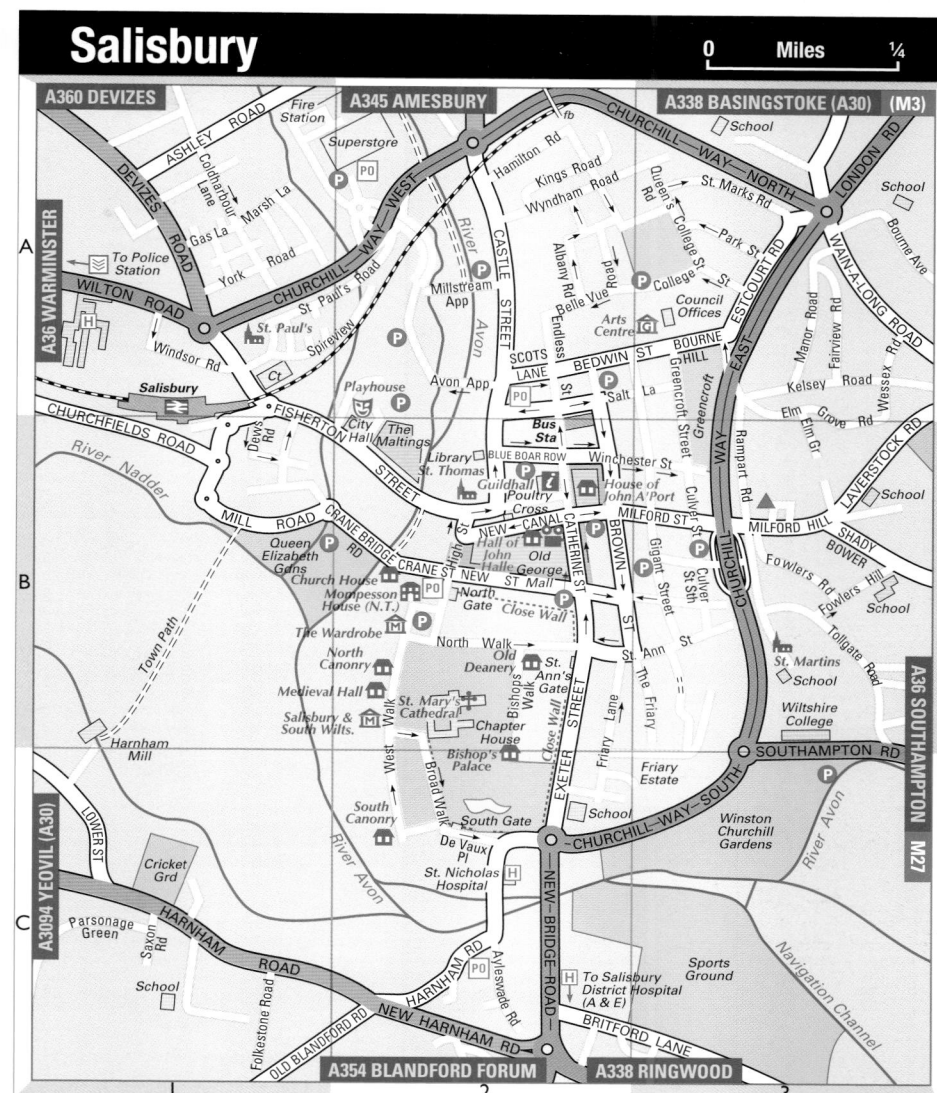

Scarborough

0 Miles ¼

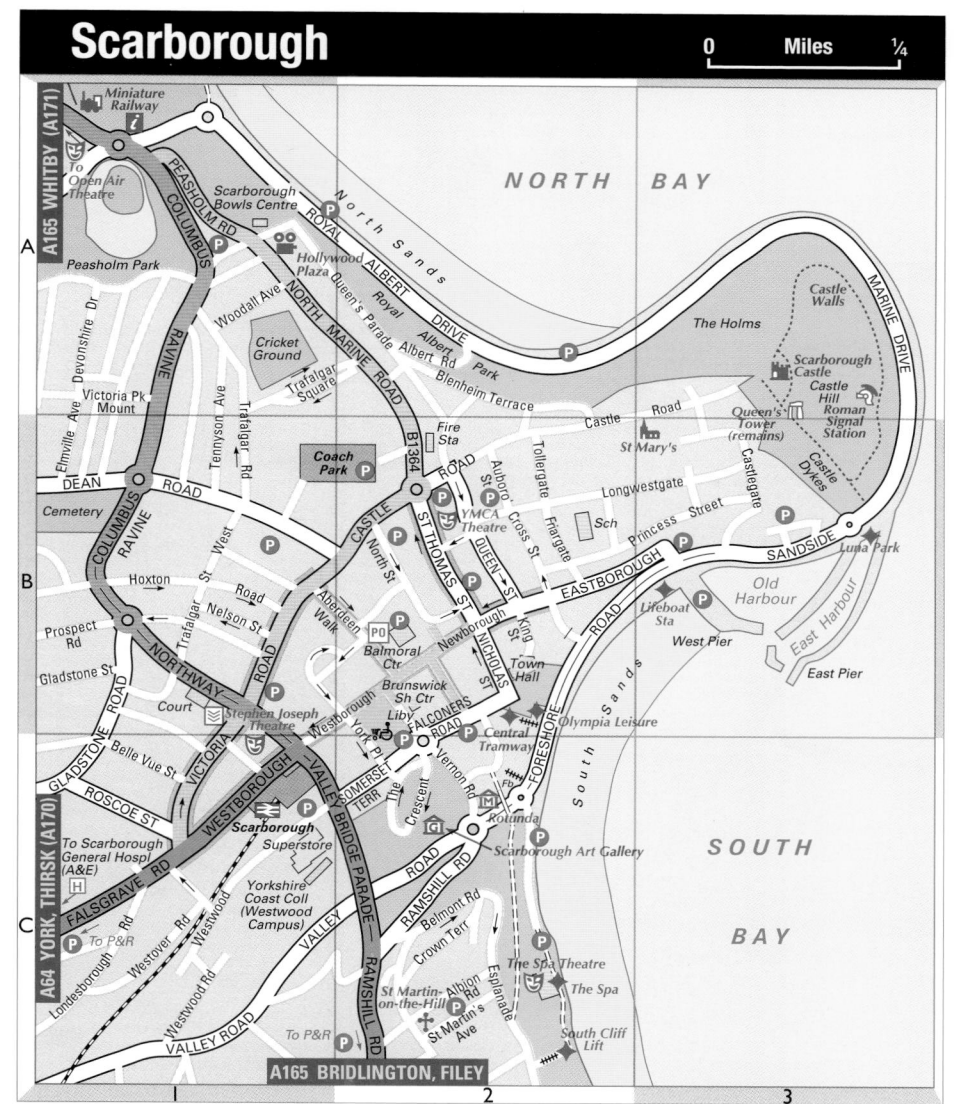

Shrewsbury

0 Miles ¼

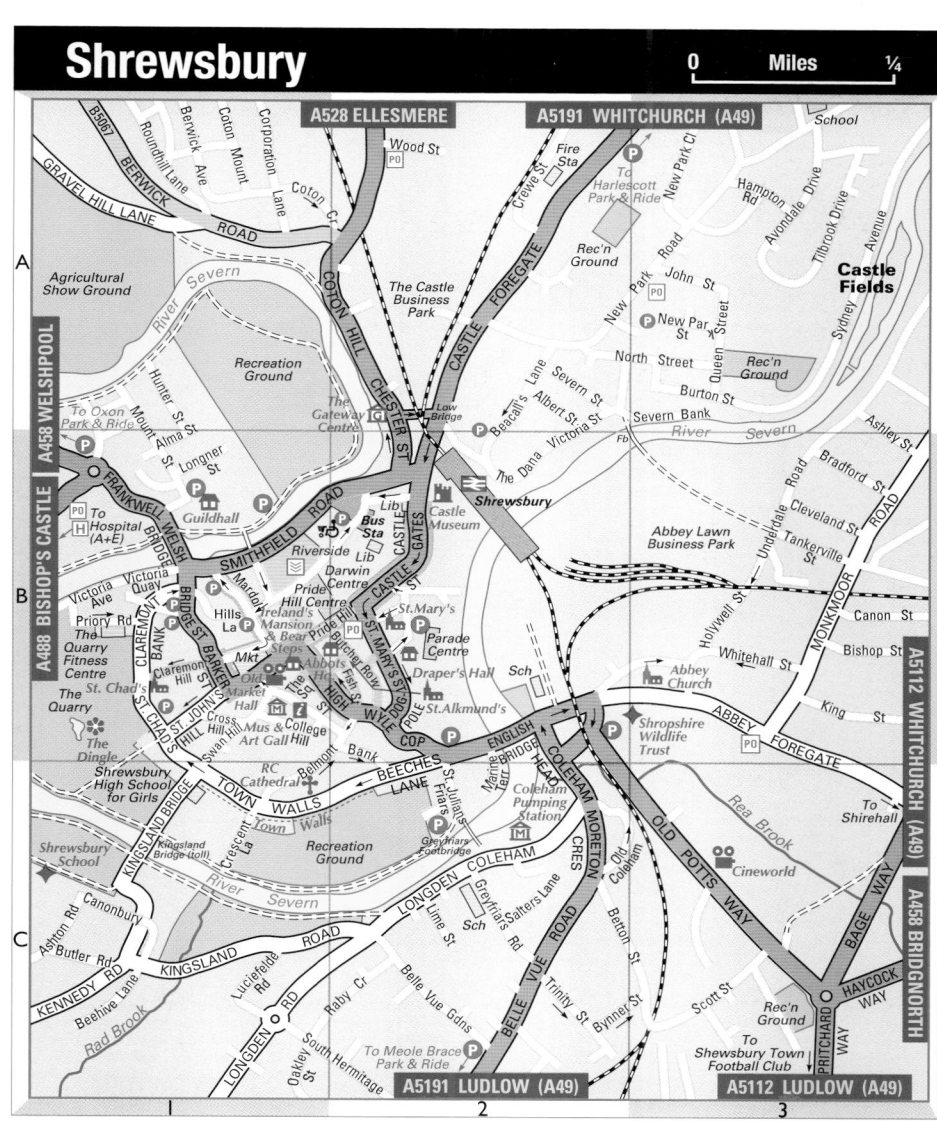

Sheffield

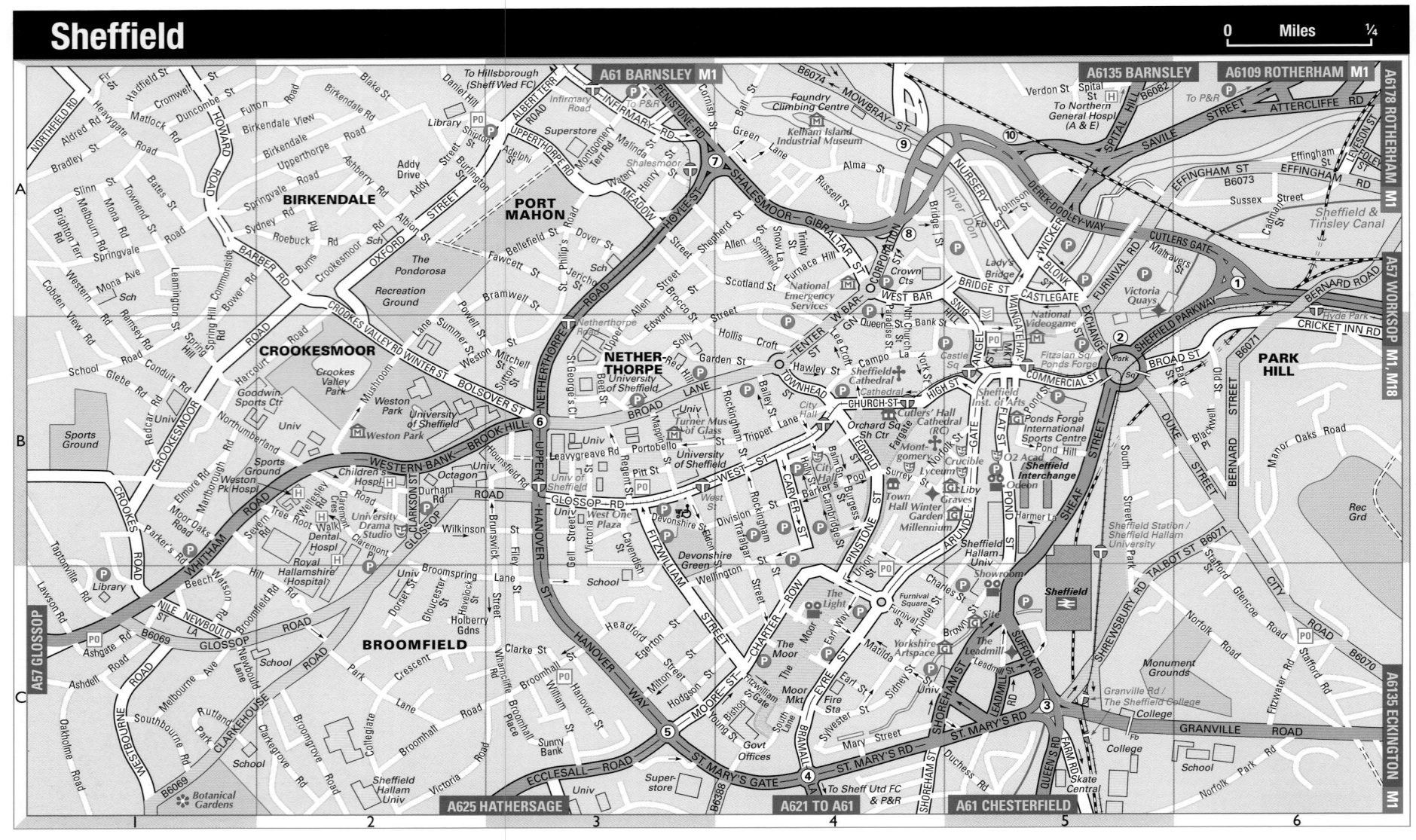

Stoke-on-Trent (Hanley)

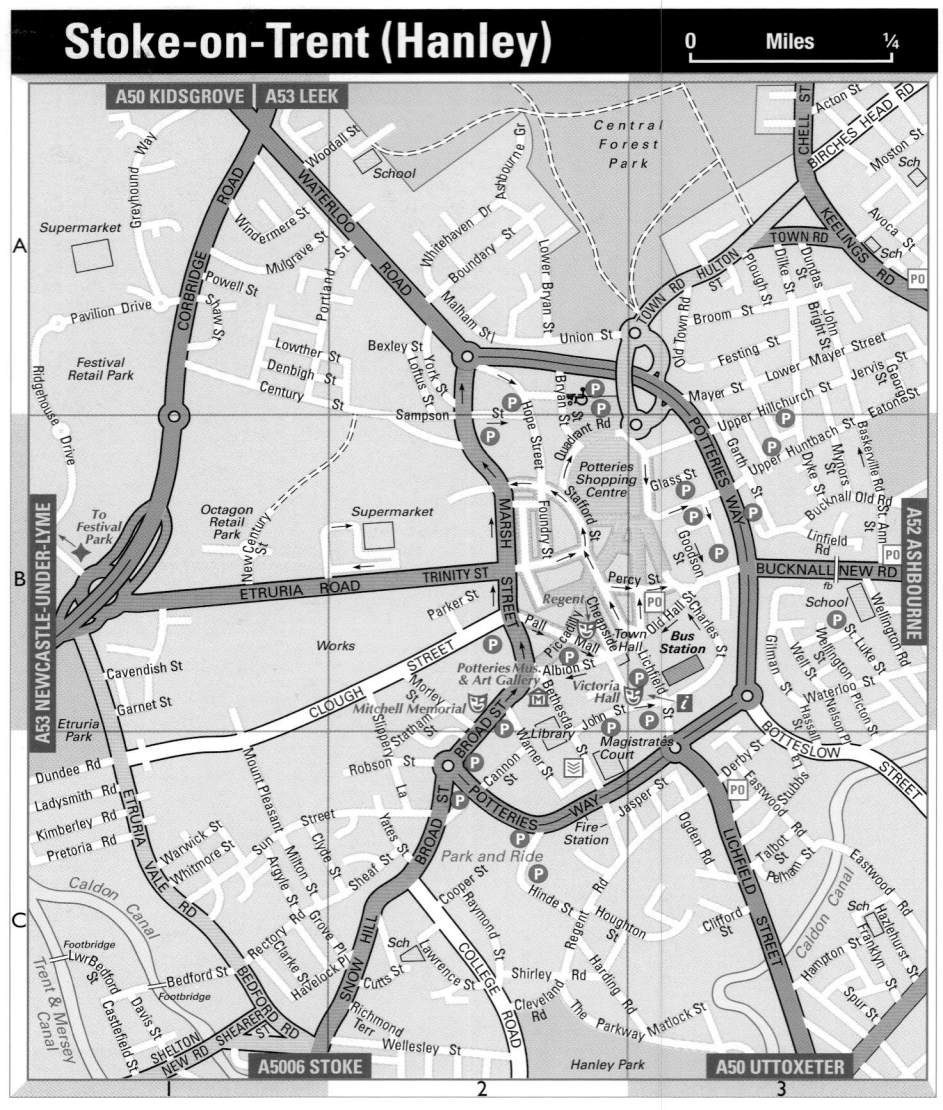

Southampton

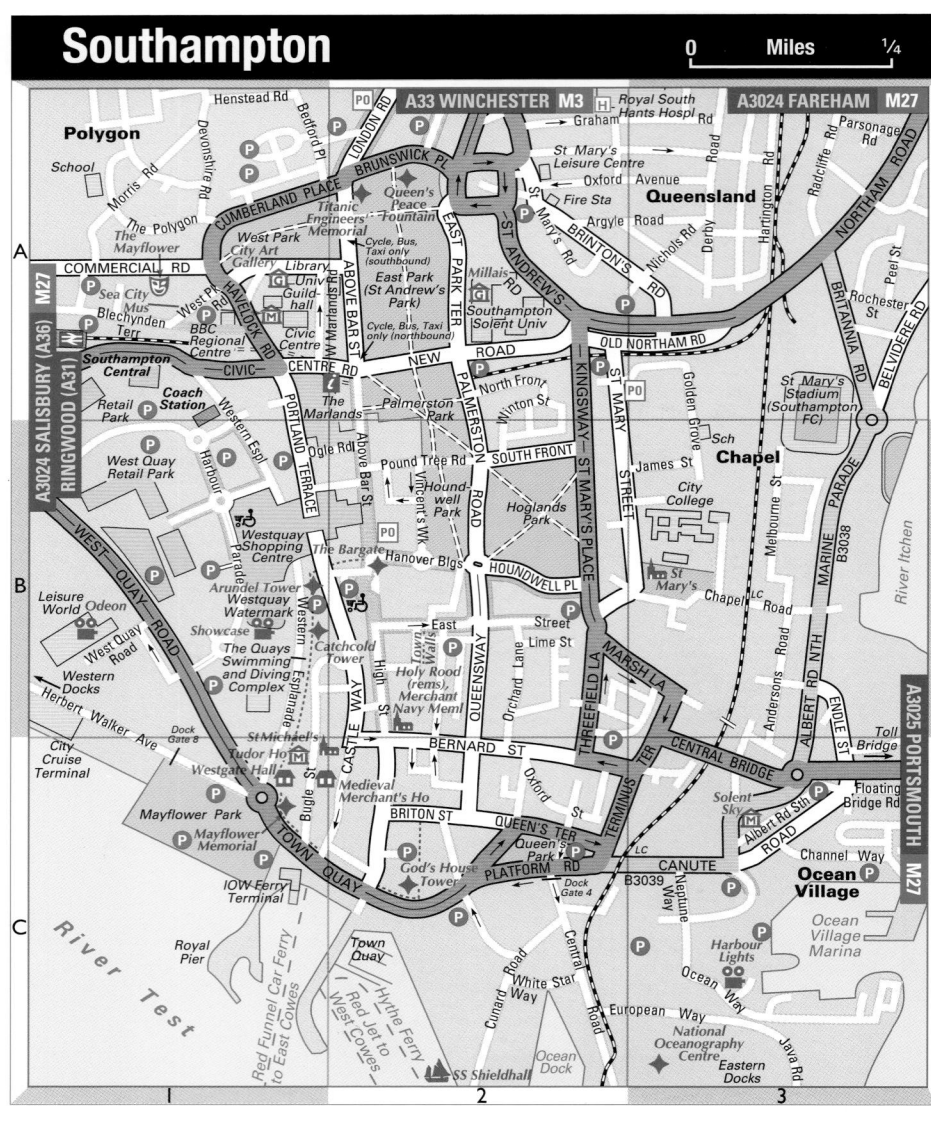

Southend-on-Sea

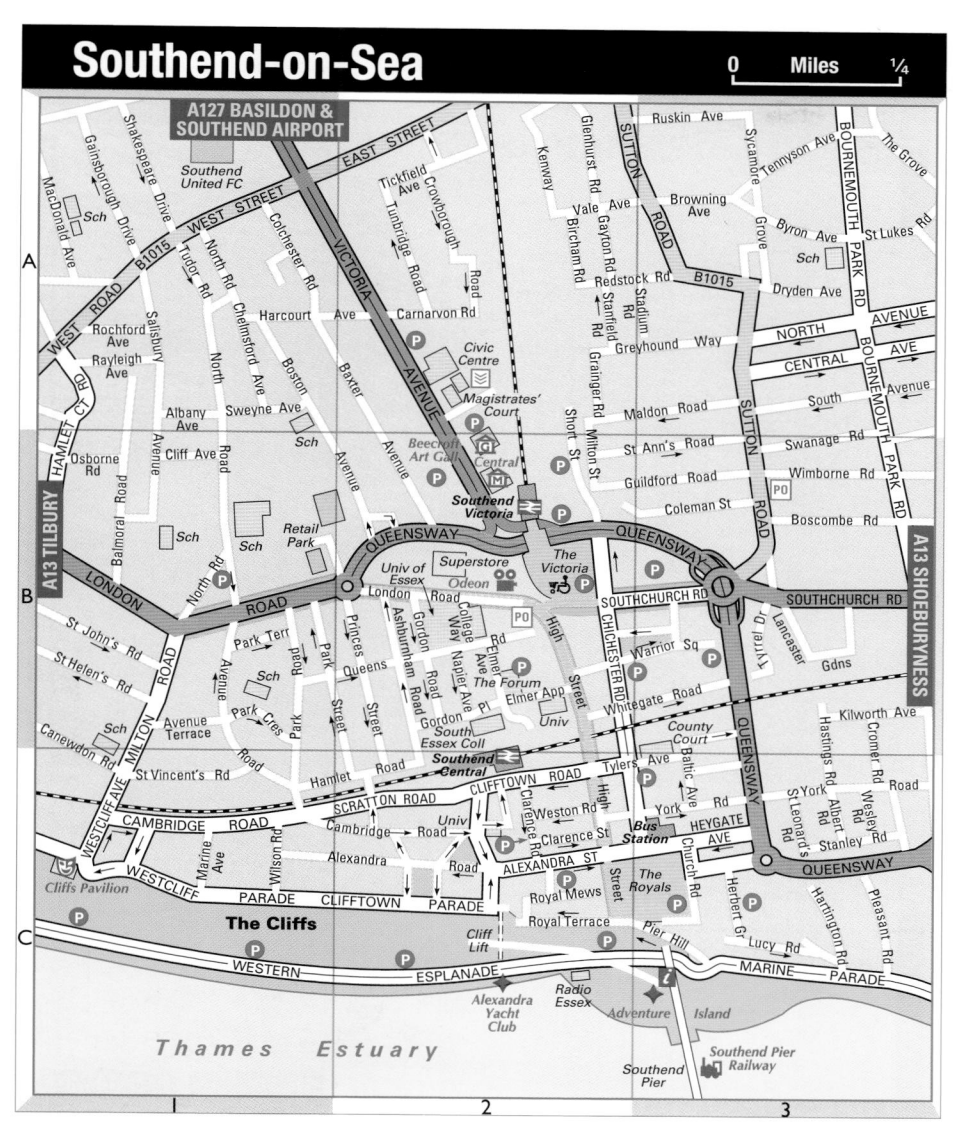

Stirling

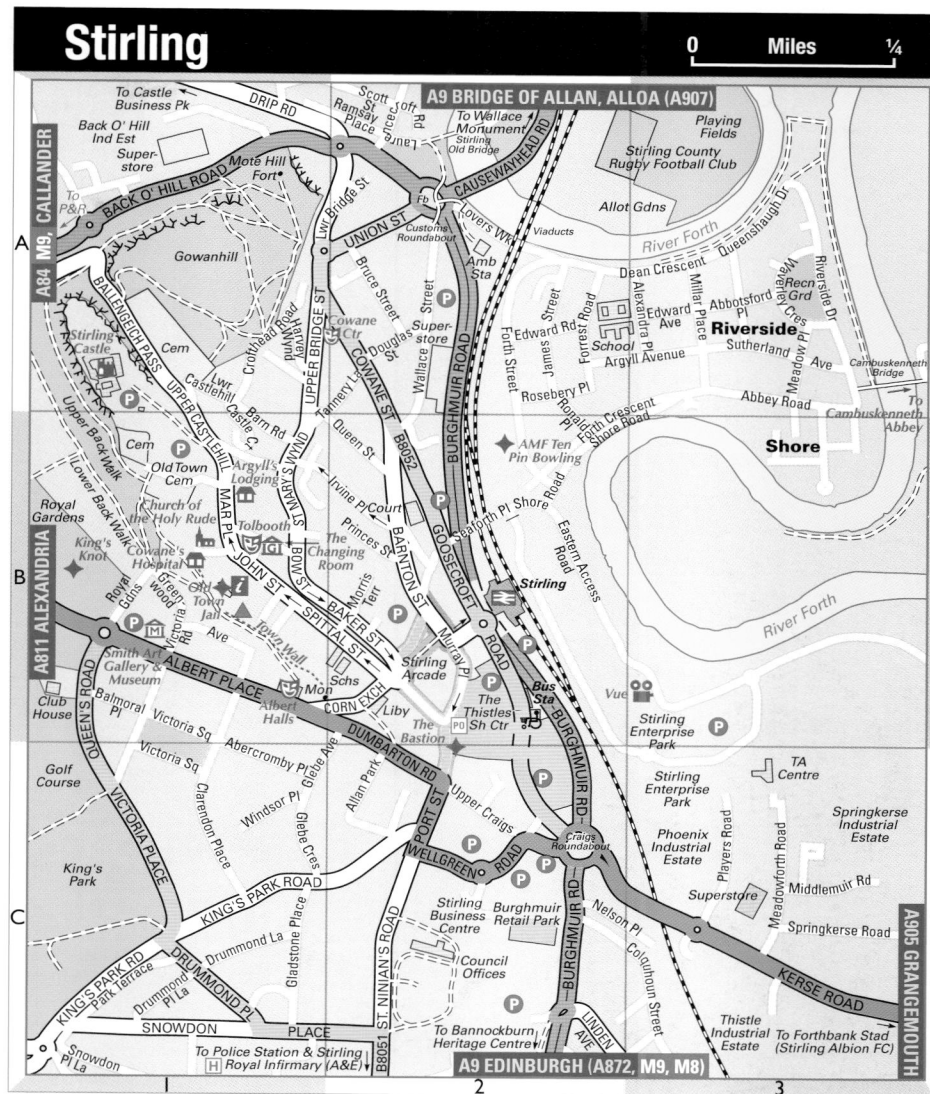

Stratford-upon-Avon

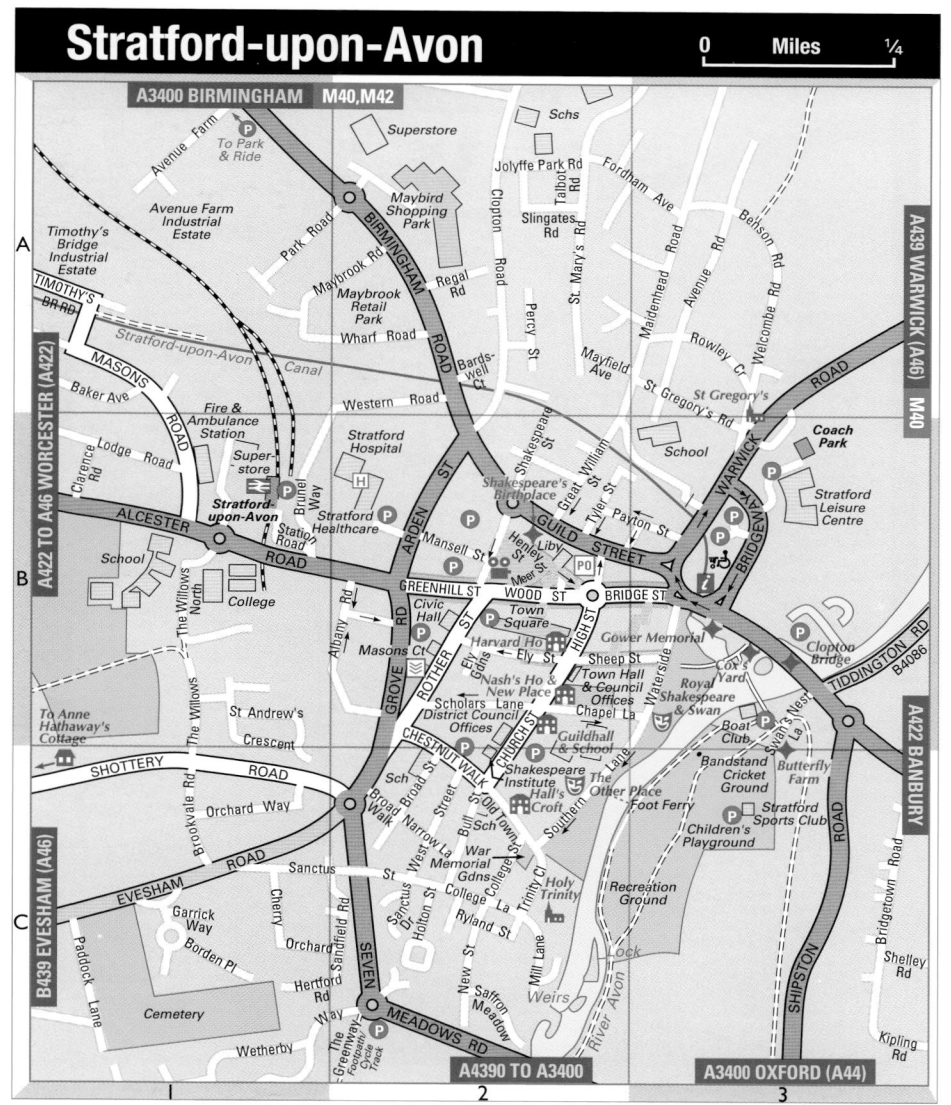

Sunderland

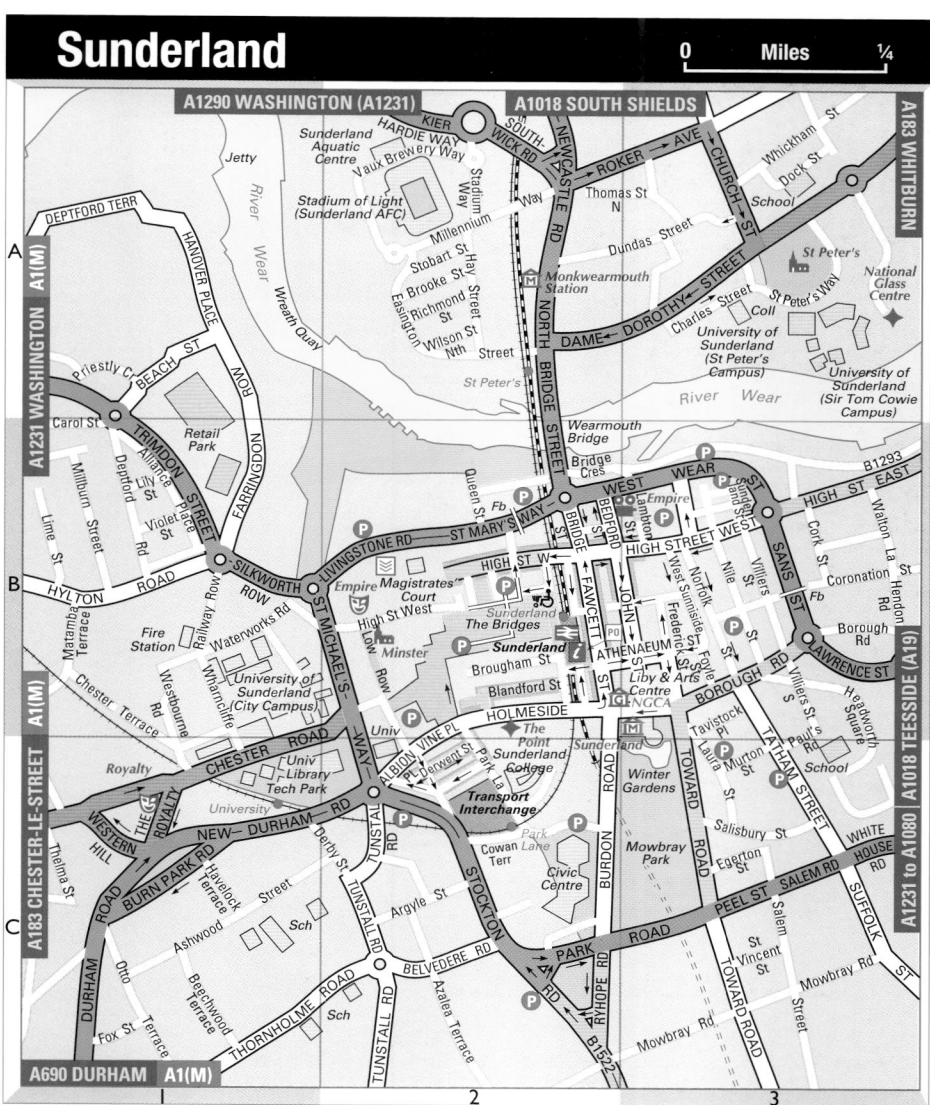

Swansea / Abertawe

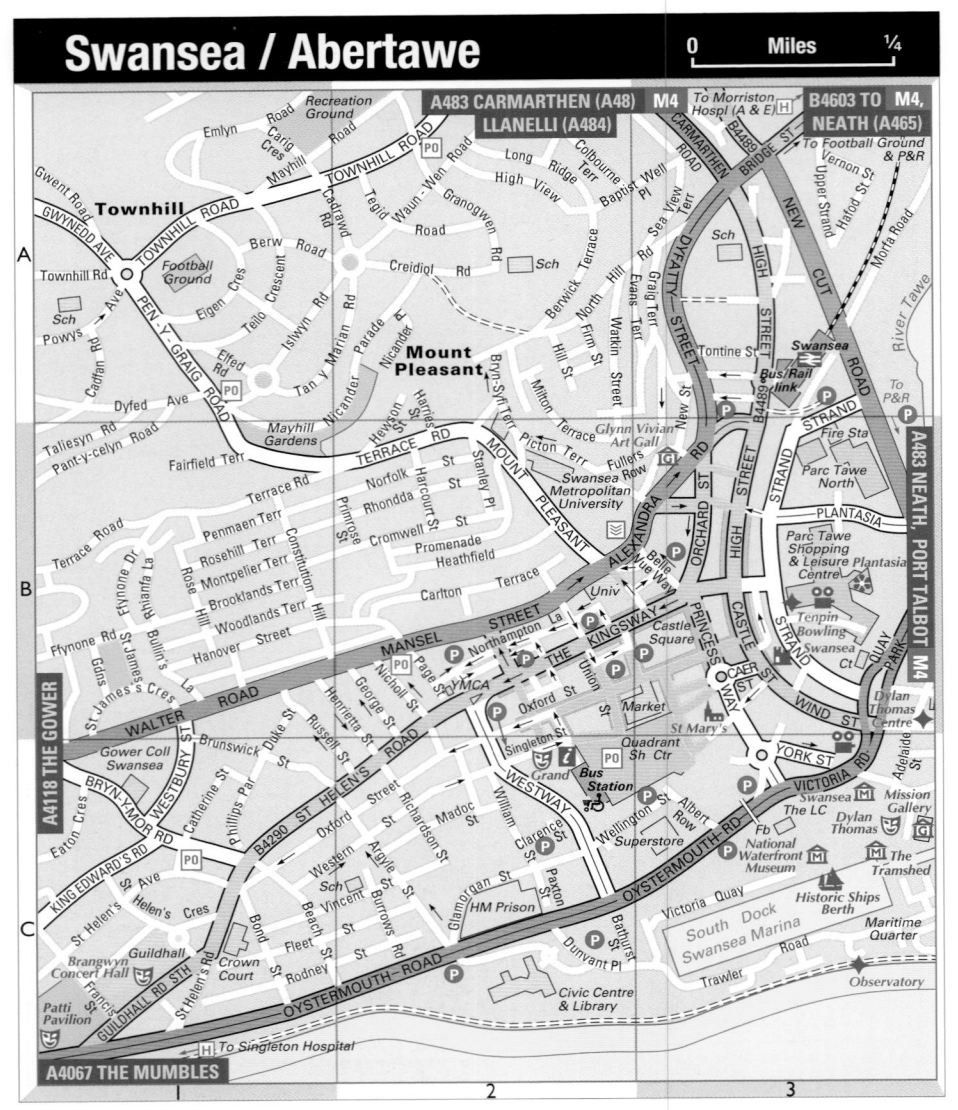

Swindon

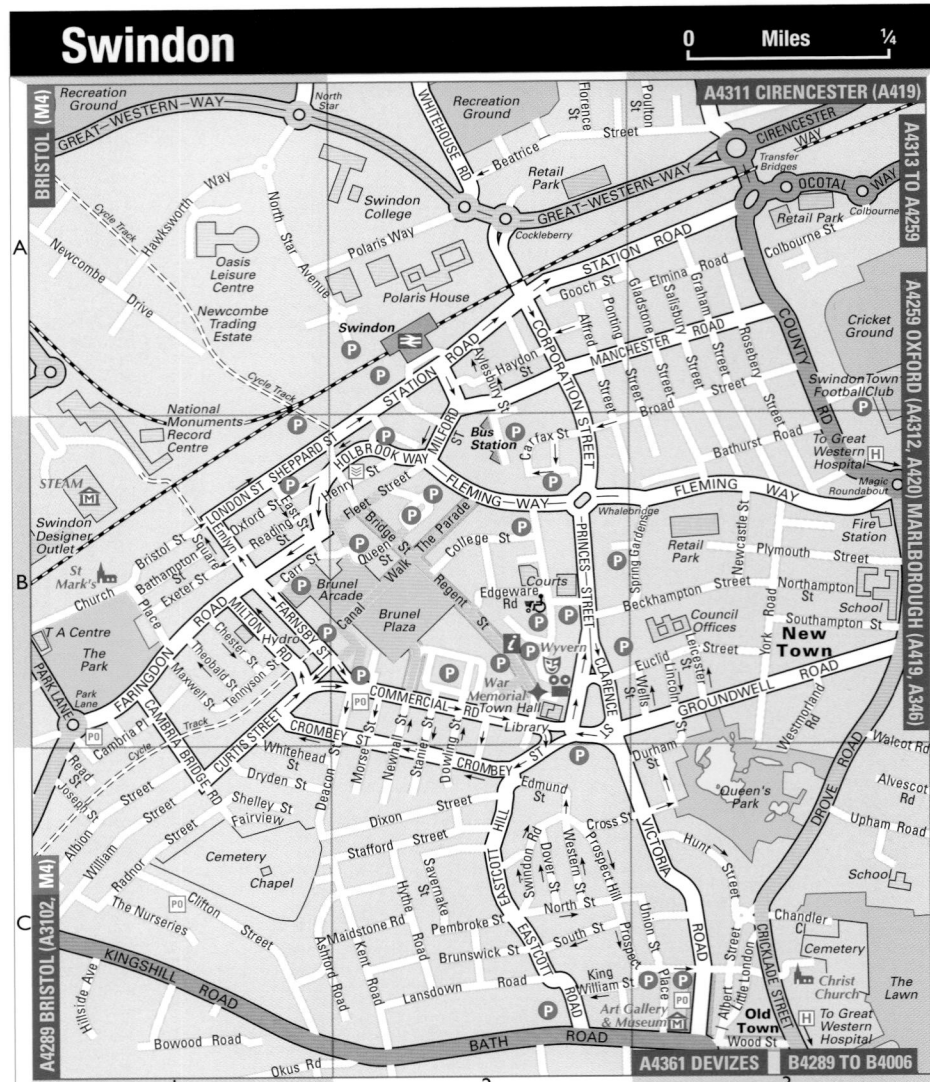

Taunton

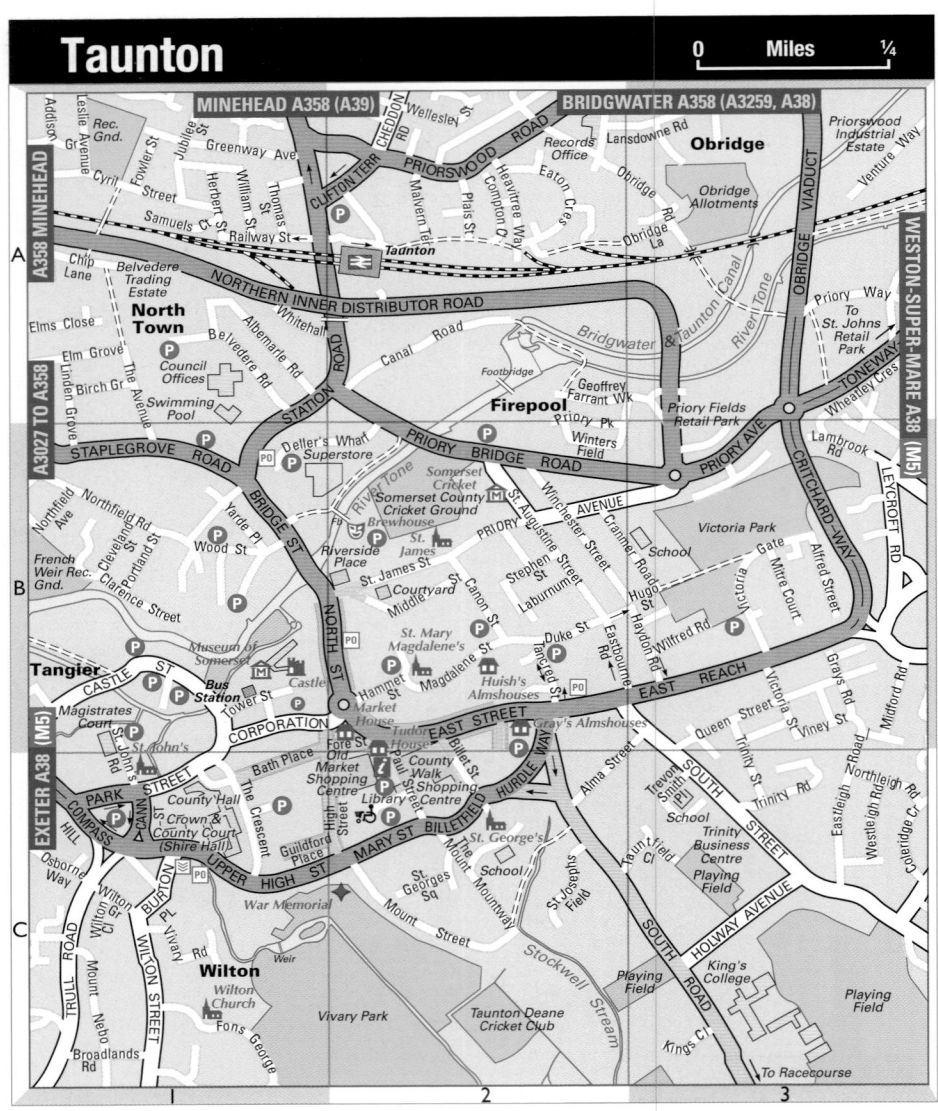

Telford

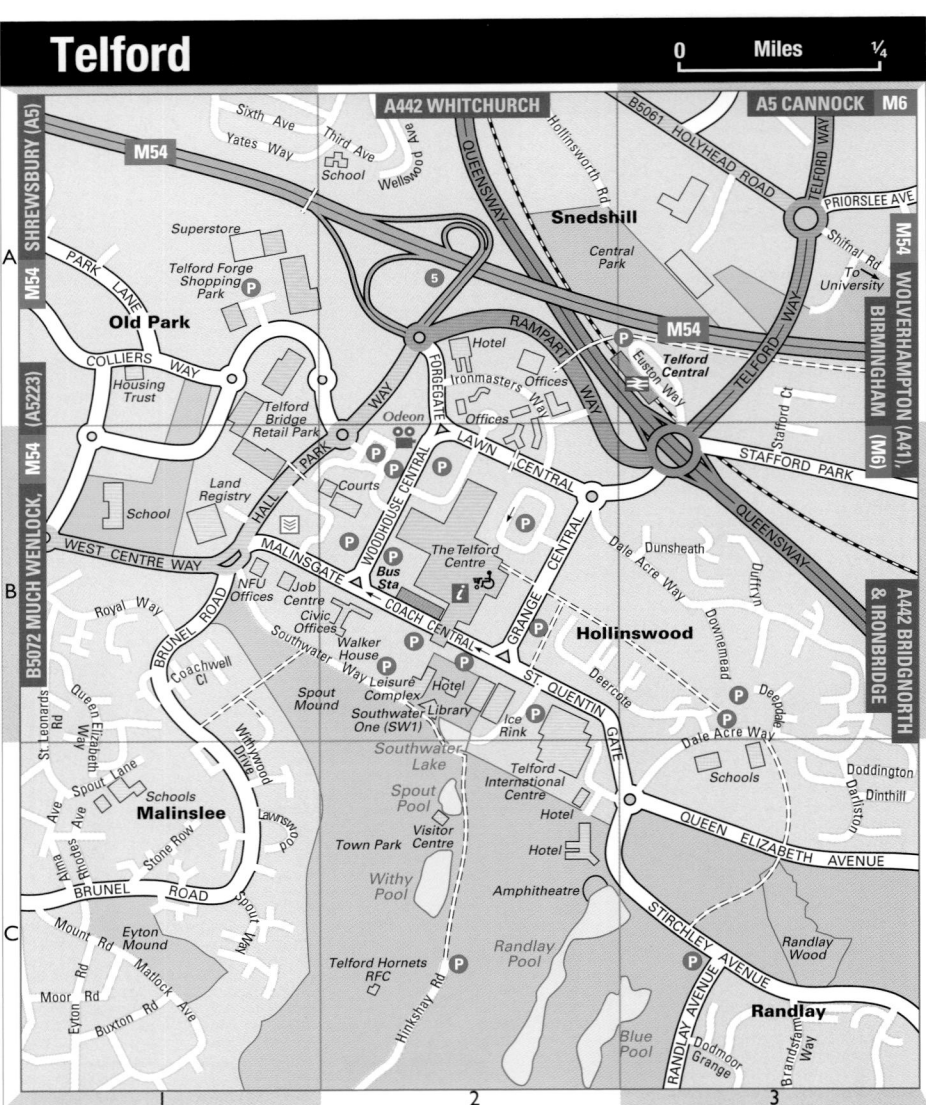

Torquay

0 Miles ¼

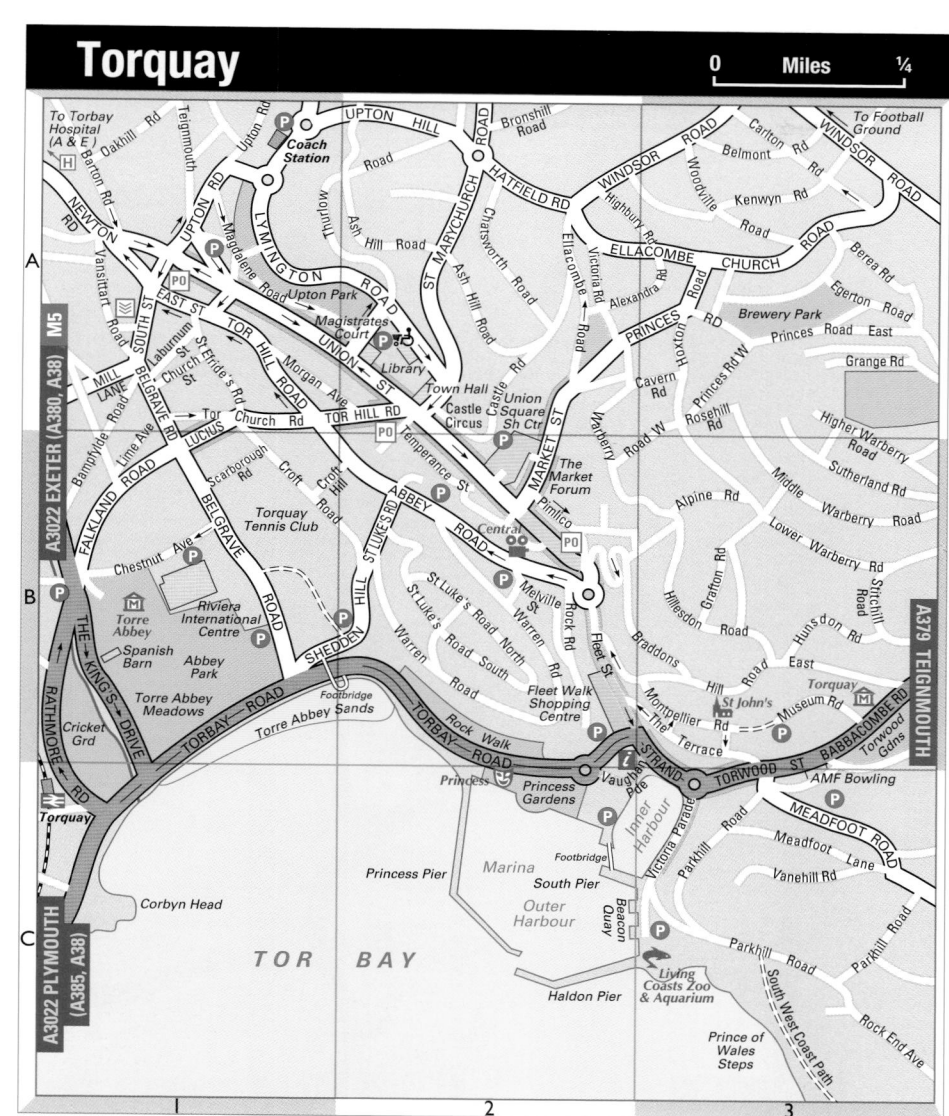

Truro

0 Miles ¼

Winchester

0 Miles ¼

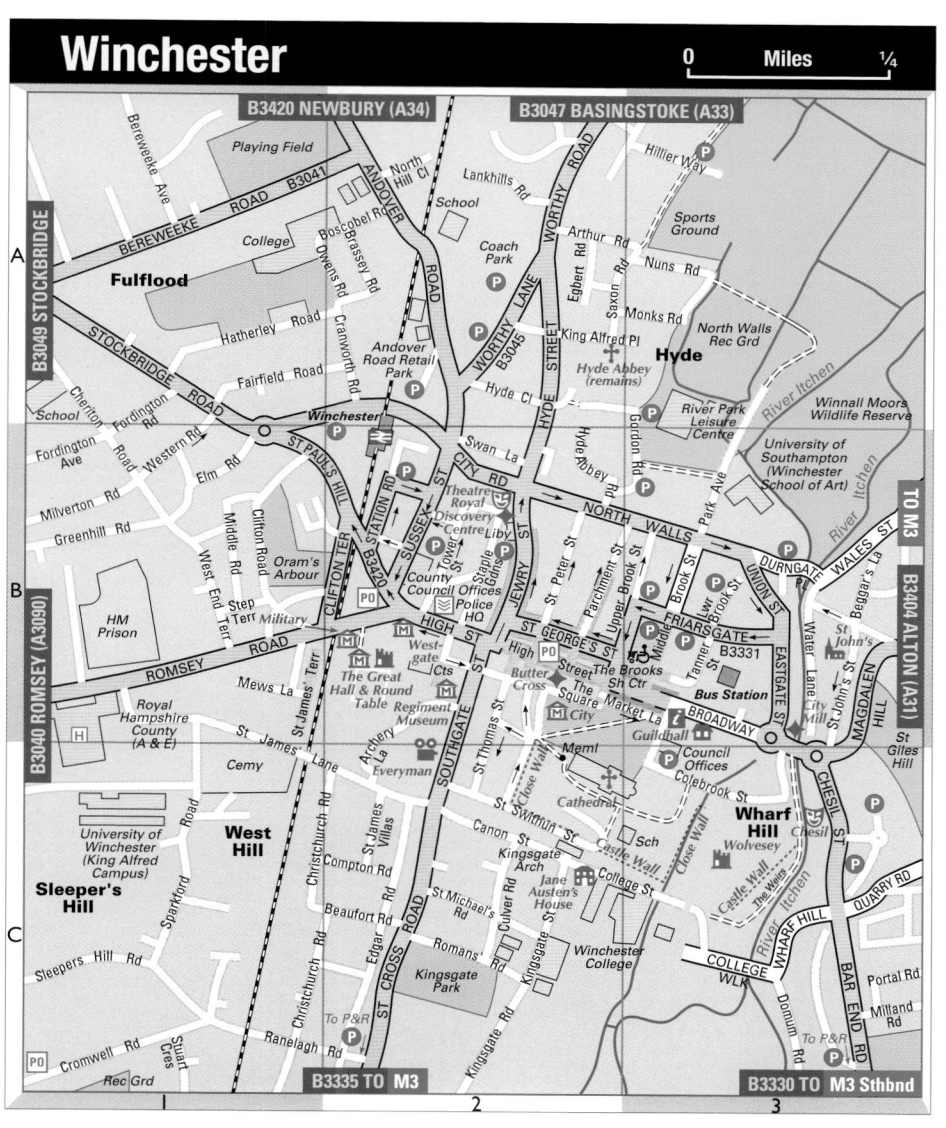

Windsor

0 Miles ¼

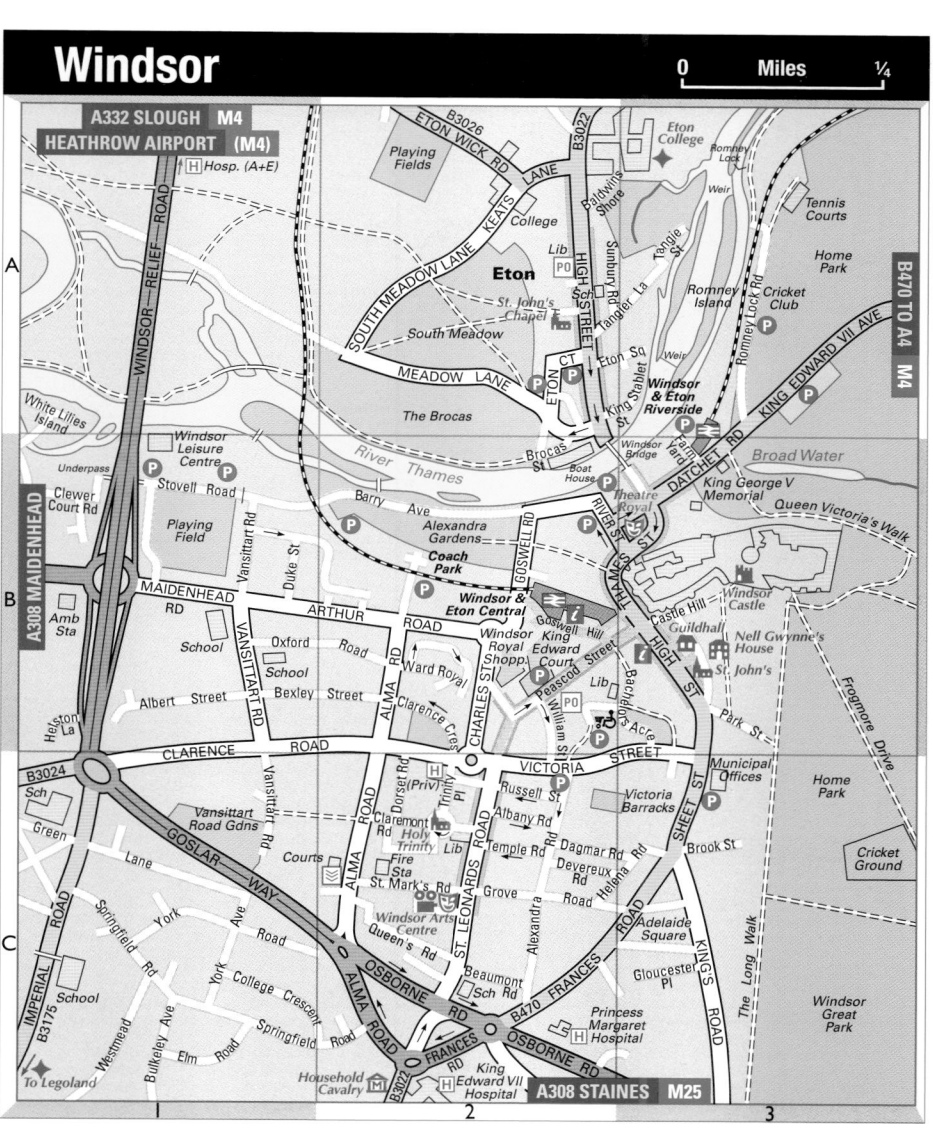

Wolverhampton

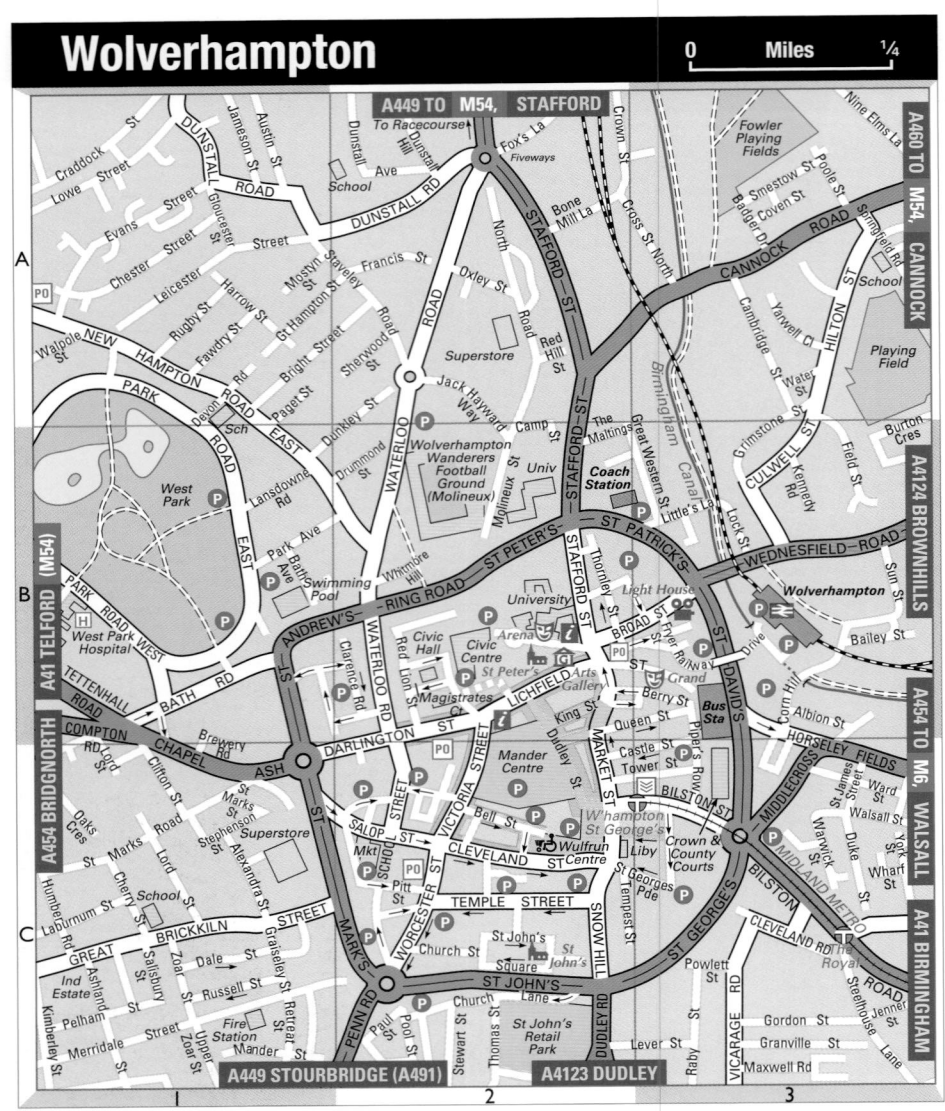

Worcester

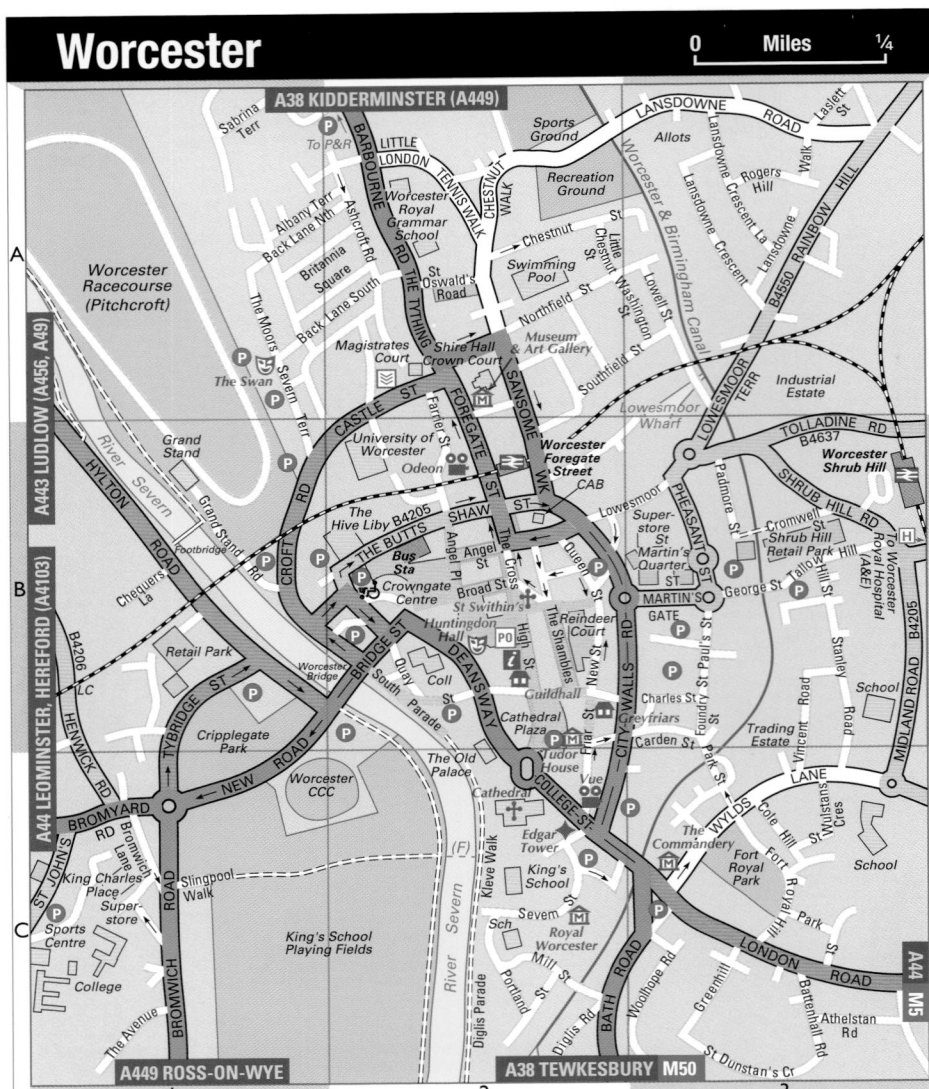

Wrexham / Wrecsam

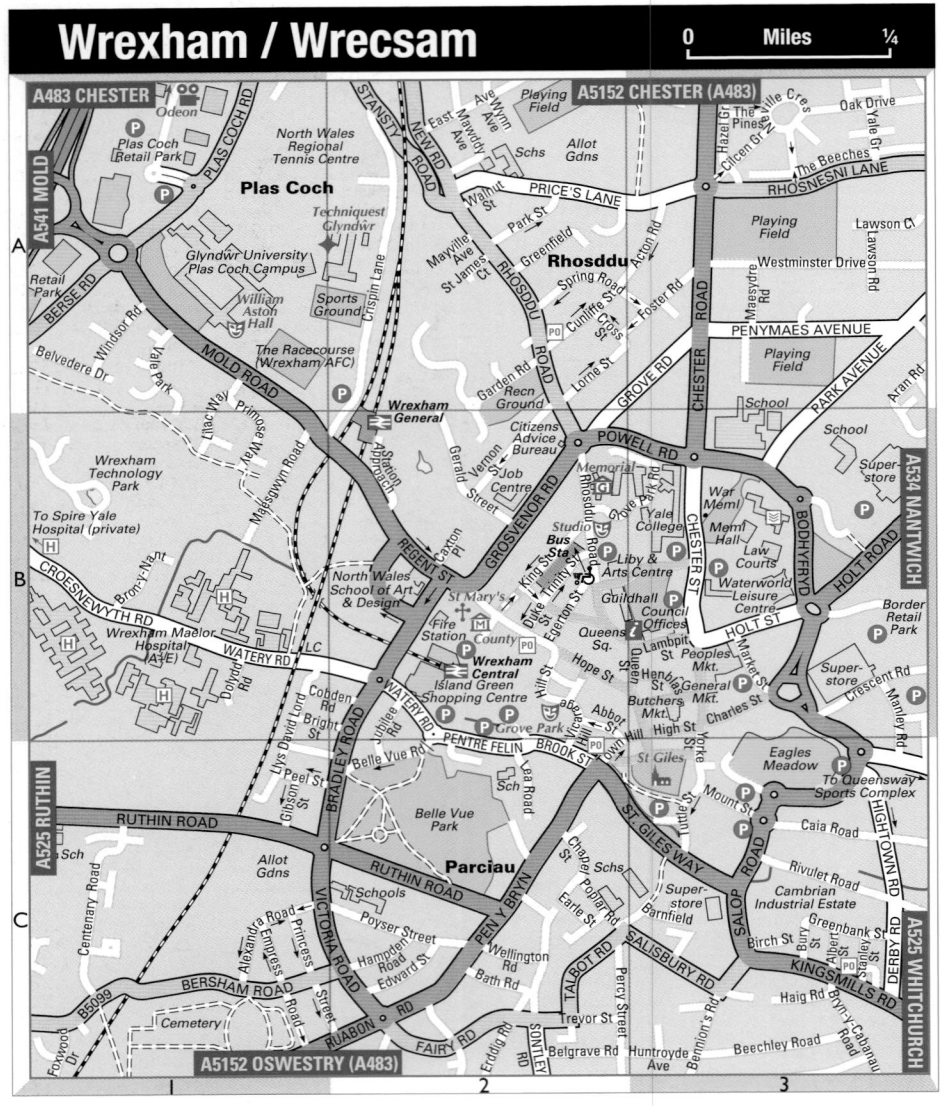

York

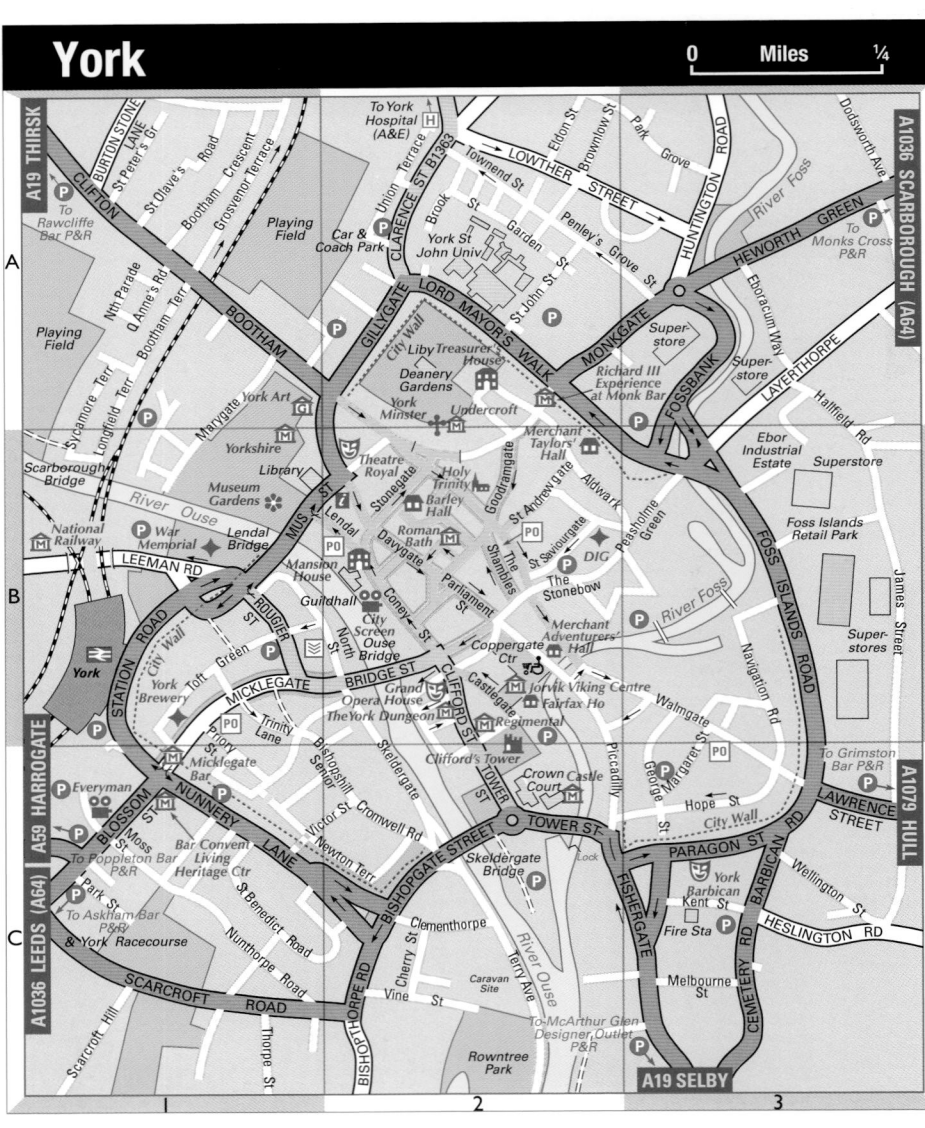

Index

Abbreviations used in the index

Aberdeen	Aberdeen City	Guern	Guernsey
Aberds	Aberdeenshire	Gwyn	Gwynedd
Ald	Alderney	Halton	Halton
Anglesey	Isle of Anglesey	Hants	Hampshire
Angus	Angus	Hereford	Herefordshire
Argyll	Argyll and Bute	Herts	Hertfordshire
Bath	Bath and North East Somerset	Highld	Highland
Bedford	Bedford	Hrtlpl	Hartlepool
Bl Gwent	Blaenau Gwent	Hull	Hull
Blackburn	Blackburn with Darwen	IoM	Isle of Man
Blackpool	Blackpool	IoW	Isle of Wight
BCP	Bournemouth, Christchurch and Poole	Invclyd	Inverclyde
		Jersey	Jersey
Borders	Scottish Borders	Kent	Kent
Brack	Bracknell	Lancs	Lancashire
Bridgend	Bridgend	Leicester	City of Leicester
Brighton	City of Brighton and Hove	Leics	Leicestershire
Bristol	City and County of Bristol	Lincs	Lincolnshire
Bucks	Buckinghamshire	London	Greater London
C Beds	Central Bedfordshire	Luton	Luton
Caerph	Caerphilly	M Keynes	Milton Keynes
Cambs	Cambridgeshire	M Tydf	Merthyr Tydfil
Cardiff	Cardiff	Mbro	Middlesbrough
Carms	Carmarthenshire	Medway	Medway
Ceredig	Ceredigion	Mers	Merseyside
Ches E	Cheshire East	Midloth	Midlothian
Ches W	Cheshire West and Chester	Mon	Monmouthshire
Clack	Clackmannanshire	Moray	Moray
Conwy	Conwy	N Ayrs	North Ayrshire
Corn	Cornwall	N Lincs	North Lincolnshire
Cumb	Cumbria	N Lanark	North Lanarkshire
Darl	Darlington	N Som	North Somerset
Denb	Denbighshire	N Yorks	North Yorkshire
Derby	City of Derby	NE Lincs	North East Lincolnshire
Derbys	Derbyshire	Neath	Neath Port Talbot
Devon	Devon	Newport	City and County of Newport
Dorset	Dorset	Norf	Norfolk
Dumfries	Dumfries and Galloway	Northants	Northamptonshire
Dundee	Dundee City	Northumb	Northumberland
Durham	Durham	Nottingham	City of Nottingham
E Ayrs	East Ayrshire	Notts	Nottinghamshire
E Dunb	East Dunbartonshire	Orkney	Orkney
E Loth	East Lothian	Oxon	Oxfordshire
E Renf	East Renfrewshire	Pboro	Peterborough
E Sus	East Sussex	Pembs	Pembrokeshire
E Yorks	East Riding of Yorkshire	Perth	Perth and Kinross
Edin	City of Edinburgh	Plym	Plymouth
Essex	Essex	Powys	Powys
Falk	Falkirk	Ptsmth	Portsmouth
Fife	Fife	Reading	Reading
Flint	Flintshire	Redcar	Redcar and Cleveland
Glasgow	City of Glasgow	Renfs	Renfrewshire
Glos	Gloucestershire	Rhondda	Rhondda Cynon Taff
Gtr Man	Greater Manchester	Rutland	Rutland
		S Ayrs	South Ayrshire
		S Glos	South Gloucestershire
		S Lanark	South Lanarkshire
		S Yorks	South Yorkshire
		Scilly	Scilly
		Shetland	Shetland
		Shrops	Shropshire
		Slough	Slough
		Som	Somerset
		Soton	Southampton
		Staffs	Staffordshire
		Southend	Southend-on-Sea
		Stirling	Stirling
		Stockton	Stockton-on-Tees
		Stoke	Stoke-on-Trent
		Suff	Suffolk
		Sur	Surrey
		Swansea	Swansea
		Swindon	Swindon
		T&W	Tyne and Wear
		Telford	Telford and Wrekin
		Thurrock	Thurrock
		Torbay	Torbay
		Torf	Torfaen
		V Glam	The Vale of Glamorgan
		W Berks	West Berkshire
		W Dunb	West Dunbartonshire
		W Isles	Western Isles
		W Loth	West Lothian
		W Mid	West Midlands
		W Sus	West Sussex
		W Yorks	West Yorkshire
		Warks	Warwickshire
		Warr	Warrington
		Wilts	Wiltshire
		Windsor	Windsor and Maidenhead
		Wokingham	Wokingham
		Worcs	Worcestershire
		Wrex	Wrexham
		York	City of York

How to use the index

Example

Charlton Mackerell Som **12** B3

- grid square
- page number
- county or unitary authority

A

Abbas Combe 12 B5
Abberley 50 C2
Abberton
 Essex 43 C6
 Worcs 50 D4
Abberwick 117 C7
Abbess Roding . . 42 C1
Abbey 11 C6
Abbey-cwm-hir . . 48 B2
Abbeydale 88 F4
Abbey Dore 49 F5
Abbey Field 43 B5
Abbey Hulton . . . 75 E6
Abbey St
 Bathans 122 C3
Abbeystead 93 D5
Abbey Town 107 D8
Abbey Village 86 B4
Abbey Wood 29 B5
Abbots Bickington . 9 C5
Abbots Bromley . . 62 B4
Abbotsbury 12 F3
Abbotsham 9 B6
Abbotskerswell . . . 7 C6
Abbots Langley . . 40 D3
Abbots Leigh 23 B7
Abbotsley 54 E3
Abbots Morton . . 50 D5
Abbots Ripton . . . 54 B3
Abbots Salford . . 51 D5
Abbotswood 14 B4
Abbotts Ann 25 E8
Abcott 49 B5
Abdon 61 F5
Aber 46 E3
Aberaeron 46 C3
Aberaman 34 D4
Aberangell 58 C5
Aber-Arad 46 F2
Aberarder 137 F7
Aberarder
 House 138 B2
Aberarder
 Lodge 137 F8
Aberargie 128 C3
Aberarth 46 C3
Aberavon 33 E8
Aber-banc 46 E2
Aberbeeg 35 D6
Abercanaid 34 D4
Abercarn 35 E6
Abercastle 44 B3
Abercegir 58 D5
Aberchirder 152 C6
Aber Cowarch . . . 59 C5
Abercraf 34 C2
Abercrombie . . . 129 D7
Abercych 45 E4
Abercynafon 34 C4
Abercynon 34 E4
Aberdalgie 128 B2
Aberdâr
 = Aberdare 34 D3
Aberdare
 = Aberdâr 34 D3
Aberdaron 70 E2
Aberdaugleddau
 = Milford Haven . . 44 E4

Aberdeen 141 D8
Aberdesach 82 F4
Aberdour 128 F3
Aberdovey 58 E3
Aberdulais 34 D1
Aberedw 48 E2
Abereiddy 44 B2
Abererch 70 D4
Aberfan 34 D4
Aberfeldy 133 E5
Aberffraw 82 E3
Aberffrwd 47 B5
Aberford 95 F7
Aberfoyle 126 D4
Abergavenny
 = Y Fenni 35 C6
Abergele 72 B3
Aber-Giâr 46 E4
Abergorlech 46 F4
Abergwaun
 = Fishguard 44 B4
Abergwesyn 47 D7
Abergwili 33 B5
Abergwynant 58 C3
Aber-gwynfi 34 E2
Abergwyngregyn 83 D6
Abergynolwyn . . . 58 D3
Aber-Hirnant 72 F3
Aberhonddu
 = Brecon 34 B4
Aberhosan 58 E5
Aberkenfig 34 F2
Aberlady 129 F6
Aberlemno 135 D5
Aberllefenni 58 D4
Abermagwr 47 B5
Abermaw
 = Barmouth 58 C3
Abermeurig 46 D4
Abermule 59 E8
Abernaint 59 B8
Abernant 32 B4
Aber-nant 34 D4
Abernethy 128 C3
Abernyte 134 F2
Aberpennar
 = Mountain Ash . . 34 E4
Aberporth 45 D4
Aber-Rhiwlech . . . 59 B6
Abersoch 70 E4
Abersychan 35 D6
Abertawe
 = Swansea 33 E7
Aberteifi
 = Cardigan 45 E3
Aberthin 22 B2
Abertillery
 = Abertyleri 35 D6
Abertridwr
 Caerph 35 F5
 Powys 59 C7
Abertyleri
 = Abertillery . . . 35 D6
Abertysswg 35 D5
Aberuthven 127 C8
Aber-Village 35 B5
Aberyscir 34 B3
Aberystwyth 58 F2
Abhainn Suidhe 154 G5
Abingdon-on-
 Thames 38 E4

Abinger Common . 28 E2
Abinger Hammer . 27 E8
Abington 114 B2
Abington Pigotts . 54 E4
Ab Kettleby 64 B4
Ab Lench 50 D5
Ablington
 Glos 37 D8
 Wilts 25 E6
Abney 75 B8
Aboyne 140 E4
Abram 86 D4
Abriachan 151 H8
Abridge 41 E7
Abronhill 119 B7
Abson 24 B2
Abthorpe 52 E4
Abune-the-Hill . . 159 F3
Aby 79 B7
Acaster Malbis . . . 95 E8
Acaster Selby . . . 95 E8
Accrington 87 B5
Acha 146 F4
Achabraid 145 E7
Achachork 149 D9
Achafolla 124 D3
Achagary 157 D10
Achahoish 144 F6
Achalader 133 E8
Achallader 131 E7
Acha Mor 155 E8
Achanalt 150 E5
Achanamara 144 E6
Achandunie 151 D9
Ach'an Todhair . . 130 B4
Achany 157 J8
Achaphubuil 130 B4
Acharacle 147 E9
Acharn
 Highld 147 F10
 Perth 132 E4
Acharole 158 E4
Achath 141 C6
Achavanich 158 F3
Achavraat 151 G12
Achddu 33 D5
Achduart 156 J3
Achentoul 157 F11
Achfary 156 F5
Achgarve 155 H13
Achiemore
 Highld 156 C6
 Highld 157 D11
A'Chill 148 H1
Achiltibuie 156 J3
Achina 157 C10
Achinduich 157 J8
Achinduin 124 B4
Achingills 158 D3
Achintee
 Highld 131 B5
 Highld 150 G2
Achintraid 149 E13
Achlean 138 E4
Achleck 146 G7
Achluachrach . . . 137 F5
Achlyness 156 D5
Achmelvich 156 G3
Achmore
 Highld 149 E13
 Stirling 132 F2

Achnaba
 Argyll 124 B5
 Argyll 145 E8
Achnabat 151 H8
Achnacarnin 156 F3
Achnacarry 136 F4
Achnacloich
 Argyll 125 B5
 Highld 149 H10
Achnaconeran . . 137 C7
Achnacraig 146 G7
Achnacroish 130 E2
Achnadrish 146 F7
Achnafalnich . . . 125 C8
Achnagarron . . . 151 E9
Achnaha 146 E7
Achnahanat 151 B8
Achnahannet . . . 139 B5
Achnairn 157 H8
Achnaluachrach . 157 J9
Achnasaul 136 F4
Achnasheen 150 F4
Achosnich 146 E7
Achranich 147 G10
Achreamie 157 C13
Achriabhach . . . 131 C5
Achriesgill 156 D5
Achrimsdale . . . 157 J12
Achtoty 157 C9
Achurch 65 F7
Achuvoldrach . . 157 D8
Achvaich 151 B10
Achvarasdal . . . 157 C12
Ackergill 158 E5
Acklam
 Mbro 102 C2
 N Yorks 96 C3
Ackleton 61 E7
Acklington 117 D8
Ackton 88 B5
Ackworth Moor
 Top 88 C5
Acle 69 C7
Acock's Green . . . 62 F5
Acol 31 C7
Acomb
 Northumb 110 C2
 York 95 D8
Aconbury 49 F7
Acre 87 B5
Acrefair 73 E6
Acre Street 15 E8
Acton
 Ches E 74 D3
 Dorset 13 G7
 London 41 F5
 Shrops 60 F3
 Suff 56 E2
 Wrex 73 D7
Acton
 Beauchamp . . . 49 D8
Acton Bridge . . . 74 B2
Acton Burnell . . . 60 D5
Acton Green 49 D8
Acton Pigott 60 D5
Acton Round 61 E6
Acton Scott 60 F4
Acton Trussell . . . 62 C3
Acton Turville . . . 37 F5
Adbaston 61 B7
Adber 12 B3

Adderley 74 E3
Adderstone 123 F7
Addiewell 120 C2
Addingham 94 E3
Addington
 Bucks 39 B7
 Kent 29 D7
 London 28 C4
Addinston 121 D8
Addiscombe 28 C4
Addlestone 27 C8
Addlethorpe 79 C8
Adel 95 F5
Adeney 61 C7
Adfa 59 D7
Adforton 49 B6
Adisham 31 D6
Adlestrop 38 B2
Adlingfleet 90 B2
Adlington 86 C4
Admaston
 Staffs 62 B4
 Telford 61 C6
Admington 51 E7
Adstock 52 F5
Adstone 52 D3
Adversane 16 B4
Advie 152 E1
Adwalton 88 B3
Adwell 39 E6
Adwick le Street . 89 D6
Adwick upon
 Dearne 89 D5
Ae Village 114 F2
Affleck 141 B7
Affpuddle 13 E6
Affric Lodge . . . 136 B4
Afon-wen 72 B5
Afton 14 F4
Agglethorpe . . . 101 F5
Agneash 84 D4
Aigburth 85 F4
Aiginis 155 D9
Aike 97 E6
Aikerness 159 C5
Aikers 159 J5
Aiketgate 108 E4
Aikton 108 D2
Ailey 48 E5
Ailstone 51 D7
Ailsworth 65 E8
Ainderby
 Quernhow 102 F1
Ainderby
 Steeple 101 E8
Aingers Green . . . 43 B7
Ainsdale 85 C4
Ainsdale-on-Sea 85 C4
Ainstable 108 E5
Ainsworth 87 C5
Ainthorpe 103 D5
Aintree 85 E4
Aird
 Argyll 124 E3
 Dumfries 104 C4
 Highld 149 A12
 W Isles 155 D10
Aird a Mhachair . 148 D2
Aird a' Mhulaidh 154 F6
Aird Asaig 154 G6

Aird Dhail 155 A9
Airdens 151 B9
Aird Mhidhinis . 148 H2
Aird Mhighe
 W Isles 154 H6
 W Isles 154 J5
Aird Mhor 148 H2
Aird of Sleat . . . 149 H10
Airdrie 119 C7
Airdtorrisdale . . 157 C9
Aird Uig 154 D5
Airidh a
 Bhruaich 154 F7
Airieland 106 D4
Airmyn 89 B8
Airntully 133 F7
Airor 149 H12
Airth 127 F7
Airton 94 D2
Airyhassen 105 E7
Aisby
 Lincs 78 F3
 Lincs 90 E2
Aisgernis 148 F2
Aiskew 101 F7
Aislaby
 N Yorks 103 D6
 N Yorks 103 F5
 Stockton 102 C2
Aisthorpe 78 A2
Aith
 Orkney 159 G3
 Shetland 160 D8
 Shetland 160 H5
Aithsetter 160 K6
Aitkenhead 112 D3
Aitnoch 151 H12
Akeld 117 B5
Akeley 52 F5
Akenham 56 E5
Albaston 6 B2
Albourne 17 C6
Albrighton
 Shrops 60 C4
 Shrops 62 D2
Alburgh 69 F5
Albury
 Herts 41 B7
 Sur 27 E8
Alby Hill 81 D7
Alcaig 151 F8
Alcaston 60 F4
Alciston 18 E2
Alcombe
 Som 21 E8
 Wilts 24 C3
Alconbury 54 B2
Alconbury
 Weston 54 B2
Aldborough
 Norf 81 D7
 N Yorks 95 C7
Aldbourne 25 B7
Aldbrough 97 F8
Aldbrough St
 John 101 C7

Aldbury 40 C2
Aldcliffe 92 C4
Aldclune 133 C6
Aldeburgh 57 D8
Aldeby 69 E7
Aldenham 40 E4
Alderbury 14 B2
Aldercar 76 E4
Alderford 68 C4
Alderholt 14 C2
Alderley 36 E4
Alderley Edge . . . 74 B5
Aldermaston 26 C3
Aldermaston
 Wharf 26 C4
Alderminster 51 E7
Alder's End 49 E8
Aldersey Green . . 73 D8
Aldershot 27 D6
Alderton
 Glos 50 F5
 Northants 52 E5
 Shrops 60 B4
 Suff 57 E7
 Wilts 37 F5
Alderwasley 76 D3
Aldfield 95 C5
Aldford 73 D8
Aldham
 Essex 43 B5
 Suff 56 E4
Aldie 151 C10
Aldingbourne . . . 16 D3
Aldingham 92 B2
Aldington
 Kent 19 B7
 Worcs 51 E5
Aldington Frith . . 19 B7
Aldochlay 126 E2
Aldreth 54 B5
Aldridge 62 D4
Aldringham 57 C8
Aldsworth 38 C1
Aldunie 140 B2
Aldwark
 Derbys 76 D2
 N Yorks 95 C7
Aldwick 16 E3
Aldwincle 65 F7
Aldworth 26 B3
Alexandria 118 B3
Alfardisworthy . . . 8 C4
Alfington 11 E6
Alfold 27 F8
Alfold Bars 27 F8
Alfold Crossways . 27 F8
Alford
 Aberds 140 C4
 Lincs 79 B7
 Som 23 F8
Alfreton 76 D4
Alfrick 50 D2
Alfrick Pound . . . 50 D2
Alfriston 18 E2
Algaltraig 145 F9
Algarkirk 79 F5
Alhampton 23 F8
Aline Lodge . . . 154 F6
Alisary 147 D10
Alkborough 90 B2
Alkerton 51 E8

Alkham 31 E6
Alkington 74 F2
Alkmonton 75 F8
Alladale Lodge . 150 C7
Allaleigh 7 D6
Allanaquoich . . . 139 E7
Allangrange
 Mains 151 F9
Allanton
 Borders 122 D4
 N Lanark 119 D8
Allathasdal 148 H1
All Cannings 25 C5
Allendale Town . 109 D8
Allenheads 109 E8
Allensford 110 D3
Allens Green 41 C7
Allensmore 49 F6
Allenton 76 F3
Aller 12 B2
Allerby 107 F7
Allerford 21 E8
Allerston 103 F6
Allerthorpe 96 E3
Allerton
 Mers 86 F2
 W Yorks 94 F4
Allerton
 Mauleverer . . . 95 D7
Allesley 63 F7
Allestree 76 F3
Allet 3 B6
Allexton 64 D5
Allgreave 75 C6
Allhallows 30 B2
Allhallows-on-
 Sea 30 B2
Alligin Shuas . . 149 C13
Allimore Green . . 62 C2
Allington
 Lincs 77 E8
 Wilts 25 C5
 Wilts 25 F7
Allithwaite 92 B3
Alloa 127 E7
Allonby 107 E7
Alloway 112 C3
All Saints South
 Elmham 69 F6
All Stretton 60 E4
Allt 33 D6
Alltchaorunn . . . 131 D5
Alltforgan 59 B6
Alltmawr 48 E2
Alltnacaillich . . . 156 E7
Allt na h-Airbhe 150 B4
Allt-nan-sùgh . . 136 B2
Alltsigh 137 C7
Alltwalis 46 F3
Alltwen 33 D8
Alltyblaca 46 E4
Allwood Green . . 56 B4
Almeley 48 D5
Almer 13 E7
Almholme 89 D6
Almington 74 F4
Alminstone Cross . 8 B5
Almondbank . . . 128 B2
Almondbury 88 C2
Almondsbury . . . 36 F3

Alne 95 C7
Alness 151 E9
Alnham 117 C5
Alnmouth 117 C8
Alnwick 117 C7
Alperton 40 F4
Alphamstone 56 F2
Alpheton 56 D2
Alphington 10 E4
Alport 76 C2
Alpraham 74 D2
Alresford 43 B6
Alrewas 63 C5
Alsager 74 D4
Alsagers Bank . . 74 E5
Alsop en le Dale . 75 D8
Alston
 Cumb 109 E7
 Devon 11 D8
Alstone 50 F4
Alstonefield 75 D8
Alswear 10 B2
Altandhu 156 H2
Altanduin 157 G11
Altarnun 8 F4
Altass 156 J7
Alterwall 158 D4
Altham 93 F7
Althorne 43 E5
Althorpe 90 D2
Alticry 105 D6
Altnabreac
 Station 157 E13
Altnacealgach
 Hotel 156 H5
Altnacraig 124 C4
Altnafeadh 131 D5
Altnaharra 157 F8
Altofts 88 B4
Alton
 Derbys 76 C3
 Hants 26 F5
 Staffs 75 E7
Alton Pancras . . . 12 D5
Alton Priors 25 C6
Altrincham 87 F5
Altrua 136 F5
Altskeith 126 D3
Altyre House . . . 151 F13
Alva 127 E7
Alvanley 73 B8
Alvaston 76 F3
Alvechurch 50 B5
Alvecote 63 D6
Alvediston 13 B7
Alveley 61 F7
Alverdiscott 9 B7
Alverstoke 15 E7
Alverstone 15 F6
Alverton 77 E7
Alves 152 B1
Alvescot 38 D2
Alveston
 S Glos 36 F3
 Warks 51 D7
Alvie 138 D4
Alvingham 91 E7
Alvington 36 D3

Abb–Alv

Alwalton 65 E8
Alweston 12 C4
Alwinton 116 D5
Alwoodley 95 E5
Alyth 134 E2
Amatnatua 150 B7
Am Baile 148 G2
Ambergate 76 D3
Amber Hill 78 E5
Amberley
Glos 37 D5
W Sus 16 C4
Amble 117 D8
Amblecote 62 F2
Ambler Thorn 87 B8
Ambleside 99 D5
Ambleston 44 C5
Ambrosden 39 C6
Am Buth 124 C4
Amcotts 90 C2
Amersham 40 E2
Amesbury 25 E6
Amington 63 D6
Amisfield 114 F2
Amlwch 82 B4
Amlwch Port 82 B4
Ammanford
=Rhydaman 33 C7
Amod 143 E8
Amotherby 96 B3
Ampfield 14 B5
Ampleforth 95 B8
Ampney Crucis 37 D7
Ampney St Mary 37 D7
Ampney St Peter 37 D7
Amport 25 E7
Ampthill 53 F8
Ampton 56 B2
Amroth 32 D2
Amulree 133 F5
Anagach 139 B6
Anaheilt 130 C2
Anancaun 150 E3
An Caol 149 C11
Ancaster 78 E2
Anchor 59 F8
Anchorsholme 92 E3
An Cnoc 155 D9
Ancroft 123 E5
Ancrum 116 B2
Anderby 79 B8
Anderson 13 E6
Anderton 74 B3
Andover 25 E8
Andover Down 25 E8
Andoversford 37 C7
Andreas 84 C4
Anfield 85 E4
Angersleigh 11 C6
Angle 44 E3
An Gleann Ur 155 D9
Angmering 16 D4
Angram
N Yorks 95 E8
N Yorks 100 E3
Anie 126 C4
Ankerville 151 D11
Anlaby 90 B4
Anmer 80 E3
Annan 107 C8
Annat
Argyll 125 C6
Highld 149 C13
Anna Valley 25 E8
Annbank 112 B4
Annesley 76 D5
Annesley
Woodhouse 76 D4
Annfield Plain 110 D4
Annifirth 160 J3
Annitsford 111 B5
Annscroft 60 D4
Ansdell 85 B4
Ansford 23 F8
Ansley 63 E6
Anslow 63 B6
Anslow Gate 63 B5
Anstey
Herts 54 F5
Leics 64 D2
Anstruther
Easter 129 D7
Anstruther
Wester 129 D7
Ansty
Hants 26 E5
Warks 63 F7
Wilts 13 B7
W Sus 17 B6
Anthill Common 15 C7
Anthorn 107 D8
Antingham 81 D8
An t-Ob
=Leverburgh 154 J5
Anton's Gowt 79 E5
Antonshill 127 F7
Antony 5 D8
Anwick 78 D4
Anwoth 106 D2
Aoradh 142 B3
Apes Hall 67 E5
Apethorpe 65 E7
Apeton 62 C2
Apley 78 B4
Apperknowle 76 B3
Apperley 37 B5
Apperley Bridge 94 F4
Appersett 100 E3
Appin 130 E3
Appin House 130 E3
Appleby 90 C3
Appleby-in-
Westmorland 100 B1
Appleby Magna 63 D7
Appleby Parva 63 D7
Applecross 149 D12
Applecross
House 149 D12
Appledore
Devon 11 C5
Devon 20 F3
Kent 19 C6
Appledore Heath 19 B6
Appleford 39 E5
Applegarthtown 114 F4
Appleshaw 25 E8
Applethwaite 98 B4
Appleton
Halton 86 F3
Oxon 38 D4
Appleton-le-
Moors 103 F5
Appleton-le-
Street 96 B3
Appleton
Roebuck 95 E8
Appleton Thorn 86 F4
Appleton Wiske 102 D1
Appletreehall 115 C8
Appletreewick 94 C3
Appley 11 B5
Appley Bridge 86 D3
Apse Heath 15 F6
Apsley End 54 F2
Apuldram 16 D2
Aquhythie 141 C6
Arabella 151 D11
Arbeadie 141 E5
Arberth
=Narberth 32 C2
Arbirlot 135 E6
Arboll 151 C11
Arborfield 27 C5
Arborfield Cross 27 C5
Arborfield
Garrison 27 C5
Arbourthorne 88 F4
Arbroath 135 E6
Arbuthnott 135 B7
Archiestown 152 D2
Arclid 74 C4
Ardachu 157 J9
Ardalanish 146 K6
Ardanaiseig 125 C6
Ardaneaskan 149 E13
Ardanstur 124 D4
Ardargie House
Hotel 128 C2
Ardarroch 149 E13
Ardbeg
Argyll 142 D5
Argyll 145 E10
Ardcharnich 150 C4
Ardchiavaig 146 K6
Ardchullarie
More 126 C4
Ardchyle 126 B4
Ard-dhubh 149 D12
Arddleen 60 C2
Ardechvie 136 E4
Ardeley 41 B6
Ardelve 149 F13
Arden 126 F2
Ardens Grafton 51 D6
Ardentinny 145 E10
Ardentraive 145 F9
Ardeonaig 132 F3
Ardersier 151 F10
Ardessie 150 C3
Ardfern 124 E4
Ardgartan 125 E8
Ardgay 151 B8
Ardgour 130 C4
Ardheslaig 149 C12
Ardiecow 152 B5
Ardindrean 150 C4
Ardingly 17 B7
Ardington 38 F4
Ardlair 140 B4
Ardlamont
House 145 G8
Ardleigh 43 B6
Ardler 134 E2
Ardley 39 B5
Ardlui 126 C2
Ardlussa 144 E5
Ardmair 150 B4
Ardmay 125 E8
Ardminish 143 D7
Ardmolich 147 D10
Ardmore
Argyll 124 C3
Highld 151 C10
Highld 156 D5
Ardnacross 147 G8
Ardnadam 145 F10
Ardnagrask 151 G8
Ardnarff 149 E13
Ardnastang 130 C2
Ardnave 142 A3
Ardno 125 E7
Ardo 153 E8
Ardoch 133 F7
Ardochy House 136 D5
Ardo House 141 B8
Ardoyne 141 B5
Ardpatrick 144 G6
Ardpatrick
House 144 H6
Ardpeaton 145 E11
Ardrishaig 145 E7
Ardross
Fife 129 D7
Highld 151 D9
Ardrossan 118 E2
Ardross Castle 151 D9
Ardshealach 147 E9
Ardsley 88 D4
Ardslignish 147 E8
Ardtalla 142 C5
Ardtalnaig 132 F4
Ardtoe 147 D9
Ardtrostan 127 B5
Arduaine 124 D3
Ardullie 151 E8
Ardvasar 149 H11
Ardvorlich 126 B5
Ardwell 104 E5
Ardwell Mains 104 E5
Ardwick 87 E6
Areley Kings 50 B3
Arford 27 F6
Argoed
Caerph 35 E5
Powys 47 C8
Arichamish 124 E5
Arichastlich 125 B8
Aridhglas 146 J6
Arileod 146 F4
Arinacrinachd 149 C12
Arinagour 146 F5
Arion 159 G3
Arisaig 147 C9
Ariundle 130 C2
Arkendale 95 C6
Arkesden 55 F5
Arkholme 93 B5
Arkleton 115 E6
Arkle Town 101 D5
Arkley 41 E5
Arksey 89 D6
Arkwright Town 76 B4
Arle 37 B6
Arlecdon 98 C2
Arlesey 54 F2
Arleston 61 C6
Arley 86 F4
Arlingham 36 C4
Arlington
Devon 20 E5
E Sus 18 E2
Glos 37 D8
Armadale
Highld 157 C10
W Loth 120 C2
Armadale
Castle 149 H11
Armathwaite 108 E5
Arminghall 69 D5
Armitage 62 C4
Armley 95 F5
Armscote 51 E7
Armthorpe 89 D7
Arnabost 146 F5
Arncliffe 94 B2
Arncroach 129 D7
Arne 13 F7
Arnesby 64 E3
Arngask 128 C3
Arnisdale 149 G13
Arnish 149 D10
Arniston Engine 121 C6
Arnol 155 C8
Arnold
E Yorks 97 E7
Notts 77 E5
Arnprior 126 E5
Arnside 92 B4
Aros Mains 147 G8
Arowry 73 F8
Arpafeelie 151 F9
Arrad Foot 99 F5
Arram 97 E6
Arrathorne 101 E7
Arreton 15 F6
Arrington 54 D4
Arrivain 125 B8
Arrochar 125 E8
Arrow 51 D5
Arthington 95 E5
Arthingworth 64 F4
Arthog 58 C3
Arthrath 153 E9
Arthurstone 134 E2
Artrochie 153 E10
Arundel 16 D4
Aryhoulan 130 C4
Asby 98 B2
Ascog 145 G10
Ascot 27 C7
Ascott 51 F8
Ascott-under-
Wychwood 38 C3
Asenby 95 B6
Asfordby 64 C4
Asfordby Hill 64 C4
Asgarby
Lincs 78 E4
Lincs 79 C6
Ash
Kent 29 C6
Kent 31 D6
Som 12 B2
Sur 27 D6
Ashampstead 26 B3
Ashbocking 57 D5
Ashbourne 75 E8
Ashbrittle 11 B5
Ash Bullayne 10 D2
Ashburton 7 C5
Ashbury
Devon 9 E7
Oxon 38 F2
Ashby 90 D3
Ashby by Partney 79 C7
Ashby cum Fenby 91 D6
Ashby de la
Launde 78 D3
Ashby-de-la-
Zouch 63 C7
Ashby Folville 64 C4
Ashby Magna 64 E2
Ashby Parva 64 F2
Ashby Puerorum 79 B6
Ashby St Ledgers 52 C3
Ashby St Mary 69 D6
Ashchurch 50 F4
Ashcombe 7 B7
Ashcott 23 F6
Ashdon 55 E6
Ashe 26 E3
Asheldham 43 D5
Ashen 55 E8
Ashendon 39 C7
Ashfield
Carms 33 B7
Stirling 127 D6
Suff 57 C6
Ashfield Green 57 B6
Ashfold
Crossways 17 B6
Ashford
Devon 20 F4
Hants 14 C2
Kent 30 E4
Sur 27 B8
Ashford Bowdler 49 B7
Ashford
Carbonell 49 B7
Ashford Hill 26 C3
Ashford in the
Water 75 C8
Ashgill 119 E7
Ash Green 63 F7
Ashill
Devon 11 C5
Norf 67 D8
Som 11 C8
Ashingdon 42 E4
Ashington
Northumb 117 F8
Ashington *continued*
Som 12 B3
W Sus 16 C5
Ashintully
Castle 133 C8
Ashkirk 115 B7
Ashlett 15 D5
Ashleworth 37 B5
Ashley
Cambs 55 C7
Ches E 87 F5
Devon 9 C8
Dorset 14 D2
Glos 37 E6
Hants 14 E3
Hants 25 F8
Northants 64 E4
Staffs 74 F4
Ashley Green 40 D2
Ashley Heath
Dorset 14 D2
Staffs 74 F4
Ash Magna 74 F2
Ashmanhaugh 69 B6
Ashmansworth 26 D2
Ashmansworthy 8 C5
Ash Mill 10 B2
Ashmore 13 C7
Ashorne 51 D8
Ashover 76 C3
Ashow 51 B8
Ashprington 7 D6
Ash Priors 11 B6
Ashreigney 9 C8
Ash Street 56 E4
Ashtead 28 D2
Ash Thomas 10 C5
Ashton
Ches W 74 C2
Corn 2 D5
Hants 15 C6
Hereford 49 C7
Involyd 118 B2
Northants 53 E5
Northants 65 F7
Ashton Common 24 D3
Ashton-in-
Makerfield 86 E3
Ashton Keynes 37 E7
Ashton under Hill 50 F4
Ashton-under-
Lyne 87 E7
Ashton upon
Mersey 87 E5
Ashurst
Hants 14 C4
Kent 18 B2
W Sus 17 C5
Ashurstwood 28 F5
Ash Vale 27 D6
Ashwater 9 E5
Ashwell
Herts 54 F3
Rutland 65 C5
Som 11 C8
Ashwellthorpe 68 E4
Ashwick 23 E8
Ashwicken 67 C7
Ashybank 115 C8
Askam in Furness 92 B2
Askern 89 C6
Askerswell 12 E3
Askett 39 D8
Askham
Cumb 99 B7
Notts 77 B7
Askham Bryan 95 E8
Askham Richard 95 E8
Asknish 145 D8
Askrigg 100 E4
Askwith 94 E4
Aslackby 78 F3
Aslacton 68 E4
Aslockton 77 F7
Asloun 140 C4
Aspatria 107 E8
Aspenden 41 B6
Asperton 79 F5
Aspley Guise 53 F7
Aspley Heath 53 F7
Aspull 86 D4
Asselby 89 B8
Asserby 79 B7
Assington 56 F3
Assynt House 151 E8
Astbury 74 C5
Astcote 52 D4
Asterley 60 D3
Asterton 60 E3
Asthall 38 C2
Asthall Leigh 38 C3
Astley
Shrops 60 C5
Warks 63 F7
Worcs 50 C2
Astley Abbotts 61 E7
Astley Bridge 86 C5
Astley Cross 50 C3
Astley Green 86 E5
Aston
Ches E 74 E3
Ches W 74 B2
Derbys 88 F2
Hereford 49 B6
Herts 41 B5
Oxon 38 D3
Shrops 60 B5
Staffs 74 E4
S Yorks 89 F5
Telford 61 D6
W Mid 62 F4
Wokingham 39 F7
Aston Abbotts 39 B8
Aston Botterell 61 F6
Aston-by-Stone 75 F6
Aston Cantlow 51 D6
Aston Clinton 40 C1
Aston Crews 36 B3
Aston Cross 50 F4
Aston End 41 B5
Aston Eyre 61 E6
Aston Fields 50 C4
Aston Flamville 63 E8
Aston Ingham 36 B3
Aston juxta
Mondrum 74 D3
Aston le Walls 52 D2
Aston Magna 51 F6
Aston Munslow 60 F5
Aston on Clun 60 F3
Aston-on-Trent 63 B8
Aston Rogers 60 D3
Aston Rowant 39 E7
Aston Sandford 39 D7
Aston Somerville 50 F5
Aston Subedge 51 E6
Aston Tirrold 39 F5
Aston Upthorpe 39 F5
Astrop 52 F3
Astwick 54 F3
Astwood
M Keynes 53 E7
Worcs 50 D3
Astwood Bank 50 C5
Aswarby 78 F3
Aswardby 79 B6
Atcham 60 D5
Atch Lench 50 D5
Athelhampton 13 E5
Athelington 57 B6
Athelney 11 B8
Athelstaneford 121 B8
Atherington 9 B7
Atherstone 63 E7
Atherstone on
Stour 51 D7
Atherton 86 D4
Atley Hill 101 D7
Atlow 76 E2
Attadale 150 H2
Attadale House 150 H2
Attenborough 76 F5
Atterby 90 E3
Attercliffe 88 F4
Attleborough
Norf 68 E3
Warks 63 E7
Attlebridge 68 C4
Atwick 97 D7
Atworth 24 C3
Aubourn 78 C2
Auchagallon 143 E9
Auchallater 139 F7
Aucharnie 153 D6
Auchattie 141 E5
Auchavan 134 C1
Auchbreck 139 B8
Auchenback 118 D5
Auchenbainzie 113 E8
Auchenblae 135 B7
Auchenbrack 113 E7
Auchenbreck 145 E9
Auchencairn
Dumfries 106 D4
Dumfries 114 F2
N Ayrs 143 F11
Auchencrosh 104 B5
Auchencrow 122 C4
Auchendinny 121 C5
Auchengray 120 D2
Auchenhalrig 152 B3
Auchenheath 119 E8
Auchenlochan 145 F8
Auchenmalg 105 D6
Auchensoul 112 E2
Auchentiber 118 E3
Auchertyre 149 F13
Auchgourish 138 C5
Auchincarroch 126 F3
Auchindrain 125 E6
Auchindrean 150 C4
Auchininna 153 D6
Auchinleck 113 B5
Auchinloch 119 B6
Auchinroath 152 C2
Auchintoul 140 C4
Auchiries 153 E10
Auchlee 141 E7
Auchleven 140 B5
Auchlochan 119 F8
Auchlossan 140 D4
Auchlunies 141 E7
Auchlyne 126 B4
Auchmacoy 153 E9
Auchmair 140 B2
Auchmantle 105 C5
Auchmillan 112 B5
Auchmithie 135 E6
Auchmuirbridge 128 D4
Auchmull 135 B5
Auchnacree 134 C4
Auchnagallin 151 H13
Auchnagatt 153 D9
Auchnaha 145 E8
Auchnashelloch 127 C6
Aucholzie 140 E2
Auchrannie 134 D2
Auchroisk 139 B6
Auchronie 140 F3
Auchterarder 127 C8
Auchteraw 137 D6
Auchterderran 128 E4
Auchterhouse 134 F3
Auchtermuchty 128 C4
Auchterneed 150 F7
Auchtertool 128 E4
Auchtertyre 152 C1
Auchtubh 126 B4
Auckengill 158 D5
Auckley 89 D7
Audenshaw 87 E7
Audlem 74 E3
Audley 74 D4
Audley End 56 F2
Auds 153 B6
Aughton
E Yorks 96 F3
Lancs 85 D4
Lancs 93 C5
S Yorks 89 F5
Wilts 25 D7
Aughton Park 86 D2
Auldearn 151 F12
Aulden 49 D6
Auldgirth 114 F2
Auldhame 129 F7
Auldhouse 119 D6
Ault a'chruinn 136 B2
Aultanrynie 156 F6
Aultbea 155 J13
Aultdearg 150 E5
Aultgrishan 155 J12
Aultguish Inn 150 D6
Aultibea 157 G13
Aultiphurst 157 C11
Aultmore 152 C4
Aultnagoire 137 B8
Aultnamain Inn 151 C9
Aultnaslat 136 D4
Aulton 140 B5
Aundorach 139 C5
Aunsby 78 F3
Auquhorthies 141 B7
Aust 36 F2
Austendike 66 B2
Austerfield 89 E7
Austrey 63 D6
Austwick 93 C7
Authorpe 91 F8
Authorpe Row 79 B8
Avebury 25 C6
Aveley 42 F1
Avening 37 E5
Averham 77 D7
Aveton Gifford 6 E4
Avielochan 138 C5
Aviemore 138 C4
Avington
Hants 26 F3
W Berks 25 C8
Avoch 151 F10
Avon 14 E2
Avonbridge 120 B2
Avon Dassett 52 E2
Avonmouth 23 B7
Avonwick 6 D5
Awbridge 14 B4
Awhirk 104 D4
Awkley 36 F2
Awliscombe 11 D6
Awre 36 D4
Awsworth 76 E4
Axbridge 23 D6
Axford
Hants 26 E4
Wilts 25 B7
Axminster 11 E7
Axmouth 11 E7
Axton 85 F2
Aycliff 31 E7
Aycliffe 101 B7
Aydon 110 C3
Aylburton 36 D3
Ayle 109 E7
Aylesbeare 10 E5
Aylesbury 39 C8
Aylesby 91 D6
Aylesford 29 D8
Aylesham 31 D6
Aylestone 64 D2
Aylmerton 81 D7
Aylsham 81 E7
Aylton 49 F8
Aymestrey 49 C6
Aynho 52 F3
Ayot St Lawrence 40 C4
Ayot St Peter 41 C5
Ayr 112 B3
Aysgarth 101 F5
Ayside 99 F5
Ayston 65 D5
Aythorpe Roding 42 C1
Ayton 122 C5
Aywick 160 E7
Azerley 95 B5

B

Babbacombe 7 C7
Babbinswood 73 F7
Babcary 12 B3
Babel 47 F7
Babell 73 B5
Babraham 55 D6
Babworth 89 F7
Bac 155 C9
Bachau 82 C4
Backaland 159 E6
Backaskaill 159 C5
Backbarrow 99 F5
Backe 32 C3
Backfolds 153 C10
Backford 73 B8
Backford Cross 73 B7
Backhill
Aberds 153 E7
Aberds 153 E10
Backhill of
Clackriach 153 D9
Backhill of
Fortree 153 D9
Backhill of
Trustach 140 E5
Backies 157 J11
Backlass 158 E4
Back of
Keppoch 147 C9
Back Rogerton 113 B5
Backwell 23 C6
Backworth 111 B6
Bacon End 42 C2
Baconsthorpe 81 D7
Bacton
Hereford 49 F5
Norf 81 D9
Suff 56 C4
Bacton Green 56 C4
Bacup 87 B6
Badachro 149 A12
Badanloch
Lodge 157 F10
Badavanich 150 F4
Badbury 38 F1
Badby 52 D3
Badcall 156 D5
Badcaul 150 B3
Baddeley Green 75 D6
Baddesley
Clinton 51 B7
Baddesley Ensor 63 E6
Baddidarach 156 G3
Baddoch 139 F7
Baddock 151 F10
Badenscoth 153 E7
Badenyon 140 C2
Badger 61 E7
Badger's Mount 29 C5
Badgeworth 37 C6
Badgworth 23 D5
Badicaul 149 F12
Badingham 57 C7
Badlesmere 30 D4
Badlipster 158 F4
Badluarach 150 B2
Badminton 37 F5
Badnaban 156 G3
Badninish 151 B10
Badrallach 150 B3
Badsey 51 E5
Badshot Lea 27 E6
Badsworth 89 C5
Badwell Ash 56 C3
Bae Colwyn
=Colwyn Bay 83 D8
Bagby 102 F2
Bag Enderby 79 B6
Bagendon 37 D7
Bagh a Chaisteil
=Castlebay 148 J1
Baghasdal 148 G2
Bagh Mor 148 C3
Bagh
Shiarabhagh 148 H2
Bagillt 73 B6
Baginton 51 B8
Baglan 33 E8
Bagley 60 B4
Bagnall 75 D6
Bagnor 26 C2
Bagshot
Sur 27 C7
Wilts 25 C8
Bagthorpe
Norf 80 D3
Notts 76 D4
Bagworth 63 D8
Bagwy Llydiart 35 B8
Bail Àrd
Bhuirgh 155 B9
Baildon 94 F4
Baile 154 J4
Baile Ailein 155 E7
Baile a
Mhanaich 148 C2
Baile an Truiseil 155 B8
Bailebeag 137 C8
Baile Boidheach 144 F6
Baile Glas 148 C3
Baile Mhartainn 148 A2
Baile Mhic Phail 148 A3
Baile Mor
Argyll 146 J5
W Isles 148 B2
Baile na Creige 148 H1
Baile nan
Cailleach 148 C2
Baile Raghaill 148 A2
Baileyhead 108 B5
Bailiesward 152 E4
Baillieston 119 C6
Bail'lochdrach 148 C3
Bail Uachdraich 148 B3
Bail'Ur
Tholastaidh 155 C10
Bainbridge 100 E4
Bainsford 127 F7
Bainshole 152 E6
Bainton
E Yorks 97 D5
Pboro 65 D7
Bairnkine 116 C2
Baker's End 41 C6
Baker Street 42 F2
Bakewell 76 C2
Bala =Y Bala 72 F3
Balachuirn 149 D10
Balavil 138 D3
Balbeg
Highld 137 B7
Highld 150 H7
Balbeggie 128 B3
Balbithan 141 C6
Balbithan House 141 C7
Balblair
Highld 151 B8
Highld 151 E10
Balby 89 D6
Balchladich 156 F3
Balchraggan
Highld 151 G8
Highld 151 H8
Balchrick 156 D4
Balchrystie 129 D6
Balcladaich 137 B5
Balcombe 28 F4
Balcombe Lane 28 F4
Balcomie 129 C8
Balcurvie 128 D5
Baldersby 95 B6
Baldersby St
James 95 B6
Balderstone 93 F6
Balderton
Ches W 73 C7
Notts 77 D8
Baldhu 3 B6
Baldinnie 129 C6
Baldock 54 F3
Baldovie 134 F4
Baldrine 84 D4
Baldslow 18 D4
Baldwin 84 D3
Baldwinholme 108 D3
Baldwin's Gate 74 E4
Bale 81 D6
Balearn 153 C10
Balemartine 146 G2
Balephuil 146 G2
Balerno 120 C4
Balevullin 146 G2
Balfield 135 C5
Balfour 159 G5
Balfron 126 F4
Balfron Station 126 F4
Balgaveny 153 D6
Balgavies 135 D5
Balgonar 128 E2
Balgove 153 E8
Balgowan 138 E2
Balgown 149 B8
Balgrochan 119 B6
Balgy 149 C13
Balhaldie 127 D7
Balhalgardy 141 B6
Balham 28 B3
Balhary 134 E2
Baliasta 160 C8
Baligill 157 C11
Balintore
Angus 134 D2
Highld 151 D11
Balintraid 151 D10
Balk 102 F2
Balkeerie 134 E3
Balkemback 134 F3
Balkholme 89 B8
Balkissock 104 A5
Ball 60 B3
Ballabeg 84 E2
Ballacannel 84 D4
Ballachulish 130 D4
Ballajora 84 C4
Ballaleigh 84 D3
Ballamodha 84 E2
Ballantrae 104 A4
Ballaquine 84 D4
Ballards Gore 43 E5
Ballasalla
IoM 84 C3
IoM 84 E2
Ballater 140 E2
Ballaugh 84 C3
Ballaveare 84 E3
Ballcorach 139 B7
Ballechin 133 D6
Balleigh 151 C10
Ballencrieff 121 B7
Ballentoul 133 C5
Ball Haye Green 75 D6
Ball Hill 26 C2
Ballidon 76 D2
Balliemore
Argyll 124 C4
Argyll 145 E9
Ballikinrain 126 F4
Ballimeanoch 125 D6
Ballimore
Argyll 145 E8
Stirling 126 C4
Ballinaby 142 B3
Ballindean 128 B4
Ballingdon 56 E2
Ballinger
Common 40 D2
Ballingham 49 F7
Ballingry 128 E3
Ballinlick 133 E6
Ballinluig 133 D6
Ballintuim 133 D8
Balloch
Angus 134 D3
Highld 151 G10
N Lanark 119 B7
W Dunb 126 F2
Ballochan 140 E4
Ballochford 152 E3
Ballochmorrie 112 F2
Balls Cross 16 B3
Balls Green 43 B6
Ballygown 146 G7
Ballygrant 142 B4
Ballyhaugh 146 F4
Balmacara 149 F13
Balmacara
Square 149 F13
Balmaclellan 106 B3
Balmacneil 133 D6
Balmacqueen 149 A9
Balmae 106 E3
Balmaha 126 E3
Balmalcolm 128 D5
Balmeanach 149 D10
Balmedie 141 C8
Balmer Heath 73 F8
Balmerino 129 B5
Balmerlawn 14 D4
Balmichael 143 E10
Balmirmer 135 F5
Balmore
Highld 149 D7
Highld 150 H6
Highld 151 G11
Perth 133 D6
Balmule 128 F4
Balmullo 129 B6
Balmungie 151 F10
Balnaboth 134 C3
Balnabruaich 151 E10
Balnabruich 158 H3
Balnacoil 157 H11
Balnacra 150 G2
Balnafoich 151 H9
Balnagall 151 C11
Balnaguard 133 D6
Balnahard
Argyll 144 D3
Argyll 146 H7
Balnain 150 H7
Balnakeil 156 C6
Balnaknock 149 B9
Balnapaling 151 E10
Balne 89 C6
Balochroy 143 C8
Balone 129 C6
Balornock 119 C6
Balquharn 133 F7
Balquhidder 126 B4
Balsall 51 B7
Balsall Common 51 B7
Balsall Heath 62 F4
Balscott 51 E8
Balsham 55 D6
Baltasound 160 C8
Balterley 74 D4
Baltersan 105 C8
Balthangie 153 C8
Baltonsborough 23 F7
Balvaird 151 F8
Balvicar 124 D3
Balvraid
Highld 149 G13
Highld 151 H11
Bamber Bridge 86 B3
Bambers Green 42 B1
Bamburgh 123 F7
Bamff 134 D2
Bamford
Derbys 88 F3
Gtr Man 87 C6
Bampton
Cumb 99 C7
Devon 10 B4
Oxon 38 D3
Bampton
Grange 99 C7
Banavie 131 B5
Banbury 52 E2
Bancffosfelen 33 C5
Banchory 141 E5
Banchory-
Devenick 141 D8
Bancycapel 33 C5
Bancyfelin 32 C4
Bancyffordd 46 F3
Bandirran 134 F2
Banff 153 B6
Bangor 83 D5
Bangor-is-y-coed
=Bangor-on-Dee 73 E7
Bangor-on-Dee
=Bangor-is-y-
coed 73 E7
Banham 68 F3
Bank 14 D3
Bankend 107 C7
Bankfoot 133 F7
Bankglen 113 C6
Bankhead
Aberdeen 141 C7
Aberds 141 D5
Bank Newton 94 D2
Banknock 119 B7
Banks
Cumb 109 C5
Lancs 85 B4
Bankshill 114 F4
Bank Street 49 C8
Banningham 81 E8
Banniskirk
House 158 E3
Bannister Green 42 B2
Bannockburn 127 E7
Banstead 28 D3
Bantham 6 E4
Banton 119 B7
Banwell 23 D5
Banyard's Green 57 B6
Bapchild 30 C3
Barabhas 155 C8
Barabhas Iarach 155 C8
Barabhas
Uarach 155 B8
Barachandroman 124 C2
Barassie 118 F3
Baravullin 124 E4
Barbaraville 151 D10
Barber Booth 88 F2
Barbieston 112 C4
Barbon 99 F8
Barbridge 74 D3
Barbrook 21 E6
Barby 52 B3
Barcaldine 130 E3
Barcheston 51 F7
Barcombe 17 C8
Barcombe Cross 17 C8
Barden 101 E6
Bardennoch 113 E5
Barden Scale 94 D3
Bardfield Saling 42 B2
Bardister 160 F5
Bardney 78 C4
Bardon 63 C8
Bardon Mill 109 C7
Bardowie 119 B5
Bardrainney 118 B3
Bardsea 92 B3
Bardsey 95 E6
Bardwell 56 B3
Bare 92 C4
Barfad 145 G7
Barford
Norf 68 D4
Warks 51 C7
Barford St John 52 F2
Barford
St Martin 25 F5
Barford St
Michael 52 F2
Barfrestone 31 D6
Bargod
=Bargoed 35 E5
Bargoed
=Bargod 35 E5
Bargrennan 105 B7
Barham
Cambs 54 B2
Kent 31 D6
Suff 56 D5
Barharrow 106 D3
Barhill 106 C5
Bar Hill 54 C4
Barholm 65 C7
Barkby 64 D3
Barkestone-le-
Vale 77 F7
Barkham 27 C5
Barking
London 41 F7
Suff 56 D4
Barkingside 41 F7
Barking Tye 56 D4
Barkisland 87 C8
Barkston
Lincs 78 E2
N Yorks 95 F7
Barkway 54 F4
Barlaston 75 F5
Barlavington 16 C3
Barlborough 76 B4
Barlby 96 F2
Barlestone 63 D8
Barley
Herts 54 F4
Lancs 93 E8
Barley Mow 111 D5
Barleythorpe 64 D5
Barling 43 F5
Barlow
Derbys 76 B3
N Yorks 89 B7
T&W 110 C4
Barmby Moor 96 E3
Barmby on the
Marsh 89 B7
Barmer 80 D4
Barmoor Castle 123 F5
Barmoor Lane
End 123 F6
Barmouth
=Abermaw 58 C3
Barmpton 101 C8
Barmston 97 D7
Barnack 65 D7
Barnacle 63 F7
Barnard Castle 101 C6

Barnard Gate 38 C4
Barnardiston 55 E8
Barnbarroch 106 D5
Barnburgh 89 D5
Barnby 69 F7
Barnby Dun 89 D7
Barnby in the Willows 77 D8
Barnby Moor 89 F7
Barnes Street 29 E7
Barnet 41 E5
Barnetby le Wold 90 D4
Barney 81 D5
Barnham
 Suff 56 B2
 W Sus 16 D3
Barnham Broom 68 D3
Barnhead 135 D6
Barnhill
 Ches W 73 D8
 Dundee 134 F4
 Moray 152 C1
Barnhills 104 B3
Barningham
 Durham 101 C5
 Suff 56 B3
Barnoldby le Beck 91 D6
Barnoldswick 93 E8
Barns Green 16 B5
Barnsley
 Glos 37 D7
 S Yorks 88 D4
Barnstaple 20 F4
Barnston
 Essex 42 C2
 Mers 85 F3
Barnstone 77 F7
Barnt Green 50 B5
Barnton
 Ches W 74 B3
 Edin 120 B4
Barnwell All Saints 65 F7
Barnwell St Andrew 65 F7
Barnwood 37 C5
Barochreal 124 C4
Barons Cross 49 D6
Barr 112 E2
Barra Castle 141 B6
Barrachan 105 E7
Barrack 153 D8
Barraglom 154 D6
Barrahormid 144 E6
Barran 124 C4
Barrapol 146 G2
Barras
 Aberds 141 F7
 Cumb 100 C3
Barrasford 110 B2
Barravullin 124 E4
Barregarrow 84 D3
Barrhead 118 D4
Barrhill 112 F2
Barrington
 Cambs 54 E4
 Som 11 C8
Barripper 2 C5
Barrmill 118 D3
Barrock 158 C4
Barrock House 158 D4
Barrow
 Lancs 93 F7
 Rutland 65 C5
 Suff 55 C8
Barroway Drove 67 D5
Barrowburn 116 C4
Barrowby 77 F8
Barrowcliff 103 F8
Barrowden 65 D6
Barrowford 93 F8
Barrow Green 30 C3
Barrow Gurney 23 C7
Barrow Haven 90 B4
Barrow-in-Furness 92 C2
Barrow Island 92 C1
Barrow Nook 86 D2
Barrows Green
 Ches E 74 D3
 Cumb 99 F7
Barrow's Green 86 F3
Barrow Street 24 F3
Barrow upon Humber 90 B4
Barrow upon Soar 64 C2
Barrow upon Trent 63 B7
Barry 135 F5
Barry = Y Barri 22 C3
Barry Island 22 C3
Barsby 64 C3
Barsham 69 F6
Barston 51 B7
Bartestree 49 E7
Barthol Chapel 153 E8
Barthomley 74 D4
Bartley 14 C4
Bartley Green 62 F4
Bartlow 55 E6
Barton
 Cambs 54 D5
 Ches W 73 D8
 Glos 37 B8
 Lancs 85 D4
 Lancs 92 F5
 N Yorks 101 D7
 Oxon 39 D5
 Torbay 7 C7
 Warks 51 D6
Barton Bendish 67 D7
Barton Hartshorn 52 F4
Barton in Fabis 76 F5
Barton in the Beans 63 D7
Barton-le-Clay 53 F8
Barton-le-Street 96 B3
Barton-le-Willows 96 C3
Barton Mills 55 B8
Barton on Sea 14 E3
Barton on the Heath 51 F7
Barton St David 23 F7
Barton Seagrave 53 B6
Barton Stacey 26 E2
Barton Turf 69 B6
Barton-under-Needwood 63 C5
Barton-upon-Humber 90 B4
Barton Waterside 90 B4
Barugh 88 D4
Barway 55 B6
Barwell 63 E8
Barwick
 Herts 41 C6
 Som 12 C3
Barwick in Elmet 95 F6
Baschurch 60 B4
Bascote 52 C2
Basford Green 75 D6
Bashall Eaves 93 E6
Bashley 14 E3
Basildon 42 F3
Basingstoke 26 D4
Baslow 76 B2
Bason Bridge 22 E5
Bassaleg 35 F6
Bassenthwaite 108 F2
Bassett 14 C5
Bassingbourn 54 E4
Bassingfield 77 F6
Bassingham 78 C2
Bassingthorpe 65 B6
Basta 160 D7
Baston 65 C8
Bastwick 69 C7
Baswick Steer 97 E6
Batchworth Heath 40 E3
Batcombe
 Dorset 12 D4
 Som 23 F8
Bate Heath 74 B3
Batford 40 C4
Bath 24 C2
Bathampton 24 C2
Bathealton 11 B5
Batheaston 24 C2
Bathford 24 C2
Bathgate 120 C2
Bathley 77 D7
Bathpool
 Corn 5 B7
 Som 11 B7
Bathville 120 C2
Batley 88 B3
Batsford 51 F6
Battersby 102 D3
Battersea 28 B3
Battisborough Cross 6 E3
Battisford 56 D4
Battisford Tye 56 D4
Battle
 E Sus 18 D4
 Powys 48 F2
Battledown 37 B6
Battlefield 60 C5
Battlesbridge 42 E3
Battlesden 40 B2
Battlesea Green 57 B6
Battleton 10 B4
Battram 63 D8
Battramsley 14 E4
Baughton 50 E3
Baughurst 26 D3
Baulking 38 E3
Baumber 78 B5
Baunton 37 D7
Baverstock 24 F5
Bawburgh 68 D4
Bawdeswell 81 E6
Bawdrip 22 F5
Bawdsey 57 E7
Bawtry 89 E7
Baxenden 87 B5
Baxterley 63 E6
Baybridge 15 B6
Baycliff 92 B2
Baydon 25 B7
Bayford
 Herts 41 D6
 Som 12 B5
Bayles 109 E7
Baylham 56 D5
Baynard's Green 39 B5
Bayston Hill 60 D4
Baythorn End 55 E8
Bayton 49 B8
Beach 130 D1
Beachampton 53 F5
Beachamwell 67 D7
Beachans 151 G13
Beacharr 143 D7
Beachborough 19 B8
Beachley 36 E2
Beacon 11 D6
Beacon End 43 B5
Beacon Hill 27 F6
Beacon's Bottom 39 E7
Beaconsfield 40 F2
Beacrabhaic 154 H6
Beadlam 102 F4
Beadlow 54 F2
Beadnell 117 B8
Beaford 9 C7
Beal
 Northumb 123 E6
 N Yorks 89 B6
Beamhurst 75 F7
Beaminster 12 D2
Beamish 110 D5
Beamsley 94 D3
Bean 29 B6
Beanacre 24 C4
Beanley 117 C6
Beaquoy 159 F4
Bear Cross 13 E8
Beardwood 86 B4
Beare Green 28 E2
Bearley 51 C6
Bearnus 146 G6
Bearpark 110 E5
Bearsbridge 109 D7
Bearsden 118 B5
Bearsted 29 D8
Bearstone 74 F4
Bearwood
 BCP 13 E8
 Hereford 49 D5
 W Mid 62 F4
Beattock 114 D3
Beauchamp Roding 42 C1
Beauchief 88 F4
Beaufort 35 C5
Beaufort Castle 151 G8
Beaulieu 14 D4
Beauly 151 G8
Beaumaris 83 D6
Beaumont
 Cumb 108 D3
 Essex 43 B7
Beaumont Hill 101 C7
Beausale 51 B7
Beauworth 15 B6
Beaworthy 9 E6
Beazley End 42 B3
Bebington 85 F4
Bebside 117 F8
Beccles 69 E7
Becconsall 86 B2
Beckbury 61 D7
Beckenham 28 C4
Beckermet 98 D2
Beckfoot
 Cumb 98 D3
 Cumb 107 E7
Beck Foot 99 E8
Beckford 50 F4
Beckhampton 25 C5
Beck Hole 103 D6
Beckingham
 Lincs 77 D8
 Notts 89 F8
Beckington 24 D3
Beckley
 E Sus 19 C5
 Hants 14 E3
 Oxon 39 C5
Beck Row 55 B7
Beck Side 98 F4
Beckton 41 F7
Beckwithshaw 95 D5
Becontree 41 F7
Bedale 101 F7
Bedburn 110 F4
Bedchester 13 C6
Beddau 34 F4
Beddgelert 71 C6
Beddingham 17 D8
Beddington 28 C4
Bedfield 57 C6
Bedford 53 D8
Bedham 16 B4
Bedhampton 15 D8
Bedingfield 57 C5
Bedlam 95 C5
Bedlington 117 F8
Bedlington Station 117 F8
Bedlinog 34 D4
Bedminster 23 B7
Bedmond 40 D3
Bednall 62 C3
Bedrule 116 C2
Bedstone 49 B5
Bedwas 35 F5
Bedworth 63 F7
Bedworth Heath 63 F7
Bed-y-coedwr 71 E8
Beeby 64 D3
Beech
 Hants 26 F4
 Staffs 75 F5
Beech Hill
 Gtr Man 86 D3
 W Berks 26 C4
Beechingstoke 25 D5
Beedon 26 B2
Beeford 97 D7
Beeley 76 C2
Beelsby 91 D6
Beenham 26 C3
Beeny 8 E3
Beer 11 F7
Beercrocombe 11 B8
Beer Hackett 12 C3
Beesands 7 E6
Beesby 91 F8
Beeson 7 E6
Beeston
 C Beds 54 E2
 Ches W 74 D2
 Norf 68 C2
 Notts 76 F5
 W Yorks 95 F5
Beeston Regis 81 C7
Beeswing 107 C5
Beetham 92 B4
Beetley 68 C2
Begbroke 38 C4
Begelly 32 D2
Beggar's Bush 48 C4
Beguildy 48 B3
Beighton
 Norf 69 D6
 S Yorks 88 F5
Beighton Hill 76 D2
Beith 118 D3
Bekesbourne 31 D5
Belaugh 69 C5
Belbroughton 50 B4
Belchamp Otten 56 E2
Belchamp St Paul 55 E8
Belchamp Walter 56 E2
Belchford 79 B5
Belford 123 F7
Belhaven 122 B2
Belhelvie 141 C8
Belhinnie 140 B3
Bellabeg 140 C2
Bellamore 112 F2
Bellanoch 144 D6
Bellaty 134 D2
Bell Bar 41 D5
Bell Busk 94 D2
Belleau 79 B7
Bellehiglash 152 E1
Bell End 50 B4
Bellerby 101 E6
Bellever 6 B4
Belliehill 135 C5
Bellingdon 40 D2
Bellingham 116 F4
Belloch 143 E7
Bellochantuy 143 E7
Bell o'th'Hill 74 E2
Bellsbank 112 D4
Bellshill
 N Lanark 119 C7
 Northumb 123 F7
Bellspool 120 F4
Bellsquarry 120 C3
Bells Yew Green 18 B3
Belmaduthy 151 F9
Belmesthorpe 65 C7
Belmont
 Blackburn 86 C4
 London 28 C3
 S Ayrs 112 B3
 Shetland 160 C7
Belnacraig 140 C2
Belowda 4 C4
Belper 76 E3
Belper Lane End 76 E3
Belsay 110 B4
Belses 115 B8
Belsford 7 D5
Belstead 56 E5
Belston 112 B3
Belstone 9 E8
Belthorn 86 B5
Beltinge 31 C5
Beltoft 90 D2
Belton
 Leics 63 B8
 Lincs 78 F2
 N Lincs 89 D8
 Norf 69 D7
Belton in Rutland 64 D5
Beltring 29 E7
Belts of Collonach 141 E5
Belvedere 29 B5
Belvoir 77 F8
Bembridge 15 F7
Bemersyde 121 F8
Bemerton 25 F6
Bempton 97 B7
Benacre 69 F8
Ben Alder Lodge 132 B2
Ben Armine Lodge 157 H10
Benbuie 113 E7
Ben Casgro 155 E9
Benderloch 124 B5
Bendronaig Lodge 150 H3
Benenden 18 B5
Benfield 105 C7
Bengate 69 B6
Bengeworth 50 E5
Benhall Green 57 C7
Benhall Street 57 C7
Benholm 135 C8
Beningbrough 95 D8
Benington
 Herts 41 B5
 Lincs 79 E6
Benllech 82 C5
Benmore
 Argyll 145 E10
 Stirling 126 B3
Benmore Lodge 156 H6
Bennacott 8 E4
Bennan 143 F10
Benniworth 91 F6
Benover 29 E8
Bensham 110 C5
Benslie 118 E3
Benson 39 E6
Bent 135 B6
Bent Gate 87 B5
Benthall
 Northumb 117 B8
 Shrops 61 D6
Bentham 37 C6
Benthoul 141 D7
Bentlawnt 60 D3
Bentley
 E Yorks 97 F6
 Hants 27 E5
 Suff 56 F5
 S Yorks 89 D6
 Warks 63 E6
 Worcs 50 C4
Bentley Heath 51 B6
Benton 21 F5
Bentpath 115 E6
Bents 120 C2
Bentworth 26 E4
Benvie 134 F3
Benwick 66 E3
Beoley 51 C5
Beoraidbeg 147 B9
Bepton 16 C2
Berden 41 B7
Bere Alston 6 C2
Bere Ferrers 6 C2
Berepper 3 D5
Bere Regis 13 E6
Bergh Apton 69 D6
Berinsfield 39 E5
Berkeley 36 E3
Berkhamsted 40 D2
Berkley 24 E3
Berkswell 51 B7
Bermondsey 28 B4
Bernera 149 F13
Bernice 145 D10
Bernisdale 149 C9
Berrick Salome 39 E6
Berriedale 158 H3
Berrier 99 B5
Berriew 59 D8
Berrington
 Northumb 123 E6
 Shrops 60 D5
Berrow 22 D5
Berrow Green 50 D2
Berry Down Cross 20 E4
Berryfield 39 C7
Berry Hill
 Glos 36 C2
 Pembs 45 E2
Berryhillock 152 B5
Berrynarbor 20 E4
Berry Pomeroy 7 C6
Bersham 73 E7
Berstane 159 G5
Berwick 18 E2
Berwick Bassett 25 B5
Berwick Hill 110 B4
Berwick St James 25 F5
Berwick St John 13 B7
Berwick St Leonard 24 F4
Berwick-upon-Tweed 123 D5
Bescar 85 C4
Besford 50 E4
Bessacarr 89 D7
Bessels Leigh 38 D4
Bessingby 97 C7
Bessingham 81 D7
Bestbeech Hill 18 B3
Besthorpe
 Norf 68 E3
 Notts 77 C8
Bestwood 77 E5
Bestwood Village 77 E5
Beswick 97 E6
Betchworth 28 E3
Bethania
 Ceredig 46 C4
 Gwyn 71 C8
 Gwyn 83 F6
Bethel
 Anglesey 82 D3
 Gwyn 72 F3
 Gwyn 82 E5
Bethersden 30 E3
Bethesda
 Gwyn 83 E6
 Pembs 32 C1
Bethlehem 33 B7
Bethnal Green 41 F6
Betley 74 E4
Betsham 29 B7
Betteshanger 31 D7
Bettiscombe 11 E8
Bettisfield 73 F8
Betton
 Shrops 60 D3
 Shrops 74 F3
Bettws
 Bridgend 34 F3
 Mon 35 C6
 Newport 35 E6
Bettws Cedewain 59 E8
Bettws Gwerfil Goch 72 E4
Bettws Ifan 46 E2
Bettws Newydd 35 D7
Bettws-y-crwyn 60 F2
Bettyhill 157 C10
Betws 33 C7
Betws Bledrws 46 D4
Betws-Garmon 82 F5
Betws-y-Coed 83 F7
Betws-yn-Rhos 72 B3
Beulah
 Ceredig 45 E4
 Powys 47 D8
Bevendean 17 D7
Bevercotes 77 B6
Beverley 97 F6
Beverston 37 E5
Bevington 36 E3
Bewaldeth 108 F2
Bewcastle 109 B5
Bewdley 50 B2
Bewerley 94 C4
Bewholme 97 D7
Bexhill 18 E4
Bexley 29 B5
Bexleyheath 29 B5
Bexwell 67 D6
Beyton 56 C3
Bhaltos 154 D5
Bhatarsaigh 148 J1
Bibury 37 D8
Bicester 39 B5
Bickenhall 11 C7
Bickenhill 63 F5
Bicker 78 F5
Bickershaw 86 D4
Bickerstaffe 86 D2
Bickerton
 Ches E 74 D2
 N Yorks 95 D7
Bickington
 Devon 7 B5
 Devon 20 F4
Bickleigh
 Devon 6 C3
 Devon 10 D4
Bickleton 20 F4
Bickley 28 C5
Bickley Moss 74 E2
Bicknacre 42 D3
Bicknoller 22 F3
Bicknor 30 D2
Bickton 14 C2
Bicton
 Shrops 60 C4
 Shrops 60 F2
Bidborough 29 E6
Biddenden 19 B5
Biddenham 53 E8
Biddestone 24 B3
Biddisham 23 D5
Biddlesden 52 E4
Biddlestone 117 D5
Biddulph 75 D5
Biddulph Moor 75 D6
Bideford 9 B6
Bidford-on-Avon 51 D6
Bidston 85 E3
Bielby 96 E3
Bieldside 141 D7
Bierley
 IoW 15 G6
 W Yorks 94 F4
Bierton 39 C8
Bigbury 6 E4
Bigbury on Sea 6 E4
Bigby 90 D4
Biggar
 Cumb 92 C1
 S Lanark 120 F3
Biggin
 Derbys 75 D8
 Derbys 76 E2
 N Yorks 95 F8
Biggings 160 G3
Biggin Hill 28 D5
Biggleswade 54 E2
Bighouse 157 C11
Bighton 26 F4
Bignor 16 C3
Big Sand 149 A12
Bigton 160 L5
Bilberry 4 C5
Bilborough 76 E5
Bilbrook 22 E2
Bilbrough 95 E8
Bilbster 158 E4
Bildershaw 101 B7
Bildeston 56 E3
Billericay 42 E2
Billesdon 64 D4
Billesley 51 D6
Billingborough 78 F4
Billinge 86 D3
Billingford 81 E6
Billingham 102 B2
Billinghay 78 D4
Billingley 88 D5
Billingshurst 16 B4
Billingsley 61 F7
Billington
 C Beds 40 B2
 Lancs 93 F7
Billockby 69 C7
Billy Row 110 F4
Bilsborrow 92 F5
Bilsby 79 B7
Bilsham 16 D3
Bilsington 19 B7
Bilson Green 36 C3
Bilsthorpe 77 C6
Bilsthorpe Moor 77 D6
Bilston
 Midloth 121 C5
 W Mid 62 E3
Bilstone 63 D7
Bilting 30 E4
Bilton
 E Yorks 97 F7
 Northumb 117 C8
 Warks 52 B2
Bilton in Ainsty 95 E7
Bimbister 159 G4
Binbrook 91 E6
Binchester Blocks 110 F5
Bincombe 12 F4
Bindal 151 C12
Binegar 23 E8
Binfield 27 B6
Binfield Heath 26 B5
Bingfield 110 B2
Bingham 77 F7
Bingley 94 F4
Bings Heath 60 C5
Binham 81 D5
Binley
 Hants 26 D2
 W Mid 51 B8
Binley Woods 51 B8
Binniehill 119 B8
Binsoe 94 B5
Binstead 15 E6
Binsted 27 E5
Binton 51 D6
Bintree 81 E6
Binweston 60 D3
Birch
 Essex 43 C5
 Gtr Man 87 D6
Bircham Newton 80 D3
Bircham Tofts 80 D3
Birchanger 41 B8
Birchencliffe 88 C2
Bircher 49 C6
Birch Green 43 C5
Birchgrove
 Cardiff 22 B3
 Swansea 33 E8
Birch Heath 74 C2
Birch Hill 74 B2
Birchington 31 C6
Birchmoor 63 D6
Birchover 76 C2
Birch Vale 87 F8
Birchwood
 Lincs 78 C2
 Warr 86 E4
Bircotes 89 E7
Birdbrook 55 E8
Birdforth 95 B7
Birdham 16 E2
Birdholme 76 C3
Birdingbury 52 C2
Birdlip 37 C6
Birdsall 96 C4
Birds Edge 88 D3
Birdsgreen 61 F7
Birdsmoor Gate 11 D8
Birdston 119 B6
Birdwell 88 D4
Birdwood 36 C4
Birgham 122 F3
Birkby 101 D8
Birkdale 85 C4
Birkenhead 85 F4
Birkenhills 153 D7
Birkenshaw
 N Lanark 119 C6
 W Yorks 88 B3
Birkhall 140 E2
Birkhill
 Angus 134 F3
 Borders 114 C5
 Borders 115 B6
Birkholme 65 B6
Birkin 89 B6
Birley 49 D6
Birling
 Kent 29 C7
 Northumb 117 D8
Birling Gap 18 F2
Birlingham 50 E4
Birmingham 62 F4
Birnam 133 E7
Birse 140 E4
Birsemore 140 E4
Birstall
 Leics 64 D2
 W Yorks 88 B3
Birstwith 94 D5
Birthorpe 78 F4
Birtley
 Hereford 49 C5
 Northumb 109 B8
 T&W 111 D5
Birts Street 50 F2
Bisbrooke 65 E5
Biscathorpe 91 F6
Biscot 40 B3
Bisham 39 F8
Bishampton 50 D4
Bish Mill 10 B2
Bishop Auckland 101 B7
Bishopbridge 90 E4
Bishopbriggs 119 C6
Bishop Burton 97 F5
Bishop Middleham 111 F6
Bishopmill 152 B2
Bishop Monkton 95 C6
Bishop Norton 90 E3
Bishopsbourne 31 D5
Bishops Cannings 24 C5
Bishop's Castle 60 F3
Bishop's Caundle 12 C4
Bishop's Cleeve 37 B6
Bishops Frome 49 E8
Bishop's Green 42 C2
Bishop's Hull 11 B7
Bishop's Itchington 51 D8
Bishops Lydeard 11 B6
Bishops Nympton 10 B2
Bishop's Offley 61 B7
Bishop's Stortford 41 B7
Bishop's Sutton 26 F4
Bishop's Tachbrook 51 C8
Bishops Tawton 20 F4
Bishopsteignton 7 B7
Bishopstoke 15 C5
Bishopston 33 F6
Bishopstone
 Bucks 39 C8
 E Sus 17 D8
 Hereford 49 E6
 Swindon 38 F2
 Wilts 13 B8
Bishopstrow 24 E3
Bishop Sutton 23 D7
Bishop's Waltham 15 C6
Bishopswood 11 C7
Bishop's Wood 62 D2
Bishopsworth 23 C7
Bishop Thornton 95 C5
Bishopthorpe 95 E8
Bishopton
 Darl 102 B1
 Dumfries 105 E8
 N Yorks 95 B6
 Renfs 118 B4
 Warks 51 D6
Bishop Wilton 96 D3
Bishton 35 F7
Bisley
 Glos 37 D6
 Sur 27 D7
Bispham 92 E3
Bispham Green 86 C2
Bissoe 3 B6
Bisterne Close 14 D3
Bitchfield 65 B6
Bittadon 20 E4
Bittaford 6 D4
Bittering 68 C2
Bitterley 49 B7
Bitterne 15 C5
Bitteswell 64 F2
Bitton 23 C8
Bix 39 F7
Bixter 160 H5
Blaby 64 E2
Blackacre 114 E3
Blackadder West 122 D4
Blackawton 7 D6
Blackborough 11 D5
Blackborough End 67 C6
Black Bourton 38 D2
Blackboys 18 C2
Blackbrook
 Derbys 76 E3
 Mers 86 E3
 Staffs 74 F4
Blackburn
 Aberds 141 C7
 Aberds 152 E5
 Blackburn 86 B4
 W Loth 120 C2
Black Callerton 110 C4
Black Clauchrie 112 F2
Black Corries Lodge 131 D6
Blackcraig 113 F7
Black Crofts 124 B5
Blackden Heath 74 B4
Blackdog 141 C8
Black Dog 10 D3
Blackfell 111 D5
Blackfield 14 D5
Blackford
 Cumb 108 C3
 Perth 127 D7
 Som 12 B4
 Som 23 E6
Blackfordby 63 C7
Blackgang 15 G5
Blackhall Colliery 111 F7
Blackhall Mill 110 D4
Blackhall Rocks 111 F7
Blackham 29 F5
Blackhaugh 121 F7
Blackheath
 Essex 43 B6
 Suff 57 B8
 Sur 27 E8
 W Mid 62 F3
Black Heddon 110 B3
Blackhill
 Aberds 153 C10
 Aberds 153 D10
 Highld 149 C8
Blackhills
 Highld 151 F12
 Moray 152 C2
Blackhorse 23 B8
Blackland 24 C5
Black Lane 87 D5
Blacklaw 153 C6
Blackley 87 D6
Blacklunans 134 C1
Black Marsh 60 E3
Blackmill 34 F3
Blackmoor 27 F5
Blackmoor Gate 21 E5
Blackmore 42 D2
Blackmore End
 Essex 55 F8
 Herts 40 C4
Black Mount 131 E6
Blackness 120 B3
Blacknest 27 E5
Black Notley 42 B3
Blacko 93 E8
Black Pill 33 E7
Blackpool
 Blackpool 92 F3
 Devon 7 E6
 Pembs 32 C1
Blackpool Gate 108 B5
Blackridge 119 C8
Blackrock
 Argyll 142 B4
 Mon 35 C6
Blackrod 86 C4
Blackshaw 107 C7
Blackshaw Head 87 B7
Blacksmith's Green 56 C5
Blackstone 17 C6
Black Tar 44 E4
Blackthorn 39 C6
Blackthorpe 56 C3
Blacktoft 90 B2
Blacktop 141 D7
Black Torrington 9 D6
Blacktown 35 F6
Blackwall Tunnel 41 F6
Blackwater
 Corn 3 B6
 Hants 27 D6
 IoW 15 F6
Blackwaterfoot 143 F9
Blackwell
 Darl 101 C7
 Derbys 75 B8
 Derbys 76 D4
 Warks 51 E7
 Worcs 50 B4
 W Sus 28 F4
Blackwood 119 E7
Blackwood = Coed Duon 35 E5
Blackwood Hill 75 D6
Blacon 73 C7
Bladnoch 105 D8
Bladon 38 C4
Blaenannerch 45 E4
Blaenau Ffestiniog 71 C8
Blaenavon 35 D6
Blaencelyn 46 D2
Blaendyryn 47 F8
Blaenffos 45 F3
Blaengarw 34 E3
Blaengwrach 34 D2
Blaen-gwynfi 34 E2
Blaenpennal 46 C5
Blaenplwyf 46 B4
Blaenporth 45 E4
Blaenrhondda 34 D3
Blaen-waun 32 B3
Blaen-y-coed 32 B4
Blaenycwm 47 B7
Blaen-y-Cwm
 Denb 72 F4
 Gwyn 71 E8
 Powys 59 B7
Blagdon
 N Som 23 D7
 Torbay 7 C6
Blagdon Hill 11 C7
Blagill 109 E7
Blaguegate 86 D2
Blaich 130 B4
Blain 147 E9
Blaina 35 D6
Blair Atholl 133 C5
Blairbeg 143 E11
Blairdaff 141 C5
Blair Drummond 127 E6
Blairglas 126 F2
Blairgowrie 134 E1
Blairhall 128 F2
Blairingone 127 E8
Blairland 118 E3
Blairlogie 127 E7
Blairlomond 125 F7
Blairmore 145 E10
Blairnamarrow 139 C8
Blairquhosh 126 F4
Blair's Ferry 145 G8
Blairskaith 119 B5
Blaisdon 36 C4
Blakebrook 50 B3
Blakedown 50 B3
Blakelaw 122 F3
Blakeley 62 E2
Blakeley Lane 75 E6
Blakemere 49 E5
Blakeney
 Glos 36 D3
 Norf 81 C6
Blakenhall
 Ches E 74 E4
 W Mid 62 E3
Blakeshall 62 F2
Blakesley 52 D4
Blanchland 110 D2
Blandford Forum 13 D6
Blandford St Mary 13 D6
Bland Hill 94 D5
Blanefield 119 B5
Blankney 78 C3
Blantyre 119 D6
Blar a'Chaorainn 131 C5
Blaran 124 D4
Blarghour 125 D5
Blarmachfoldach 130 C4
Blarnalearoch 150 B4
Blashford 14 D2
Blaston 64 E5
Blatherwycke 65 E6
Blawith 98 F4
Blaxhall 57 D7
Blaxton 89 D7
Blaydon 110 C4
Bleadon 22 D5
Bleak Hey Nook 87 D8
Blean 30 C5
Bleasby
 Lincs 90 F5
 Notts 77 E7
Bleasdale 93 E5
Bleatarn 100 C2
Blebocraigs 129 C6
Bleddfa 48 C4
Bledington 38 B2
Bledlow 39 D7
Bledlow Ridge 39 E7
Blegbie 121 C7
Blencarn 109 F6
Blencogo 107 E8
Blendworth 15 C8
Blenheim Park 80 D4
Blennerhasset 107 E8
Blervie Castle 151 F13
Bletchingdon 39 C5
Bletchingley 28 D4
Bletchley
 M Keynes 53 F6
 Shrops 74 F3
Bletherston 32 B1
Bletsoe 53 D8
Blewbury 39 F5
Blickling 81 E7
Blidworth 77 D5
Blindburn 116 C4
Blindcrake 107 F8
Blindley Heath 28 E4
Blisland 5 B6
Blissford 14 C2
Bliss Gate 50 B2
Blisworth 52 D5
Blithbury 62 B4
Blitterlees 107 D8
Blockley 51 F6
Blofield 69 D6
Blofield Heath 69 C6
Blo' Norton 56 B4
Bloomfield 115 B8
Blore 75 E8
Blount's Green 75 F7
Blowick 85 C4
Bloxham 52 F2
Bloxholm 78 D3
Bloxwich 62 D3
Bloxworth 13 E6
Blubberhouses 94 D4
Blue Anchor
 Som 22 E2
 Swansea 33 E6
Blue Row 43 C6
Blundeston 69 E8
Blunham 54 D2
Blunsdon St Andrew 37 F8
Bluntington 50 B3
Bluntisham 54 B4
Blunts 5 C8
Blyborough 90 E3
Blyford 57 B8
Blymhill 62 C2
Blyth
 Northumb 117 F9
 Notts 89 F7
Blyth Bridge 120 E4
Blythburgh 57 B8
Blythe 121 E8
Blythe Bridge 75 E6
Blyton 90 E2
Boarhills 129 C7
Boarhunt 15 D7
Boarshead 18 B2
Boars Head 86 D3
Boars Hill 38 D4
Boarstall 39 C6
Boasley Cross 9 E6
Boath 151 D8
Boat of Garten 138 C5
Bobbing 30 C2
Bobbington 62 E2
Bobbingworth 41 D8
Bocaddon 5 D6
Bochastle 126 D5
Bocking 42 B3
Bocking Churchstreet 42 B3
Boddam
 Aberds 153 D11
 Shetland 160 M5
Boddington 37 B5
Bodedern 82 C3
Bodelwyddan 72 B4
Bodenham
 Hereford 49 D7
 Wilts 14 B2
Bodenham Moor 49 D7
Bodermid 70 E2
Bodewryd 82 B3
Bodfari 72 B4
Bodffordd 82 D4
Bodham 81 C7
Bodiam 18 C4
Bodicote 52 F2
Bodieve 4 B4
Bodinnick 5 D6
Bodle Street Green 18 D3
Bodmin 5 C5
Bodney 67 E8
Bodorgan 82 E3
Bodsham 30 E5
Boduan 70 D4
Bodymoor Heath 63 E5
Bogallan 151 F9
Bogbrae 153 E10
Bogend
 Borders 122 E3
 S Ayrs 118 F3
Boghall 120 C2
Boghead 119 E7
Bogmoor 152 B3
Bogniebrae 152 D5
Bognor Regis 16 E3
Bograxie 141 C6
Bogside 119 D8
Bogton 153 C6
Bogue 113 F6
Bohenie 137 F5
Bohortha 3 C7
Bohuntine 137 F5

Boirseam 154 J5
Bojewyan 2 C2
Bolam
Durham 101 B6
Northumb 117 F6
Bolberry 6 F4
Bold Heath 86 F3
Boldon 111 C6
Boldon Colliery 111 C6
Boldre 14 E4
Boldron 101 C5
Bole 89 F8
Bolehill 76 D2
Boleside 121 F7
Bolham 10 C4
Bolham Water 11 C6
Bolingey 4 D2
Bollington 75 B6
Bollington Cross 75 B6
Bolney 17 B6
Bolnhurst 53 D8
Bolshan 135 D6
Bolsover 76 B4
Bolsterstone 88 E3
Bolstone 49 F7
Boltby 102 F2
Bolter End 39 E7
Bolton
Cumb 99 B8
E Loth 121 B8
E Yorks 96 D3
Gtr Man 86 D5
Northumb 117 C7
Bolton Abbey 94 D3
Bolton Bridge 94 D3
Bolton-by-Bowland 93 E7
Boltonfellend 108 C4
Boltongate 108 E2
Bolton-le-Sands 92 C4
Bolton Low Houses 108 E2
Bolton-on-Swale 101 E7
Bolton Percy 95 E8
Bolton Town End 92 C4
Bolton upon Dearne 89 D5
Bolventor 5 B6
Bomere Heath 60 C4
Bonar Bridge 151 B9
Bonawe 125 B6
Bonby 90 C4
Boncath 45 F4
Bonchester Bridge 115 C8
Bonchurch 15 G6
Bondleigh 9 D8
Bonehill
Devon 6 B5
Staffs 63 D5
Bo'ness 127 F8
Bonhill 118 B3
Boningale 62 D2
Bonjedward 116 B2
Bonkle 119 D8
Bonnavoulin 147 F8
Bonnington
Edin 120 C4
Kent 19 B7
Bonnybank 129 D5
Bonnybridge 127 F7
Bonnykelly 153 C8
Bonnyrigg and Lasswade 121 C6
Bonnyton
Aberds 153 E6
Angus 134 F3
Angus 135 D6
Bonsall 76 D2
Bonskeid House 133 C5
Bont 35 C7
Bontddu 58 C3
Bont-Dolgadfan 59 D5
Bont-goch 58 F3
Bonthorpe 79 B7
Bontnewydd
Ceredig 46 C5
Gwyn 82 F4
Bont-newydd 72 B4
Bont Newydd
Gwyn 71 C8
Gwyn 71 E8
Bontuchel 72 D4
Bonvilston 22 B2
Bon-y-maen 33 E7
Booker 39 E8
Boon 121 E8
Boosbeck 102 C4
Boot 98 D3
Booth 87 B8
Boothby Graffoe 78 D2
Boothby Pagnell 78 F2
Boothen 75 E5
Boothferry 89 B8
Boothville 53 C5
Booth Wood 87 C8
Bootle
Cumb 98 F3
Mers 85 E4
Booton 81 E7
Boot Street 57 E6
Boquhan 126 F4
Boraston 49 B8
Borden
Kent 30 C2
W Sus 16 B2
Bordley 94 C2
Bordon 27 F6
Bordon Camp 27 F5
Boreham
Essex 42 D3
Wilts 24 E3
Boreham Street 18 D3
Borehamwood 40 E4
Boreland
Dumfries 114 E4
Stirling 132 F2
Borgh
W Isles 148 H1
W Isles 154 J4
Borghastan 154 C7
Borgie 157 D9
Borgue
Dumfries 106 E3
Borgue *continued*
Highld 158 H3
Borley 56 E2
Bornais 148 F2
Bornesketaig 149 A8
Borness 106 E3
Boroughbridge 95 C6
Borough Green 29 D7
Borras Head 73 D7
Borreraig 148 C6
Borrobol Lodge 157 G11
Borrowash 76 F4
Borrowby 102 F2
Borrowdale 98 C4
Borrowfield 141 E7
Borth 58 E3
Borthwickbrae 115 C7
Borthwickshiels 115 C7
Borth-y-Gest 71 D6
Borve 149 D9
Borve Lodge 154 H5
Borwick 92 B5
Bosavern 2 C2
Bosbury 49 E8
Boscastle 8 E3
Boscombe
BCP 14 E2
Wilts 25 F7
Boscoppa 4 D5
Bosham 16 D2
Bosherston 44 F4
Boskenna 2 D3
Bosley 75 C6
Bossall 96 C3
Bossiney 8 F2
Bossingham 31 E5
Bossington 21 E7
Bostock Green 74 C3
Boston 79 E6
Boston Long Hedges 79 E6
Boston Spa 95 E7
Boston West 79 E5
Boswinger 3 B8
Botallack 2 C2
Botany Bay 41 E5
Botcherby 108 D4
Botcheston 63 D8
Botesdale 56 B4
Bothal 117 F8
Bothamsall 77 B6
Bothel 107 F8
Bothenhampton 12 E2
Bothwell 119 D7
Botley
Bucks 40 D2
Hants 15 C6
Oxon 38 D4
Botolph Claydon 39 B7
Botolphs 17 D5
Bottacks 150 E7
Bottesford
Leics 77 F8
N Lincs 90 D2
Bottisham 55 C6
Bottlesford 25 D6
Bottom Boat 88 B4
Bottomcraig 129 B5
Bottom House 75 D7
Bottom of Hutton 86 B2
Bottom o'th'Moor 86 C4
Botusfleming 6 C2
Botwnnog 70 D3
Bough Beech 29 E5
Boughrood 48 F3
Boughspring 36 E2
Boughton
Norf 67 D6
Northants 53 C5
Notts 77 C6
Boughton Aluph 30 E4
Boughton Lees 30 E4
Boughton Malherbe 30 E2
Boughton Monchelsea 29 D8
Boughton Street 30 D4
Boulby 103 C5
Boulden 60 F5
Boulmer 117 C8
Boulston 44 D4
Boultenstone 140 C3
Boultham 78 C2
Bourn 54 D4
Bourne 65 B7
Bourne End
Bucks 40 F1
C Beds 53 E7
Herts 40 D3
Bournemouth 13 E8
Bournes Green
Glos 37 D6
Southend 43 F5
Bournheath 50 B4
Bournmoor 111 D6
Bournville 62 F4
Bourton
Dorset 24 F2
N Som 23 C5
Oxon 38 F2
Shrops 61 E5
Bourton on Dunsmore 52 B2
Bourton on the Hill 51 F6
Bourton-on-the-Water 38 B1
Bousd 146 E5
Boustead Hill 108 D2
Bouth 99 F5
Bouthwaite 94 B4
Boveney 27 B7
Boverton 21 C8
Bovey Tracey 7 B6
Bovingdon 40 D3
Bovingdon Green
Bucks 39 F8
Herts 40 D3
Bovinger 41 D8
Bovington Camp 13 F6
Bow
Borders 121 E7
Devon 10 D2
Orkney 159 J4
Bowbank 100 B4
Bow Brickhill 53 F7
Bowburn 111 F6
Bowcombe 15 F5
Bowd 11 E6
Bowden
Borders 121 F8
Devon 7 E6
Bowden Hill 24 C4
Bowderdale 100 D1
Bowdon 87 F5
Bower 116 F3
Bowerchalke 13 B8
Bowerhill 24 C4
Bower Hinton 12 C2
Bowermadden 158 D4
Bowers Gifford 42 F3
Bowershall 128 E2
Bowertower 158 D4
Bowes 100 C4
Bowgreave 92 E4
Bowgreen 87 F5
Bowhill 115 B7
Bowhouse 107 C7
Bowland Bridge 99 F6
Bowley 49 D7
Bowlhead Green 27 F7
Bowling
W Dunb 118 B4
W Yorks 94 F4
Bowling Bank 73 E7
Bowling Green 50 D3
Bowmanstead 99 E5
Bowmore 142 C4
Bowness-on-Solway 108 C2
Bowness-on-Windermere 99 E6
Bow of Fife 128 C5
Bowsden 123 E5
Bowside Lodge 157 C11
Bowston 99 E6
Bow Street 58 F3
Bowthorpe 68 D4
Box
Glos 37 D5
Wilts 24 C3
Boxbush 36 C4
Box End 53 E8
Boxford
Suff 56 E3
W Berks 26 B2
Boxgrove 16 D3
Boxley 29 D8
Boxmoor 40 D3
Boxted
Essex 56 F4
Suff 56 D2
Boxted Cross 56 F4
Boxted Heath 56 F4
Boxworth 54 C4
Boxworth End 54 C4
Boyden Gate 31 C6
Boylestone 75 F8
Boyndie 153 B6
Boynton 97 C7
Boysack 135 E6
Boyton
Corn 8 E5
Suff 57 E7
Wilts 24 F4
Boyton Cross 42 D2
Boyton End 55 E8
Bozeat 53 D7
Braaid 84 E3
Braal Castle 158 D3
Brabling Green 57 C6
Brabourne 30 E4
Brabourne Lees 30 E4
Brabster 158 D5
Bracadale 149 E8
Bracara 147 B10
Braceborough 65 C7
Bracebridge 78 C2
Bracebridge Heath 78 C2
Bracebridge Low Fields 78 C2
Braceby 78 F3
Bracewell 93 E8
Brackenfield 76 D3
Brackenthwaite
Cumb 108 E2
N Yorks 95 D5
Bracklesham 16 E2
Brackletter 136 F4
Brackley
Argyll 143 D8
Northants 52 F3
Brackloch 156 G4
Bracknell 27 C6
Braco 127 D7
Bracobrae 152 C5
Bracon Ash 68 E4
Bracorina 147 B10
Bradbourne 76 D2
Bradbury 101 B8
Bradda 84 F1
Bradden 52 E4
Braddock 5 C6
Bradeley 75 D5
Bradenham
Bucks 39 E8
Norf 68 D2
Bradenstoke 24 B5
Bradfield
Essex 56 F5
Norf 81 D8
W Berks 26 B4
Bradfield Combust 56 D2
Bradfield Green 74 D3
Bradfield Heath 43 B7
Bradfield St Clare 56 D3
Bradfield St George 56 C3
Bradford
Corn 5 B6
Derbys 76 C2
Devon 9 D6
Northumb 123 F7
W Yorks 94 F4
Bradford Abbas 12 C3
Bradford Leigh 24 C3
Bradford-on-Avon 24 C3
Bradford-on-Tone 11 B6
Bradford Peverell 12 E4
Brading 15 F7
Bradley
Derbys 76 E2
Hants 26 E4
NE Lincs 91 D6
Staffs 62 C2
W Mid 62 E3
W Yorks 88 B2
Bradley Green 50 C4
Bradley in the Moors 75 E7
Bradley Stoke 36 F3
Bradlow 50 F2
Bradmore
Notts 77 F5
W Mid 62 E2
Bradninch 10 D5
Bradnop 75 D7
Bradpole 12 E2
Bradshaw
Gtr Man 86 C5
W Yorks 87 C8
Bradstone 9 F5
Bradwall Green 74 C4
Bradway 88 F4
Bradwell
Derbys 88 F2
Essex 42 B4
M Keynes 53 F6
Norf 69 D8
Staffs 74 E5
Bradwell Grove 38 D2
Bradwell on Sea 43 D6
Bradwell Waterside 43 D5
Bradworthy 8 C5
Bradworthy Cross 8 C5
Brae
Dumfries 107 B5
Highld 155 J13
Highld 156 J7
Shetland 160 G5
Braeantra 151 D8
Braedownie 134 B2
Braefield 150 H7
Braegrum 128 B2
Braehead
Dumfries 105 D8
Orkney 159 D5
Orkney 159 H6
S Lanark 119 F8
S Lanark 120 D2
Braehead of Lunan 135 D6
Braehoulland 160 F4
Braehungie 158 G3
Braelangwell Lodge 151 B8
Braemar 139 E7
Braemore
Highld 150 D4
Highld 158 G2
Brae of Achnahaird 156 H3
Brae Roy Lodge 137 E6
Braeside 118 B2
Braes of Enzie 152 C3
Braeswick 159 E7
Braewick 160 H5
Brafferton
Darl 101 B7
N Yorks 95 B7
Brafield-on-the-Green 53 D6
Bragar 155 C7
Bragbury End 41 B5
Bragleenmore 124 C5
Braichmelyn 83 E6
Braid 120 C5
Braides 92 D4
Braidley 101 F5
Braidwood 119 E8
Braigo 142 B3
Brailsford 76 E2
Brainshaugh 117 D8
Braintree 42 B3
Braiseworth 56 B5
Braishfield 14 B4
Braithwaite
Cumb 98 B4
S Yorks 89 C7
W Yorks 94 E3
Braithwell 89 E6
Bramber 17 C5
Bramcote
Notts 76 F5
Warks 63 F8
Bramdean 15 B7
Bramerton 69 D5
Bramfield
Herts 41 C5
Suff 57 B7
Bramford 56 E5
Bramhall 87 F6
Bramham 95 E7
Bramhope 95 E5
Bramley
Hants 26 D4
Sur 27 E8
S Yorks 89 E5
W Yorks 94 F5
Bramling 31 D6
Brampford Speke 10 E4
Brampton
Cambs 54 B3
Cumb 100 B1
Cumb 108 C5
Derbys 76 B3
Hereford 49 F6
Lincs 77 B8
Norf 81 E8
Suff 69 F7
S Yorks 88 D5
Brampton Abbotts 36 B3
Brampton Ash 64 F4
Brampton Bryan 49 B5
Brampton en le Morthen 89 F5
Bramshall 75 F7
Bramshaw 14 C3
Bramshill 26 C5
Bramshott 27 F6
Branault 147 E8
Brancaster 80 C3
Brancaster Staithe 80 C3
Brancepeth 110 F5
Branch End 110 C3
Branchill 151 F13
Branderburgh 152 A2
Brandesburton 97 E7
Brandeston 57 C6
Brand Green 36 B4
Brandhill 49 B6
Brandis Corner 9 D6
Brandiston 81 E7
Brandon
Durham 110 F5
Lincs 78 E2
Northumb 117 C6
Suff 67 F7
Warks 52 B2
Brandon Bank 67 F6
Brandon Creek 67 E6
Brandon Parva 68 D3
Brandsby 95 B8
Brandy Wharf 90 E4
Brane 2 D3
Bran End 42 B2
Branksome 13 E8
Branksome Park 13 E8
Bransby 77 B8
Branscombe 11 F6
Bransford 50 D2
Bransgore 14 E2
Branshill 127 E7
Bransholme 97 F7
Branson's Cross 51 B5
Branston
Leics 64 B5
Lincs 78 C3
Staffs 63 B6
Branston Booths 78 C3
Branstone 15 F6
Bransty 98 C1
Brant Broughton 78 D2
Brantham 56 F5
Branthwaite
Cumb 98 B2
Cumb 108 F2
Brantingham 90 B3
Branton
Northumb 117 C6
S Yorks 89 D7
Branxholme 115 C7
Branxholm Park 115 C7
Branxton 122 F4
Brassey Green 74 C2
Brassington 76 D2
Brasted 29 D5
Brasted Chart 29 D5
Brathens 141 E5
Bratoft 79 C7
Brattleby 90 F3
Bratton
Telford 61 C6
Wilts 24 D4
Bratton Clovelly 9 E6
Bratton Fleming 20 F5
Bratton Seymour 12 B4
Braughing 41 B6
Braunston 52 C3
Braunstone Town 64 D2
Braunston-in-Rutland 64 D5
Braunton 20 F3
Brawby 96 B3
Brawl 157 C11
Brawlbin 158 E2
Bray 27 B7
Braybrooke 64 F4
Braye 16
Brayford 21 F5
Bray Shop 5 B8
Braystones 98 D2
Braythorn 94 E5
Brayton 95 F9
Bray Wick 27 B6
Brazacott 8 E4
Breach 30 C2
Breachacha Castle 146 F4
Breachwood Green 40 B4
Breacleit 154 D6
Breaden Heath 73 F8
Breadsall 76 F3
Breadstone 36 D4
Breage 2 D5
Breakachy 150 G7
Bream 36 D3
Breamore 14 C2
Brean 22 D4
Breanais 154 E4
Brearton 95 C6
Breascleit 154 D7
Breaston 76 F4
Brechfa 46 F4
Brechin 135 C5
Breckan 159 H3
Breck of Cruan 159 G4
Breckrey 149 B10
Brecon = *Aberhonddu* 34 B4
Bredbury 87 E7
Brede 18 D5
Bredenbury 49 D8
Bredfield 57 D6
Bredgar 30 C2
Bredhurst 29 C8
Bredicot 50 D4
Bredon 50 F4
Bredon's Norton 50 F4
Bredwardine 48 E5
Breedon on the Hill 63 B8
Breibhig
W Isles 148 J1
W Isles 155 D9
Breich 120 C2
Breightmet 86 D5
Breighton 96 F3
Breinton 49 F6
Breinton Common 49 E6
Breiwick 160 J6
Bremhill 24 B4
Bremirehoull 160 L6
Brenchley 29 E7
Brendon 21 E6
Brenkley 110 B5
Brent Eleigh 56 E3
Brentford 28 B2
Brentingby 64 C4
Brent Knoll 22 D5
Brent Pelham 54 F5
Brentwood 42 E1
Brenzett 19 C7
Brereton 62 C4
Brereton Green 74 C4
Brereton Heath 74 C5
Bressingham 68 F3
Bretby 63 B6
Bretford 52 B2
Bretforton 51 E5
Bretherdale Head 99 D7
Bretherton 86 B2
Brettabister 160 H6
Brettenham
Norf 68 F2
Suff 56 D3
Bretton
Derbys 76 B2
Flint 73 C7
Brewer Street 28 D4
Brewlands Bridge 134 C1
Brewood 62 D2
Briach 151 F13
Briants Puddle 13 E6
Brick End 42 B1
Brickendon 41 D6
Bricket Wood 40 D4
Bricklehampton 50 E4
Bride 84 B4
Bridekirk 107 F8
Bridell 45 E3
Bridestowe 9 F7
Brideswell 152 E5
Bridford 10 F3
Bridfordmills 10 F3
Bridge 31 D5
Bridge End 78 F4
Bridgefoot
Angus 134 F3
Cumb 98 B2
Bridge Green 55 F5
Bridgehampton 12 B3
Bridge Hewick 95 B6
Bridgehill 110 D3
Bridgemary 15 D6
Bridgemont 87 F8
Bridgend
Aberds 140 C4
Aberds 152 E5
Angus 135 C5
Argyll 142 B4
Argyll 143 E8
Argyll 145 D7
Cumb 99 C5
Fife 129 C5
Moray 152 E3
N Lanark 119 B6
Pembs 45 E3
W Loth 120 B3
Bridgend = *Pen-y-Bont Ar Ogwr* 21 B8
Bridgend of Lintrathen 134 D2
Bridge of Alford 140 C4
Bridge of Allan 127 E6
Bridge of Avon 152 E1
Bridge of Awe 125 C6
Bridge of Balgie 132 E2
Bridge of Cally 133 D8
Bridge of Canny 141 E5
Bridge of Craigisla 134 D2
Bridge of Dee 106 D4
Bridge of Don 141 C8
Bridge of Dun 135 D6
Bridge of Dye 141 F5
Bridge of Earn 128 C3
Bridge of Ericht 132 D2
Bridge of Feugh 141 E6
Bridge of Forss 157 C13
Bridge of Gairn 140 E2
Bridge of Gaur 132 D2
Bridge of Muchalls 141 E7
Bridge of Oich 137 D6
Bridge of Orchy 125 B8
Bridge of Waith 159 G3
Bridge of Walls 160 H4
Bridge of Weir 118 C3
Bridgerule 8 D4
Bridges 60 E3
Bridge Sollers 49 E6
Bridge Street 56 E2
Bridgeton 119 C6
Bridgetown
Corn 8 F5
Som 21 F8
Bridge Trafford 73 B8
Bridge Yate 23 B8
Bridgham 68 F2
Bridgnorth 61 E7
Bridgtown 62 D3
Bridgwater 22 F5
Bridlington 97 C7
Bridport 12 E2
Bridstow 36 B2
Brierfield 93 F8
Brierley
Glos 36 C3
Hereford 49 D6
S Yorks 88 C5
Brierley Hill 62 F3
Briery Hill 35 D5
Brigg 90 D4
Briggswath 103 D6
Brigham
Cumb 107 F7
E Yorks 97 D6
Brighouse 88 B2
Brighstone 14 F5
Brightgate 76 D2
Brighthampton 38 D3
Brightling 18 C3
Brightlingsea 43 C6
Brighton
Brighton 17 D7
Corn 4 D4
Brighton Hill 26 E4
Brightons 120 B2
Brightwalton 26 B2
Brightwell 57 E6
Brightwell Baldwin 39 E6
Brightwell cum Sotwell 39 E5
Brignall 101 C5
Brig o'Turk 126 D4
Brigsley 91 D6
Brigsteer 99 F6
Brigstock 65 F6
Brill 39 C6
Brilley 48 E4
Brimaston 44 C4
Brimfield 49 C7
Brimington 76 B4
Brimley 7 B5
Brimpsfield 37 C6
Brimpton 26 C3
Brims 159 K3
Brimscombe 37 D5
Brimstage 85 F4
Brinacory 147 B10
Brind 96 F3
Brindister
Shetland 160 H4
Shetland 160 K6
Brindle 86 B4
Brindley Ford 75 D5
Brineton 62 C2
Bringhurst 64 E5
Brington 53 B8
Brinian 159 F5
Briningham 81 D6
Brinkhill 79 B6
Brinkley 55 D7
Brinklow 52 B2
Brinkworth 37 F7
Brinmore 138 B2
Brinscall 86 B4
Brinsea 23 C6
Brinsley 76 E4
Brinsop 49 E6
Brinsworth 88 F5
Brinton 81 D6
Brisco 108 D4
Brisley 81 E5
Brislington 23 B8
Bristol 23 B7
Briston 81 D6
Britannia 87 B6
Britford 14 B2
Brithdir 58 C4
British Legion Village 29 D8
Briton Ferry 33 E8
Britwell Salome 39 E6
Brixham 7 D7
Brixton
Devon 6 D3
London 28 B4
Brixton Deverill 24 F3
Brixworth 52 B5
Brize Norton 38 D3
Broad Blunsdon 38 E1
Broadbottom 87 E7
Broadbridge 16 D2
Broadbridge Heath 28 F2
Broad Campden 51 F6
Broad Chalke 13 B8
Broadclyst 10 E4
Broadfield
Gtr Man 87 C6
Lancs 86 B3
Pembs 32 D2
W Sus 28 F3
Broadford 149 F11
Broadford Bridge 16 B4
Broad Green
C Beds 53 E7
Essex 42 B4
Worcs 50 D2
Broadhaugh 115 D7
Broadhaven 158 E5
Broad Haven 44 D3
Broadheath 87 F5
Broad Heath 49 C8
Broadhembury 11 D6
Broadhempston 7 C6
Broad Hill 55 B6
Broad Hinton 25 B6
Broadholme
Derbys 76 E3
Lincs 77 B8
Broadland Row 18 D5
Broadlay 32 D4
Broad Laying 26 C2
Broadley
Lancs 87 C6
Moray 152 B3
Broadley Common 41 D7
Broad Marston 51 E6
Broadmayne 12 F5
Broadmeadows 121 F7
Broadmere 26 E4
Broadmoor 32 D1
Broadoak 31 C5
Broad Oak
Carms 33 B6
Cumb 98 E3
Dorset 12 E2
Dorset 13 C5
E Sus 18 C3
E Sus 18 D5
Hereford 36 B1
Mers 86 E3
Broadrashes 152 C4
Broadsea 153 B9
Broadstairs 31 C7
Broadstone
BCP 13 E8
Shrops 60 F5
Broad Street 30 D2
Broad Street Green 42 D4
Broad Town 25 B5
Broadtown Lane 25 B5
Broadwas 50 D2
Broadwater
Herts 41 B5
W Sus 17 D5
Broadway
Carms 32 D3
Pembs 44 D3
Som 11 C8
Suff 57 B7
Worcs 51 F5
Broadwell
Glos 36 C2
Glos 38 B2
Oxon 38 D2
Warks 52 C2
Broadwell House 110 D2
Broadwey 12 F4
Broadwindsor 12 D2
Broadwood Kelly 9 D8
Broadwoodwidger 9 F6
Brobury 48 E5
Brochel 149 D10
Brochloch 113 E5
Brochroy 125 B6
Brockamin 50 D2
Brockbridge 15 C7
Brockdam 117 B7
Brockdish 57 B6
Brockenhurst 14 D4
Brocketsbrae 119 F8
Brockford Street 56 C5
Brockhall 52 C4
Brockham 28 E2
Brockhampton
Glos 37 B7
Hereford 49 F7
Brockholes 88 C2
Brockhurst
Derbys 76 C3
Hants 15 D7
Brocklebank 108 E3
Brocklesby 90 C5
Brockley 23 C6
Brockley Green 56 D2
Brockleymoor 108 F4
Brockton
Shrops 60 D3
Shrops 60 F3
Shrops 61 D7
Shrops 61 E5
Telford 61 C7
Brockweir 36 D2
Brockwood 15 B7
Brockworth 37 C5
Brocton 62 C3
Brodick 143 E11
Brodsworth 89 D6
Brogaig 149 B9
Brogborough 53 F7
Brokenborough 37 F6
Broken Cross
Ches E 75 B5
Ches W 74 B3
Bromborough 85 F4
Brome 56 B5
Brome Street 57 B5
Bromeswell 57 D7
Bromfield
Cumb 107 E8
Shrops 49 B6
Bromham
Bedford 53 D8
Wilts 24 C4
Bromley
London 28 C5
W Mid 62 F3
Bromley Common 28 C5
Bromley Green 19 B6
Brompton
Medway 29 C8
N Yorks 102 E1
N Yorks 103 F7
Brompton-on-Swale 101 E7
Brompton Ralph 22 F2
Brompton Regis 21 F8
Bromsash 36 B3
Bromsberrow Heath 50 F2
Bromsgrove 50 B4
Bromyard 49 D8
Bromyard Downs 49 D8
Bronaber 71 D8
Brongest 46 E2
Bronington 73 F8
Bronllys 48 F3
Bronnant 46 C5
Bronwydd Arms 33 B5
Bronydd 48 E4
Bronygarth 73 F6
Brook
Carms 32 D3
Hants 14 B4
Hants 14 C3
IoW 14 F4
Kent 30 E4
Sur 27 E8
Sur 27 F7
Brooke
Norf 69 E5
Rutland 64 D5
Brookenby 91 E6
Brookend 36 E2
Brook End 53 C8
Brookfield 118 C4
Brook Hill 14 C3
Brookhouse 92 C5
Brookhouse Green 74 C5
Brookland 19 C6
Brooklands
Dumfries 106 B5
Gtr Man 87 E5
Shrops 74 E2
Brookmans Park 41 D5
Brooks 59 E8
Brooks Green 16 B5
Brook Street
Kent 19 B6
Kent 29 E6
W Sus 17 B7
Brookthorpe 37 C5
Brookville 67 E7
Brookwood 27 D7
Broom
C Beds 54 E2
S Yorks 88 E5
Warks 51 D5
Worcs 50 B4
Broome
Norf 69 E6
Shrops 60 F4
Broomedge 86 F5
Broome Park 117 C7
Broomer's Corner 16 B5
Broomfield
Aberds 153 E9
Essex 42 C3
Kent 30 D2
Kent 31 C5
Som 22 F4
Broomfleet 90 B2
Broom Green 81 E5
Broomhall
Ches E 74 E3
Windsor 27 C7
Broomhaugh 110 C3
Broomhill
Norf 67 D6
Northumb 117 D8
S Yorks 88 D5
Broom Hill 13 D8
Broomholm 81 D9
Broomley 110 C3
Broompark 110 E5
Broom's Green 50 F2
Broomy Lodge 14 C3
Brora 157 J12
Broseley 61 D6
Brotherhouse Bar 66 C2
Brotherstone 122 F2
Brothertoft 79 E5
Brotherton 89 B5
Brotton 102 C4
Broubster 157 C13
Brough
Cumb 100 C2
Derbys 88 F2
E Yorks 90 B3
Highld 158 C4
Notts 77 D8
Orkney 159 G4
Shetland 160 F6
Shetland 160 F7
Shetland 160 G7
Shetland 160 H6
Shetland 160 J7
Broughall 74 E2
Brough Lodge 160 D7
Brough Sowerby 100 C2
Broughton
Borders 120 F4
Cambs 54 B3
Flint 73 C7
Hants 25 F8
Lancs 92 F5
M Keynes 53 E6
N Lincs 90 D3
Northants 53 B6
N Yorks 94 D2
N Yorks 96 B3
Orkney 159 D5
Oxon 52 F2
V Glam 21 B8
Broughton Astley 64 E2
Broughton Beck 98 F4
Broughton Common 24 C3
Broughton Gifford 24 C3
Broughton Hackett 50 D4
Broughton in Furness 98 F4
Broughton Mills 98 E4
Broughton Moor 107 F7
Broughton Park 87 D6
Broughton Poggs 38 D2
Broughtown 159 D7
Broughty Ferry 134 F4
Browhouses 108 C2
Browland 160 H4
Brown Candover 26 F3
Brown Edge
Lancs 85 C4
Staffs 75 D6
Brown Heath 73 C8
Brownhill
Aberds 153 D6
Aberds 153 D8
Blackburn 93 F6
Shrops 60 B4
Brownhills
Fife 129 C7
W Mid 62 D4
Brownlow 74 C5
Brownlow Heath 74 C5
Brownmuir 135 B7
Brown's End 50 F2
Brownshill 37 D5
Brownston 6 D4
Brownyside 117 B7
Broxa 103 E7
Broxbourne 41 D6
Broxburn
E Loth 122 B2
W Loth 120 B3
Broxholme 78 B2
Broxted 42 B1
Broxton 73 D8
Broxwood 49 D5
Broyle Side 17 C8
Brù 155 C8
Bruairnis 148 H2
Bruan 158 G5
Bruar Lodge 133 B5
Brucehill 118 B3
Bruera 73 C8
Bruern Abbey 38 B2
Bruichladdich 142 B3
Bruisyard 57 C7
Brumby 90 D2
Brund 75 C8
Brundall 69 D6
Brundish 57 C6
Brundish Street 57 B6
Brunery 147 D10
Brunshaw 93 F8
Brunswick Village 110 B5
Bruntcliffe 88 B3
Bruntingthorpe 64 E3
Brunton
Fife 128 B5
Northumb 117 B8
Wilts 25 D7
Brushford
Devon 9 D8
Som 10 B4
Bruton 23 F8
Bryanston 13 D6
Brydekirk 107 B8
Bryher 2 E3
Brymbo 73 D6
Brympton 12 C3
Bryn
Carms 33 D6
Gtr Man 86 D3
Neath 34 E2

Bryn continued
Shrops 60 F2
Brynamman 33 C8
Brynberian 45 F3
Brynbryddan 34 E1
Brynbuga = Usk 35 D7
Bryncae 34 F3
Bryncethin 34 F3
Bryncir 71 C5
Bryn-coch 33 E8
Bryncroes 70 D3
Bryncrug 58 D3
Bryn Du 82 D3
Bryneglwys 72 E5
Brynford 73 B5
Bryn Gates 86 D3
Bryn-glas 83 E8
Bryn Golau 34 F3
Bryngwran 82 D3
Bryngwyn
Ceredig 45 E4
Mon 35 D7
Powys 48 E3
Brynhenllan 45 F2
Brynhoffnant 46 D2
Brynithel 35 D6
Bryn-Iwan 46 F2
Brynmawr 35 C5
Bryn-mawr 70 D3
Brynmenyn 34 F3
Brynmill 33 E7
Brynna 34 F3
Bryn-nantllech 72 C3
Bryn-penarth 59 D8
Brynrefail
Anglesey 82 C4
Gwyn 83 E5
Bryn Rhyd-yr-Arian 72 C3
Brynsadler 34 F4
Bryn Saith Marchog 72 D4
Brynsiencyn 82 E4
Bryn Sion 59 C5
Brynteg
Anglesey 82 C4
Ceredig 46 E3
Bryn-y-gwenin 35 C7
Bryn-y-maen 83 D8
Bryn-yr-eryr 70 C4
Buaile nam Bodach 148 H2
Bualintur 149 F9
Buarthmeini 72 F2
Bubbenhall 51 B8
Bubwith 96 F3
Buccleuch 115 C6
Buchanhaven 153 D11
Buchanty 127 B8
Buchlyvie 126 E4
Buckabank 108 E3
Buckden
Cambs 54 C2
N Yorks 94 B2
Buckenham 69 D6
Buckerell 11 D6
Buckfast 6 C5
Buckfastleigh 6 C5
Buckhaven 129 E5
Buckholm 121 F7
Buckholt 36 C2
Buckhorn Weston 13 B5
Buckhurst Hill 41 E7
Buckie 152 B4
Buckies 158 D3
Buckingham 52 F4
Buckland
Bucks 40 C1
Devon 6 E4
Glos 51 F5
Hants 14 E4
Herts 54 F4
Kent 31 E7
Oxon 38 E3
Sur 28 D3
Buckland Brewer 9 B6
Buckland Common 40 D2
Buckland Dinham 24 D2
Buckland Filleigh 9 D6
Buckland in the Moor 6 B5
Buckland Monachorum 6 C2
Buckland Newton 12 D4
Buckland St Mary 11 C7
Bucklebury 26 B3
Bucklegate 79 F6
Bucklerheads 134 F4
Bucklers Hard 14 E5
Bucklesham 57 E6
Buckley = Bwcle 73 C6
Bucklow Hill 86 F5
Buckminster 65 B5
Bucknall
Lincs 78 C4
Stoke 75 E6
Bucknell
Oxon 39 B5
Shrops 49 B5
Buckpool 152 B4
Bucksburn 141 D7
Buck's Cross 8 B5
Bucks Green 27 F8
Buckshaw Village 86 B3
Bucks Horn Oak 27 E6
Buckskin 26 D4
Buck's Mills 9 B5
Buckton
E Yorks 97 B7
Hereford 49 B5
Northumb 123 F6
Buckworth 54 B2
Budbrooke 51 C7
Budby 77 C6
Budd's Titson 8 D4
Bude 8 D4
Budlake 10 E4
Budle 123 F7
Budleigh Salterton 11 F5
Budock Water 3 C6
Buerton 74 E3
Buffler's Holt 52 F4
Bugbrooke 52 D4
Buglawton 75 C5
Bugle 4 D5
Bugley 24 E3
Bugthorpe 96 D3
Buildwas 61 D6
Builth Road 48 D2
Builth Wells = Llanfair-ym-Muallt 48 D2
Buirgh 154 H5
Bulby 65 B7
Bulcote 77 E6
Buldoo 157 C12
Bulford 25 E6
Bulford Camp 25 E6
Bulkeley 74 D2
Bulkington
Warks 63 F7
Wilts 24 D4
Bulkworthy 9 C5
Bullamoor 102 E1
Bullbridge 76 D3
Bullbrook 27 C6
Bulley 36 C4
Bullgill 107 F7
Bull Hill 14 E4
Bullington
Hants 26 E2
Lincs 78 B3
Bull's Green 41 C5
Bullwood 145 F10
Bulmer
Essex 56 E2
N Yorks 96 C2
Bulmer Tye 56 F2
Bulphan 42 F2
Bulverhythe 18 E4
Bulwark 153 D9
Bulwell 76 E5
Bulwick 65 E6
Bumble's Green 41 D7
Bun Abhainn Eadarra 154 G6
Bunacaimb 147 C9
Bun a'Mhuillin 148 G2
Bunarkaig 136 F4
Bunbury 74 D2
Bunbury Heath 74 D2
Bunchrew 151 G9
Bundalloch 149 F13
Buness 160 C8
Bunessan 146 J6
Bungay 69 F6
Bunkers Hill 38 C4
Bunker's Hill
Lincs 78 B2
Lincs 79 D5
Bunloit 137 B8
Bun Loyne 136 D5
Bunnahabhain 142 A5
Bunny 64 B2
Buntait 150 H6
Buntingford 41 B6
Bunwell 68 E4
Burbage
Derbys 75 B7
Leics 63 E8
Wilts 25 C7
Burchett's Green 39 F8
Burcombe 25 F5
Burcot 39 E5
Burcott 40 B1
Burdon 111 D6
Bures 56 F3
Bures Green 56 F3
Burford
Ches E 74 D3
Oxon 38 C2
Shrops 49 C7
Burg 146 G6
Burgar 159 F4
Burgate
Hants 14 C2
Suff 56 B4
Burgess Hill 17 C7
Burgh 57 D6
Burgh by Sands 108 D3
Burgh Castle 69 D7
Burghclere 26 C2
Burghead 151 E14
Burghfield 26 C4
Burghfield Common 26 C4
Burghfield Hill 26 C4
Burgh Heath 28 D3
Burghill 49 E6
Burgh le Marsh 79 C8
Burgh Muir 141 B6
Burgh next Aylsham 81 E8
Burgh on Bain 91 F6
Burgh St Margaret 69 C7
Burgh St Peter 69 E7
Burghwallis 89 C6
Burham 29 C8
Buriton 15 B8
Burland 74 D3
Burlawn 4 B4
Burleigh 27 C6
Burlescombe 11 C5
Burleston 13 E5
Burley
Hants 14 D3
Rutland 65 C5
W Yorks 95 F5
Burleydam 74 E3
Burley Gate 49 E7
Burley in Wharfedale 94 E4
Burley Lodge 14 D3
Burley Street 14 D3
Burlingjobb 48 D4
Burlow 18 D2
Burlton 60 B4
Burmarsh 19 B7
Burmington 51 F7
Burn 89 B6
Burnaston 76 F2
Burnbank 119 D7
Burnby 96 E4
Burncross 88 E4
Burneside 99 E7
Burness 159 D7
Burneston 101 F8
Burnett 23 C8
Burnfoot
Borders 115 C7
Borders 115 C8
E Ayrs 112 D4
Perth 127 D8
Burnham
Bucks 40 F2
N Lincs 90 C4
Burnham Deepdale 80 C4
Burnham Green 41 C5
Burnham Market 80 C4
Burnham Norton 80 C4
Burnham-on-Crouch 43 E5
Burnham-on-Sea 22 E5
Burnham Overy Staithe 80 C4
Burnham Overy Town 80 C4
Burnham Thorpe 80 C4
Burnhead
Dumfries 113 E8
S Ayrs 112 D2
Burnhervie 141 C6
Burnhill Green 61 D7
Burnhope 110 E4
Burnhouse 118 D3
Burniston 103 E8
Burnlee 88 D2
Burnley 93 F8
Burnley Lane 93 F8
Burnmouth 123 C5
Burn of Cambus 127 D6
Burnopfield 110 D4
Burnsall 94 C3
Burnside
Angus 135 D5
E Ayrs 113 C5
Fife 128 D3
Shetland 160 F4
S Lanark 119 C6
W Loth 120 B3
Burnside of Duntrune 134 F4
Burnswark 107 B8
Burntcommon 27 D8
Burnt Heath 76 B2
Burnthouse 3 C6
Burnt Houses 101 B6
Burntisland 128 F4
Burnton 112 D4
Burntwood 62 D4
Burnt Yates 95 C5
Burnwynd 120 C4
Burpham
Sur 27 D8
W Sus 16 D4
Burradon
Northumb 117 D5
T&W 111 B5
Burrafirth 160 B8
Burraland
Shetland 160 F5
Shetland 160 J4
Burras 3 C5
Burravoe
Shetland 160 F7
Shetland 160 G5
Burray Village 159 J5
Burrells 100 C1
Burrelton 134 F2
Burridge
Devon 20 F4
Hants 15 C6
Burrill 101 F7
Burringham 90 D2
Burrington
Devon 9 C8
Hereford 49 B6
N Som 23 D6
Burrough Green 55 D7
Burrough on the Hill 64 C4
Burrow-bridge 11 B8
Burrowhill 27 C7
Burry 33 E5
Burry Green 33 E5
Burry Port = Porth Tywyn 33 D5
Burscough 86 C2
Burscough Bridge 86 C2
Bursea 96 F4
Burshill 97 E6
Bursledon 15 D5
Burslem 75 E5
Burstall 56 E4
Burstock 12 D2
Burston
Norf 68 F4
Staffs 75 F6
Burstow 28 E4
Burstwick 91 B6
Burtersett 100 F3
Burtle 23 E5
Burton
BCP 14 E2
Ches W 73 B7
Ches W 74 C2
Lincs 78 B2
Northumb 123 F7
Pembs 44 E4
Som 22 E3
Wilts 24 B3
Burton Agnes 97 C7
Burton Bradstock 12 F2
Burton Dassett 51 D8
Burton Fleming 97 B6
Burton Green
W Mid 51 B7
Wrex 73 D7
Burton Hastings 63 E8
Burton-in-Kendal 92 B5
Burton in Lonsdale 93 B6
Burton Joyce 77 E6
Burton Latimer 53 B7
Burton Lazars 64 C4
Burton-le-Coggles 65 B6
Burton Leonard 95 C6
Burton on the Wolds 64 B2
Burton Overy 64 E3
Burton Pedwardine 78 E4
Burton Pidsea 97 F8
Burton Salmon 89 B5
Burton Stather 90 C2
Burton upon Stather 90 C2
Burton upon Trent 63 B6
Burtonwood 86 E3
Burwardsley 74 D2
Burwarton 61 F6
Burwash 18 C3
Burwash Common 18 C3
Burwash Weald 18 C3
Burwell
Cambs 55 C6
Lincs 79 B6
Burwen 82 B4
Burwick 159 K5
Bury
Cambs 66 F2
Gtr Man 87 C6
Som 10 B4
W Sus 16 C4
Bury Green 41 B7
Bury St Edmunds 56 C2
Burythorpe 96 C3
Busby 119 D5
Buscot 38 E2
Bush Bank 49 D6
Bushbury 62 D3
Bushby 64 D3
Bush Crathie 139 E8
Bushey 40 E4
Bushey Heath 40 E4
Bush Green 68 F5
Bushley 50 F3
Bushton 25 B5
Buslingthorpe 90 F4
Busta 160 G5
Butcher's Cross 18 C2
Butcombe 23 C7
Butetown 22 B3
Butleigh 23 F7
Butleigh Wootton 23 F7
Butler's Cross 39 D8
Butler's End 63 F6
Butlers Marston 51 E8
Butley 57 D7
Butley High Corner 57 E7
Butterburn 109 B6
Buttercrambe 96 D3
Butterknowle 101 B6
Butterleigh 10 D4
Buttermere
Cumb 98 C3
Wilts 25 C8
Buttershaw 88 B2
Butterstone 133 E7
Butterton 75 D7
Butterwick
Durham 102 B1
Lincs 79 E6
N Yorks 96 B3
N Yorks 97 B5
Butt Green 74 D3
Buttington 60 D2
Buttonoak 50 B2
Buttsash 14 D5
Butt's Green 14 B4
Buxhall 56 D4
Buxhall Fen Street 56 D4
Buxley 122 D4
Buxted 17 B8
Buxton
Derbys 75 B7
Norf 81 E8
Buxworth 87 F8
Bwcle = Buckley 73 C6
Bwlch 35 B5
Bwlchgwyn 73 D6
Bwlch-Llan 46 D4
Bwlchnewydd 32 B4
Bwlchtocyn 70 E4
Bwlch-y-cibau 59 C8
Bwlchyddar 59 B8
Bwlch-y-fadfa 46 E3
Bwlch-y-ffridd 59 E7
Bwlchygroes 45 F4
Bwlch-y-sarnau 48 B2
Byermoor 110 D4
Byers Green 110 F5
Byfield 52 D3
Byfleet 27 C8
Byford 49 E5
Bygrave 54 F3
Byker 111 C5
Bylchau 72 C3
Byley 74 C4
Bynea 33 E6
Byrness 116 D3
Bythorn 53 B8
Byton 49 C5
Byworth 16 B3

C

Cabharstadh 155 E8
Cablea 133 F6
Cabourne 90 D5
Cabrach
Argyll 144 G3
Moray 140 B2
Cabrich 151 G8
Cabus 92 E4
Cackle Street 17 B8
Cadbury 10 D4
Cadbury Barton 9 C8
Cadder 119 B6
Caddington 40 C3
Caddonfoot 121 F7
Cadeby
Leics 63 D8
S Yorks 89 D6
Cadeleigh 10 D4
Cade Street 18 C3
Cadgwith 3 E6
Cadham 128 D4
Cadishead 86 E5
Cadle 33 E7
Cadley
Lancs 92 F5
Wilts 25 C7
Wilts 25 D7
Cadmore End 39 E7
Cadnam 14 C3
Cadney 90 D4
Cadole 73 C6
Cadoxton 22 C3
Cadoxton-Juxta-Neath 34 E1
Cadshaw 86 C5
Cadzow 119 D7
Caeathro 82 E4
Caehopkin 34 C2
Caenby 90 F4
Caenby Corner 90 F3
Caerau
Bridgend 34 E2
Cardiff 22 B3
Caêr-bryn 33 C6
Caerdeon 58 C3
Caerdydd = Cardiff 22 B3
Caerfarchell 44 C2
Caerffili = Caerphilly 35 F5
Caerfyrddin = Carmarthen 33 B5
Caergeiliog 82 D3
Caergwrle 73 D7
Caergybi = Holyhead 82 C2
Caerleon = Caerllion 35 E7
Caer Llan 36 D1
Caerllion = Caerleon 35 E7
Caernarfon 82 E4
Caerphilly = Caerffili 35 F5
Caersws 59 E7
Caerwedros 46 D2
Caerwent 36 E1
Caerwych 71 D7
Caerwys 72 B5
Caethle 58 E3
Caim 83 C6
Caio 47 F5
Cairinis 148 B3
Cairisiadar 154 D5
Cairminis 154 J5
Cairnbaan 145 D7
Cairnbanno House 153 D8
Cairnborrow 152 D4
Cairnbrogie 141 B7
Cairnbulg Castle 153 B10
Cairncross
Angus 134 B4
Borders 122 C4
Cairndow 125 D7
Cairness 153 B10
Cairneyhill 128 F2
Cairnfield House 152 B4
Cairngaan 104 F5
Cairngarroch 104 E4
Cairnhill 153 E6
Cairnie
Aberds 141 D7
Aberds 152 D4
Cairnorrie 153 D8
Cairnpark 141 C7
Cairnryan 104 C4
Cairnton 159 H4
Caister-on-Sea 69 C8
Caistor 90 D5
Caistor St Edmund 68 D5
Caistron 117 D5
Caitha Bowland 121 E7
Calais Street 56 F3
Calanais 154 D7
Calbost 155 F9
Calbourne 14 F5
Calceby 79 B6
Calcot Row 26 B4
Calcott 31 C5
Caldback 160 C8
Caldbeck 108 F3
Caldbergh 101 F5
Caldecote
Cambs 54 D4
Cambs 65 F8
Herts 54 F3
Northants 52 D4
Caldecott
Northants 53 C7
Oxon 38 E4
Rutland 65 E5
Calderbank 119 C7
Calder Bridge 98 D2
Calderbrook 87 C7
Caldercruix 119 C8
Calder Hall 98 D2
Calder Mains 158 E2
Caldermill 119 E6
Calder Vale 92 E5
Calderwood 119 D6
Caldhame 134 E4
Caldicot 36 F1
Caldwell
Derbys 63 C6
N Yorks 101 C6
Caldy 85 F3
Caledrhydiau 46 D3
Calfsound 159 E6
Calgary 146 F6
Califer 151 F13
California
Falk 120 B2
Norf 69 C8
Calke 63 B7
Callakille 149 C11
Callaly 117 D6
Callander 126 D5
Callaughton 61 E6
Callestick 4 D2
Calligarry 149 H11
Callington 5 C8
Callow 49 F6
Callow End 50 E3
Callow Hill
Wilts 37 F7
Worcs 50 B2
Callows Grave 49 C7
Calmore 14 C4
Calmsden 37 D7
Calne 24 B5
Calow 76 B4
Calshot 15 D5
Calstock 6 C2
Calstone Wellington 24 C5
Calthorpe 81 D7
Calthwaite 108 E4
Calton
N Yorks 94 D2
Staffs 75 D8
Calveley 74 D2
Calver 76 B2
Calverhall 74 F3
Calver Hill 49 E5
Calverleigh 10 C4
Calverley 94 F5
Calvert 39 B6
Calverton
M Keynes 53 F5
Notts 77 E6
Calvine 133 C5
Calvo 107 D8
Cam 36 E4
Camas-luinie 136 B2
Camasnacroise 130 D2
Camastianavaig 149 E10
Camasunary 149 G10
Camault Muir 151 G8
Camb 160 D7
Camber 19 D6
Camberley 27 C6
Camberwell 28 B4
Camblesforth 89 B7
Cambo 117 F6
Cambois 117 F9
Camborne 3 B5
Cambourne 54 D4
Cambridge
Cambs 55 D5
Glos 36 D4
Cambridge Town 43 F5
Cambus 127 E7
Cambusavie Farm 151 B10
Cambusbarron 127 E6
Cambuskenneth 127 E7
Cambuslang 119 C6
Cambusmore Lodge 151 B10
Camden 41 F5
Camelford 8 F3
Camelsdale 27 F6
Camerory 151 H13
Camer's Green 50 F2
Camerton
Bath 23 D8
Cumb 107 F7
E Yorks 91 B6
Camghouran 132 D2
Cammachmore 141 E8
Cammeringham 90 F3
Camore 151 B10
Campbeltown 143 F8
Camperdown 111 B5
Camp Hill 63 E7
Campmuir 134 F2
Campsall 89 C6
Campsey Ash 57 D7
Campton 54 F2
Camptown 116 C2
Camrose 44 C4
Camserney 133 E5
Camster 158 F4
Camuschoirk 130 C1
Camuscross 149 G11
Camusnagaul
Highld 130 B4
Highld 150 C3
Camusrory 147 B11
Camusteel 149 D12
Camusterrach 149 D12
Camusvrachan 132 E3
Canada 14 C3
Canadia 18 D4
Canal Side 89 C7
Candacraig House 140 C2
Candlesby 79 C7
Candy Mill 120 E3
Cane End 26 B4
Canewdon 42 E4
Canford Bottom 13 D8
Canford Cliffs 13 F8
Canford Magna 13 E8
Canham's Green 56 C4
Canholes 75 B7
Canisbay 158 C5
Cann 13 B6
Cannard's Grave 23 E8
Cann Common 13 B6
Cannich 150 H6
Cannington 22 F4
Cannock 62 D3
Cannock Wood 62 C4
Canonbie 108 B3
Canon Bridge 49 E6
Canon Frome 49 E8
Canon Pyon 49 E6
Canons Ashby 52 D3
Canonstown 2 C4
Canterbury 30 D5
Cantley
Norf 69 D6
S Yorks 89 D7
Cantlop 60 D5
Canton 22 B3
Cantraybruich 151 G10
Cantraydoune 151 G10
Cantraywood 151 G10
Cantsfield 93 B6
Canvey Island 42 F3
Canwick 78 C2
Canworthy Water 8 E4
Caol 131 B5
Caolas 146 G3
Caolas Scalpaigh 154 H7
Caolas Stocinis 154 H6
Caol Ila 142 A5
Capel 28 E2
Capel Bangor 58 F3
Capel Betws Lleucu 46 D5
Capel Carmel 70 E2
Capel Coch 82 C4
Capel Curig 83 F7
Capel Cynon 46 E2
Capel Dewi
Carms 33 B5
Ceredig 46 E3
Ceredig 58 F3
Capel Garmon 83 F8
Capel-gwyn 82 D3
Capel Gwyn 33 B5
Capel Gwynfe 33 B8
Capel Hendre 33 C6
Capel Hermon 71 E8
Capel Isaac 33 B6
Capel Iwan 45 F4
Capel le Ferne 31 F6
Capel Llanilltern 34 F4
Capel Mawr 82 D4
Capel St Andrew 57 E7
Capel St Mary 56 F4
Capel Seion 46 B5
Capel Tygwydd 45 E4
Capel Uchaf 70 C5
Capelulo 83 D7
Capel-y-graig 82 E5
Capenhurst 73 B7
Capernwray 92 B5
Capheaton 117 F6
Cappercleuch 115 B5
Capplegill 114 D4
Capton 7 D6
Caputh 133 F7
Carbis Bay 2 C4
Carbost
Highld 149 D9
Highld 149 E8
Carbrook 88 F4
Carbrooke 68 D2
Carburton 77 B6
Carcant 121 D6
Carcary 135 D6
Carclaze 4 D5
Car Colston 77 E7
Carcroft 89 C6
Cardenden 128 E4
Cardeston 60 C3
Cardiff = Caerdydd 22 B3
Cardigan = Aberteifi 45 E3
Cardington
Bedford 53 E8
Shrops 60 E5
Cardinham 5 C6
Cardonald 118 C5
Cardow 152 D1
Cardrona 121 F6
Cardross 118 B3
Cardurnock 107 D8
Careby 65 C7
Careston Castle 135 D5
Carew 32 D1
Carew Cheriton 32 D1
Carew Newton 32 D1
Carey 49 F7
Carfrae 121 C8
Cargenbridge 107 B6
Cargill 134 F1
Cargo 108 D3
Cargreen 6 C2
Carham 122 F4
Carhampton 22 E2
Carharrack 3 B6
Carie
Perth 132 D3
Perth 132 F3
Carines 4 D2
Carisbrooke 15 F5
Cark 92 B3
Carlabhagh 154 C7
Carland Cross 4 D3
Carlby 65 C7
Carlecotes 88 D2
Carlesmoor 94 B4
Carleton
Cumb 99 B7
Cumb 108 D4
Lancs 92 F3
N Yorks 94 E2
Carleton Forehoe 68 D3
Carleton Rode 68 E4
Carlingcott 23 D8
Carlin How 103 C5
Carlisle 108 D4
Carlops 120 D4
Carlton
Bedford 53 D7
Cambs 55 D7
Leics 63 D7
Notts 77 E6
N Yorks 89 B7
N Yorks 101 C6
N Yorks 101 F5
N Yorks 102 F4
Stockton 102 B1
Suff 57 C7
S Yorks 88 C4
W Yorks 88 B4
Carlton Colville 69 F8
Carlton Curlieu 64 E3
Carlton Husthwaite 95 B7
Carlton in Cleveland 102 D3
Carlton in Lindrick 89 F6
Carlton le Moorland 78 D2
Carlton Miniott 102 F1
Carlton on Trent 77 C7
Carlton Scroop 78 E2
Carluke 119 D8
Carmarthen = Caerfyrddin 33 B5
Carmel
Anglesey 82 C3
Carms 33 C6
Flint 73 B5
Guern 16
Gwyn 82 F4
Carmont 141 F7
Carmunnock 119 D6
Carmyle 119 C6
Carmyllie 135 E5
Carnaby 97 C7
Carnach
Highld 136 B3
Highld 150 B3
W Isles 154 H7
Carnachy 157 D10
Càrnais 154 D5
Carnbee 129 D7
Carnbo 128 D2
Carnbrea 3 B5
Carnduff 119 E6
Carnduncan 142 B3
Carne 3 C8
Carnforth 92 B4
Carn-gorm 136 B2
Carnhedryn 44 C3
Carnhell Green 2 C5
Carnkie
Corn 3 C5
Corn 3 C6
Carno 59 E6
Carnoch
Highld 150 F5
Highld 150 H6
Carnock 128 F2
Carnon Downs 3 B6
Carnousie 153 C6
Carnoustie 135 F5
Carnwath 120 E2
Carnyorth 2 C2
Carperby 101 F5
Carpley Green 100 F4
Carr 89 E6
Carradale 143 E9
Carragraich 154 H6
Carrbridge 138 B5
Carrefour Selous 17
Carreglefn 82 C3
Carreg-wen 45 E4
Carr Hill 111 C5
Carrick
Argyll 145 E8
Fife 129 B6
Carrick Castle 145 D10
Carrick House 159 E6
Carriden 128 F2
Carrington
Gtr Man 86 E5
Lincs 79 D6
Midloth 121 C6
Carrog
Conwy 71 C8
Denb 72 E5
Carron
Falk 127 F7
Moray 152 D2
Carronbridge 113 E8
Carron Bridge 127 F6
Carronshore 127 F7
Carrshield 109 E8
Carrutherstown 107 B8
Carrville 111 E6
Carsaig
Argyll 144 E6
Argyll 147 J8
Carscreugh 105 D6
Carsegowan 105 D8
Carse Gray 134 D4
Carse Ho 144 G6
Carseriggan 105 C7
Carsethorn 107 D6
Carshalton 28 C3
Carsington 76 D2
Carskiey 143 H7
Carsluith 105 D8
Carsphairn 113 E5
Carstairs 120 E2
Carstairs Junction 120 E2
Carswell Marsh 38 E3
Carter's Clay 14 B4
Carterton 38 D2
Carterway Heads 110 D3
Carthew 4 D5
Carthorpe 101 F8
Cartington 117 D6
Cartland 119 E8
Cartmel 92 B3
Cartmel Fell 99 F6
Carway 33 D5
Cary Fitzpaine 12 B3
Cascob 48 C4
Cas-gwent = Chepstow 36 E2
Cashlie 132 E1
Cashmoor 13 C7
Casnewydd = Newport 35 F7
Cassey Compton 37 C7
Cassington 38 C4
Cassop 111 F6
Castell 72 C5
Castellau 34 F4
Castell-Howell 46 E3
Castell-Nedd = Neath 33 E8
Castell Newydd Emlyn = Newcastle Emlyn 46 E2
Castell-y-bwch 35 E6
Casterton 93 B6
Castle Acre 67 C8
Castle Ashby 53 D6
Castlebay = Bagh a Chaisteil 148 J1
Castle Bolton 101 E5
Castle Bromwich 62 F5
Castle Bytham 65 C6
Castlebythe 32 B1
Castle Caereinion 59 D8
Castle Camps 55 E7
Castle Carrock 108 D5
Castlecary 119 B7
Castle Cary 23 F8
Castle Combe 24 B3
Castlecraig 151 E11
Castle Donington 63 B8
Castle Douglas 106 C4
Castle Eaton 37 E8
Castle Eden 111 F7
Castlefairn 113 F7
Castle Forbes 140 C5
Castleford 88 B5
Castle Frome 49 E8
Castle Green 27 C7
Castle Gresley 63 C6
Castle Heaton 122 E5
Castle Hedingham 55 F8
Castlehill
Borders 120 F5
Highld 158 D3
W Dunb 118 B3
Castle Hill 29 E7
Castle Huntly 128 B5
Castle Kennedy 104 D5
Castlemaddy 113 F5
Castlemartin 44 F4
Castlemilk
Dumfries 107 B8
Glasgow 119 D6
Castlemorris 44 B4
Castlemorton 50 F2
Castle O'er 115 E5
Castle Pulverbatch 60 D4
Castle Rising 67 B6
Castleside 110 E3
Castle Stuart 151 G10
Castlethorpe 53 E6
Castleton
Angus 134 E3
Argyll 145 E7
Derbys 88 F2
Gtr Man 87 C6
Newport 35 F6
N Yorks 102 D4
Castletown
Ches W 73 D8
Highld 151 G10
Highld 158 D3
IoM 84 F2
T&W 111 D6
Castleweary 115 D7
Castley 95 E5
Caston 68 E2
Castor 65 E8
Catacol 143 D10
Catbrain 36 F2
Catbrook 36 D2
Catchall 2 D3
Catchems Corner 51 B7
Catchgate 110 D4
Catcleugh 116 D3
Catcliffe 88 F5
Catcott 23 F5
Caterham 28 D4
Catfield 69 B6
Catfirth 160 H6
Catford 28 B4
Catforth 92 F4
Cathays 22 B3
Cathcart 119 C5
Cathedine 35 B5
Catherington 15 C7
Catherton 49 B8
Catlodge 138 E2
Catlowdy 108 B4
Catmore 38 F4
Caton 92 C5
Caton Green 92 C5
Catrine 113 B5
Cat's Ash 35 E7
Catsfield 18 D4
Catshill 50 B4
Cattal 95 D7
Cattawade 56 F5
Catterall 92 E4
Catterick 101 E7
Catterick Bridge 101 E7
Catterick Garrison 101 E6
Catterlen 108 F4
Catterline 135 B8
Catterton 95 E8
Catthorpe 52 B3
Cattistock 12 E3
Catton
Northumb 109 D8
N Yorks 95 B6
Catwick 97 E7
Catworth 53 B8
Caudlesprings 68 D2
Caulcott 39 B5
Cauldcots 135 E6
Cauldhame 126 E5
Cauldmill 115 C8
Cauldon 75 E7
Caulkerbush 107 D6
Caulside 115 F7
Caunsall 62 F2
Caunton 77 D7
Causewayend 120 F3
Causeway End 105 C8
Causeway Foot 94 F3
Causewayhead
Cumb 107 D8
Stirling 127 E6
Causeyend 141 C8
Causey Park Bridge 117 E7
Cautley 100 E1
Cavendish 56 E2
Cavendish Bridge 63 B8
Cavenham 55 C8
Caversfield 39 B5
Caversham 26 B5
Caverswall 75 E6
Cavil 96 F3
Cawdor 151 F11
Cawkwell 79 B5
Cawood 95 F8
Cawsand 6 D2
Cawston 81 E7
Cawthorne 88 D3
Cawthorpe 65 B7
Cawton 96 B2
Caxton 54 D4
Caynham 49 B7
Caythorpe
Lincs 78 E2
Notts 77 E6
Cayton 103 F8
Ceann a Bhaigh 148 B2
Ceannacroc Lodge 136 C5
Ceann a Deas Loch Baghasdail 148 G2
Ceann Shiphoirt 155 F7
Ceann Tarabhaigh 154 F7
Cearsiadair 155 E8
Cefn Berain 72 C3
Cefn-brith 72 D3
Cefn Canol 73 F6
Cefn-coch 83 E8
Cefn Coch 59 B8
Cefn-coed-y-cymmer 34 D4
Cefn Cribbwr 34 F2
Cefn Cross 34 F2
Cefn-ddwysarn 72 F3
Cefn Einion 60 F2

Cefneithin.......33 C6
Cefn-gorwydd...47 E8
Cefn-mawr.......73 E6
Cefn-y-bedd.....73 D7
Cefn-y-pant......36 D3
Cei-bach..........46 D3
Ceinewydd
 =New Quay.....46 D2
Ceint..............82 D4
Cellan............46 E5
Cellarhead........75 E6
Cemaes...........82 B3
Cemmaes..........58 D5
Cemmaes Road...58 D5
Cenarth...........45 E4
Cenin.............71 C5
Central...........118 B2
Ceos.............155 E8
Ceres............129 C6
Cerne Abbas......12 D4
Cerney Wick......37 E7
Cerrigceinwen....82 D4
Cerrigydrudion...72 E3
Cessford.........116 B3
Ceunant...........82 E5
Chaceley..........50 F3
Chacewater........3 B6
Chackmore........52 F4
Chacombe.........52 E2
Chadderton........87 D7
Chadderton Fold 87 D6
Chaddesden.......76 F3
Chaddesley
 Corbett.........50 B3
Chaddleworth.....26 B2
Chadlington......38 B3
Chadshunt........51 D8
Chad Valley......62 F4
Chadwell.........64 B4
Chadwell St Mary.29 B7
Chadwick End....51 B7
Chadwick Green..86 E3
Chaffcombe.......11 C8
Chagford.........10 F2
Chailey..........17 C7
Chainbridge......66 D4
Chain Bridge.....79 E6
Chainhurst.......29 E8
Chalbury.........13 D8
Chalbury
 Common.........13 D8
Chaldon..........28 D4
Chaldon Herring..13 F5
Chale............15 G5
Chale Green......15 G5
Chalfont
 Common.........40 E3
Chalfont St Giles.40 E2
Chalfont St Peter.40 E3
Chalford.........37 D5
Chalgrove........39 E6
Chalk............29 B7
Challaborough....21 C5
Challacombe......21 E6
Challoch.........105 C7
Challock.........30 D4
Chalton
 C Beds.........40 B3
 Hants..........15 C8
Chalvington......18 E2
Chancery.........46 B4
Chandler's Ford..14 B5
Channel Tunnel...19 B8
Channerwick.....160 L6
Chantry
 Som............24 E2
 Suff...........56 E5
Chapel...........128 E4
Chapel Allerton
 Som............23 D6
 W Yorks........95 F6
Chapel Amble......4 B4
Chapel Brampton.52 C5
Chapel Chorlton..74 F5
Chapel End.......63 E7
Chapel-en-le-
 Frith..........87 F8
Chapelgate.......66 B4
Chapel Green
 Warks..........52 C2
 Warks..........63 F6
Chapel Haddlesey.89 B6
Chapelhall.......119 C7
Chapel Head......66 F3
Chapelhill
 Dumfries.......114 E3
 Highld........151 D11
 N Ayrs.........118 E4
 Perth..........128 B4
 Perth..........133 F7
Chapel Hill
 Aberds........153 E10
 Lincs..........78 D5
 Mon............36 E2
 N Yorks........95 E6
Chapelknowe.....108 B3
Chapel Lawn......48 B5
Chapel-le-Dale..93 B7
Chapel Milton...87 F8
Chapel of
 Garioch........141 B6
Chapel Row.......26 C3
Chapel St
 Leonards.......79 B8
Chapel Stile.....99 D5
Chapelton
 Angus.........135 E6
 Devon...........9 B7
 Highld........138 C5
 S Lanark......119 E6
Chapeltown
 Blackburn......86 C5
 Moray.........139 B8
 S Yorks........88 E4
Chapmanslade....24 E3
Chapmans Well....9 E5
Chapmore End....41 C6
Chappel..........42 B4
Chard............11 D8
Chardstock.......11 D8
Charfield........36 E4
Charford.........50 C4
Charing..........30 E3
Charing Cross....14 C2
Charing Heath....30 E3
Charingworth....51 F7

Charlbury........38 C3
Charlcombe.......24 C2
Charlecote.......51 D7
Charles..........21 F5
Charlesfield....107 E6
Charleston
 Angus.........134 E3
 Renfs.........118 C4
Charlestown
 Aberdeen......141 D8
 Corn............4 D5
 Derbys.........87 E8
 Dorset.........12 G4
 Fife..........128 F2
 Gtr Man........87 D6
 Highld.......149 A13
 Highld........151 G9
 W Yorks........87 B7
Charlestown of
 Aberlour.......152 D2
Charles Tye......56 D4
Charlesworth.....87 E8
Charleton.........7 E5
Charlton
 Hants..........25 E8
 Herts..........40 B4
 London.........28 B5
 Northants......52 F3
 Northumb......116 F4
 Som............23 D8
 Telford........61 C6
 Wilts..........13 B7
 Wilts..........25 D6
 Wilts..........37 E6
 Worcs..........50 D5
 W Sus..........16 C2
Charlton Abbots.37 B7
Charlton Adam...12 B3
Charlton-All-
 Saints.........14 B2
Charlton Down...12 E4
Charlton
 Horethorne.....12 B4
Charlton Kings...37 B6
Charlton
 Mackerell......12 B3
Charlton
 Marshall.......13 D6
Charlton
 Musgrove.......12 B5
Charlton on
 Otmoor.........39 C5
Charltons.......102 C4
Charlwood........28 E3
Charlynch........22 F4
Charminster......12 E4
Charmouth........11 E8
Charndon.........39 B6
Charney Bassett.38 E3
Charnock
 Richard........86 C3
Charsfield.......57 D6
Chart Corner.....29 D8
Charter Alley....26 D3
Charterhouse.....23 D6
Charterville
 Allotments.....38 C3
Chartham.........30 D5
Chartham Hatch.30 D5
Chartridge.......40 D2
Charvil..........27 B5
Charwelton.......52 D3
Chasetown........62 D4
Chastleton.......38 B2
Chasty............8 D5
Chatburn.........93 E7
Chatcull.........74 F4
Chatham..........29 C8
Chathill........117 B7
Chattenden.......29 B8
Chatteris........66 F3
Chattisham.......56 E4
Chatto..........116 C3
Chatton.........117 B6
Chawleigh........10 C2
Chawley..........38 D4
Chawston.........54 D2
Chawton..........26 F5
Cheadle
 Gtr Man........87 F6
 Staffs.........75 E7
Cheadle Heath...87 F6
Cheadle Hulme...87 F6
Cheam............28 C3
Cheapside........27 C8
Chearsley........39 C7
Chebsey..........62 B2
Checkendon.......39 F6
Checkley
 Ches E.........74 D4
 Hereford.......49 F7
 Staffs.........75 F7
Chedburgh........55 D8
Cheddar..........23 D6
Cheddington.....40 C2
Cheddleton.......75 D6
Cheddon
 Fitzpaine......11 B7
Chedglow.........37 E6
Chedgrave........69 E6
Chedington......12 D2
Chediston........57 B7
Chedworth........37 C7
Chedzoy..........22 F5
Cheeklaw........122 D3
Cheeseman's
 Green..........19 B7
Cheglinch........20 E4
Cheldon..........10 C2
Chelford.........74 B5
Chellaston.......76 F3
Chellington......53 D7
Chelmarsh........61 F7
Chelmer Village.42 D3
Chelmondiston...57 F6
Chelmorton.......75 C8
Chelmsford.......42 D3
Chelsea..........28 B3
Chelsfield.......29 C5
Chelsworth.......56 E3
Cheltenham.......37 B6
Chelveston.......53 C7
Chelvey..........23 C6
Chelwood.........23 C8
Chelwood
 Common.........17 B8

Chelwood Gate...17 B8
Chelworth........37 E6
Chelworth Green.37 E7
Chemistry........74 E2
Chenies..........40 E3
Cheny Longville..60 F4
Chepstow
 =Cas-gwent.....36 E2
Chequerfield.....89 B5
Cherhill.........24 B5
Cherington
 Glos...........37 E6
 Warks..........51 F7
Cheriton
 Devon..........21 E6
 Hants..........15 B6
 Kent...........19 B8
 Swansea........33 E5
Cheriton Bishop..10 E2
Cheriton
 Fitzpaine......10 D3
Cheriton or Stackpole
 Elidor.........44 F4
Cherrington......61 B6
Cherrybank......128 B3
Cherry Burton...97 E5
Cherry Hinton...55 D5
Cherry Orchard..50 D3
Cherry
 Willingham.....78 B3
Chertsey.........27 C8
Cheselbourne....13 E5
Chesham..........40 D2
Chesham Bois...40 E2
Cheshunt.........41 D6
Cheslyn Hay......62 D3
Chessington......28 C2
Chester..........73 C8
Chesterblade.....23 E8
Chesterfield.....76 B3
Chester-le-
 Street........111 D5
Chester Moor...111 E5
Chesters
 Borders.......116 B2
 Borders.......116 C2
Chesterton
 Cambs..........55 C5
 Cambs..........65 E8
 Glos...........37 D7
 Oxon...........39 B5
 Shrops.........61 E7
 Staffs.........74 E5
 Warks..........51 D8
Chesterwood....109 C8
Chestfield.......30 C5
Cheston...........6 D4
Cheswardine.....61 B7
Cheswick........123 E6
Chetnole.........12 D4
Chettiscombe....10 C4
Chettisham.......66 F5
Chettle..........13 C7
Chetton..........61 E6
Chetwode.........39 B6
Chetwynd Aston.61 C7
Cheveley.........55 C7
Chevening........29 D5
Chevington.......55 D8
Chevithorne......10 C4
Chew Magna......23 C7
Chew Stoke......23 C7
Chewton
 Keynsham.......23 C8
Chewton Mendip.23 D7
Chicheley........53 E7
Chichester.......16 D2
Chickerell.......12 F4
Chicklade........24 F4
Chicksgrove......24 F4
Chidden..........15 C7
Chiddingfold.....27 F7
Chiddingly.......18 D2
Chiddingstone...29 E5
Chiddingstone
 Causeway.......29 E6
Chiddingstone
 Hoath..........29 E5
Chideock.........12 E2
Chidham..........15 D8
Chidswell........88 B3
Chieveley........26 B2
Chignall St
 James..........42 D2
Chignall Smealy..42 D2
Chigwell.........41 E7
Chigwell Row....41 E7
Chilbolton.......25 F8
Chilcomb.........15 B6
Chilcombe........12 E3
Chilcompton.....23 D8
Chilcote.........63 C6
Childer Thornton.73 B7
Child Okeford...13 C6
Childrey.........38 F3
Child's Ercall...61 B6
Childswickham...51 F5
Childwall........86 F2
Childwick Green.40 C4
Chilfrome........12 E3
Chilgrove........16 C2
Chilham..........30 D4
Chilhampton.....25 F5
Chilla............9 D6
Chillaton.........9 F6
Chillenden.......31 D6
Chillerton.......15 F5
Chillesford......57 D7
Chillingham.....117 B6
Chillington
 Devon...........7 E5
 Som............11 C8
Chilmark.........24 F4
Chilson..........38 C3
Chilsworthy
 Corn............6 B2
 Devon...........8 D5
Chilthorne
 Domer..........12 C3
Chilton
 Bucks..........39 C6
 Durham........101 B7
 Oxon...........38 F4
Chilton Cantelo..12 B3
Chilton Foliat...25 B8
Chilton Lane...111 F6
Chilton Polden...23 F5

Chilton Street...55 E8
Chilton Trinity..22 F4
Chilvers Coton...63 E7
Chilwell.........76 F5
Chilworth
 Hants..........14 C5
 Sur............27 E8
Chimney..........38 D3
Chineham.........26 D4
Chingford........41 E6
Chinley..........87 F8
Chinley Head....87 F8
Chinnor..........39 D7
Chipnall.........74 F4
Chippenhall
 Green..........57 B6
Chippenham
 Cambs..........55 C7
 Wilts..........24 B4
Chipperfield.....40 D3
Chipping
 Herts..........54 F4
 Lancs..........93 E6
Chipping
 Campden........51 F6
Chipping Hill....42 C4
Chipping Norton.38 B3
Chipping Ongar..42 D1
Chipping Sodbury 36 F4
Chipping
 Warden.........52 E2
Chipstable.......10 B5
Chipstead
 Kent...........29 D5
 Sur............28 D3
Chirbury.........60 E2
Chirk =Y Waun...73 F6
Chirk Bank.......73 F6
Chirmorrie......105 B6
Chirnside.......122 D4
Chirnsidebridge 122 D4
Chirton..........25 D5
Chisbury.........25 C7
Chiselborough..12 C2
Chiseldon........25 B6
Chiserley........87 B8
Chislehampton..39 E5
Chislehurst......28 B5
Chislet..........31 C6
Chiswell Green..40 D4
Chiswick.........28 B3
Chiswick End....54 E4
Chisworth........87 E7
Chithurst........16 B2
Chittering.......55 B5
Chitterne........24 E4
Chittlehamholt...9 B8
Chittlehampton...9 B8
Chittoe..........24 C4
Chivenor.........20 F4
Chobham.........27 C7
Choicelee.......122 D3
Cholderton.......25 E7
Cholesbury.......40 D2
Chollerford.....110 B2
Chollerton......110 B2
Cholmondeston..74 C3
Cholsey..........39 F5
Cholstrey........49 D6
Chop Gate......102 E3
Choppington....117 F8
Chopwell........110 D4
Chorley
 Ches E.........74 D2
 Lancs..........86 C3
 Shrops.........61 F6
 Staffs.........62 C4
Chorleywood.....40 E3
Chorlton cum
 Hardy..........87 E6
Chorlton Lane...73 E8
Choulton.........60 F3
Chowdene.......111 D5
Chowley..........73 D8
Chrishall........54 F5
Christchurch
 BCP............14 E2
 Cambs..........66 E4
 Glos...........36 C2
 Newport........35 F7
Christian Malford.24 B4
Christleton......73 C8
Christmas
 Common.........39 E7
Christon.........23 D5
Christon Bank..117 B8
Christow.........10 F3
Chryston........119 B6
Chudleigh........7 B6
Chudleigh
 Knighton........7 B6
Chulmleigh.......9 C8
Chunal...........87 E8
Church...........86 B5
Churcham.........36 C4
Church Aston...61 C7
Churchbank......48 B4
Church
 Brampton.......52 C5
Churchbridge...62 D3
Church
 Broughton......76 F2
Church
 Crookham.......27 D6
Churchdown......37 C5
Church Eaton...62 C2
Churchend
 Essex..........42 B2
 Essex..........43 E6
 S Glos.........36 E4
Church End
 Cambs..........66 D3
 Cambs..........66 F2
 C Beds.........40 B2
 C Beds.........53 F7
 C Beds.........54 F2
 Essex..........42 B3
 Essex..........55 E6
 E Yorks........97 D6
 Hants..........26 D4
 Lincs..........78 F5
 Warks..........63 E6
 Wilts..........24 B5
Church Enstone...38 B3
Church Fenton...95 F8
Churchfield......62 E4
Churchgate
 Street.........41 C7

Church Green
 Devon..........11 E6
 Norf...........68 D3
Church Gresley...63 C6
Church
 Hanborough...38 C4
Church Hill......74 C3
Church Houses..102 E4
Churchill
 Devon..........11 D8
 Devon..........20 E4
 N Som..........23 D6
 Oxon...........38 B2
 Worcs..........50 B3
 Worcs..........50 D4
Churchinford.....11 C7
Church Knowle..13 F7
Church Laneham.77 B8
Church Langton..64 E4
Church Lawford..52 B2
Church Lawton...74 D5
Church Leigh....75 F7
Church Lench....50 D5
Church Mayfield.75 E8
Church Minshull.74 C3
Church Norton...16 E2
Churchover.......64 F2
Church Preen...60 E5
Church
 Pulverbatch...60 D4
Churchstanton...11 C6
Church Stoke...60 E2
Churchstow.......6 E5
Church Stowe...52 D4
Church Street...29 B8
Church Stretton..60 E4
Churchtown
 Derbys.........76 C2
 IoM............84 C4
 Lancs..........92 E4
 Mers...........85 F4
Church Town
 N Lincs........89 D8
 Sur............28 D4
Church Village...34 F4
Church Warsop...77 C5
Churnsike
 Lodge.........109 B6
Churston Ferrers..7 D7
Churt............27 F6
Churton..........73 D8
Churwell.........88 B3
Chute Standen...25 D8
Chwilog..........70 D5
Chyandour.........2 C3
Cilan Uchaf......70 E3
Cilcain..........73 C5
Cilcennin........46 C4
Cilfor...........71 D7
Cilfrew..........34 D1
Cilfynydd........34 E4
Cilgerran........45 E3
Cilgwyn
 Carms..........33 B8
 Gwyn...........82 F4
 Pembs..........45 F2
Ciliau Aeron....46 D3
Cill Donnain...148 F2
Cille Bhrighde..148 G2
Cille Pheadair..148 G2
Cilmery..........48 D2
Cilsan...........33 B6
Ciltalgarth......72 E2
Cilwendeg........45 F4
Cilybebyll.......33 D8
Cilycwm..........47 F6
Cimla............34 E1
Cinderford.......36 C3
Cippyn...........45 E3
Circebost.......154 D6
Cirencester......37 D7
Ciribhig........154 C6
City
 London.........41 F6
 Powys..........60 F2
City Dulas.......82 C4
Clachaig........145 E10
Clachan
 Argyll........124 D3
 Argyll........125 D7
 Argyll........130 E2
 Argyll........144 H6
 Highld.......149 E11
 W Isles.......148 D2
Clachan of
 Campsie.......119 B6
Clachan of
 Glendaruel...145 E8
Clachan-Seil..124 D3
Clachan
 Strachur......125 D6
Clachbreck......144 F6
Clachnabrain...134 C3
Clachtoll.......156 G3
Clackmannan...127 E8
Clacton-on-Sea..43 C7
Cladach
 Chireboist....148 B2
Cladach-
 knockline.....148 B2
Cladich.........125 C6
Claggan
 Highld........131 B5
 Highld.......147 E10
Claigan.........148 C7
Claines..........50 D3
Clandown.........23 D8
Clanfield
 Hants..........15 C7
 Oxon...........38 D2
Clanville........25 E8
Claonaig........145 H7
Claonel.........157 J8
Clapgate
 Dorset.........13 D8
 Herts..........41 B7
Clapham
 Bedford........53 D8
 London.........28 B3
 N Yorks........93 C7
 W Sus..........16 D4
Clap Hill........19 B7
Clappers........122 D5
Clappersgate.....99 D5
Clapton..........12 D2

Clapton-in-
 Gordano.......23 B6
Clapton-on-the-
 Hill...........38 C1
Clapworthy........9 B8
Clarach..........58 F3
Clara Vale......110 C4
Clarbeston.......32 B1
Clarbeston Road.32 B1
Clarborough......89 F8
Clardon.........158 D3
Clare............55 E8
Clarebrand......106 C4
Clarencefield...107 C7
Clarilaw........115 C8
Clark's Green...28 F2
Clarkston.......119 D5
Clashandorran..151 G8
Clashcoig.......151 B9
Clashindarroch.152 E4
Clashmore
 Highld.......151 C10
 Highld........156 F3
Clashnessie.....156 F3
Clashnoir.......139 B8
Clate...........160 G7
Clathy..........127 C8
Clatt...........140 B4
Clatter..........59 E6
Clatterford......15 F5
Clatterin Bridge 135 B6
Clatworthy.......22 F2
Claughton
 Lancs..........92 E5
 Lancs..........93 C5
 Mers...........85 F4
Claverdon........51 C6
Claverham........23 C6
Clavering........55 F5
Claverley........61 E7
Claverton........24 C2
Clawdd-newydd..72 D4
Clawthorpe.......92 B5
Clawton...........9 E5
Claxby
 Lincs..........79 B7
 Lincs..........90 E5
Claxton
 Norf...........69 D6
 N Yorks........96 C2
Claybokie.......139 E6
Claybrooke
 Magna..........63 F8
Claybrooke Parva 63 F8
Clay Common...69 F7
Clay Coton......52 B3
Clay Cross......76 C3
Claydon
 Oxon...........52 D2
 Suff...........56 D5
Claygate
 Dumfries......108 B3
 Kent...........29 E8
 Sur............28 C2
Claygate Cross..29 D7
Clayhanger
 Devon..........10 B5
 W Mid..........62 D4
Clayhidon........11 C6
Clayhill
 E Sus..........18 C5
 Hants..........14 D4
Clay Hill........26 B3
Clay Lake........66 B2
Clayock.........158 E3
Claypole.........77 E8
Clayton
 Staffs.........75 E5
 S Yorks........89 D5
 W Sus..........17 C6
 W Yorks........94 F4
Clayton Green...86 B3
Clayton-le-Moors 93 F7
Clayton-le-
 Woods.........86 B3
Clayton West...88 C3
Clayworth........89 F8
Cleadale........146 C7
Cleadon.........111 C6
Clearbrook........6 C3
Clearwell........36 D2
Cleasby.........101 C7
Cleat...........159 K5
Cleatlam........101 C6
Cleator..........98 C2
Cleator Moor....98 C2
Clebrig.........157 F8
Cleckheaton......88 B2
Cleedownton.....61 F5
Cleehill.........49 B7
Clee St Margaret.61 F5
Cleethorpes......91 D7
Cleeton St Mary.49 B8
Cleeve
 Bath...........23 D8
 Ches W.........73 D8
Cleeve Hill......37 B6
Cleeve Prior.....51 E5
Clehonger........49 F6
Cleish..........128 E2
Cleland.........119 D8
Clench Common.25 C6
Clenchwarton....67 B5
Clent............50 B4
Cleobury
 Mortimer.......49 B8
Cleobury North..61 F6
Cleongart.......143 E7
Clephanton.....151 F11
Clerklands......115 B8
Clestrain.......159 H4
Cleuch Head...115 C8
Clevancy.........25 B5
Clevedon.........23 B6
Cleveley.........38 B3
Cleveleys........92 E3
Cleverton........37 F6
Clevis...........21 B7
Clewer...........23 D6
Cley next the Sea 81 C6
Cliaid..........148 H1
Cliasmol........154 G5
Cliburn..........99 B8
Click Mill......159 F4
Cliddesden.......26 E4
Cliff...........135 E6
Cliffe
 Medway.........29 B8

Cliffe continued
 N Yorks........96 F2
Cliff End........19 D5
Cliffe Woods....29 B8
Clifford
 Hereford.......48 E4
 W Yorks........95 E7
Clifford
 Chambers.......51 D6
Clifford's Mesne..36 B4
Cliffsend........31 C7
Clifton
 Bristol........23 B7
 C Beds.........54 F2
 Cumb...........99 B7
 Derbys.........75 E8
 Lancs..........92 F4
 Nottingham.....77 F5
 N Yorks........94 E4
 Oxon...........52 F2
 Stirling......131 F7
 S Yorks........89 E6
 Worcs..........50 D3
 York...........95 D8
Clifton Campville 63 C6
Cliftoncote.....116 B4
Clifton Green...87 D5
Clifton Hampden.39 E5
Clifton Reynes...53 D7
Clifton upon
 Dunsmore.......52 B3
Clifton upon
 Teme..........50 C2
Cliftonville.....31 B7
Climaen gwyn...33 D8
Climping.........16 D4
Climpy..........120 D2
Clink............24 E2
Clint............95 D5
Clint Green.....68 C3
Clintmains......122 F2
Cliobh..........154 D5
Clippesby........69 C7
Clipsham.........65 C6
Clipston.........64 F4
Clipstone........77 C5
Clitheroe........93 E7
Cliuthar........154 H6
Clive............60 B5
Clivocast.......160 C8
Clixby...........90 D5
Clocaenog........72 D4
Clochan.........152 B4
Clock Face.......86 E3
Clockmill.......122 D3
Cloddiau.........60 D2
Clodock..........35 B7
Clola..........153 D10
Clophill.........53 F8
Clopton
 Northants......65 F7
 Suff...........57 D6
Clopton Corner..57 D6
Clopton Green...55 D8
Closeburn.......113 E8
Close Clark......84 E2
Closworth........12 C3
Clothall.........54 F3
Clotton..........74 C2
Clough Foot......87 B7
Cloughton.......103 E8
Cloughton
 Newlands......103 E8
Clousta.........160 H5
Clouston........159 G3
Clova
 Aberds........140 B3
 Angus.........134 B3
Clovelly..........8 B5
Clovenfords.....121 F7
Clovenstone.....141 C6
Clovullin.......130 C4
Clow Bridge.....87 B6
Clowne...........76 B4
Clows Top.......50 B2
Cloy.............73 E7
Cluanie Inn....136 C3
Cluanie Lodge...136 C3
Clun.............60 F3
Clunbury.........60 F3
Clunderwen......32 C2
Clune...........138 B3
Clunes..........136 F5
Clungunford.....49 B5
Clunie
 Aberds........153 C6
 Perth.........133 E8
Clunton..........60 F3
Cluny...........128 E4
Cluny Castle....138 E2
Clutton
 Bath...........23 D8
 Ches W.........73 D8
Clwt-grugoer...72 C3
Clwt-y-bont......83 E5
Clydach
 Mon............35 C6
 Swansea........33 D7
Clydach Vale....34 E3
Clydebank.......118 B4
Clydey...........45 F4
Clyffe Pypard...25 B5
Clynder.........145 E11
Clyne............34 D2
Clynelish.......157 J11
Clynnog-fawr...82 F4
Clyro............48 E4
Clyst Honiton...10 E5
Clyst Hydon.....10 D5
Clyst St George..10 F4
Clyst St
 Lawrence.......10 D5
Clyst St Mary...10 E4
Cnoc Amhlaigh 155 D10
Cnwch-coch......47 B5
Coachford.......152 D4
Coad's Green.....5 B7
Coal Aston.......76 B3
Coalbrookdale...61 D6
Coalbrookvale...35 D5
Coalburn........119 F8
Coalburns.......110 C4
Coalcleugh......109 E8
Coaley...........36 D4
Coalhall........112 C4
Coalhill.........42 E3

Coalpit Heath...36 F3
Coalport.........61 D6
Coalsnaughton.127 E8
Coaltown of
 Balgonie......128 E5
Coaltown of
 Wemyss........128 E5
Coalville........63 C8
Coalway..........36 C2
Coat.............12 B2
Coatbridge......119 C7
Coatdyke........119 C7
Coate
 Swindon........38 F1
 Wilts..........24 C5
Coates
 Cambs..........66 E3
 Glos...........37 D6
 Lancs..........93 E8
 N Yorks........94 E4
 W Sus..........16 C3
Coatham.........102 B3
Coatham
 Mundeville...101 B7
Coatsgate.......114 D3
Cobairdy........152 D5
Cobbaton..........9 B8
Cobbler's Green..69 E5
Coberley.........37 C6
Cobham
 Kent...........29 C7
 Sur............28 C2
Cobholm Island..69 D8
Cobleland.......126 E4
Cobnash..........49 C6
Coburty.........153 B9
Cockayne........102 E4
Cockayne Hatley.54 E3
Cock Bank.......73 E7
Cock Bridge.....139 D7
Cockburnspath..122 B3
Cockenzie and Port
 Seton.........121 B7
Cockerham........92 D4
Cockermouth...107 F8
Cockernhoe
 Green..........40 B4
Cockfield
 Durham........101 B6
 Suff...........56 D3
Cockfosters......41 E5
Cocking..........16 C2
Cockington........7 C6
Cocklake.........23 E6
Cockley Beck.....98 D4
Cockley Cley.....67 D7
Cockshutt........60 B4
Cockthorpe.......81 C5
Cockwood.........10 F4
Cockyard.........49 F6
Codda.............5 B6
Coddenham.......56 D5
Coddington
 Ches W.........73 D8
 Hereford.......50 E2
 Notts..........77 D8
Codford St Mary.24 F4
Codford St Peter.24 F4
Codicote.........41 C5
Codmore Hill...16 B4
Codnor...........76 E4
Codrington.......24 B2
Codsall..........62 D2
Codsall Wood...62 D2
Coed Duon
 =Blackwood...35 E5
Coedely..........34 F4
Coedkernew......35 F6
Coed Mawr.......83 D5
Coed Morgan...35 C7
Coedpoeth........73 D6
Coed-Talon......73 D6
Coedway..........60 C3
Coed-y-bryn......46 E2
Coed-y-paen......35 E7
Coed-y-ynys......35 B5
Coed
 Ystumgwern...71 E6
Coelbren.........34 C2
Coffinswell.......7 C6
Cofton Hackett..50 B5
Cogan............22 B3
Cogenhoe.........53 C6
Cogges...........38 D3
Coggeshall.......42 B4
Coggeshall
 Hamlet.........42 B4
Coggins Mill.....18 C2
Coignafearn
 Lodge.........138 C2
Coig
 Peighinnean 155 A10
Coig Peighinnean
 Bhuirgh.......155 B9
Coilacriech.....140 E2
Coilantogle.....126 D4
Coilleag........148 G2
Coillore........149 E8
Coity............34 F3
Col.............155 C9
Colaboll........157 H8
Colan.............4 C4
Colaton Raleigh..11 F5
Colbost.........148 D7
Colburn.........101 E6
Colby
 Cumb..........100 B1
 IoM............84 E2
 Norf...........81 D8
Colchester.......43 B6
Colcot...........22 C3
Cold Ash.........26 C3
Cold Ashby.......52 B4
Cold Ashton.....24 B2
Cold Aston.......37 C8
Coldbackie......157 D9
Coldbeck........100 D2
Cold Blow........32 C2
Cold Brayfield...53 D7
Coldean..........17 D7
Coldeast..........7 B6
Colden...........87 B7
Colden
 Common.........15 B5
Coldfair Green...57 C8
Coldham..........66 D4
Cold Hanworth..90 F4

Coldharbour
 Glos...........36 D2
 Kent...........29 D6
 Sur............28 E2
Cold Harbour...11 D11
Cold Hatton.....61 B6
Cold Hesledon..111 E7
Cold Higham.....52 D4
Coldingham.....122 C5
Cold Kirby......102 F3
Cold Newton.....64 D4
Cold Northcott...8 F4
Cold Norton.....42 D4
Cold Overton....64 C5
Coldrain........128 D2
Coldred..........31 E6
Coldridge.........9 D8
Coldstream
 Angus.........134 F3
 Borders.......122 F4
Coldwaltham.....16 C4
Coldwells......153 D11
Coldwells Croft.140 B4
Cole.............23 F8
Colebatch........60 F3
Colebrook........10 D5
Colebrooke.......10 E2
Coleby
 Lincs..........78 C2
 N Lincs........90 C2
Coleford
 Devon..........10 D2
 Glos...........36 C2
 Som............23 E8
Cole Green.......41 C5
Cole Henley.....26 D2
Colehill.........13 D8
Coleman's Hatch.29 F5
Colemere.........73 F8
Colemore.........26 F5
Coleorton........63 C8
Colerne..........24 B3
Colesbourne......37 C6
Colesden.........54 D2
Coles Green.....56 E4
Cole's Green....57 C6
Coleshill
 Bucks..........40 E2
 Oxon...........38 E2
 Warks..........63 F6
Colestocks.......11 D5
Colgate..........28 F3
Colgrain........126 F2
Colinsburgh.....129 D6
Colinton........120 C5
Colintraive.....145 F9
Colkirk..........80 E5
Collace.........134 F2
Collafirth......160 G6
Collaton St Mary..7 D6
College Milton..119 D6
Collessie.......128 C4
Collier Row......41 E8
Collier's End...41 B6
Collier's Green..18 B4
Collier Street...29 E8
Colliery Row...111 E6
Colliston.......141 E6
Collin..........107 B7
Collingbourne
 Ducis..........25 D7
Collingbourne
 Kingston.......25 D7
Collingham
 Notts..........77 C8
 W Yorks........95 E6
Collington.......49 C8
Collingtree......53 D5
Collins Green....86 E3
Colliston.......135 E6
Collycroft.......63 F7
Collynie........153 E8
Collyweston......65 D6
Colmonell.......104 A5
Colmworth.......54 D2
Colnabaichin...139 D8
Colnbrook.......27 B8
Colne
 Cambs..........54 B4
 Lancs..........93 E8
Colne Edge......93 E8
Colne Engaine...56 F2
Colney...........68 D4
Colney Heath...41 D5
Colney Street....40 D4
Coln Rogers.....37 D7
Coln St Aldwyn's.37 D8
Coln St Dennis..37 C7
Colpy...........153 E6
Colquhar........121 E6
Colsterdale.....101 F6
Colsterworth....65 B6
Colston Bassett..77 F6
Coltfield.......151 E13
Colthouse........99 E5
Coltishall.......69 C5
Coltness........119 D8
Colton
 Cumb...........99 F5
 Norf...........68 D4
 N Yorks........95 E8
 Staffs.........62 B4
 W Yorks........95 F6
Col Uarach......155 D9
Colva............48 D4
Colvend.........107 D5
Colvister.......160 D7
Colwall Green...50 E2
Colwall Stone...50 E2
Colwell.........110 B2
Colwich..........62 B4
Colwick..........77 E6
Colwinston.......21 B8
Colworth.........16 D3
Colwyn Bay
 =Bae Colwyn...83 D8
Colyford.........11 E7
Colyton..........11 E7
Combe
 Hereford.......48 C5
 Oxon...........38 C4
 W Berks........25 C8
Combe Common..27 F7
Combe Down......24 C2
Combe Florey....22 F3
Combe Hay.......24 D2
Combeinteignhead 7 B7

Com–Dal 207

Combe Martin 20 E4
Combe Moor 49 C5
Combe Raleigh 11 D6
Comberbach 74 B3
Comberton
Cambs 54 D4
Hereford 49 C6
Combe St Nicholas 11 C8
Combpyne 11 E7
Combridge 75 F7
Combrook 51 D8
Combs
Derbys 75 B7
Suff 56 D4
Combs Ford 56 D4
Combwich 22 E4
Comers 141 D5
Comins Coch 58 F3
Commercial End 55 C6
Commins Capel Betws 46 D5
Commins Coch 58 D5
Commondale 102 C4
Common Edge 92 F3
Commonmoor 5 C7
Commonside 74 B2
Common Side 76 B3
Compstall 87 E7
Compton
Devon 7 C6
Hants 15 B5
Sur 27 E6
Sur 27 E7
W Berks 27 B6
Wilts 25 D6
W Sus 15 C8
Compton Abbas 13 C6
Compton Abdale 37 C7
Compton Bassett 24 B5
Compton Beauchamp 38 F2
Compton Bishop 23 D5
Compton Chamberlayne 13 B8
Compton Dando 23 C8
Compton Dundon 23 F6
Compton Martin 23 D7
Compton Pauncefoot 12 B4
Compton Valence 12 E3
Comrie
Fife 128 F2
Perth 127 B6
Conaglen House 130 C4
Conchra 145 E9
Concraigie 133 E8
Conder Green 92 D4
Conderton 50 F4
Condicote 38 B1
Condorrat 119 B7
Condover 60 D4
Coneyhurst 16 B5
Coneysthorpe 96 B3
Coneythorpe 95 D6
Coney Weston 56 B3
Conford 27 F6
Congash 139 B6
Congdon's Shop 5 B7
Congerstone 63 D7
Congham 80 E3
Congleton 75 C5
Congl-y-wal 71 C8
Congresbury 23 C6
Congreve 62 C3
Conicavel 151 F12
Coningsby 78 D5
Conington
Cambs 54 C4
Cambs 65 F8
Conisbrough 89 E6
Conisby 142 B3
Conisholme 91 E8
Coniston
Cumb 99 E5
E Yorks 97 F7
Coniston Cold 94 D2
Conistone 94 C2
Connah's Quay 73 C6
Connel 124 B5
Connel Park 113 C6
Connor Downs 2 C4
Conon Bridge 151 F8
Conon House 151 F8
Cononley 94 E2
Conordan 149 E10
Consall 75 E6
Consett 110 D4
Constable Burton 101 E6
Constantine 3 D6
Constantine Bay 4 B3
Contin 150 F7
Contlaw 141 D7
Conwy 83 D7
Conyer 30 C3
Conyers Green 56 C2
Cooden 18 E4
Cooil 84 E3
Cookbury 9 D6
Cookham 40 F1
Cookham Dean 40 F1
Cookham Rise 40 F1
Cookhill 51 D5
Cookley
Suff 57 B7
Worcs 62 F2
Cookley Green 39 E6
Cookney 141 E7
Cookridge 95 E5
Cooksbridge 17 C8
Cooksmill Green 42 D2
Coolham 16 B5
Cooling 29 B8
Coombe
Corn 4 D4
Corn 8 C4
Hants 15 B7
Wilts 25 D6
Coombe Bissett 14 B2
Coombe Hill 37 B5
Coombe Keynes 13 F6
Coombes 17 D5
Coopersale Common 41 D7
Cootham 16 C4
Copdock 56 E5
Copford Green 43 B5
Copgrove 95 C6
Copister 160 F6
Cople 54 E2
Copley 101 B5
Coplow Dale 75 B8
Copmanthorpe 95 E8
Coppathorne 8 D4
Coppenhall 62 C3
Coppenhall Moss 74 D4
Copperhouse 2 C4
Coppingford 65 F8
Copplestone 10 D2
Coppull 86 C3
Coppull Moor 86 C3
Copsale 17 B5
Copster Green 93 F6
Copston Magna 63 F8
Copt Heath 51 B6
Copt Hewick 95 B6
Copthorne
Shrops 60 C4
Sur 28 F4
Copt Oak 63 C8
Copy's Green 80 D5
Copythorne 14 C4
Corbets Tey 42 F1
Corbridge 110 C2
Corby 65 F5
Corby Glen 65 B6
Cordon 143 E11
Coreley 49 B8
Cores End 40 F2
Corfe 11 C7
Corfe Castle 13 F7
Corfe Mullen 13 E7
Corfton 60 F4
Corgarff 139 D8
Corhampton 15 B7
Corlae 113 E6
Corley 63 F7
Corley Ash 63 F6
Corley Moor 63 F6
Cornaa 84 D4
Cornabus 142 D4
Cornel 83 E7
Corner Row 92 F4
Corney 98 E3
Cornforth 111 F6
Cornhill 152 C5
Cornhill-on-Tweed 122 F4
Cornholme 87 B7
Cornish Hall End 55 F7
Cornquoy 159 J6
Cornsay 110 E4
Cornsay Colliery 110 E4
Corntown
Highld 151 F8
V Glam 21 B8
Cornwell 38 B2
Cornwood 6 D4
Cornworthy 7 D6
Corpach 130 B4
Corpusty 81 D7
Corran
Highld 130 C4
Highld 149 H13
Corranbuie 145 G7
Corrany 84 D4
Corrie 143 D11
Corrie Common 114 F5
Corriecravie 143 F10
Corriemoillie 150 E6
Corriemulzie Lodge 150 B6
Corrievarkie Lodge 132 B2
Corrievorrie 138 B3
Corrimony 150 H6
Corringham
Lincs 90 E2
Thurrock 42 F3
Corris 58 D4
Corris Uchaf 58 D4
Corrour Shooting Lodge 131 C8
Corrow 125 E7
Corry 149 F11
Corrykinloch 156 G6
Corrymuckloch 133 F5
Corrynachenchy 147 G9
Corry of Ardnagrask 151 G8
Corsback 158 C4
Corscombe 12 D3
Corse
Aberds 152 D6
Glos 36 B4
Corse Lawn 50 F3
Corse of Kinnoir 152 D5
Corsewall 104 C4
Corsham 24 B3
Corsindae 141 D5
Corsley 24 E3
Corsley Heath 24 E3
Corsock 106 B4
Corston
Bath 23 C8
Wilts 37 F6
Corstorphine 120 B4
Cors-y-Gedol 71 E6
Cortachy 134 D3
Corton
Suff 69 E8
Wilts 24 E4
Corton Denham 12 B4
Coruanan Lodge 130 C4
Corunna 148 B3
Corwen 72 E4
Coryton
Devon 9 F6
Thurrock 42 F3
Cosby 64 E2
Coseley 62 E3
Cosgrove 53 E5
Cosham 15 D7
Cosheston 32 D1
Cossall 76 E4
Cossington
Leics 64 C3
Som 23 E5
Costa 159 F4
Costessey 68 C4
Costock 64 B2
Coston 64 B5
Cote 38 D3
Cotebrook 74 C2
Cotehill 108 D4
Cotes
Cumb 99 F6
Leics 64 B2
Staffs 74 F5
Cotesbach 64 F2
Cotgrave 77 F6
Cothall 141 C7
Cotham 77 E7
Cothelstone 22 F3
Cotherstone 101 C5
Cothill 38 E4
Cotleigh 11 D7
Cotmanhay 76 E4
Cotmaton 11 F6
Coton
Cambs 54 D5
Northants 52 B4
Staffs 62 B2
Staffs 75 F6
Coton Clanford 62 B2
Coton Hill
Shrops 60 C4
Staffs 75 F6
Coton in the Elms 63 C6
Cott 7 C5
Cottam
E Yorks 97 C5
Lancs 92 F5
Notts 77 B8
Cottartown 151 H13
Cottenham 54 C5
Cotterdale 100 E3
Cottered 41 B6
Cotteridge 50 B5
Cotterstock 65 E7
Cottesbrooke 52 B5
Cottesmore 65 C6
Cotteylands 10 C4
Cottingham
E Yorks 97 F6
Northants 64 E5
Cottingley 94 F4
Cottisford 52 F3
Cotton
Staffs 75 E7
Suff 56 C4
Cotton End 53 E8
Cottown
Aberds 140 B4
Aberds 141 C6
Aberds 153 D8
Cotwalton 75 F6
Couch's Mill 5 D6
Coughton
Hereford 36 B2
Warks 51 C5
Coulaghailtro 144 G6
Coulags 150 G2
Coulby Newham 102 C3
Coulderton 98 D1
Coulin 150 F3
Coull
Aberds 140 D4
Argyll 142 B3
Coulport 145 E11
Coulsdon 28 D3
Coulston 24 D4
Coulter 120 F3
Coulton 96 B2
Cound 61 D5
Coundon
Durham 101 B7
W Mid 63 F7
Coundon Grange 101 B7
Countersett 100 F4
Countess 25 E6
Countess Wear 10 F4
Countesthorpe 64 E2
Countisbury 21 E6
County Oak 28 F3
Coupar Angus 134 E2
Coup Green 86 B3
Coupland 122 F5
Cour 143 D9
Courance 114 E3
Court-at-Street 19 B7
Courteenhall 53 D5
Court Henry 33 B6
Courtsend 43 E6
Courtway 22 F4
Cousland 121 C6
Cousley Wood 18 B3
Cove
Argyll 145 E11
Borders 122 B3
Devon 10 C4
Hants 27 D6
Highld 155 H13
Cove Bay 141 D8
Cove Bottom 57 B8
Covehithe 69 F8
Coven 62 D3
Coveney 66 F4
Covenham St Bartholomew 91 E7
Covenham St Mary 91 E7
Coventry 51 B8
Coverack 3 E6
Coverham 101 F6
Covesea 152 A1
Covington
Cambs 53 B8
S Lanark 120 F2
Cowan Bridge 93 B6
Cow Ark 93 E6
Cowbeech 18 D3
Cowbit 66 C2
Cowbridge
Lincs 79 E6
Som 21 E8
Cowbridge = Y Bont-Faen 21 B8
Cowdale 75 B7
Cowden 29 E5
Cowdenbeath 128 E3
Cowdenburn 120 D5
Cowers Lane 76 E3
Cowes 15 E5
Cowesby 102 F2
Cowfold 17 B6
Cowgill 100 F2
Cowie
Aberds 141 F7
Stirling 127 F7
Cowley
Devon 10 E4
Glos 37 C6
London 40 F3
Oxon 39 D5
Cowleymoor 10 C4
Cowling
Lancs 86 C3
N Yorks 94 E2
N Yorks 101 F7
Cowlinge 55 D8
Cowpe 87 B6
Cowpen 117 F8
Cowpen Bewley 102 B2
Cowplain 15 C7
Cowshill 109 E8
Cowslip Green 23 C6
Cowstrandburn 128 E2
Cowthorpe 95 D7
Coxbank 74 E3
Coxbench 76 E3
Cox Common 69 F6
Coxford
Norf 80 E4
Soton 14 C4
Cox Green 27 B6
Coxheath 29 D8
Coxhill 31 E6
Coxhoe 111 F6
Coxley 23 E7
Cox Moor 76 D5
Coxwold 95 B8
Coychurch 21 B8
Coylton 112 B4
Coylumbridge 138 C5
Coynach 140 D3
Coynachie 152 E4
Coytrahen 34 F2
Crabadon 7 D5
Crabbs Cross 50 C5
Crabtree 17 B6
Crackenthorpe 100 B1
Crackington Haven 8 E3
Crackley 51 B7
Crackleybank 61 C7
Crackpot 100 E4
Cracoe 94 C2
Craddock 11 C5
Cradhlastadh 154 D5
Cradley 50 E2
Cradley Heath 62 F3
Crafthole 5 D8
Craggan 139 B6
Craggie
Highld 151 H10
Highld 157 H11
Cragg Vale 87 B8
Craghead 110 D5
Crai 34 B2
Craibstone 152 C4
Craichie 135 E5
Craig
Dumfries 106 B3
Dumfries 106 C3
Highld 150 G3
Craiganor Lodge 132 D3
Craig Castle 140 B3
Craig-cefn-parc 33 D7
Craigdam 153 E8
Craigdarroch
Dumfries 113 E7
Highld 150 F7
Craigdhu 150 G7
Craigearn 141 C6
Craigellachie 152 D2
Craigencross 104 C4
Craigend
Perth 128 B3
Stirling 127 F6
Craigendive 145 E9
Craigendoran 126 F2
Craigends 118 C4
Craigens
Argyll 142 B3
E Ayrs 113 C5
Craighat 126 F3
Craighead 129 D8
Craighlaw Mains 105 C7
Craighouse 144 G4
Craigie
Aberds 141 C8
Dundee 134 F4
Perth 128 B3
Perth 133 E8
S Ayrs 118 F4
Craigiefield 159 G5
Craigielaw 121 B7
Craiglockhart 120 B5
Craigmalloch 112 E4
Craigmaud 153 C8
Craigmillar 121 B5
Craigmore 145 G10
Craignant 73 F6
Craigneuk
N Lanark 119 C7
N Lanark 119 D7
Craignure 124 B3
Craigo 135 C6
Craigow 128 D2
Craig Penllyn 21 B8
Craigrothie 129 C5
Craigroy 151 F14
Craigruie 126 B3
Craigston Castle 153 C7
Craigton
Aberdeen 141 D7
Angus 134 D3
Angus 135 F5
Highld 151 B9
Craigtown 157 D11
Craig-y-don 83 C7
Craig-y-nos 34 C2
Craik 115 D6
Crail 129 D8
Crailing 116 B2
Crailinghall 116 B2
Craiselound 89 E8
Crakehill 95 B7
Crakemarsh 75 F7
Crambe 96 C3
Cramlington 111 B5
Cramond 120 B4
Cramond Bridge 120 B4
Cranage 74 C4
Cranberry 74 F5
Cranborne 13 C8
Cranbourne 27 B7
Cranbrook
Devon 10 E5
Kent 18 B4
Cranbrook Common 18 B4
Crane Moor 88 D4
Crane's Corner 68 C2
Cranfield 53 E7
Cranford 28 B2
Cranford St Andrew 53 B7
Cranford St John 53 B7
Cranham
Glos 37 C5
London 42 F1
Crank 86 E3
Crank Wood 86 D4
Cranleigh 27 F8
Cranley 57 B5
Cranmer Green 56 B4
Cranmore 14 F4
Cranna 153 C6
Crannich 147 G8
Crannoch 152 C4
Cranoe 64 E4
Cransford 57 C7
Cranshaws 122 C2
Cranstal 84 B4
Crantock 4 C2
Cranwell 78 E3
Cranwich 67 E7
Cranworth 68 D2
Craobh Haven 124 E3
Crapstone 6 C3
Crarae 125 F5
Crask Inn 157 G8
Craskins 140 D4
Crask of Aigas 150 G7
Craster 117 C8
Craswall 48 F4
Cratfield 57 B7
Crathes 141 E6
Crathie
Aberds 139 E8
Highld 137 E8
Crathorne 102 D2
Craven Arms 60 F4
Crawcrook 110 C4
Crawford
Lancs 86 D2
S Lanark 114 B2
Crawfordjohn 113 B8
Crawick 113 C7
Crawley
Hants 26 F2
Oxon 38 C3
W Sus 28 F3
Crawley Down 28 F4
Crawleyside 110 E2
Crawshawbooth 87 B6
Crawton 135 B8
Cray
N Yorks 94 B2
Perth 133 C8
Crayford 29 B6
Crayke 95 B8
Crays Hill 42 E3
Cray's Pond 39 F6
Creacombe 10 C3
Creagan 130 E3
Creag Ghoraidh 148 D2
Creaguaineach Lodge 131 C7
Creaksea 43 E5
Creaton 52 B5
Creca 108 B2
Credenhill 49 E6
Crediton 10 D3
Creebridge 105 C8
Creech Heathfield 11 B7
Creech St Michael 11 B7
Creed 3 B8
Creekmouth 41 F7
Creeting Bottoms 56 D5
Creeting St Mary 56 D4
Creeton 65 B7
Creetown 105 D8
Creggans 125 E6
Cregneash 84 F1
Creg-ny-Baa 84 D3
Cregrina 48 D3
Creich 128 B5
Creigiau 34 F4
Cremyll 6 D2
Creslow 39 B8
Cressage 61 D5
Cressbrook 75 B8
Cresselly 32 D1
Cressing 42 B3
Cresswell
Northumb 117 E8
Staffs 75 F6
Cresswell Quay 32 D1
Creswell 76 B5
Cretingham 57 C6
Cretshengan 144 G6
Crewe
Ches E 74 D4
Ches W 73 D8
Crewgreen 60 C3
Crewkerne 12 D2
Crianlarich 126 B2
Cribyn 46 D4
Criccieth 71 D5
Crich 76 D3
Crichie 153 D9
Crichton 121 C6
Crick
Mon 36 E1
Northants 52 B3
Crickadarn 48 E2
Cricket Malherbie 11 C8
Cricket St Thomas 11 D8
Crickheath 60 B2
Crickhowell 35 C6
Cricklade 37 E8
Cricklewood 41 F5
Cridling Stubbs 89 B6
Crieff 127 B7
Criggion 60 C2
Crigglestone 88 C4
Crimond 153 C10
Crimonmogate 153 C10
Crimplesham 67 D6
Crinan 144 D6
Cringleford 68 D4
Cringles 94 E3
Crinow 32 C2
Cripplesease 2 C4
Cripplestyle 13 C8
Cripp's Corner 18 C4
Croasdale 98 C2
Crockenhill 29 C6
Crockernwell 10 E2
Crockerton 24 E3
Crocketford or Ninemile Bar 106 B5
Crockey Hill 96 E2
Crockham Hill 28 D5
Crockleford Heath 43 B6
Crockness 159 J4
Crock Street 11 C8
Croeserw 34 E2
Croes-goch 44 B3
Croes-lan 46 E2
Croesor 71 C7
Croesyceiliog
Carms 33 C5
Torf 35 E7
Croes-y-mwyalch 35 E7
Croesywaun 82 F5
Croft
Leics 64 E2
Lincs 79 C8
Pembs 45 E3
Warr 86 E4
Croftamie 126 F3
Croftmalloch 120 C2
Crofton
Wilts 25 C7
W Yorks 88 C4
Croft-on-Tees 101 D7
Crofts of Benachielt 158 G3
Crofts of Haddo 153 E8
Crofts of Inverthernie 153 D7
Crofts of Meikle Ardo 153 D8
Crofty 33 E6
Croggan 124 C3
Croglin 109 E5
Croich 150 B7
Crois Dughaill 148 F2
Cromarty 151 E10
Cromblet 153 E7
Cromdale 139 B6
Cromer
Herts 41 B5
Norf 81 C8
Cromford 76 D2
Cromhall 36 E3
Cromhall Common 36 F3
Cromor 155 E9
Cromra 137 E8
Cromwell 77 C7
Cronberry 113 B6
Crondall 27 E5
Cronk-y-Voddy 84 D3
Cronton 86 F2
Crook
Cumb 99 E6
Durham 110 F4
Crookedholm 118 F4
Crookes 88 F4
Crookham
Northumb 122 F5
W Berks 26 C3
Crookham Village 27 D5
Crookhaugh 114 B4
Crookhouse 116 B3
Crooklands 99 F7
Crook of Devon 128 D2
Cropredy 52 E2
Cropston 64 C2
Cropthorne 50 E4
Cropton 103 F5
Cropwell Bishop 77 F6
Cropwell Butler 77 F6
Cros 155 A10
Crosbost 155 E8
Crosby
Cumb 107 F7
IoM 84 E3
N Lincs 90 C2
Crosby Garrett 100 D2
Crosby Ravensworth 99 C8
Crosby Villa 107 F7
Croscombe 23 E7
Cross 23 D6
Crossaig 143 C9
Crossal 149 E9
Crossapol 146 G2
Cross Ash 35 C8
Cross-at-Hand 29 E8
Crossburn 119 B8
Crossbush 16 D4
Crosscanonby 107 F7
Crossdale Street 81 D8
Crossens 85 C4
Crossflatts 94 E4
Crossford
Fife 128 F2
S Lanark 119 E8
Crossgate 66 B2
Crossgatehall 121 C6
Crossgates
Fife 128 F3
Powys 48 C2
Crossgill 93 C5
Cross Green
Devon 9 F5
Suff 56 D2
Suff 56 D3
Warks 51 D8
Cross-hands 32 B2
Cross Hands
Carms 33 C6
Pembs 32 C1
Crosshill
E Ayrs 112 B4
Fife 128 E3
S Ayrs 112 D3
Cross Hill 76 E4
Crosshouse 118 F3
Cross Houses 60 D5
Crossings 108 B5
Cross in Hand
E Sus 18 C2
Leics 64 F2
Cross Inn
Ceredig 46 C4
Ceredig 46 D2
Rhondda 34 F4
Crosskeys 35 E6
Cross Keys 29 D6
Crosskirk 157 B13
Cross Lane Head 61 E7
Crosslanes 60 C3
Cross Lanes
Corn 3 D5
N Yorks 95 C8
Wrex 73 E7
Crossle 118 C4
Crosslee 115 C6
Crossmichael 106 C4
Crossmoor 92 F4
Cross Oak 35 B5
Cross of Jackston 153 E7
Cross o'th'hands 76 E2
Crossroads
Aberds 141 E6
E Ayrs 118 F4
Cross Street 57 B5
Crossway
Hereford 49 F8
Mon 35 C8
Powys 48 D2
Crossway Green 50 C3
Crossways 13 F5
Crosswell 45 F3
Crosswood 47 B5
Crosthwaite 99 E6
Croston 86 C2
Crostwick 69 C5
Crostwight 69 B6
Crothair 154 D6
Crouch 29 D7
Croucheston 13 B8
Crouch Hill 12 C5
Crouch House Green 28 E5
Croughton 52 F3
Crovie 153 B8
Crowan 2 C5
Crowborough 18 B2
Crowcombe 22 F3
Crowdecote 75 C8
Crowden 87 E8
Crow Edge 88 D2
Crowell 39 E7
Crowfield
Northants 52 E4
Suff 56 D5
Crow Hill 36 B3
Crowhurst
E Sus 18 D4
Sur 28 E4
Crowhurst Lane End 28 E4
Crowland 66 C2
Crowlas 2 C4
Crowle
N Lincs 89 C8
Worcs 50 D4
Crowmarsh Gifford 39 F6
Crown Corner 57 B6
Crownhill 6 D2
Crownland 56 C4
Crownthorpe 68 D3
Crowntown 2 C5
Crows-an-wra 2 D2
Crowshill 68 D2
Crowsnest 60 D3
Crowthorne 27 C6
Crowton 74 B2
Croxall 63 C5
Croxby 91 E5
Croxdale 111 F5
Croxden 75 F7
Croxley Green 40 E3
Croxton
Cambs 54 C3
N Lincs 90 C4
Norf 67 F8
Staffs 74 F4
Croxtonbank 74 F4
Croxton Kerrial 64 B5
Croy
Highld 151 G10
N Lanark 119 B7
Croyde 20 F3
Croydon
Cambs 54 E4
London 28 C4
Crubenmore Lodge 138 E2
Cruckmeole 60 D4
Cruckton 60 C4
Cruden Bay 153 E10
Crudgington 61 C6
Crudwell 37 E6
Crug 48 B3
Crugmeer 4 B4
Crugybar 47 F5
Crulabhig 154 D6
Crumlin = Crymlyn 35 E6
Crumpsall 87 D6
Crundale
Kent 30 E4
Pembs 44 D4
Cruwys Morchard 10 C3
Crux Easton 26 D2
Crwbin 33 C5
Crya 159 H4
Cryers Hill 40 E1
Crymlyn 83 D6
Crymlyn = Crumlin 35 E6
Crymych 45 F3
Crynant 34 D1
Crynfryn 46 C4
Cuaig 149 C12
Cuan 124 D3
Cubbington 51 C8
Cubeck 100 F4
Cubert 4 D2
Cubley 88 D3
Cubley Common 75 F8
Cublington
Bucks 39 B8
Cublington *continued*
Hereford 49 F6
Cuckfield 17 B7
Cucklington 13 B5
Cuckney 77 B5
Cuckoo Hill 89 E8
Cuddesdon 39 D6
Cuddington
Bucks 39 C7
Ches W 74 B3
Cuddington Heath 73 E8
Cuddy Hill 92 F4
Cudham 28 D5
Cudliptown 6 B3
Cudworth
Som 11 C8
S Yorks 88 D4
Cuffley 41 D6
Cuiashader 155 B10
Cuidhir 148 H1
Cuidhtinis 154 J5
Culbo 151 E9
Culbokie 151 F9
Culburnie 150 G7
Culcabock 151 G9
Culcairn 151 E9
Culcharry 151 F11
Culcheth 86 E4
Culdrain 152 E5
Culduie 149 D12
Culford 56 B2
Culgaith 99 B8
Culham 39 E5
Culkein 156 F3
Culkein Drumbeg 156 F4
Culkerton 37 E6
Cullachie 139 B5
Cullen 152 B5
Cullercoats 111 B6
Cullicudden 151 E9
Cullingworth 94 F3
Cullipool 124 D3
Cullivoe 160 C7
Culloch 127 C6
Culloden 151 G10
Cullompton 10 D5
Culmaily 151 B11
Culmazie 105 D7
Culmington 60 F4
Culmstock 11 C6
Culnacraig 156 J3
Culnaknock 149 B10
Culpho 57 E6
Culrain 151 B8
Culross 127 F8
Culroy 112 C3
Culsh
Aberds 140 E2
Aberds 153 D8
Culshabbin 105 D7
Culswick 160 J4
Cultercullen 141 B8
Cults
Aberdeen 141 D7
Aberds 152 E5
Dumfries 105 E8
Culverstone Green 29 C7
Culverthorpe 78 E3
Culworth 52 E3
Culzie Lodge 151 D8
Cumbernauld 119 B7
Cumbernauld Village 119 B7
Cumberworth 79 B8
Cuminestown 153 C8
Cumlewick 160 L6
Cummersdale 108 D3
Cummertrees 107 C8
Cummingston 152 B1
Cumnock 113 B5
Cumnor 38 D4
Cumrew 108 D5
Cumwhinton 108 D4
Cumwhitton 108 D5
Cundall 95 B7
Cunninghamhead 118 E3
Cunnister 160 D7
Cupar 129 C5
Cupar Muir 129 C5
Cupernham 14 B4
Curbar 76 B2
Curbridge
Hants 15 C6
Oxon 38 D3
Curdridge 15 C6
Curdworth 63 E5
Curland 11 C7
Curlew Green 57 C7
Currarie 112 E1
Curridge 26 B2
Currie 120 C4
Curry Mallet 11 B8
Curry Rivel 11 B8
Curtisden Green 29 E8
Curtisknowle 6 D5
Cury 3 D5
Cushnie 153 B7
Cushuish 22 F3
Cusop 48 E4
Cutcloy 105 F8
Cutcombe 21 F8
Cutgate 87 C6
Cutiau 58 C3
Cutlers Green 55 F6
Cutnall Green 50 C3
Cutsdean 51 F5
Cutthorpe 76 B3
Cutts 160 K6
Cuxham 39 E6
Cuxton 29 C8
Cuxwold 91 D5
Cwm
Bl Gwent 35 D5
Denb 72 B4
Swansea 33 E7
Cwmafan 34 E1
Cwmaman 34 E4
Cwmann 46 E4
Cwmavon 35 D6
Cwmbach
Carms 32 B3
Carms 33 D5
Powys 48 D2
Powys 48 F3
Cwmbâch 34 D4
Cwmbelan 59 F6
Cwmbran = Cwmbrân 35 E6
Cwmbrân = Cwmbran 35 E6
Cwmbrwyno 58 F4
Cwm-byr 46 F5
Cwmcarn 35 E6
Cwmcarvan 36 D1
Cwm-Cewydd 59 C5
Cwm-cou 45 E4
Cwmcych 45 F4
Cwmdare 34 D3
Cwmderwen 59 D6
Cwmdu
Carms 46 F5
Powys 35 B5
Swansea 33 E7
Cwmduad 46 F2
Cwm-Dulais 33 D7
Cwmdwr 47 F6
Cwmfelin
Bridgend 34 F2
M Tydf 34 D4
Cwmfelin Boeth 32 C2
Cwm-felin-fach 35 E5
Cwmfelin Mynach 32 B3
Cwmffrwd 33 C5
Cwm Ffrwd-oer 35 D6
Cwmgiedd 34 C1
Cwmgors 33 C8
Cwmgwili 33 C6
Cwmgwrach 34 D2
Cwm-hesgen 71 E8
Cwmhiraeth 46 F2
Cwm-hwnt 34 D3
Cwmifor 33 B7
Cwm Irfon 47 E7
Cwmisfael 33 C5
Cwm-Llinau 58 D5
Cwmllynfell 33 C8
Cwm-mawr 33 C6
Cwmorgan 45 F4
Cwm-parc 34 E3
Cwmpengraig 46 F2
Cwm Penmachno 71 C8
Cwmrhos 35 B5
Cwmsychpant 46 E3
Cwmtillery 35 D6
Cwm-twrch Isaf 34 C1
Cwm-twrch Uchaf 34 C1
Cwmwysg 34 B2
Cwm-y-glo
Carms 33 C6
Gwyn 82 E5
Cwmyoy 35 B6
Cwmystwyth 47 B6
Cwrt 58 D3
Cwrt-newydd 46 E3
Cwrt-y-cadno 47 E5
Cwrt-y-gollen 35 C6
Cydweli = Kidwelly 33 D5
Cyffordd Llandudno = Llandudno Junction 83 D7
Cyffylliog 72 D4
Cyfronydd 59 D8
Cymer 34 E2
Cyncoed 35 F5
Cynghordy 47 E7
Cynheidre 33 D5
Cynwyd 72 E4
Cynwyl Elfed 32 B4
Cywarch 59 C5

D

Dacre
Cumb 99 B6
N Yorks 94 C4
Dacre Banks 94 C4
Daddry Shield 109 F8
Dadford 52 F4
Dadlington 63 E8
Dafarn Faig 71 C5
Dafen 33 D6
Daffy Green 68 D2
Dagenham 41 F7
Daglingworth 37 D6
Dagnall 40 C2
Dail Beag 154 C7
Dail bho Dheas 155 A9
Dail bho Thuath 155 A9
Daill 142 B4
Dailly 112 D2
Dail Mor 154 C7
Dairsie or Osnaburgh 129 C6
Daisy Hill 86 D4
Dalabrog 148 F2
Dalavich 125 D5
Dalbeattie 106 C5
Dalblair 113 C6
Dalbog 135 B5
Dalbury 76 F2
Dalby
IoM 84 E2
N Yorks 96 B2
Dalchalloch 132 C4
Dalchalm 157 J12
Dalchenna 125 E6
Dalchirach 152 E1
Dalchork 157 H8
Dalchreichart 137 C5
Dalchruin 127 C6
Dalderby 78 C5
Dale 44 E3
Dale Abbey 76 F4
Dale Head 99 C6
Dalelia 147 E10
Dale of Walls 160 H3
Daless 151 H11
Dalfaber 138 C5
Dalgarven 118 E2
Dalgety Bay 128 F3
Dalginross 127 B6
Dalguise 133 E6
Dalhalvaig 157 D11
Dalham 55 C8
Dalinlongart 145 E10
Dalkeith 121 C6

Dallam 86 E3
Dallas 151 F14
Dalleagles 113 C5
Dallinghoo 57 D6
Dallington
  E Sus 18 D3
  Northants 52 C5
Dallow 94 B4
Dalmadilly . . . 141 C6
Dalmally 125 C7
Dalmarnock . . . 119 C6
Dalmary 126 E4
Dalmellington . 112 D4
Dalmeny 120 B4
Dalmigavie . . . 138 C3
Dalmigavie
  Lodge 138 B3
Dalmore 151 E9
Dalmuir 118 B4
Dalnabreck . . . 147 E9
Dalnacardoch
  Lodge 132 B4
Dalnacroich . . 150 F6
Dalnaglar
  Castle 133 C8
Dalnahaitnach . 138 B4
Dalnaspidal
  Lodge 132 B3
Dalnavaid 133 C7
Dalnavie 151 D9
Dalnawillan
  Lodge 157 E13
Dalness 131 D5
Dalnessie 157 H9
Dalqueich 128 D2
Dalreavoch . . . 157 J10
Dalry 118 E2
Dalrymple 112 C3
Dalserf 119 D8
Dalston 108 D3
Dalswinton . . . 114 F2
Dalton
  Dumfries . . . 107 B8
  Lancs 86 D2
  Northumb . . . 110 B4
  Northumb . . . 110 D2
  N Yorks 95 B7
  N Yorks . . . 101 D6
  S Yorks 89 E5
Dalton-in-
  Furness 92 B2
Dalton-le-Dale 111 E7
Dalton-on-Tees 101 D7
Dalton Piercy 111 F7
Dalveich 126 B5
Dalvina Lodge 157 E9
Dalwhinnie . . . 138 F2
Dalwood 11 D7
Dalwyne 112 E3
Damerham 14 C2
Damgate 69 D7
Dam Green 68 F3
Damnaglaur . . . 104 F5
Damside 120 E4
Dam Side 92 E4
Danbury 42 D3
Danby 103 D5
Danby Wiske . . 101 E8
Dandaleith . . . 152 D2
Danderhall . . . 121 C6
Danebridge . . . 75 C6
Dane End 41 B6
Danehill 17 B8
Danemoor Green 68 D3
Danesford 61 E7
Daneshill 26 D4
Dangerous
  Corner 86 C3
Danskine 121 C8
Darcy Lever . . 86 C5
Darenth 29 B6
Daresbury 86 F3
Darfield 88 D5
Darfoulds 77 B5
Dargate 30 C4
Darite 5 C7
Darlaston 62 E3
Darley 94 D5
Darley Bridge 76 C2
Darley Head . . 94 D4
Darlingscott . 51 E7
Darlington . . . 101 C7
Darliston 74 F2
Darlton 77 B7
Darnall 88 F4
Darnick 121 F8
Darowen 58 D5
Darra 153 D7
Darracott 20 F3
Darras Hall . . 110 B4
Darrington . . . 89 B5
Darsham 57 C8
Dartford 29 B6
Dartford Crossing 29 B6
Dartington . . . 7 C5
Dartmeet 6 B4
Dartmouth 7 D6
Darton 88 D4
Darvel 119 F6
Darwell Hole . 18 D3
Darwen 86 B4
Datchet 27 B7
Datchworth . . . 41 C5
Datchworth
  Green 41 C5
Daubhill 86 D5
Daugh of
  Kinermony . . 152 D2
Dauntsey 37 F6
Dava 151 H13
Davenham 74 B3
Davenport Green 74 B5
Daventry 52 C3
Davidson's
  Mains 120 B5
Davidstow 8 F3
David's Well . 48 B2
Davington 115 D5
Daviot
  Aberds 141 B6
  Highld 151 H10
Davoch of
  Grange 152 C4
Davyhulme . . . 87 E5
Dawley 61 D6

Dawlish 7 B7
Dawlish Warren . 7 B7
Dawn 83 D8
Daws Heath . . . 42 F4
Daw's House
  Corn 8 F5
  Corn 8 F5
Dawsmere 79 F7
Dayhills 75 F6
Daylesford . . . 38 B2
Ddôl-Cownwy . . 82 D3
Ddrydwy 82 D3
Deadwater 116 E2
Deaf Hill 111 F6
Deal 31 D7
Deal Hall 43 E6
Dean
  Cumb 98 B2
  Devon 6 C5
  Devon 20 E4
  Dorset 13 C7
  Hants 15 C5
  Som 23 E8
Deanburnhaugh 115 C6
Deane
  Gtr Man 86 D4
  Hants 26 D3
Deanich Lodge 150 C6
Deanland 13 C7
Dean Prior . . . 6 C5
Dean Row 87 F6
Deanscales . . . 98 B2
Deanshanger . . 53 F5
Deanston 127 D6
Dearham 107 F7
Debach 57 D6
Debden
  Essex 41 E7
  Essex 55 F6
Debden Cross . 55 F6
Debenham 57 C5
Dechmont 120 B3
Deddington . . . 52 F2
Dedham 56 F4
Dedham Heath . 56 F4
Deene 65 E6
Deenethorpe . . 65 E6
Deepcar 88 E3
Deepcut 27 D7
Deepdale 100 F2
Deeping Gate . 65 D8
Deeping St
  James 65 D8
Deeping St
  Nicholas . . . 66 C2
Deerhill 152 C4
Deerhurst 37 B5
Deerness 159 H6
Defford 50 E4
Defynnog 34 B3
Deganwy 83 D7
Deighton
  N Yorks 102 D1
  W Yorks 88 C2
  York 96 E2
Deiniolen 83 E5
Delabole 8 F2
Delamere 74 C2
Delfrigs 141 B8
Delliefure . . . 151 H13
Dell Lodge . . . 139 C6
Delnabo 139 C7
Delnadamph . . . 139 D8
Delph 87 D7
Delves 110 E4
Delvine 133 E8
Dembleby 78 F3
Denaby Main . . 89 E5
Denbigh
  =Dinbych . . . 72 C4
Denbury 7 C6
Denby 76 E3
Denby Dale . . . 88 D3
Denchworth . . . 38 E3
Dendron 92 B2
Denel End 53 F8
Denend 152 E6
Denford 53 B7
Dengie 43 D5
Denham
  Bucks 40 F3
  Suff 55 C8
  Suff 57 B5
Denham Street . 57 B5
Denhead
  Aberds 153 C9
  Fife 129 C6
Denhead of
  Arbilot 135 E5
Denhead of
  Gray 134 F3
Denholm 115 C8
Denholme 94 F3
Denholme
  Clough 94 F3
Denio 70 D4
Denmead 15 C7
Denmore 141 C8
Denmoss 153 D6
Dennington . . . 57 C6
Denny 127 F7
Dennyloanhead 127 F7
Denny Lodge . . 14 D4
Denshaw 87 C7
Denside 141 E7
Densole 31 E6
Denston 55 D8
Denstone 75 E8
Dent 100 F2
Denton
  Cambs 65 F8
  Darl 101 C7
  E Sus 17 D8
  Gtr Man 87 E7
  Kent 31 E6
  Lincs 77 F8
  Norf 69 F5
  Northants . . . 53 D6
  N Yorks 94 E4
  Oxon 39 D5
Denton's Green 86 E2
Denver 67 D6
Denwick 117 C8
Deopham 68 D3
Deopham Green 68 D3
Depden 55 D8

Depden Green . 55 D8
Deptford
  London 28 B4
  Wilts 24 F5
Derby 76 F3
Derbyhaven . . . 84 F2
Dereham 68 C2
Deri 35 D5
Derril 8 D5
Derringstone . 31 E6
Derrington . . . 62 B2
Derriton 8 D5
Derryguaig . . . 146 H7
Derry Hill . . . 24 B4
Derrythorpe . . 90 D2
Dersingham . . . 80 D2
Derwen 72 D4
Derwenlas 58 E4
Desborough . . . 64 F5
Desford 63 D8
Detchant 123 F6
Detling 29 D8
Deuddwr 60 C2
Devauden 36 E1
Devil's Bridge 47 B6
Devizes 24 C5
Devol 118 B3
Devonport 6 D2
Devonside 127 E8
Devoran 3 C6
Dewar 121 E6
Dewlish 13 E5
Dewsbury 88 B3
Dewsbury Moor 88 B3
Dewshall Court 49 F6
Dhoon 84 D4
Dhoor 84 C4
Dhowin 84 B4
Dial Post 17 C5
Dibden 14 D5
Dibden Purlieu 14 D5
Dickleburgh . . 68 F4
Didbrook 51 F5
Didcot 39 F5
Diddington . . . 54 C2
Diddlebury . . . 60 F5
Didley 49 F6
Didling 16 C2
Didmarton 37 F5
Didsbury 87 E6
Didworthy 6 C4
Digby 78 D3
Diggle 87 D8
Digmoor 86 D2
Dihewyd 46 D3
Dilham 69 B6
Dilhorne 75 E6
Dillarburn . . . 119 E8
Dillington . . . 54 C2
Dilston 110 C2
Dilton Marsh . 24 E3
Dilwyn 49 D6
Dinas
  Carms 45 F4
  Gwyn 70 D3
Dinas Cross . . 45 F2
Dinas Dinlle . 82 F4
Dinas-Mawddwy 59 C5
Dinas Powys . . 22 B3
Dinbych
  =Denbigh . . . 72 C4
Dinbych-y-Pysgod
  =Tenby 32 D2
Dinder 23 E7
Dinedor 49 F7
Dingestow 36 C1
Dingle 85 F4
Dingleden 18 B5
Dingley 64 F4
Dingwall 151 F8
Dinlabyre 115 E8
Dinmael 72 E4
Dinnet 140 E3
Dinnington
  Som 12 C2
  S Yorks 89 F6
  T&W 110 B5
Dinorwic 83 E5
Dinton
  Bucks 39 C7
  Wilts 24 F5
Dinwoodie
  Mains 114 E4
Dinworthy 8 C5
Dippen 143 F11
Dippenhall . . . 27 E6
Dipple
  Moray 152 C3
  S Ayrs 112 D2
Diptford 6 D5
Dipton 110 D4
Dirdhu 139 B6
Dirleton 129 F7
Dirt Pot 109 E8
Discoed 48 C4
Diseworth 63 B8
Dishes 159 F7
Dishforth 95 B6
Disley 87 F7
Diss 56 B5
Disserth 48 D2
Distington . . . 98 B2
Ditchampton . . 25 F5
Ditcheat 23 F8
Ditchingham . . 69 E6
Ditchling 17 C7
Ditherington . 60 C5
Dittisham 7 D6
Ditton
  Halton 86 F2
  Kent 29 D8
Ditton Green . 55 D7
Ditton Priors 61 F6
Divach 137 B7
Divlyn 47 F6
Dixton
  Glos 50 F4
  Mon 36 C2
Dobcross 87 D7
Dobwalls 5 C7
Doccombe 10 F2
Dochfour House 151 H9
Dochgarroch . . 151 G9
Docking 80 D3
Docklow 49 D7

Dockray 99 B5
Dockroyd 94 F3
Doc Penfro
  =Pembroke Dock 44 E4
Dodburn 115 D7
Doddinghurst . 42 E1
Doddington
  Cambs 66 E3
  Kent 30 D3
  Lincs 78 B2
  Northumb . . . 123 F5
  Shrops 49 B8
Doddiscombsleigh 10 F3
Dodford
  Northants . . . 52 C4
  Worcs 50 B4
Dodington 24 A2
Dodleston 73 C7
Dods Leigh . . . 75 F7
Dodworth 88 D4
Doe Green 86 F3
Doe Lea 76 C4
Dogdyke 78 D5
Dogmersfield . 27 D5
Dogridge 37 F7
Dogsthorpe . . . 65 D8
Dog Village . . 10 E4
Dolanog 59 C7
Dolau
  Powys 48 C3
  Rhondda 34 F3
Dolbenmaen . . . 71 C6
Dolfach 59 D6
Dolfor 59 F8
Dol-ffor 58 D5
Dolgarrog 83 E7
Dolgellau 58 C4
Dolgran 46 F3
Dolhendre 72 F2
Doll 157 J11
Dollar 127 E8
Dolley Green . 48 C4
Dollwen 58 F3
Dolphin 73 B5
Dolphinholme . 92 D5
Dolphinton . . . 120 E4
Dolton 9 C7
Dolwen
  Conwy 83 D8
  Powys 59 D6
Dolwyd 83 D8
Dolwyddelan . . 83 F7
Dôl-y-Bont . . . 58 F3
Dôl-y-cannau . 48 E4
Dolyhir 48 D4
Doncaster 89 D6
Dones Green . . 74 B3
Donhead St
  Andrew 13 B7
Donhead St Mary 13 B7
Donibristle . 128 F3
Donington 78 F5
Donington on
  Bain 78 F5
Donington South
  Ing 78 F5
Donisthorpe . . 63 C7
Donkey Town . . 27 C7
Donnington
  Glos 38 B1
  Hereford . . . 50 F2
  Shrops 61 D5
  Telford 61 C7
  W Berks 26 C2
  W Sus 16 D2
Donnington
  Wood 61 C7
Donyatt 11 C8
Doonfoot 112 C3
Dorback Lodge 139 C6
Dorchester
  Dorset 12 E4
  Oxon 39 E5
Dordon 63 D6
Dore 88 F4
Dores 151 H8
Dorking 28 E2
Dormansland . . 28 E5
Dormanstown . . 102 B3
Dormington . . . 49 E7
Dormston 50 D4
Dornal 105 B6
Dorney 27 B7
Dornie 149 F13
Dornoch 151 C10
Dornock 108 C2
Dorrery 158 E2
Dorridge 51 B6
Dorrington
  Lincs 78 D3
  Shrops 60 D4
Dorsington . . . 51 E6
Dorstone 48 E5
Dorton 39 C6
Dorusduain . . . 136 B2
Dosthill 63 E6
Dottery 12 E2
Doublebois . . . 5 C6
Dougarie 143 E9
Doughton 37 E5
Douglas
  IoM 84 E3
  S Lanark . . . 119 F8
Douglas &
  Angus 134 F4
Douglastown . . 134 E4
Douglas
  Water 119 F8
Douglas West . 119 F8
Doulting 23 E8
Dounby 159 F3

Doune
  Highld 156 J7
  Stirling . . . 127 D6
Doune Park . . . 153 B7
Douneside 140 D3
Dounie 151 B8
Dounreay 157 C12
Dousland 6 C3
Dovaston 60 B3
Dove Holes . . . 75 B7
Dovenby 107 F7
Dover 31 E7
Dovercourt . . . 57 F6
Doverdale 50 C3
Doveridge 75 F8
Doversgreen . . 28 E3

Dowally 133 E7
Dowbridge 92 F4
Dowdeswell . . . 37 C6
Dowlais 34 D4
Dowland 9 C7
Dowlish Wake . 11 C8
Down Ampney . . 37 E8
Downcraig
  Ferry 145 H10
Downderry 5 D8
Downe 28 C5
Downend
  IoW 15 F6
  S Glos 23 B8
  W Berks 26 B2
Downfield 134 F3
Downgate 5 B8
Downham
  Essex 42 E3
  Lancs 93 E7
  Northumb . . . 122 F4
Downham
  Market 67 D6
Down Hatherley 37 B5
Downhead 23 E8
Downhill
  Perth 133 F7
  T&W 111 D6
Downholland
  Cross 85 D4
Downholme . . . 101 E6
Downies 141 E8
Downley 39 E8
Down St Mary . 10 D2
Downside
  Som 23 E8
  Sur 28 D2
Down Thomas . . 6 D3
Downton
  Hants 14 E3
  Wilts 14 B2
Downton on the
  Rock 49 B6
Dowsby 65 B8
Dowsdale 66 C2
Dowthwaitehead 99 B5
Doxey 62 B3
Doxford 117 B7
Doxford Park . 111 D6
Doynton 24 B2
Draffan 119 E7
Dragonby 90 C3
Drakeland Corner 6 D3
Drakemyre 118 D2
Drake's
  Broughton . . 50 E4
Drakes Cross . 51 B5
Drakewalls . . . 6 B2
Draughton
  Northants . . . 53 B5
  N Yorks 94 D3
Drax 89 B7
Draycote 52 B2
Draycott
  Derbys 76 F4
  Glos 51 F6
  Som 23 D6
Draycott in the
  Clay 63 B6
Draycott in the
  Moors 75 E6
Drayford 10 C2
Drayton
  Leics 64 E5
  Lincs 78 F5
  Norf 68 C4
  Oxon 38 E4
  Oxon 52 E2
  Ptsmth 15 D7
  Som 12 B2
  Worcs 50 B4
Drayton Bassett 63 D5
Drayton
  Beauchamp . . 40 C2
Drayton Parslow 39 B8
Drayton St
  Leonard 39 E5
Drebley 94 D3
Dreemskerry . . 84 C4
Dreenhill 44 D4
Drefach
  Carms 33 C6
  Carms 46 F2
Dre-fach
  Carms 33 C7
  Ceredig 46 E4
Drefelin 46 F2
Dreghorn 118 F3
Drellingore . . 31 E6
Drem 121 B8
Dresden 75 E6
Dreumasdal . . . 148 E2
Drewsteignton 10 E2
Driby 79 B6
Driffield
  E Yorks 97 D6
  Glos 37 E7
Drigg 98 E2
Drighlington . 88 B3
Drimnin 147 F8
Drimpton 12 D2
Drimsynie 125 E7
Drinisiadar . 154 H6
Drinkstone . . . 56 C3
Drinkstone
  Green 56 C3
Drishaig 125 D7
Drissaig 124 D5
Drochil 120 E4
Droitwich Spa 50 C3
Droman 156 D4
Dron 128 C3
Dronfield 76 B3
Dronfield
  Woodhouse . . 76 B3
Drongan 112 C4
Dronley 134 F3
Droxford 15 C7
Droylsden 87 E7
Druid 72 E4
Druidston 44 D3
Drimnin 147 F8
Drimmin 147 F8
Druimarbin . . . 130 B4
Druimavuic . . . 130 E4
Druimdrishaig 144 F6
Druimindarroch 147 C9
Druimyeon
  More 143 C7

Drum
  Argyll 145 F8
  Perth 128 D2
Drumbeg 156 F4
Drumblade 152 D5
Drumblair 153 D6
Drumbuie
  Dumfries . . . 113 F5
  Highld 149 E12
Drumburgh . . . 108 D2
Drumburn 107 C6
Drumchapel . . . 118 B5
Drumchardine . 151 G8
Drumchork . . . 155 J13
Drumclog 119 F6
Drumderfit . . . 151 F9
Drumeldrie . . . 129 D6
Drumelzier . . . 120 F4
Drumfearn . . . 149 G11
Drumgask 138 E2
Drumgley 134 D4
Drumguish 138 E3
Drumin 152 E1
Drumlasie 140 D5
Drumlemble . . . 143 G7
Drumligair . . . 141 C8
Drumlithie . . . 141 F6
Drummoddie . . . 105 E7
Drummond 151 E9
Drummore 104 F5
Drummuir 152 D3
Drummuir
  Castle 152 D3
Drumnadrochit 137 B8
Drumnagorrach 152 C5
Drumoak 141 E6
Drumpark 107 A5
Drumphail 105 C6
Drumrash 106 B3
Drumrunie 156 J4
Drums 141 B8
Drumsallie . . . 130 B3
Drumstinchall 107 D5
Drumsturdy . . . 134 F4
Drumtochty
  Castle 135 B6
Drumtroddan . . 105 E7
Drumuie 149 D9
Drumuillie . . . 138 B5
Drumvaich 127 D6
Drumwhindle . . 153 E9
Drunkendub . . . 135 E6
Drury 73 C6
Drury Square . 68 C2
Dry Doddington 77 E8
Dry Drayton . . 54 C4
Dryhope 115 B5
Drylaw 120 B5
Drym 2 C5
Drymen 126 F3
Drymuir 153 D9
Drynoch 149 E9
Dryslwyn 33 B6
Dryton 61 D5
Dubford 153 B8
Dubton 135 D5
Duchally 156 H6
Duchlage 126 F2
Duck Corner . . 57 E7
Duckington . . . 73 D8
Ducklington . . 38 D3
Duckmanton . . . 76 B4
Duck's Cross . 54 D2
Duddenhoe End 55 F5
Duddingston . . 121 B5
Duddington . . . 65 D6
Duddleswell . . 17 B8
Duddo 122 E5
Duddon 74 C2
Duddon Bridge 98 F4
Dudleston 73 F7
Dudleston Heath 73 F7
Dudley
  T&W 111 B5
  W Mid 62 E3
Dudley Port . . 62 E3
Duffield 76 E3
Duffryn
  Neath 34 E2
  Newport 35 F6
Dufftown 152 E3
Duffus 152 B1
Dufton 100 B1
Duggleby 96 C4
Duirinish . . . 149 E12
Duisdalemore 149 G12
Duisky 130 B4
Dukestown 35 C5
Dukinfield . . . 87 E7
Dulas 82 C4
Dulcote 23 E7
Dulford 11 D5
Dull 133 E5
Dullatur 119 B7
Dullingham . . . 55 D7
Dullingham Ley 55 D7
Dulnain Bridge 139 B5
Duloe
  Bedford 54 C2
  Corn 5 D7
Dulsie 151 G12
Dulverton 10 B4
Dulwich 28 B4
Dumbarton . . . 118 B3
Dumbleton . . . 50 F5
Dumcrieff 114 D4
Dumfries 107 B6
Dumgoyne 126 F4
Dummer 26 E3
Dumpford 16 B2
Dumpton 31 C7
Dun 135 D6
Dunain House . 151 G9
Dunalastair . 132 D4
Dunan 149 F10
Dunball 22 E5
Dunbar 122 B2
Dunbeath 158 H3
Dunbeg 124 B4
Dunblane 127 D6
Dunbog 128 C4
Duncanston . . 151 F8

Duncanstone . . 140 B4
Dun
  Charlabhaigh 154 C6
  Perth 128 D2
Dunchurch 52 B2
Duncote 52 D4
Duncow 114 F2
Duncraggan . . . 126 D4
Duncrievie . . . 128 D3
Duncton 16 C3
Dundas House . 159 K5
Dundee 134 F4
Dundeugh 113 F5
Dundon 23 F6
Dundonald . . . 118 F3
Dundonnell . . . 150 C3
Dundonnell
  Hotel 150 C3
Dundonnell
  House 150 C3
Dundraw 108 E2
Dundreggan . . . 137 C6
Dundrennan . . . 106 E4
Dundry 23 C7
Dunecht 141 D6
Dunfermline . 128 F2
Dunfield 37 E8
Dunford Bridge 88 D2
Dungworth 88 F3
Dunham 77 B8
Dunham-on-the-
  Hill 73 B8
Dunhampton . . . 50 C3
Dunham Town . . 86 F5
Dunholme 78 B3
Dunino 129 C7
Dunipace 127 F7
Dunira 127 B6
Dunkeld 133 E7
Dunkerton 24 D2
Dunkeswell . . . 11 D6
Dunkeswick . . . 95 E6
Dunkirk
  Kent 30 D4
  Norf 81 E8
Dunk's Green . 29 D7
Dunlappie 135 C5
Dunley
  Hants 26 D2
  Worcs 50 C2
Dunlichity
  Lodge 151 H9
Dunlop 118 E4
Dunmaglass
  Lodge 137 B8
Dunmore
  Argyll 144 G6
  Falk 127 F7
Dunnet 158 C4
Dunnichen . . . 135 E5
Dunninald . . . 135 D7
Dunning 128 C2
Dunnington
  E Yorks 97 D7
  Warks 51 D5
  York 96 D2
Dunnockshaw . . 87 B6
Dunollie 124 B4
Dunoon 145 F10
Dunragit 105 D5
Dunrostan 144 E6
Duns 122 D3
Dunsby 65 B8
Dunscore 113 F8
Dunscroft 89 D7
Dunsdale 102 C4
Dunsden Green 26 B5
Dunsfold 27 F8
Dunsford 10 F3
Dunshalt 128 C4
Dunshillock . . 153 D9
Dunskey House 104 D4
Dunsley 103 C6
Dunsmore 40 D1
Dunsop Bridge 93 D6
Dunstable 40 B3
Dunstall 63 B5
Dunstall Common 50 E3
Dunstall Green 55 C8
Dunstan 117 C8
Dunstan Steads 117 B8
Dunster 21 E8
Duns Tew 38 B4
Dunston
  Lincs 78 C3
  Norf 68 D5
  Staffs 62 C3
  T&W 110 C5
Dunsville 89 D7
Dunswell 97 F6
Dunsyre 120 E3
Dunterton 5 B8
Duntisbourne
  Abbots 37 D6
Duntisbourne
  Leer 37 D6
Duntisbourne
  Rouse 37 D6
Duntish 12 D4
Duntocher . . . 118 B4
Dunton
  Bucks 39 B8
  C Beds 54 E3
  Norf 80 D4
Dunton Bassett 64 E2
Dunton Green . 29 D6
Dunton Wayletts 42 E2
Duntulm 149 A9
Dunure 112 C2
Dunvant 33 E6
Dunvegan 148 D7
Dunwich 57 B8
Dunwood 75 D6
Dupplin Castle 128 C2
Durdar 108 D4
Durgates 18 B3
Durham 111 E5
Durisdeer 113 D8
Durisdeermill 113 D8
Durkar 88 C4
Durleigh 22 F4
Durley
  Hants 15 C6
  Wilts 25 C7
Durley Street . 15 C6
Durnamuck . . . 156 H3
Durness 156 C7
Durno 141 B6

Duror 130 D3
Durran
  Argyll 125 E5
  Highld 158 D3
Durrington
  Wilts 25 E6
  W Sus 16 D5
Dursley 36 E4
Durston 11 B7
Durweston 13 D6
Dury 160 G6
Duston 52 C5
Duthil 138 B5
Dutlas 48 B4
Duton Hill . . . 42 B2
Dutson 8 F5
Dutton 74 B2
Duxford
  Cambs 55 E5
  Oxon 38 E3
Dwygyfylchi . . 83 D7
Dwyran 82 E4
Dyce 141 C7
Dye House . . . 110 D2
Dyffryn
  Bridgend . . . 34 E2
  Carms 32 B4
  Pembs 44 B4
Dyffryn Ardudwy 71 E6
Dyffryn Castell 58 F4
Dyffryn Ceidrych 33 B8
Dyffryn Cellwen 34 D2
Dyke
  Lincs 65 B8
  Moray 151 F12
Dykehead
  Angus 134 C3
  N Lanark . . . 119 D8
  Stirling . . . 126 E4
Dykelands 135 C7
Dykends 134 D2
Dykeside 153 D7
Dykesmains . . . 118 E2
Dylife 59 E5
Dymchurch . . . 19 C7
Dymock 50 F2
Dyrham 24 B2
Dysart 128 E5
Dyserth 72 B4

E

Eadar Dha
  Fhadhail . . . 154 D5
Eagland Hill . 92 E4
Eagle 77 C8
Eagle Barnsdale 77 C8
Eagle Moor . . . 77 C8
Eaglescliffe . 102 C2
Eaglesfield
  Cumb 98 B2
  Dumfries . . . 108 B2
Eaglesham 119 D5
Eaglethorpe . . 65 E7
Eairy 84 E2
Eakley Lanes . 53 D6
Eakring 77 C6
Ealand 89 C8
Ealing 40 F4
Eals 109 D6
Eamont Bridge 99 B7
Earby 94 E2
Earcroft 86 B4
Eardington . . . 61 E7
Eardisland . . . 49 D6
Eardisley 48 E5
Eardiston
  Shrops 60 B3
  Worcs 49 C8
Earith 54 B4
Earle 117 B5
Earley 27 B5
Earlham 68 D5
Earlish 149 B8
Earls Barton . 53 C6
Earls Colne . . 42 B4
Earl's Croome 50 E3
Earlsdon 51 B8
Earlsferry . . . 129 E6
Earlsfield . . . 78 F2
Earlsheaton . . 88 B3
Earl Shilton . 63 E8
Earlsmill . . . 151 F12
Earl Soham . . . 57 C6
Earl Sterndale 75 C7
Earlston
  Borders . . . 121 F8
  E Ayrs 118 F4
Earl Stonham . 56 D5
Earlswood
  Mon 36 E1
  Sur 28 E3
  Warks 51 B6
Earnley 16 E2
Earsairidh . . . 148 J2
Earsdon 111 B6
Earsham 69 F6
Earswick 96 D2
Eartham 16 D3
Easby
  N Yorks 101 D6
  N Yorks 102 D3
Easdale 124 D3
Easebourne . . . 16 B2
Easenhall 52 B2
Eashing 27 E7
Easington
  Bucks 39 C6
  Durham 111 E7
  E Yorks 91 C7
  Northumb . . . 123 F7
  Oxon 39 E6
  Oxon 52 F2
  Redcar 103 C5
Easington
  Colliery . . . 111 E7
Easington Lane 111 E6
Easingwold . . . 95 C8
Easole Street . 31 D6
Eassie 134 E3
East Aberthaw 22 C3
East Adderbury 52 F2
East Allington 7 E5
East Anstey . . 10 B3
East Appleton 101 E7

East Ardsley . 88 B4
East Ashling . 16 D2
East Auchronie 141 D7
East Bank 35 D6
East Barkwith 91 F5
East Barming . 29 D8
East Barnby . . 103 C6
East Barnet . . 41 E5
East Barns . . 122 B3
East Barsham . 80 D5
East Beckham . 81 D7
East Bedfont . 27 B8
East Bergholt . 56 F4
East Bilney . . 68 C2
East Blatchington 17 D8
East Boldre . . 14 D4
Eastbourne . . 22 D5
East Brent . . 22 D5
Eastbridge . . 57 C8
East Bridgford 77 E6
East Buckland 21 F5
East Budleigh 11 F5
Eastburn 94 E3
East Burrafirth 160 H5
East Burton . . 13 F6
Eastbury
  London 40 E3
  W Berks 25 B8
East Butsfield 110 E4
East Butterwick 90 D2
Eastby 94 D3
East Cairnbeg 135 B7
East Calder . . 120 C3
East Carleton 68 D4
East Carlton
  Northants . . . 64 F5
  W Yorks 94 E5
East Chaldon . 13 F5
East Challow . 38 F3
East Chiltington 17 C7
East Chinnock 12 C2
East Chisenbury 25 D6
Eastchurch . . 30 B3
East Clandon . 27 D8
East Claydon . 39 B7
East Clyne . . 157 J12
East Coker . . 12 C3
Eastcombe . . . 37 D5
East Combe . . 22 F3
East Common . 96 F2
East Compton . 23 E8
Eastcote
  London 40 F4
  Northants . . . 52 D4
  W Mid 51 B6
Eastcott
  Corn 8 C4
  Wilts 24 D5
East Cottingwith 96 E3
Eastcourt
  Wilts 25 C7
  Wilts 37 E6
East Cowes . . 15 E6
East Cowick . . 89 B7
East Cowton . . 101 D8
East
  Cramlington 111 B5
East Cranmore 23 E8
East Creech . . 13 F7
East Croachy . 138 B2
East Croftmore 139 C5
East Curthwaite 108 E3
East Dean
  E Sus 18 F2
  Hants 14 B3
  W Sus 16 C3
East Down . . . 20 E5
East Drayton . 77 B7
East Ella . . . 90 B4
East End
  Dorset 13 E7
  E Yorks 91 B6
  Hants 14 E4
  Hants 15 B7
  Hants 26 C2
  Herts 41 B7
  Kent 18 B5
  N Som 23 B6
  Oxon 38 C3
Easter Ardross 151 D9
Easter Balmoral 139 E8
Easter
  Boleskine . . 137 B8
Easter Compton 36 F2
Easter Cringate 127 F6
Easter Davoch 140 D3
Easter Earshaig 114 D3
Easter Fearn . 151 C9
Easter
  Galcantray . 151 G11
Eastergate . . . 16 D3
Easterhouse . . 119 C6
Easter Howgate 120 C5
Easter Howlaws 122 E3
Easter Kinkell 151 F8
Easter
  Lednathie . . 134 C3
Easter Milton . 151 F12
Easter Moniack 151 G8
Eastern Green . 63 F6
Easter Ord . . 141 D7
Easter Quarff . 160 K6
Easter Rhynd . 128 C3
Easter Row . . 127 E6
Easter
  Silverford . 153 B7
Easter Skeld . 160 J5
Easterton . . . 24 D5
Eastertown of
  Auchleuchries
  . . . . 153 E10
Easter Whyntie 152 B6
East Farleigh . 29 D8
East Farndon . 64 F4
East Ferry . . 90 E2
Eastfield
  N Lanark . . . 119 C8
  N Yorks 103 F8
Eastfield Hall 117 D8
East Fortune . 121 B8
East Garston . 25 B8
Eastgate
  Durham 110 F2
  Norf 81 E7
East Ginge . . 38 F4
East Goscote . 64 C3

East Grafton 25 C7
East Grimstead . . . 14 B3
East Grinstead . . . 28 F4
East Guldeford . . . 19 C6
East Haddon 52 C4
East Hagbourne . . 39 F5
East Halton 90 C5
Eastham 85 F4
East Ham 41 F7
Eastham Ferry . . 85 F4
Easthampstead . . 27 C6
East Hanney . . . 38 E4
East Hanningfield . . 42 D3
East Hardwick . . 89 C5
East Harling . . . 68 F2
East Harlsey . . . 102 E2
East Harnham . . . 14 B2
East Harptree . . . 23 D7
East Hartford . . 111 B5
East Harting . . . 15 C8
East Hatley 54 E4
East Hauxwell . . 101 E6
East Haven . . . 135 F5
East Heath 27 C6
East Heckington . . 78 E4
East Hedleyhope . . . 110 E4
East Hendred . . . 38 F4
East Herrington 111 D6
East Heslerton . . 96 B5
East Hoathly . . . 18 D2
Easthope 61 E5
Easthorpe
  Essex 43 B5
  Leics 77 F8
  Notts 77 D7
East Horrington . . 23 E7
East Horsley . . . 27 D8
East Horton . . 123 F6
Easthouses . . . 121 C6
East Huntspill . . 22 E5
East Hyde 40 C4
East Ilkerton . . 21 E6
East Ilsley 38 F4
Eastington
  Devon 10 D2
  Glos 36 D4
  Glos 37 C8
East Keal 79 C6
East Kennett . . . 25 C6
East Keswick . . . 95 E6
East Kilbride . . 119 D6
East Kirkby . . . 79 C6
East Knapton . . 96 B4
East Knighton . . 13 F6
East Knoyle . . . 24 F3
East Kyloe . . . 123 F6
East Lambrook . . 12 C2
East Lamington . . 151 D10
East Langdon . . 31 E7
East Langton . . . 64 E4
East Langwell . . 157 J10
East Lavant . . . 16 D2
East Lavington . . 16 C3
East Layton . . . 101 D6
Eastleach Martin 38 D2
Eastleach Turville . . 38 D1
East Leake . . . 64 B2
East Learmouth 122 F4
Eastleigh
  Devon 9 B6
  Hants 14 C5
East Leigh 9 D8
East Lexham . . . 67 C8
East Lilburn . . 117 B6
Eastling 30 D3
East Linton . . . 121 B8
East Liss 15 B8
East Looe 5 D7
East Lound 89 E8
East Lulworth . . 13 F6
East Lutton . . . 96 C5
East Lydford . . . 23 F7
East Mains . . . 141 E7
East Malling . . . 29 D8
East March . . . 134 F4
East Marden . . . 16 C2
East Markham . . 77 B7
East Marton . . . 94 D2
East Meon 15 B7
East Mere 10 C4
East Mersea . . . 43 C6
East Mey 158 C5
East Molesey . . . 28 C2
Eastmoor
  Derbys 76 B3
  Norf 67 D7
East Morden . . . 13 E7
East Morton . . . 94 E4
East Ness 96 B2
East Newton . . . 97 F8
Eastney 15 E7
Eastnor 50 F2
East Norton . . . 64 D4
East Nynehead . . 11 B6
East Oakley . . . 26 D3
Eastoft 90 C2
East Ogwell . . . 7 B6
Eastoke 15 E8
Easton
  Cambs 54 B2
  Cumb 108 B4
  Cumb 108 D2
  Devon 10 F2
  Dorset 12 G4
  Hants 26 F3
  Lincs 65 B6
  Norf 68 C4
  Som 23 E7
  Suff 57 D6
  Wilts 24 B3
Easton Grey . . . 37 F5
Easton-in-Gordano . . 23 B7
Easton Maudit . . 53 D6
Easton on the Hill . . 65 D7
Easton Royal . . . 25 C7
East Orchard . . . 13 C6
East Ord 123 D5
East Panson . . . 9 E5
Eastpark 107 C7
East Peckham . . . 29 E7
East Pennard . . . 23 F7
East Perry 54 C2

East Portlemouth . . 6 F5
East Prawle 7 F5
East Preston . . . 16 D4
East Putford 9 C5
East Quantoxhead . . 22 E3
East Rainton . . 111 E6
East Ravendale . . 91 E6
East Raynham . . 80 E4
Eastrea 66 E2
East Rhidorroch Lodge 150 B5
Eastriggs 108 C2
East Rigton 95 E6
Eastrington 89 B8
East Rounton . . . 102 D2
East Row 103 C6
East Rudham . . . 80 E4
East Runton . . . 81 C7
East Ruston . . . 69 B6
Eastry 31 D7
East Saltoun . . 121 C7
East Sleekburn . . 117 F8
East Somerton . . 69 C7
East Stockwith . . 89 E8
East Stoke
  Dorset 13 F6
  Notts 77 E7
East Stour 13 B6
East Stourmouth . 31 C6
East Stowford . . 9 B8
East Stratton . . . 26 F3
East Studdal . . . 31 E7
East Suisnish . . 149 E10
East Taphouse . . . 5 C6
East-the-Water . . . 9 B7
East Thirston . . 117 E7
East Tilbury . . . 29 B7
East Tisted . . . 26 F5
East Torrington . . 90 F5
East Tuddenham 68 C3
East Tytherley . . 14 B3
East Tytherton . . 24 B4
East Village . . . 10 D3
Eastville
  Bristol 23 B8
  Lincs 79 D7
East Wall 60 E5
East Walton . . . 67 C7
Eastwell 64 B4
East Wellow . . . 14 B2
East Wemyss . . 128 E5
East Whitburn . . 120 C2
Eastwick
  Herts 41 C7
  Shetland . . 160 F5
East Williamston 32 D1
East Winch . . . 67 C6
East Winterslow . . 25 F7
East Wittering . . 15 E8
East Witton . . . 101 F6
Eastwood
  Notts 76 E4
  Southend . . . 42 F4
  W Yorks 87 B7
East Woodburn . . 116 F5
East Woodhay . . 26 C2
East Worldham . . 26 F5
East Worlington . . 10 C2
East Worthing . . 17 D5
Eathorpe 51 C8
Eaton
  Ches E 75 C5
  Ches W 74 C2
  Leics 64 B4
  Norf 68 D5
  Oxon 38 D4
  Shrops 60 F3
  Shrops 60 F5
Eaton Bishop . . 49 F6
Eaton Bray . . . 40 B2
Eaton Constantine . . 61 D5
Eaton Green . . . 40 B2
Eaton Hastings . . 38 E2
Eaton on Tern . . 61 B6
Eaton Socon . . 54 D2
Eavestone 94 C5
Ebberston . . . 103 F6
Ebbesbourne Wake 13 B7
Ebbw Vale
  = Glyn Ebwy . . . 35 D5
Ebchester . . . 110 D4
Ebford 10 F4
Ebley 37 D5
Ebnal 73 E8
Ebrington 51 E6
Ecchinswell . . . 26 D2
Ecclaw 122 C3
Ecclefechan . . . 107 B8
Eccles
  Borders 122 E3
  Gtr Man 87 E5
  Kent 29 C8
Ecclesall 88 F4
Ecclesfield . . . 88 E4
Ecclesgreig . . . 135 C7
Eccleshall 62 B2
Eccleshill 94 F4
Ecclesmachan . . 120 B3
Eccles on Sea . . 69 B7
Eccles Road . . . 68 E3
Eccleston
  Ches W 73 C8
  Lancs 86 C3
  Mers 86 E2
Eccleston Park . . 86 E2
Eccup 95 E5
Echt 141 D6
Eckford 116 B3
Eckington
  Derbys 76 B4
  Worcs 50 E4
Ecton 53 C6
Edale 88 F2
Edburton 17 C6
Edderside . . . 107 E7
Edderton . . . 151 C10
Eddistone 8 B4
Eddleston . . . 120 E5
Edenbridge . . . 28 E5
Edenfield 87 C5
Edenhall 109 F5
Edenham 65 B7
Eden Park 28 C4
Edensor 76 C2

Edentaggart . . 126 E2
Edenthorpe . . . 89 D7
Edentown . . . 108 D3
Ederline 124 E4
Edern 70 D3
Edgarley 23 F7
Edgbaston 62 F4
Edgcott
  Bucks 39 B6
  Som 21 F7
Edge 60 D3
Edgebolton . . . 61 B5
Edge End 36 C2
Edgefield 81 D6
Edgefield Street . . 81 D6
Edge Green . . . 73 D8
Edge Hill 85 F4
Edgeside 87 B6
Edgeworth 37 D6
Edgmond 61 C7
Edgmond Marsh . . 61 B7
Edgton 60 F3
Edgware 40 E4
Edgworth 86 C5
Edinample . . 126 B4
Edinbane 149 C8
Edinburgh . . . 121 B5
Edingale 63 C6
Edingight House 152 C5
Edingley 77 D6
Edingthorpe . . . 69 A6
Edingthorpe Green 69 A6
Edington
  Som 23 F5
  Wilts 24 D4
Edintore 152 D4
Edithmead 22 E5
Edith Weston . . 65 D6
Edlesborough . . 40 C2
Edlingham . . . 117 D7
Edlington 78 B5
Edmondsham . . . 13 C8
Edmondsley . . . 110 E5
Edmondthorpe . . 65 C5
Edmonstone . . 159 F6
Edmonton 41 E6
Edmundbyers . . 110 D3
Ednam 122 F3
Ednaston 76 E2
Edradynate . . 133 D5
Edrom 122 D4
Edstaston 74 F2
Edstone 51 C6
Edvin Loach . . . 49 D8
Edwalton 77 F5
Edwardstone . . . 56 E3
Edwinsford . . . 46 F5
Edwinstowe . . . 77 C6
Edworth 54 E3
Edwyn Ralph . . 49 D8
Edzell 135 C5
E Eachwick . . 110 B4
Efail Isaf 34 F4
Efailnewydd . . . 70 D4
Efailwen 32 B2
Efenechtyd . . . 72 D5
Effingham 28 D2
Effirth 160 H5
Efford 10 D3
Egdon 50 D4
Egerton
  Gtr Man 86 C5
  Kent 30 E3
Egerton Forstal . . 30 E2
Eggborough . . . 89 B6
Eggbuckland . . . 6 D3
Eggington 40 B2
Egginton 63 B6
Egglescliffe . . 102 C2
Eggleston . . . 100 B4
Egham 27 B8
Egleton 65 D5
Eglingham . . . 117 C7
Egloshayle 4 B5
Egloskerry 8 F4
Eglwys-Brewis . . 22 C2
Eglwys Cross . . 73 E8
Eglwys Fach . . . 58 E3
Eglwyswen . . . 45 F3
Eglwyswrw . . . 45 F3
Egmanton 77 C7
Egremont
  Cumb 98 C2
  Mers 85 E4
Egton 103 D6
Egton Bridge . . 103 D6
Eight Ash Green . . 43 B5
Eignaig 130 E1
Eil 138 C4
Eilanreach . . 149 G13
Eileanach Lodge 151 E8
Eilean Darach . . 150 C4
Einacleite . . . 154 E6
Eisgean 155 F8
Eisingrug 71 D7
Elan Village . . . 47 C8
Elberton 36 F3
Elburton 6 D3
Elcho 128 B3
Elcombe 37 F8
Eldernell 66 E3
Eldersfield . . . 50 F3
Eldersli 118 C4
Eldrick 112 F2
Eldroth 93 C7
Eldwick 94 E4
Elfhowe 99 E6
Elford
  Northumb . . 123 F7
  Staffs 63 C5
Elgin 152 B2
Elgol 149 G10
Elham 31 E5
Elie 129 D6
Eling 14 C4
Elishader . . 149 B10
Elishaw 116 E4
Elkesley 77 B6
Elkstone 37 C6
Ellan 138 B4
Elland 88 B2
Ellary 144 F6
Ellastone 75 E8

Ellemford . . 122 C3
Ellenbrook . . . 84 E3
Ellenhall 62 B2
Ellen's Green . . 27 F8
Ellerbeck . . . 102 E2
Ellerburn . . . 103 F6
Ellerby 103 C5
Ellerdine Heath . . 61 B6
Elleric 130 E4
Ellerker 90 B3
Ellerton
  E Yorks 96 F3
  Shrops 61 B7
Ellesborough . . 39 D8
Ellesmere 73 F8
Ellesmere Port . . 73 B8
Ellingham
  Norf 69 E6
  Northumb . . 117 B7
Ellingstring . . 101 F6
Ellington
  Cambs 54 B2
  Northumb . . 117 E8
Elliot 135 F6
Ellisfield 26 E4
Ellistown 63 C8
Ellon 153 E9
Ellonby 108 F4
Ellough 69 F7
Elloughton . . . 90 B3
Ellwood 36 D2
Elm 66 D4
Elmbridge 50 C4
Elmdon
  Essex 55 F5
  W Mid 63 F5
Elmdon Heath . . 63 F5
Elmers End . . . 28 C4
Elmesthorpe . . . 63 E8
Elmfield 15 E7
Elm Hill 13 B6
Elmhurst 62 C5
Elmley Castle . . 50 E4
Elmley Lovett . . 50 C3
Elmore 36 C4
Elmore Back . . . 36 C4
Elm Park 41 F8
Elmscott 8 B4
Elmsett 56 E4
Elmstead Market . 43 B6
Elmsted 30 E5
Elmstone 31 C6
Elmstone Hardwicke 37 B6
Elmswell
  E Yorks 97 D5
  Suff 56 C3
Elmton 76 B5
Elphin 156 H5
Elphinstone . . 121 B6
Elrick 141 D7
Elrig 105 E7
Elsdon 117 E5
Elsecar 88 E4
Elsenham 41 B8
Elsfield 39 C5
Elsham 90 C4
Elsing 68 C3
Elslack 94 E3
Elson 73 F7
Elsrickle 120 E3
Elstead 27 E7
Elsted 16 C2
Elsthorpe 65 B7
Elstob 101 B8
Elston
  Notts 77 E7
  Wilts 25 E5
Elstone 9 C8
Elstow 53 E8
Elstree 40 E4
Elstronwick . . . 97 F8
Elswick 92 F4
Elsworth 54 C4
Elterwater . . . 99 D5
Eltham 28 B5
Eltisley 54 D3
Elton
  Cambs 65 E7
  Ches W 73 B8
  Derbys 76 C2
  Glos 36 C4
  Hereford 49 B6
  Notts 77 F7
  Stockton 102 C2
Elton Green . . . 73 B8
Elvanfoot . . . 114 C2
Elvaston 76 F4
Elveden 56 B2
Elvingston . . 121 B7
Elvington
  Kent 31 D6
  York 96 E2
Elwick
  Hrtlpl 111 F7
  Northumb . . 123 F7
Elworth 74 C4
Elworthy 22 F2
Ely
  Cambs 66 F5
  Cardiff 22 B3
Emberton 53 E6
Embleton
  Cumb 107 F8
  Northumb . . 117 B8
Embo 151 B11
Emborough . . . 23 D8
Embo Street . . 151 B11
Embsay 94 D3
Emersons Green . . 23 B8
Emery Down . . . 14 D3
Emley 88 C3
Emmbrook 27 C5
Emmer Green . . 26 B5
Emmington . . . 39 D7
Emneth 66 D4
Emneth Hungate 66 D5
Empingham . . . 65 D6
Empshott 27 F5
Emstrey 60 C5
Emsworth 15 D8
Enborne 26 C2
Enborne Row . . 26 C2
Enchmarsh 60 E5
Enderby 64 E2
Endmoor 99 F7
Endon 75 D6
Endon Bank . . . 75 D6

Enfield 41 E6
Enfield Wash . . 41 E6
Enford 25 D6
Engamoor . . . 160 H4
Engine Common . . 36 F3
Englefield 26 B4
Englefield Green . . 27 B7
Englesea-brook . 74 D4
English Bicknor . . 36 C2
Englishcombe . . 24 C2
English Frankton . 60 B4
Enham Alamein . . 25 E8
Enmore 22 F4
Ennerdale Bridge 98 C2
Enoch 113 D8
Enochdhu . . . 133 C7
Ensay 146 G6
Ensbury 13 E8
Ensdon 60 C4
Ensis 9 B7
Enstone 38 B3
Enterkinfoot . . 113 D8
Enterpen 102 D2
Enville 62 F2
Eolaigearraidh . . 148 H2
Eorabus 146 J6
Eòropaidh . . . 155 A10
Epperstone . . . 77 E6
Epping 41 D7
Epping Green
  Essex 41 D7
  Herts 41 D5
Epping Upland . . 41 D7
Eppleby 101 C6
Eppleworth . . . 97 F6
Epsom 28 C3
Epwell 51 E8
Epworth 89 D8
Epworth Turbary 89 D8
Erbistock 73 E7
Erbusaig . . . 149 F12
Erchless Castle . . 150 G7
Erdington 62 E5
Eredine 125 E5
Eriboll 156 D7
Ericstane . . . 114 C3
Eridge Green . . 18 B2
Erines 145 F7
Eriswell 55 B8
Erith 29 B6
Erlestoke 24 D4
Ermine 78 B2
Ermington 6 D4
Erpingham 81 D7
Errogie 137 B8
Errol 128 B4
Erskin 118 B4
Erskine Bridg . . 118 B4
Ervie 104 C4
Erwarton 57 F6
Erwood 48 E2
Eryholme . . . 101 D8
Eryrys 73 D6
Escomb 101 B6
Escrick 96 E2
Esgairdawe . . . 46 E5
Esgairgeiliog . . 58 D4
Esh 110 E4
Esher 28 C2
Esholt 94 E4
Eshott 117 E8
Eshton 94 D2
Esh Winning . . 110 E4
Eskadale . . . 150 H7
Eskbank 121 C6
Eskdale Green . . 98 D3
Eskdalemuir . . 115 E5
Eske 97 E6
Eskham 91 E7
Esk Valley . . . 103 D6
Esprick 92 F4
Essendine 65 C7
Essendon 41 D5
Essich 151 H9
Essington 62 D3
Esslemont . . . 141 B8
Eston 102 C3
Eswick 160 H6
Etal 122 F5
Etchilhampton . . 24 C5
Etchingham . . . 18 C4
Etchinghill
  Kent 19 B8
  Staffs 62 C4
Ethie Castle . . 135 E6
Ethie Mains . . 135 E6
Etling Green . . 68 C3
Eton 27 B7
Eton Wick . . . 27 B7
Etteridge 138 E2
Ettersgill . . . 100 B3
Ettingshall . . . 62 E3
Ettington 51 E7
Etton
  E Yorks 97 E5
  Pboro 65 D8
Ettrick 115 C5
Ettrickbridge . . 115 B6
Ettrickhill . . . 115 C5
Etwall 76 F2
Euston 56 B2
Euximoor Drove . . 66 E4
Euxton 86 C3
Evanstown 34 F3
Evanton 151 E9
Evedon 78 E3
Evelix 151 B10
Evenjobb 48 C4
Evenley 52 F3
Evenlode 38 B2
Evenwood . . . 101 B6
Evenwood Gate . . 101 B6
Everbay 159 F7
Evercreech . . . 23 F8
Everdon 52 D3
Everingham . . . 96 E4
Everleigh 25 D7
Everley 103 F7
Eversholt 53 F7
Evershot 12 D3
Eversley 27 C5
Eversley Cross . . 27 C5
Everthorpe . . . 96 F5
Everton
  C Beds 54 D3
  Hants 14 E3
  Mers 85 E4
  Notts 89 E7

Evertown . . . 108 B3
Evesbatch 49 E8
Evesham 50 E5
Evington 64 D3
Ewden Village . . 88 E3
Ewell 28 C3
Ewell Minnis . . 31 E6
Ewelme 39 E6
Ewen 37 E7
Ewenny 21 B8
Ewerby 78 E4
Ewerby Thorpe . . 78 E4
Ewes 115 E6
Ewesley 117 E6
Ewhurst 27 E8
Ewhurst Green
  E Sus 18 C4
  Sur 27 F8
Ewloe 73 C7
Ewloe Green . . . 73 C6
Ewood 86 B4
Eworthy 9 E6
Ewshot 27 E6
Ewyas Harold . . 35 B7
Exbourne 9 D8
Exbury 14 E5
Exebridge 10 B4
Exelby 101 F7
Exeter 10 E4
Exford 21 F7
Exhall 51 D6
Exley Head . . . 94 F3
Exminster 10 F4
Exmouth 10 F5
Exnaboe 160 M5
Exning 55 C7
Exton
  Devon 10 F4
  Hants 15 B7
  Rutland 65 C6
  Som 21 F8
Exwick 10 E4
Eyam 76 B2
Eydon 52 D3
Eye
  Hereford 49 C6
  Pboro 66 D2
  Suff 56 B5
Eye Green 66 D2
Eyemouth . . . 122 C5
Eyeworth 54 E3
Eyhorne Street . . 30 D2
Eyke 57 D7
Eynesbury 54 D2
Eynort 149 F8
Eynsford 29 C6
Eynsham 38 D4
Eype 12 E2
Eyre
  Highld 149 C9
  Highld 149 E10
Eythorne 31 E6
Eyton
  Hereford 49 C6
  Shrops 60 F3
  Wrex 73 E7
Eyton upon the Weald Moors 61 C6

F
Faceby 102 D2
Facit 87 C6
Faddiley 74 D2
Fadmoor 102 F4
Faerdre 33 D7
Failand 23 B7
Failford 112 B4
Failsworth . . . 87 D6
Fain 150 D4
Fairbourne . . . 58 C3
Fairburn 89 B5
Fairfield
  Derbys 75 B7
  Stockton 102 C2
  Worcs 50 B4
  Worcs 50 E5
Fairford 38 D1
Fair Green . . . 67 C6
Fairhaven 85 B4
Fair Hill 108 F5
Fairlie 118 D2
Fairlight 19 D5
Fairlight Cove . . 19 D5
Fairmile 11 E5
Fairmilehead . . 120 C5
Fairoak 74 F4
Fair Oak 15 C5
Fair Oak Green . . 26 C4
Fairseat 29 C7
Fairstead
  Essex 42 C3
  Norf 67 C6
Fairwarp 17 B8
Fairy Cottage . . 84 D4
Fairy Cross . . . 9 B6
Fakenham 80 E5
Fakenham Magna 56 B3
Fala 121 C7
Fala Dam . . . 121 C7
Falahill 121 D6
Falcon 49 F8
Faldingworth . . 90 F4
Falfield 36 E3
Falkenham . . . 57 F6
Falkirk 119 B8
Falkland 128 D4
Falla 116 C3
Fallgate 76 C3
Fallin 127 E7
Fallowfield . . . 87 E6
Fallsidehill . . 122 E2
Falmer 17 D7
Falmouth 3 C5
Falsgrave . . . 103 F8
Falstone 116 F3
Fanagmore . . . 156 E4
Fangdale Beck . . 102 E3
Fangfoss 96 D3
Fankerton . . . 127 F6
Fanmore 146 G7
Fannich Lodge 150 E5
Fans 122 E2
Far Bank 89 C7
Far Bletchley . . 53 F6
Farcet 66 E2
Far Cotton . . . 52 D5

Farden 49 B7
Fareham 15 D6
Farewell 62 C4
Far Forest . . . 50 B2
Farforth 79 B6
Faringdon . . . 38 E2
Farington 86 B3
Farlam 109 D5
Farington 86 B3
Farlary 157 J10
Far Laund 76 E3
Farleigh
  N Som 23 C6
  Sur 28 C4
Farleigh Hungerford . . 24 D3
Farleigh Wallop . . 26 E4
Farlesthorpe . . 79 B7
Farleton 79 F6
Farley
  Shrops 60 D3
  Staffs 75 E7
  Wilts 14 B3
Farley Green . . 27 E8
Farley Hill
  Luton 40 B3
  Wokingham . . 26 C5
Farleys End . . . 36 C4
Farlington . . . 96 C2
Farlow 61 F6
Farmborough . . 23 C8
Farmcote
  Glos 37 B7
  Shrops 61 E7
Farmington . . . 37 C8
Farmoor 38 D4
Farmtown . . . 152 C5
Farnborough
  Hants 27 D6
  London 28 C5
  Warks 52 E2
  W Berks 38 F4
Farnborough Green 27 D6
Farncombe . . . 27 E7
Farndish 53 C7
Farndon
  Ches W 73 D8
  Notts 77 D7
Farnell 135 D6
Farnham
  Dorset 13 C7
  Essex 41 B7
  N Yorks 95 C6
  Suff 57 C7
  Sur 27 E6
Farnham Common 40 F2
Farnham Green . . 41 B7
Farnham Royal . . 40 F2
Farnhill 94 E3
Farningham . . . 29 C6
Farnley
  N Yorks 94 E5
  W Yorks 95 F5
Farnley Tyas . . 88 C2
Farnsfield . . . 77 D6
Farnworth
  Gtr Man 86 D5
  Halton 86 F3
Farr
  Highld 138 D4
  Highld 151 H9
  Highld 157 C10
Farr House . . . 151 H9
Farringdon . . . 10 E5
Farrington Gurney 23 D8
Far Sawrey . . . 99 E5
Farsley 94 F5
Farthinghoe . . . 52 F3
Farthingloe . . . 31 E6
Farthingstone . . 52 D4
Fartown 88 C2
Farway 11 E6
Fasag 149 C13
Fascadale . . . 147 D8
Faslane Port . . 145 E11
Fasnacloich . . 130 E4
Fasnakyle Ho . . 137 B6
Fassfern 130 B4
Fatfield 111 D6
Fattahead . . . 153 C6
Faugh 108 D5
Fauldhouse . . . 120 C2
Faulkbourne . . 42 C3
Faulkland 24 D2
Fauls 74 F2
Faversham . . . 30 C4
Favillar 152 E2
Fawdington . . . 95 B7
Fawfieldhead . . 75 C7
Fawkham Green . . 29 C6
Fawler 38 C3
Fawley
  Bucks 39 F7
  Hants 15 D5
  W Berks 38 F3
Fawley Chapel . . 36 B2
Faxfleet 90 B2
Faygate 28 F3
Fazakerley . . . 85 E4
Fazeley 63 D6
Fearby 101 F6
Fearn 151 D11
Fearnan 132 E4
Fearnbeg . . . 149 C12
Fearnhead 86 E4
Fearn Lodge . . 151 C9
Fearnmore . . 149 B12
Fearn Station 151 D11
Featherstone
  Staffs 62 D3
  W Yorks 88 B5
Featherwood . . 116 D4
Feckenham . . . 50 C5
Feering 42 C4
Feetham 100 E4
Feizor 93 C7
Felbridge 28 F4
Felbrigg 81 D8
Felcourt 28 E4
Felden 40 D3
Felin-Crai . . . 34 B2
Felindre
  Carms 33 B6
  Carms 33 B8

Felindre continued
  Carms 46 F2
  Carms 47 F5
  Ceredig 46 D4
  Powys 59 F8
  Swansea 33 D7
Felindre Farchog . 45 F3
Felinfach
  Ceredig 46 D4
  Powys 48 F2
Felinfoel 33 D6
Felingwmisaf . . 33 B6
Felingwmuchaf . . 33 B6
Felinwynt 45 D2
Felixkirk 102 F2
Felixstowe . . . 57 F6
Felixstowe Ferry . 57 F7
Felkington . . . 122 E5
Felkirk 88 C4
Felling 111 C5
Fell Side 108 F3
Felmersham . . . 53 D7
Felmingham . . . 81 E8
Felpham 16 E3
Felsham 56 D3
Felsted 42 B2
Feltham 28 B2
Felthorpe 68 C4
Felton
  Hereford 49 E7
  Northumb . . 117 D7
  N Som 23 C7
Felton Butler . . 60 C3
Feltwell 67 E7
Fenay Bridge . . 88 C2
Fence 93 F8
Fence Houses . . 111 D6
Fen Ditton . . . 55 C5
Fen Drayton . . 54 C4
Fen End 51 B7
Fengate 66 E2
Fenham 123 E6
Fenhouses 79 E5
Feniscliffe . . . 86 B4
Feniscowles . . . 86 B4
Feniton 11 E6
Fenlake 53 E8
Fenny Bentley . . 75 D8
Fenny Bridges . . 11 E6
Fenny Compton 52 D2
Fenny Drayton . . 63 E7
Fenny Stratford . 53 F6
Fenrother . . . 117 E7
Fen Side 79 D6
Fenstanton . . . 54 C4
Fenton
  Cambs 54 B4
  Lincs 77 B8
  Lincs 77 D8
  Stoke 75 E5
Fenton Barns . . 129 F7
Fenton Town . . 123 F5
Fenwick
  E Ayrs 118 E5
  Northumb . . 110 B3
  Northumb . . 123 E6
  S Yorks 89 C6
Feochaig . . . 143 G8
Feock 3 C7
Feolin Ferry . . 144 G3
Ferindonald . . 149 H11
Feriniquarrie . . 148 C6
Ferlochan . . . 130 E3
Fern 134 C4
Ferndale 34 E4
Ferndown 13 D8
Ferness 151 G12
Ferney Green . . 99 E6
Fernham 38 E2
Fernhill Heath . . 50 D3
Fernhurst 16 B2
Fernie 128 C5
Ferniegair . . . 119 D7
Fernilea 149 E8
Fernilee 75 B7
Ferrensby 95 C6
Ferring 16 D4
Ferrybridge . . . 89 B5
Ferryden . . . 135 D7
Ferryhill
  Aberdeen . . 141 D8
  Durham 111 F5
Ferry Hill . . . 66 F3
Ferryhill Station . 111 F5
Ferry Point . . 151 C10
Ferryside 32 C4
Fersfield 68 F3
Fersit 131 B7
Ferwig 45 E3
Feshiebridge . . 138 D4
Fetcham 28 D2
Fetterangus . . 153 C9
Fettercairn . . 135 B6
Fettes 151 F8
Fewcott 39 B5
Fewston 94 D4
F Faccombe . . . 25 D8
Ffairfach 33 B7
Ffair-Rhos . . . 47 C6
Ffaldybrenin . . 46 E5
Ffarmers 47 E5
Ffawyddog . . . 35 C6
Fforest 33 D6
Fforest-fàch . . 33 E7
Ffostrasol . . . 46 E2
Ffos-y-ffin . . . 46 C3
Ffridd-Uchaf . . 83 F5
Ffrith 73 D6
Ffrwd 82 F4
Ffynnongroyw . . 85 F2
Ffynnon-oer . . . 46 D4
Fidden 146 J6
Fiddes 141 F7
Fiddington
  Glos 50 F4
  Som 22 E4
Fiddleford . . . 13 C6
Fiddlers Hamlet . 41 D7
Field 75 F7
Field Broughton . 99 F5
Field Dalling . . 81 D6
Field Head . . . 63 D8

Fifield
  Oxon 38 C2
  Wilts 25 D6
  Windsor 27 B7
Fifield Bavant . . 13 B8
Figheldean . . . 25 E6
Filands 37 F6
Filby 69 C7
Filey 97 A7
Filgrave 53 E6
Filkins 38 D2
Filleigh
  Devon 9 B8
  Devon 10 C2
Fillingham . . . 90 F3
Fillongley . . . 63 F6
Filton 23 B8
Fimber 96 C4
Finavon 134 D4
Fincharn 124 E5
Fincham 67 D6
Finchampstead . . 27 C5
Finchdean 15 C8
Finchingfield . . 55 F7
Finchley 41 E5
Findern 76 F3
Findhorn . . . 151 E13
Findhorn Bridge 138 B4
Findochty . . . 152 B4
Findo Gask . . 128 B2
Findon
  Aberds 141 E8
  W Sus 16 D5
Findon Mains . . 151 E9
Findrack House 140 D5
Finedon 53 B7
Fingal Street . . 57 C6
Fingask 141 B6
Fingerpost . . . 50 B2
Fingest 39 E7
Finghall 101 F6
Fingland
  Cumb 108 D2
  Dumfries 113 C7
Finglesham . . . 31 D7
Fingringhoe . . . 43 B6
Finlarig 132 F2
Finmere 52 F4
Finnart 132 D2
Finningham . . . 56 C4
Finningley . . . 89 E7
Finnygaud . . . 152 C5
Finsbury 41 F6
Finstall 50 C4
Finsthwaite . . . 99 F5
Finstock 38 C3
Finstown . . . 159 G4
Fintry
  Aberds 153 C7
  Dundee 134 F4
  Stirling 126 F5
Finzean 140 E5
Fionnphort . . 146 J6
Fionnsbhagh . . 154 J5
Firbeck 89 F6
Firby
  N Yorks 96 C3
  N Yorks 101 F7
Firgrove 87 C7
Firsby 79 C7
Firsdown 25 F7
First Coast . . 150 B2
Fir Tree 110 F4
Fishbourne
  IoW 15 E6
  W Sus 16 D2
Fishburn 111 F6
Fishcross . . . 127 E7
Fisherford . . . 153 E6
Fisher Place . . 99 C5
Fisher's Pond . . 15 B5
Fisherstreet . . 27 F7
Fisherton
  Highld 151 F10
  S Ayrs 112 C2
Fishguard
  = Abergwaun . . 44 B4
Fishlake 89 C7
Fishleigh Barton . . 9 B7
Fishponds . . . 23 B8
Fishpool 36 B3
Fishtoft 79 E6
Fishtoft Drove . . 79 E6
Fishtown of Usan 135 D7
Fishwick 122 D5
Fiskavaig . . . 149 E8
Fiskerton
  Lincs 78 B3
  Notts 77 D7
Fitling 97 F8
Fittleton 25 E6
Fittleworth . . . 16 C4
Fitton End . . . 66 C4
Fitz 60 C4
Fitzhead 11 B6
Fitzwilliam . . . 88 C5
Fiunary 147 G9
Five Acres . . . 36 C2
Five Ashes . . . 18 C2
Fivecrosses . . . 74 B2
Fivehead 11 B8
Five Oak Green . . 29 E7
Five Oaks
  Jersey 17
  W Sus 16 B4
Five Roads . . . 33 D5
Flack's Green . . 42 C3
Flackwell Heath . 40 F1
Fladbury 50 E4
Fladdabister . . 160 K6
Flagg 75 C8
Flamborough . . 97 B8
Flamstead 40 C3
Flamstead End . . 41 D6
Flansham 16 D3
Flanshaw 88 B4
Flasby 94 D2
Flash 75 C7
Flashader . . . 149 C8
Flask Inn . . . 103 D7
Flaunden 40 D3
Flawborough . . 77 E7
Flawith 95 C7
Flax Bourton . . 23 C7

Flaxby 95 D6
Flaxholme 76 E3
Flaxley 36 C3
Flaxpool 22 F3
Flaxton 96 C2
Fleckney 64 E3
Flecknoe 52 C3
Fledborough 77 B8
Fleet
Hants 15 D8
Hants 27 D6
Lincs 66 B3
Fleetham 117 B7
Fleet Hargate 66 B3
Fleetlands 15 D6
Fleetville 40 D4
Fleetwood 92 E3
Flemingston 22 B2
Flemington 119 D6
Flempton 56 C2
Fleoideabhagh 154 J5
Fletchertown 108 E2
Fletching 17 B8
Flexbury 8 D4
Flexford 27 E7
Flimby 107 F7
Flimwell 18 B4
Flint = Y Fflint 73 B6
Flintham 77 E7
Flint Mountain 73 B6
Flinton 97 F8
Flintsham 48 D5
Flitcham 80 E3
Flitton 53 F8
Flitwick 53 F8
Flixborough 90 C2
Flixborough Stather 90 C2
Flixton
Gtr Man 86 E5
N Yorks 97 B6
Suff 69 F6
Flockton 88 C3
Flodaigh 148 C3
Flodden 122 F5
Flodigarry 149 A9
Flood's Ferry 66 E3
Flookburgh 92 B3
Florden 68 E4
Flore 52 C4
Flotterton 117 D5
Flowton 56 E4
Flush House 88 D2
Flushing
Aberds 153 D10
Corn 3 C7
Flyford Flavell 50 D4
Foals Green 57 B6
Fobbing 42 F3
Fochabers 152 C3
Fochriw 35 D5
Fockerby 90 C2
Fodderletter 139 B7
Fodderty 151 F8
Foel 59 C6
Foel-gastell 33 C6
Foffarty 134 E4
Foggathorpe 96 F3
Fogo 122 E3
Fogorig 122 E3
Foindle 156 E4
Folda 134 C1
Fole 75 F7
Foleshill 63 F7
Folke 12 C4
Folkestone 31 F6
Folkingham 78 F3
Folkington 18 E2
Folksworth 65 F8
Folkton 97 B6
Folla Rule 153 E7
Follifoot 95 D6
Folly Gate 9 E7
Fonthill Bishop 24 F4
Fonthill Gifford 24 F4
Fontmell Magna 13 C6
Fontwell 16 D3
Foolow 75 B8
Foots Cray 29 B5
Forbestown 140 C2
Force Mills 99 E5
Forcett 101 C6
Ford
Argyll 124 E4
Bucks 39 D7
Devon 9 B6
Glos 37 B7
Northumb 122 F5
Shrops 60 C4
Staffs 75 D7
Wilts 24 B3
W Sus 16 D3
Fordcombe 29 E6
Fordell 128 F3
Forden 60 D2
Ford End 42 C2
Forder Green 7 C5
Fordham
Cambs 55 B7
Essex 43 B5
Norf 67 E6
Fordhouses 62 D3
Fordingbridge 14 C2
Fordon 97 B6
Fordoun 135 B7
Ford's Green 56 C4
Fordstreet 43 B5
Ford Street 11 C6
Fordwells 38 C3
Fordwich 31 D5
Fordyce 152 B5
Forebridge 62 B3
Forest 109 F8
Forest Becks 93 D7
Forestburn Gate 117 E6
Foresterseat 152 C1
Forest Gate 41 F7
Forest Green 28 E2
Forest Hall 99 D7
Forest Head 109 D5
Forest Hill 39 D5
Forest Lane Head 95 D6
Forest Lodge
Argyll 131 E6
Highld 139 C6
Forest Lodge continued
Perth 133 B6
Forest Mill 127 E8
Forest Row 28 F5
Forestside 15 C8
Forest Town 77 C5
Forfar 134 D4
Forgandenny 128 C2
Forge 58 E4
Forge Side 35 D6
Forgewood 119 D7
Forgie 152 C3
Forglen House 153 C6
Formby 85 D4
Forncett End 68 E4
Forncett St Mary 68 E4
Forncett St Peter 68 E4
Forneth 133 E7
Fornham All Saints 56 C2
Fornham St Martin 56 C2
Forres 151 F13
Forrestfield 119 C8
Forrest Lodge 113 F5
Forsbrook 75 E6
Forse 158 G4
Forse House 158 G4
Forsinain 157 E12
Forsinard 157 E11
Forsinard Station 157 E11
Forston 12 E4
Fort Augustus 137 D6
Forteviot 128 C2
Fort George
Guern 16
Highld 151 F10
Forth 120 D2
Forthampton 50 F3
Forth Road Bridge 120 B4
Fortingall 132 E4
Forton
Hants 26 E2
Lancs 92 D4
Shrops 60 C4
Som 11 D8
Staffs 61 B7
Forton Heath 60 C4
Fortrie 153 D6
Fortrose 151 F10
Fortuneswell 12 G4
Fort William 131 B5
Forty Green 40 E2
Forty Hill 41 E6
Forward Green 56 D4
Fosbury 25 D8
Fosdyke 79 F6
Foss 132 D4
Foss Cross 37 D7
Fossebridge 37 C7
Fosterhouses 89 C7
Foster Street 41 D7
Foston
Derbys 75 F8
Lincs 77 E8
N Yorks 96 C2
Foston on the Wolds 97 D7
Fotherby 91 E7
Fotheringhay 65 E7
Foubister 159 H6
Foulby 88 C4
Foulden
Borders 122 D5
Norf 67 E7
Foulis Castle 151 E8
Foul Mile 18 D3
Foulridge 93 E8
Foulsham 81 E6
Fountainhall 121 E7
Four Ashes
Staffs 62 F2
Suff 56 B4
Four Crosses
Powys 59 D7
Powys 60 C2
Wrex 73 D6
Four Elms 29 E5
Four Forks 22 F4
Four Gotes 66 C4
Fourlane Ends 76 D3
Four Lane Ends 74 C2
Four Lanes 3 C5
Fourlanes End 74 D5
Four Marks 26 F4
Four Mile Bridge 82 D2
Four Oaks
E Sus 19 C5
W Mid 62 E5
W Mid 63 F6
Fourpenny 151 B11
Four Roads
Carms 33 D5
IoM 84 F2
Fourstones 109 C8
Four Throws 18 C4
Fovant 13 B8
Foveran 141 B8
Fowey 5 D6
Fowley Common 86 E4
Fowlis 134 F3
Fowlis Wester 127 B8
Fowlmere 54 E5
Fownhope 49 F7
Foxbar 118 C4
Foxcombe Hill 38 D4
Fox Corner 27 D7
Foxdale 84 E2
Foxearth 56 E2
Foxfield 98 F4
Foxham 24 B4
Foxhole
Corn 4 D4
Swansea 33 E7
Foxholes 97 B6
Foxhunt Green 18 D2
Fox Lane 27 D6
Foxley
Norf 81 E6
Wilts 37 F5
Fox Street 43 B6
Foxt 75 E7
Foxton
Cambs 54 E5
Durham 102 B1
Leics 64 E4
Foxup 93 B8
Foxwist Green 74 C3
Foxwood 49 B8
Foy 36 B2
Foyers 137 B7
Fraddam 2 C4
Fraddon 4 D4
Fradley 63 C5
Fradswell 75 F6
Fraisthorpe 97 C7
Framfield 17 B8
Framingham Earl 69 D5
Framingham Pigot 69 D5
Framlingham 57 C6
Frampton
Dorset 12 E4
Lincs 79 F6
Frampton Cotterell 36 F3
Frampton Mansell 37 D6
Frampton on Severn 36 D4
Frampton West End 79 E5
Framsden 57 D5
Framwellgate Moor 111 E5
Franche 50 B3
Frankby 85 F3
Frankley 62 F3
Frank's Bridge 48 D3
Frankton 52 B2
Frant 18 B2
Fraserburgh 153 B9
Frating Green 43 B6
Fratton 15 E7
Freathy 5 D8
Freckenham 55 B7
Freckleton 86 B2
Freeby 64 B5
Freehay 75 E7
Freeland 38 C4
Freester 160 H6
Freethorpe 69 D7
Freiston 79 E6
Fremington
Devon 20 F4
N Yorks 101 E5
Frenchay 23 B8
Frenchbeer 9 F8
Frenich 126 D3
Frensham 27 E6
Fresgoe 157 C12
Freshfield 85 D3
Freshford 24 C2
Freshwater 14 F4
Freshwater Bay 14 F4
Freshwater East 32 E1
Fressingfield 57 B6
Freston 57 F5
Freswick 158 D5
Fretherne 36 D4
Frettenham 68 C5
Freuchie 128 D4
Freuchies 134 C2
Freystrop 44 D4
Friar's Gate 29 F5
Friarton 128 B3
Friday Bridge 66 D4
Friday Street 18 E3
Fridaythorpe 96 D4
Friern Barnet 41 E5
Friesland 146 F4
Friesthorpe 90 F4
Frieston 78 E2
Frieth 39 E7
Frilford 38 E4
Frilsham 26 B3
Frimley 27 D6
Frimley Green 27 D6
Frindsbury 29 B8
Fring 80 D3
Fringford 39 B6
Frinsted 30 D2
Frinton-on-Sea 43 B8
Friockheim 135 E5
Friog 58 C3
Frisby on the Wreake 64 C3
Friskney 79 D7
Friskney Eaudike 79 D7
Friskney Tofts 79 D7
Friston
E Sus 18 F2
Suff 57 C8
Fritchley 76 D3
Fritham 14 C3
Frith Bank 79 E6
Frith Common 49 C8
Frithelstock 9 C6
Frithelstock Stone 9 C6
Frithville 79 D6
Frittenden 30 E2
Frittiscombe 7 E6
Fritton
Norf 68 E5
Norf 69 D7
Fritwell 39 B5
Frizinghall 94 F4
Frizington 98 C2
Frocester 36 D4
Frodesley 60 D5
Frodingham 90 C2
Frodsham 74 B2
Frogden 116 B3
Froggatt 76 B2
Froghall 75 E7
Frogmore
Devon 7 E5
Hants 27 D6
Frognall 65 C8
Frogshail 81 D8
Frolesworth 64 E2
Frome 24 E2
Frome St Quintin 12 D3
Fromes Hill 49 E8
Fron
Denb 72 C4
Gwyn 70 D4
Gwyn 82 F5
Powys 48 C2
Powys 59 E8
Powys 60 D2
Froncysyllte 73 E6
Frongoch 72 F3
Frostenden 69 F7
Frosterley 110 F3
Frotoft 159 F5
Froxfield 25 C7
Froxfield Green 15 B8
Froyle 27 E5
Fryerning 42 D2
Fryton 96 B2
Fulbeck 78 D2
Fulbourn 55 D6
Fulbrook 38 C2
Fulford
Som 11 B7
Staffs 75 F6
York 96 E2
Fulham 28 B3
Fulking 17 C6
Fullarton
Glasgow 119 C6
N Ayrs 118 F3
Fuller's Moor 73 D8
Fuller Street 42 C3
Fullerton 25 F8
Fulletby 79 B5
Full Sutton 96 D3
Fullwood 118 D4
Fulmer 40 F2
Fulmodestone 81 D5
Fulnetby 78 B3
Fulstow 91 E7
Fulwell 111 D6
Fulwood
Lancs 92 F5
S Yorks 88 F4
Fundenhall 68 E4
Fundenhall Street 68 E4
Funtington 15 D8
Funtley 15 D6
Funtullich 127 B6
Funzie 160 D8
Furley 11 D7
Furnace
Argyll 125 E6
Carms 33 D6
Furnace End 63 E6
Furneaux Pelham 41 B7
Furness Vale 87 F8
Furzehill 21 E6
Furze Platt 40 F1
Fyfett 11 C7
Fyfield
Essex 42 D1
Glos 38 D2
Hants 25 E7
Oxon 38 E4
Wilts 25 C6
Fylingthorpe 103 D7
Fyvie 153 E7

G

Gabhsann bho Dheas 155 B9
Gabhsann bho Thuath 155 B9
Gablon 151 B10
Gabroc Hill 118 D4
Gaddesby 64 C3
Gadebridge 40 D3
Gaer 35 B5
Gaerllwyd 35 E8
Gaerwen 82 D4
Gagingwell 38 B4
Gaick Lodge 138 F3
Gailey 62 C3
Gainford 101 C6
Gainsborough
Lincs 90 E2
Suff 57 E5
Gainsford End 55 F8
Gairloch 149 A13
Gairlochy 136 F4
Gairney Bank 128 E3
Gairnshiel Lodge 139 D8
Gaisgill 99 D8
Gaitsgill 108 E3
Galashiels 121 F7
Galgate 92 D4
Galhampton 12 B4
Gallaberry 114 F2
Gallachoille 144 E6
Gallanach
Argyll 124 C4
Argyll 146 E5
Gallantry Bank 74 D2
Gallatown 128 E4
Galley Common 63 E7
Galleyend 42 D3
Galley Hill 54 C4
Galleywood 42 D3
Gallin 132 E2
Gallowfauld 134 E4
Gallows Green 75 E7
Galltair 149 F13
Galmisdale 146 C7
Galmpton
Devon 6 E4
Torbay 7 D6
Galphay 95 B5
Galston 118 F5
Galtrigill 148 C6
Gamblesby 109 F6
Gamesley 87 E8
Gamlingay 54 D3
Gammersgill 101 F5
Gamston 77 B7
Ganarew 36 C2
Ganavan 124 B4
Gang 5 C8
Ganllwyd 71 E8
Gannochy
Angus 135 B5
Perth 128 B3
Gansclet 158 F5
Ganstead 97 F7
Ganthorpe 96 B2
Ganton 97 B5
Garbat 150 E7
Garbhallt 125 F6
Garboldisham 68 F3
Garden City 73 C7
Gardenstown 153 B7
Garden Village
Wrex 73 D7
W Yorks 95 F7
Garderhouse 160 J5
Gardham 97 E5
Gardin 160 G6
Gare Hill 24 E2
Garelochhead 145 D11
Garford 38 E4
Garforth 95 F7
Gargrave 94 D2
Gargunnock 127 E6
Garlic Street 68 F5
Garlieston 105 E8
Garlinge Green 30 D5
Garlogie 141 D6
Garmond 153 C8
Garmony 147 G9
Garmouth 152 B3
Garnant 33 C7
Garndiffaith 35 D6
Garndolbenmaen 71 C5
Garnedd 83 F7
Garnett Bridge 99 E7
Garnfadryn 70 D3
Garnkirk 119 C6
Garnlydan 35 C5
Garnswllt 33 D7
Garn-yr-erw 35 C6
Garrabost 155 D10
Garraron 124 E4
Garras 3 D6
Garreg 71 C7
Garrick 127 C7
Garrigill 109 E7
Garriston 101 E6
Garroch 113 F5
Garrogie Lodge 137 C8
Garros 149 B9
Garrow 133 E5
Garryhorn 113 E5
Garsdale 100 F2
Garsdale Head 100 E2
Garsdon 37 F6
Garshall Green 75 F6
Garsington 39 D5
Garstang 92 E4
Garston 86 F2
Garswood 86 E3
Gartcosh 119 C6
Garth
Bridgend 34 E2
Gwyn 83 D5
Powys 47 E8
Shetland 160 H4
Wrex 73 E6
Garthamlock 119 C6
Garthbrengy 48 F2
Garthdee 141 D8
Gartheli 46 D4
Garthmyl 59 E8
Garthorpe
Leics 64 B5
N Lincs 90 C2
Garth Row 99 E7
Gartly 152 E5
Gartmore 126 E4
Gartnagrenach 144 H6
Gartness
N Lanark 119 C7
Stirling 126 F4
Gartocharn 126 F3
Garton 97 F8
Garton-on-the-Wolds 97 D5
Gartsherrie 119 C7
Gartymore 157 H13
Garvald 121 B8
Garvamore 137 E8
Garvard 144 D2
Garvault Hotel 157 F10
Garve 150 E6
Garvestone 68 D3
Garvock
Aberds 135 B7
Involyd 118 B2
Garway 36 B1
Garway Hill 35 B8
Gaskan 130 B1
Gastard 24 C3
Gasthorpe 68 F2
Gatcombe 15 F5
Gateacre 86 F2
Gatebeck 99 F7
Gate Burton 90 F2
Gateford 89 F6
Gateforth 89 B6
Gatehead 118 F3
Gate Helmsley 96 D2
Gatehouse 116 F3
Gatehouse of Fleet 106 D3
Gatelawbridge 114 E2
Gateley 81 E5
Gatenby 101 F8
Gateshead 111 C5
Gatesheath 73 C8
Gateside
Aberds 140 C5
Angus 134 E4
E Renf 118 D4
Fife 128 D3
N Ayrs 118 D3
Gathurst 86 D3
Gatley 87 F6
Gattonside 121 F8
Gatwick Airport 28 E3
Gaufron 47 C8
Gaulby 64 D3
Gauldry 129 B5
Gaunt's Common 13 D8
Gautby 78 B4
Gavinton 122 D3
Gawber 88 D4
Gawcott 52 F4
Gawsworth 75 C5
Gawthorpe 88 B3
Gawthrop 100 F1
Gawthwaite 98 F4
Gaydon 51 D8
Gayfield 159 C5
Gayhurst 53 E6
Gayle 100 F3
Gayles 101 D6
Gay Street 16 B4
Gayton
Mers 85 F3
Norf 67 C7
Northants 52 D5
Staffs 62 B3
Gayton le Marsh 91 F8
Gayton le Wold 91 F6
Gayton Thorpe 67 C7
Gaywood 67 B6
Gazeley 55 C8
Geanies House 151 D11
Gearraidh Bhailteas 148 F2
Gearraidh Bhaird 155 E8
Gearraidh na h-Aibhne 154 D7
Gearraidh na Monadh 148 G2
Geary 148 B7
Geddes House 151 F11
Gedding 56 D3
Geddington 65 F5
Gedintailor 149 E10
Gedling 77 E6
Gedney 66 B4
Gedney Broadgate 66 B4
Gedney Drove End 66 B4
Gedney Dyke 66 B4
Gedney Hill 66 C3
Gee Cross 87 E7
Geilston 118 B3
Geirinis 148 D2
Geise 158 D3
Geisiadar 154 D6
Geldeston 69 E6
Gell 83 E8
Gelli
Pembs 32 C1
Rhondda 34 E3
Gellideg 34 D4
Gellifor 72 C5
Gelligaer 35 E5
Gellilydan 71 D7
Gellinudd 33 D8
Gellyburn 133 F7
Gellywen 32 B3
Gelston
Dumfries 106 D4
Lincs 78 E2
Gembling 97 D7
Gentleshaw 62 C4
Geocrab 154 H6
George Green 40 F3
Georgefield 115 E5
George Nympton 10 B2
Georgeham 20 F3
Georgetown 35 D5
Gerlan 83 E6
Germansweek 9 E6
Germoe 2 D4
Gerrans 3 C7
Gerrards Cross 40 F3
Gestingthorpe 56 F2
Geuffordd 60 C2
Gibbet Hill 64 F2
Gibbshill 106 B4
Gib Hill 74 B3
Gidea Park 41 F8
Gidleigh 9 F8
Giffnock 119 D5
Gifford 121 C8
Giffordland 118 E2
Giffordtown 128 C4
Giggleswick 93 C8
Gilberdyke 90 B2
Gilchriston 121 C7
Gilcrux 107 F8
Gildersome 88 B3
Gildingwells 89 F6
Gileston 22 C2
Gilfach 35 E5
Gilfach Goch 34 F3
Gilfachrheda 46 D3
Gillamoor 102 F4
Gillar's Green 86 E2
Gillen 148 C7
Gilling East 96 B2
Gillingham
Dorset 13 B6
Medway 29 C8
Norf 69 E7
Gilling West 101 D6
Gillock 158 E4
Gillow Heath 75 D5
Gills 158 C5
Gill's Green 18 B4
Gilmanscleuch 115 B6
Gilmerton
Edin 121 C5
Perth 127 B7
Gilmonby 100 C4
Gilmorton 64 F2
Gilmourton 119 E6
Gilsland 109 C6
Gilsland Spa 109 C6
Gilston
Borders 121 D7
Herts 41 C7
Gilwern 35 C6
Gimingham 81 D8
Giosla 154 E6
Gipping 56 C4
Gipsey Bridge 79 E5
Girdle Toll 118 E3
Girlsta 160 H6
Girsby 102 D1
Girtford 54 D2
Girthon 106 D3
Girton
Cambs 54 C5
Notts 77 C8
Girvan 112 E1
Gisburn 93 E8
Gisleham 69 F8
Gislingham 56 B4
Gissing 68 F4
Gittisham 11 E6
Gladestry 48 D4
Gladsmuir 121 B7
Glais 33 D8
Glaisdale 103 D5
Glame 149 D10
Glamis 134 E3
Glan Adda 83 D5
Glanaman 33 C7
Glan Conwy 83 D8
Glandford 81 C6
Glan-Duar 46 E4
Glandwr 32 B2
Glan-Dwyfach 71 C5
Glandy Cross 32 B2
Glandyfi 58 E3
Glan Gors 82 D4
Glangrwyney 35 C6
Glanmule 59 E8
Glanrafon 58 F3
Glanrhyd
Gwyn 70 D3
Pembs 45 E3
Glan-rhyd 82 F4
Glanton 117 C6
Glanton Pike 117 C6
Glan-traeth 82 D2
Glanvilles Wootton 12 D4
Glan-y-don 73 B5
Glan-y-nant 59 F6
Glan-yr-afon
Anglesey 83 C6
Gwyn 72 E3
Gwyn 72 E4
Glan-y-wern 71 D7
Glapthorn 65 E7
Glapwell 76 C4
Glas-allt Shiel 139 F8
Glasbury 48 F3
Glaschoil 151 H13
Glascoed
Denb 72 B3
Mon 35 D7
Powys 59 C8
Glascorrie 140 E2
Glascote 63 D6
Glascwm 48 D3
Glasdrum 130 E4
Glasfryn 72 D3
Glasgow 119 C5
Glashvin 149 B9
Glasinfryn 83 E5
Glasnacardoch 147 B9
Glasnakille 149 G10
Glasphein 148 D6
Glaspwll 58 E4
Glassburn 150 H6
Glasserton 105 F8
Glassford 119 E7
Glasshouse Hill 36 B4
Glasshouses 94 C4
Glasslie 128 D4
Glasson
Cumb 108 C2
Lancs 92 D4
Glassonby 109 F5
Glasterlaw 135 D5
Glaston 65 D5
Glastonbury 23 F7
Glatton 65 F8
Glazebrook 86 E4
Glazebury 86 E4
Glazeley 61 F7
Gleadless 88 F4
Gleadsmoss 74 C5
Gleann Tholàstaidh 155 C10
Gleaston 92 B2
Gleiniant 59 E6
Glemsford 56 E2
Glen
Dumfries 106 B5
Dumfries 106 D2
Glenamachrie 124 C5
Glen Auldyn 84 C4
Glenbarr 143 E7
Glenbeg
Highld 139 B6
Highld 147 E8
Glen Bernisdale 149 D9
Glenbervie 141 F6
Glenboig 119 C7
Glenborrodale 147 E9
Glenbranter 125 F7
Glenbreck 114 B3
Glenbrein Lodge 137 C7
Glenbrittle House 149 F9
Glenbuchat Lodge 140 C2
Glenbuck 113 B7
Glenburn 118 C4
Glencalvie Lodge 150 C7
Glencanisp Lodge 156 G4
Glencaple 107 C6
Glencarron Lodge 150 F3
Glencarse 128 B3
Glencassley Castle 156 J7
Glenceitlein 131 E5
Glencoe 130 D4
Glencraig 128 E3
Glencripesdale 147 F9
Glencrosh 113 F7
Glendavan House 140 D3
Glendevon 127 D8
Glendoebeg 137 D7
Glendoe Lodge 137 D7
Glendoick 128 B4
Glendoll Lodge 134 B2
Glenduckie 128 C4
Glendye Lodge 140 F5
Gleneagles Hotel 127 C8
Gleneagles House 127 D8
Glenegedale 142 C4
Glenelg 149 G13
Glenernie 151 G13
Glenfarg 128 C3
Glenfarquhar Lodge 141 F6
Glenferness House 151 G12
Glenfeshie Lodge 138 E4
Glenfield 64 D2
Glenfinnan 147 C11
Glenfoot 128 C3
Glenfyne Lodge 125 D8
Glengap 106 D3
Glengarnock 118 D3
Glengorm Castle 146 F7
Glengrasco 149 D9
Glenhead Farm 134 C2
Glen Ho 121 F5
Glenhoul 113 F6
Glenhurich 130 C2
Glenkerry 115 C5
Glenkiln 106 B5
Glenkindie 140 C3
Glenlatterach 152 C1
Glenlee 113 F6
Glenlichorn 127 C6
Glenlivet 139 B7
Glenlochsie 133 B7
Glenloig 143 E10
Glenluce 105 D6
Glenmallan 125 F8
Glenmarksie 150 F6
Glenmassan 145 E10
Glenmavis 119 C7
Glenmaye 84 E2
Glenmidge 113 F8
Glen Mona 84 D4
Glenmore
Argyll 124 D4
Highld 149 D9
Glenmore Lodge 139 D5
Glenmoy 134 C4
Glen Nevis House 131 B5
Glenogil 134 C4
Glen Parva 64 E2
Glenprosen Lodge 134 C2
Glenprosen Village 134 C3
Glenquiech 134 C4
Glenreasdell Mains 145 H7
Glenree 143 F10
Glenridding 99 C5
Glenrossal 156 J7
Glenrothes 128 D4
Glensanda 130 E2
Glensaugh 135 B6
Glenshero Lodge 137 E8
Glen Sluain 125 F6
Glenstockadale 104 C4
Glenstriven 145 F9
Glentaggart 113 B8
Glen Tanar House 140 E3
Glentham 90 E4
Glentirranmuir 127 E5
Glenton 140 B5
Glentress 121 F5
Glentromie Lodge 138 E3
Glen Trool Lodge 112 F4
Glentrool Village 105 B7
Glentruan 84 B4
Glentruim House 138 E2
Glentworth 90 F3
Glenuig 147 D9
Glenurquhart 151 E10
Glen Village 119 B8
Glen Vine 84 E3
Glespin 113 B8
Gletness 160 H6
Glewstone 36 B2
Glinton 65 D8
Glooston 64 E4
Glororum 123 F7
Glossop 87 E8
Gloster Hill 117 D8
Gloucester 37 C5
Gloup 160 C7
Glusburn 94 E3
Glutt Lodge 157 F12
Glutton Bridge 75 C7
Glympton 38 B4
Glynarthen 46 E2
Glynbrochan 59 F6
Glyn-Ceiriog 73 F6
Glyncoch 34 E4
Glyncorrwg 34 E2
Glyn-cywarch 71 D7
Glynde 17 D8
Glyndebourne 17 C8
Glyndyfrdwy 72 E5
Glyn Ebwy = Ebbw Vale 35 D5
Glynedd = Glynneath 34 D2
Glyn-neath = Glynedd 34 D2
Glynogwr 34 F3
Glyntaff 34 F4
Glyntawe 34 C2
Gnosall 62 B2
Gnosall Heath 62 B2
Goadby 64 E4
Goadby Marwood 64 B4
Goatacre 24 B5
Goathill 12 C4
Goathland 103 D6
Goathurst 22 F4
Goat Lees 30 E4
Gobernuisgach Lodge 156 E7
Gobhaig 154 G5
Gobowen 73 F7
Godalming 27 E7
Godley 87 E7
Godmanchester 54 B3
Godmanstone 12 E4
Godmersham 30 D4
Godney 23 E6
Godolphin Cross 2 C5
Godre'r-graig 34 D1
Godshill
Hants 14 C2
IoW 15 F6
Godstone 28 D4
Godwinscroft 14 E2
Goetre 35 D7
Goferydd 82 C2
Goff's Oak 41 D6
Gogar 120 B4
Goginan 58 F3
Golan 71 C6
Golant 5 D6
Golberdon 5 B8
Golborne 86 E4
Golcar 88 C2
Goldcliff 35 F7
Golden Cross 18 D2
Golden Green 29 E7
Golden Grove 33 C6
Goldenhill 75 D5
Golden Hill 14 E3
Golden Pot 26 E5
Golden Valley 37 B6
Golders Green 41 F5
Goldhanger 43 D5
Gold Hill 66 E5
Golding 60 D5
Goldington 53 D8
Goldsborough
N Yorks 95 D6
N Yorks 103 C6
Goldsithney 2 C4
Goldsworthy 9 B5
Goldthorpe 89 D5
Gollanfield 151 F11
Golspie 157 J11
Golval 157 C11
Gomeldon 25 F6
Gomersal 88 B3
Gomshall 27 E8
Gonalston 77 E6
Gonfirth 160 G5
Good Easter 42 C2
Gooderstone 67 D7
Goodleigh 20 F5
Goodmanham 96 E4
Goodnestone
Kent 30 C4
Kent 31 D6
Goodrich 36 C2
Goodrington 7 D6
Goodshaw 87 B6
Goodwick = Wdig 44 B4
Goodworth Clatford 25 E8
Goole 89 B8
Goonbell 3 B6
Goonhavern 4 D2
Goose Eye 94 E3
Goose Green
Gtr Man 86 D3
Norf 68 F4
W Sus 16 C5
Gooseham 8 C4
Goosey 38 E3
Goosnargh 93 F5
Goostrey 74 B4
Gorcott Hill 51 C5
Gord 160 L6
Gordon 122 E2
Gordonbush 157 J11
Gordonsburgh 152 B4
Gordonstoun 152 B1
Gordonstown
Aberds 152 C5
Aberds 153 E7
Gore 31 D7
Gorebridge 121 C6
Gore Cross 24 D5
Gorefield 66 C4
Gore Pit 42 C4
Gorey 17
Gorgie 120 B5
Goring 39 F6
Goring-by-Sea 16 D5
Goring Heath 26 B4
Gorleston-on-Sea 69 D8
Gornalwood 62 E3
Gorrachie 153 C7
Gorran Churchtown 3 B8
Gorran Haven 3 B9
Gorrenberry 115 E7
Gors 46 B5
Gorsedd 73 B5
Gorse Hill 38 F1
Gorseinon 33 E6
Gorseness 159 G5
Gorsgoch 46 D3
Gorslas 33 C6
Gorsley 36 B3
Gorstan 150 E6
Gorstanvorran 130 B2
Gorsteyhill 74 D4
Gorsty Hill 62 B5
Gortantaoid 142 A4
Gorton 87 E6
Gosbeck 57 D5
Gosberton 78 F5
Gosberton Clough 65 B8
Gosfield 42 B3
Gosford 49 C7
Gosforth
Cumb 98 D2
T&W 110 C5
Gosmore 40 B4
Gosport 15 E7
Gossabrough 160 E7
Gossington 36 D4
Goswick 123 E6
Gotham 76 F5
Gotherington 37 B6
Gott 160 J6
Goudhurst 18 B4
Goulceby 79 B5
Gourdas 153 D7
Gourdon 135 B8
Gourock 118 B2
Govan 119 C5
Govanhill 119 C5
Goveton 7 E5
Govilon 35 C6
Gowanhill 153 B10
Gowdall 89 B7
Gowerton 33 E6
Gowkhall 128 F2
Gowthorpe 96 D3
Goxhill
E Yorks 97 E7
N Lincs 90 B5
Goxhill Haven 90 B5
Goytre 34 F1
Grabhair 155 F8
Graby 65 B7
Grade 3 E6
Graffham 16 C3
Grafham
Cambs 54 C2
Sur 27 E8
Grafton
Hereford 49 F6
N Yorks 95 C7
Oxon 38 D2
Shrops 60 C4

Grafton continued
Worcs 49 C7
Grafton Flyford . . 50 D4
Grafton Regis 53 E5
Grafton
Underwood 65 F6
Grafty Green 30 E2
Graianrhyd 73 D6
Graig
Conwy 83 D8
Denb 72 B4
Graig-fechan . . . 72 D5
Grain 30 B2
Grainsby 91 E6
Grainthorpe 91 E7
Grampound 3 B8
Grampound Road . .4 D4
Gramsdal 148 C3
Granborough 39 B7
Granby 77 F7
Grandborough 52 C2
Grandtully 133 D6
Grange
Cumb 98 C4
E Ayrs 118 F4
Medway 29 C8
Mers 85 F3
Perth 128 B4
Grange
Crossroads . . . 152 C4
Grange Hall . . . 151 E13
Grange Hill 41 E7
Grangemill 76 D2
Grange Moor 88 C3
Grangemouth . . . 127 F8
Grange of
Lindores 128 C4
Grange-over-
Sands 92 B4
Grangepans 128 F2
Grangetown
Cardiff 22 B3
Redcar 102 B3
Grange Villa . . . 110 D5
Granish 138 C5
Gransmoor 97 D7
Granston 44 B3
Grantchester 54 D5
Grantham 78 F2
Grantley 94 C5
Grantlodge 141 C6
Granton
Dumfries 114 D3
Edin 120 B5
Grantown-on-
Spey 139 B6
Grantshouse 122 C4
Grappenhall 86 F4
Grasby 90 D4
Grasmere 99 D5
Grasscroft 87 D7
Grassendale 85 F4
Grassholme 100 B4
Grassington 94 C3
Grassmoor 76 C4
Grassthorpe 77 C7
Grateley 25 E7
Gratwich 75 F7
Graveley
Cambs 54 C3
Herts 41 B5
Gravelly Hill 62 E5
Gravels 60 D3
Graven 160 F6
Graveney 30 C4
Gravesend
Herts 41 B7
Kent 29 B7
Grayingham 90 E3
Grayrigg 99 E7
Grays 29 B7
Grayshott 27 F6
Grayswood 27 F7
Graythorp 102 B3
Grazeley 26 C4
Greasbrough 88 E5
Greasby 85 F3
Great Abington . . .55 E6
Great Addington . .53 B7
Great Alne 51 D6
Great Altcar 85 D4
Great Amwell 41 C6
Great Asby 100 C1
Great Ashfield . . .56 C3
Great Ayton 102 C3
Great Baddow 42 D3
Great Bardfield . . .55 F7
Great Barford 54 D2
Great Barr 62 E4
Great Barrington . .38 C2
Great Barrow 73 C8
Great Barton 56 C2
Great Barugh 96 B3
Great Bavington . 117 F5
Great Bealings . . .57 E6
Great Bedwyn 25 C7
Great Bentley 43 B7
Great Billing 53 C6
Great Bircham 80 D3
Great Blakenham . .56 D5
Great Blencow . . . 108 F4
Great Bolas 61 B6
Great Bookham . . .28 D2
Great Bourton 52 E2
Great Bowden 64 F4
Great Bradley 55 D7
Great Braxted 42 C4
Great Bricett 56 D4
Great Brickhill 53 F7
Great Bridge 62 E3
Great Bridgeford . .62 B2
Great Brington . . .52 C4
Great Bromley 43 B6
Great Broughton
Cumb 107 F7
N Yorks 102 D3
Great Budworth . . .74 B3
Great Burdon . . . 101 C8
Great Burgh 28 D3
Great Burstead . . .42 E2
Great Busby 102 D3
Great Canfield 42 C1
Great Carlton 91 F8
Great Casterton . . .65 D7
Great Chart 30 E3
Great Chatwell 61 C7
Great
Chesterford 55 E6

Great Cheverell . . 24 D4
Great Chishill 54 F5
Great Clacton 43 C7
Great Cliff 88 C4
Great Clifton 98 B2
Great Coates 91 D6
Great Comberton . .50 E4
Great Corby 108 D4
Great Cornard 56 E2
Great Cowden 97 E8
Great Coxwell 38 E2
Great Crakehall . . 101 E7
Great Cransley . . .53 B6
Great
Cressingham . . .67 D8
Great Crosby 85 E4
Great Cubley 75 F8
Great Dalby 64 C4
Great Denham 53 E8
Great
Doddington 53 C6
Great Dunham 67 C8
Great Dunmow 42 B2
Great Durnford 25 F6
Great Easton
Essex 42 B2
Leics 64 E5
Great Eccleston . . .92 E4
Great Edstone . . . 103 F5
Great Ellingham . . .68 E3
Great Elm 24 E2
Greater Doward . . .36 C2
Great Eversden . . .54 D4
Great Fencote . . . 101 E7
Great
Finborough 56 D4
Great Fransham . . .67 C7
Great Gaddesden 40 C3
Greatgate 75 E7
Great Gidding 65 F8
Great Givendale . . .96 D4
Great Glemham . . .57 C7
Great Glen 64 E3
Great Gonerby 77 F8
Great Gransden . . .54 D3
Great Green
Norf 69 F5
Suff 56 D3
Great Habton 96 B3
Great Hale 78 E4
Great Hallingbury 41 C8
Greatham
Hants 27 F5
Hrtlpl 102 B2
W Sus 16 C4
Great Hampden . . .39 D7
Great Harrowden . .53 B6
Great Harwood . . .93 F7
Great Haseley 39 D6
Great Hatfield 97 E7
Great Haywood . . .62 B4
Great Heath 63 F7
Great Heck 89 B6
Great Henny 56 F2
Great Hinton 24 D4
Great Hockham . . .68 E2
Great Holland 43 C8
Great Horkesley . . .56 F3
Great Hormead 41 B6
Great Horton 94 F4
Great Horwood 53 F5
Great Houghton
Northants 53 D5
S Yorks 88 D5
Great Hucklow 75 B8
Great Kelk 97 D7
Great Kimble 39 D8
Great Kingshill 40 E1
Great Langton . . . 101 E7
Great Leighs 42 C3
Great Lever 86 D5
Great Limber 90 D5
Great Livermere . . .56 B2
Great Longstone . . .76 B2
Great Lumley 111 E5
Great Lyth 60 D4
Great Malvern 50 E2
Great Maplestead 56 F2
Great Marton 92 F3
Great
Massingham 80 E3
Great Melton 68 D4
Great Milton 39 D6
Great Missenden 40 D1
Great Mitton 93 F7
Great Mongeham . 31 D7
Great Moulton 68 E4
Great Munden 41 B6
Great Musgrave 100 C2
Great Ness 60 C3
Great Notley 42 B3
Great Oakley
Essex 43 B7
Northants 65 F5
Great Offley 40 B4
Great Ormside . . . 100 C2
Great Orton 108 D3
Great Ouseburn . . .95 C7
Great Oxendon . . .64 F4
Great Oxney
Green 42 D2
Great Palgrave 67 C8
Great Parndon 41 D7
Great Paxton 54 C3
Great Plumpton . . .92 F3
Great Plumstead 69 C6
Great Ponton 78 F2
Great Preston 88 B5
Great Raveley 66 F2
Great Rissington . .38 C1
Great Rollright 51 F8
Great Ryburgh 81 E5
Great Ryle 117 C6
Great Ryton 60 D4
Great Saling 42 B3
Great Salkeld 109 F5
Great Sampford . . .55 F7
Great Sankey 86 F3
Great Saxham 55 C8
Great Shefford 26 B2
Great Shelford 55 D5
Great Smeaton . . . 101 D8
Great Snoring 80 D5
Great Somerford . .37 F6
Great Stainton . . . 101 B8
Great Stambridge 42 E4

Great Staughton . .54 C2
Great Steeping . . .79 C7
Great Stonar 31 D7
Greatstone on
Sea 19 C7
Great Strickland . .99 B7
Great Stukeley . . .54 B3
Great Sturton 78 B5
Great Sutton
Ches W 73 B7
Shrops 60 F5
Great
Swinburne 110 B2
Great Tew 38 B3
Great Tey 42 B4
Great Thurkleby . .95 B7
Great Thurlow 55 D7
Great Torrington . .9 C6
Great Tosson 117 D6
Great Totham
Essex 42 C4
Essex 42 C4
Great Tows 91 E6
Great Urswick 92 B3
Great Wakering . . .43 F5
Great
Waldingfield . . .56 E3
Great
Walsingham . . .80 D5
Great Waltham 42 C2
Great Warley 42 E1
Great
Washbourne . . .50 F4
Great Weldon 65 F6
Great Welnetham 56 D2
Great Wenham 56 F4
Great
Whittington . . . 110 B3
Great
Wigborough 43 C5
Great Wilbraham 55 D6
Great Wishford . . .25 F5
Great Witcombe . .37 C6
Great Witley 50 C2
Great Wolford 51 F7
Greatworth 52 E3
Great Wratting 55 E7
Great Wymondley 41 B5
Great Wyrley 62 D3
Great Wytheford .61 C5
Great Yarmouth . .69 D8
Great Yeldham 55 F8
Greave 87 B6
Greeba 84 D3
Green 72 C4
Greenbank 160 C2
Greenburn 120 C2
Greendikes 117 B6
Green End 54 D2
Greenfield
C Beds 53 F8
Flint 73 B5
Gtr Man 87 D7
Highld 136 D5
Oxon 39 E7
Greenford 40 F4
Greengairs 119 B7
Greenham 26 C2
Green
Hammerton 95 D7
Greenhaugh 116 F3
Greenhead 109 C6
Greenhill
Falk 119 B8
Kent 31 C5
Leics 63 C8
London 40 F4
Greenhills 118 D3
Greenhithe 29 B6
Greenholm 118 F5
Greenholme 99 D7
Greenhouse 115 B8
Greenhow Hill 94 C4
Greenigoe 159 H5
Greenland 158 D4
Greenlands 39 F7
Green Lane 59 E8
Greenlaw
Aberds 153 C6
Borders 122 E3
Greenlea 107 B7
Greenloaning 127 C7
Greenmount 87 C5
Greenmow 160 L6
Greenock 118 B2
Greenock West . . 118 B2
Greenodd 99 F5
Green Ore 23 D7
Greenrow 107 D8
Green St Green . . .29 C5
Greenside 110 C4
Greensidehill 117 C5
Greens Norton 52 E4
Greenstead
Green 42 B4
Greensted 41 D8
Green Street 40 E4
Greenwich 28 B4
Greet 50 F5
Greete 49 B7
Greetham
Lincs 79 B6
Rutland 65 C6
Greetland 87 B8
Gregg Hall 99 E6
Gregson Lane 86 B3
Greinetobht 148 A3
Greinton 23 F6
Gremista 160 J6
Grenaby 84 E2
Grendon
Northants 53 C6
Warks 63 D6
Grendon
Common 63 E6
Grendon Green . . .49 D7
Grendon
Underwood 39 B6
Grenofen 6 B2
Grenoside 88 E4
Greosabhagh . . . 154 H6
Gresford 73 D7
Gresham 81 D7
Greshornish 149 C8
Gressenhall 68 C2
Gressingham 93 C5
Gresty Green 74 D4
Greta Bridge 101 C5

Gretna 108 C3
Gretna Green . . . 108 C3
Gretton
Glos 50 F5
Northants 65 E5
Shrops 60 E5
Grewelthorpe 94 B5
Greygarth 94 B4
Grey Green 89 D8
Greynor 33 D6
Greysouthen 98 B2
Greystoke 108 F4
Greystone 135 E5
Greywell 26 D5
Griais 155 C9
Grianan 155 D9
Gridley Corner 9 E5
Griff 63 F7
Griffithstown 35 E6
Grimbister 159 G4
Grimblethorpe 91 F6
Grimeford
Village 86 C4
Grimethorpe 88 D5
Griminis 148 C2
Grimister 160 D6
Grimley 50 C3
Grimness 159 J5
Grimoldby 91 F7
Grimpo 60 B3
Grimsargh 93 F5
Grimsbury 52 E2
Grimsby 91 C6
Grimscote 52 D4
Grimscott 8 D4
Grimsthorpe 65 B7
Grimston
E Yorks 97 F8
Leics 64 B3
Norf 80 E3
York 96 D2
Grimstone 12 E4
Grinacombe Moor .9 E6
Grindale 97 B7
Grindigar 159 H6
Grindiscol 160 K6
Grindle 61 D7
Grindleford 76 B2
Grindleton 93 E7
Grindley 62 B4
Grindley Brook . . .74 E2
Grindlow 75 B8
Grindon
Northumb 122 E5
Staffs 75 D7
Grindonmoor
Gate 75 D7
Gringley on the
Hill 89 E8
Grinsdale 108 D3
Grinshill 60 B5
Grinton 101 E5
Griomsidar 155 E8
Grishipoll 146 F4
Grisling Common .17 B8
Gristhorpe 103 F8
Griston 68 E2
Gritley 159 H6
Grittenham 37 F7
Grittleton 37 F5
Grizebeck 98 F4
Grizedale 99 E5
Grobister 159 F7
Groby 64 D2
Groes
Conwy 72 C4
Neath 34 F1
Groes-faen 34 F4
Groesffordd
Marli 72 B4
Groeslon
Gwyn 82 E5
Gwyn 82 F4
Groes-lwyd 60 C2
Grogport 143 D9
Gromford 57 D7
Gronant 72 A4
Groombridge 18 B2
Grosmont
Mon 35 B8
N Yorks 103 D6
Groton 56 E3
Grougfoot 120 B3
Grouville 17
Grove
Dorset 12 G5
Kent 31 C6
Notts 77 B7
Oxon 38 E4
Grove Park 28 B5
Grovesend 33 D6
Grove Vale 62 E4
Grudie 150 E6
Gruids 157 J8
Gruinard House 150 B2
Grula 149 F8
Gruline 147 G8
Grunasound 160 K5
Grundisburgh 57 D6
Grunsagill 93 D7
Grutness 160 N6
Gualachulain 131 E5
Gualin House 156 D6
Guardbridge 129 C6
Guarlford 50 E3
Guay 133 E7
Guestling Green . .19 D5
Guestling Thorn . .19 D5
Guestwick 81 E6
Guestwick Green .81 E6
Guide 86 B5
Guide Post 117 F8
Guilden Morden . .54 E3
Guilden Sutton . . .73 C8
Guildford 27 E7
Guildtown 133 F8
Guilsborough 52 B4
Guilsfield 60 C2
Guilton 31 D6
Guineaford 20 F4
Guisborough 102 C4
Guiseley 94 E4
Guist 81 E5
Guith 159 E6

Guiting Power 37 B7
Gulberwick 160 K6
Gullane 129 F6
Gulval 2 C3
Gulworthy 6 B2
Gumfreston 32 D2
Gumley 64 E3
Gummow's Shop . .4 D3
Gunby
E Yorks 96 F3
Lincs 65 B6
Gundleton 26 F4
Gun Hill 18 D2
Gunn 20 F5
Gunnerside 100 E4
Gunnerton 110 B2
Gunness 90 C2
Gunnislake 6 B2
Gunnista 160 J7
Gunthorpe
Norf 81 D6
Notts 77 E6
Pboro 65 D8
Gunville 15 F5
Gunwalloe 3 D5
Gurnard 15 E5
Gurnett 75 B6
Gurney Slade 23 E8
Gurnos 34 D1
Gussage All
Saints 13 C8
Gussage St
Michael 13 C7
Gutcher 160 D7
Guthrie 135 D5
Guyhirn 66 D3
Guy's Head 66 B4
Guy's Marsh 13 B6
Guyzance 117 D8
Gwaenysgor 72 A4
Gwalchmai 82 D3
Gwaun-Cae-
Gurwen 33 C8
Gwaun-Leision . . .33 C8
Gwbert 45 E3
Gweek 3 D6
Gwehelog 35 D7
Gwenddwr 48 E2
Gwennap 3 C6
Gwenter 3 E6
Gwernaffield 73 C6
Gwernesney 35 D8
Gwernogle 46 F4
Gwernymynydd . . .73 C6
Gwersyllt 73 D7
Gwespyr 85 F2
Gwithian 2 B4
Gwredog 82 C4
Gwyddelwern 72 E4
Gwyddgrug 46 F3
Gwydyr Uchaf 83 E7
Gwynfryn 73 D6
Gwystre 48 C2
Gwytherin 83 E8
Gyfelia 73 E7
Gyffin 83 D7
Gyre 159 H4
Gyrn-goch 70 C5

H

Habberley 60 D3
Habergham 93 F8
Habrough 90 C5
Haceby 78 F3
Hacheston 57 D7
Hackbridge 28 C3
Hackenthorpe 88 F5
Hackford 68 D3
Hackforth 101 E7
Hackland 159 F4
Hackleton 53 D6
Hackness
N Yorks 103 E7
Orkney 159 J4
Hackney 41 F6
Hackthorn 90 F3
Hackthorpe 99 B7
Haconby 65 B8
Hacton 41 F8
Hadden 122 F3
Haddenham
Bucks 39 D7
Cambs 55 B5
Haddington
E Loth 121 B8
Lincs 78 C2
Haddiscoe 69 E7
Haddon
Cambs 65 E8
Ches E 75 C6
Hade Edge 88 D2
Hademore 63 D5
Hadfield 87 E8
Hadham Cross 41 C7
Hadham Ford 41 B7
Hadleigh
Essex 42 F4
Suff 56 E4
Hadley 61 C6
Hadley End 62 B5
Hadlow 29 E7
Hadlow Down 18 C2
Hadnall 60 C5
Hadstock 55 E6
Hady 76 B3
Hadzor 50 C4
Haffenden
Quarter 30 E2
Hafod-Dinbych . . .83 F8
Hafod-Iom 83 D8
Haggate 93 F8
Haggbeck 108 B4
Haggerston 123 E6
Haggrister 160 F5
Hagley
Hereford 49 E7
Worcs 62 F3
Hagworthingham 79 C6
Haigh
Gtr Man 86 D4
S Yorks 88 C3
Haigh Moor 88 B3
Haighton Green . .93 F5
Haile 98 D2

Hailes 50 F5
Hailey
Herts 41 C6
Oxon 38 C3
Hailsham 18 E2
Hail Weston 54 C2
Haimer 158 D3
Hainault 41 E7
Hainford 68 C5
Hainton 91 F5
Hairmyres 119 D6
Haisthorpe 97 C7
Hakin 44 E3
Halam 77 D6
Halbeath 128 F3
Halberton 10 C5
Halcro 158 D4
Hale
Gtr Man 87 F5
Halton 86 F2
Hants 14 C2
Hale Bank 86 F2
Halebarns 87 F5
Hales
Norf 69 E6
Staffs 74 F4
Halesfield 61 D7
Halesgate 66 B3
Halesowen 62 F3
Hales Place 30 D5
Hale Street 29 E7
Halesworth 57 B7
Halewood 86 F2
Halford
Shrops 60 F4
Warks 51 E7
Halfpenny Furze . .32 C3
Halfpenny Green .62 E2
Halfway
Carms 46 F5
Carms 47 F7
W Berks 26 C2
Halfway Bridge . . .16 B3
Halfway House . . .60 C3
Halfway Houses . .30 B3
Halifax 87 B8
Halket 118 D4
Halkirk 158 E3
Halkyn 73 B6
Halland 18 D2
Hallaton 64 E4
Hallatrow 23 D8
Hallbankgate . . . 109 D5
Hall Dunnerdale . .98 E4
Hallen 36 F2
Hall Green
W Mid 62 F5
W Yorks 88 C4
Hall Grove 41 C5
Halliburton 122 E2
Hallin 148 C7
Halling 29 C8
Hallington
Lincs 91 F7
Northumb 110 B2
Halloughton 77 D6
Hallow 50 D3
Hallrule 115 C8
Halls 122 B2
Hallsands 7 F6
Hall's Green 41 B5
Hallthwaites 98 F3
Hallworthy 8 F3
Hallyburton
House 134 F2
Hallyne 120 E4
Halmer End 74 E4
Halmore 36 D3
Halmyre Mains . . 120 E4
Halnaker 16 D3
Halsall 85 C4
Halse
Northants 52 E3
Som 11 B6
Halsetown 2 C4
Halsham 91 B6
Halsinger 20 F4
Halstead
Essex 56 F2
Kent 29 C5
Leics 64 D4
Halstock 12 D3
Haltham 78 C5
Haltoft End 79 E6
Halton
Bucks 40 C1
Halton 86 F3
Lancs 92 C5
Northumb 110 C2
Wrex 73 F7
W Yorks 95 F6
Halton East 94 D3
Halton Gill 93 B8
Halton Holegate . .79 C7
Halton Lea Gate 109 D6
Halton West 93 D8
Haltwhistle 109 C7
Halvergate 69 D7
Halwell 7 D5
Halwill 9 E6
Halwill Junction . . .9 D6
Ham
Devon 11 D7
Glos 36 E3
Highld 158 C4
Kent 31 D7
London 28 B2
Shetland 160 K1
Wilts 25 C8
Hambleden 39 F7
Hambledon
Hants 15 C7
Sur 27 F7
Hamble-le-Rice . .15 D5
Hambleton
Lancs 92 E3
N Yorks 95 F8
Hambridge 11 B8
Hambrook
S Glos 23 B8
W Sus 15 D8
Ham Common 13 B6
Hameringham 79 C6
Hamerton 54 B2

Hametoun 160 K1
Ham Green
Hereford 50 E2
Kent 19 C5
Kent 30 C2
N Som 23 B7
Worcs 50 C5
Hamilton 119 D7
Hammer 27 F6
Hammerpot 16 D4
Hammersmith 28 B3
Hammerwich 62 D4
Hammerwood 28 F5
Hammond Street 41 D6
Hammoon 13 C6
Hamnavoe
Shetland 160 E4
Shetland 160 E6
Shetland 160 F6
Shetland 160 K5
Hampden Park . . .18 E3
Hamperden End . .55 F6
Hampnett 37 C7
Hampole 89 C6
Hampreston 13 E8
Hampstead 41 F5
Hampstead
Norreys 26 B3
Hampsthwaite . . .95 D5
Hampton
London 28 C2
Shrops 61 F7
Worcs 50 E5
Hampton Bishop . .49 F7
Hampton Heath . .73 E8
Hampton in
Arden 63 F6
Hampton Loade . .61 F7
Hampton Lovett . .50 C3
Hampton Lucy . . .51 D7
Hampton on the
Hill 51 C7
Hampton Poyle . . .39 C5
Hamrow 80 E5
Hamsey 17 C8
Hamsey Green . . .28 D4
Hamstall Ridware 62 C5
Hamstead
IoW 14 E5
W Mid 62 E4
Hamstead
Marshall 26 C2
Hamsterley
Durham 110 D4
Durham 110 D4
Hamstreet 19 B7
Ham Street 23 F7
Hamworthy 13 E7
Hanbury
Staffs 63 B5
Worcs 50 C4
Hanbury
Woodend 63 B5
Hanby 78 F3
Hanchurch 74 E5
Handbridge 73 C8
Handcross 17 B6
Handforth 87 F6
Handley 73 D8
Handsacre 62 C4
Handsworth
S Yorks 88 F5
W Mid 62 E4
Handy Cross 9 B6
Hanford 75 E5
Hanging
Langford 24 F5
Hangleton 16 D4
Hanham 23 B8
Hankelow 74 E3
Hankerton 37 E6
Hankham 18 E3
Hanley 75 E5
Hanley Castle 50 E3
Hanley Child 49 C8
Hanley Swan 50 E3
Hanley William . . .49 C8
Hanlith 94 C2
Hanmer 73 F8
Hannah 79 B8
Hannington
Hants 26 D3
Northants 53 B6
Swindon 38 E1
Hannington Wick 38 E1
Hansel Village . . . 118 F3
Hanslope 53 E6
Hanthorpe 65 B7
Hanwell
London 40 F4
Oxon 52 E2
Hanwood 60 D4
Hanworth
London 28 B2
Norf 81 D7
Happendon 119 F8
Happisburgh 69 A6
Happisburgh
Common 69 B6
Hapsford 73 B8
Hapton
Lancs 93 F7
Norf 68 E4
Harberton 7 D5
Harbertonford 7 D5
Harbledown 30 D5
Harborne 62 F4
Harborough
Magna 52 B2
Harbottle 117 D5
Harbury 51 D8
Harby
Leics 77 F7
Notts 77 B8
Harcombe 11 E6
Harden
W Mid 62 D4
W Yorks 94 F3
Hardenhuish 24 B4
Hardgate 141 D6
Hardham 16 C4
Hardingham 68 D3
Hardingstone 53 D5
Hardington 24 D2
Hardington
Mandeville 12 C3
Hardington
Marsh 12 D3

Gra–Hau 211

Hardley 14 D5
Hardley Street 69 D6
Hardmead 53 E7
Hardstoft 76 C4
Hardway
Hants 15 D7
Som 24 F2
Hardwick
Bucks 39 C8
Cambs 54 D4
Norf 67 C6
Norf 68 F5
Northants 53 C6
Notts 77 B6
Oxon 38 D3
Oxon 39 B5
W Mid 62 E4
Hardwicke
Glos 36 C4
Glos 37 B6
Hereford 48 E4
Hardy's Green 43 B5
Hareby 79 C6
Hareden 93 D6
Harefield 40 E3
Hare Green 43 B6
Hare Hatch 27 B6
Harehills 95 F6
Harehope 117 B6
Haresceugh 109 E6
Harescombe 37 C5
Haresfield 37 C5
Hareshaw 119 C8
Hareshaw Head . .116 F4
Hare Street 41 B6
Harewood 95 E6
Harewood End 36 B2
Harford
Carms 46 E5
Devon 6 D4
Hargate 68 E4
Hargatewall 75 B8
Hargrave
Ches W 73 C8
Northants 53 B8
Suff 55 D8
Harker 108 C3
Harkland 160 E6
Harkstead 57 F5
Harlaston 63 C6
Harlaw House . . . 141 B6
Harlaxton 77 F8
Harle Syke 93 F8
Harlech 71 D6
Harlequin 77 F6
Harlescott 60 C5
Harlesden 41 F5
Harleston
Devon 7 E5
Norf 68 F5
Suff 56 D4
Harlestone 52 C5
Harle Wood 63 C6
Harley
Shrops 61 D5
S Yorks 88 E4
Harling Road 68 F2
Harlington
C Beds 53 F8
London 27 B8
S Yorks 89 D5
Harlosh 149 D7
Harlow 41 C7
Harlow Hill
Northumb 110 C3
N Yorks 95 D5
Harlthorpe 96 F3
Harlton 54 D4
Harman's Cross . .13 F7
Harmby 101 F6
Harmer Green 41 C5
Harmer Hill 60 B4
Harmondsworth . .27 B8
Harmston 78 C2
Harnham 110 B3
Harnhill 37 D7
Harold Hill 41 E8
Haroldston West . 44 D3
Haroldswick 160 B8
Harold Wood 41 E8
Harome 102 F4
Harpenden 40 C4
Harpford 11 E5
Harpham 97 C6
Harpley
Norf 80 E3
Worcs 49 C8
Harpole 52 C4
Harpsdale 158 E3
Harpsden 39 F7
Harpswell 90 F3
Harpurhey 87 D6
Harpur Hill 75 B7
Harraby 108 D4
Harrapool 149 F11
Harrier 160 J1
Harrietfield 127 B8
Harrietsham 30 D2
Harrington
Cumb 98 B1
Lincs 79 B6
Northants 64 F4
Harringworth 65 E6
Harris 146 B6
Harrogate 95 D6
Harrold 53 D7
Harrow 40 F4
Harrowbarrow 5 C8
Harrowden 53 E8
Harrowgate Hill 101 C7
Harrow on the
Hill 40 F4
Harrow Street 56 F3
Harrow Weald 40 E4
Harston
Cambs 54 D5
Leics 77 F8
Harswell 96 F4
Hart 111 F7
Hartburn
Northumb 117 F6
Stockton 102 C2
Hartest 56 D2
Hartfield 29 F5
Hartford
Cambs 54 B3
Ches W 74 B3

Hartfordbridge . . .27 D5
Hartford End 42 C2
Hartforth 101 D6
Harthill
Ches W 74 D2
N Lanark 120 C2
S Yorks 89 F5
Hart Hill 40 B4
Hartington 75 C8
Hartland 8 B4
Hartlebury 50 B3
Hartlepool 111 F8
Hartley
Cumb 100 D2
Kent 18 B4
Kent 29 C7
Northumb 111 B6
Hartley Westpall 26 D4
Hartley Wintney . .27 D5
Hartlip 30 C2
Hartoft End 103 E5
Harton
N Yorks 96 C3
Shrops 60 F4
T&W 111 C6
Hartpury 36 B4
Hartshead 88 B2
Hartshill 63 E7
Hartshorne 63 B7
Hartsop 99 C6
Hart Station 111 F7
Hartwell 53 D5
Hartwood 119 D8
Harvieston 126 F4
Harvington
Cross 51 E5
Harwell 38 F4
Harwich 57 F6
Harwood
Durham 109 F8
Gtr Man 86 C5
Harwood Dale . . . 103 E7
Harworth 89 E7
Hasbury 62 F3
Hascombe 27 E7
Haselbech 52 B5
Haselbury
Plucknett 12 C2
Haseley 51 C7
Haselor 51 D6
Hasfield 37 B5
Hasguard 44 E3
Haskayne 85 D4
Hasketon 57 D6
Hasland 76 C3
Haslemere 27 F7
Haslingden 87 B5
Haslingfield 54 D5
Haslington 74 D4
Hassall 74 D4
Hassall Green 74 D4
Hassell Street 30 E4
Hassendean 115 B8
Hassingham 69 D6
Hassocks 17 C6
Hassop 76 B2
Hastigrow 158 D4
Hastingleigh 30 E4
Hastings 18 E5
Hastingwood 41 D7
Hastoe 40 D2
Haswell 111 E6
Haswell Plough . . 111 E6
Hatch
C Beds 54 E2
Hants 26 D4
Wilts 13 B7
Hatch
Beauchamp 11 B8
Hatch End 40 E4
Hatchet Gate 14 D4
Hatch Green 11 C8
Hatching Green . .40 C4
Hatchmere 74 B2
Hatcliffe 91 D6
Hatfield
Hereford 49 D7
Herts 41 D5
S Yorks 89 D7
Worcs 50 D3
Hatfield Broad
Oak 41 C8
Hatfield Garden
Village 41 D5
Hatfield Heath 41 C8
Hatfield Hyde 41 C5
Hatfield Peverel . 42 C3
Hatfield
Woodhouse 89 D7
Hatford 38 E3
Hatherden 25 D8
Hatherleigh 9 D7
Hathern 64 B2
Hatherop 38 D1
Hathersage 88 F3
Hathershaw 87 D7
Hatherton
Ches E 74 E3
Staffs 62 C3
Hatley St George 54 D3
Hatt 5 C8
Hattingley 26 F4
Hatton
Aberds 153 E10
Derbys 63 B6
Lincs 78 B4
Shrops 60 E4
Warks 51 C7
Warr 86 F4
Hatton Castle . . . 153 D7
Hattoncrook 141 B7
Hatton Heath 73 C8
Hatton of
Fintray 141 C7
Haugh
E Ayrs 112 B4
Gtr Man 87 C7
Lincs 79 B7
Haugham 91 F7
Haugh Head 117 B6
Haughley 56 C4
Haughley Green . .56 C4
Haugh of Glass . . 152 E4
Haugh of Urr 106 C5

Haughs of
Clinterty 141 C7

Haughton
Notts 77 B6
Shrops 60 B3
Shrops 61 C5
Shrops 61 D7
Shrops 61 E6
Staffs 62 B2
Haughton Castle 110 E2
Haughton Green . 87 E7
Haughton Moss . 74 D2
Haultwick 41 B6
Haunn
Argyll 146 G6
W Isles 148 G2
Haunton 63 C6
Hauxley 117 D5
Hauxton 54 D5
Havant 15 D8
Haven 49 D6
Haven Bank 78 D5
Havenstreet 15 E6
Havercroft 88 C4
Haverfordwest
=Hwlffordd 44 D4
Haverhill 55 E7
Haverigg 92 B1
Havering-atte-
Bower 41 E8
Haveringland . . . 81 E7
Haversham 53 E6
Haverthwaite . . . 99 F5
Haverton Hill . . 102 B2
Hawarden
=Penarlâg 73 C7
Hawcoat 92 B2
Hawen 46 E2
Hawes 100 F3
Hawes' Green . . . 68 E5
Hawes Side 92 F3
Hawford 50 C3
Hawick 115 C8
Hawkchurch 11 D8
Hawkedon 55 D8
Hawkenbury
Kent 18 B2
Kent 30 E2
Hawkeridge 24 D3
Hawkerland 11 F5
Hawkesbury
S Glos 36 F4
Warks 63 F7
Hawkesbury
Upton 36 F4
Hawkes End 63 F7
Hawk Green 87 F7
Hawkhill 117 C8
Hawkhurst 18 B4
Hawkinge 31 F6
Hawkley 15 B8
Hawkridge 21 F7
Hawkshead 99 E5
Hawkshead Hill . 99 E5
Hawksland 119 F8
Hawkswick 94 B2
Hawksworth
Notts 77 E7
W Yorks 94 E4
W Yorks 95 F5
Hawkwell 42 E4
Hawley
Hants 27 D6
Kent 29 B6
Hawling 37 B7
Hawnby 102 F3
Haworth 94 F3
Hawstead 56 D2
Hawthorn
Durham 111 E7
Rhondda 35 F5
Wilts 24 C3
Hawthorn Hill
Brack 27 B6
Lincs 78 D5
Hawthorpe 65 B7
Hawton 77 D7
Haxby 96 D2
Haxey 89 D8
Haydock 86 E3
Haydon 12 C4
Haydon Bridge . 109 C8
Haydon Wick . . . 37 F8
Haye 5 C8
Hayes
London 28 C5
London 40 F4
Hayfield
Derbys 87 F8
Fife 128 E4
Hay Green 66 C3
Hayhill 112 C4
Hayhillock 135 E5
Hayle 2 C4
Haynes 53 E8
Haynes Church
End 53 E8
Hay-on-Wye
=Y Gelli Gandryll . 48 E4
Hayscastle 44 C4
Hayscastle Cross 44 C4
Hayshead 135 E6
Hay Street 41 B6
Hayton
Aberdeen 141 D8
Cumb 107 D8
Cumb 108 D5
E Yorks 96 E4
Notts 89 F8
Hayton's Bent . . 60 F5
Haytor Vale 7 B5
Haywards Heath . 17 B7
Haywood 89 C6
Haywood Oaks . . 77 D6
Hazelbank 119 E8
Hazelbury Bryan . 12 D5
Hazeley 26 D5
Hazel Grove 87 F7
Hazelhurst 87 D6
Hazelslade 62 C4
Hazel Street 18 B3
Hazelton 37 C7
Hazelton Walls . 128 B5
Hazelwood 76 E3

Hazlemere 40 E1
Hazlerigg 110 B5
Hazlewood 94 D3
Hazon 117 D7
Headbourne
Worthy 26 F2
Headbrook 48 D5
Headcorn 30 E2
Headingley 95 F5
Headington 39 D5
Headlam 101 C6
Headless Cross . . 50 C5
Headley
Hants 26 C3
Hants 27 F6
Sur 28 D3
Head of Muir . . 127 F7
Headon 77 B7
Heads 119 E7
Heads Nook . . . 108 D4
Heage 76 D3
Healaugh
N Yorks 95 E7
N Yorks 101 E5
Heald Green 87 F6
Heale
Devon 20 E5
Som 23 E8
Healey
Gtr Man 87 C6
Northumb 110 D3
N Yorks 101 F6
Healeyfield 110 E3
Healing 91 C6
Heamoor 2 C3
Heanish 146 G3
Heanor 76 E4
Heanton
Punchardon 20 F4
Heapham 90 F2
Hearthstone 114 B4
Heasley Mill 21 F6
Heast 149 G11
Heath
Cardiff 22 B3
Derbys 76 C4
Heath and Reach . 53 F7
Heathcote 75 C8
Heath End
Hants 26 C3
Sur 27 E6
Warks 51 C7
Heather 63 C7
Heatherfield . . . 149 D9
Heathfield
Devon 7 B6
E Sus 18 C2
Som 11 B6
Heathhall 107 B6
Heath Hayes 62 C4
Heath Hill 61 C7
Heath House 23 E6
Heathrow Airport 27 B8
Heathstock 11 D7
Heathton 62 E2
Heath Town 62 E3
Heatley 86 F5
Heaton
Lancs 92 C4
Staffs 75 C6
T&W 111 C5
W Yorks 94 F4
Heaton Moor . . . 87 E6
Heaverham 29 D6
Heaviley 87 F7
Heavitree 10 E4
Hebburn 111 C6
Hebden 94 C3
Hebden Bridge . . 87 B7
Hebron
Anglesey 82 C4
Carms 32 B2
Northumb 117 F7
Heck 114 F3
Heckfield 26 C5
Heckfield Green . 57 B5
Heckfordbridge . 43 B5
Heckington 78 E4
Heckmondwike . . 88 B3
Heddington 24 C4
Heddle 159 G4
Heddon-on-the-
Wall 110 C4
Hedenham 69 E6
Hedge End 15 C5
Hedgerley 40 F2
Hedging 11 B8
Hedley on the
Hill 110 D3
Hednesford 62 C4
Hedon 91 B5
Hedsor 40 F2
Hedworth 111 C6
Hegdon Hill 49 D7
Heggerscales . . . 100 C3
Heglibister 160 H5
Heighington
Darl 101 B7
Lincs 78 C2
Heights of Brae . 151 E8
Heights of
Kinlochewe 150 E3
Heights of
Kinlochewe 156 C7
Heilam 156 C7
Heiton 122 F3
Hele
Devon 10 D4
Devon 20 E4
Helensburgh . . . 145 E11
Helford 3 D6
Helford Passage . . 3 D6
Helhoughton 80 E4
Helions
Bumpstead 55 E7
Hellaby 89 E6
Helland 5 B5
Hellesdon 68 C5
Hellidon 52 D3
Hellifield 93 D8
Hellingly 18 D2
Hellington 69 D6
Hellister 160 J5
Helm 117 E7
Helmdon 52 E3
Helmingham 57 D5
Helmington Row 110 F4
Helmsdale 157 H13
Helmshore 87 B5
Helmsley 102 F4

Helperby 95 C7
Helperthorpe . . . 97 B5
Helpringham 78 E4
Helpston 65 D8
Helsby 73 B8
Helsey 79 B8
Helston 3 D5
Helstone 8 F2
Helton 99 B7
Helwith Bridge . . 93 C8
Hemblington 69 C6
Hemel
Hempstead 40 D3
Hemingbrough . . 96 F2
Hemingby 78 B5
Hemingford
Abbots 54 B3
Hemingford Grey . 54 B3
Hemingstone 57 D5
Hemington
Leics 63 B8
Northants 65 F7
Som 24 D2
Hemley 57 E6
Hemlington 102 C3
Hemp Green 57 C7
Hempholme 97 D6
Hempnall 68 E5
Hempnall Green . 68 E5
Hempriggs
House 158 F5
Hempstead
Essex 55 F7
Medway 29 C8
Norf 69 B7
Norf 81 D7
Hempsted 37 C5
Hempton
Norf 80 E5
Oxon 52 F2
Hemsby 69 C7
Hemswell 90 E3
Hemswell Cliff . . 90 F3
Hemsworth 88 C5
Hemyock 11 C6
Henbury
Bristol 23 B7
Ches E 75 B5
Hendon
London 41 F5
T&W 111 D7
Hendre 73 C5
Hendre-ddu 83 E8
Hendreforgan . . . 34 F3
Hendy 33 D6
Heneglwys 82 D4
Hen-feddau fawr . 45 F4
Henfield 17 C6
Henford 9 E5
Henghurst 19 B6
Hengoed
Caerph 35 E5
Powys 48 D4
Shrops 73 F6
Hengrave 56 C2
Henham 41 B8
Heniarth 59 D8
Henlade 11 B7
Henley
Shrops 49 B7
Som 23 F6
Suff 57 D5
W Sus 16 B2
Henley-in-Arden . 51 C6
Henley-on-
Thames 39 F7
Henley's Down . . 18 D4
Henllan
Ceredig 46 E2
Denb 72 C4
Henllan Amgoed . 32 B2
Henllys 35 E6
Henlow 54 F2
Hennock 10 F3
Henny Street 56 F2
Henryd 83 D7
Henry's Moat . . . 32 B1
Hensall 89 B6
Henshaw 109 C7
Hensingham 98 C1
Henstead 69 F7
Henstridge 12 C5
Henstridge Ash . . 12 C5
Henstridge Marsh 12 C5
Henton
Oxon 39 D7
Som 23 E6
Henwood 5 B7
Heogan 160 J6
Heol-las 33 E7
Heol Senni 34 B3
Heol-y-Cyw 34 F3
Hepburn 117 B6
Hepple 117 D5
Hepscott 117 F8
Heptonstall 87 B7
Hepworth
Suff 56 B3
W Yorks 88 D2
Herbrandston . . . 44 E3
Hereford 49 E7
Heriot 121 D6
Hermiston 120 B4
Hermitage
Borders 115 E8
Dorset 12 D4
W Berks 26 B3
W Sus 15 D8
Hermon
Anglesey 82 E3
Carms 33 B7
Carms 46 F2
Pembs 45 F4
Herne 31 C5
Herne Bay 31 C5
Herner 9 B7
Hernhill 30 C4
Herodsfoot 5 C7
Herongate 42 E2
Heronsford 104 A5
Herriard 26 E4
Herringfleet 69 E7
Herringswell 55 B8
Hersden 31 C6
Hersham
Corn 8 D4
Sur 28 C2
Herstmonceux . . . 18 D3

Herston 159 J5
Hertford 41 C6
Hertford Heath . . 41 C6
Hertingfordbury . 41 C6
Hesketh Bank . . . 86 B2
Hesketh Lane . . . 93 E6
Hesket
Newmarket 108 F3
Heskin Green . . . 86 C3
Hesleden 111 F7
Hesleyside 116 F4
Heslington 96 D2
Hessay 95 D8
Hessenford 5 D8
Hessett 56 C3
Hessle 90 B4
Hest Bank 92 C4
Heston 28 B2
Hestwall 159 G3
Heswall 85 F3
Hethe 39 B5
Hethersett 68 D4
Hethersgill 108 C4
Hethpool 116 B4
Hett 111 F5
Hetton 94 D2
Hetton-le-Hole . . 111 E6
Hetton Steads . . 123 F6
Heugh 110 B3
Heugh-head 140 C2
Heveningham . . . 57 B7
Hever 29 E5
Heversham 99 F6
Hevingham 81 E7
Hewas Water 3 B8
Hewelsfield 36 D2
Hewish
N Som 23 C6
Som 12 D2
Heworth 96 D2
Hexham 110 C2
Hextable 29 B6
Hexton 54 F2
Hexworthy 6 B4
Hey 93 E8
Heybridge
Essex 42 D4
Essex 42 E2
Heybridge Basin . 42 D4
Heybrook Bay 6 E3
Heydon
Cambs 54 E5
Norf 81 E7
Heydour 78 F3
Heylipol 146 G2
Heylor 160 E4
Heysham 92 C4
Heyshott 16 C2
Heyside 87 D7
Heytesbury 24 E4
Heythrop 38 B3
Heywood
Gtr Man 87 C6
Wilts 24 D3
Hibaldstow 90 D3
Hickleton 89 D5
Hickling
Norf 69 B7
Notts 64 B3
Hickling Green . . 69 B7
Hickling Heath . . 69 B7
Hickstead 17 B6
Hidcote Boyce . . . 51 E6
High Ackworth . . 88 C5
Higham
Derbys 76 D3
Kent 29 B8
Lancs 93 F8
Suff 55 C8
Suff 56 F4
Higham Dykes . . 110 B4
Higham Ferrers . . 53 C7
Higham Gobion . . 54 F2
Higham on the
Hill 63 E7
Highampton 9 D6
Higham Wood . . . 29 E6
High Angerton . . 117 F6
High Bankhill . . . 109 E5
High Barnes 111 D6
High Beach 41 E7
High Bentham . . . 93 C6
High Bickington . . 9 B8
High Birkwith . . . 93 B7
High Blantyre . . . 119 D6
High
Bonnybridge . . . 119 B8
High Bradfield . . . 88 E3
High Bray 21 F5
Highbridge
Highld 136 F4
Som 22 E5
Highbrook 28 F4
High Brooms 29 E6
High Bullen 9 B7
Highburton 88 C2
Highbury 23 E8
High Buston 117 D8
High Callerton . . 110 B4
High Catton 96 D3
Highclere 26 C2
Highcliffe 14 E3
High Cogges 38 D3
High Coniscliffe 101 C7
High Cross
Hants 15 B8
Herts 41 C6
High Easter 42 C2
High Eggborough 89 B6
High Ellington . . 101 F6
Higher Ansty 13 D5
Higher Ashton . . 10 F3
Higher Ballam . . . 92 F3
Higher Bartle . . . 92 F5
Higher Boscaswell . 2 C2
Higher
Burwardsley . . . 74 D2
High Ercall 61 C5
Higher Clovelly . . 8 B5
Higher End 86 D3
Higher Kinnerton 73 C7
Higher
Penwortham . . . 86 B3
Higher Town 2 E4
Higher Walreddon . 6 B2
Higher Walton
Lancs 86 B3
Warr 86 F3

Higher Wheelton . 86 B4
Higher Whitley . . 86 F4
Higher Wincham . 74 B3
Higher Wych . . . 73 E8
High Etherley . . 101 B6
Highfield
E Yorks 96 F3
Gtr Man 86 D5
N Ayrs 118 D3
Oxon 39 B5
S Yorks 88 F4
T&W 110 D4
Highfields
Cambs 54 D4
Northumb 123 D5
High Garrett 42 B3
Highgate 41 F5
High Grange . . . 110 F4
High Green
Norf 68 D4
S Yorks 88 E4
Worcs 50 E3
High Halden 19 B5
High Halstow . . . 29 B8
High Ham 23 F6
High Harrington . 98 B2
High Hatton 61 B6
High Hawsker . . . 103 D7
High Hesket 108 E4
High Hesleden . . 111 F7
High Hoyland . . . 88 C3
High Hunsley . . . 97 F5
High Hurstwood . 17 B8
High Hutton 96 C3
High Ireby 108 F2
High Kelling 81 C7
High Kilburn 95 B8
High Lands 101 B6
High Lane
Gtr Man 87 F7
Worcs 49 C8
High Laver 41 D8
Highlaws 107 E8
Highleadon 36 B4
High Legh 86 F5
Highleigh 16 E2
High Leven 102 C2
Highley 61 F7
High Littleton . . . 23 D8
High Lorton 98 B3
High Marishes . . . 96 B4
High Marnham . . 77 B8
High Melton 89 D6
High Mickley . . . 110 C3
High Mindork . . . 105 D7
Highmoor Cross . 39 F7
Highmoor Hill . . . 36 F1
Highnam 36 C4
Highnam Green . . 36 B4
High Newton 99 F6
High Newton-by-the-
Sea 117 B8
High Nibthwaite . 98 F4
High Offley 61 B7
High Ongar 42 D1
High Onn 62 C2
High Roding 42 C2
High Row 108 F3
High Salvington . 16 D5
High Sellafield . . 98 D2
High Shaw 100 E3
High Spen 110 D4
Highstead 31 C6
High Stoop 110 E4
High Street
Corn 4 D4
Kent 18 B4
Suff 56 E2
Suff 57 B8
Suff 57 D8
Highstreet
Green 55 F8
High Street
Green 56 D4
Hightae 107 B7
High Throston . . 111 F7
Hightown
Ches E 75 C5
Mers 85 D4
Hightown Green . 56 D3
High Toynton . . . 79 C5
High Trewhitt . . 117 D6
High Valleyfield . 128 F2
Highway 24 B5
Highweek 7 B6
High Westwood . 110 D4
Highworth 38 E2
High Wray 99 E5
High Wycombe . . 40 E2
Hilborough 67 D8
Hilcote 76 D4
Hilcott 25 D6
Hildenborough . . 29 E6
Hilden Park 29 E6
Hildersham 55 E6
Hilderstone 75 F6
Hilderthorpe 97 C7
Hilfield 12 D4
Hilgay 67 E6
Hill
Pembs 32 D2
S Glos 36 E3
W Mid 62 E5
Hillam 89 B6
Hillbeck 100 C2
Hillborough 31 C6
Hillbrae
Aberds 141 B6
Aberds 152 D6
Hill Brow 15 B8
Hillbutts 13 D7
Hillclifflane 76 E2
Hill Dale 86 C2
Hill Dyke 79 E6
Hilldyke 79 E6
Hill End
Durham 110 F3
Fife 128 E2
N Yorks 94 D3
Hillerton 10 E2
Hillesden 39 B6
Hillesley 36 F4
Hillfarrance 11 B6

Hillhead
Aberds 152 E5
Devon 7 D7
S Ayrs 112 C4
Hill Head
Hants 15 D6
Northumb 110 C2
Hillhead of
Auchentumb . . . 153 C9
Hillhead of
Cocklaw 153 D10
Hillhouse 121 D8
Hilliclay 158 D3
Hillingdon 40 F3
Hillington
Glasgow 118 C5
Norf 80 E3
Hillmorton 52 B3
Hill Mountain . . . 44 E4
Hillockhead
Aberds 140 C3
Aberds 140 D2
Hill of Beath . . . 128 E3
Hill of Fearn . . . 151 D11
Hill of
Mountblairy . . . 153 C6
Hill Ridware 62 C4
Hillside
Aberds 141 E8
Angus 135 C6
Mers 85 C4
Orkney 159 J5
Shetland 160 G6
Hillswick 160 F4
Hill Top
Durham 100 B4
Hants 14 D5
W Mid 62 E3
W Yorks 88 C4
Hill View 13 E7
Hillway 15 F7
Hillwell 160 M5
Hilmarton 24 B5
Hilperton 24 D3
Hilsea 15 D7
Hilston 97 F8
Hilton
Aberds 153 E9
Cambs 54 C3
Cumb 100 B2
Derbys 76 F2
Dorset 13 D5
Durham 101 B6
Highld 151 C10
Shrops 61 E7
Stockton 102 C2
Hilton of
Cadboll 151 D11
Himbleton 50 D4
Himley 62 E2
Hincaster 99 F7
Hinckley 63 E8
Hinderclay 56 B4
Hinderton 73 B7
Hinderwell 103 C5
Hindford 73 F7
Hindhead 27 F6
Hindley 86 D4
Hindley Green . . . 86 D4
Hindlip 50 D3
Hindolveston 81 E6
Hindon 24 F4
Hindringham 81 D5
Hingham 68 D3
Hinstock 61 B6
Hintlesham 56 E4
Hinton
Hants 14 E3
Hereford 48 F5
Northants 52 D3
S Glos 24 B2
Shrops 60 D4
Hinton Ampner . . 15 B6
Hinton Blewett . . 23 D7
Hinton
Charterhouse . . . 24 D2
Hinton-in-the-
Hedges 52 F3
Hinton Martell . . 13 D8
Hinton on the
Green 50 E5
Hinton Parva 38 F2
Hinton
St George 12 C2
Hinton St Mary . . 13 C5
Hinton Waldrist . . 38 E3
Hints
Shrops 49 B8
Staffs 63 D5
Hinwick 53 C7
Hinxhill 30 E4
Hinxton 55 E5
Hinxworth 54 E3
Hipperholme 88 B2
Hipswell 101 E6
Hirael 83 D5
Hiraeth 32 B2
Hirn 141 D6
Hirnant 59 B7
Hirst
N Lanark 119 C8
Northumb 117 F8
Hirst Courtney . . 89 B7
Hirwaen 72 C5
Hirwaun 34 D3
Hiscott 9 B7
Histon 54 C5
Hitcham 56 D3
Hitchin 54 F3
Hither Green 28 B4
Hittisleigh 10 E2
Hive 96 F4
Hixon 62 B4
Hoaden 31 D6
Hoaldalbert 35 B7
Hoar Cross 62 B5
Hoarwithy 36 B2
Hoath 31 C6
Hobarris 48 B5
Hobbister 159 H4
Hobkirk 115 C8
Hobson 110 D4
Hoby 64 C3
Hockering 68 C3
Hockerton 77 D7
Hockley 42 E4
Hockley Heath . . . 51 B6
Hockliffe 40 B2

Hockwold cum
Wilton 67 F7
Hockworthy 10 C5
Hoddesdon 41 D6
Hoddlesden 86 B5
Hoddomcross . . . 107 B8
Hoddom Mains . . 107 B8
Hodgeston 32 E1
Hodley 59 E8
Hodnet 61 B6
Hodthorpe 76 B5
Hoe
Hants 15 C6
Norf 68 C2
Hoe Gate 15 C7
Hoff 100 C1
Hoggard's Green . 56 D2
Hoggeston 39 B8
Hogha
Gearraidh 148 A2
Hoghton 86 B4
Hognaston 76 D2
Hog Patch 27 E6
Hogsthorpe 79 B8
Holbeach 66 B3
Holbeach Bank . . 66 B3
Holbeach Clough . 66 B3
Holbeach Drove . . 66 C3
Holbeach Hurn . . 66 B3
Holbeach St
Johns 66 C3
Holbeach St
Marks 79 F6
Holbeach St
Matthew 79 F7
Holbeck
Notts 76 B5
W Yorks 95 F5
Holbeck
Woodhouse 76 B5
Holberrow Green 50 D5
Holbeton 6 D4
Holborn 41 F6
Holbrook
Derbys 76 E3
Suff 57 F5
S Yorks 88 F5
Holburn 123 F6
Holbury 14 D5
Holcombe
Devon 7 B7
Som 23 E8
Holcombe Rogus . 11 C5
Holcot 53 C5
Holden 93 E7
Holdenby 52 C4
Holdenhurst 14 E2
Holdgate 61 F5
Holdingham 78 E3
Holditch 11 D8
Holefield 122 F4
Holehouses 74 B4
Holemoor 9 D6
Holestane 113 E8
Holford 22 E3
Holgate 95 D8
Holker 92 B3
Holkham 80 C4
Hollacombe 9 D5
Holland
Orkney 159 C5
Orkney 159 F7
Holland Fen 78 E5
Holland-on-Sea . . 43 C8
Hollandstoun . . . 159 C8
Hollee 108 C2
Hollesley 57 E7
Hollicombe 7 C6
Hollingbourne . . . 30 D2
Hollington
Derbys 76 F2
E Sus 18 D4
Staffs 75 F7
Hollington Grove 76 F2
Hollingworth 87 E8
Hollins 87 D6
Hollinsclough . . . 75 C7
Hollins Green . . . 86 E4
Hollins Lane 92 D4
Hollinwood
Gtr Man 87 D7
Shrops 74 F2
Hollocombe 9 C8
Holloway 76 D3
Hollowell 52 B4
Hollow Meadows . 88 F3
Holly End 66 D4
Holly Green 50 E3
Hollybush
Caerph 35 D5
E Ayrs 112 C3
Worcs 50 F2
Hollym 91 B7
Hollywood 51 B5
Holmbridge 88 D2
Holmbury St
Mary 28 E2
Holmbush 4 D5
Holmcroft 62 B3
Holme
Cambs 65 F8
Cumb 92 B5
Notts 77 D8
N Yorks 102 F1
W Yorks 88 D2
Holme Chapel . . . 87 B6
Holme Green 95 E8
Holme Hale 67 D8
Holme Lacy 49 F7
Holme Marsh 48 D5
Holme next the
Sea 80 C3
Holme-on-Spalding-
Moor 96 F4
Holme on the
Wolds 97 E5
Holme Pierrepont 77 F6
Holmer 49 E7
Holmer Green . . . 40 E2
Holme St
Cuthbert 107 E8
Holmes Chapel . . 74 C4
Holmesfield 76 B3
Holmeswood 86 C2
Holmewood 76 C4
Holme Wood 94 F4
Holmfirth 88 D2

Holmhead
Dumfries 113 F7
E Ayrs 113 B5
Holmisdale 148 D6
Holmpton 91 B7
Holmrook 98 E2
Holmsgarth 160 J6
Holmwrangle . . . 108 E5
Holne 6 C5
Holnest 12 D4
Holsworthy 8 D5
Holsworthy
Beacon 9 D5
Holt
Dorset 13 D8
Norf 81 D6
Wilts 24 C3
Worcs 50 C3
Wrex 73 D8
Holt End
Hants 26 F4
Worcs 51 C5
Holt Fleet 50 C3
Holt Heath 50 C3
Holton
Oxon 39 D6
Som 12 B4
Suff 57 B7
Holton cum
Beckering 90 F5
Holton Heath . . . 13 E7
Holton le Clay . . . 91 D6
Holton le Moor . . 90 E4
Holton St Mary . . 56 F4
Holt Park 95 E5
Holwell
Dorset 12 C5
Herts 54 F2
Leics 64 B4
Oxon 38 D2
Holwick 100 B4
Holworth 13 F5
Holybourne 26 E5
Holy Cross 50 B4
Holyhead
=Caergybi 82 C2
Holy Island 123 E7
Holymoorside . . . 76 C3
Holyport 27 B6
Holystone 117 D5
Holytown 119 C7
Holywell
Cambs 54 B4
Corn 4 D2
Dorset 12 D3
E Sus 18 F2
Northumb 111 B6
Holywell
=Treffynnon 73 B5
Holywell Green . . 87 C8
Holywell Lake . . . 11 B6
Holywell Row . . . 55 B8
Holywood 114 F2
Homer 61 D6
Homersfield 69 F5
Hom Green 36 B2
Homington 14 B2
Honeyborough . . 44 E4
Honeybourne . . . 51 E6
Honeychurch 9 D8
Honey Hill 30 C5
Honey Street 25 C6
Honey Tye 56 F3
Honiley 51 B7
Honing 69 B6
Honingham 68 C4
Honington
Lincs 78 E2
Suff 56 B3
Warks 51 E7
Honiton 11 D6
Honley 88 C2
Hood Green 88 D4
Hooe
E Sus 18 E3
Plym 6 D3
Hooe Common . . . 18 D3
Hoo Green 86 F5
Hook
E Yorks 89 B8
Hants 26 D5
London 28 C2
Pembs 44 D4
Wilts 37 F7
Hooke 12 E3
Hookgate 74 F4
Hook Green
Kent 18 B3
Kent 29 C7
Kent 29 E7
Hook Norton 51 F8
Hookway 10 E3
Hookwood 28 E3
Hoole 73 C8
Hooley 28 D3
Hoop 36 D2
Hoo St Werburgh 29 B8
Hooton 73 B7
Hooton Levitt . . . 89 E6
Hooton Pagnell . . 89 D5
Hooton Roberts . . 89 E5
Hope
Derbys 88 F2
Devon 6 F4
Highld 156 C7
Powys 60 D2
Shrops 60 D3
Staffs 75 D8
Hope =Yr Hôb . . . 73 D7
Hope Bagot 49 B7
Hope Bowdler . . . 60 E4
Hope End Green . . 42 B1
Hope Green 87 F7
Hopeman 152 B1
Hope Mansell . . . 36 C3
Hopesay 60 F3
Hope's Green 42 F3
Hope under
Dinmore 49 D7
Hopley's Green . . 48 D5
Hopperton 95 D7
Hopstone 61 E7
Hopton
Shrops 60 B3
Shrops 61 B5
Staffs 62 B3
Suff 56 B3

Hopton
Cangeford 60 F5
Hopton Castle . . . 49 B5
Hoptonheath 49 B5
Hopton on Sea . . 69 D8
Hopton Wafers . . 49 B8
Hopwas 63 D5
Hopwood
Gtr Man 87 D6
Worcs 50 B5
Horam 18 D2
Horbling 78 F4
Horbury 88 C3
Horcott 38 D1
Horden 111 E7
Horderley 60 F4
Hordle 14 E3
Hordley 73 F7
Horeb
Carms 33 B6
Carms 33 D6
Ceredig 46 E2
Horfield 23 B8
Horham 57 B6
Horkesley Heath . 43 B5
Horkstow 90 C3
Horley
Oxon 52 E2
Sur 28 E3
Hornblotton
Green 23 F7
Hornby
Lancs 93 C5
N Yorks 101 E7
N Yorks 102 D1
Horncastle 79 C5
Hornchurch 41 F8
Horncliffe 122 E5
Horndean
Borders 122 E4
Hants 15 C8
Horndon 6 B3
Horndon on the
Hill 42 F2
Horne 28 E4
Horniehaugh . . . 134 C4
Horning 69 C6
Horninghold 64 E5
Horninglow 63 B6
Horningsea 55 C5
Horningsham . . . 24 E3
Horningtoft 80 E5
Hornsby 108 D5
Horns Corner . . . 18 C4
Horns Cross
Devon 9 B5
E Sus 18 C5
Hornsea 97 E8
Hornsea Bridge . . 97 E8
Hornsey 41 F6
Hornton 51 E8
Horrabridge 6 C3
Horringer 56 C2
Horringford 15 F6
Horsebridge
Devon 6 B2
Hants 25 F8
Horse Bridge 75 D6
Horsebrook 62 C2
Horsehay 61 D6
Horseheath 55 E7
Horsehouse 101 F5
Horsell 27 D7
Horseman's
Green 73 E8
Horseway 66 F4
Horsey 69 B7
Horsford 68 C4
Horsforth 94 F5
Horsham
Worcs 50 D2
W Sus 28 F2
Horsham St Faith 68 C4
Horsington
Lincs 78 C4
Som 12 B5
Horsley
Derbys 76 E3
Glos 37 E5
Northumb 110 C3
Northumb 116 F4
Horsley Cross . . . 43 B7
Horsleycross
Street 43 B7
Horsleyhill 115 C8
Horsleyhope 110 E3
Horsley
Woodhouse 76 E3
Horsmonden 29 E7
Horspath 39 D5
Horstead 69 C5
Horsted Keynes . . 17 B7
Horton
Bucks 40 C2
Dorset 13 D8
Lancs 93 D8
Northants 53 D6
S Glos 36 F4
Shrops 60 B4
Som 11 C8
Staffs 75 D6
Swansea 33 F5
Wilts 25 C5
Windsor 27 B8
Horton-cum-
Studley 39 C5
Horton Green . . . 73 E8
Horton Heath . . . 15 C5
Horton in
Ribblesdale 93 B8
Horton Kirby 29 C6
Hortonlane 60 C4
Horwich 86 C4
Horwich End 87 F8
Horwood 9 B7
Hose 64 B4
Hoselaw 122 F4
Hoses 98 E4
Hosh 127 B7
Hosta 148 A2
Hoswick 160 L6
Hotham 96 F4
Hothfield 30 E3
Houbie 160 D8
Houdston 112 E1
Hough
Ches E 74 D4

Hough continued
Ches E....75 B5
Hougham....77 E8
Hough Green....86 F2
Hough-on-the-Hill....78 E2
Houghton
Cambs....54 B3
Cumb....108 D4
Hants....25 F8
Pembs....44 E4
W Sus....16 C4
Houghton Conquest....53 E8
Houghton Green
E Sus....19 C6
Warr....86 E4
Houghton-le-Side....101 B7
Houghton-le-Spring....111 E6
Houghton on the Hill....64 D3
Houghton Regis....40 B3
Houghton St Giles....80 D5
Houlland
Shetland....160 F7
Shetland....160 H5
Houlsyke....103 D6
Hound....15 D5
Hound Green....26 D5
Houndslow....122 E2
Houndwood....122 C4
Hounslow....39 B5
Hounslow Green....42 C2
Housay....160 F8
House of Daviot....151 G10
House of Glenmuick....140 E2
Housetter....160 E5
Houss....160 K5
Houston....118 C4
Houstry....158 G3
Houton....159 H4
Hove....17 D6
Hoveringham....77 E6
Hoveton....69 C6
Hovingham....96 B2
How....108 D5
Howbrook....88 E4
How Caple....49 F8
Howden
Borders....116 B2
E Yorks....89 B8
Howden-le-Wear....110 F4
Howe
Highld....158 D5
Norf....69 D5
N Yorks....101 F8
Howe Bridge....86 D4
Howe Green....42 D3
Howell....78 E4
How End....53 E8
Howe of Teucher....153 D7
Howe Street
Essex....42 C2
Essex....55 F7
Howey....48 D2
Howgate....120 D5
How Green....29 E5
Howick....117 C8
Howle
Durham....101 B5
Telford....61 B6
Howlett End....55 F6
Howley....11 D7
Hownam....116 C3
Hownam Mains....116 B3
Howpasley....115 D6
Howsham
N Lincs....90 D4
N Yorks....96 C3
Howslack....114 D3
Howtel....122 F4
Howton....35 B8
Howtown....99 C6
Howwood....118 C3
Hoxne....57 B5
Hoy....159 H3
Hoylake....85 F3
Hoyland....88 D4
Hoylandswaine....88 D3
Hubberholme....94 B2
Hubbert's Bridge....79 E5
Huby
N Yorks....95 C8
N Yorks....95 E6
Hucclecote....37 C5
Hucking....30 D2
Hucknall....76 E5
Huddersfield....88 C2
Huddington....50 D4
Hudswell....101 D6
Huggate....96 D4
Hugglescote....63 C8
Hughenden Valley....40 E1
Hughley....61 E5
Hugh Town....2 E4
Huish
Devon....9 C7
Wilts....25 C6
Huish Champflower....11 B5
Huish Episcopi....12 B2
Huisinis....154 F4
Hulcott....40 C1
Hulland....76 E2
Hulland Ward....76 E2
Hullavington....37 F5
Hullbridge....42 E4
Hulme....87 E6
Hulme End....75 D8
Hulme Walfield....74 C5
Hulverstone....14 F4
Hulver Street....69 F7
Humber....49 D7
Humber Bridge....90 B4
Humberston....91 D7
Humbie....121 C7
Humbleton
E Yorks....97 F8
Northumb....117 B5
Humby....78 F3

Hume....122 E3
Humshaugh....110 B2
Huna....158 C5
Huncoat....93 F7
Huncote....64 E2
Hundalee....116 C2
Hunderthwaite....100 B4
Hundleby....79 C6
Hundle Houses....79 D5
Hundleton....44 E4
Hundon....55 E8
Hundred Acres....15 C6
Hundred End....86 B2
Hundred House....48 D3
Hungarton....64 D3
Hungerford
Hants....14 C2
W Berks....25 C8
Hungerford Newtown....25 B8
Hungerton....65 B5
Hungladder....149 A8
Hunmanby....97 B6
Hunmanby Moor....97 B7
Hunningham....51 C8
Hunny Hill....15 F5
Hunsdon....41 C7
Hunsingore....95 D7
Hunslet....95 F6
Hunsonby....109 F5
Hunspow....158 C4
Hunstanton....80 C2
Hunstanworth....110 E2
Hunsterson....74 E3
Hunston
Suff....56 C3
W Sus....16 D2
Hunstrete....23 C8
Hunt End....50 C5
Hunter's Quay....145 F10
Hunthill Lodge....134 B4
Huntingdon....54 B3
Huntingfield....57 B7
Huntingford....24 F3
Huntington
E Loth....121 B7
Hereford....48 D4
Staffs....62 C3
York....96 D2
Huntingtower....128 B2
Huntley....36 C4
Huntly....152 E5
Huntlywood....122 E2
Hunton
Kent....29 E8
N Yorks....101 E6
Hunt's Corner....68 F3
Hunt's Cross....86 F2
Huntsham....10 B5
Huntspill....22 E5
Huntworth....22 F5
Hunwick....110 F4
Hunworth....81 D6
Hurdsfield....75 B6
Hurley
Warks....63 E6
Windsor....39 F8
Hurlford....118 F4
Hurliness....159 K3
Hurn....14 E2
Hurn's End....79 E7
Hursley....14 B5
Hurst
N Yorks....101 D5
Som....12 C2
Wokingham....27 B5
Hurstbourne Priors....26 E2
Hurstbourne Tarrant....25 D8
Hurst Green
E Sus....18 C4
Lancs....93 F6
Hurstpierpoint....17 C6
Hurst Wickham....17 C6
Hurstwood....93 F8
Hurtmore....27 E7
Hurworth Place....101 D7
Hury....100 C4
Husabost....148 C7
Husbands Bosworth....64 F3
Husborne Crawley....53 F7
Husthwaite....95 B8
Hutchwns....21 B7
Huthwaite....76 D4
Huttoft....79 B8
Hutton
Borders....122 D5
Cumb....99 B6
Essex....42 E2
E Yorks....97 D6
Lancs....86 B2
N Som....22 D5
Hutton Buscel....103 F7
Hutton Conyers....95 B6
Hutton Cranswick....97 D6
Hutton End....108 F4
Hutton Gate....102 C3
Hutton Henry....111 F7
Hutton-le-Hole....103 C5
Hutton Magna....101 C6
Hutton Roof
Cumb....93 B5
Cumb....108 F3
Hutton Rudby....102 D2
Hutton Sessay....95 B7
Hutton Village....67 C3
Hutton Wandesley....95 D8
Huxley....74 C2
Huxter
Shetland....160 G7
Shetland....160 H5
Huxton....122 C4
Huyton....86 E2
Hwlffordd =Haverfordwest....44 D4
Hycemoor....98 F2
Hyde
Glos....37 D5
Gtr Man....87 E7
Hants....14 C2
Hyde Heath....40 D2
Hyde Park....89 D6

Hydestile....27 E7
Hylton Castle....111 D6
Hyndford Bridge....120 E2
Hynish....146 H2
Hyssington....60 E3
Hythe
Hants....14 D5
Kent....19 B8
Hythe End....27 B8
Hythie....153 C10

I
Ibberton....13 D5
Ible....76 D2
Ibsley....14 D2
Ibstock....63 C8
Ibstone....39 E7
Ibthorpe....25 D8
Ibworth....26 D3
Ichrachan....125 B6
Ickburgh....67 E8
Ickenham....40 F3
Ickford....39 D6
Ickham....31 D6
Ickleford....54 F2
Icklesham....19 D5
Ickleton....55 E5
Icklingham....55 B8
Ickwell Green....54 E2
Icomb....38 B2
Idbury....38 C2
Ide....10 E3
Ideford....7 B6
Ide Hill....29 D5
Iden....19 C6
Iden Green
Kent....18 B4
Kent....18 B5
Idle....94 F4
Idlicote....51 E7
Idmiston....25 F6
Idole....33 C5
Idridgehay....76 E2
Idrigill....149 B8
Idstone....38 F2
Idvies....135 E5
Iffley....39 D5
Ifield....28 F3
Ifold....27 F8
Iford....17 D8
Ifton Heath....73 F7
Ightfield....74 F2
Ightham....29 D6
Iken....57 D8
Ilam....75 D8
Ilchester....12 B3
Ilderton....117 B6
Ilford....41 F7
Ilfracombe....20 E4
Ilkeston....76 E4
Ilketshall St Andrew....69 F6
Ilketshall St Lawrence....69 F6
Ilketshall St Margaret....69 F6
Ilkley....94 E4
Illey....62 F3
Illingworth....87 B8
Illogan....3 B5
Ilmer....39 D7
Ilmington....51 E7
Ilminster....11 C8
Ilsington....7 B5
Ilston....33 E6
Ilton
N Yorks....94 B4
Som....11 C8
Imachar....143 D9
Imeraval....142 D4
Immingham....91 C5
Impington....54 C5
Ince....73 B8
Ince Blundell....85 D4
Ince in Makerfield....86 D3
Inchbare....135 C6
Inchberry....152 C3
Inchbraoch....135 D7
Incheril....150 E3
Inchgrundle....134 B4
Inchina....150 B2
Inchinnan....118 C4
Inchkinloch....157 E8
Inchlaggan....136 D4
Inchlumpie....151 D8
Inchmore....150 G6
Inchnacardoch Hotel....137 C6
Inchnadamph....156 G5
Inch of Arnhall....135 B6
Inchree....130 C4
Inchture....128 B4
Inchyra....128 B3
Indian Queens....4 D4
Inerval....142 D4
Ingatestone....42 E2
Ingbirchworth....88 D3
Ingestre....62 B3
Ingham
Lincs....90 F3
Norf....69 B6
Suff....56 B2
Ingham Corner....69 B6
Ingleborough....66 C4
Ingleby
Derbys....63 B7
Lincs....77 B8
Ingleby Arncliffe....102 D2
Ingleby Barwick....102 C2
Ingleby Greenhow....102 D3
Inglemire....97 F6
Inglesbatch....24 C2
Inglesham....38 E2
Ingleton
Durham....101 B6
N Yorks....93 B6
Inglewhite....92 E5
Ingliston....120 B4
Ingoe....110 B3
Ingol....92 F5
Ingoldisthorpe....80 D2

Ingoldmells....79 C8
Ingoldsby....78 F3
Ingon....51 D7
Ingram....117 C6
Ingrow....94 F3
Ings....99 E6
Ingst....36 F2
Inham's End....66 E2
Inkberrow....50 D5
Inkpen....25 C8
Inkstack....158 C4
Inn....99 D6
Innellan....145 F10
Innerleithen....121 F6
Innerleven....129 D5
Innermessan....104 C4
Innerwick
E Loth....122 B3
Perth....132 E2
Innis Chonain....125 C7
Insch....140 B5
Insh....138 D4
Inshore....156 C6
Inskip....92 F4
Instoneville....89 C6
Instow....20 F3
Intake....89 D6
Inver
Aberds....139 E8
Highld....151 C11
Perth....133 E7
Inverailort....147 C10
Inveraldie....134 F4
Inveralligin....149 C13
Inverallochy....153 B10
Inveran....151 B8
Inveraray....125 E6
Inverarish....149 E10
Inverarity....134 E4
Inverarnan....126 C2
Inverasdale....155 J13
Inverbeg....126 E2
Inverbervie....135 B8
Inverboyndie....153 B6
Inverbroom....150 C4
Invercassley....156 J7
Invercauld House....139 E7
Inverchaolain....145 F9
Invercharnan....131 E5
Inverchoran....150 F5
Invercreran....130 E4
Inverdruie....138 C5
Inverebrie....153 E9
Invereck....145 E10
Inverernan House....140 C2
Invereshie House....138 D4
Inveresk....121 B6
Inverey....139 F6
Inverfarigaig....137 B8
Invergarry....137 D6
Invergelder....139 E8
Invergeldie....127 B6
Invergordon....151 E10
Invergowrie....134 F3
Inverguseran....149 H12
Inverhadden....132 D3
Inverharroch....152 E3
Inverherive....126 B2
Inverie....147 B10
Inverinan....125 C5
Inverinate....136 B2
Inverkeilor....135 E6
Inverkeithing....128 F3
Inverkeithny....153 D6
Inverkip....118 B2
Inverkirkaig....156 H3
Inverlael....150 C4
Inverlochlarig....126 C3
Inverlochy
Argyll....125 C7
Highld....131 B5
Inverlussa....144 E5
Inver Mallie....136 F4
Invermark Lodge....140 F3
Invermoidart....147 D9
Invermoriston....137 C7
Invernaver....157 C10
Inverneill....145 E7
Inverness....151 G9
Invernettie....153 D11
Invernoaden....125 F7
Inveroran Hotel....131 E6
Inverpolly Lodge....156 H3
Inverquharity....134 D4
Inverquhomery....153 D10
Inverroy....137 F5
Inversanda....130 D3
Invershiel....136 C2
Invershin....151 B8
Inversnaid Hotel....126 D2
Inverugie....153 D11
Inveruglas....126 D2
Inveruglass....138 D4
Inverurie....141 B6
Invervar....132 E3
Inverythan....153 D7
Inwardleigh....9 E7
Inworth....42 C4
Iochdar....148 D2
Iping....16 B2
Ipplepen....7 C6
Ipsden....39 F6
Ipsley....51 C5
Ipstones....75 D7
Ipswich....57 E5
Irby....85 F3
Irby in the Marsh....79 C7
Irby upon Humber....91 D5
Irchester....53 C7
Ireby
Cumb....108 F2
Lancs....93 B6
Ireland
Orkney....159 H4
Shetland....160 L5
Ireland's Cross....74 E4
Ireleth....92 B2
Ireshopeburn....109 F8
Irlam....86 E5
Irnham....65 B7
Iron Acton....36 F3

Ironbridge....61 D6
Iron Cross....51 D5
Irongray....107 B6
Ironmacannie....106 B3
Ironside....153 C8
Ironville....76 D4
Irstead....69 B6
Irthington....108 C4
Irthlingborough....53 B7
Irton....103 F8
Irvine....118 F3
Isauld....157 C12
Isbister
Orkney....159 F3
Orkney....159 G4
Shetland....160 D5
Shetland....160 G7
Isfield....17 C8
Isham....53 B6
Isle Abbotts....11 B8
Isle Brewers....11 B8
Isleham....55 B7
Isle of Whithorn....105 F8
Isleornsay....149 G12
Islesburgh....160 G5
Islesteps....107 B6
Isleworth....28 B2
Isley Walton....63 B8
Islibhig....154 E4
Islington....41 F6
Islip
Northants....53 B7
Oxon....39 C5
Istead Rise....29 C7
Isycoed....73 D8
Itchen....14 C5
Itchen Abbas....26 F3
Itchen Stoke....26 F3
Itchingfield....16 B5
Itchington....36 F3
Itteringham....81 D7
Itton....9 E8
Itton Common....36 E1
Ivegill....108 E4
Iver....40 F3
Iver Heath....40 F3
Iveston....110 D4
Ivinghoe....40 C2
Ivinghoe Aston....40 C2
Ivington....49 D6
Ivington Green....49 D6
Ivybridge....6 D4
Ivy Chimneys....41 D7
Ivychurch....19 C7
Ivy Cross....13 B6
Ivy Hatch....29 D6
Iwade....30 C3
Iwerne Courtney or Shroton....13 C6
Iwerne Minster....13 C6
Ixworth....56 B3
Ixworth Thorpe....56 B3

J
Jack Hill....94 D5
Jack in the Green....10 E5
Jacksdale....76 D4
Jackstown....153 E7
Jacobstow....8 D3
Jacobstowe....9 D7
Jameston....32 E1
Jamestown
Dumfries....115 C6
Highld....150 F7
W Dunb....126 F2
Jarrow....111 C6
Jarvis Brook....18 C2
Jasper's Green....42 B3
Java....124 B3
Jawcraig....119 B8
Jaywick....43 C7
Jealott's Hill....27 B6
Jedburgh....116 B2
Jeffreyston....32 D1
Jellyhill....119 B6
Jemimaville....151 E10
Jersey Farm....40 D4
Jesmond....111 C5
Jevington....18 E2
Jockey End....40 C3
Johnby....108 F4
John o'Groats....158 C5
John's Cross....18 C4
Johnshaven....135 C7
Johnston
E Renfs....118 C4
Pembs....44 D4
Johnstone....118 C4
Johnstonebridge....114 E3
Johnstown
Carms....33 C5
Wrex....73 E7
Joppa
Edin....121 B6
S Ayrs....112 C4
Jordans....40 E2
Jordanthorpe....88 F4
Jump....88 D4
Jumpers Green....14 E2
Juniper Green....120 C4
Jurby East....84 C3
Jurby West....84 C3

K
Kaber....100 C2
Kaimend....120 E2
Kaimes....121 C5
Kalemouth....116 B3
Kames
Argyll....124 D4
Argyll....145 F8
E Ayrs....113 B6
Kea....3 B7
Keadby....90 C2
Keal Cotes....79 C6
Kearsley....87 D5
Kearstwick....99 F8
Kearton....100 E4
Kearvaig....156 B5
Keasden....93 C7
Keckwick....86 F3
Keddington....91 F7
Kedington....55 E8
Kedleston....76 E3

Keelby....91 C5
Keele....74 E5
Keeley Green....53 E8
Keeston....44 D4
Keevil....24 D4
Kegworth....63 B8
Kehelland....2 B5
Keig....140 C5
Keighley....94 E3
Keil....130 D3
Keilarsbrae....127 E7
Keilhill....153 C7
Keillmore....144 E5
Keillor....134 E2
Keillour....127 B8
Keills....142 B5
Keils....144 G4
Keinton Mandeville....23 F7
Keir Mill....113 E8
Keisby....65 B7
Keiss....158 D5
Keith....152 C4
Keith Inch....153 D11
Keithock....135 C6
Kelbrook....94 E2
Kelby....78 E3
Keld
Cumb....99 C7
N Yorks....100 D3
Keldholme....103 F5
Kelfield
N Lincs....90 D2
N Yorks....95 F8
Kelham....77 D7
Kellan....147 G8
Kellas
Angus....134 F4
Moray....152 C1
Kellaton....7 F6
Kelleth....100 D1
Kelleythorpe....97 D5
Kelling....81 C6
Kellingley....89 B6
Kellington....89 B6
Kelloe....111 F6
Kelloholm....113 C7
Kelly....9 F5
Kelly Bray....5 B8
Kelmarsh....52 B5
Kelmscot....38 E2
Kelsale....57 C7
Kelsall....74 C2
Kelsall Hill....74 C2
Kelshall....54 F4
Kelsick....107 D8
Kelso....122 F3
Kelstedge....76 C3
Kelstern....91 E6
Kelsterton....73 B6
Kelton....107 B6
Kelty....128 E3
Kelvedon....42 C4
Kelvedon Hatch....42 E1
Kelvin....119 D6
Kelvinside....119 C5
Kelynack....2 C2
Kemback....129 C6
Kemberton....61 D7
Kemble....37 E6
Kemerton....50 F4
Kemeys Commander....35 D7
Kemnay....141 C6
Kempley....36 B3
Kempsey....50 E3
Kempsford....38 E1
Kemps Green....51 B6
Kempshott....26 D4
Kempston....53 E8
Kempston Hardwick....53 E8
Kempton....60 F3
Kemp Town....17 D7
Kemsing....29 D6
Kemsley....30 C3
Kenardington....19 B6
Kenchester....49 E6
Kencot....38 D2
Kendal....99 E7
Kendoon....113 F6
Kendray....88 D4
Kenfig....34 F2
Kenfig Hill....34 F2
Kenilworth....51 B7
Kenknock....132 F1
Kenley
London....28 D4
Shrops....61 D5
Kenmore
Highld....149 C12
Perth....132 E4
Kenn
Devon....10 F4
N Som....23 C6
Kennacley....154 H6
Kennacraig....145 G7
Kennerleigh....10 D3
Kennet....127 E8
Kennethmont....140 B4
Kennett....55 C7
Kennford....10 F4
Kenninghall....68 F3
Kenninghall Heath....68 F3
Kennington
Kent....30 E4
Oxon....39 D5
Kennoway....129 D5
Kenny Hill....55 B7
Kennythorpe....96 C3
Kenovay....146 G2
Kensaleyre....149 C9
Kensington....28 B3
Kensworth....40 C3
Kensworth Common....40 C3
Kentallen....130 D4
Kentchurch....35 B8
Kentford....55 C8
Kentisbeare....11 D5
Kentisbury....20 E5
Kentisbury Ford....20 E5
Kentmere....99 D6
Kenton
Devon....10 F4
Suff....57 C5

Kenton continued
T&W....110 C5
Kenton Bankfoot....110 C5
Kentra....147 E9
Kents Bank....92 B3
Kent's Green....36 B4
Kent's Oak....14 B4
Kent Street
E Sus....18 D4
Kent....29 D7
W Sus....17 B6
Kenwick....73 F8
Kenwyn....3 B7
Keoldale....156 C6
Keppanach....130 C4
Keppoch....136 B2
Keprigan....143 G7
Kepwick....102 E2
Kerchesters....122 F3
Keresley....63 F7
Kernborough....7 E5
Kerne Bridge....36 C2
Kerris....2 D3
Kerry....59 F8
Kerrycroy....145 G10
Kerry's Gate....49 F5
Kerrysdale....149 A13
Kersall....77 C7
Kersey....56 E4
Kershopefoot....115 F7
Kersoe....50 F4
Kerswell....11 D5
Kerswell Green....50 E3
Kesgrave....57 E6
Kessingland....69 F8
Kessingland Beach....69 F8
Kestle....3 B8
Kestle Mill....4 D3
Keston....28 C5
Keswick
Cumb....98 B4
Norf....68 D5
Norf....81 D9
Ketley....61 C6
Ketley Bank....61 C6
Ketsby....79 B6
Kettering....53 B6
Ketteringham....68 D4
Kettins....134 F2
Kettlebaston....56 D3
Kettlebridge....128 D5
Kettleburgh....57 C6
Kettlehill....128 D5
Kettleholm....107 B8
Kettleness....103 C6
Kettleshume....75 B6
Kettlesing Bottom....94 D5
Kettlesing Head....94 D5
Kettlestone....81 D5
Kettlethorpe....77 B8
Kettletoft....159 E7
Kettlewell....94 B2
Ketton....65 D6
Kew....28 B2
Kew Bridge....28 B2
Kewstoke....22 C5
Kexbrough....88 D4
Kexby
Lincs....90 F2
York....96 D3
Key Green....75 C5
Keyham....64 D3
Keyhaven....14 E4
Keyingham....91 B6
Keymer....17 C7
Keynsham....23 C8
Keysoe....53 C8
Keysoe Row....53 C8
Keyston....53 B8
Keyworth....77 F6
Kibblesworth....110 D5
Kibworth Beauchamp....64 E3
Kibworth Harcourt....64 E3
Kidbrooke....28 B5
Kiddemore Green....62 D2
Kidderminster....50 B3
Kiddington....38 B4
Kidlington....38 C4
Kidmore End....26 B4
Kidsgrove....74 D5
Kidstones....100 F4
Kidwelly =Cydweli....33 D5
Kiel Crofts....124 B5
Kielder....116 E2
Kierfield Ho....159 G3
Kilbagie....127 F8
Kilbarchan....118 C4
Kilbeg....149 H11
Kilberry....144 G6
Kilbirnie....118 D3
Kilbride
Argyll....124 C4
Argyll....124 C5
Highld....149 F10
Kilburn
Angus....134 C3
Derbys....76 E3
London....41 F5
N Yorks....95 B8
Kilby....64 E3
Kilchamaig....145 G7
Kilchattan....144 D2
Kilchattan Bay....145 H10
Kilchenzie....143 F7
Kilcheran....124 B4
Kilchiaran....142 B3
Kilchoan
Argyll....124 D3
Highld....146 E7
Kilchoman....142 B3
Kilchrenan....125 C6
Kilconquhar....129 D6
Kilcot....36 B3
Kilcoy....151 F8
Kilcreggan....145 E11
Kildale....102 D4
Kildalloig....143 G8
Kildary....151 D10
Kildermorie Lodge....151 D8
Kildonan....143 F11

Kildonan Lodge....157 G12
Kildonnan....146 C7
Kildrummy....140 C3
Kildwick....94 E3
Kilfinan....145 F8
Kilfinnan....137 E5
Kilgetty....32 D2
Kilgwrrwg Common....36 E1
Kilham
E Yorks....97 C6
Northumb....122 F4
Kilkenneth....146 G2
Kilkenzie....143 F7
Kilkerran....143 G8
Kilkhampton....9 E6
Killamarsh....89 F5
Killay....33 E7
Killbeg....147 G9
Killean....143 D7
Killearn....126 F4
Killen....151 F9
Killerby....101 C6
Killichonan....132 D2
Killiechonate....136 F5
Killiechronan....147 G8
Killiecrankie....133 C6
Killiemor....146 H7
Killilan....150 H2
Killimster....158 E5
Killin....132 F2
Killinallan....142 A4
Killinghall....95 D5
Killington....99 F8
Killingworth....111 B5
Killin Lodge....137 D8
Killmahumaig....144 D6
Killochyett....121 E7
Killocraw....143 E7
Killundine....147 G8
Kilmacolm....118 C3
Kilmaha....124 E5
Kilmahog....126 D5
Kilmalieu....130 D2
Kilmaluag....149 A9
Kilmany....129 B5
Kilmarie....149 G10
Kilmarnock....118 F4
Kilmaron Castle....129 C5
Kilmartin....124 E4
Kilmaurs....118 E4
Kilmelford....124 D4
Kilmeny....142 B4
Kilmersdon....23 D8
Kilmeston....15 B6
Kilmichael....143 F7
Kilmichael Glassary....145 D7
Kilmichael of Inverlussa....144 E6
Kilmington
Devon....11 E7
Wilts....24 F2
Kilmonivaig....136 F4
Kilmorack....150 G7
Kilmore
Argyll....124 C4
Highld....149 H11
Kilmory
Argyll....144 F6
Highld....147 D8
Highld....149 H8
N Ayrs....143 F10
Kilmuir
Highld....148 D7
Highld....149 A8
Highld....151 D10
Highld....151 G9
Kilmun
Argyll....124 D5
Argyll....145 E10
Kilncadzow....119 E8
Kilndown....18 B4
Kilnhurst....89 E5
Kilninian....146 G6
Kilninver....124 C4
Kiln Pit Hill....110 D3
Kilnsea....91 C8
Kilnsey....94 C2
Kilnwick....97 E5
Kilnwick Percy....96 D4
Kiloran....144 D2
Kilpatrick....143 F10
Kilpeck....49 F6
Kilphedir....157 H12
Kilpin....89 B8
Kilpin Pike....89 B8
Kilrenny....129 D7
Kilsby....52 B3
Kilspindie....128 B3
Kilsyth....119 B7
Kiltarlity....151 G8
Kilton
Notts....77 B5
Som....22 E3
Kilton Thorpe....102 C4
Kilvaxter....149 B8
Kilve....22 E3
Kilvington....77 E7
Kilwinning....118 E3
Kimberley
Norf....68 D3
Notts....76 E5
Kimberworth....88 E5
Kimblesworth....111 E5
Kimble Wick....39 D8
Kimbolton
Cambs....53 C8
Hereford....49 C7
Kimcote....64 F2
Kimmeridge....13 G7
Kimmerston....123 F5
Kimpton
Hants....25 E7
Herts....40 C4
Kinbrace....157 F11
Kinbuck....127 D6
Kincaple....129 C6
Kincardine
Fife....127 F8
Highld....151 C9
Kincardine Bridge....127 F8
Kincardine O'Neil....140 E4

Kinclaven....134 F1
Kincorth....141 D8
Kincorth House....151 E13
Kincraig....138 D4
Kincraigie....133 E6
Kindallachan....133 E6
Kineton
Glos....37 B7
Warks....51 D8
Kinfauns....128 B3
Kingairloch....130 D2
Kingarth....145 H9
Kingcoed....35 D8
King Edward....153 C7
Kingerby....90 E4
Kingham....38 B2
Kingholm Quay....107 B6
Kinghorn....128 F4
Kingie....136 D4
Kinglassie....128 E4
Kingoodie....128 B5
King's Acre....49 E6
Kingsand....6 D2
Kingsbarns....129 C7
Kingsbridge
Devon....6 E5
Som....21 F8
King's Bromley....62 C5
Kingsburgh....149 C8
Kingsbury
London....41 F5
Warks....63 E6
Kingsbury Episcopi....12 B2
King's Caple....36 B2
Kingsclere....26 D3
King's Cliffe....65 E7
Kingscote....37 E5
Kingscott....9 C7
King's Coughton....51 D5
Kingscross....143 F11
Kingsdon....12 B3
Kingsdown....31 E7
Kingseat....128 E3
Kingsey....39 D7
Kingsfold....28 F2
Kingsford
E Ayrs....118 E4
Worcs....62 F2
Kingsforth....90 C4
Kingsgate....31 B7
Kingsheanton....20 F4
King's Heath....62 F4
Kings Hedges....55 C5
King's Hill....29 D7
Kingshouse Hotel....131 D6
Kingside Hill....107 D8
Kingskerswell....7 C6
Kingskettle....128 D5
Kingsland
Anglesey....82 C2
Hereford....49 C6
Kings Langley....40 D3
Kingsley
Ches W....74 B2
Hants....27 F5
Staffs....75 E7
Kingsley Green....27 F6
Kingsley Holt....75 E7
Kingsley Park....53 C5
King's Lynn....67 B6
King's Meaburn....99 B8
Kingsmuir
Angus....134 E4
Fife....129 D7
Kings Muir....121 F5
King's Newnham....52 B2
King's Newton....63 B7
Kingsnorth....19 B7
King's Norton
Leics....64 D3
W Mid....51 B5
King's Nympton....9 D8
King's Pyon....49 D6
King's Ripton....54 B3
King's Somborne....25 F8
King's Stag....12 C5
King's Stanley....37 D5
King's Sutton....52 F2
Kingstanding....62 E4
Kingsteignton....7 B6
King Sterndale....75 B7
King's Thorn....49 F7
Kingsthorpe....53 C5
Kingston
Cambs....54 D4
Devon....6 E4
Dorset....13 D5
Dorset....13 G7
Hants....14 D2
IoW....15 F5
Kent....31 D5
Moray....152 B3
Kingston Bagpuize....38 E4
Kingston Blount....39 E7
Kingston by Sea....17 D6
Kingston Deverill....24 F2
Kingstone
Hereford....49 F6
Som....11 C8
Staffs....62 B4
Kingston Gorse....16 D4
Kingston Lisle....38 F3
Kingston Maurward....12 E5
Kingston near Lewes....17 D7
Kingston on Soar....64 B2
Kingston Russell....12 E3
Kingston St Mary....11 B7
Kingston Seymour....23 C6
Kingston upon Hull....90 B4
Kingston upon Thames....28 C2
Kingston Vale....28 B3
Kingstown....108 D3
King's Walden....40 B4
Kingswear....7 D6

Kingswells 141 D7
Kingswinford 62 F2
Kingswood
  Bucks 39 C6
  Glos 36 E4
  Hereford. 48 D4
  Kent 30 D2
  Powys 60 D2
  S Glos 23 B8
  Sur 28 D3
  Warks 51 B6
Kings Worthy 26 F2
Kingthorpe 78 B4
Kington
  Hereford. 48 D4
  Worcs 50 D4
Kington Langley 24 B4
Kington Magna 13 B5
Kington St
  Michael. 24 B4
Kingussie 138 D3
Kingweston 23 F7
Kininvie House 152 D3
Kinkell Bridge 127 C8
Kinknockie 153 D10
Kinlet 61 F7
Kinloch
  Fife 128 C4
  Highld 146 B6
  Highld 149 G11
  Highld 156 F6
  Perth 133 E8
  Perth 134 E2
Kinlochan 130 C2
Kinlochard 126 D3
Kinlochbeoraid 147 C11
Kinlochbervie 156 D5
Kinlocheil 130 B3
Kinlochewe 150 E3
Kinloch Hourn 136 D2
Kinloch Laggan . . . 137 F8
Kinlochleven 131 C5
Kinloch Lodge 157 D8
Kinlochmoidart
  . . . . 147 D10
Kinlochmorar 147 B11
Kinlochmore 131 C5
Kinloch
  Rannoch 132 D3
Kinlochspelve 124 C2
Kinloid 147 C9
Kinloss 151 E13
Kinmel Bay 72 A3
Kinmuck 141 C7
Kinmundy 141 C7
Kinnadie 153 D9
Kinnaird 128 B4
Kinnaird Castle . 135 D6
Kinneff 135 B8
Kinnelhead 114 D3
Kinnell 135 D6
Kinnerley 60 B3
Kinnersley
  Hereford. 48 E5
  Worcs 50 E4
Kinnerton 48 C4
Kinnesswood 128 D3
Kinninvie 101 B5
Kinnordy 134 D3
Kinoulton 77 F6
Kinross 128 D3
Kinrossie 134 F1
Kinsbourne
  Green 40 C4
Kinsey Heath 74 E3
Kinsham
  Hereford. 49 C5
  Worcs 50 F4
Kinsley 88 C5
Kinson 13 E8
Kintbury 25 C8
Kintessack 151 E12
Kintillo 128 C3
Kintocher 140 D4
Kinton
  Hereford. 49 B6
  Shrops 60 C3
Kintore 141 C6
Kintour 142 C5
Kintra
  Argyll 142 D4
  Argyll 146 A6
Kintraw 124 E4
Kinuachdrachd . 124 F3
Kinveachy 138 C5
Kinver 62 F2
Kippax 95 F7
Kippen 127 E5
Kippford or
  Scaur 106 D5
Kirbister
  Orkney 159 F7
  Orkney 159 H4
Kirbuster 159 F3
Kirby Bedon 69 D5
Kirby Bellars 64 C4
Kirby Cane 69 E6
Kirby Cross 43 B8
Kirby Grindalythe 96 C5
Kirby Hill
  N Yorks 95 C6
  N Yorks 101 D6
Kirby Knowle 102 F2
Kirby-le-Soken 43 B8
Kirby Misperton . . . 96 B3
Kirby Muxloe 64 D2
Kirby Row 69 E6
Kirby Sigston 102 E2
Kirby Underdale . . . 96 D4
Kirby Wiske 102 F1
Kirdford 16 B4
Kirk 158 E4
Kirkabister 160 K6
Kirkandrews 106 E3
Kirkandrews upon
  Eden 108 D3
Kirkbampton 108 D3
Kirkbean 107 D6
Kirk Bramwith 89 C7
Kirkbride 108 D2
Kirkbuddo 135 E5
Kirkburn
  Borders 121 F5
  E Yorks 97 D5
Kirkburton 88 C2

Kirkby
  Lincs 90 E4
  Mers 86 E2
  N Yorks 102 D3
Kirkby Fleetham 101 E7
Kirkby Green 78 D3
Kirkby-in-
  Ashfield 76 D5
Kirkby-in-
  Furness 98 F4
Kirkby la Thorpe . . . 78 E3
Kirkby Lonsdale . . . 93 B6
Kirkby Malham 93 C8
Kirkby Mallory 63 D8
Kirkby Malzeard . . . 94 B5
Kirkby Mills 103 F5
Kirkbymoorside 102 F4
Kirkby on Bain 78 C5
Kirkby Overflow . . . 95 E6
Kirkby Stephen 100 D2
Kirkby Thore 99 B8
Kirkby
  Underwood 65 B7
Kirkby Wharfe 95 E8
Kirkcaldy 128 E4
Kirkcambeck 108 C5
Kirkcolm 104 C4
Kirkconnel 113 C7
Kirkconnell 107 C6
Kirkcowan 105 C7
Kirkcudbright 106 D3
Kirkdale 85 E4
Kirk Deighton . 95 D6
Kirk Ella 90 B4
Kirkfieldbank 119 E8
Kirkgunzeon 107 C5
Kirk Hallam 76 E4
Kirkham
  Lancs 92 F4
  N Yorks 96 C3
Kirkhamgate 88 B3
Kirk Hammerton . 95 D7
Kirkharle 117 F6
Kirkheaton
  Northumb 110 B3
  W Yorks 88 C2
Kirkhill
  Angus 135 C6
  Highld 151 G8
  Midloth 120 C5
  Moray 152 E2
Kirkhope 115 B6
Kirkhouse 121 F6
Kirkiboll 157 D8
Kirkibost 149 G10
Kirkinch 134 E3
Kirkinner 105 D8
Kirkintilloch 119 B6
Kirk Ireton 76 D2
Kirkland
  Cumb 98 C2
  Cumb 109 F6
  Dumfries 113 C7
  Dumfries 113 E8
Kirk Langley 76 F2
Kirkleatham 102 B3
Kirklevington 102 D2
Kirkley 69 E8
Kirklington
  Notts 77 D6
  N Yorks 101 F8
Kirklinton 108 C4
Kirkliston 120 B4
Kirkmaiden 104 F5
Kirk
  Merrington 111 F5
Kirkmichael
  Perth 133 D7
  S Ayrs 112 D3
Kirk Michael 84 C3
Kirkmuirhill 119 E7
Kirknewton
  Northumb 122 F5
  W Loth. 120 C4
Kirkney 152 E5
Kirk of Shotts 119 C8
Kirkoswald
  Cumb 109 E5
  S Ayrs 112 D2
Kirkpatrick
  Durham 106 B4
Kirkpatrick-
  Fleming 108 B2
Kirk Sandall 89 D7
Kirksanton 98 F3
Kirk Smeaton 89 C6
Kirkstall 95 F5
Kirkstead 78 C4
Kirkstile 152 E5
Kirkstyle 158 C5
Kirkton
  Aberds 140 B5
  Aberds 153 D6
  Angus 134 E4
  Angus 134 F4
  Borders 115 C8
  Dumfries 114 F2
  Fife 129 B5
  Highld 149 F13
  Highld 150 G2
  Highld 151 B10
  Highld 151 F10
  Perth 127 C8
  S Lanark 114 B2
  Stirling 126 D4
Kirktonhill 121 D7
Kirkton Manor 120 F5
Kirkton of
  Airlie 134 D3
Kirkton of
  Auchterhouse . . . 134 F3
Kirkton of
  Auchterless 153 D7
Kirkton of
  Barevan 151 G11
Kirkton of
  Bourtie 141 B7
Kirkton of
  Collace 134 F1
Kirkton of Craig 135 D7
Kirkton of
  Culsalmond 153 E6
Kirkton of
  Durris 141 E6
Kirkton of
  Glenbuchat 140 C2
Kirkton of
  Glenisla 134 C1

Kirkton of
  Kingoldrum 134 D3
Kirkton of Largo 129 D6
Kirkton of
  Lethendy. 133 E8
Kirkton of Logie
  Buchan 141 B8
Kirkton of
  Maryculter 141 E7
Kirkton of
  Menmuir 135 C5
Kirkton of
  Monikie 135 F5
Kirkton of Oyne . 141 B5
Kirkton of
  Rayne 153 F6
Kirkton of
  Skene 141 D7
Kirkton of
  Tough 140 C5
Kirktown 153 C10
Kirktown of
  Alvah 153 B6
Kirktown of
  Deskford 152 B5
Kirktown of
  Fetteresso 141 F7
Kirktown of
  Mortlach 152 E3
Kirktown of
  Slains 141 B9
Kirkurd 120 E4
Kirkwall 159 G5
Kirkwhelpington 117 F5
Kirk Yetholm 116 B4
Kirmington 90 C5
Kirmond le Mire . . . 91 E5
Kirn 145 F10
Kirriemuir 134 D3
Kirstead Green 69 E5
Kirtlebridge 108 B2
Kirtleton 115 F5
Kirtling 55 D7
Kirtling Green 55 D7
Kirtlington 38 C4
Kirtomy 157 C10
Kirton
  Lincs 79 F6
  Notts 77 C6
  Suff 57 F6
Kirton End 79 E5
Kirton Holme 79 E5
Kirton in Lindsey . 90 E3
Kislingbury 52 D4
Kites Hardwick 52 C2
Kittisford 11 B5
Kittle 33 F6
Kitt's Green 63 F5
Kitt's Moss 87 F6
Kittybrewster 141 D8
Kitwood 26 F4
Kivernoll 49 F6
Kiveton Park 89 F5
Knaith 90 F2
Knaith Park 90 F2
Knap Corner 13 B6
Knaphill 27 D7
Knapp
  Perth 134 F2
  Som 11 B8
Knapthorpe 77 D7
Knapton
  Norf 81 D9
  York 95 D8
Knapton Green 49 D6
Knapwell 54 C4
Knaresborough 95 D6
Knarsdale 109 D6
Knauchland 152 C5
Knaven 153 D8
Knayton 102 F2
Knebworth 41 B5
Knedlington 89 B8
Kneesall 77 C7
Kneesworth 54 E4
Kneeton 77 E7
Knelston 33 F5
Knenhall 75 F6
Knettishall 68 F2
Knightacott 21 F5
Knightcote 51 D8
Knightley Dale 62 B2
Knighton
  Devon 6 E3
  Leicester 64 D2
  Staffs 61 B7
  Staffs 74 F4
Knighton
  =Tref-y-Clawdd . . 48 B4
Knightswood 118 C5
Knightwick 50 D2
Knill 48 C4
Knipton 77 F8
Knitsley 110 E4
Kniveton 76 D2
Knock
  Argyll 147 H8
  Cumb 100 B1
  Moray 152 C5
Knockally 158 H3
Knockan 156 H5
Knockandhu 139 B8
Knockando 152 D1
Knockando
  House. 152 D2
Knockbain 151 F9
Knockbreck 148 B7
Knockbrex 106 E2
Knockdee 158 D3
Knockdolian 104 A5
Knockenkelly 143 F11
Knockentiber 118 F3
Knockespock
  House. 140 B4
Knockfarrel 151 F8
Knockglass 104 D4
Knockholt 29 D5
Knockholt Pound 29 D5
Knockin 60 B3
Knockinlaw 118 F4
Knocklearn 106 B4
Knocknaha 143 G7
Knocknain 104 C3
Knockrome 144 F5
Knocksharry 84 D2
Knodishall 57 C8
Knolls Green 74 B5

Knolton 73 F7
Knolton Bryn 73 F7
Knook 24 E4
Knossington 64 D5
Knott End-on-
  Sea 92 E3
Knotting 53 C8
Knotting Green 53 C8
Knottingley 89 B6
Knotts
  Cumb 99 B6
  Lancs 93 D7
Knotty Ash 86 E2
Knotty Green 40 E2
Knowbury 49 B7
Knowe 105 B7
Knowehead 113 E6
Knowesgate 117 F5
Knowes of
  Elrick 152 C6
Knoweton 119 D7
Knowhead 153 C9
Knowle
  Bristol 23 B8
  Devon 10 D2
  Devon 11 F5
  Devon 20 F3
  Shrops 49 B7
  W Mid 51 B6
Knowle Green 93 F6
Knowle Park 94 E3
Knowl Hill 27 B6
Knowlton
  Dorset. 13 C8
  Kent 31 D6
Knowsley 86 E2
Knowstone 10 B3
Knox Bridge 29 E8
Knucklas 48 B4
Knuston 53 C7
Knutsford 74 B4
Knutton 74 E5
Knypersley 75 D5
Kuggar 3 E6
Kyleakin 149 F12
Kyle of
  Lochalsh 149 F12
Kylerhea 149 F12
Kylesknoydart . 147 B11
Kylesku 156 F5
Kylesmorar 147 B11
Kylestrome 156 F5
Kyllachy House . 138 B3
Kynaston 60 B3
Kynnersley 61 C6
Kyre Magna 49 C8

L

Labost 155 C7
Lacasaidh 155 E8
Lacasdal 155 D9
Laceby 91 D6
Lacey Green 39 E8
Lach Dennis 74 B4
Lackford 55 B8
Lacock 24 C4
Ladbroke 52 D2
Laddingford 29 E7
Lade Bank 79 D6
Ladock 4 D3
Lady 159 D7
Ladybank 128 C5
Ladykirk 122 E4
Ladysford 153 B9
La Fontenelle 16
Laga 147 E9
Lagalochan 124 D4
Lagavulin 142 D5
Lagg
  Argyll 144 F4
  N Ayrs 143 F10
Laggan
  Argyll 142 C3
  Highld 137 E5
  Highld 138 E2
  Highld 147 D10
  S Ayrs 112 F2
Lagganulva 146 G7
Laide 155 H13
Laigh Fenwick 118 E4
Laigh Glengall 112 C3
Laighmuir 118 E4
Laindon 42 F2
Lair 150 G3
Lairg 157 J8
Lairg Lodge 157 J8
Lairgmore 151 H8
Lairg Muir 157 J8
Laisterdyke 94 F4
Laithes 108 F4
Lake
  IoW. 15 F6
  Wilts 25 F6
Lakenham 68 D5
Lakenheath 67 F7
Lakesend 66 E5
Lakeside 99 F5
Laleham 27 C8
Laleston 21 B7
Lamarsh 56 F2
Lamas 81 E8
Lambden 122 E3
Lamberhurst 18 B3
Lamberhurst
  Quarter 18 B3
Lamberton 123 D5
Lambeth 28 B4
Lambhill 119 C5
Lambley
  Northumb 109 D6
  Notts 77 D6
Lamborough Hill 38 D4
Lambourn 25 B8
Lambourne End . 41 E7
Lambs Green 28 F3
Lambston 44 D4
Lamberton 6 B2
Lamesley 111 D5
Laminess 159 E7
Lamington
  Highld 151 D10
  S Lanark 120 F2
Lamlash 143 E11
Lamloch 112 E5
Lamonby 108 F4

Lamorna 2 D3
Lamorran 3 B7
Lampardbrook 57 C6
Lampeter =Llanbedr
  Pont Steffan. 46 E4
Lampeter Velfrey 32 C1
Lamphey 32 D1
Lamplugh 98 B2
Lamport 53 B5
Lamyatt 23 F8
Lana 8 E5
Lanark 119 E8
Lancaster 92 C4
Lanchester 110 E4
Lancing 17 D5
Landbeach 55 C5
Landcross 9 B6
Landerberry 141 D6
Landford 14 C3
Landford Manor . 14 B3
Landimore 33 E5
Landkey 20 F4
Landore 33 E7
Landrake 5 C8
Landscove 7 C5
Landshipping 32 C1
Landshipping
  Quay 32 C1
Landulph 6 C2
Landwade 55 C7
Lane 4 C3
Laneast 8 F4
Lane End
  Bucks 39 E8
  Cumb 98 E3
  Dorset. 13 E6
  Hants 15 B6
  IoW. 15 F7
  Lancs 93 E8
Lane Ends
  Lancs 93 D7
  Lancs 93 F7
  N Yorks 94 E2
Laneham 77 B8
Lanehead
  Durham 109 E8
  Northumb 116 F3
Lane Head
  Derbys 75 B8
  Durham 101 C6
  Gtr Man. 86 E4
  W Yorks 88 D2
Lanercost 109 C5
Laneshaw Bridge . 94 E2
Lane Side 87 B5
Lanfach 35 E6
Langar 77 F7
Langbank 118 B3
Langbar 94 D3
Langburnshiels 115 D8
Langcliffe 93 C8
Langdale 157 E9
Langdale End 103 E7
Langdon 8 F5
Langdon Beck 109 F8
Langdon Hills 42 F2
Langdyke 128 D5
Langenhoe 43 C6
Langford
  C Beds 54 E2
  Devon 10 D5
  Essex 42 D4
  Notts 77 D8
  Oxon 38 D2
Langford Budville 11 B6
Langham
  Essex 56 F4
  Norf 81 C6
  Rutland 64 C5
  Suff 56 C3
Langhaugh 120 F5
Langho 93 F7
Langholm 115 F6
Langleeford 117 B5
Langley
  Ches E 75 B6
  Hants 14 D5
  Herts 41 B5
  Kent 30 D2
  Northumb 109 D8
  Slough. 27 B8
  Warks 51 C6
  W Sus 16 B2
Langley Burrell . . . 24 B4
Langley Common . 76 F2
Langley Heath 30 D2
Langley Lower
  Green 54 F5
Langley Marsh 11 B5
Langley Park 110 E5
Langley Street 69 D6
Langley Upper
  Green 54 F5
Langney 18 E3
Langold 89 F6
Langore 8 F5
Langport 12 B2
Langrick 79 E5
Langridge 24 C2
Langridge Ford . . 9 B7
Langrigg 107 E8
Langrish 15 B8
Langsett 88 D3
Langshaw 121 F8
Langside 127 C6
Langskaill 159 D5
Langstone
  Hants 15 D8
  Newport 35 E7
Langthorne 101 E7
Langthorpe 95 C6
Langthwaite 101 D5
Langtoft
  E Yorks 97 C6
  Lincs 65 C8
Langton
  Durham 101 C6
  Lincs 78 C5
  Lincs 79 B6
  N Yorks 96 C3
Langton by
  Wragby 78 B4
Langton Green
  Kent 18 B2
  Suff 56 B5
Langton Herring . 12 F4
Langton
  Matravers 13 G8

Langtree 9 C6
Langwathby 109 F5
Langwell House 158 H3
Langwell Lodge 156 J4
Langwith 76 C5
Langwith
  Junction 76 C5
Langworth 78 B3
Lanivet 4 C5
Lanlivery 5 D5
Lanner 3 C6
Lanreath 5 D6
Lansallos 5 D6
Lansdown 37 B6
Lanteglos Highway 5 D6
Lanton
  Borders 116 B2
  Northumb 122 F5
Lapford 10 D2
Laphroaig 142 D4
La Planque 16
Lapley 62 C2
Lapworth 51 B6
Larachbeg 147 G9
Larbert 127 F7
Larden Green 74 D2
Largie 152 E6
Largiemore 145 E8
Largoward 129 D6
Largs 118 D2
Largybeg 143 F11
Largymore 143 F11
Larkfield 118 B2
Larkhall 119 D7
Larkhill 25 E6
Larling 68 F2
Larriston 115 E8
Lartington 101 C5
Lary 140 D2
Lasham 26 E4
Lashenden 30 E2
Lassington 36 B4
Lassodie 128 E3
Lastingham 103 E5
Latcham 23 E6
Latchford
  Herts 41 B6
  Warr 86 F4
Latchingdon 42 D4
Latchley 6 B2
Lately Common . 86 E4
Lathbury 53 E6
Latheron 158 G3
Latheronwheel 158 G3
Latheronwheel
  House. 158 G3
Lathones 129 D6
Latimer 40 E3
Latteridge 36 F3
Lattiford 12 B4
Latton 37 E7
Latton Bush 41 D7
Laudale House . 147 F9
Lauder 121 E8
Lauderdale 32 C4
Laugharne 32 C4
Laughterton 77 B8
Laughton
  E Sus 18 D2
  Leics 64 F3
  Lincs 78 F3
  Lincs 90 E2
Laughton
  Common 89 F6
Laughton en le
  Morthen 89 F6
Launcells 8 D4
Launceston 8 F5
Launton 39 B6
Laurencekirk 135 B7
Laurieston
  Dumfries 106 C3
  Falk 120 B2
Lavendon 53 D7
Lavenham 56 E3
Laverhay 114 E4
Laversdale 108 C4
Laverstock 25 F6
Laverstoke 26 E2
Laverton
  Glos 51 F5
  N Yorks 94 B5
  Som 24 D2
Lavister 73 D7
Law 119 D8
Lawers
  Perth 127 B5
  Perth 132 F3
Lawford 56 F4
Lawhitton 8 F5
Lawkland 93 C7
Lawley 61 D6
Lawnhead 62 B2
Lawrenny 32 D1
Lawshall 56 D2
Lawton 49 D6
Laxey 84 D4
Laxfield 57 B6
Laxfirth
  Shetland 160 H6
  Shetland 160 J6
Laxford Bridge . . . 156 E5
Laxo 160 G6
Laxobigging 160 F6
Laxton
  E Yorks 89 B8
  Northants 65 E6
  Notts 77 C7
Laycock 94 E3
Layer Breton 43 C5
Layer de la Haye . 43 C5
Layer Marney 43 C5
Layham 56 E4
Laylands Green . . . 25 C8
Laytham 96 F3
Layton 92 F3
Lazenby 102 B3
Lazonby 108 F5
Lea
  Derbys 76 D3
  Hereford. 36 B3
  Lincs 90 F2
  Shrops 60 D4
  Shrops 60 F3
  Wilts 37 F6
Lea Marston 63 E6
Leabrooks 76 D4
Leac a Li 154 H6
Leachkin 151 G9
Leadburn 120 D5

Leadenham 78 D2
Leaden Roding 42 C1
Leadgate
  Cumb 109 E7
  Durham 110 D4
  T&W 110 D4
Leadhills 113 C8
Leafield 38 C3
Leagrave 40 B3
Leake 102 E2
Leake
  Commonside 79 D6
  Lealholm 103 D5
Lealt
  Argyll 144 D5
  Highld 149 B10
Lea Marston 63 E6
Leamington
  Hastings 52 C2
Leamonsley 62 D5
Leamside 111 E6
Leanaig 151 F8
Leargybreck 144 F4
Leasgill 99 F6
Leasingham 78 E3
Leasingthorne 101 B7
Leasowe 85 E3
Leatherhead 28 D2
Leatherhead
  Common 28 D2
Leathley 94 E5
Leaton 60 C4
Lea Town 92 F4
Leaveland 30 D4
Leavening 96 C3
Leaves Green 28 C5
Leazes 110 D4
Lebberston 103 F8
Lechlade-on-
  Thames 38 E2
Leck 93 B6
Leckford 25 F8
Leckfurin 157 D10
Leckgruinart 142 B3
Leckhampstead
  Bucks 52 F5
  W Berks 26 B2
Leckhampstead
  Thicket 26 B2
Leckhampton 37 C6
Leckie 150 E3
Leckmelm 150 B4
Leckwith 22 B3
Leconfield 97 E6
Ledaig 124 B5
Ledburn 40 B2
Ledbury 50 F2
Ledcharrie 126 B4
Ledgemoor 49 D6
Ledicot 49 C6
Ledmore 156 H5
Lednagullin 157 C10
Ledsham
  Ches W 73 B7
  W Yorks 89 B5
Ledston 89 B5
Ledston Luck. 95 F7
Ledwell 38 B4
Lee
  Argyll 146 J7
  Devon 20 E3
  Hants 14 C4
  Lancs 93 D5
  Shrops 73 F8
Leebotten 160 L6
Leebotwood 60 E4
Lee Brockhurst . . . 60 B5
Leece 92 C2
Leechpool 44 D4
Lee Clump 40 D2
Leeds
  Kent 30 D2
  W Yorks 95 F5
Leedstown 2 C5
Leek 75 D6
Leekbrook 75 D6
Leek Wootton 51 C7
Lee Mill 6 D4
Leeming 101 F7
Leeming Bar 101 E7
Lee Moor 6 C3
Lee-on-the-
  Solent 15 D6
Lees
  Derbys 76 F2
  Gtr Man. 87 D7
  W Yorks 94 F3
Leeswood 73 C6
Legbourne 91 F7
Legerwood 121 E8
Legsby 90 F5
Leicester 64 D2
Leicester Forest
  East 64 D2
Leigh
  Dorset. 12 D4
  Glos 37 B5
  Gtr Man. 86 D4
  Kent 29 E6
  Shrops 60 D3
  Sur 28 E3
  Wilts 37 E7
  Worcs 50 D2
Leigh Beck 42 F4
Leigh Common . . . 12 B5
Leigh Delamere . 24 B3
Leigh Green 19 B6
Leigh on Sea 42 F4
Leigh Park 15 D8
Leigh Sinton 50 D2
Leighswood 62 D4
Leighterton 37 E5
Leighton
  N Yorks 94 B4
  Powys 60 D2
  Shrops 61 D6
  Som 24 E2
Leighton
  Bromswold 54 B2
Leighton Buzzard 40 B2
Leigh upon
  Mendip 23 E8
Leigh Woods 23 B7
Leinthall Earls 49 C6
Leinthall Starkes 49 C6
Leintwardine 49 B6
Leire 64 E2

Leirinmore 156 C7
Leiston 57 C8
Leitfie 134 E2
Leith 121 B5
Leitholm 122 E3
Lelant 2 C4
Lelley 97 F8
Lem Hill 50 B2
Lemmington
  Hall 117 C7
Lempitlaw 122 F3
Lenchwick 50 E5
Lendalfoot 112 F1
Lendrick Lodge . 126 D4
Lenham 30 D2
Lenham Heath. 30 E3
Lennel 122 E4
Lennoxtown 119 B6
Lenton
  Lincs 78 F3
  Nottingham 77 F5
Lentran 151 G8
Lenwade 68 C3
Leny House 126 D5
Lenzie 119 B6
Leoch 134 F3
Leochel-
  Cushnie 140 C4
Leominster 49 D6
Leonard Stanley . 37 D5
Leorin 142 D4
Lepe 15 E5
Lephin 148 D6
Lephinchapel 145 D8
Lephinmore 145 D8
Le Planel 16
Leppington 96 C3
Lepton 88 C3
Lerryn 5 D6
Lerwick 160 J6
Lesbury 117 C8
Le Skerne
  Haughton 101 C8
Leslie
  Aberds 140 B4
  Fife 128 D4
Lesmahagow 119 F8
Lesnewth 8 E3
Lessendrum 152 D5
Lessingham 69 B6
Lessonhall 108 D2
Leswalt 104 C4
Letchmore Heath . 40 E4
Letchworth 54 F3
Letcombe Bassett 38 F3
Letcombe Regis . 38 F3
Letham
  Angus 135 E5
  Falk 127 F7
  Fife 128 C5
  Perth 128 B2
Letham Grange . 135 E6
Lethenty 153 D8
Letheringham 57 D6
Letheringsett 81 D6
Lettaford 10 F2
Lettan 159 D8
Letterewe 150 D2
Letterfearn 149 F13
Letterfinlay 137 E5
Lettermorar 147 C10
Lettermore 146 G7
Letters 150 C4
Letterston 44 C4
Lettoch
  Highld 139 C6
  Highld 151 H13
Letton
  Hereford. 48 E5
  Hereford. 49 B5
Letton Green 68 D2
Letty Green 41 C5
Letwell 89 F6
Leuchars 129 B6
Leuchars House 152 B2
Leumrabhagh 155 F8
Levan 118 B2
Levaneap 160 G6
Levedale 62 C2
Leven
  E Yorks 97 E7
  Fife 129 D5
Levencorroch 143 F11
Levens 99 F6
Levens Green 41 B6
Levenshulme 87 E6
Levenwick 160 L6
Leverburgh
  =An t-Ob 154 J5
Leverington 66 C4
Leverton 79 E7
Leverton
  Highgate 79 E7
Leverton
  Lucasgate 79 E7
Leverton Outgate 79 E7
Le Villocq 16
Levington 57 F6
Levisham 103 E6
Levishie 137 C7
Lew 38 D3
Lewannick 8 F4
Lewdown 9 F6
Lewes 17 C8
Leweston 44 C4
Lewisham 28 B4
Lewiston 137 B8
Lewistown 34 F3
Lewknor 39 E7
Leworthy
  Devon 8 D5
  Devon 21 F5
Lewtrenchard 9 F6
Lexden 43 B5
Ley
  Aberds 140 C4
  Corn 5 C6
Leybourne 29 D7
Leyburn 101 E6
Leyfields 63 D6
Leyhill 40 D2
Leyland 86 B3
Leylodge 141 C6
Leymoor 88 C2
Leys
  Aberds 153 C10
  Perth 134 F2
Leys Castle 151 G9

Leysdown-on-
  Sea 30 B4
Leysmill 135 E6
Leys of Cossans 134 E3
Leysters Pole 49 C7
Leyton 41 F6
Leytonstone 41 F6
Lezant 5 B8
Leziate 67 C6
Lhanbryde 152 B2
Liatrie 150 H5
Libanus 34 B3
Libberton 120 E2
Liberton 121 C5
Liceasto 154 H6
Lichfield 62 D5
Lickey 50 B4
Lickey End 50 B4
Lickfold 16 B3
Liddel 159 K5
Liddesdale 130 D1
Liddington 38 F2
Lidgate 55 D8
Lidget 89 D7
Lidget Green 94 F4
Lidgett 77 C6
Lidlington 53 F7
Lidstone 38 B3
Lieurary 158 D2
Liff 134 F3
Lifton 9 F5
Liftondown 9 F5
Lighthorne 51 D8
Lightwater 27 C7
Lightwood 75 E6
Lightwood Green
  Ches E 74 E3
  Wrex. 73 E7
Lilbourne 52 B3
Lilburn Tower 117 B6
Lilleshall 61 C7
Lilley
  Herts 40 B4
  W Berks 26 B2
Lilliesleaf 115 B8
Lillingstone
  Dayrell 52 F5
Lillingstone
  Lovell 52 E5
Lillington
  Dorset. 12 C4
  Warks 51 C8
Lilliput 13 E8
Lilstock 22 E3
Lilyhurst 61 C7
Limbury 40 B3
Limebrook 49 C5
Limefield 87 C6
Limekilnburn 119 D7
Limekilns 128 F2
Limerigg 119 B8
Limerstone 14 F5
Limington 12 B3
Limpenhoe 69 D6
Limpley Stoke 24 C2
Limpsfield 28 D5
Limpsfield Chart 28 D5
Linby 76 D5
Linchmere 27 F6
Lincluden 107 B6
Lincoln 78 B2
Lincomb 50 C3
Lincombe 6 D5
Lindale 99 F6
Lindal in Furness 92 B2
Lindean 121 F7
Lindfield 17 B7
Lindford 27 F6
Lindifferon 128 C5
Lindley 88 C2
Lindley Green 94 E5
Lindores 128 C4
Lindridge 49 C8
Lindsell 42 B2
Lindsey 56 E3
Linford
  Hants 14 D2
  Thurrock 29 B7
Lingague 84 E2
Lingards Wood 87 C8
Lingbob 94 F3
Lingdale 102 C4
Lingen 49 C5
Lingfield 28 E4
Lingreabhagh 154 J5
Lingwood 69 D6
Linicro 149 B8
Linkenholt 25 D8
Linkhill 18 C5
Linkinhorne 5 B8
Linklater 159 K5
Linksness 159 H3
Linktown 128 E4
Linley 60 E3
Linley Green 49 D8
Linlithgow 120 B3
Linlithgow
  Bridge 120 B2
Linshiels 116 D4
Linsiadar 154 D7
Linsidemore 151 B8
Linslade 40 B2
Linstead Parva . . . 57 B7
Linstock 108 D4
Linthwaite 88 C2
Lintlaw 122 D4
Lintmill 152 B5
Linton
  Borders 116 B3
  Cambs 55 E6
  Derbys 63 C6
  Hereford. 36 B3
  Kent 29 E8
  Northumb 117 E8
  N Yorks 94 C2
  W Yorks 95 E6
Linton-on-Ouse 95 C7
Linwood
  Hants 14 D2
  Lincs 90 F5
  Renfs 118 C4
Lionacleit 148 D2
Lional 155 A10
Liphook 27 F6
Liscard 85 E4
Liscombe 21 F7
Liskeard 5 C7
L'Islet 16

Liss 15 B8
Lissett 97 D7
Liss Forest 15 B8
Lissington 90 F5
Lisvane 35 F5
Liswerry 35 F7
Litcham 67 C8
Litchborough 52 D4
Litchfield 26 D2
Litherland 85 E4
Litlington
  Cambs. 54 E4
  E Sus. 18 E2
Little Abington 54 E3
Little Addington . . .53 B7
Little Alne 51 C6
Little Altcar 85 D4
Little Asby 100 D1
Little Assynt 156 G4
Little Aston 62 D4
Little Atherfield 15 F5
Little Ayre 159 J4
Little-ayre 160 G5
Little Ayton 102 C3
Little Baddow 42 D3
Little Badminton . . .37 F5
Little Ballinluig 133 D6
Little Bampton 108 D2
Little Bardfield 55 F7
Little Barford 54 D2
Little Barningham . . .81 D7
Little Barrington 38 C2
Little Barrow 73 B8
Little Barugh 96 B3
Little Bavington 110 B2
Little Bealings 57 E6
Littlebeck 103 D6
Little Bedwyn 25 C7
Little Bentley 43 B7
Little Berkhamsted . .41 D5
Little Billing 53 C6
Little Birch 49 F7
Little Blakenham . . .56 E5
Little Blencow 108 F4
Little Bollington 86 F5
Little Bookham 28 D2
Littleborough
  Gtr Man. 87 C7
  Notts. 90 F2
Littlebourne 31 D6
Little Bowden 64 F4
Little Bradley 55 D7
Little Brampton 60 F3
Little Brechin 135 C5
Littlebredy 12 F3
Little Brickhill 53 F7
Little Brington 52 C4
Little Bromley 43 B6
Little Broughton 107 F7
Little Budworth 74 C2
Little Burstead 42 E2
Littlebury 55 F6
Littlebury Green 55 F6
Little Bytham 65 C7
Little Carlton
  Lincs. 91 F7
  Notts. 77 D7
Little Casterton 65 D7
Little Cawthorpe 91 F7
Little Chalfont 40 E2
Little Chart 30 E3
Little Chesterford . . .55 E6
Little Cheverell 24 D4
Little Chishill 54 F5
Little Clacton 43 C7
Little Clifton 98 B2
Little Colp 153 D7
Little Comberton . . .50 E4
Little Common 18 E4
Little Compton 51 F7
Little Cornard 56 F2
Little Cowarne 49 D8
Little Coxwell 38 E2
Little Crakehall 101 E7
Little Cressingham . . .67 D8
Little Crosby 85 D4
Little Dalby 64 C4
Little Dawley 61 D6
Littledean 36 C3
Little Dens 153 D10
Little Dewchurch 49 F7
Little Downham 66 F5
Little Driffield 97 D6
Little Dunham 67 C8
Little Dunkeld 133 E7
Little Dunmow 42 B2
Little Easton 42 B2
Little Eaton 76 E3
Little Eccleston 92 E4
Little Ellingham 68 E3
Little End 41 D8
Little Eversden 54 D4
Little Faringdon 38 D2
Little Fencote 101 E7
Little Fenton 95 F8
Littleferry 151 B11
Little Finborough . . .56 D4
Little Fransham 68 C2
Little Gaddesden 40 C2
Little Gidding 65 F8
Little Glemham 57 D7
Little Glenshee 133 F6
Little Gransden 54 D3
Little Green 24 E2
Little Grimsby 91 F7
Little Gruinard 150 C2
Little Habton 96 B3
Little Hadham 41 B7
Little Hale 78 E4
Little Hallingbury . . .41 C7
Littleham
  Devon 9 B6
  Devon 10 F5
Little Hampden 40 D1
Little Harrowden . . .53 B6
Little Haseley 39 D6
Little Hatfield 97 E7
Little Hautbois 81 E8
Little Haven 44 D3
Little Hay 62 D5
Little Haywood 62 B4
Little Heath 7 C6
Littlehempston 7 C6

Little Hereford 49 C7
Little Horkesley 56 F3
Little Horsted 17 C8
Little Horton 25 C5
Little Horwood 53 F5
Littlehoughton 117 C8
Little Houghton
  Northants 53 D6
  S Yorks 88 D5
Little Hucklow 75 B8
Little Hulton 86 D5
Little Humber 91 B6
Little Hungerford . . .26 B3
Little Irchester 53 C7
Little Kimble 39 D8
Little Kineton 51 D8
Little Kingshill 40 E1
Little Langdale 99 D5
Little Langford 25 F5
Little Laver 41 D8
Little Leigh 74 B3
Little Leighs 42 C3
Little Lever 87 D5
Little London
  Bucks. 39 C6
  E Sus. 18 D2
  Hants. 25 E8
  Hants. 26 D4
  Lincs. 66 B2
  Lincs. 66 B4
  Norf. 81 E7
  Powys 48 D3
Little Longstone 75 B8
Little Lynturk 140 C4
Little Malvern 50 E2
Little Maplestead . . .56 F2
Little Marcle 49 F8
Little Marlow 40 F1
Little Marsden 93 F8
Little Massingham . . .80 E3
Little Melton 68 D4
Littlemill
  Aberds. 140 E2
  E Ayrs. 112 C4
  Highld 151 F12
  Northumb 117 C8
Little Mill 35 D7
Little Milton 39 D6
Little Missenden 40 E2
Littlemoor 12 F4
Littlemore 39 D5
Little Musgrave 100 C2
Little Ness 60 C4
Little Neston 73 B6
Little Newcastle 44 C4
Little Newsham 101 C6
Little Oakley
  Essex 43 B8
  Northants 65 F5
Little Orton 108 D3
Little Ouseburn 95 C7
Littleover 76 F3
Little Paxton 54 C2
Little Petherick 4 B4
Little Pitlurg 152 D4
Little Plumpton 92 F3
Little Plumstead 69 C6
Little Ponton 78 F2
Littleport 67 F5
Little Raveley 54 B3
Little Reedness 90 B2
Little Ribston 95 D6
Little Rissington 38 C1
Little Ryburgh 81 E5
Little Ryle 117 C6
Little Salkeld 109 F5
Little Sampford 55 F7
Little Sandhurst 27 C6
Little Saxham 55 C8
Little Scatwell 150 F6
Little Sessay 95 B7
Little Shelford 54 D5
Little Singleton 92 F3
Little Skillymarno . . .153 C9
Little Smeaton 89 C6
Little Snoring 81 D5
Little Sodbury 36 F4
Little Somborne 25 F8
Little Somerford 37 F6
Little Stainforth 93 C8
Little Stainton 101 B8
Little Stanney 73 B8
Little Staughton 54 C2
Little Steeping 79 C7
Little Stoke 75 F6
Littlestone on Sea . . .19 C7
Little Stonham 56 C5
Little Stretton
  Leics 64 D3
  Shrops 60 E4
Little Strickland 99 C7
Little Stukeley 54 B3
Little Sutton 73 B7
Little Tew 38 B3
Little Thetford 55 B6
Little Thirkleby 95 B7
Littlethorpe 95 C6
Little Thurlow 55 D7
Little Thurrock 29 B7
Littleton
  Ches W 73 C8
  Hants. 26 F2
  Perth. 134 F2
  Som. 23 F6
  Sur. 27 C8
  Sur. 27 E7
Littleton Drew 37 F5
Littleton-on-Severn . .36 F2
Littleton Pannell . . .24 D5
Little Torboll 151 B10
Little Torrington 9 C6
Little Totham 42 C4
Little Toux 152 C5
Littletown 111 E6
Little Town
  Cumb 98 C4
  Lancs 93 F6
Little Urswick 92 B2
Little Wakering 43 F5
Little Walden 55 E6
Little Waldingfield . . .56 E3

Little Walsingham . . .80 D5
Little Waltham 42 C3
Little Warley 42 E2
Little Weighton 97 F5
Little Weldon 65 F6
Little Welnetham . . .56 C2
Little Wenlock 61 D6
Little Whittington Green 57 B6
Littlewick Green 27 B6
Little Wilbraham . . .55 D6
Little Wishford 25 F5
Little Witley 50 C2
Little Wittenham . . .39 E5
Little Wolford 51 F7
Littleworth
  Bedford 53 E8
  Glos 37 D5
  Oxon 38 E3
  Staffs 62 C4
  Worcs 50 D3
Little Wratting 55 E7
Little Wymington . . .53 C7
Little Wymondley . . .41 B5
Little Wyrley 62 D4
Little Yeldham 55 F8
Litton
  Derbys 75 B8
  N Yorks 94 B2
  Som. 23 D7
Litton Cheney 12 E3
Liurbost 155 E8
Liverpool 85 E4
Liverpool Airport . . .86 F2
Liversedge 88 B3
Liverton
  Devon 7 B6
  Redcar 103 C5
Livingston 120 C3
Livingston Village . . .120 C3
Lixwm 73 B5
Lizard 3 E6
Llaingoch 82 C2
Llaithddu 59 F7
Llan 59 D5
Llanaber 58 C3
Llanaelhaearn 70 C4
Llanafan 47 B5
Llanafan-fawr 47 D8
Llanallgo 82 C4
Llanandras
  = Presteigne 48 C5
Llanarmon 70 D5
Llanarmon Dyffryn Ceiriog 73 F5
Llanarmon-yn-Ial 73 D5
Llanarth
  Ceredig 46 D3
  Mon. 35 C7
Llanarthne 33 B6
Llanasa 85 F2
Llanbabo 82 C3
Llanbadarn Fawr . . .58 F3
Llanbadarn Fynydd 48 B3
Llanbadarn-y-Garreg 48 E3
Llanbadoc 35 E7
Llanbadrig 82 B3
Llanbeder 35 E7
Llanbedr
  Gwyn 71 E6
  Powys 35 B6
  Powys 48 E3
Llanbedr-Dyffryn-Clwyd 72 D5
Llanbedrgoch 82 C4
Llanbedrog 70 D4
Llanbedr Pont Steffan
  = Lampeter 46 E4
Llanbedr-y-cennin . .83 E7
Llanberis 83 E5
Llanbethêry 22 C2
Llanbister 48 B3
Llanblethian 21 B8
Llanboidy 32 B3
Llanbradach 35 E5
Llanbrynmair 59 D5
Llancarfan 22 B2
Llancayo 35 D7
Llancloudy 36 B1
Llancynfelyn 58 E3
Llandaff 22 B3
Llandanwg 71 E6
Llandarcy 33 E8
Llandawke 32 C3
Llanddaniel Fab . . .82 D4
Llanddarog 33 C6
Llanddeiniol 46 B4
Llanddeiniolen 82 E5
Llanddeusant
  Anglesey 82 C3
  Carms 34 B1
Llanddew 48 F2
Llanddewi 33 F5
Llanddewi-Brefi 47 D5
Llanddewi'r Cwm . .48 E2
Llanddewi Rhydderch 35 C7
Llanddewi Velfrey . .32 C2
Llanddoged 83 E8
Llanddona 83 D5
Llanddowror 32 C3
Llanddulas 72 B3
Llanddwywe 71 E6
Llanddyfynan 82 D5
Llandefaelog Fach . .48 F2
Llandefaelog-tre'rgraig 35 B5
Llandefalle 48 F3
Llandegai 83 D5
Llandegfan 83 D5
Llandegla 73 D5
Llandegley 48 C3
Llandegveth 35 E7
Llandegwning 70 D3
Llandeilo 33 B7
Llandeilo Graban . . .48 E2
Llandeilo'r Fan 47 F7
Llandeloy 44 C3
Llandenny 35 D8

Llandevenny 35 F8
Llandewednock 3 E6
Llandewi Ystradenny 48 C3
Llandinabo 36 B2
Llandinam 59 F7
Llandissilio 32 B2
Llandogo 36 D2
Llandough
  V Glam. 21 B8
  V Glam. 22 B3
Llandovery
  = Llanymddyfri . . .47 F6
Llandow 21 B8
Llandre
  Carms 47 E5
  Ceredig 58 F3
Llandrillo 72 F4
Llandrillo-yn-Rhos 83 C8
Llandrindod
  = Llandrindod Wells 48 C2
Llandrindod Wells
  = Llandrindod 48 C2
Llandrinio 60 C2
Llandudno 83 C7
Llandudno Junction
  = Cyffordd Llandudno 83 D7
Llandwrog 82 F4
Llandybie 33 C7
Llandyfaelog 33 C5
Llandyfan 33 C7
Llandyfriog 46 E2
Llandyfrydog 82 C4
Llandygwydd 45 E4
Llandynan 73 E5
Llandyrnog 72 C5
Llandysilio 60 C2
Llandyssil 59 E8
Llandysul 46 E3
Llanedeyrn 35 F6
Llanedi 33 D6
Llaneglwys 48 F2
Llanegryn 58 D2
Llanegwad 33 B6
Llaneilian 82 B4
Llanelian-yn-Rhos 83 D8
Llanelidan 72 D5
Llanelieu 48 F3
Llanellen 35 C7
Llanelli 33 E6
Llanelltyd 58 C4
Llanelly 35 C6
Llanelly Hill 35 C6
Llanelwedd 48 D2
Llanelwy
  = St Asaph 72 B4
Llanenddwyn 71 E6
Llanengan 70 E3
Llanerchymedd 82 C4
Llanerfyl 59 D7
Llanfachraeth 82 C3
Llanfachreth 71 E8
Llanfaelog 82 D3
Llanfaelrhys 70 E3
Llanfaenor 35 C8
Llanfaes
  Anglesey 83 D6
  Powys 34 B4
Llanfaethlu 82 C3
Llanfaglan 82 E4
Llanfair 71 E6
Llanfair-ar-y-bryn 47 F7
Llanfair Caereinion . .59 D8
Llanfair Clydogau . .46 E5
Llanfair-Dyffryn-Clwyd 72 D5
Llanfairfechan 83 D6
Llanfair Kilgheddin 35 D7
Llanfair-Nant-Gwyn 45 F3
Llanfairpwllgwyngyll 82 D5
Llanfair Talhaiarn . .72 B3
Llanfair Waterdine . .48 B4
Llanfair-ym-Muallt
  = Builth Wells 48 D2
Llanfairyneubwll . . .82 D3
Llanfairynghornwy 82 B3
Llanfallteg 32 C2
Llanfaredd 48 D2
Llanfarian 46 B4
Llanfechain 59 B8
Llanfechan 47 D8
Llanfechell 82 B3
Llanfendigaid 58 D2
Llanferres 73 C5
Llan Ffestiniog 71 C8
Llanfflewyn 82 C3
Llanfihangel-ararth 46 E3
Llanfihangel-Crucorney 35 B7
Llanfihangel Glyn Myfyr 72 D2
Llanfihangel Nant Bran 47 F8
Llanfihangel-nant-Melan 48 D3
Llanfihangel Rhydithon 48 C3
Llanfihangel Rogiet 35 F8
Llanfihangel Tal-y-llyn 35 B5
Llanfihangel-uwch-Gwili 33 B5
Llanfihangel-y-Creuddyn 47 B5
Llanfihangel-yn-Ngwynfa 59 C7
Llanfihangel yn Nhowyn 82 D3
Llanfihangel-ypennant
  Gwyn. 71 C6
  Gwyn. 58 D3
Llanfihangel-ytraethau 71 D6
Llanfilo 48 F3

Llanfoist 35 C6
Llanfor 72 F3
Llanfrechfa 35 E7
Llanfrothen 71 C7
Llanfrynach 34 B4
Llanfwrog
  Anglesey 82 C3
  Denb 72 D5
Llanfyllin 59 C8
Llanfynydd
  Carms 33 B6
  Flint 73 D6
Llanfyrnach 45 F4
Llangadfan 59 C7
Llangadog 33 B8
Llangadwaladr
  Anglesey 82 E3
  Powys 73 F5
Llangaffo 82 E4
Llangain 32 C4
Llangammarch Wells 47 E8
Llangan 21 B8
Llangarron 36 B2
Llangasty Talyllyn . . .35 B5
Llangathen 33 B6
Llangattock 35 C6
Llangattock Lingoed 35 B7
Llangattock nigh Usk 35 C7
Llangattock-Vibon-Avel 36 C1
Llangedwyn 59 B8
Llangefni 82 D4
Llangeinor 34 F3
Llangeitho 46 D5
Llangeler 46 F2
Llangelynin 58 D2
Llangendeirne 33 C5
Llangennech 33 E6
Llangennith 33 E5
Llangenny 35 C6
Llangernyw 83 E8
Llangian 70 E3
Llanglydwen 32 B2
Llangoed 83 D6
Llangoedmor 45 E3
Llangollen 73 E6
Llangolman 32 B2
Llangors 35 B5
Llangovan 36 D1
Llangower 72 F3
Llangrannog 46 D2
Llangristiolus 82 D4
Llangrove 36 C2
Llangua 35 B7
Llangunllo 48 B4
Llangunnor 33 C5
Llangurig 47 B8
Llangwm
  Conwy 72 E3
  Mon. 35 D8
  Pembs. 44 E4
Llangwnnadl 70 D3
Llangwyfan 72 C5
Llangwyfan-isaf 82 E3
Llangwyllog 82 D4
Llangwyryfon 46 B4
Llangybi
  Ceredig 46 D5
  Gwyn. 70 C5
  Mon. 35 E7
Llangyfelach 33 E7
Llangynhafal 72 C5
Llangynidr 35 C5
Llangynin 32 C3
Llangynog
  Carms 32 C4
  Powys 59 B7
Llangynwyd 34 F2
Llanhamlach 34 B4
Llanharan 34 F4
Llanharry 34 F4
Llanhennock 35 E7
Llanhiddle
  = Llanhilleth 35 D6
Llanhilleth
  = Llanhiledd 35 D6
Llaniestyn 70 D3
Llanifyny 59 F7
Llanigon 48 F4
Llanilar 46 B5
Llanilid 34 F3
Llanishen
  Cardiff. 35 F5
  Mon. 36 D1
Llanllawddog 33 B5
Llanllechid 83 E6
Llanllowell 35 E7
Llanllugan 59 D7
Llanllwch 32 C4
Llanllwchaiarn 59 E8
Llanllwni 46 E3
Llanllyfni 82 F4
Llanmadoc 33 E5
Llanmaes 21 C8
Llanmartin 35 F7
Llanmihangel 21 B8
Llanmorlais 33 E6
Llannefydd 72 B3
Llannon 33 D6
Llannor 70 D4
Llanover 35 D7
Llanpumsaint 33 B5
Llanreithan 44 C3
Llanrhaeadr 72 C4
Llanrhaeadr-ym-Mochnant 59 B8
Llanrhian 44 B3
Llanrhidian 33 E5
Llanrhos 83 C7
Llanrhyddlad 82 C3
Llanrhystud 46 C4
Llanrosser 48 F4
Llanrothal 36 C1
Llanrug 82 E5
Llanrumney 35 F6
Llanrwst 83 E8
Llansadurnen 32 C3
Llansadwrn
  Anglesey 83 D5
  Carms 47 F5

Llansaint 32 D4
Llansamlet 33 E7
Llansanffraid-ym-Mechain 60 B2
Llansannan 72 C3
Llansannor 21 B8
Llansantffraed
  Ceredig 46 C4
  Powys 35 B5
Llansantffraed Cwmdeuddwr 47 C8
Llansantffraed-in-Elvel 48 D2
Llansantffraid-in-Elvel 48 D2
Llansawel 46 F5
Llansilin 60 B2
Llansoy 35 D8
Llanspyddid 34 B4
Llanstadwell 44 E4
Llansteffan 32 C4
Llanstephan 48 E3
Llantarnam 35 E7
Llanteg 32 C2
Llanthony 35 B6
Llantilio Crossenny 35 C7
Llantilio Pertholey 35 C7
Llantood 45 E3
Llantrisant
  Anglesey 82 C3
  Mon. 35 E7
  Rhondda 34 F4
Llantrithyd 22 B2
Llantwit Fardre 34 F4
Llantwit Major
  = Llanilltud Fawr . . 21 C8
Llanuwchllyn 72 F2
Llanvaches 35 E8
Llanvair Discoed 35 E8
Llanvapley 35 C7
Llanvetherine 35 C7
Llanveynoe 48 F5
Llanvihangel Gobion 35 D7
Llanvihangel-Ystern-Llewern 35 C8
Llanwarne 36 B2
Llanwddyn 59 C7
Llanwenog 46 E3
Llanwern 35 F7
Llanwinio 32 B3
Llanwnda
  Gwyn. 82 F4
  Pembs. 44 B4
Llanwnnen 46 E4
Llanwnog 59 E7
Llanwrda 47 F6
Llanwrin 58 D4
Llanwrthwl 47 C8
Llanwrtud
  = Llanwrtyd Wells . . 47 E7
Llanwrtyd 47 E7
Llanwrtyd Wells
  = Llanwrtud 47 E7
Llanwyddelan 59 D7
Llanyblodwel 60 B2
Llanybri 32 C4
Llanybydder 46 E4
Llanycefn 32 B1
Llanychaer 44 B4
Llanycil 72 F3
Llanycrwys 46 E5
Llanymawddwy 59 C6
Llanymddyfri
  = Llandovery 47 F6
Llanymynech 60 B2
Llanynghenedl 82 C3
Llanynys 72 C5
Llan-y-pwll 73 D7
Llanyre 48 C2
Llanystumdwy 71 D5
Llanywern 35 B5
Llawhaden 32 C1
Llawnt 73 F6
Llawr Dref 70 E3
Llawryglyn 59 E6
Llay 73 D7
Llechcynfarwy 82 C3
Llecheiddior 71 C5
Llechfaen 34 B4
Llechryd
  Caerph 35 D5
  Ceredig 45 E4
Llechrydau 73 F6
Lledrod 46 B5
Llenmerewig 59 E8
Llethrid 33 E6
Llidiad Nenog 46 F4
Llidiardau 72 F2
Llidiart-y-parc 72 E5
Llithfaen 70 C4
Llong 73 C6
Llowes 48 E3
Llundain-fach 46 D4
Llwydcoed 34 D3
Llwyn 60 F2
Llwyncelyn 46 D3
Llwyndafydd 46 D2
Llwynderw 60 D2
Llwyn-du 35 C6
Llwyndyrys 70 C4
Llwyngwril 58 D2
Llwyn-hendy 33 E6
Llwynmawr 73 F6
Llwyn-têg 33 D6
Llwyn-y-brain 32 C2
Llwyn-y-groes 46 D4
Llwynypia 34 E3
Llynclys 60 B2
Llynfaes 82 D4
Llysfaen 83 D8
Llyswen 48 F3
Llysworney 21 B8
Llys-y-frân 32 B1
Llywel 47 F7
Loan 120 B2
Loanend 122 D5
Loanhead 121 C5
Loans 118 F3
Loans of Tullich 151 D11
Lobb 20 F3
Loch a Charnain 148 D3
Loch a' Ghainmh 155 E7
Lochailort 147 C10
Lochaline 147 G9

Lochanhully 138 B5
Lochans 104 D4
Locharbriggs 114 F2
Lochassynt Lodge . . .156 G4
Lochavich House 124 D5
Lochawe 125 C7
Loch Baghasdail
  = Lochboisdale 148 G2
Lochboisdale = Loch Baghasdail 148 G2
Lochbuie 124 D2
Lochcarron 149 E13
Loch Choire Lodge . . .157 F9
Lochdhu 157 E13
Lochdochart House . . .126 B3
Lochdon 124 B3
Lochdrum 150 D5
Lochead 144 F6
Lochearnhead 126 B4
Lochee 134 F3
Lochend
  Highld 151 H8
  Highld 158 C5
Locherben 114 E2
Loch Euphoirt 148 B3
Lochfoot 107 B5
Lochgair 145 D8
Lochgarthside 137 C8
Lochgelly 128 E3
Lochgilphead 145 E7
Lochgoilhead 125 E8
Loch Head 105 E7
Lochhill 152 B2
Lochindorb Lodge . . .151 H12
Lochinver 156 G3
Lochlane 127 B7
Loch Loyal Lodge . . .157 E9
Lochluichart 150 E6
Lochmaben 114 F3
Lochmaddy = Loch nam Madadh 148 B4
Lochmore Cottage . . .158 F2
Lochmore Lodge . . .156 F5
Loch nam Madadh
  = Lochmaddy 148 B4
Lochore 128 E3
Lochportain 148 A4
Lochranza 143 C10
Lochs Crofts 152 B3
Loch Sgioport 148 E3
Lochside
  Aberds 135 C7
  Highld 151 F11
  Highld 156 D7
  Highld 157 F11
Lochslin 151 C11
Lochstack Lodge . . .156 E5
Lochton 141 E6
Lochty
  Angus 135 C5
  Fife 129 D7
  Perth. 128 B2
Lochuisge 130 D1
Lochurr 113 F7
Lochwinnoch 118 D3
Lochwood
  Borders 115 B8
  Stockton 102 C1
Lockengate 4 C5
Lockerbie 114 F4
Lockeridge 25 C6
Lockerley 14 B3
Locking 23 D5
Lockington
  E Yorks 97 E5
  Leics 63 B8
Locklywood 61 B6
Locks Heath 15 D6
Lockton 103 E6
Lockwood 88 C2
Loddington
  Leics 64 D4
  Northants 53 B6
Loddiswell 6 E5
Loddon 69 E6
Lode 55 C6
Loders 12 E2
Lodsworth 16 B3
Lofthouse
  N Yorks 94 B4
  W Yorks 88 B4
Loftus 103 C5
Logan 113 B5
Loganlea 120 C2
Logan Mains 104 E4
Loggerheads 74 F4
Logie
  Angus 135 C6
  Fife 129 B6
  Moray 151 F13
Logiealmond Lodge . .133 F6
Logie Coldstone 140 D3
Logie Hill 151 D10
Logie Newton 153 E6
Logie Pert. 135 C6
Logierait 133 D6
Login 32 B2
Lolworth 54 C4
Lonbain 149 C11
Londesborough 96 E4
London Colney 40 D4
Londonderry 101 F8
Londonthorpe 78 F2
Londubh 155 J13
Lonemore 151 C10
Long Ashton 23 B7
Longbar 118 D3
Long Bennington . . .77 E8
Long Bredy 12 E3
Longbridge
  Warks. 51 C7
  W Mid 50 B5
Longbridge Deverill . .24 E3
Long Buckby 52 C4

Longburton 12 C4
Long Clawson 64 B4
Longcliffe 76 D2
Long Common 15 C6
Long Compton
  Staffs 62 B2
  Warks. 51 F7
Longcot 38 E2
Long Crendon 39 D6
Long Crichel 13 C7
Longcroft 119 B7
Longden 60 D4
Long Ditton 28 C2
Longdon
  Staffs 62 C4
  Worcs 50 F3
Longdon Green 62 C4
Longdon on Tern . . .61 C6
Longdown 10 E3
Longdowns 3 C6
Long Drax 89 B7
Long Duckmanton . .76 B4
Long Eaton 76 F4
Longfield
  Kent 29 C7
  Shetland 160 M5
Longford
  Derbys 76 F2
  Glos 37 B5
  London 27 B8
  Shrops 74 F3
  Telford 61 C7
  W Mid 63 F7
Longfordlane 76 F2
Longforgan 128 B5
Longformacus 122 D2
Longframlington 117 D7
Long Green 50 F3
Longham
  Dorset 13 E8
  Norf 68 C2
Long Hanborough . . .38 C4
Longhaven 153 E11
Longhill 153 C9
Longhirst 117 F8
Longhope
  Glos 36 C3
  Orkney 159 J4
Longhorsley 117 E7
Longhoughton 117 C8
Long Itchington 52 C2
Longlane
  Derbys 76 F2
  W Berks 26 B2
Long Lawford 52 B2
Longlevens 37 B5
Longley 88 D2
Longley Green 50 D2
Long Load 12 B2
Longmanhill 153 B7
Long Marston
  Herts. 40 C1
  N Yorks 95 D8
  Warks. 51 E6
Long Marton 100 B1
Long Melford 56 E2
Longmoor Camp . . .27 F5
Longmorn 152 C2
Long Newnton 37 E6
Long Newton
  Borders 115 B8
  Stockton 102 C1
Longnewton 121 C8
Longney 36 C4
Longniddry 121 B7
Longnor
  Shrops 60 D4
  Staffs 75 C7
Long Preston 93 D8
Longridge
  Lancs 93 F6
  Staffs 62 C3
  W Loth. 120 C2
Longriggend 119 B8
Long Riston 97 E7
Longsdon 75 D6
Longshaw 86 D3
Longside 153 D10
Long Sight 87 D7
Longstanton 54 C4
Longstock 25 F8
Longstone 32 C2
Longstowe 54 D4
Long Stratton 68 E4
Long Street 53 E5
Long Sutton
  Hants. 26 E5
  Lincs. 66 B4
  Som. 12 B2
Longthorpe 65 E8
Long Thurlow 56 C4
Longthwaite 99 B6
Longton
  Lancs 86 B2
  Stoke 75 E6
Longtown
  Cumb 108 C3
  Hereford. 35 B7
Longview 86 E2
Longville in the Dale 60 E5
Long Whatton 63 B8
Longwick 39 D7
Long Wittenham . . .39 E5
Longworth 38 E3
Longyester 121 C7
Lonmay 153 C10
Lonmore 148 D7
Loose 29 D8
Loosley Row 40 D1
Lopcombe Corner . . .25 F7
Lopen 12 C2
Loppington 60 B4
Lopwell 6 C2
Lorbottle 117 D6
Lorbottle Hall 117 D6
Lornty 134 E1
Loscoe 76 E4
Losgaintir 154 H5
Lossiemouth 152 A2

Lossit 142 C2
Lostford 74 F3
Lostock Gralam 74 B3
Lostock Green 74 B3
Lostock Hall 86 B3
Lostock Junction . . .86 D4
Lostwithiel 5 D6
Loth 159 E7
Lothbeg 157 H12
Lothersdale 94 E2
Lothmore 157 H12
Loudwater 40 E2
Loughborough 64 C2
Loughor 33 E6
Loughton
  Essex 41 E7
  M Keynes 53 F6
  Shrops 61 F6
Lound
  Lincs. 65 C7
  Notts. 89 F7
  Suff. 69 E8
Lount 63 C7
Louth 91 F7
Love Clough 87 B6
Lovedean 15 C7
Lover 14 B3
Loversall 89 E6
Loves Green 42 D2
Lovesome Hill 102 E1
Loveston 32 D1
Lovington 23 F7
Low Ackworth 89 C5
Low Barlings 78 B3
Low Bentham 93 C6
Low Bradfield 88 E3
Low Bradley 94 E3
Low Braithwaite . . .108 E4
Low Brunton 110 B2
Low Burnham 89 D8
Low Burton 101 F7
Low Buston 117 D8
Lowca 98 B1
Low Catton 96 D3
Low Clanyard 104 F5
Low Coniscliffe 101 C7
Low Crosby 108 D4
Low Dalby 103 F6
Lowdham 77 E6
Low Dinsdale 101 C8
Lowe 74 F2
Low Hill 75 D6
Low Ellington 101 F7
Lower Aisholt 22 F3
Lower Arncott 39 C6
Lower Ashton 10 F3
Lower Assendon 39 F7
Lower Badcall 156 E4
Lower Bartle 92 F4
Lower Basildon 26 B4
Lower Beeding 17 B6
Lower Benefield 65 F6
Lower Boddington . . .52 D2
Lower Brailes 51 F8
Lower Breakish 149 F11
Lower Broadheath . . .50 D3
Lower Bullingham . . .49 F7
Lower Cam 36 D4
Lower Chapel 48 F2
Lower Chute 25 D8
Lower Cragabus 142 D4
Lower Crossings 87 F8
Lower Cumberworth . .88 D3
Lower Darwen 86 B4
Lower Dean 53 C8
Lower Diabaig 149 B12
Lower Dicker 18 D2
Lower Dinchope 60 F4
Lower Down 60 F3
Lower Drift 2 D3
Lower Dunsforth . . .95 C6
Lower Egleton 49 E8
Lower Elkstone 75 D7
Lower End 40 B2
Lower Everleigh 25 D6
Lower Farringdon . . .26 F5
Lower Foxdale 84 E2
Lower Frankton 73 F7
Lower Froyle 27 E5
Lower Gledfield 151 B8
Lower Green 81 D5
Lower Hacheston . . .57 D7
Lower Halistra 148 C7
Lower Halstow 30 C2
Lower Hardres 31 D5
Lower Hawthwaite . .98 F4
Lower Heath 75 C5
Lower Hempriggs . . .151 E14
Lower Hergest 48 D4
Lower Heyford 38 B4
Lower Higham 29 B8
Lower Holbrook 57 F5
Lower Hordley 60 B3
Lower Horsebridge . .18 D2
Lower Killeyan 142 D3
Lower Kingswood . . .28 D3
Lower Kinnerton . . .73 C7
Lower Langford 23 C6
Lower Largo 129 D6
Lower Leigh 75 F7
Lower Lemington . . .51 F7
Lower Lenie 147 B8
Lower Lydbrook 36 C2
Lower Lye 49 C6
Lower Machen 35 F6
Lower Maes-coed . . .48 F5
Lower Mayland 43 D5
Lower Midway 63 B7
Lower Milovaig 148 C6
Lower Moor 50 E4
Lower Nazeing 41 D6
Lower Netchwood . . .61 E6
Lower Ollach 149 E10
Lower Penarth 22 B3

Lower Penn 62 E2
Lower
Pennington 14 E4
Lower Peover 74 E4
Lower Pexhill 75 B5
Lower Place 87 C7
Lower Quinton 51 E6
Lower Rochford .49 C6
Lower Seagry 37 F6
Lower Shelton 53 E7
Lower Shiplake . .27 B5
Lower
Shuckburgh 52 C2
Lower Slaughter .38 B1
Lower Stanton St
Quintin 37 F6
Lower Stoke 30 B2
Lower Stondon . . .54 F2
Lower Stow
Bedon 68 E2
Lower Street
Norf 69 C6
Norf 81 D8
Lower Strensham .50 E4
Lower Stretton . . .86 F4
Lower Sundon . . .40 B3
Lower Swanwick .15 D5
Lower Swell 38 B1
Lower Tean 75 F7
Lower Thurlton . . .69 E7
Lower Tote 149 B10
Lower Town 44 B4
Lower Tysoe 51 E8
Lower Upham 15 C6
Lower Vexford . . .22 F3
Lower Weare 23 D6
Lower Welson . . .48 D4
Lower Whitley . . .74 B3
Lower Wield 26 E4
Lower
Winchendon 39 C7
Lower
Withington 74 C5
Lower Woodend .39 F8
Lower Woodford .25 F6
Lower Wyche 50 E2
Lowesby 64 D4
Lowestoft 69 E8
Loweswater 98 B3
Low Etherley . .101 B6
Low Fell 111 D5
Lowford 15 C5
Low Fulney 66 B2
Low Garth 103 D5
Low Gate 110 C2
Lowgill
Cumb 99 E8
Lancs 93 C6
Low Grantley . . .94 B5
Low Habberley . .50 B3
Low Ham 12 B2
Low Hesket 108 E4
Low Hesleyhurst 117 E6
Low Hutton 96 C3
Lowick
Northants 65 F6
Northumb 123 F6
Lowick Bridge . . .98 F4
Lowick Green . . .98 F4
Low Laithe 94 C4
Lowlands 35 E6
Low Leighton . . .87 F8
Low Lorton 98 B3
Low Marishes . . .96 B4
Low Marnham . . .77 C8
Low Mill 102 E4
Low Moor
Lancs 93 E7
W Yorks 88 B2
Lowmoor Row . . .99 B8
Low Moorsley . .111 E6
Low Newton 99 F6
Low Newton-by-the-
Sea 117 B8
Lownie Moor . . .134 E4
Low Row
Cumb 108 F3
Cumb 109 C5
N Yorks 100 E4
Low Salchrie . . .104 C4
Low Smerby 143 F8
Lowsonford 51 C6
Lowther 99 B7
Lowthorpe 97 C6
Lowton 86 E4
Lowton Common .86 E4
Low Torry 128 F2
Low Worsall 102 D1
Low Wray 99 D5
Loxbeare 10 C4
Loxhill 27 F8
Loxhore 20 F5
Loxley 51 D7
Loxton 23 D5
Loxwood 27 F8
Lubcroy 156 J6
Lubenham 64 F4
Luccombe 21 E8
Luccombe
Village 15 G6
Lucker 123 F7
Luckett 5 B8
Luckington 37 F5
Lucklawhill 129 B6
Luckwell Bridge .21 F8
Lucton 49 C6
Ludag 148 G2
Ludborough 91 E6
Ludchurch 32 C2
Luddenden 87 B8
Luddenden Foot .87 B8
Luddesdown 29 C7
Luddington
N Lincs 90 C2
Warks 51 D6
Luddington in the
Brook 65 F8
Lude House 133 C5
Ludford
Lincs 91 F6
Shrops 49 B7
Ludgershall
Bucks 39 C6
Wilts 25 D7
Ludgvan 2 C4

Ludham 69 C6
Ludlow 49 B7
Ludwell 13 B7
Ludworth 111 E6
Luffincott 8 E5
Lugar 113 B5
Luggate Burn . .122 B2
Lugg Green 49 C6
Luggiebank 119 B7
Lugton 118 D4
Lugwardine 49 E7
Luib 149 F10
Lulham 49 E6
Lullenden 28 E5
Lullington
Derbys 63 C6
Som 24 D2
Lulsgate Bottom .23 C7
Lulsley 50 D2
Lumb 87 B8
Lumby 95 F7
Lumloch 119 C6
Lumphanan 140 D4
Lumphinnans . . .128 E3
Lumsdaine 122 C4
Lumsden 140 B3
Lunan 135 D6
Lunanhead 134 D4
Luncarty 128 B2
Lund
E Yorks 97 E5
N Yorks 96 F2
Shetland 160 C7
Lunderton 153 D11
Lundie
Angus 134 F2
Highld 136 C4
Lundin Links . . .129 D6
Lunga 124 E3
Lunna 160 G6
Lunning 160 G7
Lunnon 33 F6
Lunsford's Cross .18 D4
Lunt 85 D4
Luntley 49 D5
Luppitt 11 D6
Lupton 99 F7
Lurgashall 16 B3
Lusby 79 C6
Luson 6 E4
Luss 126 E2
Lussagiven 144 E5
Lusta 149 C7
Lustleigh 10 F2
Luston 49 C6
Luthermuir 135 C6
Luthrie 128 C5
Luton
Devon 7 B7
Luton 40 B3
Medway 29 C8
Lutterworth 64 F2
Lutton
Devon 6 D3
Lincs 66 B4
Northants 65 F8
Lutworthy 10 C2
Luxborough 21 F8
Luxulyan 5 D5
Lybster 158 G4
Lydbury North . . .60 F3
Lydcott 21 F5
Lydd 19 C7
Lydden 31 E6
Lyddington 65 E5
Lydd on Sea 19 C7
Lydeard St
Lawrence 22 F3
Lyde Green 26 D5
Lydford 9 F7
Lydford-on-
Fosse 23 F7
Lydgate 87 B7
Lydham 60 E3
Lydiard Green . . .37 F7
Lydiard Millicent .37 F7
Lydiate 85 D4
Lydlinch 12 C5
Lydney 36 D3
Lydstep 32 E1
Lye 62 F3
Lye Green
Bucks 40 D2
E Sus 18 B2
Lyford 38 E3
Lymbridge Green .30 E5
Lyme Regis 11 E8
Lyminge 31 E5
Lymington 14 E4
Lyminster 16 D4
Lymm 86 F4
Lymore 14 E3
Lympne 19 B8
Lympsham 22 D5
Lympstone 10 F4
Lynchat 138 D3
Lyndale House .149 C8
Lyndhurst 14 D4
Lyndon 65 D6
Lyne 27 C8
Lyne Down 49 F8
Lyneham
Oxon 38 B2
Wilts 24 B5
Lynemore 139 B6
Lynemouth 117 E8
Lyne of
Gorthleck 137 B8
Lyne of Skene . .141 C6
Lyness 159 J4
Lyng
Norf 68 C3
Som 11 B8
Lynmouth 21 E6
Lynsted 30 C3
Lynton 21 E6
Lyon's Gate 12 D4
Lyonshall 48 D5
Lytchett
Matravers 13 E7
Lytchett Minster .13 E7
Lyth 158 D4
Lytham 85 B4
Lytham St Anne's .85 B4
Lythe 103 C6
Lythes 159 K5

M

Mabe Burnthouse .3 C6
Mabie 107 B6
Mablethorpe 91 F9
Macclesfield 75 B6
Macclesfield
Forest 75 B6
Macduff 153 B7
Mace Green 56 E5
Macharioch 143 H8
Machen 35 F6
Machrihanish . .143 F7
Machynlleth 58 D4
Machynys 33 E6
Mackerel's
Common 16 B4
Mackworth 76 F3
Macmerry 121 B7
Madderty 127 B8
Maddiston 120 B2
Madehurst 16 C3
Madeley
Staffs 74 E4
Telford 61 D6
Madeley Heath . .74 E4
Madeley Park . . .74 E4
Madingley 54 C4
Madley 49 F6
Madresfield 50 E3
Madron 2 C3
Maen-y-groes . . .46 D2
Maenaddwyn 82 C4
Maenclochog 32 B1
Maendy 22 B2
Maentwrog 71 C7
Maer 74 F4
Maerdy
Conwy 72 E4
Rhondda 34 E3
Maes-y-groes . . .46 D2
Maesbrook 60 B2
Maesbury 60 B3
Maesbury Marsh .60 B3
Maesgwyn-Isaf. .59 C8
Maesgwynne 32 B3
Maeshafn 73 C6
Maesllyn 46 E2
Maesteg 34 E2
Maesybont 33 C6
Maesycrugiau . . .46 E3
Maesymeillion . .46 E3
Magdalen Laver .41 D8
Maggieknockater
. . . . .152 D3
Magham Down . .18 D3
Maghull 85 D4
Magor 35 F8
Magpie Green . . .68 F4
Maiden Bradley . .24 F3
Maidencombe. . . .7 C7
Maidenhall 57 E5
Maidenhead 40 F1
Maiden Law 110 E4
Maiden Newton .12 E3
Maidens 112 D2
Maidensgrave . . .57 E6
Maiden's Green . .27 B6
Maidenwell
Corn 5 B6
Lincs 79 B6
Maiden Wells 44 F4
Maidford 52 D4
Maids Moreton . .52 F5
Maidstone 29 D8
Maidwell 52 B5
Mail 160 L6
Main 59 C8
Maindee 35 F7
Mainsforth 111 F6
Mains of Airies .104 C3
Mains of
Allardice 135 B8
Mains of
Annochie 153 D9
Mains of
Ardestie 135 F5
Mains of Balhall 135 C5
Mains of
Ballindarg 134 D4
Mains of
Balnakettle . . .135 B6
Mains of
Birness 153 E9
Mains of
Burgie 151 F13
Mains of
Clunas 151 G11
Mains of
Crichie 153 D9
Mains of
Dalvey 151 H14
Mains of
Dellavaird 141 F6
Mains of Drum .141 E7
Mains of
Edingight 152 C5
Mains of
Fedderate 153 D8
Mains of
Inkhorn 153 E9
Mains of Mayen 152 D5
Mains of
Melgund 135 D5
Mains of
Thornton 135 B6
Mains of
Watten 158 E4
Mainsriddle 107 D6
Mainstone 60 F2
Maisemore 37 B5
Malacleit 148 A2
Malborough. 6 F5
Malcoff 87 F8
Maldon 42 D4
Malham 94 C2
Maligar 149 B9
Mallaig 147 B9
Malleny Mills . . .120 C4
Malling 126 C4
Mallwyd 59 C5
Malmesbury 37 F6
Malmsmead 21 E6

Malpas
Ches W 73 E8
Corn 3 B7
Newport 35 E7
Malswick 36 B4
Maltby
Stockton 102 C2
S Yorks 89 E6
Maltby le Marsh .91 F8
Malting Green . . .43 B5
Maltman's Hill . . .30 E3
Malton 96 B3
Malvern Link 50 E2
Malvern Wells . . .50 E2
Mamble 49 B8
Mamhead 7 B8
Mamhilad 35 D7
Manaccan 3 D6
Manafon 59 D8
Manais 154 J6
Manar House . . .141 B6
Manaton 10 F2
Manby 91 F7
Mancetter 63 E7
Manchester 87 E6
Manchester
Airport 87 F6
Mancot 73 C7
Mandally 137 D5
Manea 66 F4
Manfield 101 C7
Mangaster 160 F5
Mangotsfield. . . .23 B8
Mangurstadh . . .154 D5
Mankinholes 87 B7
Manley 74 B2
Manmoel 35 D5
Mannal 146 G2
Mannerston 120 B3
Manningford
Bohune 25 D6
Manningford
Bruce 25 D6
Manningham 94 F4
Mannings Heath. .17 B6
Mannington 81 D7
Manningtree 56 F4
Mannofield 141 D8
Manor 41 F7
Manorbier 32 E1
Manordeilo 33 B7
Manor Estate. . . .88 F4
Manorhill 122 F2
Manorowen 44 B4
Mansel Curdge . .33 F6
Mansell Gamage .49 E5
Mansergh 99 F8
Mansfield
E Ayrs 113 C6
Notts 76 C5
Mansfield
Woodhouse 76 C5
Mansriggs 98 F4
Manston
Dorset 13 C6
Kent 31 C7
W Yorks 95 F6
Manswood 13 D7
Manthorpe
Lincs 65 C7
Lincs 78 F2
Manton
N Lincs 90 D3
Notts 77 B5
Rutland 65 D5
Wilts 25 C6
Manuden 41 B7
Maperton 12 B4
Maplebeck 77 C7
Maple Cross 40 E3
Mapledurham . . .26 B4
Mapledurwell . . .26 D4
Maplehurst 17 B5
Maplescombe . . .29 C6
Mapperley 76 E4
Mapperley Park . .77 E5
Mapperton 12 E3
Mappleborough
Green 51 C5
Mappleton 97 E8
Mappowder 12 D5
Maraig 154 G6
Marazanvose 4 D3
Marazion 2 C4
Marbhig 155 F9
Marbury 74 E2
March
Cambs 66 E4
S Lanark 114 C2
Marcham 38 E4
Marchamley 61 B5
Marchington 75 F8
Marchington
Woodlands 62 B5
Marchroes 70 E4
Marchwiel 73 E7
Marchwood 14 C4
Marcross 21 C8
Marden
Hereford 49 E7
Kent 29 E8
T&W 111 B6
Wilts 25 D5
Marden Beech . . .29 E8
Marden Thorn. . . .29 E8
Mardy 35 C7
Marefield 64 D4
Mareham le Fen .79 C5
Mareham on the
Hill 79 C5
Marehay 76 E3
Marehill 16 C4
Maresfield 17 B8
Marfleet 90 B5
Marford 73 D7
Margam 34 F1
Margaret Marsh .13 C6
Margaret Roding .42 C1
Margaretting 42 D2
Margate 31 B7
Margnaheglish 143 E11
Margrove Park . .102 C4
Marham 67 C7
Marhamchurch. . .8 A4
Marholm 65 D8
Mariandyrys 83 C6
Marianglas 82 C5
Mariansleigh 10 B2

Marionburgh . . .141 D6
Marishader 149 B9
Marjoriebanks . .114 F3
Mark
Dumfries 104 D5
S Ayrs 104 B4
Som 23 E5
Markbeech. 29 E5
Markby 79 B7
Mark Causeway .23 E5
Mark Cross
E Sus 17 C8
E Sus 18 B2
Market Bosworth 63 D8
Market Deeping . .65 D8
Market Drayton . .74 F3
Market
Harborough 64 F4
Markethill 134 F2
Market Lavington 24 D5
Market Overton . .65 C5
Market Rasen . . .90 F5
Market Stainton .78 B5
Market Warsop . .77 C5
Market Weighton .96 E4
Market Weston . .56 B3
Markfield 63 C8
Markham 35 D5
Markham Moor . .77 B7
Markinch 128 D4
Markington 95 C5
Marksbury 23 C8
Marks Tey 43 B5
Markyate 40 C3
Marland 87 C6
Marlborough 25 C6
Marlbrook
Hereford 49 D7
Worcs 50 B4
Marlcliff 51 D5
Marldon 7 C6
Marlesford 57 D7
Marley Green. . . .74 E2
Marley Hill 110 D5
Marley Mount . . .14 E3
Marlingford 68 D4
Marloes 44 E2
Marlow
Bucks 39 F8
Hereford 49 B6
Marlow Bottom . .40 F1
Marlpit Hill 28 E5
Marlpool 76 E4
Marnhull 13 C5
Marnock 152 C5
Marnoch 119 C7
Marple 87 F7
Marple Bridge . . .87 F7
Marr 89 D6
Marrel 157 H13
Marrick 101 E5
Marrister 160 G7
Marros 32 D3
Marsden
T&W 111 C6
W Yorks 87 C8
Marsett 100 F4
Marsh
Devon 11 C7
W Yorks 94 F3
Marshall's Heath 40 C4
Marshalsea 11 D8
Marshalswick . . .40 D4
Marsham 81 E7
Marshaw 93 D5
Marsh Baldon . . .39 E5
Marshborough . .31 D7
Marshbrook 60 F4
Marshchapel 91 E7
Marshfield
Newport 35 F6
S Glos 24 B2
Marsh Gibbon . . .39 B6
Marsh Green
Devon 10 E5
Kent 28 E5
Staffs 75 D5
Marshland St
James 66 D5
Marsh Lane 76 B4
Marshside 85 C4
Marsh Street 21 E8
Marshwood 11 E8
Marske 101 D6
Marske-by-the-
Sea 102 B4
Marston
Ches W 74 B3
Hereford 49 D5
Lincs 77 E8
Oxon 39 D5
Staffs 62 B3
Staffs 62 C2
Warks 63 E6
Wilts 24 C4
Marston Doles . . .52 D2
Marston Green . .63 F5
Marston Magna . .12 B3
Marston Meysey .37 E8
Marston
Montgomery . . .75 F8
Marston
Moretaine 53 E7
Marston on Dove .63 B6
Marston St
Lawrence 52 E3
Marston Stannett .49 D7
Marston Trussell .64 F3
Marstow 36 C2
Marsworth 40 C2
Marten 25 D7
Marthall 74 B5
Martham 69 C7
Martin
Hants 13 C8
Kent 31 E7
Lincs 78 C4
Lincs 78 D4
Martin Dales 78 C4
Martin Drove End .13 B8
Martinhoe 21 E5
Martinhoe Cross .21 E5
Martin
Hussingtree 50 C3
Martin Mill 31 E7
Martinscroft 86 F4

Martinstown 12 F4
Martlesham 57 E6
Martlesham
Heath 57 E6
Martletwy 32 C1
Martley 50 D2
Martock 12 C2
Marton
Ches E 75 C5
E Yorks 97 F7
Lincs 90 F2
Mbro 102 C3
N Yorks 95 C7
N Yorks 103 F5
Shrops 60 B4
Shrops 60 D2
Warks 52 C2
Marton-le-Moor .95 B6
Martyr's Green . .27 D8
Martyr Worthy . . .26 F3
Marwick 159 F3
Marwood 20 F4
Marybank 150 F7
Maryburgh 151 F8
Maryhill 119 C5
Marykirk 135 C6
Marylebone 86 D3
Marypark 152 E1
Maryport
Cumb 107 F7
Dumfries 104 F5
Mary Tavy 6 B3
Maryton 135 D6
Marywell
Aberds 140 E4
Aberds 141 E8
Angus 135 E6
Masham 101 F7
Mashbury 42 C2
Masongill 93 B6
Masonhill 112 B3
Mastin Moor 76 B4
Mastrick 141 D7
Matching 41 C8
Matching Green . .41 C8
Matching Tye 41 C8
Matfen 110 B3
Matfield 29 E7
Mathern 36 E2
Mathon 50 E2
Mathry 44 B3
Matlaske 81 D7
Matlock 76 C2
Matlock Bath 76 D2
Matson 37 C5
Matterdale End. . .99 B5
Mattersey 89 F7
Mattersey Thorpe 89 F7
Mattingley 26 D5
Mattishall 68 C3
Mattishall Burgh .68 C3
Mauchline 112 B4
Maud 153 D9
Maugersbury. . . .38 B2
Maughold 84 C4
Mauld 150 H7
Maulden 53 F8
Maulds Meaburn .99 C8
Maunby 102 F1
Maund Bryan . . .49 D7
Maundown 11 B5
Mautby 69 C7
Mavis Enderby . .79 C6
Mawbray 107 E7
Mawdesley 86 C2
Mawdlam 34 F2
Mawgan 3 D6
Maw Green 74 D4
Mawla 4 D2
Mawnan 3 D6
Mawnan Smith . . .3 D6
Mawsley 53 B6
Maxey 65 D8
Maxstoke 63 F6
Maxton
Borders 122 F2
Kent 31 E7
Maxwellheugh . .122 F3
Maxwelltown . . .107 B6
Maxworthy 8 E4
Mayals 33 E7
May Bank 75 E5
Maybole 112 D3
Mayfield
E Sus 18 C2
Midloth 121 C6
Staffs 75 E8
W Loth 120 C2
Mayford 27 D7
Mayland 43 D5
Maynard's Green 18 D2
Maypole
Mon. 36 C1
Scilly 2 E4
Maypole Green
Essex 43 B5
Norf 69 E7
Suff 57 C6
Maywick 160 L5
Meadle 39 D8
Meadowtown 60 D3
Meaford 75 F5
Mealabost 155 D9
Mealabost
Bhuirgh 155 B9
Meal Bank 99 E7
Mealsgate 108 E2
Meanwood 95 F5
Mearbeck 93 C8
Meare 23 E6
Meare Green
Som 11 B8
Som 11 B8
Mears Ashby 53 C6
Measham 63 C7
Meath Green 28 E3
Meathop 99 F6
Meaux 97 F6
Meavy 6 C3
Medbourne 64 E4
Medburn 110 B4
Meddon 8 C4
Meden Vale 77 C6
Medlam 79 D6
Medmenham 39 F8
Medomsley 110 D4
Medstead 26 F4
Meer End 51 B7
Meerbrook 75 C6
Meers Bridge 91 F8

Meesden 54 F5
Meeth 9 D7
Meggethead 114 B4
Meidrim 32 B3
Meifod
Denb 72 D4
Powys 59 C8
Meigle
N Ayrs 118 C1
Perth 134 E2
Meikle Earnock 119 D7
Meikle Ferry . . .151 C10
Meikle Forter . . .134 C2
Meikle Gluich . .151 C9
Meikleour 134 F1
Meikle
Pinkerton 122 B3
Meikle Strath . . .135 B6
Meikle Tarty 141 B8
Meikle Wartle . . .153 E7
Meinciau 33 C5
Meir 75 E6
Meir Heath 75 E6
Melbourn 54 E4
Melbourne
Derbys 63 B7
E Yorks 96 E3
S Lanark 120 E3
Melbury Abbas . .13 B6
Melbury Bubb . . .12 D3
Melbury Osmond 12 D3
Melbury
Sampford 12 D3
Melby 160 H3
Melchbourne 53 C8
Melcombe
Bingham 13 D5
Melcombe Regis .12 F4
Meldon
Devon 9 E7
Northumb 117 F7
Meldreth 54 E4
Meldrum House .141 B7
Melfort 124 D4
Melgarve 137 E7
Meliden 72 A4
Melin-y-coed 83 E8
Melin-y-ddôl 59 D7
Melin-y-grug 59 D7
Melin-y-Wig 72 E4
Melinbyrhedyn . .58 D5
Melincourt 34 D2
Melincryddan 34 E1
Melkinthorpe 99 B7
Melkridge 109 C7
Melksham 24 C4
Melldalloch 145 E8
Melling
Lancs 93 B5
Mers 85 D4
Melling Mount . . .86 D2
Mellis 56 B5
Mellon Charles 155 H13
Mellon Udrigle 155 H13
Mellor
Gtr Man 87 F7
Lancs 93 F6
Mellor Brook 93 F6
Mells 24 E2
Melmerby
Cumb 109 F6
N Yorks 95 B6
N Yorks 101 F6
Melplash 12 E2
Melrose 121 F8
Melsetter 159 K3
Melsonby 101 D6
Meltham 88 C2
Melton 57 D6
Meltonby 96 D3
Melton Constable 81 D6
Melton Mowbray 64 C4
Melton Ross 90 C4
Melvaig 155 J12
Melverley 60 C3
Melverley Green . 60 C3
Melvich 157 C11
Membury 11 D7
Memsie 153 B9
Memus 134 D4
Menabilly 5 D5
Menai Bridge
= Porthaethwy . .83 D5
Mendham 69 F6
Mendlesham 56 C5
Mendlesham
Green 56 C4
Menheniot 5 C7
Mennock 113 D8
Menston 94 E4
Menstrie 127 E7
Menthorpe 96 F2
Mentmore 40 C2
Meoble 147 C10
Meole Brace 60 C4
Meols 85 E3
Meonstoke 15 C7
Meopham 29 C7
Meopham Station 29 C7
Mepal 66 F4
Meppershall 54 F2
Merbach 48 E5
Mere
Ches E 86 F5
Wilts 24 F3
Mere Brow 86 C2
Mereclough 93 F8
Mere Green 62 E5
Mereside 92 F3
Mereworth 29 D7
Mergie 141 F6
Meriden 63 F7
Merkadale 149 E8
Merkland
Dumfries 106 B4
S Ayrs 112 E2
Merkland Lodge 156 G7
Merley 13 E8
Merlin's Bridge . .44 D4
Merrington 60 B4
Merrion 44 F4
Merriott 12 C2
Merrivale 6 B3
Merrow 27 D8
Merrymeet 5 C7
Mersham 19 B7
Merstham 28 D3
Merston 16 D2
Merstone 15 F6

Merther 3 B7
Merthyr 32 B4
Merthyr Cynog . . 47 F8
Merthyr-Dyfan . .22 C3
Merthyr Mawr . . .21 B7
Merthyr Tudful
= Merthyr Tydfil . 34 D4
Merthyr Tydfil
= Merthyr Tudful . 34 D4
Merthyr Vale 34 D4
Merton
Devon 9 C7
London 28 B3
Norf 68 E2
Oxon 39 C5
Mervinslaw 116 C2
Meshaw 10 C2
Messing 42 C4
Messingham 90 D2
Metfield 69 F5
Metheringham . . .78 C3
Methil 129 E5
Methlem 70 D2
Methley 88 B4
Methlick 153 E8
Methven 128 B2
Methwold 67 E7
Methwold Hythe .67 E7
Mettingham 69 F6
Mevagissey 3 B9
Mewith Head 93 C7
Mexborough 89 D5
Mey 158 C4
Meysey Hampton 37 E8
Miabhag
W Isles 154 G5
W Isles 154 H6
Miabhig 154 D5
Michaelchurch . .36 B2
Michaelchurch
Escley 48 F5
Michaelchurch on
Arrow 48 D4
Michaelston-le-
Pit 22 B3
Michaelston-y-
Fedw 35 F6
Michaelstow 5 B5
Michaelston-super-
Ely 22 B3
Micheldever 26 F3
Michelmersh 14 B4
Mickfield 56 C5
Micklebring 89 E6
Mickleby 103 C6
Micklefield 95 F7
Mickleham 28 D2
Mickleover 76 F3
Micklethwaite . . .94 E4
Mickleton
Durham 100 B4
Glos 51 E6
Mickletown 88 B4
Mickle Trafford . .73 C8
Mickley 95 B5
Mickley Square . 110 C3
Mid Ardlaw 153 B9
Mid Auchinlech 118 B3
Midbea 159 D5
Mid Beltie 140 D5
Mid Calder 120 C3
Mid Cloch
Forbie 153 C7
Mid Clyth 158 G4
Middle
Assendon 39 F7
Middlebie 108 B2
Middle
Cairncake 153 D8
Middle Claydon . .39 B7
Middle Drums . . .135 D5
Middleforth
Green 86 B3
Middleham 101 F6
Middle Handley . .76 B4
Middlehope 60 F4
Middle Littleton . .51 E5
Middle Maes-
coed 48 F5
Middlemarsh 12 D4
Middlemuir 141 B8
Middle Rasen . . .90 F4
Middlesbrough .102 B2
Middleshaw
Cumb 99 F7
Middlesmoor 94 B3
Middlestone 111 F5
Middlestone
Moor 110 F5
Middlestown 88 C3
Middlethird 122 E2
Middleton
Aberds 141 C7
Argyll 146 G2
Cumb 99 F8
Derbys 75 C8
Derbys 76 D2
Essex 56 F2
Gtr Man 87 D6
Hants 26 E2
Hereford 49 C7
Lancs 92 D4
Midloth 121 D6
Norf 67 C6
Northants 64 F5
Northumb 117 F6
Northumb 123 F7
N Yorks 94 E4
N Yorks 103 F5
Perth 128 D3
Perth 133 E8
Shrops 49 B7
Shrops 60 B3
Suff 57 C8
Swansea 33 F5
Warks 63 E5
W Yorks 88 B3
Middleton
Cheney 52 E2
Middleton Green .75 F6
Middleton Hall . .117 B5
Middleton-in-
Teesdale 100 B4

Middleton Moor .57 C8
Middleton One
Row 102 C1
Middleton-on-
Leven 102 D2
Middleton-on-
Sea 16 D3
Middleton on the
Hill 49 C7
Middleton-on-the-
Wolds 96 E5
Middleton Priors .61 E6
Middleton
Quernhow 95 B6
Middleton St
George 101 C8
Middleton
Scriven 61 F6
Middleton Stoney 39 B5
Middleton Tyas .101 D7
Middletown
Cumb 98 D1
Powys 60 C3
Middle Tysoe 51 E8
Middle Wallop . . .25 F7
Middlewich 74 C3
Middle
Winterslow 25 F7
Middle Woodford 25 F6
Middlewood
Green 56 C4
Middlezoy 23 F5
Middridge 101 B7
Midfield 157 C8
Midge Hall 86 B3
Midgeholme 109 D6
Midgham 26 C3
Midgley
W Yorks 87 B8
W Yorks 88 C3
Midhopestones . .88 E3
Midhurst 16 B2
Mid Lavant 16 D2
Midlem 115 B8
Mid Main 150 H7
Midmar 141 D5
Midsomer Norton 23 D8
Midton 118 B2
Midtown
Highld 155 J13
Highld 157 C8
Midtown of
Buchromb 152 D3
Mid Urchany . . .151 G11
Midville 79 D6
Mid Walls 160 H4
Mid Yell 160 D7
Migdale 151 B9
Migvie 140 D3
Milarrochy 126 E3
Milborne St
Andrew 13 E6
Milborne Port . . .12 C4
Milborne St
Andrew 13 E6
Milborne Wick . .12 B4
Milbourne 110 B4
Milburn 100 B1
Milbury Heath . . .36 E3
Milcombe 52 F2
Milden 56 E3
Mildenhall
Suff 55 B8
Wilts 25 C7
Milebrook 48 B5
Milebush 29 E8
Mile Cross 68 C5
Mile Elm 24 C4
Mile End
Essex 43 B5
Glos 36 C2
Mileham 68 C2
Mile Oak 17 D6
Milesmark 128 F2
Milfield 122 F5
Milford
Derbys 76 E3
Devon 8 B4
Powys 59 E7
Staffs 62 B3
Sur 27 E7
Wilts 14 B2
Milford Haven
= Aberdaugleddau
. . . . .44 E4
Milford on Sea . .14 E3
Milkwall 36 D2
Milkwell 13 B7
Milland 16 B2
Millarston 118 C4
Millbank
Aberds 153 D11
Highld 158 D3
Mill Bank 87 B8
Millbeck 98 B4
Millbounds 159 E6
Millbreck 153 D10
Millbridge 27 E6
Millbrook
C Beds 53 F8
Corn 6 D2
Soton 14 C4
Millburn 112 B4
Millcombe 7 E6
Mill Common 69 F7
Millcorner 18 C5
Milldale 75 D8
Millden Lodge . .135 B5
Milldens 135 D5
Mill End
Bucks 39 F7
Herts 54 F4
Millerhill 121 C6
Miller's Dale 75 B8
Miller's Green . . .76 D2
Millgreen 61 B6
Mill Green
Essex 42 D2
Norf 68 F4
Suff 56 E3
Millhalf 48 E4
Millhayes 11 D7
Millhead 92 B4
Millheugh 119 D7
Mill Hill 41 E5
Millholme 99 E7
Millhouse
Argyll 145 E8
Cumb 108 F3

Mil–New 217

Millhousebridge 114 F4
Millhouse Green 88 D3
Millhouses 88 F4
Millikenpark 118 C4
Millin Cross 44 D4
Millington 96 D4
Mill Lane 27 D5
Millmeece 74 F5
Mill of Kingoodie 141 B7
Mill of Muiresk 153 D6
Mill of Sterin 140 E2
Mill of Uras 141 F7
Millom 98 F3
Millook 8 E3
Mill Place 90 D3
Millpool 5 B6
Millport 145 H10
Millquarter 113 F6
Mill Side 99 F6
Mill Street 68 C3
Millthorpe 78 F4
Millthrop 100 E1
Milltimber 141 D7
Milltown
Corn 5 D6
Derbys 76 C3
Devon 20 F4
Dumfries 108 B3
Milltown of Aberdalgie 128 B2
Milltown of Auchindoun 152 D3
Milltown of Craigston 153 C7
Milltown of Edinvillie 152 D2
Milltown of Kildrummy 140 C3
Milltown of Rothiemay 152 D5
Milltown of Towie 140 C3
Milnathort 128 D3
Milner's Heath 73 C8
Milngavie 119 B5
Milnrow 87 C7
Milnshaw 87 B5
Milnthorpe 99 F6
Milo 33 C6
Milson 49 B8
Milstead 30 D3
Milston 25 E6
Milton
Angus 134 E3
Cambs 55 C5
Cumb 109 C5
Derbys 63 B7
Dumfries 105 D6
Dumfries 106 B5
Dumfries 113 F8
Highld 150 F6
Highld 150 H7
Highld 151 D10
Highld 151 G8
Highld 158 E5
Moray 152 B5
Notts 77 B7
N Som 22 C5
Oxon 38 E4
Oxon 52 F2
Pembs 32 D1
Perth 127 C8
Ptsmth 15 E7
Stirling 126 D4
Stoke 75 D6
W Dunb 118 B4
Milton Abbas 13 D6
Milton Abbot 6 B2
Milton Bridge 120 C5
Milton Bryan 53 F7
Milton Clevedon 23 F8
Milton Coldwells 153 E9
Milton Combe 6 C2
Milton Damerel 9 C5
Miltonduff 152 B1
Milton End 37 D8
Milton Ernest 53 D8
Milton Green 73 D8
Miltonhill 151 E13
Milton Hill 38 E4
Miltonise 105 B5
Milton Keynes 53 F6
Milton Keynes Village 53 F6
Milton Lilbourne 25 C6
Milton Malsor 52 D5
Milton Morenish 132 F3
Milton of Auchinhove 140 D4
Milton of Balgonie 128 D5
Milton of Buchanan 126 E3
Milton of Campfield 140 D5
Milton of Campsie 119 B6
Milton of Corsindae 141 D5
Milton of Cushnie 140 C4
Milton of Dalcapon 133 D6
Milton of Edradour 133 D6
Milton of Gollanfield 151 F10
Milton of Lesmore 140 B3
Milton of Logie 140 D3
Milton of Murtle 141 D7
Milton of Noth 140 B4
Milton of Tullich 140 E2
Milton on Stour 24 F2
Milton Regis 30 C3
Milton under Wychwood 38 C2
Milverton
Som 11 B6
Warks 51 C8
Milwich 75 F6
Minard 125 F5
Minchinhampton 37 D5
Mindrum 122 F4
Minehead 21 E8
Minera 73 D6
Minety 37 E7
Minffordd
Gwyn 58 C4
Gwyn 71 D6
Gwyn 83 D5
Miningsby 79 C6
Minions 5 B7
Minishant 112 C3
Minllyn 59 C5
Minnes 141 B8
Minngearraidh 148 F2
Minnigaff 105 C8
Minnonie 153 B7
Minskip 95 C6
Minstead 14 C3
Minsted 16 B2
Minster
Kent 30 B3
Kent 31 C7
Minsterley 60 D3
Minster Lovell 38 C3
Minsterworth 36 C4
Minterne Magna 12 D4
Minting 78 B4
Mintlaw 153 D9
Minto 115 B8
Minton 60 E4
Minwear 32 C1
Minworth 63 E5
Mirbister 159 F4
Mirehouse 98 C1
Mireland 158 D5
Mirfield 88 C3
Miserden 37 D6
Miskin 34 F4
Misson 89 E7
Misterton
Leics 64 F2
Notts 89 E8
Som 12 D2
Mistley 56 F5
Mitcham 28 C3
Mitcheldean 36 C3
Mitchell 4 D3
Mitchel Troy 36 C1
Mitcheltroy Common 36 D1
Mitford 117 F7
Mithian 4 D2
Mitton 62 C2
Mixbury 52 F4
Moat 108 B4
Moats Tye 56 D4
Mobberley
Ches E 74 B4
Staffs 75 E7
Moccas 49 E5
Mochdre
Conwy 83 D8
Powys 59 F7
Mochrum 105 E7
Mockbeggar 14 D2
Mockerkin 98 B2
Modbury 6 D4
Moddershall 75 F6
Moelfre
Anglesey 82 C5
Powys 59 B8
Moffat 114 D3
Moggerhanger 54 E2
Moira 63 C7
Molash 30 D4
Mol-chlach 149 G9
Mold = Yr Wyddgrug 73 C6
Moldgreen 88 C2
Molehill Green 42 B1
Molescroft 97 E6
Molesden 117 F7
Molesworth 53 B8
Moll 149 E10
Molland 10 B3
Mollington
Ches W 73 B7
Oxon 52 E2
Mollinsburn 119 B7
Monachty 46 C4
Monachylemore 126 C3
Monar Lodge 150 G5
Monaughty 48 C4
Monboddo House 135 B7
Mondynes 135 B7
Monevechadan 125 E7
Monewden 57 D6
Moneydie 128 B2
Moniaive 113 E7
Monifieth 134 F4
Monikie 135 F4
Monimail 128 C4
Monington 45 E3
Monk Bretton 88 D4
Monken Hadley 41 E5
Monk Fryston 89 B6
Monkhopton 61 E6
Monkland 49 D6
Monkleigh 9 B6
Monknash 21 B8
Monkokehampton 9 D7
Monkseaton 111 B6
Monks Eleigh 56 E3
Monk's Gate 17 B6
Monks Heath 74 B5
Monk Sherborne 26 D4
Monkshill 153 D7
Monksilver 22 F2
Monks Kirby 63 F8
Monk Soham 57 C6
Monkspath 51 B6
Monks Risborough 39 D8
Monk Street 42 B2
Monkswood 35 D7
Monkton
Devon 11 D6
Kent 31 C6
Pembs 44 E4
S Ayrs 112 B3
Monkton Combe 24 C2
Monkton Deverill 24 F3
Monkton Farleigh 24 C3
Monkton Heathfield 11 B7
Monkton Up Wimborne 13 C8
Monkwearmouth 111 D6
Monkwood 26 F4
Monmouth = Trefynwy 36 C2
Monmouth Cap 35 B7
Monnington on Wye 49 E5
Monreith 105 E7
Monreith Mains 105 E7
Montacute 12 C2
Montcoffer House 153 B6
Montford
Argyll 145 G10
Shrops 60 C4
Montford Bridge 60 C4
Montgarrie 140 C4
Montgomery = Trefaldwyn 60 E2
Montrave 129 D5
Montrose 135 D7
Mont Saint 16
Montsale 43 E6
Monxton 25 E8
Monyash 75 C8
Monymusk 141 C5
Monzie 127 B7
Monzie Castle 127 B7
Moodiesburn 119 B6
Moonzie 128 C5
Moor Allerton 95 F5
Moorby 79 C5
Moor Crichel 13 D7
Moordown 13 E8
Moore 86 F3
Moorend 36 D4
Moor End
E Yorks 96 F4
York 96 D2
Moorends 89 C7
Moorgate 88 E5
Moorgreen 76 E4
Moorhall 76 B3
Moorhampton 49 E5
Moorhead 94 F4
Moorhouse
Cumb 108 D3
Notts 77 C7
Moorlinch 23 F5
Moor Monkton 95 D8
Moor of Granary 151 F13
Moor of Ravenstone 105 E7
Moor Row 98 C2
Moorsholm 102 C4
Moorside 87 D7
Moor Street 30 C2
Moorthorpe 89 C5
Moortown
Hants 14 D2
IoW 14 F5
Lincs 90 E4
Morangie 151 C10
Morar 147 B9
Morborne 65 E8
Morchard Bishop 10 D2
Morcombelake 12 E2
Morcott 65 D6
Morda 60 B2
Morden
Dorset 13 E7
London 28 C3
Mordiford 49 F7
Mordon 101 B8
More 60 E3
Morebath 10 B4
Morebattle 116 B3
Morecambe 92 C4
Morefield 150 B4
Moreleigh 7 D5
Morenish 132 F2
Moresby 98 B1
Moresby Parks 98 C1
Morestead 15 B6
Moreton
Dorset 13 F6
Essex 41 D8
Mers 85 E3
Oxon 39 D6
Staffs 61 C7
Moreton Corbet 61 B5
Moretonhampstead 10 F2
Moreton-in-Marsh 51 F7
Moreton Jeffries 49 E8
Moreton Morrell 51 D8
Moreton on Lugg 49 E7
Moreton Pinkney 52 E3
Moreton Say 74 F3
Moreton Valence 36 D4
Morfa
Carms 33 C6
Carms 33 E6
Morfa Bach 32 C4
Morfa Bychan 71 D6
Morfa Dinlle 82 F4
Morfa Glas 34 D2
Morfa Nefyn 70 C3
Morfydd 72 E5
Morgan's Vale 14 B2
Moriah 46 B5
Morland 99 B7
Morley
Derbys 76 E3
Durham 101 B6
W Yorks 88 B3
Morley Green 87 F6
Morley St Botolph 68 E3
Morningside
Edin 120 B5
N Lanark 119 D8
Morningthorpe 68 E5
Morpeth 117 F8
Morphie 135 C7
Morrey 62 C5
Morris Green 55 F8
Morriston 33 E7
Morston 81 C6
Mortehoe 20 E3
Mortimer 26 C4
Mortimer's Cross 49 C6
Mortimer West End 26 C4
Mortlake 28 B3
Morton
Cumb 108 D3
Morton *continued*
Derbys 76 C4
Lincs 65 B7
Lincs 77 C8
Lincs 90 E2
Norf 68 C4
Notts 77 D7
S Glos 36 E3
Shrops 60 B2
Morton Bagot 51 C6
Morton-on-Swale 101 E8
Morvah 2 C3
Morval 5 D7
Morvich
Highld 136 B2
Highld 157 J10
Morville 61 E6
Morville Heath 61 E6
Morwenstow 8 C4
Mosborough 88 F5
Moscow 118 E4
Mosedale 108 F3
Moseley
W Mid 62 E3
W Mid 62 F4
Worcs 50 D3
Moss
Argyll 146 G2
Highld 147 E9
S Yorks 89 C6
Wrex 73 D7
Mossat 140 C3
Mossbank 160 F6
Moss Bank 86 E3
Mossbay 98 B1
Mossblown 112 B4
Mossbrow 86 F5
Mossburnford 116 C2
Mossdale 106 B3
Moss Edge 92 E4
Mossend 119 C7
Moss End 27 B6
Mosser 98 B3
Mossfield 151 D9
Mossgiel 112 B4
Mosside 134 D4
Mossley
Ches E 75 C5
Gtr Man 87 D7
Mossley Hill 85 F4
Moss of Barmuckity 152 B2
Moss Pit 62 B3
Moss-side 151 F11
Moss Side 92 F3
Mosstodloch 152 B3
Mosston 135 E5
Mossy Lea 86 C3
Mosterton 12 D2
Moston
Gtr Man 87 D6
Shrops 61 B5
Moston Green 74 C4
Mostyn 85 F2
Mostyn Quay 85 F2
Motcombe 13 B6
Mothecombe 6 E4
Motherby 99 B6
Motherwell 119 D7
Mottingham 28 B5
Mottisfont 14 B4
Mottistone 14 F5
Mottram in Longdendale 87 E7
Mottram St Andrew 75 B5
Mouilpied 16
Mouldsworth 74 B2
Moulin 133 D6
Moulsecoomb 17 D7
Moulsford 39 F5
Moulsoe 53 E7
Moulton
Ches W 74 C3
Lincs 66 B3
Northants 53 C5
N Yorks 101 D7
Suff 55 C7
V Glam 22 B2
Moulton Chapel 66 C2
Moulton Eaugate 66 C3
Moulton St Mary 69 D6
Moulton Seas End 66 B3
Mounie Castle 141 B6
Mount
Corn 4 D2
Corn 5 C6
Highld 151 G12
Mountain 94 F3
Mountain Ash = Aberpennar 34 E4
Mountain Cross 120 E4
Mountain Water 44 C4
Mountbenger 115 B6
Mount Bures 56 F3
Mount Canisp 151 D10
Mountfield 18 C4
Mountgerald 151 E8
Mount Hawke 3 B6
Mountjoy 4 C3
Mountnessing 42 E2
Mounton 36 E2
Mount Pleasant
Ches E 74 D5
Derbys 63 C6
Derbys 76 E3
Flint 73 B6
Hants 14 E3
W Yorks 88 B3
Mountsorrel 64 C2
Mount Sorrel 13 B8
Mount Tabor 87 B8
Mousehole 2 D3
Mousen 123 F7
Mouswald 107 B7
Mow Cop 75 D5
Mowhaugh 116 B4
Mowsley 64 F3
Moxley 62 E3
Moy
Highld 137 F7
Highld 151 H10
Moy Hall 151 H10
Moy House 151 E13
Moyles Court 14 D2
Moylgrove 45 E3
Moy Lodge 137 F7
Muasdale 143 D7
Muchalls 141 E8
Much Birch 49 F7
Much Cowarne 49 E8
Much Dewchurch 49 F6
Muchelney 12 B2
Much Hadham 41 C7
Much Hoole 86 B2
Muchlarnick 5 D7
Much Marcle 49 F8
Muchrachd 150 H5
Much Wenlock 61 D6
Muckernich 151 F8
Mucking 42 F2
Muckleford 12 E4
Mucklestone 74 F4
Muckleton 61 B5
Muckletown 140 B4
Muckley Corner 62 D4
Muckton 91 F7
Mudale 157 F8
Muddiford 20 F4
Mudeford 14 E2
Mudford 12 C3
Mudgley 23 E6
Mugdock 119 B5
Mugeary 149 E9
Mugginton 76 E2
Muggleswick 110 E3
Muie 157 J9
Muir 139 F6
Muirden 153 C7
Muirdrum 135 F5
Muirhead
Angus 134 F3
Fife 128 D4
N Lanark 119 C6
S Ayrs 118 F3
Muirhouselaw 116 B2
Muirhouses 128 F2
Muirkirk 113 B6
Muirmill 127 F6
Muir of Fairburn 150 F7
Muir of Fowlis 140 C4
Muir of Ord 151 F8
Muir of Pert 134 F4
Muirshearlich 136 F4
Muirskie 141 E7
Muirtack 153 E9
Muirton
Highld 151 E10
Perth 127 C8
Perth 128 B3
Muirton Mains 150 F7
Muirton of Ardblair 134 E1
Muirton of Ballochy 135 C6
Muiryfold 153 C7
Muker 100 E4
Mulbarton 68 D4
Mulben 152 C3
Mulindry 142 C4
Mullardoch House 150 H5
Mullion 3 E5
Mullion Cove 3 E5
Mumby 79 B8
Munderfield Row 49 D8
Munderfield Stocks 49 D8
Mundesley 81 D9
Mundford 67 E8
Mundham 69 E6
Mundon 42 D4
Mundurno 141 C8
Munerigie 137 D5
Muness 160 C8
Mungasdale 150 B2
Mungrisdale 108 F3
Munlochy 151 F9
Munsley 49 E8
Munslow 60 F5
Murchington 9 F8
Murcott 39 C5
Murkle 158 D3
Murlaggan
Highld 136 E3
Highld 137 F6
Murra 159 H3
Murrayfield 120 B5
Murrow 66 D3
Mursley 39 B8
Murthill 134 D4
Murthly 133 F7
Murton
Cumb 100 B2
Durham 111 E6
Northumb 123 E5
York 96 D2
Musbury 11 E7
Muscoates 102 F4
Musdale 124 C5
Musselburgh 121 B6
Muston
Leics 77 F8
N Yorks 97 B6
Mustow Green 50 B3
Mutehill 106 E3
Mutford 69 F7
Muthill 127 C7
Mutterton 10 D5
Muxton 61 C7
Mybster 158 E3
Myddfai 34 B1
Myddle 60 B4
Mydroilyn 46 D3
Myerscough 92 F4
Mylor Bridge 3 C7
Mynachlog-ddu 45 F3
Myndtown 60 F3
Mynydd Bach 47 B6
Mynydd-bach 36 E1
Mynydd Bodafon 82 C4
Mynydd Isa 73 C6
Mynyddygarreg 33 D5
Mynytho 70 D4
Myrebird 141 E6
Myrelandhorn 158 E4
Myreside 128 B4
Myrtle Hill 47 F6
Mytchett 27 D6
Mytholm 87 B7
Mytholmroyd 87 B8
Myton-on-Swale 95 C7
Mytton 60 C4

N

Naast 155 J13
Naburn 95 E8
Nackington 31 D5
Nacton 57 E6
Nafferton 97 D6
Na Gearrannan 154 C6
Nailbridge 36 C3
Nailsbourne 11 B7
Nailsea 23 B6
Nailstone 63 D8
Nailsworth 37 E5
Nairn 151 F11
Nalderswood 28 E3
Nancegollan 2 C5
Nancledra 2 C3
Nanhoron 70 D3
Nannau 71 E8
Nannerch 73 C5
Nanpantan 64 C2
Nanpean 4 D4
Nanstallon 4 C5
Nant-ddu 34 C4
Nanternis 46 D2
Nantgaredig 33 B5
Nantgarw 35 F5
Nant-glas 47 C8
Nantglyn 72 C4
Nantgwyn 47 B8
Nantlle 82 F5
Nantmawr 60 B2
Nantmel 48 C2
Nantmor 71 C7
Nant Peris 83 F6
Nant Uchaf 72 D4
Nantwich 74 D3
Nant-y-Bai 47 E6
Nant-y-cafn 34 D2
Nantycaws 33 C5
Nant-y-derry 35 D7
Nant-y-ffi 46 F4
Nantyffyllon 34 E2
Nantyglo 35 C5
Nant-y-moel 34 E3
Nant-y-pandy 83 D6
Naphill 39 E8
Nappa 93 D8
Napton on the Hill 52 C2
Narberth = Arberth 32 C2
Narborough
Leics 64 E2
Norf 67 C7
Nasareth 82 F4
Naseby 52 B4
Nash
Bucks 53 F5
Hereford 48 C5
Newport 35 F7
Shrops 49 B8
Nash Lee 39 D8
Nassington 65 E7
Nasty 41 B6
Nateby
Cumb 100 D2
Lancs 92 E4
Natland 99 F7
Naughton 56 E4
Naunton
Glos 37 B8
Worcs 50 F3
Naunton Beauchamp 50 D4
Navenby 78 D2
Navestock Heath 41 E8
Navestock Side 42 E1
Navidale 157 H13
Nawton 102 F4
Nayland 56 F3
Nazeing 41 D7
Neacroft 14 E2
Neal's Green 63 F7
Neap 160 H7
Near Sawrey 99 E5
Neasham 101 C8
Neath = Castell-Nedd 33 E8
Neath Abbey 33 E8
Neatishead 69 B6
Nebo
Anglesey 82 B4
Ceredig 46 C4
Conwy 83 F8
Gwyn 82 F4
Necton 67 D8
Nedd 156 F4
Nedderton 117 F8
Nedging Tye 56 E4
Needham 68 F5
Needham Market 56 D4
Needingworth 54 B4
Needwood 63 B5
Neen Savage 49 B8
Neen Sollars 49 B8
Neenton 61 F6
Nefyn 70 C4
Neilston 118 D4
Neinthirion 59 D6
Neithrop 52 E2
Nelly Andrews Green 60 D2
Nelson
Caerph 35 E5
Lancs 93 F8
Nelson Village 111 B5
Nemphlar 119 E8
Nempnett Thrubwell 23 C7
Nene Terrace 66 D2
Nenthall 109 E7
Nenthead 109 E7
Nenthorn 122 F2
Nerabus 142 C3
Nercwys 73 C6
Nerston 119 D6
Nesbit 123 F5
Ness 73 B7
Nesscliffe 60 C3
Neston
Ches W 73 B6
Wilts 24 C3
Nether Alderley 74 B5
Netheravon 25 E6
Nether Blainslie 121 E8
Nether Booth 88 F2
Netherbrae 153 C7
Netherbrough 159 G4
Nether Broughton 64 B3
Netherburn 119 E8
Nether Burrow 93 B6
Netherbury 12 E2
Netherby
Cumb 108 B3
N Yorks 95 E6
Nether Cerne 12 E4
Nether Compton 12 C3
Nethercote 52 C3
Nethercott 20 F3
Nether Crimond 141 B7
Nether Dalgliesh 115 D5
Nether Dallachy 152 B3
Netherend 36 D2
Nether Exe 10 D4
Netherfield 18 D4
Nether Glasslaw 153 C8
Netherhampton 14 B2
Nether Handwick 134 E3
Nether Haugh 88 E5
Nether Heage 76 D3
Nether Heyford 52 D4
Nether Hindhope 116 C3
Nether Howecleuch 114 C3
Nether Kellet 92 C5
Nether Kinmundy 153 D10
Nether Langwith 76 B5
Netherlaw 106 E4
Nether Leask 153 E10
Nether Lenshie 153 D6
Netherley
Aberds 141 E7
Mers 86 F2
Nethermill 114 F3
Nether Monynut 122 C3
Nethermuir 153 D9
Nether Padley 76 B2
Nether Park 153 C10
Netherplace 118 D5
Nether Poppleton 95 D8
Netherseal 63 C6
Nether Silton 102 E2
Nether Stowey 22 F3
Netherthird 113 C5
Netherthong 88 D2
Netherthorpe 89 F6
Netherton
Angus 135 D5
Devon 7 B6
Hants 25 D8
Mers 85 D4
Northumb 117 D5
Oxon 38 E4
Perth 133 D8
Stirling 119 B5
W Mid 62 F3
Worcs 50 E4
W Yorks 88 C2
W Yorks 88 C3
Nethertown
Cumb 98 D1
Highld 158 C5
Nether Urquhart 128 D3
Nether Wallop 25 F8
Nether Wasdale 98 D3
Nether Whitacre 63 E6
Netherwitton 117 E7
Netherwood 113 B6
Nether Worton 52 F2
Nethy Bridge 139 B6
Netley 15 D5
Netley Marsh 14 C4
Netteswell 41 C7
Nettlebed 39 F7
Nettlebridge 23 E8
Nettlecombe 12 E3
Nettleden 40 C3
Nettleham 78 B3
Nettlestead 29 D7
Nettlestead Green 29 D7
Nettlestone 15 E7
Nettlesworth 111 E5
Nettleton
Lincs 90 D5
Wilts 24 B3
Neuadd 33 B7
Nevendon 42 E3
Nevern 45 E2
New Abbey 107 C6
New Aberdour 153 B8
New Addington 28 C4
Newall 94 E4
New Alresford 26 F3
New Alyth 134 E2
Newark
Orkney 159 D8
Pboro 66 D2
Newark-on-Trent 77 D7
New Arley 63 F6
Newarthill 119 D7
New Ash Green 29 C7
New Barn 29 C7
New Barnetby 90 C4
Newbarns 92 B2
New Barton 53 C6
Newbattle 121 C6
New Bewick 117 B6
Newbiggin
Cumb 92 C2
Cumb 98 E2
Cumb 99 B6
Cumb 99 B8
Cumb 109 E5
Durham 100 B4
N Yorks 100 E4
N Yorks 100 F4
Newbiggin-by-the-Sea 117 F9
Newbigging
Angus 134 E2
Angus 134 F4
Angus 134 F4
S Lanark 120 E3
Newbiggin-on-Lune 100 D2
New Bilton 52 B2
Newbold
Derbys 76 B3
Leics 63 C8
Newbold on Avon 52 B2
Newbold on Stour 51 E7
Newbold Pacey 51 D7
Newbold Verdon 63 D8
New Bolingbroke 79 D6
Newborough
Anglesey 82 E4
Pboro 66 D2
Staffs 62 B5
Newbottle
Northants 52 F3
T&W 111 D6
New Boultham 78 B2
Newbourne 57 E6
New Bradwell 53 E6
New Brancepeth 110 E5
Newbridge
Caerph 35 E6
Ceredig 46 D4
Corn 2 C3
Corn 5 C8
Dumfries 107 B6
Edin 120 B4
Hants 14 C3
IoW 14 F5
Pembs 44 B4
New Bridge 73 E6
Newbridge Green 50 F3
Newbridge-on-Usk 35 E7
Newbridge on Wye 48 D2
New Brighton
Flint 73 C6
Mers 85 E4
New Brinsley 76 D4
Newbrough 109 C8
New Broughton 73 D7
New Buckenham 68 E3
Newbuildings 10 D2
Newburgh
Aberds 141 B8
Aberds 153 C9
Borders 115 C6
Fife 128 C4
Lancs 86 C2
Newburn 110 C4
Newbury 26 C2
Newbury Park 41 F7
Newby
Cumb 99 B7
Lancs 93 E8
N Yorks 93 B7
N Yorks 102 C3
N Yorks 103 E8
Newby Bridge 99 F5
Newby East 108 D4
New Byth 153 C8
Newby West 108 D3
Newby Wiske 102 F1
Newcastle
Mon 35 C8
Shrops 60 F2
Newcastle Emlyn = Castell Newydd Emlyn 46 E2
Newcastleton or Copshaw Holm 115 F7
Newcastle-under-Lyme 74 E5
Newcastle upon Tyne 110 C5
New Catton 68 C5
Newchapel
Pembs 45 F4
Powys 59 F6
Staffs 75 D5
Sur 28 E4
New Cheriton 15 B6
Newchurch
Carms 32 B4
IoW 15 F6
Kent 19 B7
Lancs 93 F8
Mon 36 E1
Powys 48 D4
Staffs 62 B5
New Costessey 68 C4
Newcott 11 D7
New Cowper 107 E8
Newcraighall 121 B6
New Cross
Ceredig 46 B5
London 28 B4
New Cumnock 113 C6
New Deer 153 D8
New Delaval 111 B5
Newdigate 28 E2
New Duston 52 C5
New Earswick 96 D2
New Edlington 89 E6
New Elgin 152 B2
New Ellerby 97 F7
Newell Green 27 B6
New Eltham 28 B5
New End 51 D5
Newenden 18 C5
Newent 36 B4
Newerne 36 D3
New Farnley 94 F5
New Ferry 85 F4
Newfield
Durham 110 F5
Highld 151 D10
Newford 2 E4
Newfound 26 D3
New Fryston 89 B5
Newgale 44 C3
New Galloway 106 B3
Newgate 81 C6
Newgate Street 41 D6
New Gilston 129 D6
New Grimsby 2 E3
New Hainford 68 C5
Newhall
Ches E 74 E3
Derbys 63 B6
Newhall House 151 E9
Newhall Point 151 E10
Newham 117 B7
Newham Hall 117 B7
New Hartley 111 B6
Newhaven
Derbys 75 D8
Edin 121 B5
E Sus 17 D8
New Haw 27 C8
New Hedges 32 D2
New Herrington 111 D6
Newhey 87 C7
New Hinksey 39 D5
New Holkham 80 D4
New Holland 90 B4
Newholm 103 C6
New Houghton
Derbys 76 C4
Norf 80 E3
Newhouse 119 C7
New Houses 93 B8
New Humberstone 64 D3
New Hutton 99 E7
New Hythe 29 D8
Newick 17 B8
Newingreen 19 B8
Newington
Kent 19 B8
Kent 30 C2
Kent 31 C7
Notts 89 E7
Oxon 39 E6
Shrops 60 F4
New Inn
Carms 46 F3
Mon 36 D1
Pembs 45 F2
Torf 35 E7
New Invention
Shrops 48 B4
W Mid 62 D3
New Kelso 150 G2
New Kingston 64 B2
New Lanark 119 E8
Newland
Glos 36 D2
Hull 97 F6
N Yorks 89 B7
Worcs 50 E2
Newlandrig 121 C6
Newlands
Borders 115 E8
Highld 151 G10
Moray 152 C3
Northumb 110 D3
Newland's Corner 27 E8
Newlandsmuir 119 D6
Newlands of Geise 158 D2
Newlands of Tynet 152 B3
Newlands Park 82 C2
New Lane 86 C2
New Lane End 86 E4
New Leake 79 D7
New Leeds 153 C9
New Longton 86 B3
Newlot 159 G6
New Luce 105 C5
Newlyn 2 D3
Newmachar 141 C7
Newmains 119 D8
New Malden 28 C3
Newmarket
Suff 55 C7
W Isles 155 D9
New Marske 102 B4
New Marton 73 F7
New Micklefield 95 F7
Newmill
Borders 115 C7
Corn 2 C3
Moray 152 C4
New Mill
Aberds 141 F6
Herts 40 C2
Wilts 25 C6
W Yorks 88 D2
Newmill of Inshewan 134 C4
New Mills
Ches E 87 F5
Corn 4 D3
Derbys 87 F7
Powys 59 D7
Newmills of Boyne 152 C5
Newmiln 133 F8
Newmilns 118 F5
New Milton 14 E3
New Moat 32 B1
Newnham
Cambs 54 D5
Glos 36 C3
Hants 26 D5
Herts 54 F3
Kent 30 D3
Northants 52 D3
Newnham Bridge 49 C8
New Ollerton 77 C6
New Oscott 62 E4
Newpark 129 C6
New Park 95 D5
New Pitsligo 153 C8
New Polzeath 4 B4
Newport
Devon 20 F4
Essex 55 F6
E Yorks 96 F4
Highld 158 H3
IoW 15 F6
Norf 69 C8
Telford 61 C7
Newport = Casnewydd 35 F7
Newport = Trefdraeth 45 F2
Newport-on-Tay 129 B6
Newport Pagnell 53 E6
Newpound Common 16 B4
Newquay = Ceinewydd 46 D2
New Rackheath 69 C5
New Radnor 48 C4

New Rent 108 F4
New Ridley 110 D3
New Road Side 94 E2
New Romney 19 C7
New Rossington 89 E7
New Row
  Ceredig 47 B6
  Lancs 93 F6
  N Yorks 102 C4
New Sarum 25 F6
Newsbank 74 C5
Newseat
  Aberds 153 D10
  Aberds 153 E7
Newsham
  Northumb 111 B6
  N Yorks 101 C6
  N Yorks 102 F1
Newsholme
  E Yorks 89 B8
  Lancs 93 D8
Newsome 88 C2
Newstead
  Borders 121 F8
  Northumb 117 B7
  Notts 76 D5
New Stevenston 119 D7
New Street 75 D7
New Street Lane 74 F3
New Swanage 13 F8
Newthorpe 95 F7
Newton
  Argyll 125 F6
  Borders 116 B2
  Bridgend 21 B8
  Cambs 54 E5
  Cambs 66 C4
  Cardiff 22 B4
  Ches W 73 C8
  Ches W 74 B2
  Ches W 74 D2
  Cumb 92 B2
  Derbys 76 D4
  Dorset 13 C5
  Dumfries 108 B2
  Dumfries 114 E4
  Gtr Man 87 E7
  Hereford 48 F5
  Hereford 49 D7
  Highld 151 E10
  Highld 151 G10
  Highld 156 F5
  Highld 158 F5
  Lancs 92 F4
  Lancs 93 B5
  Lancs 93 D6
  Lincs 78 F3
  Moray 152 B1
  Norf 67 C8
  Northants 65 F5
  Northumb 110 C3
  Notts 77 E6
  Perth 133 F5
  S Lanark 119 C6
  S Lanark 120 F2
  Staffs 62 B4
  Suff 56 E3
  Swansea 33 F7
  S Yorks 89 D6
  Warks 52 B3
  Wilts 14 B3
  W Loth 120 B3
Newton Abbot 7 B6
Newtonairds 113 F6
Newton Arlosh 107 D8
Newton Aycliffe 101 B7
Newton Bewley 102 B2
Newton Blossomville 53 D7
Newton Bromswold 53 C7
Newton Burgoland 63 D7
Newton by Toft 90 F4
Newton Ferrers 6 E3
Newton Flotman 68 E5
Newtongrange 121 C6
Newton Hall 110 C3
Newton Harcourt 64 E3
Newton Heath 87 D6
Newtonhill
  Aberds 141 E8
  Highld 151 G8
Newton House 141 B5
Newton Kyme 95 E7
Newton-le-Willows
  Mers 86 E3
  N Yorks 101 F7
Newton Longville 53 F6
Newton Mearns 118 D5
Newtonmill 135 C6
Newtonmore 138 E3
Newton Morrell 101 D7
Newton Mulgrave 103 C5
Newton of Ardtoe 147 D9
Newton of Balcanquhal 128 C3
Newton of Falkland 128 D4
Newton on Ayr 112 B3
Newton on Ouse 95 D8
Newton-on-Rawcliffe 103 E6
Newton-on-the-Moor 117 D7
Newton on Trent 77 B8
Newton Park 145 G10
Newton Poppleford 11 F5
Newton Purcell 52 F4
Newton Reigny 108 F4
Newton Regis 63 D6
Newton St Cyres 10 E3
Newton St Faith 68 C5
Newton St Loe 24 C2
Newton St Petrock 9 C6
Newton Solney 63 B6
Newton Stacey 26 E2
Newton Stewart 105 C8
Newton Tony 25 E7
Newton Tracey 9 B7

Newton under Roseberry 102 C3
Newton upon Derwent 96 E3
Newton Valence 26 F5
New Totley 76 B3
Newtown
  Argyll 125 E6
  BCP 13 E8
  Ches W 74 B2
  Corn 3 D6
  Cumb 107 E7
  Cumb 108 C5
  Derbys 87 F7
  Devon 10 B2
  Glos 36 D3
  Glos 50 F4
  Hants 14 B4
  Hants 14 C3
  Hants 15 C6
  Hants 15 C7
  Hants 15 D5
  Hants 26 C2
  Hereford 49 E8
  Highld 137 D6
  IoM 84 E3
  IoW 14 E5
  Northumb 117 B6
  Northumb 117 D6
  Northumb 123 E5
  Shrops 73 F8
  Staffs 75 C6
  Staffs 75 C7
  Wilts 13 B7
Newtown = Y Drenewydd 59 E8
Newtown Linford 64 D2
Newtown St Boswells 121 F8
Newtown Unthank 63 D8
New Tredegar = Tredegar Newydd 35 D5
New Trows 119 F8
Newtyle 134 E2
New Ulva 144 E6
New Walsoken 66 D4
New Waltham 91 D6
New Whittington 76 B3
New Wimpole 54 E4
New Winton 121 B7
New Yatt 38 C3
New York
  Lincs 78 D5
  N Yorks 94 C4
Neyland 44 E4
Niarbyl 84 E2
Nibley 36 F3
Nibley Green 36 E4
Nibon 160 F5
Nicholashayne 11 C6
Nicholaston 33 F6
Nidd 95 C6
Nigg
  Aberdeen 141 D8
  Highld 151 D11
Nigg Ferry 151 E10
Nightcott 10 B3
Nilig 72 D4
Nine Ashes 42 D1
Ninebanks 109 D7
Nine Mile Burn 120 D4
Nine Wells 44 C2
Ninfield 18 D4
Ningwood 14 F4
Nisbet 116 B2
Nisthouse
  Orkney 159 G4
  Shetland 160 G7
Niton 15 G6
Nitshill 118 C5
Noak Hill 41 E8
Noblethorpe 88 D3
Nobottle 52 C4
Nocton 78 C3
Noke 39 C5
Nolton 44 D3
Nolton Haven 44 D3
No Man's Heath
  Ches W 74 E2
  Warks 63 D6
Nomansland
  Devon 10 C3
  Wilts 14 C3
Noneley 60 B4
Nonikiln 151 D9
Nonington 31 D6
Noonsbrough 160 H4
Norbreck 92 E3
Norbridge 50 E2
Norbury
  Ches E 74 E2
  Derbys 75 E8
  Shrops 60 E3
  Staffs 61 B7
Nordelph 67 D5
Norden 87 C6
Norden Heath 13 F7
Nordley 61 E6
Norham 122 E5
Norley 74 B2
Norleywood 14 E4
Normanby
  N Lincs 90 C2
  N Yorks 103 F5
  Redcar 102 C3
Normanby-by-Spital 90 F4
Normanby le Wold 90 E5
Norman Cross 65 E8
Normandy 27 D7
Norman's Bay 18 E3
Norman's Green 11 D5
Normanston 69 E8
Normanton
  Derby 76 F3
  Leics 77 E8
  Lincs 78 E2
  Notts 77 D7
  Rutland 65 D7
  W Yorks 88 B4
Normanton le Heath 63 C7

Normanton on Soar 64 B2
Normanton-on-the-Wolds 77 F6
Normanton on Trent 77 C7
Normoss 92 F3
Norney 27 E7
Norrington Common 24 C3
Norris Green 85 E4
Norris Hill 63 C7
Northacre 68 E2
Northallerton 102 E1
Northam
  Devon 9 B6
  Soton 14 C5
Northampton 53 C5
North Anston 89 F6
North Aston 38 B4
North Baddesley 14 C4
North Ballachulish 130 C4
North Barrow 12 B4
North Barsham 80 D5
Northbeck 79 A3
North Benfleet 42 F3
North Bersted 16 D3
North Berwick 129 F7
North Boarhunt 15 C7
North Bovey 10 F2
North Bradley 24 D3
North Brentor 9 F7
North Brewham 24 F2
Northbridge Street 18 C4
North Buckland 20 E3
North Burlingham 69 C6
North Cadbury 12 B4
North Cairn 104 B3
North Carlton 78 B2
North Carrine 143 H7
North Cave 96 F4
North Cerney 37 D7
Northchapel 16 B3
North Charford 14 C2
North Charlton 117 B7
North Cheriton 12 B4
North Cliff 97 E8
North Cliffe 96 F4
North Clifton 77 B8
North Cockerington 91 E7
North Coker 12 C3
North Collafirth 160 E5
North Common 17 B7
North Connel 124 B5
North Cornelly 34 F2
North Cotes 91 D7
North Cove 69 F7
North Cowton 101 D7
North Crawley 53 E7
North Cray 29 B5
North Creake 80 D4
North Curry 11 B8
North Dalton 96 D5
North Dawn 159 H5
North Deighton 95 D6
North Dell 160 A3
North Duffield 96 F2
Northdyke 159 F3
North Elkington 91 E6
North Elmham 81 E5
North Elmsall 89 C5
Northend
  Bucks 39 E7
  Warks 51 D8
Northenden 87 E6
North Erradale 155 J12
North Fambridge 42 E4
North Fearns 149 E10
North Featherstone 88 B5
North Ferriby 90 B3
Northfield
  Aberden 141 D8
  Borders 122 C5
  E Yorks 90 B4
  W Mid 50 B5
Northfields 65 D7
Northfleet 29 B7
North Frodingham 97 D7
Northgate 65 D8
North Gluss 160 F5
North Gorley 14 C2
North Green
  Norf 68 F5
  Suff 57 C7
North Greetwell 78 B3
North Grimston 96 C4
North Halley 159 H6
North Halling 29 C8
North Hayling 15 D8
North Hazelrigg 123 F6
North Heasley 21 F6
North Heath 16 B4
North Hill
  Cambs 55 B5
  Corn 5 B7
North Hinksey 38 D4
North Holmwood 28 E2
Northhouse 115 D7
North Howden 96 F3
North Huish 6 E5
North Hykeham 78 C2
Northiam 18 C5
Northill 54 E2
Northington 26 F3
North Johnston 44 D4
North Kelsey 90 D4

North Kelsey Moor 90 D4
North Kessock 151 G9
North Killingholme 90 C5
North Kilvington 102 F2
North Kilworth 64 F3
North Kirkton 153 C11
North Kiscadale 143 F11
North Kyme 78 D4
North Lancing 17 D5
Northlands 79 D6
Northlea 111 D7
Northleach 37 C8
North Lee 39 D8
Northleigh 11 E6
North Leigh 38 C3
North Leverton with Habblesthorpe 89 F8
Northlew 9 E7
North Littleton 51 E5
North Lopham 68 F3
North Luffenham 65 D6
North Marden 16 C2
North Marston 39 B7
North Middleton
  Midloth 121 D6
  Northumb 117 B6
North Molton 10 B2
Northmoor 38 D4
Northmoor Green or Moorland 22 F5
North Moreton 39 F5
North Mundham 16 D2
North Muskham 77 D7
North Newbald 96 F5
North Newington 52 F2
North Newnton 25 D6
North Newton 22 F4
Northney 15 D8
North Nibley 36 E4
North Oakley 26 D3
North Ockendon 42 F1
Northolt 40 F4
Northop 73 C6
Northop Hall 73 C6
North Ormesby 102 C3
North Ormsby 91 E6
Northorpe
  Lincs 65 C7
  Lincs 78 F5
  Lincs 90 E2
North Otterington 102 F1
Northover
  Som 12 B3
  Som 23 F6
North Owersby 90 E4
Northowram 88 B2
North Perrott 12 D2
North Petherton 22 F4
North Petherwin 8 F4
North Pickenham 67 D8
North Piddle 50 D4
North Poorton 12 E3
Northport 13 F7
North Port 125 C6
Northpunds 160 L6
North Queensferry 128 F3
North Radworthy 21 F6
North Rauceby 78 E3
Northrepps 81 D8
North Reston 91 F7
North Rigton 95 D5
North Rode 75 C5
North Roe 160 E5
North Runcton 67 C6
North Sandwick 160 D7
North Scale 92 C1
North Scarle 77 C8
North Seaton 117 F8
North Shian 130 E3
North Shields 111 C6
North Shoebury 43 F5
North Shore 92 F3
North Side
  Cumb 98 B2
  Pboro 66 E2
North Skelton 102 C4
North Somercotes 91 E8
North Stainley 95 B5
North Stainmore 100 C3
North Stifford 42 F2
North Stoke
  Bath 24 C2
  Oxon 39 F6
  W Sus 16 C4
North Street
  Hants 26 F4
  Kent 30 D2
  Medway 30 B2
  W Berks 26 B4
North Sunderland 123 F8
North Tamerton 8 E5
North Tawton 9 D8
North Thoresby 91 E6
North Tidworth 25 E7
North Togston 117 D8
Northtown 159 J5
North Tuddenham 68 C3
North Walbottle 110 C4
North Walsham 81 D8
North Waltham 26 E3
North Warnborough 26 D5
North Water Bridge 135 C6
North Watten 158 E4
Northway 50 F4
North Weald Bassett 41 D7
North Wheatley 89 F8
North Whilborough 7 C6
Northwich 74 B3
Northwick 36 F2
North Wick 23 C7
North Wingfield 76 C4
North Witham 65 B6

Northwold 67 E7
Northwood
  Derbys 76 C2
  IoW 15 E5
  Kent 31 C7
  London 40 E3
  Shrops 73 F8
Northwood Green 36 C4
North Woolwich 28 B5
North Wootton
  Dorset 13 C6
  Norf 67 B6
  Som 23 E7
North Wraxall 24 B3
North Wroughton 38 F1
Norton
  E Sus 17 D8
  Glos 37 B5
  Halton 86 F3
  Herts 54 F3
  IoW 14 F4
  Mon 35 C8
  Northants 52 C4
  Notts 77 B5
  Powys 48 C5
  Shrops 60 F4
  Shrops 61 D5
  Shrops 61 D7
  Stockton 102 B2
  Suff 56 C3
  S Yorks 89 C6
  Wilts 37 F5
  Worcs 50 D3
  Worcs 50 E5
  W Sus 16 D3
  W Sus 16 E2
Norton Bavant 24 E4
Norton Bridge 75 F5
Norton Canes 62 D4
Norton Canon 49 E5
Norton Corner 81 E6
Norton Disney 77 D8
Norton East 62 D4
Norton Ferris 24 F2
Norton Fitzwarren 11 B6
Norton Green 14 F4
Norton Hawkfield 23 C7
Norton Heath 42 D2
Norton in Hales 74 F4
Norton-in-the-Moors 75 D5
Norton-Juxta-Twycross 63 D7
Norton-le-Clay 95 B7
Norton Lindsey 51 C7
Norton Malreward 23 C8
Norton Mandeville 42 D1
Norton-on-Derwent 96 B3
Norton St Philip 24 D2
Norton sub Hamdon 12 C2
Norton Woodseats 88 F4
Norwell 77 C7
Norwell Woodhouse 77 C7
Norwich 68 D5
Norwick 160 B8
Norwood 89 F5
Norwood Hill 28 E3
Norwoodside 66 E4
Noseley 64 E4
Noss 160 M5
Noss Mayo 6 E3
Nosterfield 101 F7
Nostie 149 F13
Notgrove 37 B8
Nottage 21 B7
Notting Hill 41 F5
Nottingham 77 F5
Nottington 12 F4
Notton
  Wilts 24 C4
  W Yorks 88 C4
Nounsley 42 C3
Noutard's Green 50 C2
Novar House 151 E9
Nox 60 C4
Nuffield 39 F6
Nunburnholme 96 E4
Nuncargate 76 D5
Nuneaton 63 E7
Nuneham Courtenay 39 E5
Nun Hills 87 B6
Nun Monkton 95 D8
Nunney 24 E2
Nunnington 96 B2
Nunnykirk 117 E6
Nunsthorpe 91 D6
Nunthorpe
  Mbro 102 C3
  York 96 D2
Nunton 14 B2
Nunwick 95 B6
Nupend 36 D4
Nursling 14 C4
Nursted 15 B8
Nutbourne
  W Sus 15 D8
  W Sus 16 C4
Nutfield 28 D4
Nuthall 76 E5
Nuthampstead 54 F5
Nuthurst 17 B5
Nutley
  E Sus 17 B8
  Hants 26 E3
Nutwell 89 D7
Nybster 158 D5
Nyetimber 16 E2
Nyewood 16 B2
Nymet Rowland 10 D2
Nymet Tracey 10 D2
Nympsfield 37 D5
Nynehead 11 B6
Nyton 16 D3

O
Oadby 64 D3
Oad Street 30 C2
Oakamoor 75 E7
Oakbank 120 C3
Oak Cross 9 E7
Oakdale 35 E6
Oake 11 B6
Oaken 62 D2
Oakenclough 92 E5
Oakengates 61 C7
Oakenholt 73 B6
Oakenshaw
  Durham 110 F5
  W Yorks 88 B2
Oakerthorpe 76 D3
Oakes 88 C2
Oakfield 35 C7
Oakford
  Ceredig 46 D3
  Devon 10 B4
Oakfordbridge 10 B4
Oakgrove 75 C6
Oakham 65 D5
Oakhanger 27 F5
Oakhill 23 E8
Oakhurst 29 D6
Oakington 54 C5
Oaklands
  Herts 41 C5
  Powys 48 D2
Oakle Street 36 C4
Oakley
  BCP 13 E8
  Bedford 53 D8
  Fife 128 F2
  Hants 26 D3
  Oxon 39 D7
  Suff 57 B5
Oakley Green 27 B7
Oakley Park 59 F7
Oakmere 74 C2
Oakridge
  Glos 37 D6
  Hants 26 D4
Oaks 60 D4
Oaksey 37 E6
Oaks Green 75 F8
Oakthorpe 63 C7
Oakwoodhill 28 F2
Oakworth 94 F3
Oape 156 J7
Oare
  Kent 30 C4
  Som 21 E7
  W Berks 26 B3
  Wilts 25 C6
Oasby 78 F3
Oathlaw 134 D4
Oatlands 95 D6
Oban
  Argyll 124 C4
  Highld 147 C11
Oborne 12 C4
Obthorpe 65 C7
Occlestone Green 74 C3
Occold 57 B5
Ochiltree 112 B5
Ochtermuthill 127 C7
Ochtertyre 127 B7
Ockbrook 76 F4
Ockham 27 D8
Ockle 147 D8
Ockley 28 E2
Ocle Pychard 49 E7
Octon 97 C6
Octon Cross Roads 97 C6
Odcombe 12 C3
Odd Down 24 C2
Oddendale 99 C7
Odder 78 B2
Oddingley 50 D4
Oddington
  Glos 38 B2
  Oxon 39 C5
Odell 53 D7
Odie 159 F7
Odiham 26 D5
Odstock 14 B2
Odstone 63 D7
Offchurch 51 C8
Offenham 51 E5
Offham
  E Sus 17 C7
  Kent 29 D7
  W Sus 16 D4
Offord Cluny 54 C3
Offord Darcy 54 C3
Offton 56 E4
Offwell 11 E6
Ogbourne Maizey 25 B6
Ogbourne St Andrew 25 B6
Ogbourne St George 25 B7
Ogil 134 C4
Ogle 110 B4
Ogmore 21 B7
Ogmore-by-Sea 21 B7
Ogmore Vale 34 E3
Okeford Fitzpaine 13 C6
Okehampton 9 E7
Okehampton Camp 9 E7
Okraquoy 160 K6
Old 53 B5
Old Aberdeen 141 D8
Old Alresford 26 F3
Oldany 156 F4
Old Arley 63 E6
Old Basford 76 E5
Old Basing 26 D4
Olderberrow 51 C6
Old Bewick 117 B6
Old Bolingbroke 79 C6
Oldborough 10 D2
Old Brampton 76 B3
Old Bridge of Tilt 133 C5
Old Bridge of Urr 106 C4
Old Buckenham 68 E3

Old Burghclere 26 D2
Oldbury
  Shrops 61 E7
  Warks 63 E7
  W Mid 62 F3
Oldbury-on-Severn 36 E3
Oldbury on the Hill 37 F5
Old Byland 102 F3
Old Cassop 111 F6
Oldcastle
  Bridgend 21 B8
  Mon 35 B7
Old Castleton 115 E8
Old Catton 68 C5
Old Clee 91 D6
Old Cleeve 22 E2
Old Clipstone 77 C6
Old Colwyn 83 D8
Oldcotes 89 F6
Old Coulsdon 28 D4
Old Crombie 152 C5
Old Dailly 112 E2
Old Dalby 64 B3
Old Deer 153 D9
Old Denaby 89 E5
Old Edlington 89 E6
Old Eldon 101 B7
Old Ellerby 97 F7
Oldfallow 62 C3
Old Felixstowe 57 F7
Oldfield 50 C3
Old Fletton 65 E8
Oldford 24 D2
Old Glossop 87 E8
Old Goole 89 B8
Old Hall 59 F6
Oldham 87 D7
Oldhamstocks 122 B3
Old Heath 43 B6
Old Heathfield 18 C2
Old Hill 62 F3
Old Hunstanton 80 C2
Old Hurst 54 B3
Old Hutton 99 F7
Old Kea 3 B7
Old Kilpatrick 118 B4
Old Kinnernie 141 D6
Old Knebworth 41 B5
Old Langho 93 F7
Old Laxey 84 D4
Old Leake 79 D7
Old Malton 96 B3
Oldmeldrum 141 B7
Old Micklefield 95 F7
Old Milton 14 E3
Old Milverton 51 C7
Old Monkland 119 C2
Old Netley 15 D5
Old Philpstoun 120 B3
Old Quarrington 111 F6
Old Radnor 48 D4
Old Rattray 153 C10
Old Rayne 141 B5
Old Romney 19 C7
Oldshore Beg 156 D4
Oldshoremore 156 D5
Old Sodbury 36 F4
Old Somerby 78 F2
Oldstead 102 F3
Old Stratford 53 E5
Old Thirsk 102 F2
Otford 29 D6
Old Town
  Cumb 99 F7
  Cumb 108 E4
  Northumb 116 E4
  Scilly 2 E4
Oldtown of Ord 152 C6
Old Trafford 87 E6
Old Tupton 76 C3
Old Warden 54 E2
Old Weston 53 B8
Oldway 33 F6
Oldways End 10 B3
Old Whittington 76 B3
Old Wick 158 E5
Old Windsor 27 B7
Old Wives Lees 30 D4
Old Woking 27 D8
Old Woodhall 78 C5
Olgrinmore 158 E2
Oliver's Battery 15 B5
Ollaberry 160 E5
Ollerton
  Ches E 74 B4
  Notts 77 C6
  Shrops 61 B6
Olmarch 46 D5
Olney 53 D6
Olrig House 158 D3
Olton 62 F5
Olveston 36 F3
Olwen 46 E4
Ombersley 50 C3
Ompton 77 C6
Onchan 84 E3
Onecote 75 D7
Onen 35 C8
Ongar Hill 67 B5
Ongar Street 49 C6
Onibury 49 B6
Onich 130 C4
Onllwyn 34 C2
Onneley 74 E4
Onslow Village 27 E7
Onthank 118 E4
Openwoodgate 76 E3
Opinan
  Highld 149 A12
  Highld 155 H13
Orange Lane 122 E3
Orange Row 66 B5
Orasaigh 155 F8
Orbliston 152 C3
Orbost 148 D7
Orby 79 C7
Orchard Hill 9 B6
Orchard Portman 11 B7
Orcheston 25 E5
Orcop 36 B1
Orcop Hill 36 B1
Ord 149 G11
Ordhead 141 C5
Ordie 140 D3

Ordiequish 152 C3
Ordsall 89 F7
Ore 18 D5
Oreton 61 F6
Orford
  Suff 57 E8
  Warr 86 E4
Orgreave 63 C5
Orlestone 19 B6
Orleton
  Hereford 49 C6
  Worcs 49 C8
Orlingbury 53 B6
Ormesby 102 C3
Ormesby St Margaret 69 C7
Ormesby St Michael 69 C7
Ormiclate Castle 148 E2
Ormiscaig 155 H13
Ormiston 121 C7
Ormsaigmore 146 E7
Ormsary 144 F6
Ormsgill 92 B1
Ormskirk 86 D2
Orpington 29 C5
Orrell
  Gtr Man 86 D3
  Mers 85 E4
Orrisdale 84 C3
Orroland 106 E4
Orsett 42 F2
Orslow 62 C2
Orston 77 E7
Orthwaite 108 F2
Orton
  Cumb 99 D8
  Northants 53 B6
Orton Longueville 65 E8
Orton-on-the-Hill 63 D7
Orton Waterville 65 E8
Orwell 54 D4
Osbaldeston 93 F6
Osbaldwick 96 D2
Osbaston 60 B3
Osbournby 78 F3
Oscroft 74 C2
Ose 149 D8
Osgathorpe 63 C8
Osgodby
  Lincs 90 E4
  N Yorks 103 F8
  N Yorks 96 F2
Oskaig 149 E10
Oskamull 146 G7
Osmaston
  Derby 76 E2
  Derbys 76 E2
Osmington 12 F5
Osmington Mills 12 F5
Osmotherley 102 E2
Ospisdale 151 C10
Ospringe 30 C4
Ossett 88 B3
Ossington 77 C7
Ostend 43 E5
Oswaldkirk 96 B2
Oswaldtwistle 86 B5
Oswestry 60 B2
Otham 29 D8
Othery 23 F5
Otley
  Suff 57 D6
  W Yorks 94 E5
Otterbourne 15 B5
Otterburn
  Northumb 116 E4
  N Yorks 93 D8
Otterburn Camp 116 E4
Otter Ferry 145 E8
Otterham 8 E3
Otterhampton 22 E4
Ottershaw 27 C8
Otterswick 160 E7
Otterton 11 F5
Ottery St Mary 11 E6
Ottinge 31 E5
Ottringham 91 B6
Oughterby 108 D2
Oughtershaw 100 F3
Oughterside 107 E8
Oughtibridge 88 E4
Oughtrington 86 F4
Oulston 95 B8
Oulton
  Cumb 108 D2
  Norf 81 E7
  Staffs 75 F6
  Suff 69 E8
  W Yorks 88 B4
Oulton Broad 69 E8
Oulton Street 81 E7
Oundle 65 F7
Ousby 109 F6
Ousdale 158 H2
Ousden 55 D8
Ousefleet 90 B2
Ouston
  Durham 111 D5
  Northumb 110 B3
Outertown 159 G3
Outgate 99 E5
Outhgill 100 D2
Outlane 87 C8
Out Newton 91 B7
Out Rawcliffe 92 E4
Outwell 66 D5
Outwick 14 C2
Outwood
  Sur 28 E4
  W Yorks 88 B4
Outwoods 61 C7
Ovenden 87 B8
Ovenscloss 121 F7
Over
  Cambs 54 B4
  Ches W 74 C3
  S Glos 36 F2
Overbister 159 D7
Overbury 50 F4
Overcombe 12 F4
Over Compton 12 C3

Overgreen 76 B3
Over Green 63 E5
Over Haddon 76 C2
Over Hulton 86 D4
Over Kellet 92 B5
Over Kiddington 38 B4
Over Knutsford 74 B4
Overleigh 23 F6
Overley Green 51 D5
Over Monnow 36 C2
Over Norton 38 B3
Over Peover 74 B4
Overpool 73 B7
Overscaig Hotel 156 G7
Overseal 63 C6
Over Silton 102 E2
Oversland 30 D4
Overstone 53 C6
Over Stowey 22 F3
Overstrand 81 C8
Over Stratton 12 C2
Over Tabley 86 F5
Overthorpe 52 E2
Overton
  Aberdeen 141 C7
  Ches W 74 B2
  Dumfries 107 C6
  Hants 26 E3
  Lancs 92 D4
  N Yorks 95 D8
  Shrops 49 B7
  Swansea 33 F5
  W Yorks 88 B4
Overton = Owrtyn 73 E7
Overton Bridge 73 E7
Overtown 119 D8
Over Wallop 25 F7
Over Whitacre 63 E6
Over Worton 38 B4
Oving
  Bucks 39 B7
  W Sus 16 D3
Ovingdean 17 D7
Ovingham 110 C3
Ovington
  Durham 101 C6
  Essex 55 E8
  Hants 26 F3
  Norf 68 D2
  Northumb 110 C3
Ower 14 C4
Owermoigne 13 F5
Owlbury 60 E3
Owler Bar 76 B2
Owlerton 88 F4
Owl's Green 57 C6
Owlswick 39 D7
Owmby 90 D4
Owmby-by-Spital 90 F4
Owrtyn = Overton 73 E7
Owslebury 15 B6
Owston
  Leics 64 D4
  S Yorks 89 C6
Owston Ferry 90 D2
Owstwick 97 F8
Owthorne 91 B7
Owthorpe 77 F6
Oxborough 67 D7
Oxcombe 79 B6
Oxen End 42 B2
Oxenholme 99 F7
Oxenhope 94 F3
Oxen Park 99 F5
Oxenton 50 F4
Oxenwood 25 D8
Oxford 39 D5
Oxhey 40 E4
Oxhill 51 E8
Oxley 62 D3
Oxley Green 43 C5
Oxley's Green 18 C3
Oxnam 116 C2
Oxshott 28 C2
Oxspring 88 D3
Oxted 28 D4
Oxton
  Borders 121 D7
  Notts 77 D6
Oxwich 33 F5
Oxwick 80 E5
Oykel Bridge 156 J6
Oyne 141 B5

P
Pabail Iarach 155 D10
Pabail Uarach 155 D10
Pace Gate 94 D4
Packington 63 C7
Padanaram 134 D4
Padbury 52 F5
Paddington 41 F5
Paddlesworth 19 B8
Paddock Wood 29 E7
Paddockhole 115 F5
Padfield 87 E8
Padiham 93 F7
Padog 83 F8
Padside 94 D4
Padstow 4 B4
Padworth 26 C4
Page Bank 110 F5
Pagelsham Eastend 43 E5
Pagham 16 E2
Paglesham Churchend 43 E5
Paibeil 148 B2
Paible 154 H5
Paignton 7 C6
Pailton 63 F8
Painscastle 48 E3
Painshawfield 110 C3
Painsthorpe 96 D4
Painswick 37 D5
Pairc Shiaboist 154 C7
Paisley 118 C4
Pakefield 69 E8
Pakenham 56 C3
Pale 72 F3
Palestine 25 E7
Paley Street 27 B7
Palfrey 62 E4
Palgowan 112 F3
Palgrave 56 B5
Pallion 111 D6

Palmarsh 19 B8
Palnackie 106 D5
Palnure 105 C8
Palterton 76 C4
Pamber End 26 D4
Pamber Green . .26 D4
Pamber Heath . .26 D4
Pamphill 13 D7
Pampisford 55 E5
Pan 159 J4
Panbride 135 F5
Pancrasweek. 8 D4
Pandy
  Gwyn. 58 D3
  Mon. 35 B7
  Powys 59 D6
  Wrex. 73 F5
Pandy Tudur . . .83 E8
Panfield 42 B3
Pangbourne 26 B4
Pannal 95 D6
Panshanger 41 C5
Pant 60 B2
Pant-glas
  Carms 33 B6
  Gwyn. 71 C5
Pant-glâs 58 E4
Pant-glas 73 F6
Pantgwyn
  Carms 33 B6
  Ceredig. 45 E4
Pant-lasau 33 E7
Pant Mawr 59 F5
Panton 78 B4
Pantperthog 58 D4
Pant-teg 33 B5
Pant-y-Caws . . .32 B2
Pant-y-dwr 47 B8
Pant-y-ffridd . .59 D8
Pantyffynnon . .33 C7
Pantymwyn 73 C5
Pant-yr-awel . .34 F3
Pant-y-Wacco . .72 B5
Panxworth 69 C6
Papcastle 107 F8
Papigoe 158 E5
Papil 160 K5
Papley 159 J5
Papple 121 B8
Papplewick 76 D5
Papworth
  Everard 54 C3
Papworth St
  Agnes. 54 C3
Par 5 D5
Parbold 86 C2
Parbrook
  Som. 23 F7
  W Sus 16 B4
Parc 72 F2
Parcllyn 45 D4
Parc-Seymour . .35 E8
Pardshaw 98 B2
Parham 57 C7
Park 114 E2
Park Corner
  Oxon 39 F6
  Windsor 40 F1
Parkend 36 D3
Park End
  Mbro 102 C3
  Northumb . . .109 B8
Parkeston 57 F6
Parkgate
  Ches W 73 B6
  Dumfries . . .114 F3
  Kent 19 B5
  Sur 28 E3
Park Gate 15 D6
Parkham 9 B5
Parkham Ash . . .9 B5
Park Hill
  Notts. 77 D6
  N Yorks 95 C6
Parkhill House 141 C7
Parkhouse 36 D1
Parkhouse Green 76 C4
Parkhurst 15 E5
Parkmill 33 F6
Parkneuk 135 B7
Parkstone 13 E8
Park Street 28 F2
Parley Cross . . .13 E8
Parracombe 21 E5
Parrog 45 F2
Parsley Hay 75 C8
Parsonage Green 42 D3
Parsonby 107 F8
Parson Cross . .88 E4
Parson Drove . .66 D3
Parson's Heath .43 B6
Partick 119 C5
Partington 86 E5
Partney 79 C7
Parton
  Cumb 98 B1
  Dumfries . . .106 A3
  Glos 37 B5
Partridge Green 17 C5
Parwich 75 D8
Passenham 53 F5
Paston 81 D9
Patchacott 9 E6
Patcham 17 D7
Patching 16 D4
Patchole 20 E5
Pateley Bridge 94 C4
Paternoster
  Heath 43 C5
Pathe 23 F7
Pathhead
  Aberds 135 C7
  E Ayrs 113 C6
  Fife 128 E4
  Midloth 121 C6
Path of Condie 128 C2
Pathstruie 128 C2
Patna 112 C4
Patney 25 D5
Patrick 84 D2
Patrick
  Brompton . . .101 E7
Patrington 91 B7
Patrixbourne . .31 D5
Patterdale 99 C5
Pattingham 62 E2
Pattishall 52 D4

Pattiswick Green .42 B4
Patton Bridge . .99 E7
Paul 2 D3
Paulerspury 52 E5
Paull 91 B5
Paulton 23 D8
Pavenham 53 D7
Pawlett 22 E5
Pawston 122 F4
Paxford 51 F6
Paxton 122 E5
Payhembury . . .11 D5
Paythorne 93 D8
Peacehaven 17 D8
Peak Dale 75 B7
Peak Forest . . .75 B8
Peakirk 65 D8
Pearsie 134 D3
Peasedown St
  John. 24 D2
Peasemore 26 B2
Peasenhall 57 C7
Pease Pottage . .28 F3
Peaslake 27 E8
Peasley Cross . .86 E3
Peasmarsh 19 C5
Peaston 121 C7
Peastonbank . .121 C7
Peathill 153 B9
Peat Inn 129 D6
Peatling Magna .64 E2
Peatling Parva . .64 F2
Peaton 60 F5
Peats Corner . . .57 C5
Pebmarsh 56 F2
Pebworth 51 E6
Pecket Well 87 B7
Peckforton 74 D2
Peckham 28 B4
Peckleton 63 D8
Pedlinge 19 B8
Pedmore 62 F3
Pedwell 23 F6
Peebles 121 E5
Peel 84 D2
Peel Common . .15 D6
Peel Park 17 B8
Peening Quarter .19 C5
Pegsdon 54 F2
Pegswood 117 F8
Pegwell 31 C7
Peinchorran . .149 E10
Peinlich 149 C9
Pelaw 111 C5
Pelcomb Bridge 44 D4
Pelcomb Cross .44 D4
Peldon 43 C5
Pellon 87 B8
Pelsall 62 D4
Pelton 111 D5
Pelutho 107 E8
Pelynt 6 D4
Pemberton 86 D3
Pembrey 33 D5
Pembridge 49 D5
Pembroke
  =Penfro 44 E4
Pembroke Dock
  = Doc Penfro .44 E4
Pembury 29 E7
Penallt 36 C2
Penally 32 E2
Penalt 36 B2
Penare 3 B8
Penarlâg
  =Hawarden . .73 C7
Penarth 22 B3
Pen-bont
  Rhydybeddau . .58 F3
Penbryn 45 D4
Pencader 46 F3
Pencaenewydd .70 C5
Pencaitland . .121 C7
Pencarnisiog . . .82 D3
Pencarreg 46 E4
Pencelli 34 B4
Pen-clawdd 33 E6
Pencoed 34 F3
Pencombe 49 D7
Pencoyd 36 B2
Pencraig
  Hereford 36 B2
  Powys 59 B7
Pendeen 2 C2
Penderyn 34 D3
Pendine 32 D3
Pendlebury 87 D5
Pendleton 93 F7
Pendock 50 F2
Pendoggett 4 B5
Pendomer 12 C3
Pendoylan 22 B2
Pendre 34 F3
Penegoes 58 D4
Pen-ffordd 32 B1
Penfro
  =Pembroke . .44 E4
Pengam 35 E5
Penge 28 B4
Pengenffordd . .48 F3
Pengorffwysfa .82 B4
Pengover Green .5 C7
Pen-groes-oped 35 D7
Penhale
  Corn 3 E5
  Corn 4 D4
Penhalvaen 3 C6
Penhill 38 F1
Penhow 35 E8
Penhurst 18 D3
Peniarth 58 D3
Penicuik 120 C5
Peniel
  Carms 33 B5
  Denb. 72 C4
Penifiler 149 D9
Peninver 143 F8
Penisarwaun . . .83 E5
Penistone 88 D3
Penjerrick 3 C6
Penketh 86 F3
Penkill 112 E2
Penkridge 62 D3
Penley 73 F8
Penllergaer . . .33 E7
Penllyn 21 B8
Pen-llyn 82 C3
Pen-lôn 82 E4

Penmachno 83 F7
Penmaen 33 F6
Penmaenan 83 D7
Penmaenmawr . .83 D7
Penmaenpool . .58 C3
Penmark 22 C2
Penmarth 3 C6
Penmon 83 C6
Penmore Mill .146 F7
Penmorfa
  Ceredig. 46 C4
  Gwyn. 71 C6
Penmynydd 82 D5
Penn
  Bucks 40 E2
  W Mid 62 E2
Pennal 58 D4
Pennan 153 B8
Pennant
  Ceredig. 46 C4
  Denb. 72 D4
  Denb. 72 F4
  Powys 59 E5
Pennant
  Melangell 59 B7
Pennar 44 E4
Pennard 33 F6
Pennerley 60 E3
Pennington
  Cumb 92 B2
  Gtr Man. 86 E4
  Hants 14 E4
Penn Street 40 E2
Penny Bridge . .99 F5
Pennycross . . .147 J8
Pennygate 69 B6
Pennygown . . .147 G8
Pennymoor 10 C3
Pennywell 111 D6
Penparc
  Ceredig. 45 E4
  Pembs. 44 B3
Penparcau 58 F2
Penperlleni . . .35 D7
Penpillick 5 D5
Penpol 3 C7
Penpoll 5 D6
Penpont
  Dumfries . . .113 E8
  Powys 34 B3
Penprysg 34 F3
Penquit 6 D4
Penrherber 45 F4
Penrhiwceiber .34 E4
Penrhiw goch . .33 C6
Penrhiw-llan . .46 E2
Penrhiw-pâl . . .46 E2
Penrhos 70 D4
Penrhôs 35 C8
Penrhos 34 C1
Penrhosfeilw . .82 C2
Penrhyn Bay . . .83 C8
Penrhyn-coch . .58 F3
Penrhyndeudraeth
  . . . . .71 D7
Penrhynside . . .83 C8
Penrice 33 F5
Penrith 108 F5
Penrose 4 B3
Penruddock 99 B6
Penryn 3 C6
Pensarn
  Carms 33 C5
  Conwy 72 B3
Pen-sarn
  Gwyn. 70 C5
  Gwyn. 71 C6
Pensax 50 C2
Pensby 85 F3
Penselwood 24 F2
Pensford 23 C8
Penshaw 111 D6
Penshurst 29 E6
Pensilva 5 C7
Penston 121 B7
Pentewan 3 B9
Pentir 83 E5
Pentire 4 C2
Pentlow 56 E2
Pentney 67 C7
Penton Mewsey .25 E8
Pentraeth 82 D5
Pentre
  Carms 33 C6
  Powys 59 F7
  Powys 60 E2
  Rhondda 34 E3
  Shrops 60 C3
  Wrex. 73 E6
  Wrex. 73 E6
Pentrebach
  M Tydf 34 D4
  Swansea 33 D7
Pentre-bâch . . .46 E4
Pentre-bach . . .47 F8
Pentrebeirdd . .59 C8
Pentre Berw . . .82 D4
Pentre-bont . . .83 F7
Pentrecagal . . .46 E2
Pentre-celyn
  Denb. 72 D5
  Powys 59 D5
Pentre-chwyth .33 E7
Pentre-cwrt . . .46 F2
Pentre Dolau-
  Honddu 47 E8
Pentredwr 72 E5
Pentre-dwr 33 E7
Pentrefelin
  Carms 33 B6
  Ceredig. 46 E3
  Conwy 83 D8
  Gwyn. 71 D6
Pentrefoelas . .83 F8
Pentre-galar . .45 F3
Pentregat 46 D2
Pentre-Gwenlais 33 C7
Pentre Gwynfryn 71 E6
Pentre Halkyn .73 B6
Pentreheyling .60 E2
Pentre-Isaf . . .83 E8
Pentre
  Llanrhaeadr .72 C4
Pentre-llwyn-
  llwyd 47 D8
Pentre-llyn . . .46 B5
Pentre-llyn
  cymmer 72 D3
Pentre Meyrick .21 B8
Pentre-poeth . .35 F6

Pentre'r Felin .83 E8
Pentre'r-felin .47 F8
Pentre-rhew . . .47 D5
Pentre-tafarn-
  yfedw 83 E8
Pentre-ty-gwyn .47 F7
Pentrich 76 D3
Pentridge 13 C8
Pen-twyn 36 D2
Pentyrch 35 F5
Penuchadre 21 B7
Penuwch 46 C4
Penwithick 4 D5
Penwyllt 34 C2
Penybanc 33 C7
Pen-y-banc 33 B7
Penybont 48 C3
Pen-y-bont
  Carms 32 B4
  Gwyn. 58 D4
  Gwyn. 71 E7
  Powys 60 B2
Pen-y-Bont Ar Ogwr
  =Bridgend . . .21 B8
Penybontfawr . .59 B7
Pen-y-bryn
  Gwyn. 58 C3
  Pembs. 45 E3
Penycae 73 E6
Pen-y-cae 34 C2
Pen-y-cae-mawr 35 E8
Pen-y-cefn 72 B5
Pen-y-clawdd . .36 D1
Pen-y-coedcae .34 F4
Penycwm 44 C3
Pen-y-fai 34 F2
Penyffordd 73 C7
Pen-y-ffridd . .82 F5
Pen-y-garn
  Carms 46 A4
  Ceredig. 58 F3
Penygarnedd . . .59 B8
Pen-y-garnedd .82 D5
Pen-y-gop 72 E3
Penygraig 34 E3
Pen-y-graig . . .70 D2
Penygroes
  Gwyn. 82 F4
  Pembs. 45 F3
Pen-y-groes . . .33 C6
Pen-y-groeslon 70 D3
Pen-y-Gwryd
  Hotel 83 F6
Penyrheol 35 F5
Pen-yr-heol . . .35 C8
Pen-yr-
  Heolgerrig . . .34 D4
Penysarn 82 B4
Pen-y-stryt . . .73 D5
Penywaun 34 D3
Penzance 2 C3
Peopleton 50 D4
Peover Heath . .74 B4
Peper Harow . . .27 E7
Perceton 118 E3
Percie 140 E4
Percyhorner . .153 B9
Periton 21 E8
Perivale 40 F4
Perkinsville . .111 D5
Perlethorpe . . .77 B6
Perranarworthal .3 C6
Perranporth 4 D2
Perranuthnoe . . .2 D4
Perranzabuloe . .4 D2
Perry Barr 62 E4
Perryfoot 88 F2
Perry Green
  Herts. 41 C7
  Wilts. 37 F6
Perry Street . . .29 B7
Pershall 74 F5
Pershore 50 E4
Pert 135 C6
Pertenhall 53 C8
Perth 128 B3
Perthy 73 F7
Perton 62 E2
Pertwood 24 F3
Peter's Green .40 C4
Peters Marland .9 C6
Peterstone
  Wentlooge . . .35 F6
Peterston-super-
  Ely 22 B2
Peterstow 36 B2
Peter Tavy 6 B3
Petertown 159 H4
Petham 30 D5
Petrockstow 9 D7
Pett 19 D5
Pettaugh 57 D5
Petteridge 29 E7
Pettinain 120 E2
Pettistree 57 D6
Petton
  Devon 10 B5
  Shrops 60 B4
Petts Wood 28 C5
Petty 153 E7
Pettycur 128 F4
Pettymuick . . .141 B8
Petworth 16 B3
Pevensey 18 E3
Pevensey Bay . .18 E3
Pewsey 25 C6
Pexham 8 B4
Philham 8 B4
Philiphaugh . .115 B7
Phillack 2 C4
Philleigh 3 C7
Philpstoun . . .120 B3
Phocle Green . .36 B3
Phoenix Green .27 D5
Pica 98 B2
Piccotts End . . .40 D3
Pickering 103 F5
Picket Piece . . .25 E8
Picket Post 14 D2
Pickhill 101 F8
Picklescott . . .60 E4
Pickletillem . .129 B6

Pickmere 74 B3
Pickney 11 B6
Pickstock 61 B7
Pickwell
  Devon 20 E3
  Leics. 64 C4
Pickworth
  Lincs. 78 F3
  Rutland 65 C6
Picton
  Ches W 73 B8
  Flint 85 F2
  N Yorks 102 D2
Piddinghoe 17 D8
Piddington
  Northants . . .53 D6
  Oxon 39 C6
Piddletrenthide .12 E5
Pidley 54 B4
Piercebridge . .101 C7
Pierowall 159 D5
Pigdon 117 F7
Pikehall 75 D8
Pilgrims Hatch .42 E1
Pilham 90 E2
Pill 23 B7
Pillaton 6 C2
Pillerton Hersey 51 E8
Pillerton Priors 51 E7
Pilleth 48 C4
Pilley
  Hants 14 E4
  S Yorks 88 D4
Pilling 92 E4
Pilling Lane . . .92 E3
Pillowell 36 D3
Pillwell 13 C5
Pilning 36 F2
Pilsbury 75 C8
Pilsdon 12 E2
Pilsgate 65 D7
Pilsley
  Derbys 76 B2
  Derbys 76 C4
Pilton
  Devon 20 F4
  Northants . . .65 F7
  Rutland 65 D6
  Som. 23 E7
Pilton Green . . .33 F5
Pimperne 13 D7
Pinchbeck 66 B2
Pinchbeck Bars 66 B1
Pinchbeck West .66 B2
Pincheon Green .89 C7
Pinehurst 38 F1
Pinfold 85 C4
Pinged 33 D5
Pinhoe 10 E4
Pinkneys Green .40 F1
Pinley 51 B8
Pin Mill 57 F6
Pinminnoch . . .112 E1
Pinmore 112 E2
Pinmore Mains 112 E2
Pinner 40 F4
Pinvin 50 E4
Pinwherry 112 F1
Pinxton 76 D4
Pipe and Lyde .49 E7
Pipe Gate 74 E4
Piperhill 151 F11
Piper's Pool 8 F4
Pipewell 64 F5
Pippacott 20 F4
Pipton 48 F3
Pirbright 27 D7
Pirnmill 143 D9
Pirton
  Herts. 54 F2
  Worcs 50 E3
Pisgah
  Ceredig. 47 B5
  Stirling 127 D6
Pishill 39 F7
Pistyll 70 C4
Pitagowan 133 C5
Pitblae 153 B9
Pitcairngreen 128 B2
Pitcalnie 151 D11
Pitcaple 141 B6
Pitchcombe 37 D5
Pitchcott 39 B7
Pitchford 60 D5
Pitch Green . . .39 D7
Pitch Place 27 D7
Pitcombe 23 F8
Pitcorthie 129 D7
Pitcox 122 B2
Pitcur 134 F2
Pitfichie 141 C5
Pitforthie 135 B8
Pitgrudy 151 B10
Pitkennedy . . .135 D5
Pitkevy 128 D4
Pitkierie 129 D7
Pitlessie 128 D5
Pitlochry 133 D6
Pitmachie 141 B5
Pitmain 138 D3
Pitmedden 141 B7
Pitminster 11 C7
Pitmunie 141 C5
Pitney 12 B2
Pitscottie 129 C6
Pitsea 42 F3
Pitsford 53 C5
Pitsmoor 88 F4
Pitstone 40 C2
Pitstone Green 40 C2
Pitt Court 36 E4
Pittendreich . .152 B1
Pittentrail . . .157 J10
Pittington 111 E6
Pittodrie 141 B5
Pitton 25 F7
Pittswood 29 E7
Pittulie 153 B9
Pityme 4 B4
Pityoulish 138 C5
Pixey Green . . .57 B6
Pixham 28 E2
Pixley 49 E8
Place Newton . .96 B4
Plaidy 153 C7

Plains 119 C7
Plaish 60 E5
Plaistow 27 F8
Plaitford 14 C3
Plank Lane 86 E4
Plas-canol 58 C2
Plas Gogerddan .58 F3
Plas Llwyngwern 58 D4
Plas Nantyr . . .73 F5
Plas-yn-Cefn . .72 B4
Plastow Green .26 C3
Platt 29 D7
Platt Bridge . . .86 D4
Platts Common .88 D4
Plawsworth . . .111 E5
Plaxtol 29 D7
Playden 19 C5
Playford 57 E6
Play Hatch 26 B5
Playing Place . . .3 B7
Playley Green .50 F2
Plealey 60 D4
Pleasington . . .86 B4
Pleasley 76 C5
Pleckgate 93 F6
Plenmeller . . .109 C7
Pleshey 42 C2
Plockton 149 E13
Plocrapol 154 H6
Ploughfield . . .49 E5
Plowden 60 F3
Ploxgreen 60 D3
Pluckley 30 E3
Pluckley Thorne 30 E3
Plumbland 107 F8
Plumley 74 B4
Plumpton
  Cumb 108 F4
  E Sus 17 C7
Plumpton Green 17 C7
Plumpton Head 108 F5
Plumstead
  London 29 B5
  Norf 81 D7
Plumtree 77 F6
Plungar 77 F7
Plush 12 D5
Plwmp 46 D2
Plymouth 6 D2
Plympton 6 D3
Plymstock 6 D3
Plymtree 11 D5
Pockley 102 F4
Pocklington . . .96 E4
Pockthorpe 68 C2
Pode Hole 66 B2
Podimore 12 B3
Podington 53 C7
Podmore 74 F4
Point Clear 43 C6
Pointon 78 F4
Pokesdown 14 E2
Pol a Charra . .148 G2
Polbae 105 B6
Polbain 156 H2
Polbathic 6 D2
Polbeth 120 C3
Polchar 138 D4
Polebrook 65 F7
Pole Elm 50 E3
Polegate 18 E2
Poles 151 B10
Polesworth 63 D6
Polglass 156 H3
Polgooth 3 D8
Poling 16 D4
Polkerris 5 D5
Polla 156 D6
Pollington 89 C7
Polloch 130 C1
Pollok 118 C5
Pollokshields 119 C5
Polmassick 3 B8
Polmont 120 B2
Polnessan 112 C4
Polnish 147 C10
Polperro 5 D7
Polruan 5 D7
Polsham 23 E7
Polstead 56 F3
Poltalloch 124 F4
Poltimore 10 E4
Polton 121 C5
Polwarth 122 D3
Polyphant 8 F4
Polzeath 4 B4
Ponders End . . .41 E6
Pondtail 27 D6
Ponsanooth 3 C6
Ponsonby 98 D2
Ponsworthy 6 B5
Pont Aber 33 B8
Pont Aber-Geirw 71 E8
Pontamman 33 C7
Pontantwn 33 C5
Pontardawe 33 D8
Pontarddulais .33 D6
Pont-ar-gothi .33 B6
Pont ar Hydfer .34 B2
Pont-ar-llechau 33 B8
Pontarsais 33 B5
Pontblyddyn . . .73 C7
Pontbren Araeth 33 B7
Pontbren Llwyd 34 D3
Pont Cwm Pydew 72 F4
Pont Cyfyng . . .83 F7
Pont Cysyllte . .73 E6
Pont Dolydd
  Prysor 71 D8
Pontefract 89 B5
Ponteland 110 B4
Ponterwyd 58 F4
Pontesbury 60 D3
Pontfadog 73 F6
Pontfaen 47 F8
Pont-faen 34 B3
Pont Fronwydd .58 B5
Pont-gareg 45 E3
Pontgarreg 46 D2
Pont-Henri 33 D5
Ponthir 35 E7
Ponthirwaun . . .45 E4
Pontllanfraith .35 E5
Pontlliw 33 D7
Pont-Llogel . . .59 C7
Pontllyfni 82 F4
Pontlottyn 35 D5

Pontneddfechan 34 D3
Pontnewydd 35 E6
Pont Pen-y-
  benglog 83 E6
Pontrhydfendigaid
  . . . . .47 C6
Pont Rhyd-goch .83 E6
Pont-Rhyd-sarn .59 B5
Pont Rhyd-y-cyff 34 F2
Pont-rhyd-y-
  groes 47 B6
Pontrilas 35 B7
Pontrobert 59 C8
Pont-rug 82 E5
Pont Senni
  =Sennybridge .34 B3
Ponts Green . . .18 D3
Pontshill 36 B3
Pont-siân 46 E3
Pontsticill 34 C4
Pontwgan 83 D7
Pontyates 33 D5
Pontyberem 33 C6
Pontyclun 34 F4
Pontycymer 34 E3
Pontyglasier . .45 F3
Pont-y-gwaith .34 E4
Pont-y-pant . . .83 F7
Pont y Pennant 59 B6
Pontypool
  =Pont-y-pŵl .35 D6
Pontypridd 34 F4
Pont-y-pŵl
  =Pontypool . .35 D6
Pont yr Afon-
  Gam 71 C8
Pont-yr-hafod .44 C4
Pontywaun 35 E6
Pooksgreen 14 C4
Pool
  Corn 3 B5
  W Yorks 94 E5
Poole 13 E8
Poole Keynes . .37 E6
Poolend 75 D6
Poolewe 155 J13
Pooley Bridge .99 B6
Poolfold 75 D5
Poolhill 36 B4
Pool
  o'Muckhart .128 D2
Pool Quay 60 D2
Poolsbrook 76 B4
Pootings 29 E5
Pope Hill 44 D4
Popeswood 27 C6
Popham 26 E3
Poplar 41 F6
Popley 26 D4
Porchester 77 E5
Porchfield 14 E5
Porin 150 F6
Poringland 69 D5
Porkellis 3 C5
Porlock 21 E7
Porlock Weir . .21 E7
Portachoillan 144 H6
Port Ann 145 E8
Port Appin . . .130 E3
Port Arthur . .160 K5
Port Askaig . .142 B5
Portavadie . . .145 G8
Port Bannatyne 145 G9
Port Carlisle 108 C2
Port Charlotte 142 C3
Portchester . . .15 D7
Portclair 137 C7
Port Clarence 102 B2
Port Driseach 145 F8
Port Ellen . . .142 D4
Port
  Elphinstone 141 C6
Portencalzie . .104 B4
Portencross . .118 E1
Port Erin 84 F1
Port Erroll . .153 E10
Porteshan 12 F4
Portessie 152 B4
Port e Vullen .84 C4
Port-Eynon 33 F5
Portfield Gate 44 D4
Portgate 9 F6
Port Gaverne . . .8 F2
Port Glasgow 118 B3
Portgordon . . .152 B3
Portgower 157 H13
Porth
  Corn 4 C3
  Rhondda 34 E4
Porthaethwy
  =Menai Bridge 83 D5
Porthallow
  Corn 3 D6
  Corn 5 D7
Porthcawl 21 B7
Porthcothan . . .4 C3
Porthcurno 2 D2
Port
  Henderson 149 A12
Porthgain 44 B3
Porthill 60 C4
Porthkerry 22 C2
Porthleven 2 D5
Porthllechog . .82 B4
Porthmadog . . .71 D6
Porthmeor 2 C3
Portholland 3 B8
Porthoustock . .3 D7
Porthtowan 3 B5
Porth Tywyn
  =Burry Port .33 D5
Porthyrhyd
  Carms 33 C6
  Carms 47 F6
Porth-y-waen . .60 B2
Portincaple . .145 D11
Portington 96 F3
Portinnisherrich 125 D5
Portinscale 98 B4
Portishead 23 B7
Portkil 145 E11
Portknockie . .152 B4
Port Lamont . .145 F9

Portlethen . . .141 E8
Portling 107 D5
Port Lion 44 E4
Portloe 3 C8
Portmahomack 151 C12
Portmeirion . . .71 D6
Portmellon 3 B9
Port Mholair .155 D10
Port Mor 146 D7
Portmore 14 E4
Portnacroish .130 E3
Portnahaven . .142 C2
Portnalong . . .149 E8
Portnaluchaig 147 C9
Portnancon . . .156 C7
Port Nan
  Giùran 155 D10
Port nan Long 148 A3
Portnellan . . .126 B3
Port Nis 155 A10
Portobello 121 B6
Port of
  Menteith . . .126 D4
Porton 25 F6
Portpatrick . .104 D4
Port Quin 4 A4
Port Ramsay . .130 E2
Portreath 3 B5
Portree 149 D9
Port St Mary . .84 F2
Portscatho 3 C7
Portsea 15 D7
Portskerra . . .157 C11
Portskewett . . .36 F2
Portslade 17 D6
Portslade-by-
  Sea 17 D6
Portsmouth
  Ptsmth 15 D7
  W Yorks 87 B7
Portsonachan 125 C6
Portsoy 152 B5
Port Sunlight .85 F4
Portswood 14 C5
Port Talbot . . .34 E1
Porttanachy . .152 B3
Port Tennant . .33 E7
Portuairk 146 E7
Portway
  Hereford 49 F6
  Worcs 51 B5
Port Wemyss . .142 C2
Port William .105 E7
Portwrinkle 5 D8
Poslingford . . .55 E8
Postbridge 6 B4
Postcombe 39 E7
Postling 19 B8
Postwick 69 D5
Potholm 115 F6
Potsgrove 40 B2
Potten End 40 D3
Potter Brompton 97 B5
Potterhanworth 78 C3
Potterhanworth
  Booths 78 C3
Potter Heigham 69 C7
Potterne 24 D4
Potterne Wick .24 D5
Potternewton . .95 F6
Potters Bar . . .41 D5
Potter's Cross 62 F2
Potterspury . . .53 E5
Potter Street . .41 D7
Potterton
  Aberds 141 C8
  W Yorks 95 F7
Potto 102 D2
Potton 54 E3
Pott Row 80 E3
Pott Shrigley . .75 B6
Poughill
  Corn 8 D4
  Devon 10 D3
Poulshot 24 D4
Poulton
  Glos 37 D8
  Mers 85 E4
Poulton-le-Fylde 92 F3
Pound Bank 50 B2
Poundbury 12 E4
Poundfield 18 B2
Pound Green
  E Sus 18 C2
  IoW 14 F4
  Worcs 50 B2
Pound Hill 28 F3
Poundland 112 F1
Poundon 39 B6
Poundsgate 6 B5
Poundstock 8 E4
Powburn 117 C6
Powderham 10 F4
Powerstock 12 E3
Powfoot 107 C8
Powick 50 D3
Powmill 128 E2
Poxwell 12 F5
Poyle 27 B8
Poynings 17 C6
Poyntington . . .12 C4
Poynton 87 F7
Poynton Green 61 C5
Poystreet Green 56 D3
Praa Sands 2 D4
Pratt's Bottom 29 C5
Praze 3 C6
Praze-an-Beeble .2 C5
Predannack
  Wollas 3 E5
Prees 74 F2
Preesall 92 E3
Prees Green . . .74 F2
Preesgweene . . .73 F6
Prees Heath . . .74 F2
Prees Higher
  Heath 74 F2
Prees Lower
  Heath 74 F2
Prendergast . .122 D5
Prendwick 117 C6
Prengwyn 46 E3
Prenteg 71 C6
Prenton 85 F4
Prescot 86 E2
Prescott 60 B4

Pressen 122 F4
Prestatyn 72 A4
Prestbury
  Ches E. 75 B6
  Glos 37 B6
Presteigne
  =Llanandras .48 C5
Presthope 61 E5
Prestleigh 23 E8
Preston
  Borders 122 D3
  Brighton 17 D7
  Devon 7 B6
  Dorset 12 F5
  E Loth 121 B8
  E Yorks 97 F7
  Glos 37 D7
  Glos 49 F8
  Herts. 40 B4
  Kent 30 C4
  Kent 31 C6
  Lancs. 86 B3
  Northumb . . .117 B7
  Rutland 65 D5
  Shrops 60 C5
  Wilts. 24 B5
  Wilts. 25 B7
Preston Bagot .51 C6
Preston Bissett 39 B6
Preston Bowyer 11 B6
Preston
  Brockhurst . .60 B5
Preston Brook .86 F3
Preston
  Candover 26 E4
Preston Capes .52 D3
Preston
  Crowmarsh . . .39 E6
Preston Gubbals 60 C4
Prestonmill . . .107 D6
Preston on Stour .51 E7
Preston on the
  Hill 86 F3
Preston on Wye .49 E5
Prestonpans . .121 B6
Preston
  Plucknett . . .12 C3
Preston St Mary . 56 D3
Preston-under-
  Scar 101 E5
Preston upon the
  Weald Moors .61 C6
Preston Wynne .49 E7
Prestwich 87 D6
Prestwick
  Northumb . . .110 B4
  S Ayrs 112 B3
Prestwood 40 D1
Price Town 34 E3
Prickwillow . . .67 F5
Priddy 23 D7
Priesthaugh . .115 D7
Priest Hutton .92 B5
Priest Weston . .60 E2
Primethorpe . . .64 E2
Primrose Green 68 C3
Primrosehill . .40 D3
Primrose Valley .97 B7
Princes Gate . .32 C2
Princes
  Risborough . .39 D8
Princethorpe . .52 B2
Princetown
  Caerph 35 C5
  Devon 6 B3
Prion 72 C4
Prior Muir . . .129 C7
Prior Park . . .123 D5
Priors Frome . .49 F7
Priors Hardwick 52 D2
Priorslee 61 C7
Priors Marston 52 D2
Priory Wood . . .48 E4
Priston 23 C8
Pristow Green .68 F4
Prittlewell . . .42 F4
Privett 15 B7
Prixford 20 F4
Probus 3 B7
Proncy 151 B10
Prospect 107 E8
Prudhoe 110 C3
Ptarmigan
  Lodge 126 D2
Pubil 132 E1
Puckeridge 41 B6
Puckington 11 C8
Pucklechurch . .23 B8
Pucknall 14 B4
Puckrup 50 F3
Puddinglake . . .74 C4
Puddington
  Ches W 73 B7
  Devon 10 C3
Puddledock 68 E3
Puddletown 12 E5
Pudleston 49 D7
Pudsey 94 F5
Pulborough 16 C4
Pulford 73 D7
Pulham 12 D5
Pulham Market 68 F4
Pulham St Mary 68 F5
Pulloxhill 53 F8
Pumpherston .120 C3
Pumsaint 47 E5
Puncheston 32 B1
Punnett's Town 18 C3
Purbrook 15 D7
Purewell 14 E2
Purfleet 29 B6
Puriton 22 E5
Purleigh 42 D4
Purley
  London 28 C4
  W Berks 26 B4
Purlogue 48 B4
Purls Bridge . .66 F4
Purse Caundle .12 C4
Purslow 60 F3
Purston Jaglin 88 C5
Purton
  Glos 36 D3

220 Pur–St D

Purton *continued*
Glos 36 D3
Wilts 37 F7
Purton Stoke 37 E7
Pury End 52 E5
Pusey 38 E3
Putley 49 F8
Putney 28 B3
Putsborough 20 E3
Puttenham
  Herts. 40 C1
  Sur 27 E7
Puxton 23 C6
Pwll 33 D5
Pwllcrochan 44 E4
Pwll-glas 72 D5
Pwllgloyw 48 F2
Pwllheli 70 D4
Pwllmeyric 36 E2
Pwll-trap 32 C3
Pwll-y-glaw 34 E1
Pyecombe 17 C6
Pye Corner 35 F7
Pye Green 62 C3
Pyewipe 91 C6
Pyle 15 G5
Pyle = Y Pîl 34 F2
Pylle 23 F8
Pymoor 66 F4
Pyrford 27 D8
Pyrton 39 E6
Pytchley 53 B6
Pyworthy 8 D5

Q

Quabbs 60 F2
Quadring 78 F5
Quainton 39 C7
Quarley 25 E7
Quarndon 76 E3
Quarrier's
  Homes 118 C3
Quarrington 78 E3
Quarrington Hill.111 F6
Quarry Bank 62 F3
Quarryford 121 C8
Quarryhill 151 C10
Quarrywood 152 B1
Quarter 119 D7
Quatford 61 E7
Quatt 61 F7
Quebec 110 E4
Quedgeley 37 C5
Queen Adelaide . . .67 F5
Queenborough . . .30 B3
Queen Camel 12 B3
Queen Charlton . . .23 C8
Queen Dart 10 C3
Queenhill 50 F3
Queen Oak 24 F2
Queensbury 94 F4
Queensferry
  Edin. 120 B3
  Flint 73 C7
Queensferry
  Crossing 120 B4
Queen's Head 60 B3
Queen's Park
  Bedford. 53 E8
  Northants 53 C5
Queenstown 92 F3
Queen Street
  Kent 29 E7
  Wilts 37 F7
Queenzieburn . . .119 B6
Quemerford 24 C5
Quendale 160 M5
Quendon 55 F6
Queniborough 64 C3
Quenington 37 D8
Quernmore 92 D5
Quethiock 5 C8
Quholm 159 G3
Quicks Green 26 B3
Quidenham 68 F3
Quidhampton
  Hants 26 D3
  Wilts 25 F6
Quilquox 153 E9
Quina Brook 74 F2
Quindry 159 J5
Quinton
  Northants 53 D5
  W Mid 62 F3
Quintrell Downs . . .4 C3
Quixhill 75 E8
Quoditch 9 E6
Quoig 127 B7
Quorndon 64 C2
Quothquan 120 F2
Quoyloo 159 F3
Quoyness 159 H3
Quoys
  Shetland 160 B8
  Shetland 160 G6

R

Raasay House . 149 E10
Rabbit's Cross 29 E8
Raby 73 B7
Rachan Mill 120 F4
Rachub 83 E6
Rackenford 10 C3
Rackham 16 C4
Rackheath 69 C5
Racks 107 B7
Rackwick
  Orkney 159 D5
  Orkney 159 J3
Radbourne 76 F2
Radcliffe
  Gtr Man. 87 D5
  Northumb 117 D8
Radcliffe on
  Trent 77 F6
Radclive 52 F4
Radcot 38 E2
Raddery 151 F10
Radernie 129 D6
Radford Semele .51 C8
Radipole 12 F4

Radlett 40 E4
Radley 39 E5
Radmanthwaite . .76 C5
Radmoor 61 B6
Radmore Green . .74 D2
Radnage 39 E7
Radstock 23 D8
Radstone 52 E3
Radway 51 E8
Radway Green . . .74 D4
Radwell
  Bedford. 53 D8
  Herts. 54 F3
Radwinter 55 F7
Radyr 35 F5
Rafford 151 F13
Ragdale 64 C3
Raglan 35 D8
Ragnall 77 B8
Rahane 145 E11
Rainford 86 D2
Rainford
  Junction 86 D2
Rainham
  London 41 F8
  Medway 30 C2
Rainhill 86 E2
Rainhill Stoops . . .86 E3
Rainow 75 B6
Rainton 95 B6
Rainworth 77 D5
Raisbeck 99 D8
Raise 109 E7
Rait 128 B4
Raithby
  Lincs 79 C6
  Lincs 91 F7
Rake 16 B2
Rakewood 87 C7
Ram 46 E4
Ramasaig 148 D6
Rame
  Corn 3 C6
  Corn 6 E2
Rameldry Mill
  Bank 128 D5
Ram Lane 30 E3
Ramnageo 160 C8
Rampisham 12 D3
Rampside 92 C2
Rampton
  Cambs. 54 C5
  Notts. 77 B7
Ramsbottom 87 C5
Ramsbury 25 B7
Ramscraigs 158 H3
Ramsdean 15 B8
Ramsdell 26 D3
Ramsden 38 C3
Ramsden
  Bellhouse 42 E3
Ramsden Heath . .42 E3
Ramsey
  Cambs. 66 F2
  Essex 57 F6
  IoM 84 C4
Ramseycleuch . . .115 C5
Ramsey Forty
  Foot 66 F3
Ramsey Heights .66 F2
Ramsey Island . . .43 D5
Ramsey Mereside 66 F2
Ramsey St Mary's.66 F2
Ramsgate 31 C7
Ramsgill 94 B4
Ramshorn 75 E7
Ramsnest
  Common 27 F7
Ranais 155 E9
Ranby
  Lincs 78 B5
  Notts. 89 F7
Rand 78 B4
Randwick 37 D5
Ranfurly 118 C3
Rangag 158 F3
Rangemore 63 B5
Rangeworthy 36 F3
Rankinston 112 C4
Ranmoor 88 F4
Ranmore
  Common 28 D2
Rannerdale 98 C3
Rannoch
  Station 131 D8
Ranochan 147 C11
Ranskill 89 F7
Ranton 62 B2
Ranworth 69 C6
Raploch 127 E6
Rapness 159 D6
Rascal Moor 96 F4
Rascarrel 106 E4
Rashierieve 141 B8
Raskelf 95 B7
Rassau 35 C5
Rastrick 88 B2
Ratagan 136 C2
Ratby 64 D2
Ratcliffe Culey . . .63 E7
Ratcliffe on Soar .63 B8
Ratcliffe on the
  Wreake 64 C2
Rathen 153 B10
Rathillet 129 B5
Rathmell 93 D8
Ratho 120 B4
Ratho Station 120 B4
Rathven 152 B4
Ratley 51 E8
Ratlinghope 60 E4
Rattar 158 C4
Ratten Row 92 E4
Rattery 6 C5
Rattlesden 56 D3
Rattray 134 E1
Raughton Head .108 E3
Raunds 53 B7
Ravenfield 89 E5
Ravenglass 98 E2
Raveningham 69 E6
Ravenscar 103 D7
Ravenscraig 118 B2
Ravensdale 84 C3
Ravenseat 100 D3
Ravenshead 77 D5
Ravensmoor 74 D3

Ravensthorpe
  Northants 52 B4
  W Yorks. 88 B3
Ravenstone
  Leics 63 C8
  M Keynes 53 E6
Ravenstonedale 100 D2
Ravenstown 92 B3
Ravenstruther . . .120 E2
Ravensworth 101 D6
Raw 103 D7
Rawcliffe
  E Yorks 89 B7
  York 95 D8
Rawcliffe Bridge .89 B7
Rawdon 94 F5
Rawmarsh 88 E5
Rawreth 42 E3
Rawridge 11 D7
Rawtenstall 87 B6
Raxton 153 E8
Raydon 56 F4
Raylees 117 E5
Rayleigh 42 E4
Rayne 42 B3
Rayners Lane 40 F4
Raynes Park 28 C3
Reach 55 C6
Read 93 F7
Reading 26 B5
Reading Street . . .19 B6
Reagill 99 C8
Rearquhar 151 B10
Rearsby 64 C3
Reaster 158 D4
Reawick 160 J5
Reay 157 C12
Rechullin 149 C13
Reculver 31 C6
Redberth 32 D1
Redbourn 40 C4
Redbourne 90 E3
Redbrook
  Mon. 36 C2
  Wrex. 74 E2
Redburn
  Highld 151 E8
  Highld 151 G12
  Northumb 109 C7
Redcar 102 B4
Redcastle
  Angus 135 D6
  Highld 151 G8
Redcliff Bay 23 B6
Red Dial 108 E2
Redding 120 B2
Reddingmuirhead
  . . . . .120 B2
Reddish 87 E6
Redditch 50 C5
Rede 56 D2
Redenhall 69 F5
Redesdale
  Camp 116 E4
Redesmouth 116 F4
Redford
  Aberds 135 B7
  Angus 135 E6
  Durham 110 F3
Redfordgreen 115 C6
Redgorton 128 B2
Redgrave 56 B4
Redhill
  Aberds 141 D6
  Aberds 153 E6
  N Som 23 C7
  Sur 28 D3
Red Hill 50 D3
Redhouse 145 G7
Redhouses 142 B4
Red Houses 17
Redisham 69 F7
Redland
  Bristol. 23 B7
  Orkney 159 F4
Redlingfield 57 B5
Red Lodge 55 B7
Redlynch
  Som. 23 F9
  Wilts 14 B3
Redmarley
  D'Abitot 50 F2
Redmarshall 102 B1
Redmile 77 F7
Redmire 101 E5
Redmoor 5 C5
Rednal 60 B3
Redpath 121 F8
Red Rail 36 B2
Redpoint 149 B12
Red Rock 86 D3
Red Roses 32 C3
Red Row 117 E8
Red Street 74 D5
Redvales 87 D6
Red Wharf Bay . .82 C5
Redwick
  Newport 35 F8
  S Glos 36 F2
Redworth 101 B7
Reed 54 F4
Reedham 69 D7
Reedness 89 B8
Reeds Beck 78 C5
Reepham
  Lincs 78 B3
  Norf 81 E6
Reeth 101 E5
Regaby 84 C4
Regoul 151 F11
Reiff 156 H2
Reigate 28 D3
Reighton 97 B7
Reighton Gap 97 B7
Reinigeadal 154 G7
Reiss 158 E5
Rejerrah 4 D2
Releath 3 C5
Relubbus 2 C4
Relugas 151 G12
Remenham 39 F7
Remenham Hill. . .39 F7
Remony 132 E4
Rempstone 64 B2
Rendcomb 37 D7
Rendham 57 C7
Rendlesham 57 D7

Renfrew 118 C5
Renhold 53 D8
Renishaw 76 B4
Rennington 117 C8
Renton 118 B3
Renwick 109 E5
Repps 69 C7
Repton 63 B7
Reraig 149 F13
Rescobie 135 D5
Resipole 147 E10
Resolis 151 E9
Resolven 34 D2
Reston 122 C4
Reswallie 135 D5
Retew 4 D4
Retford 89 F8
Rettendon 42 E3
Rettendon Place .42 E3
Revesby 79 D5
Revesby Bridge. . .79 C6
Rewe 10 E4
Rew Street 15 E5
Reydon 57 B8
Reydon Smear. . . .57 B8
Reymerston 68 D3
Reynalton 32 D1
Reynoldston 33 E5
Rezare 5 B8
Rhaeadr Gwy
  = Rhayader 47 C8
Rhandirmwyn 47 E6
Rhayader
  = Rhaeadr Gwy . .47 C8
Rhedyn 70 D3
Rhemore 147 F8
Rhencullen 84 C3
Rhes-y-cae 73 B5
Rhewl
  Denb 72 C5
  Denb 73 E5
Rhian 157 H8
Rhicarn 156 G3
Rhiconich 156 D5
Rhicullen 151 D9
Rhidorroch
  House. 150 B4
Rhifail 157 E10
Rhigos 34 D3
Rhilochan 157 J10
Rhiroy 150 C4
Rhisga = Risca . . .35 E6
Rhiw 70 E3
Rhiwabon
  = Ruabon 73 E7
Rhiwbina 35 F5
Rhiwbryfdir 71 C7
Rhiwderin 35 F6
Rhiwlas
  Gwyn 72 F3
  Gwyn 83 E5
  Powys 73 F5
Rhodes 87 D6
Rhodesia 77 B5
Rhodes Minnis . . .31 E5
Rhodiad 44 C2
Rhondda 34 E3
Rhonehouse or Kelton
  Hill 106 D4
Rhoose = Y Rhws .22 C2
Rhôs
  Carms 46 F2
  Neath 33 D8
Rhosaman 33 C8
Rhosbeirio 82 B3
Rhoscefnhir 82 D5
Rhoscolyn 82 D2
Rhoscrowther 44 E4
Rhosesmor 73 C6
Rhos-fawr 70 D4
Rhosgadfan 82 F5
Rhosgoch 82 C4
Rhos-goch 48 E3
Rhos-hill 45 E3
Rhoshirwaun 70 E2
Rhoslan 71 C5
Rhoslefain 58 D2
Rhosllanerchrugog
  . . . . .73 E6
Rhosmaen 33 B7
Rhosmeirch 82 D4
Rhosneigr 82 D3
Rhosnesni 73 D7
Rhos-on-Sea 83 C8
Rhosrobin 73 D7
Rhossili 33 F5
Rhosson 44 C2
Rhostryfan 82 F4
Rhostyllen 73 E7
Rhosybol 82 C4
Rhos-y-brithdir . .59 B8
Rhos-y-garth 46 B5
Rhos-y-gwaliau . .72 F3
Rhos-y-llan 70 D3
Rhos-y-Madoc . . .73 E7
Rhos-y-meirch . . .48 C4
Rhu
  Argyll 145 E11
  Argyll 145 G7
Rhuallt 72 B4
Rhuddall Heath. .74 C2
Rhuddlan
  Ceredig 46 E3
  Denb 72 B4
Rhue 150 B3
Rhulen 48 E3
Rhunahaorine . . .143 D8
Rhuthun = Ruthin 72 D5
Rhyd
  Gwyn 71 C7
  Powys 59 D6
Rhydaman
  = Ammanford . .33 C7
Rhydargaeau 33 B5
Rhydcymerau 46 F4
Rhydd 50 E3
Rhyd-Ddu 83 F5
Rhydding 33 E8
Rhydfudr 46 C4
Rhydlewis 46 E2
Rhydlios 70 D2
Rhydlydan 83 F8
Rhyd-moel-ddu . .48 B2
Rhydness 48 E3
Rhydowen 46 E3
Rhyd-Rosser 46 C4
Rhydspence 48 E4
Rhydtalog 73 D6

Rhyd-uchaf 72 F3
Rhyd-wen 58 C4
Rhydwyn 82 C3
Rhyd-y-clafdy 70 D4
Rhydycroesau 73 F6
Rhydyfelin
  Ceredig 46 B4
  Rhondda 34 F4
Rhyd-y-foel 72 B3
Rhyd-y-fro 33 D8
Rhyd-y-gwin 33 D7
Rhydymain 58 B5
Rhyd-y-meirch . . .35 D7
Rhyd-y-meudwy . .72 D5
Rhydymwyn 73 C6
Rhyd-y-pandy 33 D7
Rhyd-y-sarn 71 C7
Rhyl = Y Rhyl 72 A4
Rhymney
  = Rhymni 35 D5
Rhymni
  = Rhymney 35 D5
Rhynd
  Fife 129 B6
  Perth. 128 B3
Rhynie
  Aberds 140 B3
  Highld 151 D11
Ribbesford 50 B2
Ribblehead 93 B3
Ribbleton 93 F5
Ribchester 93 F6
Ribigill 157 D8
Riby 91 D5
Riby Cross Roads 91 D5
Riccall 96 F2
Riccarton 118 F4
Richards Castle . .49 C6
Richings Park 27 B8
Richmond
  London 28 B2
  N Yorks 101 D6
Rickarton 141 F7
Rickinghall 56 B4
Rickleton 111 D5
Rickling 55 F5
Rickmansworth . .40 E3
Riddings
  Cumb 108 B4
  Derbys 76 D4
Riddlecombe 9 C8
Riddlesden 94 E3
Riddrie 119 C6
Ridge
  Dorset 13 F7
  Hants 14 C4
  Wilts 24 F4
Ridgebourne 48 C2
Ridge Green 28 E4
Ridgehill 23 C7
Ridge Lane 63 E6
Ridgeway Cross . .50 E2
Ridgewell 55 E8
Ridgewood 17 C8
Ridgmont 53 F7
Riding Mill 110 C3
Ridleywood 73 D8
Ridlington
  Norf 69 A6
  Rutland 64 D5
Ridsdale 116 F5
Riechip 133 E7
Riemore 133 E7
Rienachait 156 F3
Rievaulx 102 F3
Rift House 111 F7
Rigg 108 C2
Riggend 119 B7
Rigsby 79 B7
Rigside 119 F8
Riley Green 86 B4
Rileyhill 62 C5
Rilla Mill 5 B7
Rillington 96 B4
Rimington 93 E8
Rimpton 12 B4
Rimswell 91 B7
Rinaston 44 C4
Ringasta 160 M5
Ringford 106 D3
Ringinglow 88 F3
Ringland 68 C4
Ringles Cross 17 B8
Ringmer 17 C8
Ringmore 6 E4
Ring's End 66 D3
Ringsfield 69 F7
Ringshall
  Herts. 40 C2
  Suff. 56 D4
Ringshall Stocks . 56 D4
Ringstead
  Norf 80 C3
  Northants 53 B7
Ringwood 14 D2
Ringwould 31 E7
Rinmore 140 C3
Rinnigill 159 J4
Rinsey 2 D4
Riof 154 D6
Ripe 18 D2
Ripley
  Derbys 76 D3
  Hants 14 E2
  N Yorks 95 C5
  Sur 27 D8
Riplingham 97 F5
Ripon 95 B6
Rippingale 65 B7
Ripple
  Kent 31 E7
  Worcs 50 F3
Ripponden 87 C8
Rireavach 150 B3
Risabus 142 D4
Risbury 49 D7
Risby 55 C8
Risca = Rhisga . . .35 E6
Rise 97 E7
Riseden 18 B3
Risegate 66 B2
Riseholme 78 B2
Riseley
  Bedford. 53 C8
  Wokingham 26 C5

Rishangles 57 C5
Rishton 93 F7
Rishworth 87 C8
Rising Bridge 87 B5
Risley
  Derbys 76 F4
  Warr. 86 E4
Risplith 94 C5
Rispond 156 C7
Rivar 25 C8
Rivenhall End 42 C4
River Bank 55 C6
Riverhead 29 D6
Rivington 86 C4
Roachill 10 B3
Roade 53 D5
Road Green 69 E5
Roadhead 108 B5
Roadmeetings . . .119 D8
Roadside 158 D3
Roadside of
  Catterline 135 B8
Roadside of
  Kinneff 135 B8
Roadwater 22 F2
Roag 149 D7
Roa Island 92 C2
Roath 22 B3
Roberton
  Borders 115 C7
  S Lanark 114 B2
Robertsbridge . . .18 C4
Roberttown 88 B2
Robeston Cross . .44 E3
Robeston Wathen 32 C1
Robin Hood 88 B4
Robin Hood's
  Bay 103 D7
Roborough
  Devon 6 C3
  Devon 9 C7
Roby 86 E2
Roby Mill 86 D3
Rocester 75 F8
Roch 44 C3
Rochdale 87 C6
Roche 4 C4
Rochester
  Medway 29 C8
  Northumb 116 E4
Rochford 42 E4
Rock
  Corn 4 B4
  Northumb 117 B8
  Worcs 50 B2
  W Sus 16 C5
Rockbeare 10 E5
Rockbourne 14 C2
Rockcliffe
  Cumb 108 C3
  Dumfries. 107 D5
Rock Ferry 85 F4
Rockfield
  Highld 151 C12
  Mon. 36 C1
Rockford 14 D2
Rockhampton 36 E3
Rockingham 65 E5
Rockland All
  Saints. 68 E2
Rockland St Mary 69 D6
Rockland St
  Peter. 68 E2
Rockley 25 B6
Rockwell End 39 F7
Rockwell Green . .11 B6
Rodborough 37 D5
Rodbourne
  Swindon 37 F8
  Wilts 37 F6
Rodbourne
  Cheney 37 F8
Rodd 48 C5
Roddam 117 B6
Rodden 12 F4
Rode 24 D3
Rodeheath 75 C5
Rode Heath 74 D5
Roden 61 C5
Rodhuish 22 F2
Rodington 61 C5
Rodley
  Glos 36 C4
  W Yorks 94 F5
Rodmarton 37 E6
Rodmell 17 D8
Rodmersham 30 C3
Rodney Stoke 23 D6
Rodsley 76 E2
Rodway 22 F4
Rodwell 12 G4
Roecliffe 95 C6
Roe Green 54 F4
Roehampton 28 B3
Roesound 160 G5
Roffey 28 F2
Rogart 157 J10
Rogart Station . .157 J10
Rogate 16 B2
Rogerstone 35 F6
Roghadal 154 J5
Rogiet 36 F1
Rogue's Alley 66 D3
Roke 39 E6
Roker 111 D7
Rollesby 69 C7
Rolleston
  Leics 64 D4
  Notts 77 D7
Rolleston-on-
  Dove 63 B6
Rolston 97 E8
Rolvenden 19 B5
Rolvenden Layne .19 B5
Romaldkirk 100 B4
Romanby 102 E1
Romannobridge 120 E4
Romansleigh 10 B2
Romford 41 F8
Romiley 87 E7
Romsey 14 B4
Romsey Town 55 D5
Romsley
  Shrops 61 F7
  Worcs 50 B4
Ronague 84 E2
Rookhope 110 E2

Rookley 15 F6
Rooks Bridge 23 D5
Roos 97 F8
Roosebeck 92 C2
Rootpark 120 D2
Ropley 26 F4
Ropley Dean 26 F4
Ropsley 78 F2
Rora 153 C10
Rorandle 141 C5
Rorrington 60 D3
Roscroggan 3 B5
Rose 4 D2
Roseacre
  Kent 29 D8
  Lancs 92 F4
Rose Ash 10 B2
Rosebank 119 E8
Rosebrough 117 B7
Rosebush 32 B1
Rosecare 8 E3
Rosedale Abbey .103 E5
Roseden 117 B6
Rosefield 151 F11
Rose Green 16 E3
Rose Grove 93 F8
Rosehall 156 J7
Rosehaugh
  Mains 151 F9
Rosehearty 153 B9
Rosehill 74 F3
Rose Hill
  E Sus 17 C8
  Lancs 86 D2
Roseisle 152 B1
Roybridge 137 F5
Roydhouse 88 C3
Roseland 18 E3
Rosemarket 44 E4
Rosemarkie 151 F10
Rosemary Lane . .11 C6
Rosemount 134 E1
Rosenannon 4 C4
Rosewell 121 C5
Roseworth 102 B2
Roseworthy 2 C5
Rosgill 99 C7
Roshven 147 D10
Roskhill 149 D7
Roskill House . . .151 F9
Rosley 108 E3
Roslin 121 C5
Rosliston 63 C6
Rosneath 145 E11
Ross
  Dumfries. 106 E3
  Northumb 123 F7
  Perth. 127 B6
Rossett 73 D7
Rossett Green 95 D6
Rossie Ochill 128 C2
Rossie Priory . . .134 F2
Rossington 89 E7
Rosskeen 151 E9
Rossland 118 B4
Ross-on-Wye 36 B3
Roster 158 G4
Rostherne 86 F5
Rosthwaite 98 C4
Roston 75 E8
Rosyth 128 F3
Rothbury 117 D6
Rotherby 64 C3
Rotherfield 18 C2
Rotherfield Greys 39 F7
Rotherfield
  Peppard 39 F7
Rotherham 88 E5
Rotherstorpe 52 D5
Rotherwick 26 D5
Rothes 152 D2
Rothesay 145 G9
Rothiebrisbane . .153 E7
Rothienorman . . .153 E7
Rothiesholm 159 F7
Rothley
  Leics 64 C2
  Northumb 117 F6
Rothley Shield
  East. 117 E6
Rothmaise 153 E6
Rothwell
  Lincs 91 E5
  Northants 64 F5
  W Yorks 88 B4
Rothwell Haigh . .88 B4
Rotsea 97 D6
Rottal 134 C3
Rotten End 57 C7
Rottingdean 17 D7
Rottington 98 C1
Roud 15 F6
Rough Common . .30 D5
Roughburn 137 F6
Rough Close 75 F6
Rough Common . .30 D5
Roughlee 93 E8
Roughley 62 E5
Roughsike 108 B5
Roughton
  Lincs 78 C5
  Norf 81 D8
  Shrops 61 E7
Roughton Moor . .78 C5
Roundhay 95 F6
Roundstonefoot 114 D4
Roundstreet
  Common 16 B4
Roundway 24 C5
Rousdon 11 E7
Rous Lench 50 D5
Routenburn 118 C1
Routh 97 E6
Row
  Corn 5 B5
  Cumb 99 F6
Rowanburn 108 B4
Rowardennan . . .126 E2
Rowde 24 C4
Rowen 83 D7
Rowfoot 109 C6
Row Heath 43 C7
Rowhedge 43 B6
Rowhook 28 F2
Rowington 51 C7

Rowland 76 B2
Rowlands Castle. 15 C8
Rowlands Gill . . .110 D4
Rowledge 27 E6
Rowlestone 35 B7
Rowley
  E Yorks 97 F5
  Shrops 60 D3
Rowley Hill 88 C2
Rowley Regis 62 F3
Rowly 27 E8
Rowney Green . . .50 B5
Rownhams 14 C4
Rowrah 98 C2
Rowsham 39 C8
Rowsley 76 C2
Rowstock 38 F4
Rowston 78 D3
Rowton
  Ches W 73 C8
  Shrops 60 C3
  Telford 61 C6
Roxburgh 122 F3
Roxby
  N Lincs 90 C3
  N Yorks 103 C5
Roxton 54 D2
Roxwell 42 D2
Royal Leamington
  Spa 51 C8
Royal Oak
  Darl. 101 B7
  Lancs 86 D2
Royal Tunbridge
  Wells 18 B2
Royal Wootton
  Bassett 37 F7
Roydon
  Essex 41 D7
  Norf 68 F3
  Norf 80 E3
Roydon Hamlet. .41 D7
Royston
  Herts. 54 E4
  S Yorks 88 C4
Royton 87 D7
Rozel 17
Ruabon
  = Rhiwabon 73 E7
Ruaig 146 G3
Ruan Lanihorne . . .3 B7
Ruan Minor 3 E6
Ruarach 136 B2
Ruardean 36 C3
Ruardean
  Woodside 36 C3
Rubery 50 B4
Ruckcroft 108 E5
Ruckhall 49 F6
Ruckinge 19 B7
Ruckland 79 B6
Ruckley 60 D5
Rudbaxton 44 C4
Rudby 102 D2
Ruddington 77 F5
Rudford 36 B4
Rudge
  Shrops 62 E2
  Som. 24 D3
Rudgeway 36 F3
Rudgwick 27 F8
Rudhall 36 B3
Rudheath 74 B3
Rudley Green 42 D4
Rudry 35 F5
Rudston 97 C6
Rudyard 75 D6
Rufford 86 C2
Rufforth 95 D8
Rugby 52 B3
Rugeley 62 C4
Ruglen 112 D2
Ruilick 151 G8
Ruishton 11 B7
Ruisigearraidh . .154 J4
Ruislip 40 F3
Ruislip Common . .40 F3
Rumbling
  Bridge 128 E2
Rumburgh 69 F6
Rumford 4 B3
Rumney 22 B4
Runcorn 86 F3
Runcton 16 D2
Runcton Holme . .67 D6
Rundlestone 6 B3
Runfold 27 E6
Runhall 68 D3
Runham
  Norf 69 C7
  Norf 69 D8
Runnington 11 B6
Runsell Green 42 D3
Runswick Bay . . .103 C6
Runwell 42 E3
Ruscombe 27 B5
Rushall
  Hereford. 49 F8
  Norf 68 F4
  Wilts 25 D6
  W Mid 62 D4
Rushbrooke 56 C2
Rushbury 60 E5
Rushden
  Herts. 54 F4
  Northants 53 C7
Rushenden 30 B3
Rushford 68 F2
Rush Green 41 F8
Rush-head 153 D8
Rushlake Green . .18 D3
Rushmere 69 F7
Rushmere St
  Andrew 57 E6
Rushmoor 27 E6
Rushock 50 B3
Rusholme 87 E6
Rushton
  Ches W 74 C2
  Northants 64 F5
  Shrops 61 D6
Rushton Spencer 75 C6
Rushwick 50 D3
Rushyford 101 B7
Ruskie 126 D5
Ruskington 78 D3

Rusland 99 F5
Rusper 28 F3
Ruspidge 36 C3
Russell's Water . .39 F7
Russel's Green . . .57 B6
Rusthall 18 B2
Rustington 16 D4
Ruston 103 F7
Ruston Parva 97 C6
Ruswarp 103 D6
Rutherford 122 F2
Rutherglen 119 C6
Ruthernbridge 4 C5
Ruthin = Rhuthun 72 D5
Ruthrieston 141 D8
Ruthven
  Aberds 152 D5
  Angus 134 E2
  Highld 138 E3
  Highld 151 H11
Ruthven House . .134 E3
Ruthvoes 4 C4
Ruthwell 107 C7
Ruyton-XI-Towns.60 B3
Ryal 110 B3
Ryal Fold 86 B4
Ryall 12 E2
Ryarsh 29 D7
Rydal 99 D5
Ryde 15 E6
Rye 19 C6
Ryecroft Gate 75 C6
Rye Foreign 19 C5
Rye Harbour 19 D6
Ryehill 91 B6
Rye Park 41 C6
Rye Street 50 F2
Ryhall 65 C7
Ryhill 88 C4
Ryhope 111 D7
Rylstone 94 D2
Ryme Intrinseca . .12 C3
Ryther 95 F8
Ryton
  Glos 50 F2
  N Yorks 96 B3
  Shrops 61 D7
  T&W 110 C4
Ryton-on-
  Dunsmore. 51 B8

S

Sabden 93 F7
Sacombe 41 C6
Sacriston 110 E5
Sadberge 101 C8
Saddell 143 E8
Saddington 64 E3
Saddle Bow 67 C6
Saddlescombe . . .17 C6
Sadgill 99 D6
Saffron Walden . .55 F6
Sageston 32 D1
Saham Hills 68 D2
Saham Toney 68 D2
Saighdinis 148 B3
Saighton 73 C8
St Abbs 122 C5
St Abb's Haven . .122 C5
St Agnes
  Corn 4 D2
  Scilly 2 F3
St Albans 40 D4
St Allen 4 D3
St Andrews 129 C7
St Andrew's
  Major 22 B3
St Anne 16
St Annes 85 B4
St Ann's 114 E3
St Ann's Chapel
  Corn 6 B2
  Devon 6 E4
St Anthony-in-
  Meneage. 3 D6
St Anthony's Hill .18 E3
St Arvans 36 E2
St Asaph
  = Llanelwy 72 B4
St Athan 22 C2
St Aubin 17
St Austell 4 D5
St Bees 98 C1
St Blazey 5 D5
St Boswells 121 F8
St Brelade 17
St Breock 4 B4
St Breward 5 B5
St Briavels 36 D2
St Bride's 44 D3
St Brides Major . .21 B7
St Bride's
  Netherwent 35 F8
St Brides-super-
  Ely 22 B2
St Brides
  Wentlooge 35 F6
St Budeaux 6 D2
Saintbury 51 F6
St Buryan 2 D3
St Catherine 24 B2
St Catherine's . . .125 E7
St Clears
  = Sanclêr 32 C3
St Cleer 5 C7
St Clement 3 B7
St Clements 17
St Clether 8 F4
St Colmac 145 G9
St Columb Major . .4 C4
St Columb Minor . .4 C3
St Columb Road . . .4 D4
St Combs 153 B10
St Cross South
  Elmham. 69 F5
St Cyrus 135 C7
St David's 127 B8
St David's
  = Tyddewi 44 C2
St Day 3 B6
St Dennis 4 D4
St Devereux 49 F6
St Dogmaels 45 E3
St Dogwells 44 C4
St Dominick 6 C2
St Donat's 21 C8

St Edith's 24 C4
St Endellion 4 B4
St Enoder 4 D3
St Erme 4 D3
St Erney 5 D8
St Erth 2 C4
St Ervan 4 B3
St Eval 4 C3
St Ewe 3 B8
St Fagans 153 C10
St Fergus 153 C10
St Fillans 127 B5
St Florence 32 D1
St Genny's 8 E3
St George 72 B3
St George's 22 B2
St Germans 5 D8
St Giles 78 B2
St Giles in the
  Wood 9 C7
St Giles on the
  Heath 9 E5
St Harmon 47 B8
St Helena 63 D6
St Helen
  Auckland 101 B6
St Helens
  IoW 15 F7
  Mers 86 E3
St Helen's 18 D5
St Helier
  Jersey 17
  London 28 C3
St Hilary
  Corn 2 C4
  V Glam 22 B2
Saint Hill 28 F4
St Illtyd 35 D6
St Ippollytts . . . 40 B4
St Ishmael's . . . 44 E3
St Issey 4 B4
St Ive 5 C8
St Ives
  Cambs 54 B4
  Corn 2 B4
  Dorset 14 D2
St James South
  Elmham 69 F6
St Jidsey 4 C4
St John 6 D2
St John's
  IoM 84 D2
  Jersey 17
  Sur 27 D7
  Worcs 50 D3
St John's
  Chapel 109 F8
St John's Fen
  End 66 C5
St John's
  Highway 66 C5
St John's Town of
  Dalry 113 F6
St Judes 84 C3
St Just 2 C2
St Just in
  Roseland 3 C7
St Katherine's . 153 E7
St Keverne 3 D6
St Kew 4 B5
St Kew Highway . 4 B5
St Keyne 5 C7
St Lawrence
  Corn 4 C5
  Essex 43 D5
  IoW 15 G6
St Leonards
  Dorset 14 D2
  E Sus 18 E4
  S Lanark 119 D6
St Leonard's . . 40 D2
St Levan 2 D2
St Lythans . . . 22 B3
St Mabyn 4 B5
St Madoes . . . 128 B3
St Margarets . . 41 C6
St Margaret's . 49 F5
St Margaret's at
  Cliffe 31 E7
St Margaret's
  Hope 159 J5
St Margaret South
  Elmham 69 F6
St Mark's 84 E2
St Martin 5 D7
St Martins
  Corn 3 D6
  Perth 134 F1
St Martin's
  Jersey 17
  Shrops 73 F7
St Mary Bourne . 26 D2
St Mary
  Church 22 B2
St Mary Cray . . 29 C5
St Mary Hill . . 21 B8
St Mary Hoo . . 30 B2
St Mary in the
  Marsh 19 C7
St Mary's
  Jersey 17
  Orkney 159 H5
St Mary's Bay . 19 C7
St Maughans . . 36 C1
St Mawes 3 C7
St Mawgan . . . 4 C3
St Mellion . . . 5 C8
St Mellons . . . 35 F6
St Merryn . . . 4 B3
St Mewan . . . 4 D4
St Michael
  Caerhays . . . 3 B8
St Michael
  Penkevil . . . 3 B7
St Michaels . . 49 C7
St Michael's . . 19 B5
St Michael's on
  Wyre 92 E4
St Michael South
  Elmham 69 F6
St Minver . . . 4 B4
St Monans . . 129 D7
St Neot 5 C6
St Neots . . . 54 C2
St Newlyn East . 4 D3
St Nicholas
  Pembs 44 B3
  V Glam 22 B2

St Nicholas at
  Wade 31 C6
St Ninians . . 127 E6
St Osyth 43 C7
St Osyth Heath . 43 C7
St Ouens 17
St Owens Cross . 36 B2
St Paul's Cray . 29 C5
St Paul's Walden . 40 B4
St Peter's
  Jersey 17
  Kent 31 C7
St Petrox 44 F4
St Pinnock . . . 5 C7
St Quivox . . . 112 B3
St Ruan 3 E6
St Sampson . . 16
St Stephen . . . 4 D4
St Stephens
  Corn 6 D2
  Herts 40 D4
St Stephen's . . 8 F5
St Teath 8 F2
St Thomas . . . 10 E4
St Tudy 5 B5
St Twynnells . . 44 F4
St Veep 5 D6
St Vigeans . . 135 E6
St Wenn 4 C4
St Weonards . . 36 B1
Salcombe . . . 6 F5
Salcombe Regis . 11 F6
Salcott 43 C5
Sale 87 E5
Saleby 79 B7
Sale Green . . . 50 D4
Salehurst 18 C4
Salem
  Carms 33 B7
  Ceredig 58 F3
Salen
  Argyll 147 G8
  Highld 147 E9
Salesbury . . . 93 F6
Salford
  C Beds 53 F7
  Gtr Man 87 E6
  Oxon 38 B2
Salford Priors . 51 D5
Salfords 28 E3
Salhouse . . . 69 C6
Saline 128 E2
Salisbury . . . 14 B2
Sallachan . . 130 C3
Sallachy
  Highld 150 H2
  Highld 157 J8
Salle 81 E7
Salmonby . . . 79 B6
Salmond's Muir . 135 F5
Salperton . . . 37 B7
Salph End . . . 53 D8
Salsburgh . . . 119 C8
Saltaire 94 F4
Saltash 5 D8
Saltburn . . . 151 E10
Saltburn-by-the-
  Sea 102 B4
Saltby 65 B5
Saltcoats
  Cumb 98 E2
  N Ayrs . . . 118 E2
Saltdean . . . 17 D7
Salt End . . . 91 B5
Salter 93 C6
Salterforth . . 93 E8
Salterswall . . 74 C3
Saltfleet . . . 91 E8
Saltfleetby All
  Saints 91 E8
Saltfleetby St
  Clements . . 91 E8
Saltfleetby St
  Peter 91 F8
Saltford . . . 23 C8
Salthouse . . . 81 C6
Saltmarshe . . 89 B8
Saltney 73 C7
Salton 96 B3
Saltwick . . . 110 B4
Saltwood . . . 19 B8
Salum 146 G3
Salvington . . 16 D5
Salwarpe . . . 50 C3
Salwayash . . 12 E2
Sambourne . . 51 C5
Sambrook . . 61 B7
Samhla . . . 148 B2
Samlesbury . . 93 F5
Samlesbury
  Bottoms . . . 86 B4
Sampford
  Arundel . . . 11 C6
Sampford Brett . 22 E2
Sampford
  Courtenay . . 9 D8
Sampford
  Peverell . . . 10 C5
Sampford Spiney . 6 B3
Sampool Bridge . 99 F6
Samuelston . 121 B7
Sanachan . . 149 D13
Sanaigmore . 142 A3
Sancler
  = St Clears . 32 C3
Sancreed . . . 2 D3
Sancton 96 F5
Sand
  Highld . . . 150 B2
  Shetland . . 160 J5
Sandaig . . . 149 H12
Sandale . . . 108 E2
Sandal Magna . 88 C4
Sandbach . . . 74 C4
Sandbank . . 145 E10
Sandbanks . . 13 F8
Sandend . . . 152 B5
Sanderstead . 28 C4
Sandfields . . 37 B6
Sandford
  Cumb 100 C2
  Devon 10 D3
  Dorset 13 F7
  IoW 15 F6
  N Som 23 D6
  Shrops 74 F2

Sandford *continued*
  S Lanark . . . 119 E7
Sandfordhill . . 153 D11
Sandford on
  Thames 39 D5
Sandford Orcas . 12 B4
Sandford St
  Martin 38 B4
Sandgate 19 B8
Sandgreen . . 106 D2
Sandhaven . . 153 B9
Sandhead . . . 104 E4
Sandhills . . . 27 F7
Sandhoe . . . 110 C2
Sand Hole . . . 96 F4
Sandholme
  E Yorks 96 F4
  Lincs 79 F6
Sandhurst
  Brack 27 C6
  Glos 37 B5
  Kent 18 C4
Sandhurst Cross . 18 C4
Sandhutton . . 102 F1
Sand Hutton . . 96 D2
Sandiacre . . . 76 F4
Sandilands
  Lincs 91 F9
  S Lanark . . . 119 F8
Sandiway . . . 74 B3
Sandleheath . . 14 C2
Sandling . . . 29 D8
Sandlow Green . 74 C4
Sandness . . . 160 H3
Sandon
  Essex 42 D3
  Herts 54 F4
  Staffs 75 F6
Sandown 15 F6
Sandplace . . . 5 D7
Sandridge
  Herts 40 C4
  Wilts 24 C4
Sandringham . 67 B6
Sandsend . . 103 C6
Sandside
  House 157 C12
Sandsound . . 160 J5
Sandtoft . . . 89 D8
Sandway . . . 30 D2
Sandwell . . . 62 F4
Sandwich . . . 31 D7
Sandwick
  Cumb 99 C6
  Orkney . . . 159 K5
  Shetland . . 160 L6
Sandwith . . . 98 C1
Sandy
  Carms 33 D5
  C Beds . . . 54 E2
Sandy Bank . . 79 D5
Sandycroft . . 73 C7
Sandyford
  Dumfries . . 114 E5
  Stoke 75 D5
Sandygate . . 84 C3
Sandy Haven . 44 E3
Sandyhills . . 107 D5
Sandylands . . 92 C4
Sandy Lane
  Wilts 24 C4
  Wrex 73 E7
Sandypark . . 10 F2
Sandysike . . 108 C3
Sangobeg . . 156 C7
Sangomore . . 156 C7
Sanna 146 E7
Sanndabhaig
  W Isles . . . 148 D3
  W Isles . . . 155 D9
Sannox . . . 143 D11
Sanquhar . . 113 D7
Santon 90 C3
Santon Bridge . 98 D3
Santon Downham 67 F8
Sapcote . . . 63 E8
Sapey Common . 50 C2
Sapiston . . . 56 B3
Sapley 54 B3
Sapperton
  Glos 37 D6
  Lincs 78 F3
Saracen's Head . 66 B3
Sarclet . . . 158 F5
Sardis 33 D6
Sarn
  Bridgend . . 34 F3
  Powys 60 D2
Sarnau
  Carms 32 C4
  Ceredig . . . 46 D2
  Gwyn 72 F3
  Powys 48 F2
  Powys 60 C2
Sarn Bach . . 70 E4
Sarnesfield . . 49 D5
Sarn Meyllteyrn . 70 D3
Saron
  Carms 33 C7
  Carms 46 F2
  Denb 72 C4
  Gwyn 82 E5
  Gwyn 82 F4
Sarratt 40 E3
Sarre 31 C6
Sarsden . . . 38 B2
Sarsgrum . . 156 C6
Satley 110 E4
Satron 100 E4
Satterleigh . . 9 B8
Satterthwaite . 99 E5
Satwell . . . 39 F7
Sauchen . . . 141 C5
Saucher . . . 134 F1
Sauchie . . . 127 E7
Sauchieburn . 135 C6
Saughall . . . 73 B7
Saughtree . . 115 D9
Saul 36 D4
Saundby . . . 89 F8
Saundersfoot . 32 D2
Saunderton . . 39 D7
Saunton . . . 20 F3
Sausthorpe . . 79 C6
Saval 157 J8
Savary . . . 147 G9
Savile Park . . 87 B8
Sawbridge . . 52 C2

Sawbridgeworth . 41 C7
Sawdon . . . 103 F7
Sawley
  Derbys . . . 76 F4
  Lancs 93 E7
  N Yorks . . . 94 C5
Sawston . . . 55 E5
Sawtry 65 F8
Saxby
  Leics 64 C5
  Lincs 90 F4
Saxby All Saints . 90 C3
Saxelbye . . . 64 B4
Saxham Street . 56 C4
Saxilby . . . 77 B8
Saxlingham . . 81 D6
Saxlingham
  Green 68 E5
Saxlingham
  Nethergate . . 68 E5
Saxlingham
  Thorpe 68 E5
Saxmundham . 57 C7
Saxon Street . 55 D7
Saxondale . . 77 F6
Saxtead . . . 57 C6
Saxtead Green . 57 C6
Saxthorpe . . 81 D7
Saxton . . . 95 F7
Sayers Common . 17 C6
Scackleton . . 96 B2
Scadabhagh . 154 H6
Scaftworth . . 89 E7
Scagglethorpe . 96 B4
Scaitcliffe . . 87 B5
Scalasaig . . 144 D2
Scalby
  E Yorks . . . 90 B2
  N Yorks . . 103 F8
Scaldwell . . 53 B5
Scale Houses . 109 E5
Scales
  Cumb 92 B2
  Cumb 99 B5
  Lancs 92 F4
Scalford . . . 64 B4
Scaling . . . 103 C5
Scallastle . . 124 B2
Scalloway . . 160 K6
Scalpay . . . 154 H7
Scalpay House . 149 F11
Scalpsie . . . 145 H9
Scamadale . . 147 B10
Scamblesby . . 79 B5
Scamodale . . 130 B2
Scampston . . 96 B4
Scampton . . 78 B2
Scapa 159 H5
Scapegoat Hill . 87 C8
Scar 159 D7
Scarborough . 103 F8
Scarcliffe . . 76 C4
Scarcroft . . . 95 E6
Scarcroft Hill . 95 E6
Scardroy . . . 150 F5
Scarff 160 E4
Scarfskerry . . 158 C4
Scargill . . . 101 C5
Scarinish . . 146 G3
Scarisbrick . . 85 C4
Scarning . . . 68 C2
Scarrington . . 77 E7
Scartho . . . 91 D6
Scarwell . . . 159 F3
Scatness . . 160 M5
Scatraig . . . 151 H10
Scawby . . . 90 D3
Scawsby . . . 89 D6
Scawton . . 102 F3
Scayne's Hill . 17 B7
Scethrog . . . 35 B5
Scholar Green . 74 D5
Scholes
  W Yorks . . . 88 B2
  W Yorks . . . 88 D3
  W Yorks . . . 95 F6
School Green . 74 C3
Scleddau . . . 44 B4
Scofton . . . 89 F7
Scole 56 B5
Scolpaig . . 148 A2
Scone 128 B3
Sconser . . . 149 E10
Scoonie . . . 129 D5
Scoor . . . 146 K7
Scopwick . . 78 D3
Scoraig . . . 150 B3
Scorborough . 97 E6
Scorrier . . . 3 B6
Scorton
  Lancs 92 E5
  N Yorks . . 101 D7
Sco Ruston . . 81 E8
Scotbheinn . . 148 C3
Scotby 108 D4
Scotch Corner . 101 D7
Scotforth . . 92 D4
Scothern . . 78 B3
Scotland Gate . 117 F8
Scotlandwell . 128 D3
Scotsburn . . 151 D10
Scotscalder
  Station . . . 158 E2
Scotscraig . . 129 B6
Scot's Gap . . 117 F6
Scotston
  Aberds . . . 135 B7
  Perth 133 E6
Scotstoun . . 118 C5
Scotstown . . 130 C2
Scottas . . . 149 H12
Scotter . . . 90 D2
Scotterthorpe . 90 D2
Scottlethorpe . 65 B7
Scotton
  Lincs 90 E2
  N Yorks . . . 95 D6
  N Yorks . . 101 E6
Scottow . . . 81 E8
Scoughall . . 129 F8
Scoulag . . . 145 H10
Scoulton . . 68 D2
Scourie . . . 156 E4
Scourie More . 156 E4
Scousburgh . 160 M5

Scrabster . . 158 C2
Scrafield . . . 79 C6
Scrainwood . . 117 D5
Scrane End . . 79 E6
Scraptoft . . . 64 D3
Scratby . . . 69 C8
Scrayingham . 96 C3
Scredington . 78 E3
Scremby . . . 79 C7
Scremerston . 123 E6
Screveton . . 77 E7
Scrivelsby . . 79 C5
Scriven . . . 95 D6
Scrooby . . . 89 E7
Scropton . . . 75 F8
Scrub Hill . . 78 D5
Scruton . . . 101 E7
Sculcoates . . 97 F6
Sculthorpe . . 80 D4
Scunthorpe . . 90 C2
Scurlage . . . 33 F5
Sea 11 C8
Seaborough . . 12 D2
Seacombe . . 85 E4
Seacroft
  Lincs 79 C8
  W Yorks . . . 95 F6
Seadyke . . . 79 F6
Seafield
  S Ayrs . . . 112 B3
  W Loth . . . 120 C3
Seaford . . . 17 E8
Seaforth . . . 85 E4
Seagrave . . 64 C3
Seaham . . . 111 E7
Seahouses . . 123 F8
Seal 29 D6
Sealand . . . 73 C7
Seale 27 E6
Seamer
  N Yorks . . 102 C2
  N Yorks . . 103 F8
Seamill . . . 118 E2
Sea Palling . . 69 B7
Searby . . . 90 D4
Seasalter . . 30 C4
Seascale . . 98 D2
Seathorne . . 79 C8
Seathwaite
  Cumb 98 C4
  Cumb 98 E4
Seatoller . . 98 C4
Seaton
  Corn 5 D8
  Cumb 107 F7
  Devon 11 F7
  Durham . . 111 D6
  E Yorks . . . 97 E7
  Northumb . 111 B6
  Rutland . . 65 E5
Seaton Burn . 110 B5
Seaton Carew . 102 B3
Seaton Delaval . 111 B6
Seaton Ross . 96 E3
Seaton Sluice . 111 B6
Seatown
  Aberds . . . 152 B5
  Dorset 12 E2
Seave Green . 102 D3
Seaview . . . 15 E7
Seaville . . . 107 D8
Seavington St
  Mary 12 C2
Seavington St
  Michael . . . 12 C2
Sebergham . . 108 E3
Seckington . . 63 D6
Second Coast . 150 B2
Sedbergh . . 100 E1
Sedbury . . . 36 E2
Sedbusk . . . 100 E3
Sedgeberrow . 50 F5
Sedgebrook . . 77 F8
Sedgefield . . 102 B1
Sedgeford . . 80 D3
Sedgehill . . 13 B6
Sedgley . . . 62 E3
Sedgwick . . 99 F7
Sedlescombe . 18 D4
Sedlescombe
  Street 18 D4
Seend 24 C4
Seend Cleeve . 24 C4
Seer Green . . 40 E2
Seething . . . 69 E6
Sefton 85 D4
Seghill . . . 111 B5
Seifton . . . 60 F4
Seighford . . 62 B2
Seilebost . . 154 H5
Seion 82 E5
Seisdon . . . 62 E2
Seisiadar . . 155 D10
Selattyn . . . 73 F6
Selborne . . . 26 F5
Selby 96 F2
Selham . . . 16 B3
Selhurst . . . 28 C4
Selkirk . . . 115 B7
Sellack . . . 36 B2
Sellafirth . . 160 D7
Sellibister . . 159 D8
Sellindge . . 19 B8
Sellindge Lees . 19 B8
Selling . . . 30 D4
Sells Green . . 24 C4
Selly Oak . . 62 F4
Selmeston . . 18 E2
Selsdon . . . 28 C4
Selsey 16 E2
Selsfield
  Common . . 28 F4
Selside . . . 93 C8
Selsted . . . 31 E6
Selston . . . 76 D4
Selworthy . . 21 E8
Sembribge . . 156 C4
Semer 56 E3
Semington . . 24 C3
Semley . . . 13 B6
Send 27 D8
Send Marsh . 27 D8
Senghenydd . 35 E5
Sennen . . . 2 D2
Sennen Cove . 2 D2
Sennybridge
  = Pont Senni . 34 B3
Serlby 89 F7
Sessay . . . 95 B7
Setchey . . . 67 C6

Setley 14 D4
Setter 160 E6
Settiscarth . . 159 G4
Settle 93 C8
Settrington . . 96 B4
Sevenhampton . 37 B7
Seven Kings . 41 F7
Sevenoaks . . 29 D6
Sevenoaks Weald 29 D6
Seven Sisters . 34 D2
Severn Beach . 36 F2
Severnhampton . 38 E2
Severn Stoke . 50 E3
Sewards End . . 55 F6
Sewardstone . 41 E6
Sewardstonebury 41 E6
Sewerby . . . 97 C7
Seworgan . . 3 C6
Sewstern . . 65 B5
Sezincote . . 51 F6
Sgarastaigh . 154 J5
Sgarasta Mhor . 154 H5
Sgiogarstaigh 155 A10
Shabbington . 39 D6
Shackerstone . 63 D7
Shackleford . 27 E7
Shade 87 B7
Shadforth . . 111 E6
Shadingfield . 69 F7
Shadoxhurst . 19 B6
Shadsworth . 86 B5
Shadwell
  Norf 68 F2
  W Yorks . . . 95 F6
Shaftesbury . 13 B6
Shafton . . . 88 C4
Shalbourne . . 25 C8
Shalcombe . . 14 F4
Shalden . . . 26 E4
Shaldon . . . 7 B7
Shalfleet . . . 14 F5
Shalford
  Essex 42 B3
  Sur 27 E8
Shalford Green . 42 B3
Shallowford . . 21 E6
Shalmsford
  Street 30 D4
Shalstone . . 52 F4
Shamley Green . 27 E8
Shandon . . 145 E11
Shandwick . 151 D11
Shangton . . 64 E4
Shankhouse . 111 B5
Shanklin . . . 15 F6
Shanquhar . . 152 E5
Shanzie . . . 134 D2
Shap 99 C7
Shapwick
  Dorset 13 D7
  Som 23 F6
Shardlow . . 76 F4
Shareshill . . 62 D3
Sharlston . . 88 C4
Sharlston
  Common . . 88 C4
Sharnbrook . 53 D7
Sharnford . . 63 E8
Sharoe Green . 92 F5
Sharow . . . 95 B6
Sharpenhoe . 53 F8
Sharperton . 117 D5
Sharpness . . 36 D3
Sharp Street . 69 B6
Sharpthorne . 28 F4
Sharrington . 81 D6
Shatterford . 61 F7
Shaugh Prior . 6 C3
Shavington . . 74 D4
Shaw
  Gtr Man . . . 87 D7
  W Berks . . . 26 C2
  Wilts 24 C3
Shawbury . . 61 B5
Shawdon Hall . 117 C6
Shawell . . . 64 F2
Shawford . . 15 B5
Shawforth . . 87 B6
Shaw Green . 86 C3
Shawhead . . 107 B5
Shaw Mills . . 95 C5
Shawton . . 119 E6
Shawtonhill . 119 E6
Shear Cross . 24 E3
Shearington . 107 C7
Shearsby . . 64 E3
Shebbear . . 9 D6
Shebdon . . 61 B7
Shebster . . 157 C13
Sheddens . . 119 D5
Shedfield . . 15 C6
Sheen 75 C8
Sheepscar . . 95 F6
Sheepscombe . 37 C5
Sheepstor . . 6 C3
Sheepwash . 9 D6
Sheepway . . 23 B6
Sheepy Magna . 63 D7
Sheepy Parva . 63 D7
Sheering . . 41 C8
Sheerness . . 30 B3
Sheet 15 B8
Sheffield
  Bottom . . . 26 C4
Sheffield Green . 17 B8
Shefford . . 54 F2
Shefford
  Woodlands . 25 B8
Sheigra . . . 156 C4
Sheinton . . 61 D6
Shelderton . . 49 B6
Sheldon
  Derbys . . . 75 C8
  Devon 11 D6
  W Mid 63 F5
Sheldwich . . 30 D4
Shelf 88 B2
Shelfanger . . 68 F4
Shelfield
  Warks 51 C6
  W Mid 62 D4
Shelford . . . 77 E6
Shellacres . . 122 E4

Shelley
  Essex 42 D1
  Suff 56 F4
  W Yorks . . . 88 C3
Shellingford . 38 E3
Shellow Bowells . 42 D2
Shelsley
  Beauchamp . 50 C2
Shelsley Walsh . 50 C2
Shelthorpe . . 64 C2
Shelton
  Bedford . . . 53 C8
  Norf 68 E5
  Notts 77 E7
  Shrops . . . 60 C4
Shelton Green . 68 E5
Shelve 60 E3
Shelwick . . 49 E7
Shenfield . . 42 E2
Shenington . 51 E8
Shenley . . . 40 D4
Shenley Brook
  End 53 F6
Shenleybury . 40 D4
Shenley Church
  End 53 F6
Shenmore . . 49 F5
Shennanton . 105 C7
Shenstone
  Staffs 62 D5
  Worcs 50 B3
Shenton . . . 63 D7
Shenval
  Highld . . . 137 B7
  Moray . . . 139 B8
Shepeau Stow . 66 C3
Shephall . . . 41 B5
Shepherd's Green 39 F7
Shepherd's Port . 80 D2
Shepherdswell . 31 E6
Shepley . . . 88 D2
Shepperdine . 36 E3
Shepperton . 28 C5
Shepreth . . 54 E4
Shepshed . . 63 C8
Shepton
  Beauchamp . 12 C2
Shepton Mallet . 23 E8
Shepton
  Montague . . 23 F8
Shepway . . . 29 D8
Sheraton . . 111 F7
Sherborne
  Dorset 12 C4
  Glos 38 C1
Sherborne St
  John 26 D4
Sherbourne . . 51 C7
Sherburn
  Durham . . 111 E6
  N Yorks . . . 97 B5
Sherburn Hill . 111 E6
Sherburn in
  Elmet 95 F7
Shere 27 E8
Shereford . . 80 E4
Sherfield English 14 B3
Sherfield on
  Loddon . . . 26 D4
Sherford . . 7 E5
Sheriffhales . 61 C7
Sheriff Hutton . 96 C2
Sheringham . 81 C7
Sherington . . 53 E6
Shernal Green . 50 C4
Shernborne . 80 D3
Sherrington . 24 F4
Sherston . . 37 F5
Sherwood Green . 9 B7
Shettleston . 119 C6
Shevington . . 86 D3
Shevington Moor 86 C3
Shevington Vale . 86 D3
Sheviock . . 5 D8
Shide 15 F5
Shiel Bridge . 136 C2
Shieldaig
  Highld . . . 149 A13
  Highld . . . 149 C13
Shieldhill
  Dumfries . . 114 F3
  Falk 119 B8
  S Lanark . . 120 F3
Shielfoot . . 147 E9
Shielhill
  Angus . . . 134 D4
  Involyd . . . 118 B2
Shifford . . . 38 D3
Shifnal . . . 61 D7
Shilbottle . . 117 D7
Shildon . . . 101 B7
Shillingford
  Devon 10 B4
  Oxon 39 E5
Shillingford
  St George . . 10 F4
Shillingstone . 13 C6
Shillington . . 54 F2
Shillmoor . . 116 D4
Shilton
  Oxon 38 D2
  Warks 63 F8
Shilvinghton . 117 F7
Shimpling
  Norf 68 F4
  Suff 56 D2
Shimpling
  Street 56 D2
Shincliffe . . 111 E5
Shiney Row . 111 D6
Shinfield . . 26 C5
Shingham . . 67 D7
Shingle Street . 57 E7
Shinner's Bridge . 7 C5
Shinness . . 157 H8
Shipbourne . 29 D6
Shipdham . . 68 D2
Shipham . . 23 D6
Shiplake . . 27 B5
Shiplake . . 27 B5
Shipley
  Derbys . . . 76 E4
  Northumb . 117 C7
  Shrops . . . 62 E2
  W Sus . . . 16 B5
  W Yorks . . . 94 F4
Shipley Shiels . 116 E3
Shipmeadow . 69 F6

Shippea Hill
  Station . . . 67 F6
Shippon . . . 38 E4
Shipston-on-
  Stour 51 E7
Shipton
  Glos 37 C7
  N Yorks . . . 95 D8
  Shrops . . . 61 E5
Shipton Bellinger 25 E7
Shipton Gorge . 12 E2
Shipton Green . 16 D2
Shipton Moyne . 37 F5
Shipton on
  Cherwell . . 38 C4
Shipton Solers . 37 C7
Shiptonthorpe . 96 E4
Shipton-under-
  Wychwood . 38 C2
Shirburn . . . 39 E6
Shirdley Hill . 85 C4
Shirebrook . . 76 C5
Shiregreen . . 88 E4
Shirehampton . 23 B7
Shiremoor . . 111 B6
Shirenewton . 36 E1
Shireoaks . . 89 F6
Shirkoak . . 19 B6
Shirland . . . 76 D3
Shirley
  Derbys . . . 76 E2
  London . . . 28 C4
  Soton 14 C5
  W Mid . . . 51 B6
Shirl Heath . 49 D6
Shirrell Heath . 15 C6
Shirwell . . . 20 F4
Shirwell Cross . 20 F4
Shiskine . . 143 F10
Shobdon . . 49 C6
Shobnall . . . 63 B6
Shobrooke . . 10 D3
Shoby 64 C3
Shocklach . . 73 E8
Shoeburyness . 43 F5
Sholden . . . 31 D7
Sholing . . . 14 C5
Shoot Hill . . 60 C4
Shop
  Corn 4 B3
  Corn 8 C4
Shop Corner . 57 F6
Shoreditch . . 41 F6
Shoreham . . 29 C6
Shoreham-by-
  Sea 17 D6
Shore Mill . . 151 E10
Shoresdean . 123 E5
Shoreswood . 122 E5
Shoreton . . 151 E9
Shorncote . . 37 E7
Shorne . . . 29 B7
Shortacombe . 9 F7
Shortgate . . 17 C8
Short Heath . 62 D3
Shortlanesend . 3 B7
Shortlees . . 118 F4
Shortstown . 53 E8
Shorwell . . 15 F5
Shoscombe . . 24 D2
Shotatton . . 60 B3
Shotesham . . 69 E5
Shotgate . . 42 E3
Shotley . . . 57 F6
Shotley Bridge . 110 D3
Shotleyfield . 110 D3
Shotley Gate . 57 F6
Shottenden . . 30 D4
Shottermill . . 27 F6
Shottery . . 51 D6
Shotteswell . 52 E2
Shottisham . . 57 E7
Shottle . . . 76 E3
Shottlegate . . 76 E3
Shotton
  Durham . . 111 F7
  Flint 73 C7
  Northumb . 122 F4
Shotton Colliery 111 E6
Shotts 119 C8
Shotwick . . 73 B7
Shouldham . 67 D6
Shouldham
  Thorpe . . . 67 D6
Shoulton . . 50 D3
Shover's Green . 18 B3
Shrawardine . 60 C4
Shrawley . . 50 C3
Shrewley
  Common . . 51 C7
Shrewsbury . 60 C4
Shrewton . . 25 E5
Shripney . . 16 D3
Shrivenham . 38 F2
Shropham . . 68 E2
Shrub End . . 43 B5
Shucknall . . 49 E7
Shudy Camps . 55 E7
Shulishadermor 149 D9
Shurdington . 37 C6
Shurlock Row . 27 B6
Shurrery . . 157 D13
Shurrery
  Lodge . . . 157 D13
Shurton . . . 22 E4
Shustoke . . 63 E6
Shute
  Devon 10 D3
  Devon 11 E7
Shutford . . 51 E8
Shuthonger . 50 F3
Shutlanger . . 52 D5
Shuttington . 63 D6
Shuttlewood . 76 B4
Siabost bho
  Dheas . . . 155 C7
Siabost bho
  Thuath . . . 155 C7
Siadar . . . 155 B8
Siadar Iarach . 155 B8
Siadar Uarach . 155 B8
Sibbaldbie . . 114 F4
Sibbertoft . . 64 F3
Sibdon Carwood 60 F4
Sibford Ferris . 51 F8
Sibford Gower . 51 F8

Sibsey . . . 79 D6
Sibson
  Cambs . . . 65 E7
  Leics 63 D7
Sibthorpe . . 77 E7
Sibton . . . 57 C7
Sibton Green . 57 B7
Sicklesmere . 56 C2
Sicklinghall . 95 E6
Sid 11 F6
Sidbury
  Devon . . . 11 E6
  Shrops . . . 61 F6
Sidcot . . . 23 D6
Sidcup . . . 29 B5
Siddick . . . 107 F7
Siddington
  Ches E . . . 74 B5
  Glos 37 E7
Sidemoor . . 50 B4
Sidestrand . . 81 D8
Sidford . . . 11 E6
Sidlesham . . 16 E2
Sidley 18 E4
Sidlow . . . 28 E3
Sidmouth . . 11 F6
Sigford . . . 7 B5
Sigglesthorne . 97 E7
Sighthill . . 120 B4
Sigingstone . 21 B8
Signet . . . 38 C2
Silchester . . 26 C4
Sildinis . . 155 F7
Sileby . . . 64 C2
Silecroft . . 98 F3
Silfield . . . 68 E4
Silian . . . 46 D4
Silkstone . . 88 D3
Silkstone
  Common . . 88 D3
Silk Willoughby 78 E3
Silloth . . . 107 D8
Sills 116 D4
Sillyearn . . 152 C5
Siloh 47 F6
Silpho . . . 103 E7
Silsden . . 94 E3
Silsoe . . . 53 F8
Silverburn . 120 C5
Silverdale
  Lancs 92 B4
  Staffs . . . 74 E5
Silver End . . 42 C4
Silvergate . . 81 E7
Silverhill . . 18 D4
Silverley's Green 57 B6
Silverstone . . 52 E4
Silverton . . 10 D4
Silvington . . 49 B8
Silwick . . . 160 J4
Simmondley . 87 E8
Simonburn . . 109 B8
Simonsbath . 21 F6
Simonstone . 93 F7
Simprim . . 122 E4
Simpson . . 53 F6
Simpson Cross . 44 D3
Sinclair's Hill . 122 D4
Sinclairston . 112 C4
Sinderby . . 101 F8
Sinderhope . 109 D8
Sindlesham . 27 C5
Singdean . . 115 D8
Singleborough . 53 F6
Singleton
  Lancs 92 F3
  W Sus . . . 16 C2
Singlewell . . 29 B7
Sinkhurst Green . 30 E2
Sinnahard . . 140 C3
Sinnington . 103 F5
Sinton Green . 50 C3
Sipson . . . 27 B8
Sirhowy . . . 35 C5
Sisland . . . 69 E6
Sissinghurst . 18 B4
Sisterpath . . 122 E3
Siston . . . 23 B8
Sithney . . . 2 D5
Sittingbourne . 30 C2
Six Ashes . . 61 F7
Sixhills . . . 91 F5
Six Hills . . . 64 B3
Six Mile Bottom . 55 D6
Sixpenny Handley 13 C7
Sizewell . . . 57 C8
Skail 157 E10
Skaill
  Orkney . . . 159 E5
  Orkney . . . 159 H6
Skares . . . 113 C5
Skateraw . . 122 B3
Skaw 160 G7
Skeabost . . 149 D9
Skeabrae . . 159 F3
Skeeby . . . 101 D7
Skeffington . 64 D4
Skeffling . . 91 C7
Skegby . . . 76 C4
Skegness . . 79 C8
Skelberry . . 160 M5
Skelbo . . . 151 B10
Skelbrooke . . 89 C6
Skeldyke . . 79 F6
Skellingthorpe . 78 B2
Skellister . . 160 H6
Skellow . . . 89 C6
Skelmanthorpe 88 C3
Skelmersdale . 86 D2
Skelmonae . 153 E8
Skelmorlie . . 118 C1
Skelmuir . . 153 D9
Skelpick . . 157 D10
Skelton
  Cumb . . . 108 F4
  E Yorks . . . 89 B8
  N Yorks . . 101 C5
  Redcar . . . 102 C4
  York 95 D8
Skelton-on-Ure . 95 C6
Skelwick . . 159 D5
Skelwith Bridge . 99 D5
Skendleby . . 79 C7
Skene House . 141 D6
Skenfrith . . 36 B1

Skerne 97 D6
Skeroblingarry 143 F8
Skerray 157 C9
Skerton 92 C4
Sketchley 63 E8
Sketty 33 E7
Skewen 33 E8
Skewsby 96 B2
Skeyton 81 E8
Skiag Bridge 156 G5
Skibo Castle 151 C10
Skidbrooke 91 E8
Skidbrooke North End 91 E8
Skidby 97 F6
Skilgate 10 B4
Skillington 65 B5
Skinburness 107 D8
Skinflats 127 F8
Skinidin 148 D7
Skinnet 157 C8
Skinningrove 103 B5
Skipness 145 H7
Skippool 92 E3
Skipsea 97 D7
Skipsea Brough 97 D7
Skipton 94 D2
Skipton-on-Swale 95 B6
Skipwith 96 F2
Skirbeck 79 E6
Skirbeck Quarter 79 E6
Skirlaugh 97 F7
Skirling 120 F3
Skirmett 39 F7
Skirpenbeck 96 D3
Skirwith 109 F6
Skirza 158 D5
Skulamus 149 F11
Skullomie 157 C9
Skyborry Green 48 B4
Skye of Curr 139 B5
Skyreholme 94 C3
Slackhall 87 F8
Slackhead 152 B4
Slad 37 D5
Slade
Devon 20 E4
Pembs 44 D4
Slade Green 29 B6
Slaggyford 109 D6
Slaidburn 93 D7
Slaithwaite 87 C8
Slaley 110 D2
Slamannan 119 B8
Slapton
Bucks 40 B2
Devon 7 E6
Northants 52 E4
Slatepit Dale 76 C3
Slattocks 87 D6
Slaugham 17 B6
Slaughterford 24 B3
Slawston 64 E4
Sleaford
Hants 27 F6
Lincs 78 E3
Sleagill 99 C7
Sleapford 61 C6
Sledge Green 50 F3
Sledmere 96 C5
Sleightholme 100 C4
Sleights 103 D6
Slepe 13 E7
Slickly 158 D4
Sliddery 143 F10
Sligachan Hotel 149 F9
Slimbridge 36 D4
Slindon
Staffs 74 F5
W Sus 16 D3
Slinfold 28 F2
Sling 83 E6
Slingsby 96 B2
Slioch 152 E5
Slip End
C Beds 40 C3
Herts 54 F3
Slipton 53 B7
Slitting Mill 62 C4
Slochd 138 B4
Slockavullin 124 F4
Sloley 81 E8
Sloothby 79 B7
Slough 27 B7
Slough Green 17 B6
Sluggan 138 B4
Slumbay 149 E13
Slyfield 27 D7
Slyne 92 C4
Smailholm 122 F2
Smallbridge 87 C7
Smallburgh 69 B6
Smallburn
Aberds 153 D10
E Ayrs 113 B6
Small Dole 17 C6
Smalley 76 E4
Smallfield 28 E4
Small Hythe 19 B5
Smallridge 11 D8
Smannell 25 E8
Smardale 100 D2
Smarden 30 E2
Smarden Bell 30 E2
Smeatharpe 11 C6
Smeeth 19 B7
Smeeton Westerby 64 E3
Smercleit 148 G2
Smerral 158 G3
Smethwick 62 F4
Smirisary 147 D9
Smisby 63 C7
Smithfield 108 C4
Smith Green 92 D4
Smithincott 11 C5
Smith's Green 42 B1
Smithstown 149 A12
Smithton 151 G10
Smithy Green 74 B4
Smockington 63 F8
Smoogro 159 H4
Smythe's Green 43 C5
Snaigow House 133 E7
Snailbeach 60 D3
Snailwell 55 C7
Snainton 103 F7
Snaith 89 B7
Snape
N Yorks 101 F7
Suff 57 D7
Snape Green 85 C4
Snarestone 63 D7
Snarford 90 F4
Snargate 19 C6
Snave 19 C7
Snead 60 E3
Sneath Common 68 F4
Sneaton 103 D6
Sneatonthorpe 103 D7
Snelland 90 F4
Snelston 75 E8
Snettisham 80 D2
Sniseabhal 148 E2
Snitter 117 D6
Snitterby 90 E3
Snitterfield 51 D7
Snitton 49 B7
Snodhill 48 E5
Snodland 29 C7
Snowden Hill 88 D3
Snowdown 31 D6
Snowshill 51 F5
Snydale 88 C5
Soar
Anglesey 82 D3
Carms 33 B7
Devon 6 F5
Soar-y-Mynydd 47 D6
Soberton 15 C7
Soberton Heath 15 C7
Sockbridge 99 B7
Sockburn 101 D8
Soham 55 B6
Soham Cotes 55 B6
Solas 148 A3
Soldon Cross 8 C5
Soldridge 26 F4
Sole Street
Kent 29 C7
Kent 30 E4
Solihull 51 B6
Sollers Dilwyn 49 D6
Sollers Hope 49 F8
Sollom 86 C2
Solva 44 C2
Somerby
Leics 64 C4
Lincs 90 D4
Somercotes 76 D4
Somerford 14 E2
Somerford Keynes 37 E7
Somerley 16 E2
Somerleyton 69 E7
Somersal Herbert 75 F8
Somersby 79 B6
Somersham
Cambs 54 B4
Suff 56 E4
Somerton
Oxon 38 B4
Som 12 B2
Sompting 17 D5
Sonning 27 B5
Sonning Common 39 F7
Sonning Eye 27 B5
Sontley 73 E7
Sopley 14 E2
Sopwell 40 D4
Sopworth 37 F5
Sorbie 105 E8
Sordale 158 D3
Sorisdale 146 E5
Sorn 113 B5
Sornhill 118 F5
Sortat 158 D4
Sotby 78 B5
Sots Hole 78 C4
Sotterley 69 F7
Soudley 61 B7
Soughton 73 C6
Soulbury 40 B1
Soulby 100 C2
Souldern 52 F3
Souldrop 53 C7
Sound
Ches E 74 E3
Shetland 160 H5
Shetland 160 J6
Sound Heath 74 E3
Soundwell 23 B8
Sourhope 116 B4
Sourin 159 E5
Sourton 9 E7
Soutergate 98 F4
South Acre 67 C8
Southall 40 F4
South Allington 7 F5
South Alloa 127 E7
Southam
Glos 37 B6
Warks 52 C2
South Ambersham 16 B3
Southampton 14 C5
South Anston 89 F6
South Ascot 27 C7
South Ballachulish 130 D4
South Balloch 112 E3
South Bank 102 B3
South Barrow 12 B4
South Beach 70 D4
South Benfleet 42 F3
South Bersted 16 D3
Southborough 29 E6
Southbourne
BCP 14 E2
W Sus 15 D8
South Brent 6 C4
South Brewham 24 F2
South Broomhill 117 E8
Southburgh 68 D2
South Burlingham 69 D6
Southburn 97 D5
South Cadbury 12 B4
South Cairn 104 C3
South Carlton 78 B2
South Cave 96 F5
South Cerney 37 E7
South Chard 11 D8
South Charlton 117 B7
South Cheriton 12 B4
Southchurch 43 F5
South Cliffe 96 F4
South Clifton 77 B8
South Cockerington 91 F7
South Cornelly 34 F2
Southcott 25 D6
Southcourt 39 C8
South Cove 69 F7
South Creagan 130 E3
South Creake 80 D4
South Croxton 64 C3
South Croydon 28 C4
South Dalton 97 E5
South Darenth 29 C6
Southdean 116 D2
Southdene 86 E2
South Duffield 96 F2
Southease 17 D8
South Elkington 91 F6
South Elmsall 89 C5
Southend
Argyll 143 H7
W Berks 26 B3
Wilts 25 B6
South End
Bucks 40 B1
Cumb 92 C2
N Lincs 90 B5
Southend-on-Sea 42 F4
Southernden 30 E2
Southerndown 21 B7
Southerness 107 D6
South Erradale 149 A12
Southery 67 E6
South Fambridge 42 E4
South Fawley 38 F3
South Ferriby 90 B3
Southfield 111 B5
Southfleet 29 B7
South Garth 160 D7
South Garvan 130 B3
Southgate
Ceredig 46 B4
London 41 E5
Norf 81 E7
Swansea 33 F6
South Glendale 148 G2
South Godstone 28 E4
South Gorley 14 C2
South Green
Essex 42 E2
Kent 30 C2
South-haa 160 E5
South Ham 26 D4
South Hanningfield 42 E3
South Harting 15 C8
South Hatfield 41 D5
South Hayling 15 E8
South Hazelrigg 123 F6
South Heath 40 D2
South Heighton 17 D8
South Hetton 111 E6
South Hiendley 88 C4
South Hill 5 B8
South Hinksey 39 D5
South Hole 8 B4
South Holme 96 B2
South Holmwood 28 E2
South Hornchurch 41 F8
South Hykeham 78 C2
South Hylton 111 D6
Southill 54 E2
South Kelsey 90 E4
South Kessock 151 G9
South Killingholme 91 C5
South Kilvington 102 F2
South Kilworth 64 F3
South Kirkby 88 C5
South Kirkton 141 D6
South Kiscadale 143 F11
South Kyme 78 E4
South Lancing 17 D5
Southleigh 11 E7
South Leigh 38 D3
South Leverton 89 F8
South Littleton 51 E5
South Lopham 68 F3
South Luffenham 65 D6
South Malling 17 C8
South Marston 38 F1
South Middleton 117 B5
South Milford 95 F7
South Millbrex 153 D8
South Milton 6 E5
South Mimms 41 D5
Southminster 43 E5
South Molton 10 B2
Southmoor 38 E3
South Moreton 39 F5
South Mundham 16 D2
South Muskham 77 D7
South Newbald 96 F5
South Newington 52 F2
South Newton 25 F5
South Normanton 76 D4
South Norwood 28 C4
South Nutfield 28 E4
South Ockendon 42 F1
Southoe 54 C2
Southolt 57 C5
South Ormsby 79 B6
Southorpe 65 D7
South Otterington 102 F1
South Owersby 90 E4
Southowram 88 B2
South Oxhey 40 E4
South Perrott 12 D2
South Petherton 12 C2
South Petherwin 8 F5
South Pickenham 67 D8
South Pool 7 E5
Southport 85 C4
South Port 125 C6
Southpunds 160 L6
South Radworthy 21 F6
South Rauceby 78 E3
South Raynham 80 E4
Southrepps 81 D8
South Reston 91 F8
Southrey 78 C4
Southrop 38 D1
Southrope 26 E4
South Runcton 67 D6
South Scarle 77 C8
Southsea 15 E7
South Shian 130 E3
South Shields 111 C6
South Shore 92 F3
South Somercotes 91 E8
South Stainley 95 C6
South Stainmore 100 C3
South Stifford 29 B7
Southstoke 24 C2
South Stoke
Oxon 39 F5
W Sus 16 D4
South Street
E Sus 17 C7
Kent 30 C5
Kent 30 D4
London 28 D5
South Tawton 9 E8
South Thoresby 79 B7
South Tidworth 25 E7
Southtown
Norf 69 D8
Orkney 159 J5
South Town 26 F4
South View 26 D4
Southwaite 108 E4
South Walsham 69 C6
Southwark 28 B4
South Warnborough 26 E5
Southwater 17 B5
Southwater Street 17 B5
Southway 23 E7
South Weald 42 E1
Southwell
Dorset 12 G4
Notts 77 D6
South Weston 39 E7
South Wheatley
Corn 8 E4
Notts 89 F8
South Whiteness 160 J5
Southwick
Hants 15 D7
Northants 65 E7
T&W 111 D6
Wilts 24 D3
W Sus 17 D6
South Widcombe 23 D7
South Wigston 64 E2
South Willingham 91 F5
South Wingfield 76 D3
South Witham 65 C6
Southwold 57 B9
South Wonston 26 F2
Southwood
Norf 69 D6
Som 23 F7
South Woodham Ferrers 42 E4
South Wootton 67 B6
South Wraxall 24 C3
South Zeal 9 E8
Soval Lodge 155 E8
Sowber Gate 102 F1
Sowerby
N Yorks 102 F2
W Yorks 87 B8
Sowerby Bridge 87 B8
Sowerby Row 108 F3
Sowood 87 C8
Sowton 10 E4
Soyal 151 B8
Spacey Houses 95 D6
Spa Common 81 D8
Spadeadam Farm 109 B5
Spalding 66 B2
Spaldington 96 F3
Spaldwick 54 B2
Spalford 77 C8
Spanby 78 F3
Sparham 68 C3
Spark Bridge 99 F5
Sparkford 12 B4
Sparkhill 62 F4
Sparkwell 6 D3
Sparrow Green 68 C2
Sparrowpit 87 F8
Sparsholt
Hants 26 F2
Oxon 38 F3
Spartylea 109 E8
Spaunton 103 F5
Spaxton 22 F4
Spean Bridge 136 F5
Spear Hill 16 C5
Speen
Bucks 39 E8
W Berks 26 C2
Speeton 97 B7
Speke 86 F2
Speldhurst 29 E6
Spellbrook 41 C7
Spelsbury 38 B3
Spelter 34 E2
Spencers Wood 26 C5
Spennithorne 101 F6
Spennymoor 111 F5
Spetchley 50 D3
Spetisbury 13 D7
Spexhall 69 F6
Spey Bay 152 B3
Speybridge 139 B6
Speyview 152 D2
Spilsby 79 C7
Spindlestone 123 F7
Spinkhill 76 B4
Spinningdale 151 C9
Spirthill 24 B4
Spital Hill 89 E7
Spital in the Street 90 F3
Spithurst 17 C8
Spittal
Dumfries 105 D7
Spittal *continued*
E Loth 121 B7
Highld 158 E3
Northumb 123 D6
Pembs 44 C4
Stirling 126 F4
Spittalfield 133 E8
Spittal of Glenmuick 140 F2
Spittal of Glenshee 133 B8
Spixworth 68 C5
Splayne's Green 17 B8
Spofforth 95 D6
Spondon 76 F4
Spon End 51 B8
Spon Green 73 C6
Spooner Row 68 E3
Sporle 67 C8
Spott 122 B2
Spratton 52 B5
Spreakley 27 E6
Spreyton 9 E8
Spridlington 90 F4
Springburn 119 C6
Springfield
Dumfries 108 C3
Essex 42 D3
Fife 128 C5
Moray 151 F13
W Mid 62 F4
Springhill 62 D3
Springholm 106 C5
Springkell 108 B2
Springside 118 F3
Springthorpe 90 F2
Spring Vale 88 D3
Spring Valley 84 E3
Springwell 111 D5
Sproatley 97 F7
Sproston Green 74 C4
Sprotbrough 89 D6
Sproughton 56 E5
Sprouston 122 F3
Sprowston 68 C5
Sproxton
Leics 65 B5
N Yorks 102 F4
Spurstow 74 D2
Spynie 152 B2
Squires Gate 92 F3
Srannda 154 J5
Sronphadruig Lodge 132 B4
Stableford
Shrops 61 E7
Staffs 74 F5
Stacey Bank 88 E3
Stackhouse 93 C8
Stackpole 44 F4
Staddiscombe 6 D3
Staddlethorpe 90 B2
Stadhampton 39 E6
Stadhlaigearraidh 148 E2
Staffi 149 B9
Staffield 108 E5
Stafford 62 B3
Stagsden 53 E7
Stainburn
Cumb 98 B2
N Yorks 94 E5
Stainby 65 B6
Staincross 88 C4
Staindrop 101 B6
Staines-upon-Thames 27 B8
Stainfield
Lincs 65 B7
Lincs 78 B4
Stainforth
N Yorks 93 C8
S Yorks 89 C7
Staining 92 F3
Stainland 87 C8
Stainsacre 103 D7
Stainsby 76 C4
Stainton
Cumb 99 B6
Cumb 99 F7
Durham 101 C5
Mbro 102 C2
N Yorks 101 E6
S Yorks 89 E6
Stainton by Langworth 78 B3
Staintondale 103 E7
Stainton le Vale 91 E5
Stainton with Adgarley 92 B2
Stair
Cumb 98 B4
E Ayrs 112 B4
Stairhaven 105 D6
Staithes 103 C5
Stakeford 117 F8
Stake Pool 92 E4
Stalbridge 12 C5
Stalbridge Weston 12 C5
Stalham 69 B6
Stalham Green 69 B6
Stalisfield Green 30 D3
Stallingborough 91 C5
Stalling Busk 100 F4
Stalmine 92 E3
Stalybridge 87 E7
Stambourne 55 F8
Stambourne Green 55 F8
Stamford 65 D7
Stamford Bridge
Ches W 73 C8
E Yorks 96 D3
Stamfordham 110 B3
Stanah 99 C5
Stanborough 41 C5
Stanbridge
C Beds 40 B2
Dorset 13 D8
Stanbrook 50 E3
Stanbury 94 F3
Stand
Gtr Man 87 D5
N Lanark 119 C7
Standburn 120 B2
Standeford 62 D3
Standen 30 E2
Standford 27 F6
Standingstone 107 F7
Standish 86 C3
Standlake 38 D3
Standon
Hants 14 B5
Herts 41 B6
Staffs 74 F5
Stane 119 D8
Stanfield 80 E5
Stanford
C Beds 54 E2
Kent 19 B8
Stanford Bishop 49 D8
Stanford Bridge 50 C2
Stanford Dingley 26 B3
Stanford in the Vale 38 E3
Stanford-le-Hope 42 F2
Stanford on Avon 52 B3
Stanford on Soar 64 B2
Stanford on Teme 50 C2
Stanford Rivers 41 D8
Stanfree 76 B4
Stanghow 102 C4
Stanground 66 E2
Stanhoe 80 D4
Stanhope
Borders 114 B4
Durham 110 F2
Stanion 65 F6
Stanley
Derbys 76 E4
Durham 110 D4
Lancs 86 D2
Perth 133 F8
Staffs 75 D6
W Yorks 88 B4
Stanley Common 76 E4
Stanley Gate 86 D2
Stanley Hill 49 E8
Stanlow 73 B8
Stanmer 17 D7
Stanmore
Hants 15 B5
London 40 E4
W Berks 26 B2
Stannergate 134 F4
Stanningley 94 F5
Stannington
Northumb 110 B5
S Yorks 88 F4
Stansbatch 48 C5
Stansfield 55 D8
Stanstead 56 E2
Stanstead Abbotts 41 C6
Stansted 29 C7
Stansted Airport 42 B1
Stansted Mountfitchet 41 B8
Stanton
Glos 51 F5
Mon 35 B7
Northumb 117 F7
Staffs 75 E8
Suff 56 B3
Stanton by Bridge 63 B7
Stanton-by-Dale 76 F4
Stanton Drew 23 C7
Stanton Fitzwarren 38 E1
Stanton Harcourt 38 D4
Stanton Hill 76 C4
Stanton in Peak 76 C2
Stanton Lacy 49 B6
Stanton Long 61 E5
Stanton-on-the-Wolds 77 F6
Stanton Prior 23 C8
Stanton St Bernard 25 C5
Stanton St John 39 D5
Stanton St Quintin 24 B4
Stanton Street 56 C3
Stanton under Bardon 63 C8
Stanton upon Hine Heath 61 B5
Stanton Wick 23 C8
Stanwardine in the Fields 60 B4
Stanwardine in the Wood 60 B4
Stanway
Essex 43 B5
Glos 51 F5
Stanway Green 57 B6
Stanwell 27 B8
Stanwell Moor 27 B8
Stanwick 53 B7
Stanwick-St-John 101 C6
Stanwix 108 D4
Stanydale 160 H4
Staoinebrig 148 E2
Stape 103 E5
Stapehill 13 D8
Stapeley 74 E3
Stapenhill 63 B6
Staple
Kent 31 D6
Som 22 E3
Staple Cross 18 C4
Staplefield 17 B6
Staple Fitzpaine 11 C7
Stapleford
Cambs 55 D5
Herts 41 C6
Leics 64 C5
Lincs 77 D8
Notts 76 F4
Wilts 25 F5
Stapleford Abbotts 41 E8
Stapleford Tawney 41 E8
Staplegrove 11 B7
Staplehay 11 B7
Staplehurst 29 E8
Staplers 15 F6
Stapleton
Bristol 23 B8
Cumb 108 B5
Stapleton *continued*
Hereford 48 C5
Leics 63 E8
N Yorks 101 C7
Shrops 60 D4
Som 12 B2
Stapley 11 C6
Staploe 54 C2
Staplow 49 E8
Star
Fife 128 D5
Pembs 45 F4
Som 23 D6
Stara 159 F3
Starbeck 95 D6
Starbotton 94 B2
Starcross 10 F4
Stareton 51 B8
Starkholmes 76 D3
Starlings Green 55 F5
Starston 68 F5
Startforth 101 C5
Startley 37 F6
Stathe 11 B8
Stathern 77 F7
Station Town 111 F7
Staughton Green 54 C2
Staughton Highway 54 C2
Staunton
Glos 36 B4
Glos 36 C2
Staunton in the Vale 77 E8
Staunton on Arrow 49 C5
Staunton on Wye 49 E5
Staveley
Cumb 99 E6
Cumb 99 F5
Derbys 76 B4
N Yorks 95 C6
Staverton
Devon 7 C5
Glos 37 B5
Northants 52 C3
Wilts 24 C3
Staverton Bridge 37 B5
Stawell 23 F5
Staxigoe 158 E5
Staxton 97 B6
Staylittle 59 E5
Staynall 92 E3
Staythorpe 77 D7
Stean 94 B3
Stearsby 96 B2
Steart 22 E4
Stebbing 42 B2
Stebbing Green 42 B2
Stedham 16 B2
Steele Road 115 E8
Steen's Bridge 49 D7
Steep 15 B8
Steeple
Dorset 13 F7
Essex 43 D5
Steeple Ashton 24 D4
Steeple Aston 38 B4
Steeple Barton 38 B4
Steeple Bumpstead 55 E7
Steeple Claydon 39 B6
Steeple Gidding 65 F8
Steeple Langford 24 F5
Steeple Morden 54 E3
Steep Marsh 15 B8
Steeton 94 E3
Stein 148 C7
Steinmanhill 153 D7
Stelling Minnis 30 E5
Stemster 158 D3
Stemster House 158 D3
Stenalees 4 D5
Stenhousemuir 127 F7
Stenigot 91 F6
Stenness 160 F4
Stenscholl 149 B9
Stenso 159 F4
Stenson 63 B7
Stenton
E Loth 122 B2
Fife 128 E4
Stenwith 77 F8
Stepaside 32 D2
Stepping Hill 87 F7
Steppingley 53 F8
Stepps 119 C6
Sterndale Moor 75 C8
Sternfield 57 C7
Sterridge 20 E4
Stert 24 D5
Stetchworth 55 D7
Stevenage 41 B5
Stevenston 118 E2
Steventon
Hants 26 E3
Oxon 38 E4
Stevington 53 D7
Stewartby 53 E8
Stewarton
Argyll 143 G7
E Ayrs 118 E4
Stewkley 40 B1
Stewton 91 F7
Steyne Cross 15 F7
Steyning 17 C5
Steynton 44 E4
Stibb 8 C4
Stibbard 81 E5
Stibb Cross 9 C6
Stibb Green 25 C7
Stibbington 65 E7
Stichill 122 F3
Sticker 4 D4
Stickford 79 D6
Sticklepath 9 E8
Stickney 79 D6
Stiffkey 81 C5
Stifford's Bridge 50 E2
Stillingfleet 95 E8
Stillington
N Yorks 95 C8
Stockton 102 B1
Stilton 65 F8
Stinchcombe 36 E4
Stinsford 12 E5
Stirchley 61 D7
Stirkoke House 158 E5
Stirling
Aberds 153 D11
Stirling 127 E6
Stisted 42 B3
Stithians 3 C6
Stittenham 151 D9
Stivichall 51 B8
Stixwould 78 C4
Stoak 73 B8
Stobieside 119 F6
Stobo 120 F4
Stoborough 13 F7
Stoborough Green 13 F7
Stobshiel 121 C7
Stobswood 117 E8
Stock 42 E2
Stockbridge 25 F8
Stockbury 30 C2
Stockcross 26 C2
Stockdalewath 108 E3
Stockerston 64 E5
Stock Green 50 D4
Stockheath 15 D8
Stockiemuir 126 F4
Stockingford 63 E7
Stocking Pelham 41 B7
Stockland 11 D7
Stockland Bristol 22 E4
Stockleigh English 10 D3
Stockleigh Pomeroy 10 D3
Stockley 24 C5
Stocklinch 11 C8
Stockport 87 E6
Stocksbridge 88 E3
Stocksfield 110 C3
Stockton
Hereford 49 C7
Norf 69 E6
Shrops 60 D2
Shrops 61 E7
Warks 52 C2
Wilts 24 F4
Stockton Heath 86 F4
Stockton-on-Tees 102 C2
Stockton on Teme 50 C2
Stockton on the Forest 96 D2
Stock Wood 50 D5
Stodmarsh 31 C6
Stody 81 D6
Stoer 156 G3
Stoford
Som 12 C3
Wilts 25 F5
Stogumber 22 F2
Stogursey 22 E4
Stoke
Devon 8 B4
Hants 15 D8
Hants 26 D2
Medway 30 B2
Suff 57 E5
Stoke Abbott 12 D2
Stoke Albany 64 F5
Stoke Ash 56 B5
Stoke Bardolph 77 E6
Stoke Bliss 49 C8
Stoke Bruerne 52 E5
Stoke by Clare 55 E8
Stoke-by-Nayland 56 F3
Stoke Canon 10 E4
Stoke Charity 26 F2
Stoke Climsland 5 B8
Stoke D'Abernon 28 D2
Stoke Doyle 65 F7
Stoke Dry 65 E5
Stoke Farthing 13 B8
Stoke Ferry 67 E7
Stoke Fleming 7 E6
Stokeford 13 F6
Stoke Gabriel 7 D6
Stoke Gifford 23 B8
Stoke Golding 63 E7
Stoke Goldington 53 E6
Stoke Green 40 F2
Stokeham 77 B7
Stoke Hammond 40 B1
Stoke Heath 61 B6
Stoke Holy Cross 68 D5
Stokeinteignhead 7 B7
Stoke Lacy 49 E8
Stoke Lyne 39 B5
Stoke Mandeville 39 C8
Stokenchurch 39 E7
Stoke Newington 41 F6
Stokenham 7 E6
Stoke on Tern 61 B6
Stoke-on-Trent 75 E5
Stoke Orchard 37 B6
Stoke Poges 40 F2
Stoke Prior
Hereford 49 D7
Worcs 50 C4
Stoke Rivers 20 F5
Stoke Rochford 65 B6
Stoke Row 39 F6
Stoke St Gregory 11 B8
Stoke St Mary 11 B7
Stoke St Michael 23 E8
Stoke St Milborough 61 F5
Stokesay 60 F4
Stokesby 69 C7
Stokesley 102 D3
Stoke sub Hamdon 12 C2
Stoke Talmage 39 E6
Stoke Trister 12 B5
Stoke Wake 13 D5
Stolford 22 E4
Stondon Massey 42 D1
Stone
Bucks 39 C7
Glos 36 E3
Kent 19 C6
Kent 29 B6
Staffs 75 F6
S Yorks 89 F6
Worcs 50 B3
Stone Allerton 23 D6
Ston Easton 23 D8
Stone Bridge Corner 66 D2
Stonebroom 76 D4
Stone Chair 88 B2
Stone Cross
E Sus 18 E3
Kent 31 D7
Stone-edge Batch 23 B6
Stoneferry 97 F7
Stonefield 119 D6
Stonegate
E Sus 18 C3
N Yorks 103 D5
Stonegrave 96 B2
Stonehaugh 109 B7
Stonehaven 141 F7
Stonehouse
Glos 37 D5
Northumb 109 D6
S Lanark 119 E7
Stone House 100 F2
Stoneleigh 51 B8
Stonely 54 C2
Stoner Hill 15 B8
Stonesby 64 B5
Stonesfield 38 C3
Stone's Green 43 B7
Stone Street
Kent 29 D6
Suff 56 F3
Suff 69 F6
Stonethwaite 98 C4
Stoneybreck 160 N8
Stoneyburn 120 C2
Stoney Cross 14 C3
Stoneygate
Aberds 153 E10
Leicester 64 D3
Stoneyhills 43 E5
Stoneykirk 104 D4
Stoney Middleton 76 B2
Stoney Stanton 63 E8
Stoney Stoke 24 F2
Stoney Stratton 23 F8
Stoney Stretton 60 D3
Stoneywood
Aberdeen 141 C7
Falk 127 F6
Stonganess 160 C7
Stonham Aspal 56 D5
Stonnall 62 D4
Stonor 39 F7
Stonton Wyville 64 E4
Stony Cross 50 E2
Stonyfield 151 D9
Stony Stratford 53 E5
Stoodleigh 10 C4
Stopes 88 F3
Stopham 16 C4
Stopsley 40 B4
Stores Corner 57 E7
Storeton 85 F4
Stornoway 155 D9
Storridge 50 E2
Storrington 16 C4
Storrs 99 E5
Storth 99 F6
Storwood 96 E3
Stotfield 152 A2
Stotfold 54 F3
Stottesdon 61 F6
Stoughton
Leics 64 D3
Sur 27 D7
W Sus 16 C2
Stoul 147 B10
Stoulton 50 E4
Stourbridge 62 F3
Stourpaine 13 D6
Stourport on Severn 50 B3
Stour Provost 13 B5
Stour Row 13 B6
Stourton
Staffs 62 F2
Warks 51 F7
Wilts 24 F2
Stourton Caundle 12 C5
Stove
Orkney 159 E7
Shetland 160 L6
Stoven 69 F7
Stow
Borders 121 E7
Lincs 78 F3
Lincs 90 F2
Stow Bardolph 67 D6
Stow Bedon 68 E2
Stowbridge 67 D6
Stow cum Quy 55 C6
Stowe 48 B5
Stowe-by-Chartley 62 B4
Stowe Green 36 D2
Stowell 12 B4
Stowford 9 F6
Stowlangtoft 56 C3
Stow Longa 54 B2
Stow Maries 42 E4
Stowmarket 56 D4
Stow-on-the-Wold 38 B1
Stowting 30 E5
Stowupland 56 D4
Straad 145 G9
Strachan 141 E5
Stradbroke 57 B6
Stradishall 55 D8
Stradsett 67 D6
Stragglethorpe 78 D2
Straid 112 E1
Straith 113 F8
Straiton
Edin 121 C5
S Ayrs 112 D3
Straloch
Aberds 141 B7
Perth 133 C7
Stramshall 75 F7
Strang 84 E3
Stranraer 104 C4
Stratfield Mortimer 26 C4
Stratfield Saye 26 C4
Stratfield Turgis 26 D4
Stratford 41 F6

Stratford St
Andrew 57 C7
Stratford St Mary .56 F4
Stratford Sub
Castle. 25 F6
Stratford Tony. . .13 B8
Stratford-upon-
Avon 51 D6
Strath
Highld 149 A12
Highld 158 E4
Strathan
Highld 136 E2
Highld 156 G3
Highld 157 C8
Strathaven 119 E7
Strathblane 119 B5
Strathcanaird . . 156 J4
Strathcarron . . .150 G2
Strathcoil 124 B2
Strathdon 140 C2
Strathellie 153 B10
Strathkinness . . 129 C6
Strathmashie
House. 137 E8
Strathmiglo 128 C4
Strathmore
Lodge. 158 F3
Strathpeffer . . .150 F7
Strathrannoch . .150 D6
Strathtay. 133 D6
Strathvaich
Lodge. 150 D3
Strathwhillan . . 143 E11
Strathy. 157 C11
Strathyre 126 C4
Stratton
Corn 8 D4
Dorset. 12 E4
Glos 37 D7
Stratton Audley . .39 B6
Stratton on the
Fosse. 23 D8
Stratton St
Margaret. 38 F1
Stratton St
Michael 68 E5
Stratton
Strawless 81 E8
Stravithie 129 C7
Streat. 17 C7
Streatham 28 B4
Streatley
C Beds. 40 B3
W Berks 39 F5
Street
Lancs 92 D5
N Yorks 103 D5
Som. 23 F6
Street Dinas . . .73 F7
Street End
Kent 30 D5
W Sus 16 E2
Street Gate. . . .110 D5
Streethay 62 C5
Streetlam 101 E8
Streetly 62 E4
Street Lydan . . .73 F8
Streetly End. . . .55 E7
Strefford. 60 F4
Strelley 76 E5
Strensall 96 C2
Stretcholt 22 E4
Strete. 7 E6
Stretford. 87 E6
Strethall 55 F5
Stretham 55 B6
Strettington . . 16 D2
Stretton
Ches W 73 D8
Derbys 76 C3
Rutland. 65 C6
Staffs 62 C2
Staffs 63 B6
Warr 86 F4
Stretton
Grandison. 49 E8
Stretton-on-
Dunsmore. . . .52 B2
Stretton-on-
Fosse 51 F7
Stretton Sugwas .49 E6
Stretton under
Fosse. 63 F8
Stretton
Westwood. 61 E5
Strichen 153 C9
Strines. 87 F7
Stringston 22 E3
Strixton 53 C7
Stroat. 36 E2
Stromeferry. . . 149 E13
Stromemore . . . 149 E13
Stromness 159 H3
Stronaba. 136 F5
Stronachlachar . 126 C3
Stronchreggan . 130 B4
Stronchrubie . . .156 H5
Strone
Argyll 145 E10
Highld 136 F4
Highld 137 B8
Invclyd 118 B2
Stronmilchan . .125 C7
Strontian 130 C2
Strood 29 C8
Strood Green
Sur 28 E3
W Sus 16 B4
W Sus 28 F2
Stroud
Glos 37 D5
Hants 15 B8
Stroud Green. . .42 E4
Stroxton 78 F2
Struan
Highld 149 E8
Perth. 133 C5
Strubby 91 F8
Strumpshaw . . .69 D6
Strutherhill . . .119 E7
Struy 150 H6
Stryt-issa 73 E6
Stuartfield . . . 153 D9
Stubbington . . .15 G3
Stubbins 87 C5
Stubbs Cross . . .19 B6
Stubbs Green . . .69 E6

Stubb's Green . . .69 E5
Stubhampton . . .13 C7
Stub Place 98 E2
Stubton 77 E8
Stuckgowan . . . 126 D2
Stuckton 14 C2
Stud Green 27 B6
Studham 40 C3
Studland 13 F8
Studley
Works. 51 C5
Wilts 24 B4
Studley Roger . .95 B5
Stump Cross . . .55 E6
Stuntney 55 B6
Sturbridge 74 F5
Sturmer. 55 E7
Sturminster
Marshall 13 D7
Sturminster
Newton 13 C5
Sturry 31 C5
Sturton 90 D3
Sturton by Stow . .90 F2
Sturton le
Steeple 89 F8
Stuston 56 B5
Stutton
N Yorks 95 E7
Suff 57 F5
Styal 87 F6
Styrrup 89 E7
Suainebost. . . . 155 A10
Suardail 155 D9
Succoth
Aberds 152 E4
Argyll 125 E8
Suckley 50 D2
Suckquoy 159 K5
Sudborough 65 F6
Sudbourne 57 D8
Sudbrook
Lincs 78 E2
Mon. 36 F2
Sudbrooke 78 B3
Sudbury
Derbys 75 F8
London 40 F4
Suff 56 E2
Suddie 151 F9
Sudgrove 37 D6
Suffield
Norf 81 D8
N Yorks 103 E7
Sugnall 74 F4
Sugwas Pool . . .49 E6
Suladale 149 C8
Sulaisiadar 155 D10
Sulby 84 C3
Sulgrave 52 E3
Sulham 26 B4
Sulhamstead . . .26 C4
Sulland 159 D6
Sullington 16 C4
Sullom 160 F5
Sullom Voe Oil
Terminal 160 F5
Sully 22 C3
Sumburgh 160 N6
Summer Bridge . 94 C5
Summercourt . . .4 D3
Summerfield 80 D3
Summergangs . .97 F7
Summer-house 101 C7
Summerleaze . . .35 F8
Summersdale . . .16 D2
Summerseat . . .87 C5
Summertown . . .39 D5
Summit 87 D7
Sunbury-on-
Thames 28 C2
Sundaywell 113 F8
Sunderland
Argyll 142 B3
Cumb 107 F8
T&W 111 D6
Sunderland
Bridge 111 F5
Sundhope. 115 B6
Sundon Park . . .40 B3
Sundridge 29 D5
Sunipol 146 F6
Sunk Island . . .91 C6
Sunningdale . . .27 C7
Sunninghill 27 C7
Sunningwell . . .38 D4
Sunniside
Durham. 110 F4
T&W 110 D5
Sunnyhurst 86 B4
Sunnylaw 127 E6
Sunnyside. 28 F4
Sunton 25 D7
Surby 84 E2
Surfleet 66 B2
Surfleet Seas End 66 B2
Surlingham 69 D6
Sustead 81 D7
Susworth 90 D2
Sutcombe 8 C5
Suton 68 E3
Sutors of
Cromarty . . . 151 E11
Sutterby 79 B6
Sutterton 79 F5
Sutton
Cambs 54 B5
C Beds. 54 E3
Kent 31 E7
London 28 C3
Mers 86 E2
Norf 69 B6
Notts 77 F7
N Yorks 89 F7
N Yorks 89 B5
Oxon 38 D4
Pboro 65 E7
Shrops 61 F7
Shrops 74 F3
Som. 23 H8
Staffs 61 B7
Suff 57 E7
S Yorks 89 C6
W Sus 16 C3
Sutton at Hone . .29 B6
Sutton Bassett . .64 E4
Sutton Benger . .24 B4

Sutton Bonington 64 B2
Sutton Bridge . . .66 B4
Sutton Cheney . . 63 D8
Sutton Coldfield . .62 E5
Sutton Courtenay 39 E5
Sutton Crosses. . 66 B4
Sutton Grange . . .95 B5
Sutton Green. . . .27 D8
Sutton Howgrave .95 B6
Sutton In
Ashfield. 76 D4
Sutton-in-Craven 94 E3
Sutton Ings 97 F7
Sutton in the
Elms 64 E2
Sutton Lane Ends .75 B6
Sutton Leach. . . .86 E3
Sutton Maddock . .61 D7
Sutton Mallet . . .23 F5
Sutton
Mandeville. 13 B7
Sutton Manor . . .86 E3
Sutton Montis . . .12 B4
Sutton on Hull . . .97 F7
Sutton on Sea . . .91 F9
Sutton-on-the-
Forest 95 C8
Sutton on the Hill .76 F2
Sutton on Trent . .77 C7
Sutton St
Edmund. 66 C3
Sutton St James . 66 C3
Sutton St
Nicholas 49 E7
Sutton Scarsdale .76 C4
Sutton Scotney. . .26 F2
Sutton under
Brailes. 51 F8
Sutton-under-
Whitestonecliffe
. . . . .102 F2
Sutton upon
Derwent. 96 E3
Sutton Valence . . 30 E2
Sutton Veny 24 E3
Sutton Waldron . 13 C6
Sutton Weaver . . 74 B2
Sutton Wick 23 D7
Swaby 79 B6
Swadlincote. 63 C7
Swaffham. 67 D8
Swaffham
Bulbeck 55 C6
Swaffham Prior . . 55 C6
Swafield 81 D8
Swainby 102 D2
Swainshill 49 E6
Swainsthorpe . . . 68 D5
Swainswick 24 C2
Swalcliffe. 51 F8
Swalecliffe. 30 C5
Swallow 91 D5
Swallowcliffe . . 13 B7
Swallowfield . . .26 C5
Swallownest 89 F5
Swallows Cross . .42 E2
Swanage 13 G8
Swanbister 159 H4
Swanbourne 39 B8
Swan Green
Ches W 74 B4
Suff 57 B6
Swanland 90 B3
Swanley 29 C6
Swanley Village . 29 C6
Swanmore 15 C6
Swannington
Leics 63 C8
Norf 68 C4
Swanscombe . . . 29 B7
Swansea
= Abertawe 33 E7
Swanton Abbott .81 E8
Swanton Morley . 68 C3
Swanton Novers .81 D6
Swanton Street. . 30 D2
Swanwick
Derbys 76 D4
Hants 15 D6
Swarby 78 E3
Swardeston 68 D5
Swarister 160 E7
Swarkestone. . . .63 B7
Swarland 117 D7
Swarland Estate 117 D7
Swarthmoor 92 B2
Swathwick 76 C3
Swaton 78 F4
Swavesey 54 C4
Sway. 14 E3
Swayfield 65 B6
Swaythling 14 C5
Sweet Green . . . 49 C8
Sweetham 10 E3
Sweethouse 5 C5
Sweffling 57 C7
Swepstone 63 C7
Swerford 51 F8
Swettenham 74 C5
Swetton 94 B4
Swffryd 35 E6
Swiftsden 18 C4
Swilland 57 D5
Swillington 95 F6
Swimbridge 9 B8
Swimbridge
Newland 20 F5
Swinbrook 38 C2
Swinderby 77 C8
Swindon
Glos 37 B6
Staffs 62 E2
Swindon 38 F1
Swine. 97 F7
Swinefleet 89 B8
Swineshead
Bedford. 53 C8
Lincs 78 E5
Swineshead
Bridge 78 E5
Swiney. 158 G4
Swinford
Leics 52 B3
Oxon 38 D4
Swingate 76 E5
Swingfield
Minnis 31 E6
Swingfield Street .31 E6

Swinhoe 117 B8
Swinhope. 91 E6
Swining 160 G6
Swinithwaite . . .101 F5
Swinnow Moor . . .94 F5
Swinscoe 75 E8
Swinside Hall . . .116 C3
Swinstead. 65 B7
Swinton
Borders. 122 E4
Gtr Man 87 D5
N Yorks 94 B5
N Yorks 96 B3
S Yorks 88 E5
Swintonmill 122 E4
Swithland 64 C2
Swordale 151 E8
Swordland 147 B10
Swordly. 157 C10
Sworton Heath . .86 F4
Swydffynnon . . .47 C5
Swynnerton 75 F5
Swyre. 12 F3
Sychtyn 59 D6
Syde 37 C6
Sydenham
London 28 B4
Oxon 39 D7
Sydenham
Damerel 6 B2
Syderstone 80 D4
Sydling St
Nicholas 12 E4
Sydmonton 26 D2
Syerston 77 E7
Syke 87 C6
Sykehouse 89 C7
Sykes 93 D6
Syleham 57 B6
Sylen 33 E6
Symbister 160 G7
Symington
S Ayrs 118 F3
S Lanark 120 F2
Symonds Green .12 E2
Symonds Yat . . .36 C2
Synod Inn 46 D3
Syre 157 E9
Syreford 37 B7
Syresham 52 E4
Syston
Leics 64 C3
Lincs 78 E2
Sytchampton . . .50 C3
Sywell 53 C6

T

Taagan. 150 E3
Tabost 155 A10
Tabost 155 F8
Tackley 38 B4
Tacleit 154 D6
Tacolneston. . . .68 E4
Tadcaster 95 E7
Taddington. 75 B8
Taddiport 9 C6
Tadley 26 C4
Tadlow. 54 E3
Tadmarton 51 F8
Tadworth 28 D3
Tafarnau-bach . .35 C5
Tafarn-y-gelyn . .73 C5
Taff's Well 35 F4
Tafolwern 59 D5
Tai. 83 E7
Taibach 34 F1
Tai-bach 59 B8
Taigh a
Ghearraidh . . . 148 A2
Tai-mawr 72 E3
Tain
Highld 151 C10
Highld 158 D4
Tainant 73 E6
Tainlon 82 F4
Tairbeart
= Tarbert 154 G6
Tai'r-Bull 34 B3
Tairgwaith 33 C8
Tai-Ucha 72 D4
Takeley 42 B1
Takeley Street . .41 B8
Talachddu 48 F2
Talacre 85 E2
Talardd 59 B5
Talaton 11 E5
Talbenny 44 D3
Talbot Green . . .34 F4
Talbot Village . .13 E8
Tale. 11 D5
Talerddig 59 D6
Talgarreg 46 D3
Talgarth 48 F3
Talisker 149 E8
Talke 74 D5
Talkin. 109 D5
Talladale 150 D2
Talla Linnfoots . 114 B4
Tallarn Green . . .73 E8
Tallentire 107 F8
Talley. 46 F5
Tallington 65 D7
Talmine 157 C8
Talog 32 B4
Talsarn 34 B1
Tal-sarn 46 D4
Talsarnau. 71 D7
Talskiddy 4 C4
Talwrn
Anglesey 82 D4
Wrex 73 E6
Tal-y-bont
Ceredig 58 F3
Conwy 83 E7
Gwyn. 71 E6
Gwyn. 83 D6
Talybont-on-Usk .35 B5
Tal-y-cafn 83 D7
Talygarn 34 F4
Talyllyn 35 B5
Tal-y-llyn 58 D4
Talysarn 82 F4
Talywain 35 D6
Tal-y-wern 58 D5
Tame Bridge . . .102 D3
Tamerton Foliot . .6 C2

Tamworth 63 D6
Tandem 88 C2
Tanden 19 B6
Tandridge. 28 D4
Tanerdy 33 B5
Tanfield. 110 D4
Tanfield Lea. . . . 110 D4
Tangasdal. 148 J1
Tangiers 44 D4
Tangley 25 D8
Tanglwst 46 F2
Tangmere. 16 D3
Tangwick 160 F4
Tan Hinon 59 F5
Tankersley 88 D4
Tankerton 30 C5
Tan-lan
Conwy 83 E7
Gwyn. 71 C7
Tannach 158 F5
Tannachie 141 F6
Tannadice 134 D4
Tannington 57 C6
Tansley 76 D3
Tansley Knoll . . .76 C3
Tansor 65 E7
Tantobie 110 D4
Tanton 102 C3
Tanworth-in-
Arden. 51 B6
Tan-y-bwlch 71 C7
Tan-y-fron 72 C3
Tan-y-graig
Anglesey 82 D5
Gwyn. 70 D4
Tanygrisiau 71 C7
Tan-y-groes 45 E4
Tan-y-pistyll 59 B7
Tan-yr-allt 82 F4
Tanyrhydiau. . . .47 C6
Taobh a
Chaolais 148 G2
Taobh a'Ghlinne 155 F8
Taobh a Thuath Loch
Aineort 148 F2
Taobh a Tuath Loch
Baghasdail 148 F2
Taobh Tuath 154 J4
Taplow. 40 F2
Tapton. 76 B3
Tarbat House. . . 151 D10
Tarbert
Argyll 143 C7
Argyll 144 E5
Argyll 145 G7
Tarbert
= Tairbeart 154 G6
Tarbet
Argyll 126 D2
Highld 147 B10
Highld 156 E4
Tarbock Green . .86 F2
Tarbolton 112 B4
Tarbrax 120 D3
Tardebigge 50 C5
Tarfside. 134 B4
Tarland 140 D3
Tarleton 86 B2
Tarlogie. 151 C10
Tarlscough 86 C2
Tarlton. 37 E6
Tarnbrook 93 D5
Tarporley 74 C2
Tarr. 22 F3
Tarrant Crawford .13 D7
Tarrant Gunville . .13 C7
Tarrant Hinton . .13 C7
Tarrant
Keynston 13 D7
Tarrant
Launceston 13 D7
Tarrant Monkton .13 D7
Tarrant Rawston . .13 D7
Tarrant Rushton . .13 D7
Tarrel 151 C11
Tarring Neville . . 17 D8
Tarrington 49 E8
Tarsappie 128 B3
Tarskavaig 149 H10
Tarves 153 E8
Tarvie
Highld 150 F7
Perth. 133 C7
Tarvin 73 C8
Tasburgh 68 E5
Tasley. 61 E6
Taston 38 B3
Tatenhill 63 B6
Tathall End. 53 E6
Tatham 93 C6
Tathwell 91 F7
Tatling End. 40 F3
Tatsfield 28 D5
Tattenhall 73 D8
Tattenhoe. 53 F6
Tatterford 80 E4
Tattersett 80 D4
Tattershall 78 D5
Tattershall
Bridge 78 D4
Tattershall
Thorpe. 78 D5
Tattingstone . . .56 F5
Tatworth 11 D8
Taunton. 11 B7
Taverham 68 C4
Tavernspite 32 C2
Tavistock 6 B2
Taw Green 9 E8
Tawstock 9 B7
Taxal 75 B7
Tay Bridge 129 B6
Tayinloan 143 D7
Taymouth
Castle. 132 E4
Taynish 144 E6
Taynton
Glos 36 B4
Oxon 38 C2
Taynuilt 125 B6
Tayport 129 B6
Tayvallich 144 E6
Tealby 91 E5
Tealing 134 F4
Teangue 149 H11
Teanna
Mhachair 148 B2
Tebay 99 D8

Tebworth 40 B2
Tedburn St Mary . .10 E3
Teddington
Glos 50 F4
London 28 B2
Tedstone
Delamere 49 D8
Tedstone Wafre . 49 D8
Teeton 52 B4
Teffont Evias . . .24 F4
Teffont Magna . .24 F4
Tegryn 45 F4
Teigh 65 C5
Teigncombe 9 F8
Teigngrace. 7 B6
Teignmouth 7 B7
Telford. 61 D6
Telham 18 D4
Tellisford 24 D3
Telscombe 17 D8
Telscombe Cliffs 17 D7
Templand 114 F3
Temple
Corn 5 B6
Glasgow 118 C5
Midloth 121 D6
Temple Balsall . .51 B7
Temple Bar
Carms 33 C6
Ceredig. 46 D4
Temple Cloud . . 23 D8
Temple Combe . .12 B5
Temple Ewell . . .31 E6
Temple Grafton . 51 D6
Temple Guiting . .37 B7
Templehall 128 E4
Temple
Herdewyke 51 D8
Temple Hirst . . .89 B7
Temple
Normanton. . . .76 C4
Temple Sowerby .99 B8
Templeton
Devon 10 C3
Pembs. 32 C2
Templeton
Bridge 10 C3
Templetown. . . .110 D4
Tempsford 54 D2
Tenbury Wells . . .49 C7
Tenby = Dinbych-y-
Pysgod 32 D2
Tendring 43 B7
Tendring Green . .43 B7
Ten Mile Bank . .67 E6
Tenston 159 G3
Tenterden 19 B5
Terling 42 C3
Ternhill 74 F3
Terregles Banks 107 B6
Terrick. 39 D8
Terrington 96 B2
Terrington St
Clement 66 C5
Terrington St
John 66 C5
Teston 29 D8
Testwood 14 C4
Tetbury 37 E5
Tetbury Upton. . .37 E5
Tetchill 73 F7
Tetcott. 8 E5
Tetford 79 B6
Tetney 91 D7
Tetney Lock 91 D7
Tetsworth. 39 D6
Tettenhall. 62 E2
Teuchan 153 E10
Teversal 76 C4
Teversham 55 D5
Teviothead 115 D7
Tewel 141 F7
Tewin 41 C5
Tewkesbury. . . .50 F3
Teynham 30 C3
Thackthwaite . . .98 B3
Thainston 135 B6
Thakeham 16 C5
Thame 39 D7
Thames Ditton . .28 C2
Thames Haven . .42 F3
Thamesmead . . .41 F7
Thanington 30 D5
Thankerton 120 F2
Tharston 68 E5
Thatcham 26 C3
Thatto Heath . . .86 E3
Thaxted. 55 F7
The Aird 149 C9
Theakston 101 F8
Thealby 90 C2
Theale
Som. 23 E6
W Berks 26 B4
The Arms 67 E8
Thearne 97 F6
The Bage. 48 E4
The Balloch . . . 127 C6
The Barony 159 F3
Theberton 57 C8
The Bog. 60 E3
The Bourne 27 E6
The Braes 149 E10
The Broad. 49 C6
The Butts 24 E2
The Camp
Glos 37 D6
Herts. 40 D4
The Chequer . . .73 E8
The City. 39 E7
The Common . . .25 F7
The Craigs 150 B7
The Cronk 84 C3
Theddingworth . .64 F3
Theddlethorpe All
Saints. 91 F8
Theddlethorpe St
Helen 91 F8
The Dell. 69 E7
The Den. 118 D3
The Eals 116 F3
The Eaves 36 D3
The Flatt 109 B5
The Four Alls . . .74 F3
The Garths 160 B8
The Green
Cumb 98 F3

The Grove. 107 B6
The Hall. 160 D8
The Haven 27 F8
The Heath
Norf 81 E7
Suff 56 F5
The Hill 98 F3
The Howe
Cumb 99 F6
IoM 84 F1
The Hundred . . .49 C7
Thelbridge
Barton 10 C2
The Lee 40 D2
The Lhen. 84 B3
Thelnetham. . . .56 B4
Thelveton. 68 F4
Thelwall 86 F4
The Marsh
Powys. 60 E3
Wilts 37 F7
Themelthorpe. . .81 E6
The Middles. . . .110 D5
The Moor 18 C4
The Mumbles
= Y Mwmbwls. . . .33 F7
The Murray. 119 D6
The Neuk 141 E6
Thenford. 52 E3
The Oval 24 C2
The Pole of
Itlaw 153 C6
The Quarry 36 E4
Therfield. 54 F4
The Rhos. 32 C1
The Rock. 61 D6
The Ryde. 41 D5
The Sands. 27 E6
The Stocks 19 C6
Thetford
Lincs 65 C8
Norf 67 F8
The Throat 27 C6
The Vauld 49 E7
The Wyke 61 D7
Theydon Bois. . . .41 E7
Thickwood 24 B3
Thimbleby
Lincs 78 C5
N Yorks 102 E2
Thingwall 85 F3
Thirdpart 118 C1
Thirlby 102 F2
Thirlestane 121 E8
Thirn 101 F7
Thirsk 102 F2
Thirtleby 97 F7
Thistleton
Lancs 92 F4
Rutland. 65 C6
Thistley Green . .55 B7
Thixendale 96 C4
Thockrington . . .110 B2
Tholomas Drove . 66 D3
Tholthorpe. 95 C7
Thomas Chapel. .32 D2
Thomas Close . . 108 E4
Thomastown . . .152 E5
Thompson 68 E2
Thomshill 152 C2
Thong 29 B7
Thongsbridge . . .88 D2
Thoralby 101 F5
Thoresway 91 E5
Thorganby
Lincs 91 E6
N Yorks 96 E2
Thorgill 103 E5
Thorington 57 B8
Thorington Street 56 F4
Thorlby 94 D2
Thorley 41 C7
Thorley Street
Herts. 41 C7
IoW 14 F4
Thormanby 95 B7
Thornaby-on-
Tees 102 C2
Thornage 81 D6
Thornborough
Bucks 52 F5
N Yorks 95 B5
Thornbury
Devon 9 D6
Hereford. 49 D8
S Glos 36 E3
W Yorks 94 F4
Thornby 52 B4
Thorncliffe. 75 D7
Thorncombe
Dorset. 11 D8
Dorset. 13 D6
Thorncombe
Street 27 E8
Thorncote Green .54 E2
Thorncross 14 F5
Thorndon 56 C5
Thorndon Cross . .9 E7
Thorne. 89 C7
Thorner 95 E6
Thorne St
Margaret. 11 B5
Thorney
Notts 77 B8
Pboro 66 D2
Thorney Crofts . .91 B6
Thorney Green . .56 C4
Thorney Hill. . . .14 E2
Thorney Toll. . . .66 D3
Thornfalcon. . . .11 B7
Thornford. 12 C4
Thorngumbald . .91 B6
Thornham 80 C3
Thornham
Magna 56 B5
Thornham Parva .56 B5
Thornhaugh. . . .65 D7
Thornhill
Cardiff. 35 F5
Cumb 98 D2
Derbys 88 F2
Dumfries 113 E8
Soton 15 C5
Stirling 127 C6
W Yorks 88 C3
Thornhill Edge . .88 C3
Thornhill Lees . .88 C3
Thornholme. . . .97 C7

Thornley
Durham. 110 F4
Durham. 111 F6
Thornliebank . . .118 D5
Thorns 55 D8
Thornsett. 87 F8
Thorns Green . . .87 F5
Thornthwaite
Cumb 98 B4
N Yorks 94 D4
Thornton
Angus 134 E3
Bucks 53 F5
E Yorks 96 E3
Fife 128 E4
Lancs 92 E3
Leics 63 D8
Lincs 78 C5
Mbro 102 C2
Mers 85 D4
Northumb 123 E6
Pembs. 44 E4
W Yorks 94 F4
Thornton Curtis . 90 C4
Thornton Heath . 28 C4
Thornton Hough. .85 F4
Thornton in
Craven. 94 E2
Thornton-le-
Beans. 102 E1
Thornton-le-Clay 96 C2
Thornton-le-
Dale. 103 F6
Thornton le Moor.90 E4
Thornton-le-
Moor 102 F1
Thornton-le-
Moors 73 B8
Thornton-le-
Street. 102 F2
Thorntonloch . . 122 B3
Thorntonpark . . 122 E5
Thornton Rust. . 100 F4
Thornton
Steward 101 F6
Thornton
Watlass. 101 F7
Thornwood
Common 41 D7
Thornydykes . . . 122 E2
Thoroton 77 E7
Thorp Arch. 95 E7
Thorpe
Derbys 75 D8
E Yorks 97 E5
Lincs 91 F8
Norf 69 E7
N Yorks 94 C3
Notts 77 F7
Sur 27 C8
Thorpe Abbotts .57 B5
Thorpe Acre. . . .64 B2
Thorpe Arnold. . .64 B4
Thorpe Audlin . .89 C5
Thorpe Bassett. .96 B4
Thorpe Bay. 43 F5
Thorpe by Water. .65 E5
Thorpe Common .57 F6
Thorpe
Constantine . . .63 D6
Thorpe Culvert . .79 C7
Thorpe End 69 C5
Thorpe Fendykes 79 C7
Thorpe Green
Essex 43 B7
Suff 56 D3
Thorpe Hesley. . .88 E4
Thorpe in Balne . 89 C6
Thorpe in the
Fallows 90 F3
Thorpe Langton .64 E4
Thorpe Larches 102 B1
Thorpe-le-Soken.43 B7
Thorpe-le-Street .96 E4
Thorpe Malsor . .53 B6
Thorpe
Mandeville. 52 E3
Thorpe Market . .81 D8
Thorpe Marriot . .68 C4
Thorpe Morieux .56 D3
Thorpeness 57 D8
Thorpe on the
Hill 78 C2
Thorpe St
Andrew 69 D5
Thorpe St Peter . 79 C7
Thorpe Salvin . .89 F6
Thorpe Satchville 64 C4
Thorpe Thewles 102 B2
Thorpe Tilney . . 78 D4
Thorpe
Underwood 95 D7
Thorpe Waterville 65 F7
Thorpe
Willoughby. . . .95 F8
Thorrington. . . .43 C6
Thorverton 10 D4
Thrandeston. . . .56 B5
Thrapston. 53 B7
Thrashbush 119 C7
Threapland
Cumb 107 F8
N Yorks 94 C2
Threapwood
Ches W 73 E8
Staffs 75 E7
Three Ashes. . . .36 B2
Three Bridges . .28 F3
Three Burrows . .3 B6
Three Chimneys .18 B5
Three Cocks . . .48 F3
Three Crosses . .33 E6
Three Cups
Corner 18 C3
Three Holes 66 D5
Threekingham . .78 F3
Three Leg Cross .18 B3
Three Legged
Cross 13 D8
Threemile Cross. 26 C5
Threemilestone . .3 B6
Threemiletown. 120 B3
Three Oaks 18 D5
Threlkeld 99 B5
Threshfield 94 C2

Thrigby 69 C7
Thringarth 100 B4
Thringstone 63 C8
Thrintoft 101 E8
Thriplow. 54 E5
Throckenholt . . .66 D3
Throcking. 54 F4
Throckley. 110 C4
Throckmorton . .50 E4
Throphill 117 F7
Thropton 117 D6
Throsk. 127 E7
Throwleigh 9 E8
Throwley. 30 D3
Thrumpton. 76 F5
Thrumster 158 F5
Thrunton 117 C6
Thrupp
Glos 37 D5
Oxon 38 C4
Thrushelton. 9 F6
Thrussington . . .64 C3
Thruxton
Hants 25 E7
Hereford. 49 F6
Thrybergh. 89 E5
Thulston 76 F4
Thundergay . . . 143 D9
Thundersley 42 F3
Thundridge 41 C6
Thurcaston 64 C2
Thurcroft 89 F5
Thurgarton
Norf 81 D7
Notts 77 E6
Thurgoland 88 D3
Thurlaston
Leics 64 E2
Warks 52 B2
Thurlbear 11 B7
Thurlby
Lincs 65 C8
Lincs 78 C2
Thurleigh 53 D8
Thurlestone. 6 E4
Thurloxton 22 F4
Thurlstone. 88 D3
Thurlton 69 E7
Thurlwood. 74 D5
Thurmaston 64 D3
Thurnby. 64 D3
Thurne. 69 C7
Thurnham
Kent 30 D2
Lancs 92 D4
Thurning
Norf 81 E6
Northants 65 F7
Thurnscoe 89 D5
Thurnscoe
East. 89 D5
Thursby 108 D3
Thursford 81 D5
Thursley 27 F7
Thurso 158 D3
Thurso East . . .158 D3
Thurstaston. . . .85 F3
Thurston 56 C3
Thurstonfield . . 108 D3
Thurstonland . . .88 C2
Thurton. 69 D6
Thurvaston 76 F2
Thuxton 68 D3
Thwaite
N Yorks 100 E3
Suff 56 C5
Thwaite St Mary .69 E6
Thwaites 94 E3
Thwaites Brow . .94 E3
Thwing 97 B6
Tibbermore . . . 128 B2
Tibberton
Glos 36 B4
Telford 61 B6
Worcs 50 D4
Tibenham 68 F4
Tibshelf. 76 C4
Tibthorpe 97 D5
Ticehurst. 18 B3
Tichborne 26 F3
Tickencote 65 D6
Tickenham 23 B6
Tickhill 89 E6
Ticklerton 60 E4
Ticknall 63 B7
Tickton 97 E6
Tidcombe 25 D7
Tiddington
Oxon 39 D6
Warks 51 D7
Tidebrook 18 C3
Tideford 5 D8
Tideford Cross . . .5 C8
Tidenham 36 E2
Tideswell 75 B8
Tidmarsh 26 B4
Tidmington 51 F7
Tidpit 13 C8
Tidworth 25 E7
Tiers Cross 44 D4
Tiffield 52 D4
Tifty 153 D7
Tigerton 135 C5
Tigh-na-Blair . . 127 C6
Tighnabruaich . .145 F8
Tighnafiline . . . 155 J13
Tigley 7 C5
Tilbrook 53 C8
Tilbury. 29 B7
Tilbury Juxta
Clare 55 E8
Tile Cross 63 F5
Tile Hill 51 B7
Tilehurst. 26 B4
Tilford 27 E6
Tilgate. 28 F3
Tilgate Forest
Row 28 F3
Tillathrowie. . . .152 E4
Tilley 60 B5
Tillicoultry 127 E8
Tillingham 43 D5
Tillington
Hereford. 49 E6
W Sus 16 B3

Tillington
  Common......49 E6
Tillyarblet......135 C5
Tillybirloch......141 D5
Tillycorthie......141 B8
Tillydrine......140 C4
Tillyfour......140 C4
Tillyfourie......140 C5
Tillygarmond......140 D4
Tillygreig......141 B7
Tillykerrie......141 B7
Tilmanstone......31 D7
Tilney All Saints......67 C5
Tilney High End......67 C5
Tilney St
  Lawrence......66 C5
Tilshead......24 E5
Tilstock......74 F2
Tilston......73 D8
Tilstone Fearnall......74 C2
Tilsworth......40 B2
Tilton on the Hill......64 D4
Timberland......78 D4
Timbersbrook......75 C5
Timberscombe......21 E8
Timble......94 D4
Timperley......87 F5
Timsbury
  Bath......23 D8
  Hants......14 B4
Timsgearraidh......154 D5
Timworth Green......56 C2
Tincleton......13 E5
Tindale......109 D6
Tingewick......52 F4
Tingley......88 B3
Tingrith......53 F8
Tingwall......159 F4
Tinhay......9 F5
Tinshill......95 F5
Tinsley......88 E5
Tintagel......8 F2
Tintern Parva......36 D2
Tintinhull......12 C3
Tintwistle......87 E8
Tinwald......114 F3
Tinwell......65 D7
Tipperty......141 B8
Tipsend......66 E5
Tipton......62 E3
Tipton St John......11 E5
Tiptree......42 C4
Tirabad......47 E7
Tiraghoil......146 J6
Tirley......37 B5
Tirphil......35 D5
Tirril......99 B7
Tir-y-dail......33 C7
Tisbury......13 B7
Tisman's
  Common......27 F8
Tissington......75 D8
Titchberry......8 B4
Titchfield......15 D6
Titchmarsh......53 B8
Titchwell......80 C3
Tithby......77 F6
Titley......48 C5
Titlington......117 C7
Titsey......28 D5
Tittensor......75 F5
Tittleshall......80 E4
Tiverton
  Ches W......74 C2
  Devon......10 C4
Tivetshall St
  Margaret......68 F4
Tivetshall St Mary 68 F4
Tividale......62 E3
Tivy Dale......88 D3
Tixall......62 B3
Tixover......65 D6
Toab
  Orkney......159 H6
  Shetland......160 M5
Toadmoor......76 D3
Tobermory......147 F8
Toberonochy......124 E3
Tobha Mor......148 E2
Tobhtarol......154 D6
Tobson......154 D6
Tocher......153 E6
Tockenham......24 B5
Tockenham Wick......37 F7
Tockholes......86 B4
Tockington......36 F3
Tockwith......95 D7
Todber......13 B6
Todding......49 B6
Toddington
  C Beds......40 B3
  Glos......50 F5
Todenham......51 F7
Todhills......108 C3
Todlachie......141 C5
Todmorden......87 B7
Todrig......115 C7
Todwick......89 F5
Toft
  Cambs......54 D4
  Lincs......65 C7
Toft Hill
  Durham......101 B6
  Lincs......78 C5
Toft Monks......69 E7
Toft next Newton......90 F4
Toftrees......80 E4
Tofts......158 D5
Toftwood......68 C2
Togston......117 D8
Tokavaig......149 G11
Tokers Green......26 B5
Tolastadh a
  Chaolais......154 D6
Tolastadh bho
  Thuath......155 C10
Tolland......22 F3
Tollard Royal......13 C7
Toll Bar......89 D6
Tollbar End......51 B8
Toll End......62 E3
Toller Fratrum......12 E3
Toller Porcorum......12 E3
Tollerton
  Notts......77 F6

Tollerton continued
  N Yorks......95 C8
Tollesbury......43 C5
Tolleshunt
  D'Arcy......43 C5
Tolleshunt Major......43 C5
Toll of Birness......153 E10
Tolm......155 D9
Tolpuddle......13 E5
Tolvah......138 E4
Tolworth......28 C2
Tomatin......138 B4
Tombreck......151 H9
Tomdoun......136 D4
Tomich
  Highld......137 B6
  Highld......151 D9
Tomich House......151 G8
Tomintoul
  Aberds......139 E7
  Moray......139 C7
Tomnaven......152 E4
Tomnavoulin......139 B8
Tondu......34 F2
Tonfanau......58 D2
Tong
  Shrops......61 D7
  W Yorks......94 F5
Tonge......63 B8
Tongham......27 E6
Tongland......106 D3
Tong Norton......61 D7
Tongue......157 D8
Tongue End......65 C8
Tongwynlais......35 F5
Tonna......34 E1
Ton-Pentre......34 E3
Tonwell......41 C6
Tonypandy......34 E3
Tonyrefail......34 F4
Toot Baldon......39 D5
Toothill......14 C4
Toot Hill......41 D8
Topcliffe......95 B7
Topcroft......69 E5
Topcroft Street......69 E5
Top of Hebers......87 D6
Toppesfield......55 F8
Toppings......86 C5
Topsham......10 F4
Torbay......7 D7
Torbeg......143 F10
Torboll Farm......151 B10
Torbrex......127 E6
Torbryan......7 C6
Torcross......7 E6
Tore......151 F9
Torinturk......145 G7
Torksey......77 B8
Torlum......148 C2
Torlundy......131 B5
Tormarton......24 B2
Tormisdale......142 C2
Tormitchell......112 E2
Tornagrain......151 G10
Tornahaish......139 D8
Tornaveen......140 D5
Torness......137 B8
Toronto......110 F4
Torpenhow......108 F2
Torphichen......120 B2
Torphins......140 D5
Torpoint......6 D2
Torquay......7 C7
Torquhan......121 E7
Torran
  Argyll......124 E4
  Highld......149 D10
  Highld......151 D10
Torrance......119 B6
Torrans......146 J7
Torranyard......118 E3
Torre......7 C7
Torridon......150 F2
Torridon
  House......149 C13
Torrin......149 F10
Torrisdale......157 C9
Torrisdale-
  Square......143 E8
Torrish......157 H12
Torrisholme......92 C4
Torroble......157 J8
Torry
  Aberdeen......141 D8
  Aberds......152 E4
Torryburn......128 F2
Torterston......153 D10
Torthorwald......107 B7
Tortington......16 D4
Tortworth......36 E4
Torvaig......149 D9
Torver......98 E4
Torwood......127 F7
Torworth......89 F7
Tosberry......8 B4
Toscaig......149 E12
Toseland......54 C3
Tosside......93 D7
Tostock......56 C3
Totaig
  Highld......148 C2
  Highld......149 F13
Totegan......157 C11
Tothill......91 F8
Totland......14 F4
Totnes......7 C6
Toton......76 F5
Totronald......146 F4
Totscore......149 B8
Tottenham......41 E6
Tottenhill......67 C6
Tottenhill Row......67 C6
Totteridge......41 E5
Totternhoe......40 B2
Tottington......87 C5
Totton......14 C4
Touchen End......27 B6
Tournaig......155 J13
Toux......153 C9
Toward......145 G10
Towcester......52 E4
Towednack......2 C3

Tower End......67 C6
Towersey......39 D7
Towie
  Aberds......140 C3
  Aberds......153 B8
Towiemore......152 D3
Tow Law......110 F4
Townend......118 B4
Town End
  Cambs......66 E4
  Cumb......99 F6
Towngate......65 C8
Townhead
  Cumb......108 F5
  Dumfries......106 E3
  S Ayrs......112 D2
  S Yorks......88 D3
Townhead of
  Greenlaw......106 C4
Townhill......128 F3
Town Row......18 B2
Townsend
  Bucks......39 D7
  Herts......40 D4
Townshend......2 C4
Town Yetholm......116 B4
Towthorpe......96 D2
Towton......95 F7
Towyn......72 B3
Toxteth......85 F4
Toynton All
  Saints......79 C6
Toynton Fen Side 79 C6
Toynton St Peter. 79 C7
Toy's Hill......29 D5
Trabboch......112 B4
Traboe......3 D6
Tradespark
  Highld......151 F11
  Orkney......159 H5
Trafford Park......87 E5
Trallong......34 B3
Tranent......121 B7
Tranmere......85 F4
Trantlebeg......157 D11
Trantlemore......157 D11
Tranwell......117 F7
Trapp......33 C7
Traprain......121 B8
Traquair......121 F6
Trawden......94 F2
Trawsfynydd......71 D8
Trealaw......34 E4
Treales......92 F4
Trearddur......82 D2
Treaslane......149 C8
Trebanog......34 E4
Trebanos......33 D8
Trebartha......5 B7
Trebarwith......8 F2
Trebetherick......4 B4
Treborough......22 F2
Trebudannon......4 C3
Trebullett......5 B8
Treburley......5 B8
Trebyan......5 C5
Trecastle......34 B2
Trecenydd......35 F5
Trecwn......44 B4
Trecynon......34 D3
Tredavoe......2 D3
Treddiog......44 C3
Tredegar = Newydd
  New Tredegar......35 D5
Tredington
  Glos......37 B6
  Warks......51 E7
Tredinnick......4 B4
Tredomen......48 F3
Tredunnock......35 E7
Tredustan......48 F3
Treen......2 D2
Treeton......88 F5
Trefaldwyn
  =Montgomery......60 E2
Trefasser......44 B3
Trefdraeth......82 D4
Trefeglwys......59 E6
Trefenter......46 C5
Treffgarne......44 C4
Treffynnon
  =Holywell......73 B5
Treffynnon......44 C3
Trefgarn Owen......44 C3
Trefi......35 C5
Trefil......35 C5
Trefilan......46 D4
Treflach......60 B2
Trefnanney......60 C2
Trefnant......72 B4
Trefonen......60 B2
Trefor
  Anglesey......82 C3
  Gwyn......70 C4
Treforest......34 F4
Trefriw......83 E7
Tref-y-Clawdd
  =Knighton......48 B4
Trefynwy
  =Monmouth......36 C2
Tregadillett......8 F4
Tregaian......82 D4
Tregare......35 C8
Tregaron......47 D5
Tregarth......83 E6
Tregeare......8 F4
Tregeiriog......73 F5
Tregele......82 B3
Tre-Gibbon......34 D3
Tregidden......3 D6
Treglemais......44 C3
Tregole......8 E3
Tregonetha......4 C4
Tregony......3 B8
Tregoss......4 C4
Tregoyd......48 F4
Tregroes......46 E3
Tregurrian......4 C3
Tregynon......59 E7
Trehafod......34 E4
Treharris......34 E4
Treherbert......34 E3

Treknow......8 F2
Trelan......3 E6
Trelash......8 E3
Trelassick......4 D3
Trelawnyd......72 B4
Trelech......45 F4
Treleddyd-fawr......44 C2
Trelewis......35 E5
Treligga......8 F2
Trelights......4 B4
Trelill......4 B5
Trelissick......3 C7
Trellech......36 D2
Trelleck Grange......36 D1
Trelogan......85 D2
Trelystan......60 D2
Tremadog......71 C6
Tremail......8 F3
Tremaine......45 E4
Tremar......5 C7
Trematon......5 D8
Tremeirchion......72 B4
Trenance......4 C3
Trenarren......3 B9
Trench......61 C6
Treneglos......8 F4
Trenewan......5 D7
Trent......12 C3
Trentham......75 E5
Trentishoe......20 E5
Trent Vale......75 E5
Treoes......21 B8
Treorchy
  =Treorci......34 E3
Treorci
  =Treorchy......34 E3
Tre'r-ddôl......58 E3
Trerulefoot......5 D8
Tresaith......45 D4
Tresawle......3 B7
Trescott......62 E2
Trescowe......2 C4
Tresham......36 E4
Tresillian......3 B7
Tresinwen......44 A4
Treskinnick Cross.8 E4
Tresmeer......8 F4
Tresparrett......8 E3
Tresparrett Posts......8 E3
Tressait......133 C5
Tresta
  Shetland......160 D8
  Shetland......160 H5
Treswell......77 B7
Tre-Taliesin......58 E3
Trethosa......4 D4
Trethurgy......4 D5
Tretio......44 C2
Tretire......36 B2
Tretower......35 B5
Treuddyn......73 D6
Trevalga......8 F2
Trevalyn......73 D7
Trevanson......4 B4
Trevarren......4 C4
Trevarrian......4 C3
Trevarrick......3 B8
Trevaughan......32 C2
Tre-vaughan......32 B4
Treveighan......5 B5
Trevellas......4 D2
Treverva......3 C6
Trevethin......35 D6
Trevigro......5 C8
Treviscoe......4 D4
Trevone......4 B3
Trewarmett......8 F2
Trewassa......8 F3
Trewellard......2 C2
Trewen......8 F4
Trewennack......3 D5
Trewern......60 C2
Trewethern......4 B5
Trewidland......5 D7
Trewint......8 E3
Trewithian......3 C7
Trewoofe......2 D3
Trewoon......4 D4
Treworga......3 B7
Treworlas......3 C7
Tre-wyn......35 B7
Treyarnon......4 C3
Treyford......16 C2
Trezaise......4 D4
Triangle......87 B8
Trickett's Cross......13 D8
Triffleton......44 C4
Trimdon......111 F6
Trimdon
  Colliery......111 F6
Trimdon Grange.111 F6
Trimingham......81 D8
Trimley Lower
  Street......57 F6
Trimley St Martin......57 F6
Trimley St Mary......57 F6
Trimpley......50 B2
Trimsaran......33 D5
Trimstone......20 E3
Trinafour......132 C4
Trinant......35 D6
Tring......40 C2
Tring Wharf......40 C2
Trinity
  Angus......135 C6
  Jersey......17
Trisant......47 B6
Trislaig......130 B4
Trispen......4 D3
Tritlington......117 E8
Trochry......133 E6
Trodigal......143 F7
Troed-rhiwdalar 47 D8
Troedyraur......46 E2
Troedyrhiw......34 D4
Tromode......84 E3
Trondavoe......160 F5
Troon
  Corn......3 C5
  S Ayrs......118 F3
Trosaraidh......148 G2
Trossachs Hotel 126 D4
Troston......56 B2
Trottiscliffe......29 C7
Trotton......16 B2

Troutbeck
  Cumb......99 B5
  Cumb......99 D6
Troutbeck Bridge 99 D6
Trowbridge......24 D3
Trowell......76 F4
Trow Green......36 D2
Trowle Common......24 D3
Trowley Bottom......40 C3
Trows......122 F2
Trowse Newton......68 D5
Trudoxhill......24 E2
Trull......11 B7
Trumaisgearraidh
  ......148 A3
Trumpan......148 B7
Trumpet......49 F8
Trumpington......54 D5
Trunch......81 D8
Trunnah......92 E3
Truro......3 B7
Trusham......10 F3
Trusley......76 F2
Trusthorpe......91 F9
Trysull......62 E2
Tubney......38 E4
Tuckenhay......7 D6
Tuckhill......61 F7
Tuckingmill......3 B5
Tuddenham......55 B8
Tuddenham St
  Martin......57 E5
Tudeley......29 E7
Tudhoe......111 F5
Tudorville......36 B2
Tudweiliog......70 D3
Tuesley......27 E7
Tuffley......37 C5
Tufton
  Hants......26 E2
  Pembs......32 B1
Tugby......64 D4
Tugford......61 F5
Tullibardine......127 C8
Tullibody......127 E7
Tullich
  Argyll......125 D6
  Highld......138 B2
Tullich Muir......151 D10
Tulliemet......133 D6
Tulloch
  Aberds......135 B7
  Aberds......153 E8
  Perth......128 B2
Tulloch Castle......151 E8
Tullochgorm......125 F5
Tulloes......135 E5
Tullybannocher 127 B6
Tullybelton......133 F7
Tullyfergus......134 E2
Tullymurdoch......134 D1
Tullynessle......140 C4
Tumble......33 C6
Tumby Woodside 79 D5
Tummel Bridge.132 D4
Tunga......155 D9
Tunstall
  E Yorks......97 F9
  Kent......30 C2
  Lancs......93 B6
  Norf......69 D7
  N Yorks......101 E7
  Stoke......75 D5
  Suff......57 D7
  T&W......111 D6
Tunstead
  Derbys......75 B8
  Gtr Man......87 D8
  Norf......81 E8
Tunworth......26 E4
Tupsley......49 E7
Tupton......76 C3
Turgis Green......26 D4
Turin......135 D5
Turkdean......37 C8
Tur Langton......64 E4
Turleigh......24 C3
Turn......87 C6
Turnastone......49 F5
Turnberry......112 D2
Turnditch......76 E2
Turners Hill......28 F4
Turners Puddle......13 E6
Turnford......41 D6
Turnhouse......120 B4
Turnworth......13 D6
Turriff......153 C7
Turton Bottoms......86 C5
Turves......66 E3
Turvey......53 D7
Turville......39 E7
Turville Heath......39 E7
Turweston......52 F4
Tushielaw......115 C6
Tutbury......63 B6
Tutnall......50 B4
Tutshill......36 E2
Tuttington......81 E8
Tutts Clump......26 B3
Tuxford......77 B7
Twatt
  Orkney......159 F3
  Shetland......160 H5
Twechar......119 B7
Tweedmouth......123 D5
Tweedsmuir......114 B3
Twelve Heads......3 B6
Twelvewood......5 C7
Twemlow Green......74 C4
Twenty......65 B8
Twerton......24 C2
Twickenham......28 B2
Twigworth......37 B5
Twineham......17 C6
Twinhoe......24 D2
Twinstead......56 F2
Twinstead Green.56 F2
Twiss Green......86 E4
Twiston......93 E8
Twitchen
  Devon......21 F6
  Shrops......49 B5
Twitton......29 D5
Two Bridges......6 B4
Two Dales......76 C2
Two Mills......73 B7
Twycross......63 D7
Twyford
  Bucks......39 B6
  Derbys......63 B7

Twyford continued
  Hants......15 B5
  Leics......64 C4
  Lincs......65 B6
  Norf......81 E6
  Wokingham......27 B5
Twyford Common 49 F7
Twynholm......106 D3
Twyning......50 F3
Twyning Green......50 F3
Twynllanan......34 B1
Twynmynydd......33 C7
Twyn-y-Sheriff......35 D8
Twywell......53 B7
Tyberton......49 F5
Tyburn......62 E5
Tycroes......33 C7
Tycrwyn......59 C8
Tyddewi
  =St David's......44 C2
Tydd Gote......66 C4
Tydd St Giles......66 C4
Tydd St Mary......66 C4
Tyddyn-mawr......71 C6
Ty-draw......83 F8
Tye Green
  Essex......41 D7
  Essex......42 B3
  Essex......55 F6
Ty-hen
  Carms......32 B4
  Gwyn......70 D2
Ty-mawr......82 C4
Ty Mawr Cwm......72 E3
Ty-nant
  Conwy......72 E3
  Gwyn......59 B6
Tyncelyn......46 C5
Tyndrum......131 F7
Tyneham......13 F6
Tynehead......121 D6
Tynemouth......111 C6
Tyne Tunnel......111 C6
Tynewydd......34 E3
Tyninghame......122 B2
Tynron......113 E8
Tyn-y-celyn......73 F5
Tyn-y-coed......72 F5
Tyn-y-fedwen......72 F5
Tyn-y-ffridd......72 F5
Tyn-y-graig......48 D2
Tyn-y-groes......83 E7
Tyn-y-maes......83 E6
Tyn-y-pwll......82 C4
Tyn-y-r-eithin......47 C5
Tyringham......53 E6
Tythecott......9 C6
Tythegston......21 B7
Tytherington
  Ches E......75 B6
  S Glos......36 F3
  Som......24 E2
  Wilts......24 E4
Tytherleigh......11 D8
Tywardreath......5 D5
Tywyn
  Conwy......83 D7
  Gwyn......58 D2

U

Uachdar......148 C2
Uags......149 E12
Ubbeston Green......57 B7
Ubley......23 D7
Uckerby......101 D7
Uckfield......17 B8
Uckington......37 B6
Uddingston......119 C6
Uddington......119 F8
Udimore......19 D5
Udny Green......141 B7
Udny Station......141 B8
Udston......119 D6
Udstonhead......119 E7
Uffcott......25 B6
Uffculme......11 C5
Uffington
  Lincs......65 D7
  Oxon......38 F3
  Shrops......60 C5
Ufford
  Pboro......65 D7
  Suff......57 D6
Ufton......51 C8
Ufton Nervet......26 C4
Ugadale......143 F8
Ugborough......6 D4
Uggeshall......69 F7
Ugglebarnby......103 D6
Ughill......88 E3
Ugley......41 B8
Ugley Green......41 B8
Ugthorpe......103 C5
Uidh......148 J1
Uig
  Argyll......145 E10
  Highld......149 B8
  Highld......149 B8
Uigen......154 D5
Uigshader......149 D9
Uisken......146 K6
Ulbster......158 F5
Ulceby
  Lincs......79 B7
  N Lincs......90 C5
Ulceby Skitter......90 C5
Ulcombe......30 E2
Uldale......108 F2
Uley......36 E4
Ulgham......117 E8
Ullapool......150 B4
Ullenhall......51 C6
Ulleskelf......95 E8
Ullesthorpe......64 F2

Ulley......89 F5
Ullingswick......49 E7
Ullinish......149 E8
Ullock......98 B2
Ulnes Walton......86 C3
Ulpha......98 E3
Ulrome......97 D7
Ulsta......160 E6
Ulva House......146 H7
Ulverston......92 B2
Ulwell......13 F8
Umberleigh......9 B8
Unapool......156 F5
Unasary......148 F2
Underbarrow......99 E6
Undercliffe......94 F4
Underhoull......160 C7
Underriver......29 D6
Underwood......76 D4
Undy......35 F8
Unifirth......160 H4
Union Cottage......141 E7
Union Mills......84 E3
Union Street......18 B4
Unstone......76 B3
Unstone Green......76 B3
Unthank
  Cumb......108 F4
  Cumb......109 E6
Unthank End......108 F4
Upavon......25 D6
Up Cerne......12 D4
Upchurch......30 C2
Upcott......48 D5
Upend......55 D7
Up Exe......10 D4
Upgate......68 C4
Uphall......120 B3
Uphall Station......120 B3
Upham
  Devon......10 D3
  Hants......15 B6
Uphampton......50 C3
Up Hatherley......37 B6
Uphill......22 D5
Up Holland......86 D3
Uplawmoor......118 D4
Upleadon......36 B4
Upleatham......102 C4
Uplees......30 C3
Uploders......12 E3
Uplowman......10 C5
Uplyme......11 E8
Up Marden......15 C8
Up Nately......26 D4
Upnor......29 B8
Upottery......11 D7
Upper Affcot......60 F4
Upper
  Ardchronie......151 C9
Upper Arley......61 F7
Upper Arncott......39 C6
Upper Astrop......52 F3
Upper Badcall......156 E4
Upper Basildon......26 B3
Upper Beeding......17 C5
Upper Benefield......65 F6
Upper
  Bighouse......157 D11
Upper
  Boddington......52 D2
Upper Borth......58 F3
Upper Boyndlie 153 B9
Upper Brailes......51 F8
Upper Breakish 149 F11
Upper Breinton......49 E6
Upper
  Broadheath......50 D3
Upper Broughton.64 B3
Upper
  Bucklebury......26 C3
Upper
  Burnhaugh......141 E7
Upperby......108 D4
Upper Caldecote.54 E2
Upper Catesby......52 D3
Upper Chapel......48 E2
Upper Church
  Village......34 F4
Upper Chute......25 D7
Upper Clatford......25 E8
Upper Clynnog......71 C5
Upper
  Cumberworth......88 D3
Upper Cwmbran......35 E6
Upper Dallachy 152 B3
Upper Dean......53 C8
Upper Denby......88 D3
Upper Denton......109 C6
Upper Derraid......151 H13
Upper Dicker......18 E2
Upper Dovercourt 57 F6
Upper Druimfin......147 F8
Upper Dunsforth.95 C7
Upper Eathie......151 E10
Upper Elkstone......75 D7
Upper End......75 B7
Upper Farringdon 26 F5
Upper Framilode 36 C4
Upper
  Glenfintaig......137 F5
Upper Gornal......62 E3
Upper
  Gravenhurst......54 F2
Upper Green
  Mon......35 C7
  W Berks......25 C8
Upper Grove
  Common......36 B2
Upper Hackney......76 C2
Upper Hale......27 E6
Upper Halistra......148 C7
Upper Halling......29 C7
Upper
  Hambleton......65 D6
Upper Hardres
  Court......31 D5
Upper Hartfield......29 F5
Upper Haugh......88 E5
Upper Heath......61 F5
Upper Hellesdon 68 C5
Upper Helmsley......96 D2
Upper Hergest......48 D4
Upper Heyford
  Northants......52 D4
  Oxon......38 B4
Upper Hill......49 D6

Upper Hopton......88 C2
Upper
  Horsebridge......18 D2
Upper Hulme......75 C7
Upper Inglesham......38 E2
Upper
  Inverbrough......151 H11
Upper Killay......33 E6
Upper
  Knockando......152 D1
Upper Lambourn......38 F3
Upper Leigh......75 F7
Upper Lenie......137 B8
Upper Lochton......141 E5
Upper Longdon......62 C4
Upper Lybster......158 G4
Upper Lydbrook......36 C3
Upper Maes-
  coed......48 F5
Upper Midway......63 B6
Uppermill......87 D7
Upper Milovaig......148 D6
Upper Minety......37 E7
Upper Mitton......50 B3
Upper North
  Dean......39 E8
Upper Obney......133 F7
Upper Ollach......149 E10
Upper Padley......76 B2
Upper Pollicott......39 C7
Upper Poppleton 95 D8
Upper Quinton......51 E6
Upper Ratley......14 B4
Upper Rissington 38 C2
Upper Rochford......49 C8
Upper Sandaig 149 G12
Upper Sanday......159 H6
Upper Sapey......49 C8
Upper Saxondale 77 F6
Upper Seagry......37 F6
Upper Shelton......53 E7
Upper
  Sheringham......81 C7
Upper
  Skelmorlie......118 C2
Upper Slaughter......38 B1
Upper Soudley......36 C3
Uppersound......160 J6
Upper Stondon......54 F2
Upper Stowe......52 D4
Upper Stratton......38 F1
Upper Street
  Hants......14 C2
  Norf......69 C6
  Norf......69 C6
  Suff......56 F5
Upper Strensham 50 F4
Upper Sundon......40 B3
Upper Swell......38 B1
Upper Tean......75 F7
Upperthong......88 D2
Upperthorpe......89 D8
Upper Tillyrie......128 D3
Upperton......16 B3
Upper Tooting......28 B3
Upper Tote......149 C10
Upper Town
  Derbys......76 C3
  Highld......158 C5
  Orkney......159 J5
Upper Town......23 C7
Upper
  Treverward......48 B4
Upper Tysoe......51 E8
Upper Upham......25 B7
Upper
  Wardington......52 E2
Upper Weald......53 F5
Upper Weedon......52 D4
Upper Wield......26 F4
Upper
  Winchendon......39 C7
Upper Witton......62 E4
Upper Woodend 141 C6
Upper Woodford......25 F6
Upper Wootton......26 D3
Upper Wyche......50 E2
Uppingham......65 E5
Uppington......61 D6
Upsall......102 F2
Upshire......41 D7
Up Somborne......25 F8
Upstreet......31 C6
Up Sydling......12 D4
Upthorpe......56 B3
Upton
  Cambs......54 B2
  Ches W......73 C8
  Corn......8 D4
  Dorset......12 F5
  Dorset......13 E7
  Hants......14 C4
  Hants......25 D8
  Leics......63 E7
  Lincs......90 F2
  Mers......85 F3
  Norf......69 C6
  Notts......77 B7
  Notts......77 D7
  Oxon......39 F5
  Pboro......65 D8
  Slough......27 B7
  Som......10 B4
  Som......23 D6
  W Yorks......89 C5
Upton Bishop......36 B3
Upton Cheyney......23 C8
Upton Cressett......61 E6
Upton Cross......5 B7
Upton Grey......26 E4
Upton Hellions......10 D3
Upton Lovell......24 E4
Upton Magna......61 C5
Upton Noble......24 F2
Upton Pyne......10 E4
Upton St
  Leonard's......37 C5
Upton
  Scudamore......24 E3
Upton Snodsbury 50 D4
Upton upon
  Severn......50 E3
Upton Warren......50 C4
Upwaltham......16 C3
Upware......55 B6
Upwell......66 D5
Upwey......12 F4
Upwood......66 F2

Uradale......160 K6
Urafirth......160 F5
Urchfont......24 D5
Urdimarsh......49 E7
Ure......160 F4
Ure Bank......95 B6
Urgha......154 H6
Urishay Common......48 F5
Urlay Nook......102 C1
Urmston......87 E5
Urpeth......110 D5
Urquhart
  Highld......151
  Moray......152 B2
Urra......102 D3
Urray......151 F8
Ushaw Moor......110 E5
Usk =Brynbuga......35 D7
Usselby......90 E4
Usworth......111 D6
Utkinton......74 C2
Utley......94 E3
Uton......10 E3
Utterby......91 E7
Uttoxeter......75 F7
Uwchmynydd......70 E2
Uxbridge......40 F3
Uyeasound......160 C7
Uzmaston......44 D4

V

Valley......82 D2
Valleyfield......106 D3
Valley Truckle......8 F2
Valtos......149 B10
Valsgarth......160 B8
Van......59 F6
Vange......42 F3
Varteg......35 D6
Vatten......149 D7
Vaul......146 G3
Vaynor......34 C4
Veensgarth......160 J6
Velindre......48 F3
Vellow......22 F2
Veness......159 F6
Venn Green......9 C6
Vennington......60 D3
Venn Ottery......11 E5
Venny Tedburn......10 E3
Ventnor......15 G6
Vernham Dean......25 D8
Vernham Street......25 D8
Vernolds
  Common......60 F4
Verwood......13 D8
Veryan......3 C8
Vicarage......11 F7
Vickerstown......92 C1
Victoria
  Corn......4 C4
  S Yorks......88 D2
Vidlin......160 G6
Viewpark......119 C7
Vigo Village......29 C7
Vinehall Street......18 C4
Vine's Cross......18 D2
Viney Hill......36 D3
Virginia Water......27 C8
Virginstow......9 E5
Vobster......24 E2
Voe
  Shetland......160 E6
  Shetland......160 G6
Vowchurch......49 F5
Voxter......160 F5
Voy......159 G3

W

Wackerfield......101 B6
Wacton......68 E4
Wadbister......160 J6
Wadborough......50 E4
Wadborough......39 C7
Waddingham......90 E3
Waddington
  Lancs......93 E7
  Lincs......78 C2
Wadebridge......4 B4
Wadeford......11 C8
Wadenhoe......65 F7
Wadesmill......41 C6
Wadhurst......18 B3
Wadshelf......76 B3
Wadsley......88 E4
Wadsley Bridge......88 E4
Wadworth......89 E6
Waen
  Denb......72 C3
  Denb......72 C5
Waen Fach......60 C2
Waen Goleugoed......72 B4
Wag......157 G13
Wainfleet All
  Saints......79 D7
Wainfleet Bank......79 D7
Wainfleet St
  Mary......79 D7
Wainfleet Tofts......79 D7
Wainhouse Corner.8 E3
Wainscott......29 B8
Wainstalls......87 B8
Waithe......91 D6
Wakefield......88 B4
Wake Lady
  Green......102 E4
Wakerley......65 E6
Wakes Colne......42 B4
Walberswick......57 B8
Walberton......16 D3
Walbottle......110 C4
Walcot
  Lincs......78 F3
  N Lincs......90 B2
  Shrops......60 F3
  Swindon......38 F1
  Telford......61 C5
Walcote
  Leics......64 F2
  Warks......51 D6
Walcot Green......68 F4
Walcott
  Lincs......78 D4

Walcott continued
Norf 69 A6
Walden 101 F5
Walden Head . . 100 F4
Walden Stubbs . . 89 C6
Waldersey 66 D4
Walderslade 29 C8
Walderton 15 C8
Walditch 12 E2
Waldley 75 F8
Waldridge 111 D5
Waldringfield 57 D6
Waldringfield
Heath 57 E6
Waldron 18 D2
Wales 89 F5
Walesby
Lincs 90 E5
Notts 77 B6
Walford
Hereford 36 B2
Hereford 49 B5
Shrops 60 B4
Walford Heath . . 60 C4
Walgherton 74 E3
Walgrave 53 B6
Walhampton 14 E4
Walkden 86 D5
Walker 111 C5
Walker Barn 75 B6
Walkerburn 121 F6
Walker Fold 93 E6
Walkeringham . . . 89 E8
Walkerith 89 E8
Walkern 41 B5
Walker's Green . . . 49 E7
Walkerville 101 E7
Walkford 14 E3
Walkhampton 6 C3
Walkington 97 F5
Walkley 88 F4
Walk Mill 93 F8
Wall
Northumb 110 C2
Staffs 62 D5
Wallaceton 113 F8
Wallacetown
S Ayrs 112 A3
S Ayrs 112 D2
Wallands Park . . 17 C8
Wallasey 85 E4
Wall Bank 60 E5
Wallcrouch 18 B3
Wall Heath 62 F2
Wallingford 39 F6
Wallington
Hants 15 D6
Herts 54 F3
London 28 C3
Wallis 32 B1
Walliswood 28 F2
Walls 160 J4
Wallsend 111 C5
Wallston 22 B3
Wall under
Heywood 60 E5
Wallyford 121 B6
Walmer 31 D7
Walmer Bridge . . 86 B2
Walmersley 87 C6
Walmley 62 E5
Walpole 57 B7
Walpole Cross
Keys 66 C5
Walpole Highway 66 C5
Walpole Marsh . . 66 C4
Walpole St
Andrew 66 C5
Walpole St Peter . 66 C5
Walsall 62 E4
Walsall Wood . . . 62 D4
Walsden 87 B7
Walsgrave on
Sowe 63 F7
Walsham le
Willows 56 B3
Walshaw 87 C5
Walshford 95 D7
Walsoken 66 C4
Walston 120 E3
Walsworth 54 F3
Walters Ash 39 E8
Walterston 22 B2
Walterstone 35 B7
Waltham
Kent 30 E5
NE Lincs 91 D6
Waltham Abbey . . 41 D6
Waltham Chase . . 15 C6
Waltham Cross . . 41 D6
Waltham on the
Wolds 64 B5
Waltham St
Lawrence 27 B6
Walthamstow . . . 41 F6
Walton
Cumb 108 C5
Derbys 76 C3
Leics 64 F2
Mers 85 E4
M Keynes 53 F6
Pboro 65 D8
Powys 48 D4
Som 23 F6
Staffs 75 F5
Suff 57 F6
Telford 61 C5
Warks 51 D7
W Yorks 88 C4
W Yorks 95 E7
Walton Cardiff . . 50 F4
Walton East 32 B1
Walton-in-
Gordano 23 B6
Walton-le-Dale . . 86 B3
Walton-on-
Thames 28 C2
Walton on the Hill
Staffs 62 B3
Sur 28 D3
Walton-on-the-
Naze 43 B8
Walton on the
Wolds 64 C2
Walton-on-Trent 63 C6
Walton West 44 D3
Walwen 73 B6
Walwick 110 B2

Walworth 101 C7
Walworth Gate . 101 B7
Walwyn's Castle . 44 D3
Wambrook 11 D7
Wanborough
Sur 27 E7
Swindon 38 F2
Wandsworth 28 B3
Wangford 57 B8
Wanlockhead . . . 113 C8
Wansford
E Yorks 97 D6
Pboro 65 E7
Wanstead 41 F7
Wanstrow 24 E2
Wanswell 36 D3
Wantage 38 F3
Wapley 24 B2
Wappenbury 51 C8
Wappenham 52 E4
Warbleton 18 D3
Warblington 15 D8
Warborough 39 E5
Warboys 66 F3
Warbreck 92 F3
Warbstow 8 E4
Warburton 86 F5
Warcop 100 C2
Warden
Kent 30 B4
Northumb 110 C2
Ward End 62 F5
Warden Hill 37 B6
Wardhill 159 F7
Wardington 52 E2
Wardlaw 115 C5
Wardle
Ches E 74 D3
Gtr Man 87 C7
Wardley 64 D5
Wardlow 75 B8
Wardy Hill 66 F4
Ware
Herts 41 C6
Kent 31 C6
Wareham 13 F7
Warehorne 19 B6
Waren Mill 123 F7
Warenford 117 B7
Warenton 123 F7
Wareside 41 C6
Waresley
Cambs 54 D3
Worcs 50 B3
Warfield 27 B6
Warfleet 7 D6
Wargrave 27 B5
Warham 80 C5
Warhill 87 E7
Wark
Northumb 109 B8
Northumb 122 F4
Warkleigh 9 B8
Warkton 53 B6
Warkworth
Northants 52 E2
Northumb 117 D8
Warlaby 101 E8
Warland 87 B7
Warleggan 5 C6
Warlingham 28 D4
Warmfield 88 B4
Warmingham 74 C4
Warmington
Northants 65 E7
Warks 52 E2
Warminster 24 E3
Warmlake 30 D2
Warmley 23 B8
Warmley Tower . . 23 B8
Warmonds Hill . . 53 C7
Warmsworth 89 D6
Warmwell 13 F5
Warndon 50 D3
Warnford 15 B7
Warnham 28 F2
Warninglid 17 B6
Warren
Ches E 75 B5
Pembs 44 F4
Warren Heath . . 57 E6
Warren Row 39 F8
Warren Street . . 30 D3
Warrington
M Keynes 53 D6
Warr 86 F4
Warsash 15 D5
Warslow 75 D7
Warter 96 D4
Warthermarske . . 94 B5
Warthill 96 D2
Wartling 18 E3
Wartnaby 64 B4
Warton
Lancs 86 B2
Lancs 92 B4
Northumb 117 D6
Warks 63 D6
Warwick 51 C7
Warwick Bridge 108 D4
Warwick on
Eden 108 D4
Wasbister 159 E4
Wasdale Head . . . 98 D3
Washaway 4 C5
Washbourne 7 D5
Wash Common . . 26 C2
Washfield 10 C4
Washfold 101 D5
Washford 22 E2
Washford Pyne . . 10 C3
Washingborough 78 B3
Washington
T&W 111 D6
W Sus 16 C5
Wasing 26 C3
Waskerley 110 E3
Wasperton 51 D7
Wasps Nest 78 C3
Wass 95 B8
Watchet 22 E2
Watchfield
Oxon 38 E2
Som 22 E5
Watchgate 99 E7
Watchhill 107 E8
Watcombe 7 C7
Watendlath 98 C4

Water
Devon 10 F2
Lancs 87 B6
Waterbeach 55 C5
Waterbeck 108 B2
Waterden 80 D4
Water End
E Yorks 96 F3
Herts 40 C3
Herts 41 D5
Waterfall 75 D7
Waterfoot
E Renf 119 D5
Lancs 87 B6
Waterford
Hants 14 E4
Herts 41 C6
Waterhead
Cumb 99 D5
Dumfries 114 E4
Waterheads 120 D5
Waterhouses
Durham 110 E4
Staffs 75 D7
Wateringbury . . . 29 D7
Waterloo
BCP 13 E8
Gtr Man 87 D7
Highld 149 F11
Mers 85 E4
N Lanark 119 D8
Norf 68 C5
Perth 133 F7
Shrops 74 E2
Waterloo Port . . 82 E4
Waterlooville . . . 15 D7
Watermeetings . 114 C2
Watermillock . . . 99 B6
Water Newton . . 65 E8
Water Orton 63 E5
Waterperry 39 D6
Waterrow 11 B5
Watersfield 16 C4
Waterside
Aberds 141 B9
Blackburn 86 B5
Cumb 108 E2
E Ayrs 112 D4
E Ayrs 118 E4
E Dunb 119 B6
E Renf 118 D5
Water's Nook . . . 86 D4
Waterstock 39 D6
Waterston 44 E4
Water Stratford . 52 F4
Waters Upton . . . 61 C6
Water Yeat 98 F4
Watford
Herts 40 E4
Northants 52 C4
Watford Gap 62 D5
Wath
N Yorks 94 C4
N Yorks 95 B6
N Yorks 95 B6
Wath Brow 98 C2
Wath upon
Dearne 88 D5
Watlington
Norf 67 C6
Oxon 39 E6
Watnall 76 E5
Watten 158 E4
Wattisfield 56 B4
Wattisham 56 D4
Wattlesborough
Heath 60 C3
Watton
E Yorks 97 D6
Norf 68 D2
Watton at Stone . 41 C6
Wattston 119 B7
Wattstown 34 E4
Wauchan 136 F2
Waulkmill
Lodge 159 H4
Waun 59 D5
Waunarlwydd . . . 33 E7
Waunclunda 47 F5
Waunfawr 82 F5
Waungron 33 D6
Waunlwyd 35 D5
Waun-y-clyn 33 D5
Wavendon 53 F7
Waverbridge . . . 108 E2
Waverton
Ches W 73 C8
Cumb 108 E2
Wavertree 85 F4
Wawne 97 F6
Waxham 69 B7
Waxholme 91 B7
Way 31 C7
Wayfield 29 C8
Wayford 12 D2
Waymills 74 E2
Way Village 10 C3
Wdig = Goodwick . 44 B4
Weachyburn . . . 153 C6
Weald 38 D3
Wealdstone 40 F4
Weardley 95 E5
Weare 23 D6
Weare Giffard . . . 9 B6
Wearhead 109 F8
Weasdale 100 D1
Weasenham All
Saints 80 E4
Weasenham St
Peter 80 E4
Weatheroak Hill . 51 B5
Weaverham 74 B3
Weaverthorpe . . 97 B5
Webheath 50 C5
Wedderlairs . . . 153 E8
Wedderlie 122 D2
Weddington 63 E7
Wedhampton . . . 25 D5
Wedmore 23 E6
Wednesbury 62 E3
Wednesfield 62 D3
Weedon 39 C8
Weedon Bec 52 D4
Weedon Lois 52 E4
Weeford 63 D5
Week
Devon 10 C2
Week St Mary . . . 8 E4

Weekley 65 F5
Week St Mary . . . 8 E4
Weel 97 F6
Weeley 43 B7
Weeley Heath . . . 43 B7
Weem 133 E5
Weeping Cross . . 62 B3
Weethley Gate . . 51 D5
Weeting 67 F7
Weeton
E Yorks 91 B7
Lancs 92 F3
N Yorks 95 E5
Weetwood Hall . 117 B6
Weir 87 B6
Weir Quay 6 C2
Welborne 68 D3
Welbourn 78 D2
Welburn
N Yorks 96 C3
N Yorks 102 F4
Welbury 102 D1
Welby 78 F2
Welches Dam . . . 66 F4
Welcombe 8 C4
Weld Bank 86 C3
Weldon 117 E7
Welford
Northants 64 F3
W Berks 26 B2
Welford-on-
Avon 51 D6
Welham
Leics 64 E4
Notts 89 F8
Welham Green . . 41 D5
Well
Hants 27 E5
Lincs 79 B7
N Yorks 101 F7
Welland 50 E2
Wellbank 134 F4
Welldale 107 C8
Well End 40 F1
Wellesbourne . . . 51 D7
Well Heads 94 F3
Well Hill 29 C5
Welling 29 B5
Wellingborough . 53 C6
Wellingham 80 E4
Wellingore 78 D2
Wellington
Cumb 98 D2
Hereford 49 E6
Som 11 B6
Telford 61 C6
Wellington Heath 50 E2
Wellington Hill . . 95 F6
Wellow
Bath 24 D2
IoW 14 F4
Notts 77 C6
Wellpond Green . 41 B7
Wells 23 E7
Wellsborough . . . 63 D7
Wells Green 74 D3
Wells-next-the-
Sea 80 C5
Wellswood 7 C7
Well Town 10 D4
Wellwood 128 F2
Welney 66 E5
Welshampton . . . 73 F8
Welsh Bicknor . . 36 C2
Welsh End 74 F2
Welsh Frankton . 73 F7
Welsh Hook 44 C4
Welsh Newton . . 36 C1
Welshpool
= Y Trallwng 60 D2
Welsh St Donats . 22 B2
Welton
Cumb 108 E3
E Yorks 90 B3
Lincs 78 B3
Northants 52 C3
Welton le Marsh . 79 C7
Welton le Wold . 91 F6
Welwick 91 B7
Welwyn 41 C5
Welwyn Garden
City 41 C5
Wem 60 B5
Wembdon 22 F4
Wembley 40 F4
Wembury 6 E3
Wembworthy 9 D8
Wemyss Bay . . . 118 C1
Wenallt
Ceredig 47 B5
Gwyn 72 E3
Wendens Ambo . 55 F6
Wendlebury 39 C5
Wendling 68 C2
Wendover 40 D1
Wendron 3 C5
Wendy 54 E4
Wenfordbridge . . 5 B5
Wenhaston 57 B8
Wennington
Cambs 54 B3
Lancs 93 B6
London 41 F8
Wensley
Derbys 76 C2
N Yorks 101 F5
Wentbridge 89 C5
Wentnor 60 E3
Wentworth
Cambs 55 B5
S Yorks 88 E4
Wenvoe 22 B3
Weobley 49 D6
Weobley Marsh . . 49 D6
Wereham 67 D6
Wergs 62 D2
Wern
Powys 59 C6
Powys 60 C2
Wernffrwd 33 E6
Wernyrheolydd . 35 C7
Werrington
Corn 8 F5
Pboro 65 D8
Staffs 75 E6
Weeford 63 D5
Wervin 73 B8
Wesham 92 F4
Weeke 26 F2

Wessington 76 D3
West Acre 67 C7
West Adderbury . 52 F2
West Allerdean . 123 E5
West Alvington . . . 6 E5
West Amesbury . . 25 E6
West Anstey 10 B3
West Ashby 79 B5
West Ashling 16 D2
West Ashton 24 D3
West Auckland . 101 B6
West Bagborough 22 F3
West Barkwith . . 91 F5
West Barnby . . . 103 C6
West Barsham . . . 80 D5
West Bay 12 E2
West Beckham . . 81 D7
West Bedfont . . . 27 B8
West Benhar . . . 119 C8
Westbere 31 C5
West Bergholt . . . 43 B5
West Bexington . . 12 F3
West Bilney 67 C7
West
Blatchington . . 17 D6
Westborough 77 E8
Westbourne
BCP 13 E8
Suff 56 E5
W Sus 15 D8
West Bowling . . . 94 F4
West Bradford . . . 93 E7
West Bradley 23 F7
West Bretton 88 C3
West Bridgford . . 77 F5
West Bromwich . . 62 E4
Westbrook 26 B2
West Buckland
Devon 21 F5
Som 11 B6
West Burrafirth . 160 H4
West Burton
N Yorks 101 F5
W Sus 16 C3
Westbury
Bucks 52 F4
Shrops 60 D3
Wilts 24 D3
Westbury Leigh . . 24 D3
Westbury-on-
Severn 36 C4
Westbury on
Trym 23 B7
Westbury-sub-
Mendip 23 E7
West Butterwick . 90 D2
Westby 92 F3
West Byfleet 27 C8
West Caister 69 C8
West Calder 120 C3
West Camel 12 B3
West Challow . . . 38 F3
West
Chelborough . . 12 D3
West
Chevington . . . 117 E8
West Chiltington 16 C4
West Chiltington
Common 16 C4
West Chinnock . . 12 C2
West Chisenbury 25 D6
West Clandon . . . 27 D8
West Cliffe 31 E7
Westcliff-on-Sea 42 F4
West Clyne 157 J11
West Clyth 158 G4
West Coker 12 C3
Westcombe 23 F8
West Compton
Dorset 12 E3
Som 23 E7
Westcote 38 B2
Westcott
Bucks 39 C7
Devon 10 D5
Sur 28 E2
Westcott Barton . 38 B4
West Cowick 89 B7
West Cranmore . . 23 E8
West Cross 33 F7
West Cullery . . . 141 D6
West Curry 8 E4
West
Curthwaite . . . 108 E3
West Darlochan . 143 F7
Westdean 18 F2
West Dean
Wilts 14 B3
W Sus 16 C2
West Deeping . . . 65 D8
West Dene 17 D6
West Derby 85 E4
West Dereham . . 67 D6
West Didsbury . . 87 E6
West Ditchburn . 117 B7
West Down 20 E4
West Drayton
London 27 B8
Notts 77 B7
West Ella 90 B4
West End
Bedford 53 D7
E Yorks 96 F5
E Yorks 97 F7
Hants 15 C5
Lancs 86 B5
Norf 69 C8
N Som 23 C6
N Yorks 94 D4
Oxon 38 D4
S Lanark 120 C2
Suff 69 F7
Sur 27 C7
S Yorks 89 D7
Wilts 13 B7
Wilts 24 B4
W Sus 16 C5
West End Green . 26 C4
Wester
Aberchalder . . 137 B8
Wester
Balgedie 128 D3
Wester
Culbeuchly . . . 153 B6

Westerdale
Highld 158 E3
N Yorks 102 D4
Wester
Dechmont 120 C3
Wester Denoon . 134 E3
Westergate 16 D3
Wester
Gruinards 151 B8
Westerham 28 D5
Westerhope 110 C4
Wester Lealty . . 151 D9
Wester
Milton 151 F12
Wester Newburn 129 D6
Westerleigh 23 B9
Wester Quarff . . 160 K6
Wester Skeld . . . 160 J4
Westerton
Angus 135 D6
Durham 110 F5
W Sus 16 D2
Westerwick 160 J4
West Farleigh . . . 29 D8
West Felton 60 B3
West Fenton . . . 129 F6
West Ferry 134 F4
West
Firle 17 D8
Westfield
Cumb 98 B1
E Sus 18 D5
Hereford 50 E2
Highld 158 D2
N Lanark 119 B7
Norf 68 D2
W Loth 120 B2
Westfields 12 D5
Westfields of
Rattray 134 E1
Westgate
Durham 110 F2
N Lincs 89 D8
Norf 80 C4
Westgate on Sea . 31 B7
West Ginge 38 F4
West Grafton . . . 25 C7
West Green 26 D5
West
Greenskares . . 153 B7
West Grimstead . 14 B3
West Grinstead . . 17 B5
West Haddlesey . 89 B6
West Haddon . . . 52 B4
West Hagbourne 39 F5
West Hagley 62 F3
Westhall
Aberds 141 B5
Suff 57 B8
West Hall 109 C5
West Hallam 76 E4
West Halton 90 B3
Westham
Dorset 12 G4
E Sus 18 E3
Som 23 E6
West Ham 41 F7
Westhampnett . . 16 D2
West Handley . . . 76 B3
West Hanney . . . 38 E4
West
Hanningfield . . 42 E3
West Hardwick . . 88 C5
West Harnham . . 14 B2
West Harptree . . . 23 D7
West Hatch 11 B7
Westhay 23 E6
West Head 67 D5
West Heath
Ches E 74 C5
Hants 26 D3
Hants 27 D6
West
Helmsdale . . . 157 H13
West Hendred . . 38 F4
West Heslerton . 96 B5
Westhide 49 E7
Westhill
Aberds 141 D7
Highld 151 G10
West Hill
Devon 11 E5
E Yorks 97 C7
N Som 23 B6
West Hoathly . . . 28 F4
West Holme 13 F6
Westhope
Hereford 49 D6
Shrops 60 F4
West Horndon . . 42 F2
Westhorpe
Lincs 78 F5
Suff 56 C4
West Horrington . 23 E7
West Horsley . . . 27 D8
West Horton . . . 123 F6
West Hougham . . 31 E6
Westhoughton . . 86 D4
West Houlland . . 160 H4
Westhouse 93 B6
Westhouses 76 D4
Westhumble 28 D2
West Huntington 96 D2
West Hythe 19 B8
West Ilsley 38 F4
Westing 160 C7
West Itchenor . . . 15 D8
West Keal 79 C6
West Kennett . . . 25 C6
West Kilbride . . 118 E2
West Kingsdown 29 C6
West Kington . . . 24 B3
West
Kinharrachie . 153 E8
West Kirby 85 F3
West Knapton . . . 96 B4
West Knighton . . 12 F5
West Knoyle 24 F3
West Kyloe 123 E6
Westlake 6 E4
West Langdon . . 31 E7
West Langwell . 157 J9

West Lavington
Wilts 24 D5
W Sus 16 B2
West Layton . . . 101 D6
West Lea 111 E7
West Leake 64 B2
West Learmouth 122 F4
Westleigh
Devon 9 B6
Devon 11 C5
Gtr Man 86 D4
West Leigh 9 D8
Westleton 57 C8
West Lexham . . . 67 C8
Westley
Shrops 60 D3
Suff 56 C2
Westley
Waterless 55 D7
West Lilling 96 C2
Westlington 39 C7
Westlinton 108 C3
West Linton 120 D4
West Liss 15 B8
West Littleton . . 24 B2
West Looe 5 D7
West Luccombe . 21 E7
West Lulworth . . 13 F6
West Lutton 96 C5
West Lydford . . . 23 F7
West Lyng 11 B8
West Lynn 67 B6
West Malling . . . 29 D7
West Malvern . . . 50 E2
West Marden . . . 15 C8
West Marina 18 E4
West Markham . . 77 B7
Westmarsh 31 C6
West Marsh 91 C6
West Marton . . . 93 D8
West Meon 15 B7
West Mersea 43 C6
Westmeston 17 C7
Westmill 41 B6
West Milton 12 E3
Westminster 28 B3
West Minster . . . 30 B3
West Molesey . . . 28 C2
West Monkton . . 11 B7
West Moors 13 D8
West Morriston . 122 E2
Westmuir 134 D3
West Muir 135 C5
Westness 159 F4
West Ness 96 B2
West Newham . . 110 B3
Westnewton
Cumb 107 E8
Northumb 122 F5
West Newton
E Yorks 97 F7
Norf 67 B6
West Norwood . . 28 B4
Westoe 111 C6
Weston
Bath 24 C2
Ches E 74 D4
Devon 11 F6
Dorset 12 G4
Halton 86 F3
Hants 15 B8
Herts 54 F3
Lincs 66 B2
Northants 52 E3
Notts 77 C7
N Yorks 94 E4
Shrops 60 C5
Shrops 61 B5
Staffs 62 B3
W Berks 26 B2
Weston Beggard . 49 E7
Westonbirt 37 F5
Weston by
Welland 64 E4
Weston Colville . 55 D7
Westoncommon . 60 B4
Weston Coyney . . 75 E6
Weston Favell . . . 53 C5
Weston Green
Cambs 55 D7
Norf 68 C4
Weston Heath . . . 61 C7
Weston Hills 66 B2
Westoning 53 F8
Weston-in-
Gordano 23 B6
Weston Jones . . . 61 B7
Weston Longville 68 C4
Weston
Lullingfields . . 60 B4
Weston-on-the-
Green 39 C5
Weston-on-Trent 63 B8
Weston Patrick . . 26 E4
Weston Rhyn . . . 73 F6
Weston-sub-
Edge 51 E6
Weston-super-
Mare 22 C5
Weston Turville . 40 C1
Weston under
Lizard 62 C2
Weston under
Penyard 36 B3
Weston Underwood
Derbys 76 E2
M Keynes 53 D6
Westonzoyland . . 23 F5
West Orchard . . . 13 C6
West Overton . . . 25 C6
Westow 96 C3
West Park 111 F7
West Parley 13 E8
West Peckham . . 29 D7
West Pelton 110 D5
West Pennard . . . 23 F7
West Pentire 4 C2
West Perry 54 C2
Westport
Argyll 143 F7
Som 11 C8
West Putford 9 C5
Westra 22 B3
West Rainton . . 111 E6

West Rasen 90 F4
West Raynham . . 80 E4
West Retford 89 F7
Westrigg 120 C2
West Rounton . . 102 D2
West Row 55 B7
West Rudham . . . 80 E4
West Runton 81 C7
West Saltoun . . . 121 C7
West Sandwick . 160 E6
West Scrafton . . 101 F5
West Sleekburn . 117 F8
West Somerton . . 69 C7
West Stafford . . . 12 F5
West Stockwith . 89 E8
West Stoke 16 D2
West
Stonesdale . . . 100 D3
West Stoughton . 23 E6
West Stour 13 B5
West Stourmouth 31 C6
West Stow 56 B2
West Stowell . . . 25 C6
West Strathan . . 157 C8
West Stratton . . . 26 E3
West Street 30 D3
Westland 38 E1
West Tanfield . . . 95 B5
West Taphouse . . . 5 C6
West Tarbert . . . 145 G7
West Thirston . . 117 E7
West Thorney . . . 15 D8
West Thurrock . . 29 B6
West Tilbury 29 B7
West Tisted 15 B7
West Tofts
Norf 67 E8
Perth 133 F8
West Torrington . 90 F5
West Town
Hants 15 E8
N Som 23 C6
West Tytherley . . 14 B3
West Tytherton . . 24 B4
Westville 76 E5
West Walton 66 C4
West Walton
Highway 66 C4
Westward 108 E2
Westward Ho! . . . 9 B6
Westwell
Kent 30 E3
Oxon 38 D2
Westwell Leacon 30 E3
West Wellow 14 C3
West Wemyss . . 128 E5
Westwick
Cambs 54 C5
Durham 101 C5
Norf 81 E8
West Wick 23 C5
West Wickham
Cambs 55 E7
London 28 C4
West Williamston 32 D1
West Willoughby 78 E2
West Winch 67 C6
West Winterslow . 25 F7
West Wittering . . 15 E8
West Witton . . . 101 F5
Westwood
Devon 10 E5
Wilts 24 D3
West Woodburn 116 F4
West Woodhay . . 25 C8
West Woodlands . 24 E2
Westwoodside . . 89 E8
West Worldham . 26 F5
West Worlington . 10 C2
West Worthing . . 16 D5
West Wratting . . 55 D7
West Wycombe . 39 E8
West Wylam . . . 110 C4
West Yell 160 E6
Wetheral 108 D4
Wetherby 95 E7
Wetherden 56 C4
Wetheringsett . . 56 C5
Wethersfield 55 F8
Wethersta 160 G5
Wetherup Street . 56 C5
Wetley Rocks . . . 75 E6
Wettenhall 74 C3
Wetton 75 D8
Wetwang 96 D5
Wetwood 74 F4
Wexcombe 25 D7
Wexham Street . . 40 F2
Weybourne
Norf 81 C7
Sur 27 E6
Weybread 68 F5
Weybridge 27 C8
Weycroft 11 E8
Weydale 158 D3
Weyhill 25 E8
Weymouth 12 G4
Whaddon
Bucks 53 F6
Cambs 54 E4
Glos 37 C5
Wilts 14 B2
Whale 99 B7
Whaley 76 B5
Whaley Bridge . . 87 F8
Whaley Thorns . . 76 B5
Whaligoe 158 F5
Whalley 93 F7
Whalton 117 F7
Wham 93 C7
Whaplode 66 B3
Whaplode Drove 66 C3
Whaplode St
Catherine 66 B3
Wharfe 93 C7
Wharles 92 F4
Wharncliffe Side . 88 E3
Wharram le
Street 96 C4
Wharton 74 C3
Wharton Green . . 74 C3
Whashton 101 D6
Whatcombe 13 D6
Whatcote 51 E8
Whatfield 56 E4
Whatley
Som 11 D8
Som 24 E2
West Lackington 12 E5

Whatstandwell . . 76 D3
Whatton 77 F7
Whauphill 105 E8
Whaw 100 D4
Wheatacre 69 E7
Wheatcroft 76 D3
Wheathampstead 40 C4
Wheathill 61 F6
Wheatley
Devon 10 E4
Hants 27 E5
Oxon 39 D5
S Yorks 89 D6
W Yorks 87 B8
Wheatley Hill . . 111 F6
Wheatley Aston . 62 C2
Wheddon Cross . . 21 F8
Wheedlemont . . 140 B3
Wheelerstreet . . . 27 E7
Wheelock 74 D4
Wheelock Heath . 74 D4
Wheelton 86 B4
Wheen 134 B3
Wheldrake 96 E2
Whelford 38 E1
Whelpley Hill . . . 40 D2
Whempstead . . . 41 B6
Whenby 96 C2
Whepstead 56 D2
Wherstead 57 E5
Wherwell 25 E8
Wheston 75 B8
Whetsted 29 E7
Whetstone 64 E2
Whicham 98 F3
Whichford 51 F8
Whickham 110 C5
Whiddon Down . 10 E5
Whigstreet 134 E4
Whilton 52 C4
Whimble 9 D5
Whim Farm . . . 120 D5
Whimple 10 E5
Whimpwell
Green 69 B6
Whinburgh 68 D3
Whinnieliggate . 106 D4
Whinnyfold . . . 153 E10
Whippingham . . 15 E6
Whipsnade 40 C3
Whipton 10 E4
Whirlow 88 F4
Whisby 78 C2
Whissendine . . . 64 C5
Whissonsett 80 E5
Whistlefield
Argyll 145 D10
Argyll 145 D11
Whistley Green . . 27 B5
Whiston
Mers 86 E2
Northants 53 C6
Staffs 62 C4
Staffs 75 E7
S Yorks 88 F5
Whitbeck 98 F3
Whitbourne 50 D2
Whitburn
T&W 111 C7
W Loth 120 C2
Whitburn
Colliery 111 C7
Whitby
Ches W 73 B7
N Yorks 103 C6
Whitbyheath . . . 73 B7
Whitchurch
Bath 23 C8
Bucks 39 B7
Cardiff 35 F5
Devon 6 B2
Hants 26 E2
Hereford 36 C2
Oxon 26 B4
Pembs 44 C2
Shrops 74 E2
Whitchurch
Canonicorum . . 11 E8
Whitchurch Hill . 26 B4
Whitcombe 12 F5
Whitcott Keysett 60 F2
Whiteacen 152 D2
Whiteacre Heath 63 E6
Whitebridge . . . 137 C7
Whitebrook 36 D2
Whiteburn 121 E8
Whitecairn 105 D6
Whitecairns . . . 141 C8
Whitecastle 120 E3
Whitechapel 93 E5
Whitecleat 159 H6
White Coppice . . 86 C4
Whitecraig 121 B6
Whitecroft 36 D3
Whitecross
Corn 4 B4
Falk 120 B2
Staffs 62 B2
Whiteface 151 C10
Whitefarland . . . 143 D9
Whitefaulds . . . 112 D2
Whitefield
Gtr Man 87 D6
Perth 134 F1
Whiteford 141 B6
Whitegate 74 C3
Whitehall
Blackburn 86 B4
W Sus 16 B5
Whitehall
Village 159 F7
Whitehaven 98 C1
Whitehill 27 F5
Whitehills
Aberds 153 B6
S Lanark 119 D6
Whitehough 87 F8
Whitehouse
Aberds 140 C5
Argyll 145 G7
Whiteinch 118 C5
Whitekirk 129 F7
White Lackington 12 E5
White Ladies
Aston 50 D4

Whitelaw 119 E6
Whiteleas 111 C6
Whiteley Bank ... 15 F6
Whiteley Green ... 75 B6
Whiteley Village . 27 C5
White Lund 92 C4
Whitemans Green ... 17 B7
White Mill 33 B5
Whitemire ... 151 F12
Whitemoor 4 D4
Whitemore 75 C5
Whitenap 14 B4
White Ness 160 J5
White Notley ... 42 C3
Whiteoak Green . 38 C3
Whiteparish 14 B3
White Pit 79 B6
White Post 77 D6
Whiterashes ... 141 B7
White Rocks 35 B8
White Roding ... 42 C1
Whiterow 158 F5
Whiteshill 37 D5
Whiteside
  Northumb ... 109 C7
  W Loth 120 C2
Whitesmith 18 D2
Whitestaunton ... 11 C7
Whitestone
  Devon 10 E3
  Devon 20 E3
  Warks 63 F7
Whitestones ... 153 C8
Whitestreet Green ... 56 F3
Whitewall Corner .. 96 B3
White Waltham ... 27 B6
Whiteway
  Glos 37 C6
  Glos 37 E5
Whitewell
  Aberds 153 B9
  Lancs 93 E6
Whitewell Bottom ... 87 B6
Whiteworks 6 B4
Whitfield
  Kent 31 E7
  Northants 52 F4
  Northumb ... 109 D7
  S Glos 36 E3
Whitford
  Devon 11 E7
  Flint 72 B5
Whitgift 90 B2
Whitgreave 62 B2
Whithorn 105 E8
Whiting Bay ... 143 F11
Whitkirk 95 F6
Whitland 32 C2
Whitletts 112 B3
Whitley
  N Yorks 89 B6
  Reading 26 B5
  Wilts 24 C3
Whitley Bay ... 111 B6
Whitley Chapel . 110 D2
Whitley Lower ... 88 C3
Whitley Row ... 29 D5
Whitlock's End ... 51 B6
Whitminster ... 36 D4
Whitmore 74 E5
Whitnage 10 C5
Whitnash 51 C8
Whitney-on-Wye .. 48 E4
Whitrigg
  Cumb 108 D2
  Cumb 108 F2
Whitsbury 14 C2
Whitsome 122 D4
Whitson 35 F7
Whitstable 30 C5
Whitstone 8 E4
Whittingham ... 117 C6
Whittingslow ... 60 F4
Whittington
  Glos 37 B7
  Lancs 93 B6
  Norf 67 E7
  Shrops 73 F7
  Staffs 62 F2
  Staffs 63 D5
  Worcs 50 D3
Whittlebury ... 52 E4
Whittle-le-Woods ... 86 B3
Whittlesey 66 E2
Whittlesford ... 55 E5
Whittlestone Head ... 86 C5
Whitton
  Borders 116 B3
  N Lincs 90 B3
  Northumb ... 117 D6
  Powys 48 C4
  Shrops 49 B7
  Stockton 102 B1
  Suff 56 E5
Whittonditch ... 25 B7
Whittonstall ... 110 D3
Whitway 26 D2
Whitwell
  Derbys 76 B5
  Herts 40 B4
  IoW 15 G6
  N Yorks 101 E7
  Rutland 65 D6
Whitwell-on-the-Hill ... 96 C3
Whitwell Street .. 81 E7
Whitwick 63 C8
Whitwood 88 B5
Whitworth 87 C6
Whixall 74 F2
Whixley 95 D7
Whoberley 51 B8
Whorlton
  Durham 101 C6
  N Yorks 102 D2
Whygate 109 B7
Whyle 49 C7
Whyteleafe 28 D4
Wibdon 36 E2
Wibsey 88 A2

Wibtoft 63 F8
Wichenford 50 C2
Wichling 30 D3
Wick
  BCP 14 E2
  Devon 11 D6
  Highld 158 E5
  S Glos 24 B2
  Shetland 160 K6
  V Glam 21 B8
  Wilts 14 E2
  Worcs 50 E4
  W Sus 16 D4
Wicken
  Cambs 55 B6
  Northants 52 F5
Wicken Bonhunt .. 55 F6
Wickenby 90 F4
Wicken Green Village ... 80 D4
Wickersley 89 E5
Wickford 42 E3
Wickham
  Hants 15 C6
  W Berks 25 B8
Wickham Bishops ... 42 C4
Wickhambreux .. 31 D6
Wickhambrook .. 55 D8
Wickhamford .. 51 E5
Wickham Market .. 57 D7
Wickhampton .. 69 D7
Wickham St Paul .. 56 F2
Wickham Skeith . 56 C4
Wickham Street
  Suff 55 D8
  Suff 56 C4
Wick Hill 27 C5
Wicklewood ... 68 D3
Wickmere 81 D7
Wick St Lawrence ... 23 C5
Wickwar 36 F4
Widdington ... 55 F6
Widdrington .. 117 E8
Widdrington Station ... 117 E8
Widecombe in the Moor ... 6 B5
Widegates 5 D7
Widemouth Bay .. 8 D4
Wide Open ... 110 B5
Widewall 159 J5
Widford
  Essex 42 D2
  Herts 41 C7
Widham 37 F7
Widmer End ... 40 E1
Widmerpool ... 64 B3
Widnes 86 F3
Wigan 86 D3
Wiggaton 11 E6
Wiggenhall St Germans ... 67 C5
Wiggenhall St Mary Magdalen ... 67 C5
Wiggenhall St Mary the Virgin ... 67 C5
Wigginton
  Herts 40 C2
  Oxon 51 F8
  Staffs 63 D6
  York 95 D8
Wigglesworth .. 93 D8
Wiggonby 108 D2
Wiggonholt 16 C4
Wighill 95 E7
Wighton 80 D5
Wigley 14 C4
Wigmore
  Hereford 49 C6
  Medway 30 C2
Wigsley 77 B8
Wigsthorpe ... 65 F7
Wigston 64 E3
Wigthorpe 89 F6
Wigtoft 79 F5
Wigton 108 E2
Wigtown 105 D8
Wigtwizzle 88 E3
Wike 95 E6
Wike Well End .. 89 C7
Wilbarston 64 F5
Wilberfoss 96 D3
Wilberlee 87 C8
Wilburton 55 B5
Wilby
  Norf 68 F3
  Northants 53 C6
  Suff 57 B6
Wilcot 25 C6
Wilcott 60 C3
Wilcrick 35 F8
Wilday Green .. 76 B3
Wildboarclough . 75 C6
Wilden
  Bedford 53 D8
  Worcs 50 B3
Wildhern 25 D8
Wildhill 41 D5
Wildmoor 50 B4
Wildsworth ... 90 E2
Wilford 77 F5
Wilkesley 74 E3
Wilkhaven ... 151 C12
Wilkieston .. 120 C4
Willand 10 C5
Willaston
  Ches E 74 D3
  Ches W 73 B7
Willen 53 E6
Willenhall
  W Mid 51 B8
  W Mid 62 E3
Willerby
  E Yorks 97 F6
  N Yorks 97 B6
Willersey 51 F6
Willersley 48 E5
Willesborough . 30 E4
Willesborough Lees ... 30 E4
Willesden 41 F5
Willett 22 F3
Willey
  Shrops 61 E6
  Warks 63 F8
Willey Green .. 27 D7

Williamscott ... 52 E2
Willian 54 F3
Willingale 42 D1
Willingdon 18 E2
Willingham ... 54 B5
Willingham by Stow ... 90 F2
Willington
  Bedford 54 E2
  Derbys 63 B6
  Durham 110 F4
  T&W 111 C6
  Warks 51 F7
Willington Corner ... 74 C2
Willisham Tye .. 56 D4
Willitoft 96 F3
Williton 22 E2
Willoughbridge .. 74 E4
Willoughby
  Lincs 79 B7
  Warks 52 C3
Willoughby-on-the-Wolds ... 64 B3
Willoughby Waterleys ... 64 E2
Willoughton ... 90 E3
Willows Green . 42 C3
Willsbridge ... 23 B8
Willsworthy 9 F7
Wilmcote 51 D6
Wilmington
  Devon 11 E7
  E Sus 18 E2
  Kent 29 B6
Wilminstone 6 B2
Wilmslow 87 F6
Wilnecote 63 D6
Wilpshire 93 F6
Wilsden 94 F3
Wilsford
  Lincs 78 E3
  Wilts 25 D6
  Wilts 25 F6
Wilsill 94 C4
Wilsley Pound .. 18 B4
Wilsom 26 F5
Wilson 63 B8
Wilsontown .. 120 D2
Wilstead 53 E8
Wilsthorpe ... 65 C7
Wilstone 40 C2
Wilton
  Borders 115 C7
  Cumb 98 C2
  N Yorks 103 F6
  Redcar 102 C3
  Wilts 25 C7
  Wilts 25 F5
Wimbish 55 F6
Wimbish Green .. 55 F7
Wimblebury ... 62 C4
Wimbledon 28 B3
Wimblington .. 66 E4
Wimborne Minster ... 13 E8
Wimborne St Giles ... 13 C8
Wimbotsham .. 67 D6
Wimpson 14 C4
Wimpstone ... 51 E7
Wincanton 12 B5
Wincham 74 B3
Winchburgh .. 120 B3
Winchcombe ... 37 B7
Winchelsea ... 19 D6
Winchelsea Beach ... 19 D6
Winchester ... 15 B5
Winchet Hill .. 29 E8
Winchfield 27 D5
Winchmore Hill
  Bucks 40 E2
  London 41 E6
Wincle 75 C6
Wincobank 88 E4
Windermere ... 99 E6
Winderton 51 E8
Windhill 151 G8
Windhouse ... 160 D6
Windlehurst ... 87 F7
Windlesham ... 27 C7
Windley 76 E3
Windmill Hill
  E Sus 18 D3
  Som 11 C8
Windrush 38 C1
Windsor
  N Lincs 89 C8
  Windsor 27 B7
Windsoredge .. 37 D5
Windygates ... 128 D5
Windyknowe .. 120 C2
Windywalls .. 122 F3
Wineham 17 B6
Winestead 91 B6
Winewall 94 E2
Winfarthing .. 68 F4
Winford
  IoW 15 F6
  N Som 23 C7
Winforton 48 E4
Winfrith Newburgh ... 13 F6
Wing
  Bucks 40 B1
  Rutland 65 D5
Wingate 111 F7
Wingates
  Gtr Man 86 D4
  Northumb ... 117 E7
Wingerworth .. 76 C3
Wingfield
  C Beds 40 B2
  Suff 57 B6
  Wilts 24 D3
Wingham 31 D6
Wingmore 31 E5
Wingrave 40 C1
Winkburn 77 D7
Winkfield 27 B6
Winkfield Row .. 27 B6
Winkhill 75 D7
Winklebury ... 26 D4
Winkleigh 9 D8
Winksley 95 B5
Winkton 14 E2
Winlaton 110 C4

Winless 158 E5
Winmarleigh .. 92 E4
Winnal 49 F6
Winnall 15 B5
Winnersh 27 B5
Winscales 98 B2
Winscombe ... 23 D6
Winsford
  Ches W 74 C3
  Som 21 F8
Winsham 11 D8
Winshill 63 B6
Winskill 109 F5
Winslade 26 E4
Winsley 24 C3
Winslow 39 B7
Winson 37 D7
Winson Green .. 62 F4
Winsor 14 C4
Winster
  Cumb 99 E6
  Derbys 76 C2
Winston
  Durham 101 C6
  Suff 57 C5
Winstone 37 D6
Winston Green .. 57 C5
Winswell 9 C6
Winterborne Clenston ... 13 D6
Winterborne Herringston .. 12 F4
Winterborne Houghton ... 13 D6
Winterborne Kingston 13 E6
Winterborne Monkton 12 F4
Winterborne Stickland 13 D6
Winterborne Whitechurch . 13 D6
Winterborne Zelston 13 E6
Winterbourne
  S Glos 36 F3
  W Berks 26 B2
Winterbourne Abbas 12 E4
Winterbourne Bassett 25 B6
Winterbourne Dauntsey 25 F6
Winterbourne Down 23 B8
Winterbourne Earls 25 F6
Winterbourne Gunner 25 F6
Winterbourne Monkton 25 B6
Winterbourne Steepleton .. 12 F4
Winterbourne Stoke 25 C5
Winter Gardens .. 42 F3
Winteringham .. 90 B3
Winterley 74 D4
Wintersett 88 C4
Wintershill ... 15 C6
Winterton 90 C3
Winterton-on-Sea ... 69 C7
Winthorpe
  Lincs 79 C8
  Notts 77 D8
Winton
  BCP 13 E8
  Cumb 100 C2
  N Yorks 102 E2
Wintringham .. 96 B4
Winwick
  Cambs 65 F8
  Northants 52 B4
  Warr 86 E4
Wirksworth ... 76 D2
Wirksworth Moor 76 D2
Wirswall 74 E2
Wisbech 66 D4
Wisbech St Mary 66 D4
Wisborough Green ... 16 B4
Wiseton 89 F8
Wishaw
  N Lanark ... 119 D7
  Warks 63 E5
Wisley 27 D8
Wispington ... 78 B5
Wissenden ... 30 E3
Wissett 57 B7
Wistanstow ... 60 F4
Wistanswick .. 61 B6
Wistaston 74 D3
Wistaston Green .. 74 D3
Wiston
  Pembs 32 C1
  S Lanark ... 120 F2
  W Sus 16 C5
Wistow
  Cambs 66 F2
  N Yorks 95 F8
Wiswell 93 F7
Witcham 66 F4
Witchampton .. 13 D7
Witchford 55 B6
Witham 42 C4
Witham Friary .. 24 E2
Witham on the Hill ... 65 C7
Withcall 91 F6
Withdean 17 D7
Witherenden Hill 18 C3
Witheridge 10 C3
Witherley 63 E7
Withern 91 F8
Withernsea ... 91 B7
Withernwick .. 97 E7
Withersdale Street ... 69 F5
Withersfield .. 55 E7
Witherslack .. 99 F6
Withiel 4 C4
Withiel Florey .. 21 F8
Withington
  Glos 37 C7
  Gtr Man 87 E6
  Hereford 49 E7

Withington continued
  Staffs 75 F7
Withington Green 74 B5
Withleigh 10 C4
Withnell 86 B4
Withybrook 63 F8
Withycombe ... 22 E2
Withycombe Raleigh ... 10 F5
Withyham 29 F5
Withypool 21 F7
Witley 27 F7
Witnesham ... 57 D5
Witney 38 C3
Wittering 65 D7
Wittersham ... 19 C5
Witton
  Angus 135 B5
  Worcs 50 C3
Witton Bridge .. 69 A6
Witton Gilbert . 110 E5
Witton-le-Wear 110 F4
Witton Park .. 110 F4
Wiveliscombe .. 11 B5
Wivelrod 26 F4
Wivelsfield ... 17 B7
Wivelsfield Green 17 B7
Wivenhoe 43 B6
Wivenhoe Cross 43 B6
Wiveton 81 C6
Wix 43 B7
Wixford 51 D5
Wixhill 61 B5
Wixoe 55 E8
Woburn 53 F7
Woburn Sands . 53 F7
Wokefield Park . 26 C4
Woking 27 D8
Wokingham ... 27 C6
Wolborough 7 B6
Woldingham .. 28 D4
Wold Newton
  E Yorks 97 B6
  NE Lincs 91 E6
Wolfclyde 120 F3
Wolferton 67 B6
Wolfhill 134 F1
Wolf's Castle .. 44 C4
Wolfsdale 44 C4
Woll 115 B7
Wollaston
  Northants 53 C7
  Shrops 60 C3
Wollaton 76 F5
Wollerton 74 F3
Wollescote 62 F3
Wolsingham .. 110 F3
Wolstanton ... 75 E5
Wolston 52 B2
Wolvercote .. 38 D4
Wolverhampton .. 62 E3
Wolverley
  Shrops 73 F8
  Worcs 50 B3
Wolverton
  Hants 26 D3
  M Keynes 53 E6
  Warks 51 C7
Wolverton Common ... 26 D3
Wolvesnewton . 36 E1
Wolvey 63 F8
Wolviston ... 102 B2
Wombleton ... 102 F4
Wombourne ... 62 E2
Wombwell 88 D4
Womenswold .. 31 D6
Womersley ... 89 C6
Wonastow 36 C1
Wonersh 27 E8
Wonson 9 F8
Wonston 26 F2
Wooburn 40 F2
Wooburn Green .. 40 F2
Woodacott 9 D5
Woodale 94 B3
Woodbank ... 143 G2
Woodbastwick . 69 C6
Woodbeck 77 B7
Woodborough
  Notts 77 E6
  Wilts 25 D6
Woodbridge
  Dorset 12 C5
  Suff 57 E6
Woodbury 10 F5
Woodbury Salterton ... 10 F5
Woodchester .. 37 D5
Woodchurch
  Kent 19 B6
  Mers 85 F3
Woodcombe ... 21 E8
Woodcote 39 F6
Woodcott 26 D2
Woodcroft 36 E2
Woodcutts 13 C7
Wood Dalling . 81 E6
Woodditton ... 55 D7
Woodeaton ... 39 C5
Woodend
  Cumb 98 E3
  Northants 52 E4
  W Sus 16 D2
Wood End
  Herts 41 B6
  Warks 51 B6
Wood Enderby .. 79 C5
Woodend Green .. 42 B1
Woodfalls 14 B2
Woodfield
  Oxon 39 B5
  S Ayrs 112 B3
Wood Field ... 28 D2
Woodford
  Corn 8 C4
  Devon 7 D5
  Glos 36 E3
  Gtr Man 87 F6
  London 41 E7
  Northants 53 B7
Woodford Bridge 41 E7
Woodford Halse .. 52 D3
Woodgate

Woodgate continued
  W Sus 16 D3
Woodgreen 14 C2
Wood Green .. 41 E6
Woodhall
  Herts 41 C5
  Invclyd 118 B3
  N Yorks 100 E4
Woodhall Spa . 78 C4
Woodham 27 C8
Woodham Ferrers ... 42 E3
Woodham Mortimer ... 42 D4
Woodham Walter 42 D4
Woodhaven .. 129 B6
Wood Hayes ... 62 D3
Woodhead ... 153 E7
Woodhey 87 C5
Woodhill 61 F7
Woodhorn ... 117 F8
Woodhouse
  Leics 64 C2
  S Lincs 89 D8
  S Yorks 88 F5
  W Yorks 95 F5
Woodhouse Eaves ... 64 C2
Woodhouselee .. 120 C4
Woodhouselees 108 B3
Woodhouse Park 87 F6
Woodhouses ... 63 C5
Woodhurst 53 D5
Woodingdean .. 17 D7
Woodkirk 88 B3
Woodland
  Devon 7 C5
  Durham 101 B6
Woodlands
  Aberds 141 E6
  Dorset 13 D8
  Hants 14 C4
  Highld 151 E8
  N Yorks 95 D6
  S Yorks 89 D6
Woodlands Park .. 27 B6
Woodlands St Mary ... 25 B8
Wood Lanes ... 87 F7
Woodleigh 6 E5
Woodlesford .. 88 B4
Woodley
  Gtr Man 87 E7
  Wokingham .. 27 B5
Woodmancote
  Glos 36 E4
  Glos 37 B6
  Glos 37 D7
  W Sus 15 D8
  W Sus 17 C6
Woodmancott .. 26 E3
Woodmansey .. 97 F6
Woodmansterne 28 D3
Woodminton .. 13 B8
Woodnesborough . 31 D7
Woodnewton .. 65 E7
Wood Norton .. 81 E6
Woodplumpton .. 92 F5
Woodrising ... 68 D2
Woodseaves
  Shrops 74 F3
  Staffs 61 B7
Woodsend 25 B7
Woodsetts 89 F6
Woodsford ... 13 E5
Wood's Green . 18 B3
Woodside
  Aberdeen ... 141 D8
  Aberds 153 D10
  Brack 27 B7
  Fife 129 D6
  Hants 14 E4
  Herts 41 D5
  Perth 134 F2
Woodside of Arbeadie ... 141 E6
Woodstock
  Oxon 38 C4
  Pembs 32 B1
Wood Street
  Norf 69 B6
  Sur 27 D7
Woodthorpe
  Derbys 76 B4
  Leics 64 C2
  Lincs 91 F8
  York 95 F8
Woodton 69 E5
Woodtown
  Devon 9 B6
  Devon 9 B6
Woodvale 85 C4
Woodville 63 C7
Woodwalton .. 66 F2
Woofferton ... 49 C7
Wookey 23 E7
Wookey Hole .. 23 E7
Wool 13 F6
Woolacombe .. 20 E3
Woolage Green .. 31 E6
Woolaston 36 E2
Woolavington .. 22 E5
Woolbeding ... 16 B2
Wooldale 88 D2
Wooler 117 B5
Woolfardisworthy
  Devon 8 B5
  Devon 10 D3
Woolfords Cottages ... 120 D3
Woolhampton .. 26 C3
Woolhope 49 F8
Woolhope Cockshoot ... 49 F8
Woolland 13 D5
Woollaton 9 C6
Woolley
  Bath 24 C2
  Cambs 54 B2
  Corn 8 C4
  Derbys 76 D3
  W Yorks 88 C4
Woolmere Green 50 C4
Woolmer Green .. 41 C5

Woolpit 56 C3
Woolscott 52 C2
Woolsington . 110 C4
Woolstanwood .. 74 D3
Woolstaston .. 60 E4
Woolsthorpe
  Lincs 65 B6
  Lincs 77 F8
Woolston
  Devon 6 E5
  Shrops 60 B3
  Shrops 60 F3
  Soton 14 C5
  Warr 86 F4
Woolstone
  M Keynes 53 F6
  Oxon 38 F2
Woolton 86 F2
Woolton Hill .. 26 C2
Woolverstone .. 57 F5
Woolverton ... 24 D2
Woolwich 28 B5
Woolwich Ferry .. 28 B5
Woonton 49 D5
Wooperton ... 117 B6
Woore 74 E4
Wootten Green .. 57 B6
Wootton
  Bedford 53 E8
  Hants 14 E3
  Hereford 48 D5
  Kent 31 E6
  N Lincs 90 C4
  Northants 53 D5
  Oxon 38 C4
  Oxon 38 D4
  Shrops 49 B6
  Shrops 60 B3
  Staffs 62 B2
  Staffs 75 E8
Wootton Bridge .. 15 E6
Wootton Common ... 15 E6
Wootton Courtenay ... 21 E8
Wootton Fitzpaine 11 E8
Wootton Rivers . 25 C6
Wootton St Lawrence ... 26 D3
Wootton Wawen .. 51 C6
Worcester 50 D3
Worcester Park .. 28 C3
Wordsley 62 F2
Worfield 61 E7
Work 159 G5
Workington ... 98 B1
Worksop 77 B5
Worlaby 90 C4
Worlds End ... 26 B2
Worle 23 C5
Worleston 74 D3
Worlingham ... 69 F7
Worlington ... 55 B7
Worlingworth . 57 C6
Wormald Green 95 C6
Wormbridge .. 49 F6
Wormegay 67 C6
Wormelow Tump .. 49 F6
Wormhill 75 B8
Wormingford .. 56 F3
Worminghall .. 39 D6
Wormington .. 50 F5
Worminster .. 23 E7
Wormit 129 B5
Wormleighton . 52 D2
Wormley
  Herts 41 D6
  Sur 27 F7
Wormley West End ... 41 D6
Wormshill 30 D2
Wormsley 49 E6
Worplesdon ... 27 D7
Worrall 88 E4
Worsbrough .. 88 D4
Worsbrough Common ... 88 D4
Worsley 86 D5
Worstead 69 B6
Worsthorne ... 93 F8
Worston 93 E7
Worswell 6 E3
Worth
  Kent 31 D7
  W Sus 28 F4
Wortham 56 B4
Worthen 60 D3
Worthenbury .. 73 E8
Worthing
  Norf 68 C2
  W Sus 16 D5
Worthington . 63 B8
Worth Matravers 13 G7
Worting 26 D4
Wortley
  S Yorks 88 E4
  W Yorks 95 F5
Worton
  N Yorks 100 E4
  Wilts 24 D4
Wortwell 69 F5
Wotherton 60 D2
Wotter 6 C3
Wotton 28 E2
Wotton-under-Edge ... 36 E4
Wotton Underwood ... 39 C6
Woughton on the Green ... 53 F6
Wouldham 29 C8
Wrabness 57 F5
Wrafton 20 F3
Wragby
  Lincs 78 B4
  W Yorks 88 C5
Wragholme ... 91 E7
Wramplingham 68 D4
Wrangbrook .. 89 C5
Wrangham ... 153 E6
Wrangle 79 D7
Wrangle Bank . 79 D7
Wrangle Lowgate ... 79 D7
Wrangway 11 C6
Wrantage 11 B8
Wrawby 90 D4

Wraxall
  Dorset 12 D3
  N Som 23 B6
  Som 23 F8
Wray 93 C6
Wraysbury ... 27 B8
Wrayton 93 B6
Wrea Green ... 92 F3
Wreay
  Cumb 99 B6
  Cumb 108 E4
Wrecclesham .. 27 E6
Wrecsam =Wrexham ... 73 D7
Wrekenton ... 111 D5
Wrelton 103 F5
Wrenbury 74 E2
Wrench Green .. 103 F7
Wreningham .. 68 E4
Wrentham 69 F7
Wrenthorpe ... 88 B4
Wrentnall 60 D4
Wressle
  E Yorks 96 F3
  N Lincs 90 D3
Wrestlingworth 54 E3
Wretham 68 F2
Wretton 67 E6
Wrexham =Wrecsam ... 73 D7
Wrexham Industrial Estate ... 73 E7
Wribbenhall .. 50 B2
Wrightington Bar 86 C3
Wrinehill 74 E4
Wrington 23 C6
Writhlington .. 24 D2
Writtle 42 D2
Wrockwardine .. 61 C6
Wroot 89 D8
Wrotham 29 D7
Wrotham Heath 29 D7
Wroughton 37 F8
Wroxall
  IoW 15 G6
  Warks 51 B7
Wroxeter 61 D5
Wroxham 69 C6
Wroxton 52 E2
Wyaston 75 E8
Wyberton 79 E6
Wyboston 54 D2
Wybunbury ... 74 E4
Wychbold 50 C4
Wych Cross ... 28 F5
Wyck 27 F5
Wyck Rissington 38 B1
Wycoller 94 F2
Wycomb 64 B4
Wycombe Marsh 40 E1
Wyddial 54 F4
Wye 30 E4
Wyesham 36 C2
Wyfordby 64 C4
Wyke
  Dorset 13 B5
  Shrops 61 D6
  Sur 27 D7
  W Yorks 88 B2
Wykeham
  N Yorks 96 B4
  N Yorks 103 F7
Wyken 63 F7
Wyke Regis ... 12 G4
Wykey 60 B3
Wylam 110 C4
Wylde Green .. 62 E5
Wyllie 35 E5
Wylye 24 F5
Wymering 15 D7
Wymeswold ... 64 B3
Wymington ... 53 C7
Wymondham
  Leics 65 C5
  Norf 68 D4
Wyndham 34 E3
Wynford Eagle .. 12 E3
Wyng 159 J4
Wynyard Village 102 B2
Wyre Piddle .. 50 E4
Wysall 64 B3
Wythall 51 B5
Wytham 38 D4
Wythburn ... 99 C5
Wythenshawe .. 87 F6
Wythop Mill .. 98 B3
Wyton 54 B3
Wyverstone .. 56 C4
Wyverstone Street ... 56 C4
Wyville 65 B5
Wyvis Lodge . 150 D7

Y

Yaddlethorpe . 90 D2
Yafford 14 F5
Yafforth 101 E8
Yalding 29 D7
Yanworth 37 C7
Yapham 96 D3
Yapton 16 D3
Yarburgh 91 E7
Yarcombe 11 D7
Yard 22 F2
Yardley 62 F5
Yardley Gobion 53 E5
Yardley Hastings 53 D6
Yardro 48 D4
Yarkhill 49 E8
Yarlet 62 B3
Yarlington 12 B4
Yarlside 92 C2
Yarm 102 C2
Yarmouth 14 F4
Yarnbrook ... 24 D3
Yarnfield 75 F5
Yarnscombe .. 9 B7
Yarnton 38 C4
Yarpole 49 C6
Yarrow 115 B6
Yarrow Feus . 115 B6
Yarsop 49 E6
Yarwell 65 E7
Yate 36 F4
Yateley 27 C6
Yatesbury ... 25 B5

Yattendon 26 B3
Yatton
  Hereford 49 C6
  N Som 23 C6
Yatton Keynell .. 24 B3
Yaverland 15 F7
Yaxham 68 C3
Yaxley
  Cambs 65 E8
  Suff 56 B5
Yazor 49 E6
Y Bala =Bala .. 72 F3
Y Barri =Barry . 22 C3
Y Bont-Faen =Cowbridge .. 21 B8
Y Drenewydd =Newtown ... 59 E8
Yeading 40 F4
Yeadon 94 E5
Yealand Conyers .. 92 B5
Yealand Redmayne .. 92 B5
Yealmpton 6 D3
Yearby 102 B4
Yearsley 95 B8
Yeaton 60 C4
Yeaveley 75 E8
Yedingham ... 96 B4
Yeldon 53 C8
Yelford 38 D3
Yelland 20 F3
Yelvertoft ... 52 B3
Yelverton
  Devon 6 C3
  Norf 69 D5
Yenston 12 B5
Yeoford 10 E2
Yeolmbridge ... 8 F5
Yeo Mill 10 B3
Yeovil 12 C3
Yeovil Marsh . 12 C3
Yeovilton 12 B3
Yerbeston 32 D1
Yesnaby 159 G3
Yetlington .. 117 D6
Yetminster ... 12 C3
Yettington ... 11 F5
Yetts o'Muckhart . 128 D2
Y Felinheli ... 82 E5
Y Fenni =Abergavenny 35 C6
Y Fflint =Flint .. 73 B6
Y Ffôr 70 D4
Y Ffrith 72 A4
Y Gelli Gandryll =Hay-on-Wye .. 48 E4
Yieldshields . 119 D8
Yiewsley 40 F3
Y Mwmbwls =The Mumbles 33 F7
Ynysboeth ... 34 E4
Ynysddu 35 E5
Ynysgyfflog .. 58 C3
Ynyshir 34 E4
Ynyslas 58 E3
Ynys-meudwy .. 33 D8
Ynystawe 33 D7
Ynysybwl 34 E4
Yockenthwaite 94 B2
Yockleton 60 C3
Yokefleet 90 B2
Yoker 118 C5
Yonder Bognie 152 D5
York 95 D8
Yorkletts 30 C4
Yorkley 36 D3
York Town 27 C6
Yorton 60 B5
Youlgreave ... 76 C2
Youlstone 8 C4
Youlthorpe ... 96 D3
Youlton 95 C7
Young's End .. 42 C3
Young Wood .. 78 B4
Yoxall 62 C5
Yoxford 57 C7
Y Pîl =Pyle ... 34 F2
Yr Hôb =Hope . 73 D7
Y Rhws =Rhoose. 22 C2
Y Rhyl =Rhyl .. 72 A4
Yr Wyddgrug =Mold 73 C6
Ysbyty-Cynfyn 47 B6
Ysbyty Ifan .. 72 E2
Ysbyty Ystwyth .. 47 B6
Ysceifiog 73 B5
Yspitty 33 E6
Ystalyfera ... 34 D1
Ystrad 34 E3
Ystrad Aeron .. 46 D4
Ystradfellte .. 34 C3
Ystradffin ... 47 E6
Ystradgynlais . 34 C1
Ystradmeurig . 47 C6
Ystrad-mynach .. 35 E5
Ystradowen
  Carms 33 C8
  V Glam 22 B2
Ystumtuen ... 47 B6
Ythanbank .. 153 E9
Ythanwells .. 153 E6
Ythsie 153 E8
Y Trallwng =Welshpool .. 60 D2
Y Waun =Chirk .. 73 F6

Z

Zeal Monachorum . 10 D2
Zeals 24 F2
Zelah 4 D3
Zennor 2 C3